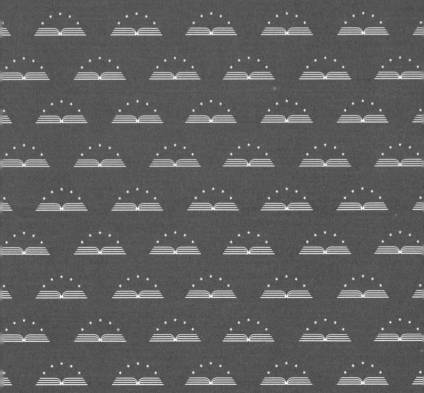

ROBERT FROST

# ROBERT FROST

## COLLECTED POEMS, PROSE, & PLAYS

*Complete Poems 1949*
*In the Clearing*
*Uncollected Poems*
*Plays*
*Lectures, Essays, Stories, and Letters*

THE LIBRARY OF AMERICA

*Complete Poems of Robert Frost 1949*, copyright 1916, 1923, 1928, 1930, 1934,
1939, 1943, 1945, 1947, 1949, © 1967 by Henry Holt and Co., copyright
1936, 1942, 1944, 1945, 1947, 1948, 1951, © 1956, 1958, 1962 by Robert Frost,
and copyright © 1964, 1967 by Lesley Frost Ballantine. *In the Clearing*,
copyright 1942, 1948, 1950, 1951, 1952, 1953, © 1955, 1956, 1958, 1959, 1960,
1961, 1962 by Robert Frost and copyright © 1970 by Lesley Frost Ballantine.
Reprinted by arrangement with Henry Holt and Co. For further
information on copyright holders and publication rights, see pages 956–67.

The paper used in this publication meets the
minimum requirements of the American National Standard for
Information Sciences—Permanence of Paper for Printed
Library Materials, ANSI Z39.48—1984.

Distributed to the trade in the United States
by Penguin Books USA Inc
and in Canada by Penguin Books Canada Ltd.

Library of Congress Catalog Number: 94–43693
For cataloging information, see end of Index.
ISBN: 1–883011–06–x

First Printing
The Library of America—81

Manufactured in the United States of America

RICHARD POIRIER AND MARK RICHARDSON
SELECTED THE CONTENTS AND WROTE THE NOTES
FOR THIS VOLUME

*The texts of most of the prose included in this
volume have been established by
Mark Richardson.*

# Contents

# COMPLETE POEMS
## OF
## ROBERT FROST

### 1949

## The Pasture

I'm going out to clean the pasture spring;
I'll only stop to rake the leaves away
(And wait to watch the water clear, I may):
I sha'n't be gone long.—You come too.

I'm going out to fetch the little calf
That's standing by the mother. It's so young,
It totters when she licks it with her tongue.
I sha'n't be gone long.—You come too.

# Contents

## MOUNTAIN INTERVAL

## NEW HAMPSHIRE

## WEST-RUNNING BROOK

## A FURTHER RANGE

### TAKEN DOUBLY

  *Read before the Phi Beta Kappa Society at William and Mary College, December 5, 1941.

  †Read before the Phi Beta Kappa Society at Harvard University, June 20, 1941.

## A MASQUE OF REASON

## A MASQUE OF MERCY

# A BOY'S WILL

## Into My Own

One of my wishes is that those dark trees,
So old and firm they scarcely show the breeze,
Were not, as 'twere, the merest mask of gloom,
But stretched away unto the edge of doom.

I should not be withheld but that some day
Into their vastness I should steal away,
Fearless of ever finding open land,
Or highway where the slow wheel pours the sand.

I do not see why I should e'er turn back,
Or those should not set forth upon my track
To overtake me, who should miss me here
And long to know if still I held them dear.

They would not find me changed from him they knew—
Only more sure of all I thought was true.

## Ghost House

I dwell in a lonely house I know
That vanished many a summer ago,
   And left no trace but the cellar walls,
   And a cellar in which the daylight falls,
And the purple-stemmed wild raspberries grow.

O'er ruined fences the grapevines shield
The woods come back to the mowing field;
   The orchard tree has grown one copse
   Of new wood and old where the woodpecker chops;
The footpath down to the well is healed.

I dwell with a strangely aching heart
In that vanished abode there far apart
   On that disused and forgotten road
   That has no dust-bath now for the toad.
Night comes; the black bats tumble and dart;

The whippoorwill is coming to shout
And hush and cluck and flutter about:
   I hear him begin far enough away
   Full many a time to say his say
Before he arrives to say it out.

It is under the small, dim, summer star.
I know not who these mute folk are
   Who share the unlit place with me—
   Those stones out under the low-limbed tree
Doubtless bear names that the mosses mar.

They are tireless folk, but slow and sad,
Though two, close-keeping, are lass and lad,—
   With none among them that ever sings,
   And yet, in view of how many things,
As sweet companions as might be had.


## My November Guest

My Sorrow, when she's here with me,
   Thinks these dark days of autumn rain
Are beautiful as days can be;
She loves the bare, the withered tree;
   She walks the sodden pasture lane.

Her pleasure will not let me stay.
   She talks and I am fain to list:
She's glad the birds are gone away,
She's glad her simple worsted gray
   Is silver now with clinging mist.

The desolate, deserted trees,
 The faded earth, the heavy sky,
The beauties she so truly sees,
She thinks I have no eye for these,
 And vexes me for reason why.

Not yesterday I learned to know
 The love of bare November days
Before the coming of the snow,
But it were vain to tell her so,
 And they are better for her praise.

## Love and a Question

A Stranger came to the door at eve,
 And he spoke the bridegroom fair.
He bore a green-white stick in his hand,
 And, for all burden, care.
He asked with the eyes more than the lips
 For a shelter for the night,
And he turned and looked at the road afar
 Without a window light.

The bridegroom came forth into the porch
 With 'Let us look at the sky,
And question what of the night to be,
 Stranger, you and I.'
The woodbine leaves littered the yard,
 The woodbine berries were blue,
Autumn, yes, winter was in the wind;
 'Stranger, I wish I knew.'

Within, the bride in the dusk alone
 Bent over the open fire,
Her face rose-red with the glowing coal
 And the thought of the heart's desire.

The bridegroom looked at the weary road,
 Yet saw but her within,
And wished her heart in a case of gold
 And pinned with a silver pin.

The bridegroom thought it little to give
 A dole of bread, a purse,
A heartfelt prayer for the poor of God,
 Or for the rich a curse;
But whether or not a man was asked
 To mar the love of two
By harboring woe in the bridal house,
 The bridegroom wished he knew.

## A Late Walk

When I go up through the mowing field,
 The headless aftermath,
Smooth-laid like thatch with the heavy dew,
 Half closes the garden path.

And when I come to the garden ground,
 The whir of sober birds
Up from the tangle of withered weeds
 Is sadder than any words.

A tree beside the wall stands bare,
 But a leaf that lingered brown,
Disturbed, I doubt not, by my thought,
 Comes softly rattling down.

I end not far from my going forth
 By picking the faded blue
Of the last remaining aster flower
 To carry again to you.

## Stars

How countlessly they congregate
　O'er our tumultuous snow,
Which flows in shapes as tall as trees
　When wintry winds do blow!—

As if with keenness for our fate,
　Our faltering few steps on
To white rest, and a place of rest
　Invisible at dawn,—

And yet with neither love nor hate,
　Those stars like some snow-white
Minerva's snow-white marble eyes
　Without the gift of sight.


## Storm Fear

When the wind works against us in the dark,
And pelts with snow
The lower chamber window on the east,
And whispers with a sort of stifled bark,
The beast,
'Come out! Come out!'—
It costs no inward struggle not to go,
Ah, no!
I count our strength,
Two and a child,
Those of us not asleep subdued to mark
How the cold creeps as the fire dies at length,—
How drifts are piled,
Dooryard and road ungraded,
Till even the comforting barn grows far away,
And my heart owns a doubt
Whether 'tis in us to arise with day
And save ourselves unaided.

## Wind and Window Flower

Lovers, forget your love,
  And list to the love of these,
She a window flower,
  And he a winter breeze.

When the frosty window veil
  Was melted down at noon,
And the cagèd yellow bird
  Hung over her in tune,

He marked her through the pane,
  He could not help but mark,
And only passed her by,
  To come again at dark.

He was a winter wind,
  Concerned with ice and snow,
Dead weeds and unmated birds,
  And little of love could know.

But he sighed upon the sill,
  He gave the sash a shake,
As witness all within
  Who lay that night awake.

Perchance he half prevailed
  To win her for the flight
From the firelit looking-glass
  And warm stove-window light.

But the flower leaned aside
  And thought of naught to say,
And morning found the breeze
  A hundred miles away.

## To the Thawing Wind

Come with rain, O loud Southwester!
Bring the singer, bring the nester;
Give the buried flower a dream;
Make the settled snowbank steam;
Find the brown beneath the white;
But whate'er you do tonight,
Bathe my window, make it flow,
Melt it as the ice will go;
Melt the glass and leave the sticks
Like a hermit's crucifix;
Burst into my narrow stall;
Swing the picture on the wall;
Run the rattling pages o'er;
Scatter poems on the floor;
Turn the poet out of door.

## A Prayer in Spring

Oh, give us pleasure in the flowers today;
And give us not to think so far away
As the uncertain harvest; keep us here
All simply in the springing of the year.

Oh, give us pleasure in the orchard white,
Like nothing else by day, like ghosts by night;
And make us happy in the happy bees,
The swarm dilating round the perfect trees.

And make us happy in the darting bird
That suddenly above the bees is heard,
The meteor that thrusts in with needle bill,
And off a blossom in mid air stands still.

For this is love and nothing else is love,
The which it is reserved for God above
To sanctify to what far ends He will,
But which it only needs that we fulfill.


## Flower-Gathering

I left you in the morning,
And in the morning glow,
You walked a way beside me
To make me sad to go.
Do you know me in the gloaming,
Gaunt and dusty gray with roaming?
Are you dumb because you know me not,
Or dumb because you know?

All for me? And not a question
For the faded flowers gay
That could take me from beside you
For the ages of a day?
They are yours, and be the measure
Of their worth for you to treasure,
The measure of the little while
That I've been long away.


## Rose Pogonias

A saturated meadow,
    Sun-shaped and jewel-small,
A circle scarcely wider
    Than the trees around were tall;
Where winds were quite excluded,
    And the air was stifling sweet
With the breath of many flowers,—
    A temple of the heat.

There we bowed us in the burning,
    As the sun's right worship is,
To pick where none could miss them
    A thousand orchises;
For though the grass was scattered,
    Yet every second spear
Seemed tipped with wings of color,
    That tinged the atmosphere.

We raised a simple prayer
    Before we left the spot,
That in the general mowing
    That place might be forgot;
Or if not all so favored,
    Obtain such grace of hours,
That none should mow the grass there
    While so confused with flowers.


## Waiting

### A field at dusk

What things for dream there are when specter-like,
Moving along tall haycocks lightly piled,
I enter alone upon the stubble field,
From which the laborers' voices late have died,
And in the antiphony of afterglow
And rising full moon, sit me down
Upon the full moon's side of the first haycock
And lose myself amid so many alike.

I dream upon the opposing lights of the hour,
Preventing shadow until the moon prevail;
I dream upon the nighthawks peopling heaven,
Each circling each with vague unearthly cry,
Or plunging headlong with fierce twang afar;
And on the bat's mute antics, who would seem
Dimly to have made out my secret place,

Only to lose it when he pirouettes,
And seek it endlessly with purblind haste;
On the last swallow's sweep; and on the rasp
In the abyss of odor and rustle at my back,
That, silenced by my advent, finds once more,
After an interval, his instrument,
And tries once—twice—and thrice if I be there;
And on the worn book of old-golden song
I brought not here to read, it seems, but hold
And freshen in this air of withering sweetness;
But on the memory of one absent most,
For whom these lines when they shall greet her eye.

## In a Vale

When I was young, we dwelt in a vale
    By a misty fen that rang all night,
And thus it was the maidens pale
I knew so well, whose garments trail
    Across the reeds to a window light.

The fen had every kind of bloom,
    And for every kind there was a face,
And a voice that has sounded in my room
Across the sill from the outer gloom.
    Each came singly unto her place,

But all came every night with the mist;
    And often they brought so much to say
Of things of moment to which, they wist,
One so lonely was fain to list,
    That the stars were almost faded away

Before the last went, heavy with dew,
    Back to the place from which she came—
Where the bird was before it flew,
Where the flower was before it grew,
    Where bird and flower were one and the same.

And thus it is I know so well
   Why the flower has odor, the bird has song.
You have only to ask me, and I can tell.
No, not vainly there did I dwell,
   Nor vainly listen all the night long.


## A Dream Pang

I had withdrawn in forest, and my song
Was swallowed up in leaves that blew alway;
And to the forest edge you came one day
(This was my dream) and looked and pondered long,
But did not enter, though the wish was strong:
You shook your pensive head as who should say,
'I dare not—too far in his footsteps stray—
He must seek me would he undo the wrong.'

Not far, but near, I stood and saw it all
Behind low boughs the trees let down outside;
And the sweet pang it cost me not to call
And tell you that I saw does still abide.
But 'tis not true that thus I dwelt aloof,
For the wood wakes, and you are here for proof.


## In Neglect

They leave us so to the way we took,
   As two in whom they were proved mistaken,
That we sit sometimes in the wayside nook,
With mischievous, vagrant, seraphic look,
   And *try* if we cannot feel forsaken.

## The Vantage Point

If tired of trees I seek again mankind,
  Well I know where to hie me—in the dawn,
  To a slope where the cattle keep the lawn.
There amid lolling juniper reclined,
Myself unseen, I see in white defined
  Far off the homes of men, and farther still,
  The graves of men on an opposing hill,
Living or dead, whichever are to mind.

And if by noon I have too much of these,
  I have but to turn on my arm, and lo,
  The sun-burned hillside sets my face aglow,
My breathing shakes the bluet like a breeze,
  I smell the earth, I smell the bruisèd plant,
  I look into the crater of the ant.

## Mowing

There was never a sound beside the wood but one,
And that was my long scythe whispering to the ground.
What was it it whispered? I knew not well myself;
Perhaps it was something about the heat of the sun,
Something, perhaps, about the lack of sound—
And that was why it whispered and did not speak.
It was no dream of the gift of idle hours,
Or easy gold at the hand of fay or elf:
Anything more than the truth would have seemed too weak
To the earnest love that laid the swale in rows,
Not without feeble-pointed spikes of flowers
(Pale orchises), and scared a bright green snake.
The fact is the sweetest dream that labor knows.
My long scythe whispered and left the hay to make.

## Going for Water

The well was dry beside the door,
  And so we went with pail and can
Across the fields behind the house
  To seek the brook if still it ran;

Not loth to have excuse to go,
  Because the autumn eve was fair
(Though chill), because the fields were ours,
  And by the brook our woods were there.

We ran as if to meet the moon
  That slowly dawned behind the trees,
The barren boughs without the leaves,
  Without the birds, without the breeze.

But once within the wood, we paused
  Like gnomes that hid us from the moon,
Ready to run to hiding new
  With laughter when she found us soon.

Each laid on other a staying hand
  To listen ere we dared to look,
And in the hush we joined to make
  We heard, we knew we heard the brook.

A note as from a single place,
  A slender tinkling fall that made
Now drops that floated on the pool
  Like pearls, and now a silver blade.

## Revelation

We make ourselves a place apart
  Behind light words that tease and flout,
But oh, the agitated heart
  Till someone really find us out.

'Tis pity if the case require
 (Or so we say) that in the end
We speak the literal to inspire
 The understanding of a friend.

But so with all, from babes that play
 At hide-and-seek to God afar,
So all who hide too well away
 Must speak and tell us where they are.

## The Trial by Existence

Even the bravest that are slain
 Shall not dissemble their surprise
On waking to find valor reign,
 Even as on earth, in paradise;
And where they sought without the sword
 Wide fields of asphodel fore'er,
To find that the utmost reward
 Of daring should be still to dare.

The light of heaven falls whole and white
 And is not shattered into dyes,
The light forever is morning light;
 The hills are verdured pasture-wise;
The angel hosts with freshness go,
 And seek with laughter what to brave;—
And binding all is the hushed snow
 Of the far-distant breaking wave.

And from a cliff-top is proclaimed
 The gathering of the souls for birth,
The trial by existence named,
 The obscuration upon earth.
And the slant spirits trooping by
 In streams and cross- and counter-streams
Can but give ear to that sweet cry
 For its suggestion of what dreams!

And the more loitering are turned
   To view once more the sacrifice
Of those who for some good discerned
   Will gladly give up paradise.
And a white shimmering concourse rolls
   Toward the throne to witness there
The speeding of devoted souls
   Which God makes his especial care.

And none are taken but who will,
   Having first heard the life read out
That opens earthward, good and ill,
   Beyond the shadow of a doubt;
And very beautifully God limns,
   And tenderly, life's little dream,
But naught extenuates or dims,
   Setting the thing that is supreme.

Nor is there wanting in the press
   Some spirit to stand simply forth,
Heroic in its nakedness,
   Against the uttermost of earth.
The tale of earth's unhonored things
   Sounds nobler there than 'neath the sun;
And the mind whirls and the heart sings,
   And a shout greets the daring one.

But always God speaks at the end:
   'One thought in agony of strife
The bravest would have by for friend,
   The memory that he chose the life;
But the pure fate to which you go
   Admits no memory of choice,
Or the woe were not earthly woe
   To which you give the assenting voice.'

And so the choice must be again,
   But the last choice is still the same;
And the awe passes wonder then,
   And a hush falls for all acclaim.

And God has taken a flower of gold
   And broken it, and used therefrom
The mystic link to bind and hold
   Spirit to matter till death come.

'Tis of the essence of life here,
   Though we choose greatly, still to lack
The lasting memory at all clear,
   That life has for us on the wrack
Nothing but what we somehow chose;
   Thus are we wholly stripped of pride
In the pain that has but one close,
   Bearing it crushed and mystified.

## The Tuft of Flowers

I went to turn the grass once after one
Who mowed it in the dew before the sun.

The dew was gone that made his blade so keen
Before I came to view the leveled scene.

I looked for him behind an isle of trees;
I listened for his whetstone on the breeze.

But he had gone his way, the grass all mown,
And I must be, as he had been,—alone,

'As all must be,' I said within my heart,
'Whether they work together or apart.'

But as I said it, swift there passed me by
On noiseless wing a bewildered butterfly,

Seeking with memories grown dim o'er night
Some resting flower of yesterday's delight.

And once I marked his flight go round and round,
As where some flower lay withering on the ground.

And then he flew as far as eye could see,
And then on tremulous wing came back to me.

I thought of questions that have no reply,
And would have turned to toss the grass to dry;

But he turned first, and led my eye to look
At a tall tuft of flowers beside a brook,

A leaping tongue of bloom the scythe had spared
Beside a reedy brook the scythe had bared.

The mower in the dew had loved them thus,
By leaving them to flourish, not for us,

Nor yet to draw one thought of ours to him,
But from sheer morning gladness at the brim.

The butterfly and I had lit upon,
Nevertheless, a message from the dawn,

That made me hear the wakening birds around,
And hear his long scythe whispering to the ground,

And feel a spirit kindred to my own;
So that henceforth I worked no more alone;

But glad with him, I worked as with his aid,
And weary, sought at noon with him the shade;

And dreaming, as it were, held brotherly speech
With one whose thought I had not hoped to reach.

'Men work together,' I told him from the heart,
'Whether they work together or apart.'

## Pan with Us

Pan came out of the woods one day,—
His skin and his hair and his eyes were gray,
The gray of the moss of walls were they,—
    And stood in the sun and looked his fill
    At wooded valley and wooded hill.

He stood in the zephyr, pipes in hand,
On a height of naked pasture land;
In all the country he did command
    He saw no smoke and he saw no roof.
    That was well! and he stamped a hoof.

His heart knew peace, for none came here
To this lean feeding save once a year
Someone to salt the half-wild steer,
    Or homespun children with clicking pails
    Who see so little they tell no tales.

He tossed his pipes, too hard to teach
A new-world song, far out of reach,
For a sylvan sign that the blue jay's screech
    And the whimper of hawks beside the sun
    Were music enough for him, for one.

Times were changed from what they were:
Such pipes kept less of power to stir
The fruited bough of the juniper
    And the fragile bluets clustered there
    Than the merest aimless breath of air.

They were pipes of pagan mirth,
And the world had found new terms of worth.
He laid him down on the sun-burned earth
    And raveled a flower and looked away—
    Play? Play?—What should he play?

## The Demiurge's Laugh

It was far in the sameness of the wood;
   I was running with joy on the Demon's trail,
Though I knew what I hunted was no true god.
   It was just as the light was beginning to fail
That I suddenly heard—all I needed to hear:
It has lasted me many and many a year.

The sound was behind me instead of before,
   A sleepy sound, but mocking half,
As of one who utterly couldn't care.
   The Demon arose from his wallow to laugh,
Brushing the dirt from his eye as he went;
And well I knew what the Demon meant.

I shall not forget how his laugh rang out.
   I felt as a fool to have been so caught,
And checked my steps to make pretense
   It was something among the leaves I sought
(Though doubtful whether he stayed to see).
Thereafter I sat me against a tree.

## Now Close the Windows

Now close the windows and hush all the fields:
   If the trees must, let them silently toss;
No bird is singing now, and if there is,
   Be it my loss.

It will be long ere the marshes resume,
   It will be long ere the earliest bird:
So close the windows and not hear the wind,
   But see all wind-stirred.

## In Hardwood Groves

The same leaves over and over again!
They fall from giving shade above
To make one texture of faded brown
And fit the earth like a leather glove.

Before the leaves can mount again
To fill the trees with another shade,
They must go down past things coming up.
They must go down into the dark decayed.

They *must* be pierced by flowers and put
Beneath the feet of dancing flowers.
However it is in some other world
I know that this is the way in ours.

## A Line-Storm Song

The line-storm clouds fly tattered and swift.
    The road is forlorn all day,
Where a myriad snowy quartz stones lift,
    And the hoof-prints vanish away.
The roadside flowers, too wet for the bee,
    Expend their bloom in vain.
Come over the hills and far with me,
    And be my love in the rain.

The birds have less to say for themselves
    In the wood-world's torn despair
Than now these numberless years the elves,
    Although they are no less there:
All song of the woods is crushed like some
    Wild, easily shattered rose.
Come, be my love in the wet woods, come,
    Where the boughs rain when it blows.

There is the gale to urge behind
   And bruit our singing down,
And the shallow waters aflutter with wind
   From which to gather your gown.
What matter if we go clear to the west,
   And come not through dry-shod?
For wilding brooch shall wet your breast
   The rain-fresh goldenrod.

Oh, never this whelming east wind swells
   But it seems like the sea's return
To the ancient lands where it left the shells
   Before the age of the fern;
And it seems like the time when after doubt
   Our love came back amain.
Oh, come forth into the storm and rout
   And be my love in the rain.


## October

O hushed October morning mild,
Thy leaves have ripened to the fall;
Tomorrow's wind, if it be wild,
Should waste them all.
The crows above the forest call;
Tomorrow they may form and go.
O hushed October morning mild,
Begin the hours of this day slow.
Make the day seem to us less brief.
Hearts not averse to being beguiled,
Beguile us in the way you know.
Release one leaf at break of day;
At noon release another leaf;
One from our trees, one far away.
Retard the sun with gentle mist;
Enchant the land with amethyst.
Slow, slow!

For the grapes' sake, if they were all,
Whose leaves already are burnt with frost,
Whose clustered fruit must else be lost—
For the grapes' sake along the wall.

## My Butterfly

Thine emulous fond flowers are dead, too,
And the daft sun-assaulter, he
That frighted thee so oft, is fled or dead:
Save only me
(Nor is it sad to thee!)
Save only me
There is none left to mourn thee in the fields.

The gray grass is scarce dappled with the snow;
Its two banks have not shut upon the river;
But it is long ago—
It seems forever—
Since first I saw thee glance,
With all thy dazzling other ones,
In airy dalliance,
Precipitate in love,
Tossed, tangled, whirled and whirled above,
Like a limp rose-wreath in a fairy dance.

When that was, the soft mist
Of my regret hung not on all the land,
And I was glad for thee,
And glad for me, I wist.

Thou didst not know, who tottered, wandering on high,
That fate had made thee for the pleasure of the wind,
With those great careless wings,
Nor yet did I.

And there were other things:
It seemed God let thee flutter from his gentle clasp:
Then fearful he had let thee win
Too far beyond him to be gathered in,
Snatched thee, o'ereager, with ungentle grasp.

Ah! I remember me
How once conspiracy was rife
Against my life—
The languor of it and the dreaming fond;
Surging, the grasses dizzied me of thought,
The breeze three odors brought,
And a gem-flower waved in a wand!

Then when I was distraught
And could not speak,
Sidelong, full on my cheek,
What should that reckless zephyr fling
But the wild touch of thy dye-dusty wing!

I found that wing broken today!
For thou art dead, I said,
And the strange birds say.
I found it with the withered leaves
Under the eaves.

## *Reluctance*

Out through the fields and the woods
    And over the walls I have wended;
I have climbed the hills of view
    And looked at the world, and descended;
I have come by the highway home,
    And lo, it is ended.

The leaves are all dead on the ground,
    Save those that the oak is keeping
To ravel them one by one
    And let them go scraping and creeping
Out over the crusted snow,
    When others are sleeping.

And the dead leaves lie huddled and still,
    No longer blown hither and thither;
The last lone aster is gone;
    The flowers of the witch-hazel wither;
The heart is still aching to seek,
    But the feet question 'Whither?'

Ah, when to the heart of man
    Was it ever less than a treason
To go with the drift of things,
    To yield with a grace to reason,
And bow and accept the end
    Of a love or a season?

# NORTH OF BOSTON

## *Mending Wall*

Something there is that doesn't love a wall,
That sends the frozen-ground-swell under it,
And spills the upper boulders in the sun;
And makes gaps even two can pass abreast.
The work of hunters is another thing:
I have come after them and made repair
Where they have left not one stone on a stone,
But they would have the rabbit out of hiding,
To please the yelping dogs. The gaps I mean,
No one has seen them made or heard them made,
But at spring mending-time we find them there.
I let my neighbor know beyond the hill;
And on a day we meet to walk the line
And set the wall between us once again.
We keep the wall between us as we go.
To each the boulders that have fallen to each.
And some are loaves and some so nearly balls
We have to use a spell to make them balance:
'Stay where you are until our backs are turned!'
We wear our fingers rough with handling them.
Oh, just another kind of outdoor game,
One on a side. It comes to little more:
There where it is we do not need the wall:
He is all pine and I am apple orchard.
My apple trees will never get across
And eat the cones under his pines, I tell him.
He only says, 'Good fences make good neighbors.'
Spring is the mischief in me, and I wonder
If I could put a notion in his head:
'*Why* do they make good neighbors? Isn't it
Where there are cows? But here there are no cows.
Before I built a wall I'd ask to know
What I was walling in or walling out,

And to whom I was like to give offense.
Something there is that doesn't love a wall,
That wants it down.' I could say 'Elves' to him,
But it's not elves exactly, and I'd rather
He said it for himself. I see him there
Bringing a stone grasped firmly by the top
In each hand, like an old-stone savage armed.
He moves in darkness as it seems to me,
Not of woods only and the shade of trees.
He will not go behind his father's saying,
And he likes having thought of it so well
He says again, 'Good fences make good neighbors.'

## The Death of the Hired Man

Mary sat musing on the lamp-flame at the table
Waiting for Warren. When she heard his step,
She ran on tip-toe down the darkened passage
To meet him in the doorway with the news
And put him on his guard. 'Silas is back.'
She pushed him outward with her through the door
And shut it after her. 'Be kind,' she said.
She took the market things from Warren's arms
And set them on the porch, then drew him down
To sit beside her on the wooden steps.

'When was I ever anything but kind to him?
But I'll not have the fellow back,' he said.
'I told him so last haying, didn't I?
If he left then, I said, that ended it.
What good is he? Who else will harbor him
At his age for the little he can do?
What help he is there's no depending on.
Off he goes always when I need him most.
He thinks he ought to earn a little pay,
Enough at least to buy tobacco with,
So he won't have to beg and be beholden.
"All right," I say, "I can't afford to pay

Any fixed wages, though I wish I could."
"Someone else can." "Then someone else will have to."
I shouldn't mind his bettering himself
If that was what it was. You can be certain,
When he begins like that, there's someone at him
Trying to coax him off with pocket-money,—
In haying time, when any help is scarce.
In winter he comes back to us. I'm done.'

'Sh! not so loud: he'll hear you,' Mary said.

'I want him to: he'll have to soon or late.'

'He's worn out. He's asleep beside the stove.
When I came up from Rowe's I found him here,
Huddled against the barn-door fast asleep,
A miserable sight, and frightening, too—
You needn't smile—I didn't recognize him—
I wasn't looking for him—and he's changed.
Wait till you see.'

                    'Where did you say he'd been?'

'He didn't say. I dragged him to the house,
And gave him tea and tried to make him smoke.
I tried to make him talk about his travels.
Nothing would do: he just kept nodding off.'

'What did he say? Did he say anything?'

'But little.'

                    'Anything? Mary, confess
He said he'd come to ditch the meadow for me.'

'Warren!'

                    'But did he? I just want to know.'

'Of course he did. What would you have him say?
Surely you wouldn't grudge the poor old man

Some humble way to save his self-respect.
He added, if you really care to know,
He meant to clear the upper pasture, too.
That sounds like something you have heard before?
Warren, I wish you could have heard the way
He jumbled everything. I stopped to look
Two or three times—he made me feel so queer—
To see if he was talking in his sleep.
He ran on Harold Wilson—you remember—
The boy you had in haying four years since.
He's finished school, and teaching in his college.
Silas declares you'll have to get him back.
He says they two will make a team for work:
Between them they will lay this farm as smooth!
The way he mixed that in with other things.
He thinks young Wilson a likely lad, though daft
On education—you know how they fought
All through July under the blazing sun,
Silas up on the cart to build the load,
Harold along beside to pitch it on.'

'Yes, I took care to keep well out of earshot.'

'Well, those days trouble Silas like a dream.
You wouldn't think they would. How some things linger!
Harold's young college boy's assurance piqued him.
After so many years he still keeps finding
Good arguments he sees he might have used.
I sympathize. I know just how it feels
To think of the right thing to say too late.
Harold's associated in his mind with Latin.
He asked me what I thought of Harold's saying
He studied Latin like the violin
Because he liked it—that an argument!
He said he couldn't make the boy believe
He could find water with a hazel prong—
Which showed how much good school had ever done him.
He wanted to go over that. But most of all
He thinks if he could have another chance
To teach him how to build a load of hay—'

'I know, that's Silas' one accomplishment.
He bundles every forkful in its place,
And tags and numbers it for future reference,
So he can find and easily dislodge it
In the unloading. Silas does that well.
He takes it out in bunches like big birds' nests.
You never see him standing on the hay
He's trying to lift, straining to lift himself.'

'He thinks if he could teach him that, he'd be
Some good perhaps to someone in the world.
He hates to see a boy the fool of books.
Poor Silas, so concerned for other folk,
And nothing to look backward to with pride,
And nothing to look forward to with hope,
So now and never any different.'

Part of a moon was falling down the west,
Dragging the whole sky with it to the hills.
Its light poured softly in her lap. She saw it
And spread her apron to it. She put out her hand
Among the harp-like morning-glory strings,
Taut with the dew from garden bed to eaves,
As if she played unheard some tenderness
That wrought on him beside her in the night.
'Warren,' she said, 'he has come home to die:
You needn't be afraid he'll leave you this time.'

'Home,' he mocked gently.

                         'Yes, what else but home?
It all depends on what you mean by home.
Of course he's nothing to us, any more
Than was the hound that came a stranger to us
Out of the woods, worn out upon the trail.'

'Home is the place where, when you have to go there,
They have to take you in.'

                        'I should have called it
Something you somehow haven't to deserve.'

Warren leaned out and took a step or two,
Picked up a little stick, and brought it back
And broke it in his hand and tossed it by.
'Silas has better claim on us you think
Than on his brother? Thirteen little miles
As the road winds would bring him to his door.
Silas has walked that far no doubt today.
Why doesn't he go there? His brother's rich,
A somebody—director in the bank.'

'He never told us that.'

                           'We know it though.'

'I think his brother ought to help, of course.
I'll see to that if there is need. He ought of right
To take him in, and might be willing to—
He may be better than appearances.
But have some pity on Silas. Do you think
If he had any pride in claiming kin
Or anything he looked for from his brother,
He'd keep so still about him all this time?'

'I wonder what's between them.'

                           'I can tell you.
Silas is what he is—we wouldn't mind him—
But just the kind that kinsfolk can't abide.
He never did a thing so very bad.
He don't know why he isn't quite as good
As anybody. Worthless though he is,
He won't be made ashamed to please his brother.'

'*I* can't think Si ever hurt anyone.'

'No, but he hurt my heart the way he lay
And rolled his old head on that sharp-edged chair-back.
He wouldn't let me put him on the lounge.
You must go in and see what you can do.
I made the bed up for him there tonight.

You'll be surprised at him—how much he's broken.
His working days are done; I'm sure of it.'

'I'd not be in a hurry to say that.'

'I haven't been. Go, look, see for yourself.
But, Warren, please remember how it is:
He's come to help you ditch the meadow.
He has a plan. You mustn't laugh at him.
He may not speak of it, and then he may.
I'll sit and see if that small sailing cloud
Will hit or miss the moon.'

                             It hit the moon.
Then there were three there, making a dim row,
The moon, the little silver cloud, and she.

Warren returned—too soon, it seemed to her,
Slipped to her side, caught up her hand and waited.

'Warren?' she questioned.

                             'Dead,' was all he answered.


## The Mountain

The mountain held the town as in a shadow.
I saw so much before I slept there once:
I noticed that I missed stars in the west,
Where its black body cut into the sky.
Near me it seemed: I felt it like a wall
Behind which I was sheltered from a wind.
And yet between the town and it I found,
When I walked forth at dawn to see new things,
Were fields, a river, and beyond, more fields.
The river at the time was fallen away,
And made a widespread brawl on cobblestones;
But the signs showed what it had done in spring:

Good grassland gullied out, and in the grass
Ridges of sand, and driftwood stripped of bark.
I crossed the river and swung round the mountain.
And there I met a man who moved so slow
With white-faced oxen in a heavy cart,
It seemed no harm to stop him altogether.

'What town is this?' I asked.

                    'This? Lunenburg.'

Then I was wrong: the town of my sojourn,
Beyond the bridge, was not that of the mountain,
But only felt at night its shadowy presence.
'Where is your village? Very far from here?'

'There is no village—only scattered farms.
We were but sixty voters last election.
We can't in nature grow to many more:
That thing takes all the room!' He moved his goad.
The mountain stood there to be pointed at.
Pasture ran up the side a little way,
And then there was a wall of trees with trunks;
After that only tops of trees, and cliffs
Imperfectly concealed among the leaves.
A dry ravine emerged from under boughs
Into the pasture.

                    'That looks like a path.
Is that the way to reach the top from here?—
Not for this morning, but some other time:
I must be getting back to breakfast now.'

'I don't advise your trying from this side.
There is no proper path, but those that *have*
Been up, I understand, have climbed from Ladd's.
That's five miles back. You can't mistake the place:
They logged it there last winter some way up.
I'd take you, but I'm bound the other way.'

'You've never climbed it?'

                              'I've been on the sides,
Deer-hunting and trout-fishing. There's a brook
That starts up on it somewhere—I've heard say
Right on the top, tip-top—a curious thing.
But what would interest you about the brook,
It's always cold in summer, warm in winter.
One of the great sights going is to see
It steam in winter like an ox's breath,
Until the bushes all along its banks
Are inch-deep with the frosty spines and bristles—
You know the kind. Then let the sun shine on it!'

'There ought to be a view around the world
From such a mountain—if it isn't wooded
Clear to the top.' I saw through leafy screens
Great granite terraces in sun and shadow,
Shelves one could rest a knee on getting up—
With depths behind him sheer a hundred feet.
Or turn and sit on and look out and down,
With little ferns in crevices at his elbow.

'As to that I can't say. But there's the spring,
Right on the summit, almost like a fountain.
That ought to be worth seeing.'

                              'If it's there.
You never saw it?'

                    'I guess there's no doubt
About its being there. I never saw it.
It may not be right on the very top:
It wouldn't have to be a long way down
To have some head of water from above,
And a *good distance* down might not be noticed
By anyone who'd come a long way up.
One time I asked a fellow climbing it
To look and tell me later how it was.'

'What did he say?'

                        'He said there was a lake
Somewhere in Ireland on a mountain top.'

'But a lake's different. What about the spring?'

'He never got up high enough to see.
That's why I don't advise your trying this side.
He tried this side. I've always meant to go
And look myself, but you know how it is:
It doesn't seem so much to climb a mountain
You've worked around the foot of all your life.
What would I do? Go in my overalls,
With a big stick, the same as when the cows
Haven't come down to the bars at milking time?
Or with a shotgun for a stray black bear?
'Twouldn't seem real to climb for climbing it.'

'I shouldn't climb it if I didn't want to—
Not for the sake of climbing. What's its name?'

'We call it Hor: I don't know if that's right.'

'Can one walk around it? Would it be too far?'

'You can drive round and keep in Lunenburg,
But it's as much as ever you can do,
The boundary lines keep in so close to it.
Hor is the township, and the township's Hor—
*And* a few houses sprinkled round the foot,
Like boulders broken off the upper cliff,
Rolled out a little farther than the rest.'

'Warm in December, cold in June, you say?'

'I don't suppose the water's changed at all.
You and I know enough to know it's warm
Compared with cold, and cold compared with warm.
But all the fun's in how you say a thing.'

'You've lived here all your life?'

                       'Ever since Hor
Was no bigger than a—' What, I did not hear.
He drew the oxen toward him with light touches
Of his slim goad on nose and offside flank,
Gave them their marching orders and was moving.

## A Hundred Collars

Lancaster bore him—such a little town,
Such a great man. It doesn't see him often
Of late years, though he keeps the old homestead
And sends the children down there with their mother
To run wild in the summer—a little wild.
Sometimes he joins them for a day or two
And sees old friends he somehow can't get near.
They meet him in the general store at night,
Preoccupied with formidable mail,
Rifling a printed letter as he talks.
They seem afraid. He wouldn't have it so:
Though a great scholar, he's a democrat,
If not at heart, at least on principle.
Lately when coming up to Lancaster,
His train being late, he missed another train
And had four hours to wait at Woodsville Junction
After eleven o'clock at night. Too tired
To think of sitting such an ordeal out,
He turned to the hotel to find a bed.

'No room,' the night clerk said. 'Unless—'

Woodsville's a place of shrieks and wandering lamps
And cars that shock and rattle—and *one* hotel.

'You say "unless." '

                              'Unless you wouldn't mind
Sharing a room with someone else.'

                                        'Who is it?'

'A man.'

          'So I should hope. What kind of man?'

'I know him: he's all right. A man's a man.
Separate beds, of course, you understand.'
The night clerk blinked his eyes and dared him on.

'Who's that man sleeping in the office chair?
Has he had the refusal of my chance?'

'He was afraid of being robbed or murdered.
What do you say?'

                    'I'll have to have a bed.'

The night clerk led him up three flights of stairs
And down a narrow passage full of doors,
At the last one of which he knocked and entered.
'Lafe, here's a fellow wants to share your room.'

'Show him this way. I'm not afraid of him.
I'm not so drunk I can't take care of myself.'

The night clerk clapped a bedstead on the foot.
'This will be yours. Good-night,' he said, and went.

'Lafe was the name, I think?'

                              'Yes, *Lay*fayette.
You got it the first time. And yours?'

'Magoon.
Doctor Magoon.'

'A Doctor?'

'Well, a teacher.'

'Professor Square-the-circle-till-you're-tired?
Hold on, there's something I don't think of now
That I had on my mind to ask the first
Man that knew anything I happened in with.
I'll ask you later—don't let me forget it.'

The Doctor looked at Lafe and looked away.
A man? A brute. Naked above the waist,
He sat there creased and shining in the light,
Fumbling the buttons in a well-starched shirt.
'I'm moving into a size-larger shirt.
I've felt mean lately; mean's no name for it.
I just found what the matter was tonight:
I've been a-choking like a nursery tree
When it outgrows the wire band of its name tag.
I blamed it on the hot spell we've been having.
'Twas nothing but my foolish hanging back,
Not liking to own up I'd grown a size.
Number eighteen this is. What size do you wear?'

The Doctor caught his throat convulsively.
'Oh—ah—fourteen—fourteen.'

'Fourteen! You say so!
I can remember when I wore fourteen.
And come to think I must have back at home
More than a hundred collars, size fourteen.
Too bad to waste them all. You ought to have them.
They're yours and welcome; let me send them to you.
What makes you stand there on one leg like that?
You're not much furtherer than where Kike left you.
You act as if you wished you hadn't come.
Sit down or lie down, friend; you make me nervous.'

The Doctor made a subdued dash for it,
And propped himself at bay against a pillow.

'Not that way, with your shoes on Kike's white bed.
You can't rest that way. Let me pull your shoes off.'

'Don't touch me, please—I say, don't touch me, please.
I'll not be put to bed by you, my man.'

'Just as you say. Have it your own way then.
"My man" is it? You talk like a professor.
Speaking of who's afraid of who, however,
I'm thinking I have more to lose than you
If anything should happen to be wrong.
Who wants to cut your number fourteen throat!
Let's have a showdown as an evidence
Of good faith. There is ninety dollars.
Come, if you're not afraid.'

                              '*I'*m not afraid.
There's five: that's all I carry.'

                              'I can search you?
Where are you moving over to? Stay still.
You'd better tuck your money under you
And sleep on it the way I always do
When I'm with people I don't trust at night.'

'Will you believe me if I put it there
Right on the counterpane—that I do trust you?'

'You'd say so, Mister Man.—I'm a collector.
My ninety isn't mine—you won't think that.
I pick it up a dollar at a time
All round the country for the *Weekly News*,
Published in Bow. You know the *Weekly News*?'

'Known it since I was young.'

                              'Then you know me.

Now we are getting on together—talking.
I'm sort of Something for it at the front.
My business is to find what people want:
They pay for it, and so they ought to have it.
Fairbanks, he says to me—he's editor—
"Feel out the public sentiment"—he says.
A good deal comes on me when all is said.
The only trouble is we disagree
In politics: I'm Vermont Democrat—
You know what that is, sort of double-dyed;
The *News* has always been Republican.
Fairbanks, he says to me, "Help us this year,"
Meaning by us their ticket. "No," I says,
"I can't and won't. You've been in long enough:
It's time you turned around and boosted us.
You'll have to pay me more than ten a week
If I'm expected to elect Bill Taft.
I doubt if I could do it anyway." '

'You seem to shape the paper's policy.'

'You see I'm in with everybody, know 'em all.
I almost know their farms as well as they do.'

'You drive around? It must be pleasant work.'

'It's business, but I can't say it's not fun.
What I like best's the lay of different farms,
Coming out on them from a stretch of woods,
Or over a hill or round a sudden corner.
I like to find folks getting out in spring,
Raking the dooryard, working near the house.
Later they get out further in the fields.
Everything's shut sometimes except the barn;
The family's all away in some back meadow.
There's a hay load a-coming—when it comes.
And later still they all get driven in:
The fields are stripped to lawn, the garden patches
Stripped to bare ground, the maple trees
To whips and poles. There's nobody about.

The chimney, though, keeps up a good brisk smoking.
And I lie back and ride. I take the reins
Only when someone's coming, and the mare
Stops when she likes: I tell her when to go.
I've spoiled Jemima in more ways than one.
She's got so she turns in at every house
As if she had some sort of curvature,
No matter if I have no errand there.
She thinks I'm sociable. I maybe am.
It's seldom I get down except for meals, though.
Folks entertain me from the kitchen doorstep,
All in a family row down to the youngest.'

'One would suppose they might not be as glad
To see you as you are to see them.'

                                    'Oh,
Because I want their dollar? I don't want
Anything they've not got. I never dun.
I'm there, and they can pay me if they like.
I go nowhere on purpose: I happen by.
Sorry there is no cup to give you a drink.
I drink out of the bottle—not your style.
Mayn't I offer you—?'

                      'No, no, no, thank you.'

'Just as you say. Here's looking at you then.—
And now I'm leaving you a little while.
You'll rest easier when I'm gone, perhaps—
Lie down—let yourself go and get some sleep.
But first—let's see—what was I going to ask you?
Those collars—who shall I address them to,
Suppose you aren't awake when I come back?'

'Really, friend, I can't let you. You—may need them.'

'Not till I shrink, when they'll be out of style.'

'But really I—I have so many collars.'

'I don't know who I rather would have have them.
They're only turning yellow where they are.
But you're the doctor as the saying is.
I'll put the light out. Don't you wait for me:
I've just begun the night. You get some sleep.
I'll knock so-fashion and peep round the door
When I come back so you'll know who it is.
There's nothing I'm afraid of like scared people.
I don't want you should shoot me in the head.
What am I doing carrying off this bottle?
There now, you get some sleep.'

        He shut the door.
The Doctor slid a little down the pillow.

## Home Burial

He saw her from the bottom of the stairs
Before she saw him. She was starting down,
Looking back over her shoulder at some fear.
She took a doubtful step and then undid it
To raise herself and look again. He spoke
Advancing toward her: 'What is it you see
From up there always—for I want to know.'
She turned and sank upon her skirts at that,
And her face changed from terrified to dull.
He said to gain time: 'What is it you see,'
Mounting until she cowered under him.
'I will find out now—you must tell me, dear.'
She, in her place, refused him any help
With the least stiffening of her neck and silence.
She let him look, sure that he wouldn't see,
Blind creature; and awhile he didn't see.
But at last he murmured, 'Oh,' and again, 'Oh.'

'What is it—what?' she said.

      'Just that I see.'

'You don't,' she challenged. 'Tell me what it is.'

'The wonder is I didn't see at once.
I never noticed it from here before.
I must be wonted to it—that's the reason.
The little graveyard where my people are!
So small the window frames the whole of it.
Not so much larger than a bedroom, is it?
There are three stones of slate and one of marble,
Broad-shouldered little slabs there in the sunlight
On the sidehill. We haven't to mind *those*.
But I understand: it is not the stones,
But the child's mound—'

       'Don't, don't, don't, don't,' she cried.

She withdrew shrinking from beneath his arm
That rested on the bannister, and slid downstairs;
And turned on him with such a daunting look,
He said twice over before he knew himself:
'Can't a man speak of his own child he's lost?'

'Not you! Oh, where's my hat? Oh, I don't need it!
I must get out of here. I must get air.
I don't know rightly whether any man can.'

'Amy! Don't go to someone else this time.
Listen to me. I won't come down the stairs.'
He sat and fixed his chin between his fists.
'There's something I should like to ask you, dear.'

'You don't know how to ask it.'

       'Help me, then.'

Her fingers moved the latch for all reply.

'My words are nearly always an offense.
I don't know how to speak of anything
So as to please you. But I might be taught

I should suppose. I can't say I see how.
A man must partly give up being a man
With women-folk. We could have some arrangement
By which I'd bind myself to keep hands off
Anything special you're a-mind to name.
Though I don't like such things 'twixt those that love.
Two that don't love can't live together without them.
But two that do can't live together with them.'
She moved the latch a little. 'Don't—don't go.
Don't carry it to someone else this time.
Tell me about it if it's something human.
Let me into your grief. I'm not so much
Unlike other folks as your standing there
Apart would make me out. Give me my chance.
I do think, though, you overdo it a little.
What was it brought you up to think it the thing
To take your mother-loss of a first child
So inconsolably—in the face of love.
You'd think his memory might be satisfied—'

'There you go sneering now!'

                              'I'm not, I'm not!
You make me angry. I'll come down to you.
God, what a woman! And it's come to this,
A man can't speak of his own child that's dead.'

'You can't because you don't know how to speak.
If you had any feelings, you that dug
With your own hand—how could you?—his little grave;
I saw you from that very window there,
Making the gravel leap and leap in air,
Leap up, like that, like that, and land so lightly
And roll back down the mound beside the hole.
I thought, Who is that man? I didn't know you.
And I crept down the stairs and up the stairs
To look again, and still your spade kept lifting.
Then you came in. I heard your rumbling voice
Out in the kitchen, and I don't know why,
But I went near to see with my own eyes.

You could sit there with the stains on your shoes
Of the fresh earth from your own baby's grave
And talk about your everyday concerns.
You had stood the spade up against the wall
Outside there in the entry, for I saw it.'

'I shall laugh the worst laugh I ever laughed.
I'm cursed. God, if I don't believe I'm cursed.'

'I can repeat the very words you were saying.
"Three foggy mornings and one rainy day
Will rot the best birch fence a man can build."
Think of it, talk like that at such a time!
What had how long it takes a birch to rot
To do with what was in the darkened parlor.
You *couldn't* care! The nearest friends can go
With anyone to death, comes so far short
They might as well not try to go at all.
No, from the time when one is sick to death,
One is alone, and he dies more alone.
Friends make pretense of following to the grave,
But before one is in it, their minds are turned
And making the best of their way back to life
And living people, and things they understand.
But the world's evil. I won't have grief so
If I can change it. Oh, I won't, I won't!'

'There, you have said it all and you feel better.
You won't go now. You're crying. Close the door.
The heart's gone out of it: why keep it up.
Amy! There's someone coming down the road!'

'*You*—oh, you think the talk is all. I must go—
Somewhere out of this house. How can I make you—'

'If—you—do!' She was opening the door wider.
'Where do you mean to go? First tell me that.
I'll follow and bring you back by force. I *will!*—'

## *The Black Cottage*

We chanced in passing by that afternoon
To catch it in a sort of special picture
Among tar-banded ancient cherry trees,
Set well back from the road in rank lodged grass,
The little cottage we were speaking of,
A front with just a door between two windows,
Fresh painted by the shower a velvet black.
We paused, the minister and I, to look.
He made as if to hold it at arm's length
Or put the leaves aside that framed it in.
'Pretty,' he said. 'Come in. No one will care.'
The path was a vague parting in the grass
That led us to a weathered window-sill.
We pressed our faces to the pane. 'You see,' he said,
'Everything's as she left it when she died.
Her sons won't sell the house or the things in it.
They say they mean to come and summer here
Where they were boys. They haven't come this year.
They live so far away—one is out west—
It will be hard for them to keep their word.
Anyway they won't have the place disturbed.'
A buttoned hair-cloth lounge spread scrolling arms
Under a crayon portrait on the wall,
Done sadly from an old daguerreotype.
'That was the father as he went to war.
She always, when she talked about the war,
Sooner or later came and leaned, half knelt
Against the lounge beside it, though I doubt
If such unlifelike lines kept power to stir
Anything in her after all the years.
He fell at Gettysburg or Fredericksburg,
I ought to know—it makes a difference which:
Fredericksburg wasn't Gettysburg, of course.
But what I'm getting to is how forsaken
A little cottage this has always seemed;
Since she went more than ever, but before—
I don't mean altogether by the lives

That had gone out of it, the father first,
Then the two sons, till she was left alone.
(Nothing could draw her after those two sons.
She valued the considerate neglect
She had at some cost taught them after years.)
I mean by the world's having passed it by—
As we almost got by this afternoon.
It always seems to me a sort of mark
To measure how far fifty years have brought us.
Why not sit down if you are in no haste?
These doorsteps seldom have a visitor.
The warping boards pull out their own old nails
With none to tread and put them in their place.
She had her own idea of things, the old lady.
And she liked talk. She had seen Garrison
And Whittier, and had her story of them.
One wasn't long in learning that she thought
Whatever else the Civil War was for,
It wasn't just to keep the States together,
Nor just to free the slaves, though it did both.
She wouldn't have believed those ends enough
To have given outright for them all she gave.
Her giving somehow touched the principle
That all men are created free and equal.
And to hear her quaint phrases—so removed
From the world's view today of all those things.
That's a hard mystery of Jefferson's.
What did he mean? Of course the easy way
Is to decide it simply isn't true.
It may not be. I heard a fellow say so.
But never mind, the Welshman got it planted
Where it will trouble us a thousand years.
Each age will have to reconsider it.
You couldn't tell her what the West was saying,
And what the South to her serene belief.
She had some art of hearing and yet not
Hearing the latter wisdom of the world.
White was the only race she ever knew.
Black she had scarcely seen, and yellow never.
But how could they be made so very unlike

By the same hand working in the same stuff?
She had supposed the war decided that.
What are you going to do with such a person?
Strange how such innocence gets its own way.
I shouldn't be surprised if in this world
It were the force that would at last prevail.
Do you know but for her there was a time
When to please younger members of the church,
Or rather say non-members in the church,
Whom we all have to think of nowadays,
I would have changed the Creed a very little?
Not that she ever had to ask me not to;
It never got so far as that; but the bare thought
Of her old tremulous bonnet in the pew,
And of her half asleep was too much for me.
Why, I might wake her up and startle her.
It was the words "descended into Hades"
That seemed too pagan to our liberal youth.
You know they suffered from a general onslaught.
And well, if they weren't true why keep right on
Saying them like the heathen? We could drop them.
Only—there was the bonnet in the pew.
Such a phrase couldn't have meant much to her.
But suppose she had missed it from the Creed
As a child misses the unsaid Good-night,
And falls asleep with heartache—how should *I* feel?
I'm just as glad she made me keep hands off,
For, dear me, why abandon a belief
Merely because it ceases to be true.
Cling to it long enough, and not a doubt
It will turn true again, for so it goes.
Most of the change we think we see in life
Is due to truths being in and out of favor.
As I sit here, and oftentimes, I wish
I could be monarch of a desert land
I could devote and dedicate forever
To the truths we keep coming back and back to.
So desert it would have to be, so walled
By mountain ranges half in summer snow,
No one would covet it or think it worth

The pains of conquering to force change on.
Scattered oases where men dwelt, but mostly
Sand dunes held loosely in tamarisk
Blown over and over themselves in idleness.
Sand grains should sugar in the natal dew
The babe born to the desert, the sand storm
Retard mid-waste my cowering caravans—
There are bees in this wall.' He struck the clapboards,
Fierce heads looked out; small bodies pivoted.
We rose to go. Sunset blazed on the windows.


## Blueberries

'You ought to have seen what I saw on my way
To the village, through Patterson's pasture today:
Blueberries as big as the end of your thumb,
Real sky-blue, and heavy, and ready to drum
In the cavernous pail of the first one to come!
And all ripe together, not some of them green
And some of them ripe! You ought to have seen!'

'I don't know what part of the pasture you mean.'

'You know where they cut off the woods—let me see—
It was two years ago—or no!—can it be
No longer than that?—and the following fall
The fire ran and burned it all up but the wall.'

'Why, there hasn't been time for the bushes to grow.
That's always the way with the blueberries, though:
There may not have been the ghost of a sign
Of them anywhere under the shade of the pine,
But get the pine out of the way, you may burn
The pasture all over until not a fern
Or grass-blade is left, not to mention a stick,
And presto, they're up all around you as thick
And hard to explain as a conjuror's trick.'

'It must be on charcoal they fatten their fruit.
I taste in them sometimes the flavor of soot.
And after all really they're ebony skinned:
The blue's but a mist from the breath of the wind,
A tarnish that goes at a touch of the hand,
And less than the tan with which pickers are tanned.'

'Does Patterson know what he has, do you think?'

'He may and not care and so leave the chewink
To gather them for him—you know what he is.
He won't make the fact that they're rightfully his
An excuse for keeping us other folk out.'

'I wonder you didn't see Loren about.'

'The best of it was that I did. Do you know,
I was just getting through what the field had to show
And over the wall and into the road,
When who should come by, with a democrat-load
Of all the young chattering Lorens alive,
But Loren, the fatherly, out for a drive.'

'He saw you, then? What did he do? Did he frown?'

'He just kept nodding his head up and down.
You know how politely he always goes by.
But he thought a big thought—I could tell by his eye—
Which being expressed, might be this in effect:
"I have left those there berries, I shrewdly suspect,
To ripen too long. I am greatly to blame." '

'He's a thriftier person than some I could name.'

'He seems to be thrifty; and hasn't he need,
With the mouths of all those young Lorens to feed?
He has brought them all up on wild berries, they say,
Like birds. They store a great many away.
They eat them the year round, and those they don't eat
They sell in the store and buy shoes for their feet.'

'Who cares what they say? It's a nice way to live,
Just taking what Nature is willing to give,
Not forcing her hand with harrow and plow.'

'I wish you had seen his perpetual bow—
And the air of the youngsters! No one of them turned,
And they looked so solemn-absurdly concerned.'

'I wish I knew half what the flock of them know
Of where all the berries and other things grow,
Cranberries in bogs and raspberries on top
Of the boulder-strewn mountain, and when they will crop.
I met them one day and each had a flower
Stuck into his berries as fresh as a shower;
Some strange kind—they told me it hadn't a name.'

'I've told you how once not long after we came,
I almost provoked poor Loren to mirth
By going to him of all people on earth
To ask if he knew any fruit to be had
For the picking. The rascal, he said he'd be glad
To tell if he knew. But the year had been bad.
There *had* been some berries—but those were all gone.
He didn't say where they had been. He went on:
"I'm sure—I'm sure"—as polite as could be.
He spoke to his wife in the door, "Let me see,
Mame, *we* don't know any good berrying place?"
It was all he could do to keep a straight face.'

'If he thinks all the fruit that grows wild is for him,
He'll find he's mistaken. See here, for a whim,
We'll pick in the Pattersons' pasture this year.
We'll go in the morning, that is, if it's clear,
And the sun shines out warm: the vines must be wet.
It's so long since I picked I almost forget
How we used to pick berries: we took one look round,
Then sank out of sight like trolls underground,
And saw nothing more of each other, or heard,
Unless when you said I was keeping a bird
Away from its nest, and I said it was you.

"Well, one of us is." For complaining it flew
Around and around us. And then for a while
We picked, till I feared you had wandered a mile,
And I thought I had lost you. I lifted a shout
Too loud for the distance you were, it turned out,
For when you made answer, your voice was as low
As talking—you stood up beside me, you know.'

'We sha'n't have the place to ourselves to enjoy—
Not likely, when all the young Lorens deploy.
They'll be there tomorrow, or even tonight.
They won't be too friendly—they may be polite—
To people they look on as having no right
To pick where they're picking. But we won't complain.
You ought to have seen how it looked in the rain,
The fruit mixed with water in layers of leaves,
Like two kinds of jewels, a vision for thieves.'

## A Servant to Servants

I didn't make you know how glad I was
To have you come and camp here on our land.
I promised myself to get down some day
And see the way you lived, but I don't know!
With a houseful of hungry men to feed
I guess you'd find. . . . It seems to me
I can't express my feelings any more
Than I can raise my voice or want to lift
My hand (oh, I can lift it when I have to).
Did ever you feel so? I hope you never.
It's got so I don't even know for sure
Whether I *am* glad, sorry, or anything.
There's nothing but a voice-like left inside
That seems to tell me how I ought to feel,
And would feel if I wasn't all gone wrong.
You take the lake. I look and look at it.
I see it's a fair, pretty sheet of water.
I stand and make myself repeat out loud

The advantages it has, so long and narrow,
Like a deep piece of some old running river
Cut short off at both ends. It lies five miles
Straight away through the mountain notch
From the sink window where I wash the plates,
And all our storms come up toward the house,
Drawing the slow waves whiter and whiter and whiter.
It took my mind off doughnuts and soda biscuit
To step outdoors and take the water dazzle
A sunny morning, or take the rising wind
About my face and body and through my wrapper,
When a storm threatened from the Dragon's Den,
And a cold chill shivered across the lake.
I see it's a fair, pretty sheet of water,
Our Willoughby! How did you hear of it?
I expect, though, everyone's heard of it.
In a book about ferns? Listen to that!
You let things more like feathers regulate
Your going and coming. And you like it here?
I can see how you might. But I don't know!
It would be different if more people came,
For then there would be business. As it is,
The cottages Len built, sometimes we rent them,
Sometimes we don't. We've a good piece of shore
That ought to be worth something, and may yet.
But I don't count on it as much as Len.
He looks on the bright side of everything,
Including me. He thinks I'll be all right
With doctoring. But it's not medicine—
Lowe is the only doctor's dared to say so—
It's rest I want—there, I have said it out—
From cooking meals for hungry hired men
And washing dishes after them—from doing
Things over and over that just won't stay done.
By good rights I ought not to have so much
Put on me, but there seems no other way.
Len says one steady pull more ought to do it.
He says the best way out is always through.
And I agree to that, or in so far
As that I can see no way out but through—

Leastways for me—and then they'll be convinced.
It's not that Len don't want the best for me.
It was his plan our moving over in
Beside the lake from where that day I showed you
We used to live—ten miles from anywhere.
We didn't change without some sacrifice,
But Len went at it to make up the loss.
His work's a man's, of course, from sun to sun,
But he works when he works as hard as I do—
Though there's small profit in comparisons.
(Women and men will make them all the same.)
But work ain't all. Len undertakes too much.
He's into everything in town. This year
It's highways, and he's got too many men
Around him to look after that make waste.
They take advantage of him shamefully,
And proud, too, of themselves for doing so.
We have four here to board, great good-for-nothings,
Sprawling about the kitchen with their talk
While I fry their bacon. Much they care!
No more put out in what they do or say
Than if I wasn't in the room at all.
Coming and going all the time, they are:
I don't learn what their names are, let alone
Their characters, or whether they are safe
To have inside the house with doors unlocked.
I'm not afraid of them, though, if they're not
Afraid of me. There's two can play at that.
I have my fancies: it runs in the family.
My father's brother wasn't right. They kept him
Locked up for years back there at the old farm.
I've been away once—yes, I've been away.
The State Asylum. I was prejudiced;
I wouldn't have sent anyone of mine there;
You know the old idea—the only asylum
Was the poorhouse, and those who could afford,
Rather than send their folks to such a place,
Kept them at home; and it does seem more human.
But it's not so: the place is the asylum.
There they have every means proper to do with,

And you aren't darkening other people's lives—
Worse than no good to them, and they no good
To you in your condition; you can't know
Affection or the want of it in that state.
I've heard too much of the old-fashioned way.
My father's brother, he went mad quite young.
Some thought he had been bitten by a dog,
Because his violence took on the form
Of carrying his pillow in his teeth;
But it's more likely he was crossed in love,
Or so the story goes. It was some girl.
Anyway all he talked about was love.
They soon saw he would do someone a mischief
If he wa'n't kept strict watch of, and it ended
In father's building him a sort of cage,
Or room within a room, of hickory poles,
Like stanchions in the barn, from floor to ceiling,—
A narrow passage all the way around.
Anything they put in for furniture
He'd tear to pieces, even a bed to lie on.
So they made the place comfortable with straw,
Like a beast's stall, to ease their consciences.
Of course they had to feed him without dishes.
They tried to keep him clothed, but he paraded
With his clothes on his arm—all of his clothes.
Cruel—it sounds. I s'pose they did the best
They knew. And just when he was at the height,
Father and mother married, and mother came,
A bride, to help take care of such a creature,
And accommodate her young life to his.
That was what marrying father meant to her.
She had to lie and hear love things made dreadful
By his shouts in the night. He'd shout and shout
Until the strength was shouted out of him,
And his voice died down slowly from exhaustion.
He'd pull his bars apart like bow and bowstring,
And let them go and make them twang until
His hands had worn them smooth as any oxbow.
And then he'd crow as if he thought that child's play—
The only fun he had. I've heard them say, though,

They found a way to put a stop to it.
He was before my time—I never saw him;
But the pen stayed exactly as it was
There in the upper chamber in the ell,
A sort of catch-all full of attic clutter.
I often think of the smooth hickory bars.
It got so I would say—you know, half fooling—
'It's time I took my turn upstairs in jail'—
Just as you will till it becomes a habit.
No wonder I was glad to get away.
Mind you, I waited till Len said the word.
I didn't want the blame if things went wrong.
I was glad though, no end, when we moved out,
And I looked to be happy, and I was,
As I said, for a while—but I don't know!
Somehow the change wore out like a prescription.
And there's more to it than just window-views
And living by a lake. I'm past such help—
Unless Len took the notion, which he won't,
And I won't ask him—it's not sure enough.
I s'pose I've got to go the road I'm going:
Other folks have to, and why shouldn't I?
I almost think if I could do like you,
Drop everything and live out on the ground—
But it might be, come night, I shouldn't like it,
Or a long rain. I should soon get enough,
And be glad of a good roof overhead.
I've lain awake thinking of you, I'll warrant,
More than you have yourself, some of these nights.
The wonder was the tents weren't snatched away
From over you as you lay in your beds.
I haven't courage for a risk like that.
Bless you, of course, you're keeping me from work,
But the thing of it is, I need to *be* kept.
There's work enough to do—there's always that;
But behind's behind. The worst that you can do
Is set me back a little more behind.
I sha'n't catch up in this world, anyway.
I'd *rather* you'd not go unless you must.

## *After Apple-Picking*

My long two-pointed ladder's sticking through a tree
Toward heaven still,
And there's a barrel that I didn't fill
Beside it, and there may be two or three
Apples I didn't pick upon some bough.
But I am done with apple-picking now.
Essence of winter sleep is on the night,
The scent of apples: I am drowsing off.
I cannot rub the strangeness from my sight
I got from looking through a pane of glass
I skimmed this morning from the drinking trough
And held against the world of hoary grass.
It melted, and I let it fall and break.
But I was well
Upon my way to sleep before it fell,
And I could tell
What form my dreaming was about to take.
Magnified apples appear and disappear,
Stem end and blossom end,
And every fleck of russet showing clear.
My instep arch not only keeps the ache,
It keeps the pressure of a ladder-round.
I feel the ladder sway as the boughs bend.
And I keep hearing from the cellar bin
The rumbling sound
Of load on load of apples coming in.
For I have had too much
Of apple-picking: I am overtired
Of the great harvest I myself desired.
There were ten thousand thousand fruit to touch,
Cherish in hand, lift down, and not let fall.
For all
That struck the earth,
No matter if not bruised or spiked with stubble,
Went surely to the cider-apple heap
As of no worth.
One can see what will trouble

This sleep of mine, whatever sleep it is.
Were he not gone,
The woodchuck could say whether it's like his
Long sleep, as I describe its coming on,
Or just some human sleep.


## The Code

There were three in the meadow by the brook
Gathering up windrows, piling cocks of hay,
With an eye always lifted toward the west
Where an irregular sun-bordered cloud
Darkly advanced with a perpetual dagger
Flickering across its bosom. Suddenly
One helper, thrusting pitchfork in the ground,
Marched himself off the field and home. One stayed.
The town-bred farmer failed to understand.

'What is there wrong?'

                          'Something you just now said.'

'What did I say?'

                          'About our taking pains.'

'To cock the hay?—because it's going to shower?
I said that more than half an hour ago.
I said it to myself as much as you.'

'You didn't know. But James is one big fool.
He thought you meant to find fault with his work.
That's what the average farmer would have meant.
James would take time, of course, to chew it over
Before he acted: he's just got round to act.'

'He is a fool if that's the way he takes me.'

'Don't let it bother you. You've found out something.
The hand that knows his business won't be told
To do work better or faster—those two things.
I'm as particular as anyone:
Most likely I'd have served you just the same.
But I know you don't understand our ways.
You were just talking what was in your mind,
What was in all our minds, and you weren't hinting.
Tell you a story of what happened once:
I was up here in Salem at a man's
Named Sanders with a gang of four or five
Doing the haying. No one liked the boss.
He was one of the kind sports call a spider,
All wiry arms and legs that spread out wavy
From a humped body nigh as big's a biscuit.
But work! that man could work, especially
If by so doing he could get more work
Out of his hired help. I'm not denying
He was hard on himself. I couldn't find
That he kept any hours—not for himself.
Daylight and lantern-light were one to him:
I've heard him pounding in the barn all night.
But what he liked was someone to encourage.
Them that he couldn't lead he'd get behind
And drive, the way you can, you know, in mowing—
Keep at their heels and threaten to mow their legs off.
I'd seen about enough of his bulling tricks
(We call that bulling). I'd been watching him.
So when he paired off with me in the hayfield
To load the load, thinks I, Look out for trouble.
I built the load and topped it off; old Sanders
Combed it down with a rake and says, "O.K."
Everything went well till we reached the barn
With a big jag to empty in a bay.
You understand that meant the easy job
For the man up on top of throwing *down*
The hay and rolling it off wholesale,
Where on a mow it would have been slow lifting.
You wouldn't think a fellow'd need much urging
Under those circumstances, would you now?

But the old fool seizes his fork in both hands,
And looking up bewhiskered out of the pit,
Shouts like an army captain, "Let her come!"
Thinks I, D'ye mean it? "What was that you said?"
I asked out loud, so's there'd be no mistake,
"Did you say, Let her come?" "Yes, let her come."
He said it over, but he said it softer.
Never you say a thing like that to a man,
Not if he values what he is. God, I'd as soon
Murdered him as left out his middle name.
I'd built the load and knew right where to find it.
Two or three forkfuls I picked lightly round for
Like meditating, and then I just dug in
And dumped the rackful on him in ten lots.
I looked over the side once in the dust
And caught sight of him treading-water-like,
Keeping his head above. "Damn ye," I says,
"That gets ye!" He squeaked like a squeezed rat.
That was the last I saw or heard of him.
I cleaned the rack and drove out to cool off.
As I sat mopping hayseed from my neck,
And sort of waiting to be asked about it,
One of the boys sings out, "Where's the old man?"
"I left him in the barn under the hay.
If ye want him, ye can go and dig him out."
They realized from the way I swabbed my neck
More than was needed something must be up.
They headed for the barn; I stayed where I was.
They told me afterward. First they forked hay,
A lot of it, out into the barn floor.
Nothing! They listened for him. Not a rustle.
I guess they thought I'd spiked him in the temple
Before I buried him, or I couldn't have managed.
They excavated more. "Go keep his wife
Out of the barn." Someone looked in a window,
And curse me if he wasn't in the kitchen
Slumped way down in a chair, with both his feet
Against the stove, the hottest day that summer.
He looked so clean disgusted from behind
There was no one that dared to stir him up,

Or let him know that he was being looked at.
Apparently I hadn't buried him
(I may have knocked him down); but my just trying
To bury him had hurt his dignity.
He had gone to the house so's not to meet me.
He kept away from us all afternoon.
We tended to his hay. We saw him out
After a while picking peas in his garden:
He couldn't keep away from doing something.'

'Weren't you relieved to find he wasn't dead?'

'No! and yet I don't know—it's hard to say.
I went about to kill him fair enough.'

'You took an awkward way. Did he discharge you?'

'Discharge me? No! He knew I did just right.'


## The Generations of Men

A governor it was proclaimed this time,
When all who would come seeking in New Hampshire
Ancestral memories might come together.
And those of the name Stark gathered in Bow,
A rock-strewn town where farming has fallen off,
And sprout-lands flourish where the ax has gone.
Someone had literally run to earth
In an old cellar hole in a by-road
The origin of all the family there.
Thence they were sprung, so numerous a tribe
That now not all the houses left in town
Made shift to shelter them without the help
Of here and there a tent in grove and orchard.
They were at Bow, but that was not enough:
Nothing would do but they must fix a day
To stand together on the crater's verge

That turned them on the world, and try to fathom
The past and get some strangeness out of it.
But rain spoiled all. The day began uncertain,
With clouds low trailing and moments of rain that misted.
The young folk held some hope out to each other
Till well toward noon when the storm settled down
With a swish in the grass. 'What if the others
Are there,' they said. 'It isn't going to rain.'
Only one from a farm not far away
Strolled thither, not expecting he would find
Anyone else, but out of idleness.
One, and one other, yes, for there were two.
The second round the curving hillside road
Was a girl; and she halted some way off
To reconnoiter, and then made up her mind
At least to pass by and see who he was,
And perhaps hear some word about the weather.
This was some Stark she didn't know. He nodded.
'No fête today,' he said.

                    'It looks that way.'

She swept the heavens, turning on her heel.
'I only idled down.'

                    'I idled down.'

Provision there had been for just such meeting
Of stranger cousins, in a family tree
Drawn on a sort of passport with the branch
Of the one bearing it done in detail—
Some zealous one's laborious device.
She made a sudden movement toward her bodice,
As one who clasps her heart. They laughed together.
'Stark?' he inquired. 'No matter for the proof.'

'Yes, Stark. And you?'

                    'I'm Stark.' He drew his passport.

'You know we might not be and still be cousins:
The town is full of Chases, Lowes, and Baileys,
All claiming some priority in Starkness.
My mother was a Lane, yet might have married
Anyone upon earth and still her children
Would have been Starks, and doubtless here today.'

'You riddle with your genealogy
Like a Viola. I don't follow you.'

'I only mean my mother was a Stark
Several times over, and by marrying father
No more than brought us back into the name.'

'One ought not to be thrown into confusion
By a plain statement of relationship,
But I own what you say makes my head spin.
You take my card—you seem so good at such things—
And see if you can reckon our cousinship.
Why not take seats here on the cellar wall
And dangle feet among the raspberry vines?'

'Under the shelter of the family tree.'

'Just so—that ought to be enough protection.'

'Not from the rain. I think it's going to rain.'

'It's raining.'

         'No, it's misting; let's be fair.
Does the rain seem to you to cool the eyes?'

The situation was like this: the road
Bowed outward on the mountain halfway up,
And disappeared and ended not far off.
No one went home that way. The only house
Beyond where they were was a shattered seedpod.
And below roared a brook hidden in trees,

The sound of which was silence for the place.
This he sat listening to till she gave judgment.

'On father's side, it seems, we're—let me see—'

'Don't be too technical.—You have three cards.'

'Four cards, one yours, three mine, one for each branch
Of the Stark family I'm a member of.'

'D'you know a person so related to herself
Is supposed to be mad.'

                          'I may be mad.'

'You look so, sitting out here in the rain
Studying genealogy with me
You never saw before. What will we come to
With all this pride of ancestry, we Yankees?
I think we're all mad. Tell me why we're here
Drawn into town about this cellar hole
Like wild geese on a lake before a storm?
What do we see in such a hole, I wonder.'

'The Indians had a myth of Chicamoztoc,
Which means The Seven Caves that We Came out of.
This is the pit from which we Starks were digged.'

'You must be learned. That's what you see in it?'

'And what do you see?'

                          'Yes, what *do* I see?
First let me look. I see raspberry vines—'

'Oh, if you're going to use your eyes, just hear
What *I* see. It's a little, little boy,
As pale and dim as a match flame in the sun;
He's groping in the cellar after jam,
He thinks it's dark and it's flooded with daylight.'

'He's nothing. Listen. When I lean like this
I can make out old Grandsir Stark distinctly,—
With his pipe in his mouth and his brown jug—
Bless you, it isn't Grandsir Stark, it's Granny,
But the pipe's there and smoking and the jug.
She's after cider, the old girl, she's thirsty;
Here's hoping she gets her drink and gets out safely.'


'Tell me about her. Does she look like me?'


'She should, shouldn't she, you're so many times
Over descended from her. I believe
She does look like you. Stay the way you are.
The nose is just the same, and so's the chin—
Making allowance, making due allowance.'


'You poor, dear, great, great, great, great Granny!'


'See that you get her greatness right. Don't stint her.'


'Yes, it's important, though you think it isn't.
I won't be teased. But see how wet I am.'


'Yes, you must go; we can't stay here for ever.
But wait until I give you a hand up.
A bead of silver water more or less
Strung on your hair won't hurt your summer looks.
I wanted to try something with the noise
That the brook raises in the empty valley.
We have seen visions—now consult the voices.
Something I must have learned riding in trains
When I was young. I used to use the roar
To set the voices speaking out of it,
Speaking or singing, and the band-music playing.
Perhaps you have the art of what I mean.
I've never listened in among the sounds
That a brook makes in such a wild descent.
It ought to give a purer oracle.'

'It's as you throw a picture on a screen:
The meaning of it all is out of you;
The voices give you what you wish to hear.'

'Strangely, it's anything they wish to give.'

'Then I don't know. It must be strange enough.
I wonder if it's not your make-believe.
What do you think you're like to hear today?'

'From the sense of our having been together—
But why take time for what I'm like to hear?
I'll tell you what the voices really say.
You will do very well right where you are
A little longer. I mustn't feel too hurried,
Or I can't give myself to hear the voices.'

'Is this some trance you are withdrawing into?'

'You must be very still; you mustn't talk.'

'I'll hardly breathe.'

                    'The voices seem to say—'

'I'm waiting.'

            'Don't! The voices seem to say:
Call her Nausicaä, the unafraid
Of an acquaintance made adventurously.'

'I let you say that—on consideration.'

'I don't see very well how you can help it.
You want the truth. I speak but by the voices.
You see they know I haven't had your name,
Though what a name should matter between us—'

'I shall suspect—'

                'Be good. The voices say:
Call her Nausicaä, and take a timber
That you shall find lies in the cellar charred
Among the raspberries, and hew and shape it
For a door-sill or other corner piece
In a new cottage on the ancient spot.
The life is not yet all gone out of it.
And come and make your summer dwelling here,
And perhaps she will come, still unafraid,
And sit before you in the open door
With flowers in her lap until they fade,
But not come in across the sacred sill—'

'I wonder where your oracle is tending.
You can see that there's something wrong with it,
Or it would speak in dialect. Whose voice
Does it purport to speak in? Not old Grandsir's
Nor Granny's, surely. Call up one of them.
They have best right to be heard in this place.'

'You seem so partial to our great-grandmother
(Nine times removed. Correct me if I err.)
You will be likely to regard as sacred
Anything she may say. But let me warn you,
Folks in her day were given to plain speaking.
You think you'd best tempt her at such a time?'

'It rests with us always to cut her off.'

'Well then, it's Granny speaking: "I dunnow!
Mebbe I'm wrong to take it as I do.
There ain't no names quite like the old ones though,
Nor never will be to my way of thinking.
One mustn't bear too hard on the newcomers,
But there's a dite too many of them for comfort.
I should feel easier if I could see
More of the salt wherewith they're to be salted.
Son, you do as you're told! You take the timber—

It's as sound as the day when it was cut—
And begin over—" There, she'd better stop.
You can see what is troubling Granny, though.
But don't you think we sometimes make too much
Of the old stock? What counts is the ideals,
And those will bear some keeping still about.'

'I can see we are going to be good friends.'

'I like your "going to be." You said just now
It's going to rain.'

     'I know, and it was raining.
I let you say all that. But I must go now.'

'You let me say it? on consideration?
How shall we say good-by in such a case?'

'How shall we?'

     'Will you leave the way to me?'

'No, I don't trust your eyes. You've said enough.
Now give me your hand up.—Pick me that flower.'

'Where shall we meet again?'

      'Nowhere but here
Once more before we meet elsewhere.'

        'In rain?'

'It ought to be in rain. Sometime in rain.
In rain tomorrow, shall we, if it rains?
But if we must, in sunshine.' So she went.

## *The Housekeeper*

I let myself in at the kitchen door.

'It's you,' she said. 'I can't get up. Forgive me
Not answering your knock. I can no more
Let people in than I can keep them out.
I'm getting too old for my size, I tell them.
My fingers are about all I've the use of
So's to take any comfort. I can sew:
I help out with this beadwork what I can.'

'That's a smart pair of pumps you're beading there.
Who are they for?'

         'You mean?—oh, for some miss.
I can't keep track of other people's daughters.
Lord, if I were to dream of everyone
Whose shoes I primped to dance in!'

                'And where's John?'

'Haven't you seen him? Strange what set you off
To come to his house when he's gone to yours.
You can't have passed each other. I know what:
He must have changed his mind and gone to Garland's.
He won't be long in that case. You can wait.
Though what good you can be, or anyone—
It's gone so far. You've heard? Estelle's run off.'

'Yes, what's it all about? When did she go?'

'Two weeks since.'

         'She's in earnest, it appears.'

'I'm sure she won't come back. She's hiding somewhere.
I don't know where myself. John thinks I do.
He thinks I only have to say the word,

And she'll come back. But, bless you, I'm her mother—
I can't talk to her, and, Lord, if I could!'

'It will go hard with John. What will he do?
He can't find anyone to take her place.'

Oh, if you ask me that, what *will* he do?
He gets some sort of bakeshop meals together,
With me to sit and tell him everything,
What's wanted and how much and where it is.
But when I'm gone—of course I can't stay here:
Estelle's to take me when she's settled down.
He and I only hinder one another.
I tell them they can't get me through the door, though:
I've been built in here like a big church organ.
We've been here fifteen years.'

                                        'That's a long time
To live together and then pull apart.
How do you see him living when you're gone?
Two of you out will leave an empty house.'

'I don't just see him living many years,
Left here with nothing but the furniture.
I hate to think of the old place when we're gone,
With the brook going by below the yard,
And no one here but hens blowing about.
If he could sell the place, but then, he can't:
No one will ever live on it again.
It's too run down. This is the last of it.
What I think he will do, is let things smash.
He'll sort of swear the time away. He's awful!
I never saw a man let family troubles
Make so much difference in his man's affairs.
He's just dropped everything. He's like a child.
I blame his being brought up by his mother.
He's got hay down that's been rained on three times.
He hoed a little yesterday for me:
I thought the growing things would do him good.
Something went wrong. I saw him throw the hoe

Sky-high with both hands. I can see it now—
Come here—I'll show you—in that apple tree.
That's no way for a man to do at his age:
He's fifty-five, you know, if he's a day.'

'Aren't you afraid of him? What's that gun for?'

'Oh, that's been there for hawks since chicken-time.
John Hall touch me! Not if he knows his friends.
I'll say that for him, John's no threatener
Like some menfolk. No one's afraid of him;
All is, he's made up his mind not to stand
What he has got to stand.'

                              'Where is Estelle?
Couldn't one talk to her? What does she say?
You say you don't know where she is.'

                                        'Nor want to!
She thinks if it was bad to live with him,
It must be right to leave him.'

                              'Which is wrong!'

'Yes, but he should have married her.'

                                        'I know.'

'The strain's been too much for her all these years:
I can't explain it any other way.
It's different with a man, at least with John:
He knows he's kinder than the run of men.
Better than married ought to be as good
As married—that's what he has always said.
I know the way he's felt—but all the same!'

'I wonder why he doesn't marry her
And end it.'

                  'Too late now: she wouldn't have him.

He's given her time to think of something else.
That's his mistake. The dear knows my interest
Has been to keep the thing from breaking up.
This is a good home: I don't ask for better.
But when I've said, "Why shouldn't they be married,"
He'd say, "Why should they?" no more words than that.'

'And after all why should they? John's been fair
I take it. What was his was always hers.
There was no quarrel about property.'

'Reason enough, there was no property.
A friend or two as good as own the farm,
Such as it is. It isn't worth the mortgage.'

'I mean Estelle has always held the purse.'

'The rights of that are harder to get at.
I guess Estelle and I have filled the purse.
'Twas we let him have money, not he us.
John's a bad farmer. I'm not blaming him.
Take it year in, year out, he doesn't make much.
We came here for a home for me, you know,
Estelle to do the housework for the board
Of both of us. But look how it turns out:
She seems to have the housework, and besides
Half of the outdoor work, though as for that,
He'd say she does it more because she likes it.
You see our pretty things are all outdoors.
Our hens and cows and pigs are always better
Than folks like us have any business with.
Farmers around twice as well off as we
Haven't as good. They don't go with the farm.
One thing you can't help liking about John,
He's fond of nice things—too fond, some would say.
But Estelle don't complain: she's like him there.
She wants our hens to be the best there are.
You never saw this room before a show,
Full of lank, shivery, half-drowned birds
In separate coops, having their plumage done.

The smell of the wet feathers in the heat!
You spoke of John's not being safe to stay with.
You don't know what a gentle lot we are:
We wouldn't hurt a hen! You ought to see us
Moving a flock of hens from place to place.
We're not allowed to take them upside down,
All we can hold together by the legs.
Two at a time's the rule, one on each arm,
No matter how far and how many times
We have to go.'

      'You mean that's John's idea.'

'And we live up to it; or I don't know
What childishness he wouldn't give way to.
He manages to keep the upper hand
On his own farm. He's boss. But as to hens:
We fence our flowers in and the hens range.
Nothing's too good for them. We say it pays.
John likes to tell the offers he has had,
Twenty for this cock, twenty-five for that.
He never takes the money. If they're worth
That much to sell, they're worth as much to keep.
Bless you, it's all expense, though. Reach me down
The little tin box on the cupboard shelf,
The upper shelf, the tin box. That's the one.
I'll show you. Here you are.'

      'What's this?'

         'A bill—

For fifty dollars for one Langshang cock—
Receipted. And the cock is in the yard.'

'Not in a glass case, then?'

      'He'd need a tall one:
He can eat off a barrel from the ground.
He's been in a glass case, as you may say,
The Crystal Palace, London. He's imported.

John bought him, and we paid the bill with beads—
Wampum, I call it. Mind, we don't complain.
But you see, don't you, we take care of him.'

'And like it, too. It makes it all the worse.'

'It seems as if. And that's not all: he's helpless
In ways that I can hardly tell you of.
Sometimes he gets possessed to keep accounts
To see where all the money goes so fast.
You know how men will be ridiculous.
But it's just fun the way he gets bedeviled—
If he's untidy now, what will he be—?'

'It makes it all the worse. You must be blind.'

'Estelle's the one. You needn't talk to me.'

'Can't you and I get to the root of it?
What's the real trouble? What will satisfy her?'

'It's as I say: she's turned from him, that's all.'

'But why, when she's well off? Is it the neighbors,
Being cut off from friends?'

                              'We have our friends.
That isn't it. Folks aren't afraid of us.'

'She's let it worry her. You stood the strain,
And you're her mother.'

                              'But I didn't always.
I didn't relish it along at first.
But I got wonted to it. And besides—
John said I was too old to have grandchildren.
But what's the use of talking when it's done?
She won't come back—it's worse than that—she can't.'

'Why do you speak like that? What do you know?
What do you mean?—she's done harm to herself?'

'I mean she's married—married someone else.'

'Oho, oho!'

                    'You don't believe me.'

                                        'Yes, I do,
Only too well. I knew there must be something!
So that was what was back. She's bad, that's all!'

'Bad to get married when she had the chance?'

'Nonsense! See what she's done! But who, but who—'

'Who'd marry her straight out of such a mess?
Say it right out—no matter for her mother.
The man was found. I'd better name no names.
John himself won't imagine who he is.'

'Then it's all up. I think I'll get away.
You'll be expecting John. I pity Estelle;
I suppose she deserves some pity, too.
You ought to have the kitchen to yourself
To break it to him. You may have the job.'

'You needn't think you're going to get away.
John's almost here. I've had my eye on someone
Coming down Ryan's Hill. I thought 'twas him.
Here he is now. This box! Put it away.
And this bill.'

                    'What's the hurry? He'll unhitch.'

'No, he won't, either. He'll just drop the reins
And turn Doll out to pasture, rig and all.
She won't get far before the wheels hang up

On something—there's no harm. See, there he is!
My, but he looks as if he must have heard!'

John threw the door wide but he didn't enter.
'How are you, neighbor? Just the man I'm after.
Isn't it Hell,' he said. 'I want to know.
Come out here if you want to hear me talk.
I'll talk to you, old woman, afterward.
I've got some news that maybe isn't news.
What are they trying to do to me, these two?'

'Do go along with him and stop his shouting.'
She raised her voice against the closing door:
'Who wants to hear your news, you—dreadful fool?'


## The Fear

A lantern light from deeper in the barn
Shone on a man and woman in the door
And threw their lurching shadows on a house
Nearby, all dark in every glossy window.
A horse's hoof pawed once the hollow floor,
And the back of the gig they stood beside
Moved in a little. The man grasped a wheel,
The woman spoke out sharply, 'Whoa, stand still!
I saw it just as plain as a white plate,'
She said, 'as the light on the dashboard ran
Along the bushes at the roadside—a man's face.
You *must* have seen it too.'

                                  'I didn't see it.
Are you sure—'

                    'Yes, I'm sure!'

                                      '—it was a face?'

'Joel, I'll have to look. I can't go in,
I can't, and leave a thing like that unsettled.

Doors locked and curtains drawn will make no difference.
I always have felt strange when we came home
To the dark house after so long an absence,
And the key rattled loudly into place
Seemed to warn someone to be getting out
At one door as we entered at another.
What if I'm right, and someone all the time—
Don't hold my arm!'

        'I say it's someone passing.'

'You speak as if this were a traveled road.
You forget where we are. What is beyond
That he'd be going to or coming from
At such an hour of night, and on foot too?
What was he standing still for in the bushes?'

'It's not so very late—it's only dark.
There's more in it than you're inclined to say.
Did he look like—?'

        'He looked like anyone.
I'll never rest tonight unless I know.
Give me the lantern.'

        'You don't want the lantern.'

She pushed past him and got it for herself.

'You're not to come,' she said. 'This is my business.
If the time's come to face it, I'm the one
To put it the right way. He'd never dare—
Listen! He kicked a stone. Hear that, hear that!
He's coming towards us. Joel, *go* in—please.
Hark!—I don't hear him now. But please go in.'

'In the first place you can't make me believe it's—'

'It is—or someone else he's sent to watch.
And now's the time to have it out with him

While we know definitely where he is.
Let him get off and he'll be everywhere
Around us, looking out of trees and bushes
Till I sha'n't dare to set a foot outdoors.
And I can't stand it. Joel, let me go!'

'But it's nonsense to think he'd care enough.'

'You mean you couldn't understand his caring.
Oh, but you see he hadn't had enough—
Joel, I won't—I won't—I promise you.
We mustn't say hard things. You mustn't either.'

'I'll be the one, if anybody goes!
But you give him the advantage with this light.
What couldn't he do to us standing here!
And if to see was what he wanted, why,
He has seen all there was to see and gone.'

He appeared to forget to keep his hold,
But advanced with her as she crossed the grass.

'What do you want?' she cried to all the dark.
She stretched up tall to overlook the light
That hung in both hands hot against her skirt.

'There's no one; so you're wrong,' he said.

                                    'There is.—
What do you want?' she cried, and then herself
Was startled when an answer really came.

'Nothing.' It came from well along the road.

She reached a hand to Joel for support:
The smell of scorching woolen made her faint.
'What are you doing round this house at night?'

'Nothing.' A pause: there seemed no more to say.

And then the voice again: 'You seem afraid.
I saw by the way you whipped up the horse.
I'll just come forward in the lantern light
And let you see.'

    'Yes, do.—Joel, go back!'

She stood her ground against the noisy steps
That came on, but her body rocked a little.

'You see,' the voice said.

      'Oh.' She looked and looked.

'You don't see—I've a child here by the hand.
A robber wouldn't have his family with him.'

'What's a child doing at this time of night—?'

'Out walking. Every child should have the memory
Of at least one long-after-bedtime walk.
What, son?'

'Then I should think you'd try to find
Somewhere to walk—'

     'The highway, as it happens—
We're stopping for the fortnight down at Dean's.'

'But if that's all—Joel—you realize—
You won't think anything. You understand?
You understand that we have to be careful.
This is a very, very lonely place.
Joel!' She spoke as if she couldn't turn.
The swinging lantern lengthened to the ground,
It touched, it struck, it clattered and went out.

## The Self-Seeker

'Willis, I didn't want you here today:
The lawyer's coming for the company.
I'm going to sell my soul, or, rather, feet.
Five hundred dollars for the pair, you know.'

'With you the feet have nearly been the soul;
And if you're going to sell them to the devil,
I want to see you do it. When's he coming?'

'I half suspect you knew, and came on purpose
To try to help me drive a better bargain.'

'Well, if it's true! Yours are no common feet.
The lawyer don't know what it is he's buying:
So many miles you might have walked you won't walk.
You haven't run your forty orchids down.
What does he think?—How *are* the blessed feet?
The doctor's sure you're going to walk again?'

'He thinks I'll hobble. It's both legs and feet.'

'They must be terrible—I mean to look at.'

'I haven't dared to look at them uncovered.
Through the bed blankets I remind myself
Of a starfish laid out with rigid points.'

'The wonder is it hadn't been your head.'

'It's hard to tell you how I managed it.
When I saw the shaft had me by the coat,
I didn't try too long to pull away,
Or fumble for my knife to cut away,
I just embraced the shaft and rode it out—
Till Weiss shut off the water in the wheel-pit.
That's how I think I didn't lose my head.
But my legs got their knocks against the ceiling.'

'Awful. Why didn't they throw off the belt
Instead of going clear down in the wheel-pit?'

'They say some time was wasted on the belt—
Old streak of leather—doesn't love me much
Because I make him spit fire at my knuckles,
The way Ben Franklin used to make the kite-string.
That must be it. Some days he won't stay on.
That day a woman couldn't coax him off.
He's on his rounds now with his tail in his mouth
Snatched right and left across the silver pulleys.
Everything goes the same without me there.
You can hear the small buzz saws whine, the big saw
Caterwaul to the hills around the village
As they both bite the wood. It's all our music.
One ought as a good villager to like it.
No doubt it has a sort of prosperous sound,
And it's our life.'

                'Yes, when it's not our death.'

'You make that sound as if it wasn't so
With everything. What we live by we die by.
I wonder where my lawyer is. His train's in.
I want this over with; I'm hot and tired.'

'You're getting ready to do something foolish.'

'Watch for him, will you, Will? You let him in.
I'd rather Mrs. Corbin didn't know;
I've boarded here so long, she thinks she owns me.
You're bad enough to manage without her.'

'I'm going to be worse instead of better.
You've got to tell me how far this is gone:
Have you agreed to any price?'

'Five hundred.
Five hundred—five—five! One, two, three, four, five.
You needn't look at me.'

'I don't believe you.'

'I told you, Willis, when you first came in.
Don't you be hard on me. I have to take
What I can get. You see they have the feet,
Which gives them the advantage in the trade.
I can't get back the feet in any case.'

'But your flowers, man, you're selling out your flowers.'

'Yes, that's one way to put it—all the flowers
Of every kind everywhere in this region
For the next forty summers—call it forty.
But I'm not selling those, I'm giving them,
They never earned me so much as one cent:
Money can't pay me for the loss of them.
No, the five hundred was the sum they named
To pay the doctor's bill and tide me over.
It's that or fight, and I don't want to fight—
I just want to get settled in my life,
Such as it's going to be, and know the worst,
Or best—it may not be so bad. The firm
Promise me all the shooks I want to nail.'

'But what about your flora of the valley?'

'You have me there. But that—you didn't think
That was worth money to me? Still I own
It goes against me not to finish it
For the friends it might bring me. By the way,
I had a letter from Burroughs—did I tell you?—
About my *Cyprepedium reginæ*;
He says it's not reported so far north.
There! there's the bell. He's rung. But you go down
And bring him up, and don't let Mrs. Corbin.—
Oh, well, we'll soon be through with it. I'm tired.'

Willis brought up besides the Boston lawyer
A little barefoot girl who in the noise
Of heavy footsteps in the old frame house,
And baritone importance of the lawyer,
Stood for a while unnoticed with her hands
Shyly behind her.

     'Well, and how is Mister—'

The lawyer was already in his satchel
As if for papers that might bear the name
He hadn't at command. 'You must excuse me,
I dropped in at the mill and was detained.'

'Looking round, I suppose,' said Willis.

         'Yes,
Well, yes.'

   'Hear anything that might prove useful?'

The Broken One saw Anne. 'Why, here is Anne.
What do you want, dear? Come, stand by the bed;
Tell me what is it?' Anne just wagged her dress
With both hands held behind her. 'Guess,' she said.

'Oh, guess which hand? My, my! Once on a time
I knew a lovely way to tell for certain
By looking in the ears. But I forget it.
Er, let me see. I think I'll take the right.
That's sure to be right even if it's wrong.
Come, hold it out. Don't change.—A Ram's Horn orchid!
A Ram's Horn! What would I have got, I wonder,
If I had chosen left. Hold out the left.
Another Ram's Horn! Where did you find those,
Under what beech tree, on what woodchuck's knoll?'

Anne looked at the large lawyer at her side,
And thought she wouldn't venture on so much.

'Were there no others?'

                    'There were four or five.
I knew you wouldn't let me pick them all.'

'I wouldn't—so I wouldn't. You're the girl!
You see Anne has her lesson learned by heart.'

'I wanted there should be some there next year.'

'Of course you did. You left the rest for seed,
And for the backwoods woodchuck. You're the girl!
A Ram's Horn orchid seedpod for a woodchuck
Sounds something like. Better than farmer's beans
To a discriminating appetite,
Though the Ram's Horn is seldom to be had
In bushel lots—doesn't come on the market.
But, Anne, I'm troubled; have you told me all?
You're hiding something. That's as bad as lying.
You ask this lawyer man. And it's not safe
With a lawyer at hand to find you out.
Nothing is hidden from some people, Anne.
You don't tell me that where you found a Ram's Horn
You didn't find a Yellow Lady's Slipper.
What did I tell you? What? I'd blush, I would.
Don't you defend yourself. If it was there,
Where is it now, the Yellow Lady's Slipper?'

'Well, wait—it's common—it's too *common*.'

                              'Common?
The Purple Lady's Slipper's commoner.'

'I didn't bring a Purple Lady's Slipper.
To *You*—to you I mean—they're both too common.'

The lawyer gave a laugh among his papers
As if with some idea that she had scored.

'I've broken Anne of gathering bouquets.
It's not fair to the child. It can't be helped though:
Pressed into service means pressed out of shape.
Somehow I'll make it right with her—she'll see.
She's going to do my scouting in the field,
Over stone walls and all along a wood
And by a river bank for water flowers,
The floating Heart, with small leaf like a heart,
And at the *sinus* under water a fist
Of little fingers all kept down but one,
And that thrust up to blossom in the sun
As if to say, "You! You're the Heart's desire."
Anne has a way with flowers to take the place
Of what she's lost: she goes down on one knee
And lifts their faces by the chin to hers
And says their names, and leaves them where they are.'

The lawyer wore a watch the case of which
Was cunningly devised to make a noise
Like a small pistol when he snapped it shut
At such a time as this. He snapped it now.

'Well, Anne, go, dearie. Our affair will wait.
The lawyer man is thinking of his train.
He wants to give me lots and lots of money
Before he goes, because I hurt myself,
And it may take him I don't know how long.
But put our flowers in water first. Will, help her:
The pitcher's too full for her. There's no cup?
Just hook them on the inside of the pitcher.
Now run.—Get out your documents! You see
I have to keep on the good side of Anne.
I'm a great boy to think of number one.
And you can't blame me in the place I'm in.
Who will take care of my necessities
Unless I do?'

                    'A pretty interlude,'
The lawyer said. 'I'm sorry, but my train—
Luckily terms are all agreed upon.
You only have to sign your name. Right—there.'

'You, Will, stop making faces. Come round here
Where you can't make them. What is it you want?
I'll put you out with Anne. Be good or go.'

'You don't mean you will sign that thing unread?'

'Make yourself useful then, and read it for me.
Isn't it something I have seen before?'

'You'll find it is. Let your friend look at it.'

'Yes, but all that takes time, and I'm as much
In haste to get it over with as you.
But read it, read it. That's right, draw the curtain:
Half the time I don't know what's troubling me.—
What do you say, Will? Don't you be a fool,
You, crumpling folks's legal documents.
Out with it if you've any real objection.'

'Five hundred dollars!'

                              'What would you think right?'

'A thousand wouldn't be a cent too much;
You know it, Mr. Lawyer. The sin is
Accepting anything before he knows
Whether he's ever going to walk again.
It smells to me like a dishonest trick.'

'I think—I think—from what I heard today—
And saw myself—he would be ill-advised—'

'What did you hear, for instance?' Willis said.

'Now the place where the accident occurred—'

The Broken One was twisted in his bed.
'This is between you two apparently.
Where I come in is what I want to know.
You stand up to it like a pair of cocks.

Go outdoors if you want to fight. Spare me.
When you come back, I'll have the papers signed.
Will pencil do? Then, please, your fountain pen.
One of you hold my head up from the pillow.'

Willis flung off the bed. 'I wash my hands—
I'm no match—no, and don't pretend to be—'

The lawyer gravely capped his fountain pen.
'You're doing the wise thing: you won't regret it.
We're very sorry for you.'

                              Willis sneered:
'Who's *we?*—some stockholders in Boston?
I'll go outdoors, by gad, and won't come back.'

'Willis, bring Anne back with you when you come.
Yes. Thanks for caring. Don't mind Will: he's savage.
He thinks you ought to pay me for my flowers.
You don't know what I mean about the flowers.
Don't stop to try to now. You'll miss your train.
Good-by.' He flung his arms around his face.


## The Wood-Pile

Out walking in the frozen swamp one gray day,
I paused and said, 'I will turn back from here.
No, I will go on farther—and we shall see.'
The hard snow held me, save where now and then
One foot went through. The view was all in lines
Straight up and down of tall slim trees
Too much alike to mark or name a place by
So as to say for certain I was here
Or somewhere else: I was just far from home.
A small bird flew before me. He was careful
To put a tree between us when he lighted,
And say no word to tell me who he was
Who was so foolish as to think what *he* thought.

He thought that I was after him for a feather—
The white one in his tail; like one who takes
Everything said as personal to himself.
One flight out sideways would have undeceived him.
And then there was a pile of wood for which
I forgot him and let his little fear
Carry him off the way I might have gone,
Without so much as wishing him good-night.
He went behind it to make his last stand.
It was a cord of maple, cut and split
And piled—and measured, four by four by eight.
And not another like it could I see.
No runner tracks in this year's snow looped near it.
And it was older sure than this year's cutting,
Or even last year's or the year's before.
The wood was gray and the bark warping off it
And the pile somewhat sunken. Clematis
Had wound strings round and round it like a bundle.
What held it though on one side was a tree
Still growing, and on one a stake and prop,
These latter about to fall. I thought that only
Someone who lived in turning to fresh tasks
Could so forget his handiwork on which
He spent himself, the labor of his ax,
And leave it there far from a useful fireplace
To warm the frozen swamp as best it could
With the slow smokeless burning of decay.

## Good Hours

I had for my winter evening walk—
No one at all with whom to talk,
But I had the cottages in a row
Up to their shining eyes in snow.

And I thought I had the folk within:
I had the sound of a violin;
I had a glimpse through curtain laces
Of youthful forms and youthful faces.

I had such company outward bound.
I went till there were no cottages found.
I turned and repented, but coming back
I saw no window but that was black.

Over the snow my creaking feet
Disturbed the slumbering village street
Like profanation, by your leave,
At ten o'clock of a winter eve.

# MOUNTAIN INTERVAL

## The Road Not Taken

Two roads diverged in a yellow wood,
And sorry I could not travel both
And be one traveler, long I stood
And looked down one as far as I could
To where it bent in the undergrowth;

Then took the other, as just as fair,
And having perhaps the better claim,
Because it was grassy and wanted wear;
Though as for that the passing there
Had worn them really about the same,

And both that morning equally lay
In leaves no step had trodden black.
Oh, I kept the first for another day!
Yet knowing how way leads on to way,
I doubted if I should ever come back.

I shall be telling this with a sigh
Somewhere ages and ages hence:
Two roads diverged in a wood, and I—
I took the one less traveled by,
And that has made all the difference.

## Christmas Trees

### A Christmas Circular Letter

The city had withdrawn into itself
And left at last the country to the country;
When between whirls of snow not come to lie

And whirls of foliage not yet laid, there drove
A stranger to our yard, who looked the city,
Yet did in country fashion in that there
He sat and waited till he drew us out
A-buttoning coats to ask him who he was.
He proved to be the city come again
To look for something it had left behind
And could not do without and keep its Christmas.
He asked if I would sell my Christmas trees;
My woods—the young fir balsams like a place
Where houses all are churches and have spires.
I hadn't thought of them as Christmas trees.
I doubt if I was tempted for a moment
To sell them off their feet to go in cars
And leave the slope behind the house all bare,
Where the sun shines now no warmer than the moon.
I'd hate to have them know it if I was.
Yet more I'd hate to hold my trees except
As others hold theirs or refuse for them,
Beyond the time of profitable growth,
The trial by market everything must come to.
I dallied so much with the thought of selling.
Then whether from mistaken courtesy
And fear of seeming short of speech, or whether
From hope of hearing good of what was mine,
I said, 'There aren't enough to be worth while.'

'I could soon tell how many they would cut,
You let me look them over.'

                              'You could look.
But don't expect I'm going to let you have them.'
Pasture they spring in, some in clumps too close
That lop each other of boughs, but not a few
Quite solitary and having equal boughs
All round and round. The latter he nodded 'Yes' to,
Or paused to say beneath some lovelier one,
With a buyer's moderation, 'That would do.'
I thought so too, but wasn't there to say so.

We climbed the pasture on the south, crossed over,
And came down on the north.

                              He said, 'A thousand.'

'A thousand Christmas trees!—at what apiece?'

He felt some need of softening that to me:
'A thousand trees would come to thirty dollars.'

Then I was certain I had never meant
To let him have them. Never show surprise!
But thirty dollars seemed so small beside
The extent of pasture I should strip, three cents
(For that was all they figured out apiece),
Three cents so small beside the dollar friends
I should be writing to within the hour
Would pay in cities for good trees like those,
Regular vestry trees whole Sunday Schools
Could hang enough on to pick off enough.
A thousand Christmas trees I didn't know I had!
Worth three cents more to give away than sell
As may be shown by a simple calculation.
Too bad I couldn't lay one in a letter.
I can't help wishing I could send you one
In wishing you herewith a Merry Christmas.


## An Old Man's Winter Night

All out-of-doors looked darkly in at him
Through the thin frost, almost in separate stars,
That gathers on the pane in empty rooms.
What kept his eyes from giving back the gaze
Was the lamp tilted near them in his hand.
What kept him from remembering what it was
That brought him to that creaking room was age.
He stood with barrels round him—at a loss.
And having scared the cellar under him

In clomping here, he scared it once again
In clomping off;—and scared the outer night,
Which has its sounds, familiar, like the roar
Of trees and crack of branches, common things,
But nothing so like beating on a box.
A light he was to no one but himself
Where now he sat, concerned with he knew what,
A quiet light, and then not even that.
He consigned to the moon, such as she was,
So late-arising, to the broken moon
As better than the sun in any case
For such a charge, his snow upon the roof,
His icicles along the wall to keep;
And slept. The log that shifted with a jolt
Once in the stove, disturbed him and he shifted,
And eased his heavy breathing, but still slept.
One aged man—one man—can't keep a house,
A farm, a countryside, or if he can,
It's thus he does it of a winter night.


## The Exposed Nest

You were forever finding some new play.
So when I saw you down on hands and knees
In the meadow, busy with the new-cut hay,
Trying, I thought, to set it up on end,
I went to show you how to make it stay,
If that was your idea, against the breeze,
And, if you asked me, even help pretend
To make it root again and grow afresh.
But 'twas no make-believe with you today,
Nor was the grass itself your real concern,
Though I found your hand full of wilted fern,
Steel-bright June-grass, and blackening heads of clover.
'Twas a nest full of young birds on the ground
The cutter-bar had just gone champing over
(Miraculously without tasting flesh)
And left defenseless to the heat and light.

You wanted to restore them to their right
Of something interposed between their sight
And too much world at once—could means be found.
The way the nest-full every time we stirred
Stood up to us as to a mother-bird
Whose coming home has been too long deferred,
Made me ask would the mother-bird return
And care for them in such a change of scene
And might our meddling make her more afraid.
That was a thing we could not wait to learn.
We saw the risk we took in doing good,
But dared not spare to do the best we could
Though harm should come of it; so built the screen
You had begun, and gave them back their shade.
All this to prove we cared. Why is there then
No more to tell? We turned to other things.
I haven't any memory—have you?—
Of ever coming to the place again
To see if the birds lived the first night through,
And so at last to learn to use their wings.


## A Patch of Old Snow

There's a patch of old snow in a corner
 That I should have guessed
Was a blow-away paper the rain
 Had brought to rest.

It is speckled with grime as if
 Small print overspread it,
The news of a day I've forgotten—
 If I ever read it.

## *In the Home Stretch*

She stood against the kitchen sink, and looked
Over the sink out through a dusty window
At weeds the water from the sink made tall.
She wore her cape; her hat was in her hand.
Behind her was confusion in the room,
Of chairs turned upside down to sit like people
In other chairs, and something, come to look,
For every room a house has—parlor, bedroom,
And dining room—thrown pell-mell in the kitchen.
And now and then a smudged, infernal face
Looked in a door behind her and addressed
Her back. She always answered without turning.

'Where will I put this walnut bureau, lady?'

'Put it on top of something that's on top
Of something else,' she laughed. 'Oh, put it where
You can tonight, and go. It's almost dark;
You must be getting started back to town.'

Another blackened face thrust in and looked
And smiled, and when she did not turn, spoke gently,
'What are you seeing out the window, *lady?*'

'Never was I beladied so before.
Would evidence of having been called lady
More than so many times make me a lady
In common law, I wonder.'

                              'But I ask,
What are you seeing out the window, lady?'

'What I'll be seeing more of in the years
To come as here I stand and go the round
Of many plates with towels many times.'

'And what is that? You only put me off.'

'Rank weeds that love the water from the dishpan
More than some women like the dishpan, Joe;

A little stretch of mowing-field for you;
Not much of that until I come to woods
That end all. And it's scarce enough to call
A view.'

          'And yet you think you like it, dear?'

'That's what you're so concerned to know! You hope
I like it. Bang goes something big away
Off there upstairs. The very tread of men
As great as those is shattering to the frame
Of such a little house. Once left alone,
You and I, dear, will go with softer steps
Up and down stairs and through the rooms, and none
But sudden winds that snatch them from our hands
Will ever slam the doors.'

                              'I think you see
More than you like to own to out that window.'

'No; for besides the things I tell you of,
I only see the years. They come and go
In alternation with the weeds, the field,
The wood.'

          'What kind of years?'

                              'Why, latter years—
Different from early years.'

                              'I see them, too.
You didn't count them?'

                              'No, the further off
So ran together that I didn't try to.
It can scarce be that they would be in number
We'd care to know, for we are not young now.
And bang goes something else away off there.
It sounds as if it were the men went down,
And every crash meant one less to return
To lighted city streets we, too, have known,
But now are giving up for country darkness.'

'Come from that window where you see too much,
And take a livelier view of things from here.
They're going. Watch this husky swarming up
Over the wheel into the sky-high seat,
Lighting his pipe now, squinting down his nose
At the flame burning downward as he sucks it.'

'See how it makes his nose-side bright, a proof
How dark it's getting. Can you tell what time
It is by that? Or by the moon? The new moon!
What shoulder did I see her over? Neither.
A wire she is of silver, as new as we
To everything. Her light won't last us long.
It's something, though, to know we're going to have her
Night after night and stronger every night
To see us through our first two weeks. But, Joe,
The stove! Before they go! Knock on the window;
Ask them to help you get it on its feet.
We stand here dreaming. Hurry! Call them back!'

'They're not gone yet.'

                              'We've got to have the stove,
Whatever else we want for. And a light.
Have we a piece of candle if the lamp
And oil are buried out of reach?'

                              Again
The house was full of tramping, and the dark,
Door-filling men burst in and seized the stove.
A cannon-mouth-like hole was in the wall,
To which they set it true by eye; and then
Came up the jointed stovepipe in their hands,
So much too light and airy for their strength
It almost seemed to come ballooning up,
Slipping from clumsy clutches toward the ceiling.
'A fit!' said one, and banged a stovepipe shoulder.
'It's good luck when you move in to begin
With good luck with your stovepipe. Never mind,
It's not so bad in the country, settled down,

When people're getting on in life. You'll like it.'
Joe said: 'You big boys ought to find a farm,
And make good farmers, and leave other fellows
The city work to do. There's not enough
For everybody as it is in there.'
'God!' one said wildly, and, when no one spoke:
'Say that to Jimmy here. He needs a farm.'
But Jimmy only made his jaw recede
Fool-like, and rolled his eyes as if to say
He saw himself a farmer. Then there was a French boy
Who said with seriousness that made them laugh,
'Ma friend, you ain't know what it is you're ask.'
He doffed his cap and held it with both hands
Across his chest to make as 'twere a bow:
'We're giving you our chances on de farm.'
And then they all turned to with deafening boots
And put each other bodily out of the house.
'Good-by to them! We puzzle them. They think—
I don't know what they think we see in what
They leave us to: that pasture slope that seems
The back some farm presents us; and your woods
To northward from your window at the sink,
Waiting to steal a step on us whenever
We drop our eyes or turn to other things,
As in the game "Ten-step" the children play.'

'Good boys they seemed, and let them love the city.
All they could say was "God!" when you proposed
Their coming out and making useful farmers.'

'Did they make something lonesome go through you?
It would take more than them to sicken you—
Us of our bargain. But they left us so
As to our fate, like fools past reasoning with.
They almost shook *me*.'

                              'It's all so much
What we have always wanted, I confess
It's seeming bad for a moment makes it seem
Even worse still, and so on down, down, down.

It's nothing; it's their leaving us at dusk.
I never bore it well when people went.
The first night after guests have gone, the house
Seems haunted or exposed. I always take
A personal interest in the locking up
At bedtime; but the strangeness soon wears off.'
He fetched a dingy lantern from behind
A door. 'There's that we didn't lose! And these!'—
Some matches he unpocketed. 'For food—
The meals we've had no one can take from us.
I wish that everything on earth were just
As certain as the meals we've had. I wish
The meals we haven't had were, anyway.
What have you you know where to lay your hands on?'

'The bread we bought in passing at the store.
There's butter somewhere, too.'

                              'Let's rend the bread.
I'll light the fire for company for you;
You'll not have any other company
Till Ed begins to get out on a Sunday
To look us over and give us his idea
Of what wants pruning, shingling, breaking up.
He'll know what he would do if he were we,
And all at once. He'll plan for us and plan
To help us, but he'll take it out in planning.
Well, you can set the table with the loaf.
Let's see you find your loaf. I'll light the fire.
I like chairs occupying other chairs
Not offering a lady—'

                    'There again, Joe!
*You're tired.*'

                    'I'm drunk-nonsensical tired out;
Don't mind a word I say. It's a day's work
To empty one house of all household goods
And fill another with 'em fifteen miles away,
Although you do no more than dump them down.'

'Dumped down in paradise we are and happy.'

'It's all so much what I have always wanted,
I can't believe it's what you wanted, too.'

'Shouldn't you like to know?'

                          'I'd like to know
If it is what you wanted, then how much
You wanted it for me.'

                          'A troubled conscience!
You don't want me to tell if *I* don't know.'

'I don't want to find out what can't be known.
But who first said the word to come?'

                          'My dear,
It's who first thought the thought. You're searching, Joe,
For things that don't exist; I mean beginnings.
Ends and beginnings—there are no such things.
There are only middles.'

                    'What is this?'

                              'This life?
Our sitting here by lantern-light together
Amid the wreckage of a former home?
You won't deny the lantern isn't new.
The stove is not, and you are not to me,
Nor I to you.'

                    'Perhaps you never were?'

'It would take me forever to recite
All that's not new in where we find ourselves.
New is a word for fools in towns who think
Style upon style in dress and thought at last
Must get somewhere. I've heard you say as much.
No, this is no beginning.'

                          'Then an end?'

'End is a gloomy word.'

              'Is it too late
To drag you out for just a good-night call
On the old peach trees on the knoll to grope
By starlight in the grass for a last peach
The neighbors may not have taken as their right
When the house wasn't lived in? I've been looking:
I doubt if they have left us many grapes.
Before we set ourselves to right the house,
The first thing in the morning, out we go
To go the round of apple, cherry, peach,
Pine, alder, pasture, mowing, well, and brook.
All of a farm it is.'

              'I know this much:
I'm going to put you in your bed, if first
I have to make you build it. Come, the light.'

When there was no more lantern in the kitchen,
The fire got out through crannies in the stove
And danced in yellow wrigglers on the ceiling,
As much at home as if they'd always danced there.


## The Telephone

'When I was just as far as I could walk
From here today,
There was an hour
All still
When leaning with my head against a flower
I heard you talk.
Don't say I didn't, for I heard you say—
You spoke from that flower on the window sill—
Do you remember what it was you said?'

'First tell me what it was you thought you heard.'

'Having found the flower and driven a bee away,
I leaned my head,
And holding by the stalk,

I listened and I thought I caught the word—
What was it? Did you call me by my name?
Or did you say—
*Someone* said "Come"—I heard it as I bowed.'

'I may have thought as much, but not aloud.'

'Well, so I came.'


## Meeting and Passing

As I went down the hill along the wall
There was a gate I had leaned at for the view
And had just turned from when I first saw you
As you came up the hill. We met. But all
We did that day was mingle great and small
Footprints in summer dust as if we drew
The figure of our being less than two
But more than one as yet. Your parasol
Pointed the decimal off with one deep thrust.
And all the time we talked you seemed to see
Something down there to smile at in the dust.
(Oh, it was without prejudice to me!)
Afterward I went past what you had passed
Before we met and you what I had passed.


## Hyla Brook

By June our brook's run out of song and speed.
Sought for much after that, it will be found
Either to have gone groping underground
(And taken with it all the Hyla breed
That shouted in the mist a month ago,
Like ghost of sleigh-bells in a ghost of snow)—
Or flourished and come up in jewel-weed,
Weak foliage that is blown upon and bent

Even against the way its waters went.
Its bed is left a faded paper sheet
Of dead leaves stuck together by the heat—
A brook to none but who remember long.
This as it will be seen is other far
Than with brooks taken otherwhere in song.
We love the things we love for what they are.

## The Oven Bird

There is a singer everyone has heard,
Loud, a mid-summer and a mid-wood bird,
Who makes the solid tree trunks sound again.
He says that leaves are old and that for flowers
Mid-summer is to spring as one to ten.
He says the early petal-fall is past
When pear and cherry bloom went down in showers
On sunny days a moment overcast;
And comes that other fall we name the fall.
He says the highway dust is over all.
The bird would cease and be as other birds
But that he knows in singing not to sing.
The question that he frames in all but words
Is what to make of a diminished thing.

## Bond and Free

Love has earth to which she clings
With hills and circling arms about—
Wall within wall to shut fear out.
But Thought has need of no such things,
For Thought has a pair of dauntless wings.

On snow and sand and turf, I see
Where Love has left a printed trace
With straining in the world's embrace.

And such is Love and glad to be.
But Thought has shaken his ankles free.

Thought cleaves the interstellar gloom
And sits in Sirius' disc all night,
Till day makes him retrace his flight,
With smell of burning on every plume,
Back past the sun to an earthly room.

His gains in heaven are what they are.
Yet some say Love by being thrall
And simply staying possesses all
In several beauty that Thought fares far
To find fused in another star.

## Birches

When I see birches bend to left and right
Across the lines of straighter darker trees,
I like to think some boy's been swinging them.
But swinging doesn't bend them down to stay
As ice-storms do. Often you must have seen them
Loaded with ice a sunny winter morning
After a rain. They click upon themselves
As the breeze rises, and turn many-colored
As the stir cracks and crazes their enamel.
Soon the sun's warmth makes them shed crystal shells
Shattering and avalanching on the snow-crust—
Such heaps of broken glass to sweep away
You'd think the inner dome of heaven had fallen.
They are dragged to the withered bracken by the load,
And they seem not to break; though once they are bowed
So low for long, they never right themselves:
You may see their trunks arching in the woods
Years afterwards, trailing their leaves on the ground
Like girls on hands and knees that throw their hair
Before them over their heads to dry in the sun.

But I was going to say when Truth broke in
With all her matter-of-fact about the ice-storm
I should prefer to have some boy bend them
As he went out and in to fetch the cows—
Some boy too far from town to learn baseball,
Whose only play was what he found himself,
Summer or winter, and could play alone.
One by one he subdued his father's trees
By riding them down over and over again
Until he took the stiffness out of them,
And not one but hung limp, not one was left
For him to conquer. He learned all there was
To learn about not launching out too soon
And so not carrying the tree away
Clear to the ground. He always kept his poise
To the top branches, climbing carefully
With the same pains you use to fill a cup
Up to the brim, and even above the brim.
Then he flung outward, feet first, with a swish,
Kicking his way down through the air to the ground.
So was I once myself a swinger of birches.
And so I dream of going back to be.
It's when I'm weary of considerations,
And life is too much like a pathless wood
Where your face burns and tickles with the cobwebs
Broken across it, and one eye is weeping
From a twig's having lashed across it open.
I'd like to get away from earth awhile
And then come back to it and begin over.
May no fate willfully misunderstand me
And half grant what I wish and snatch me away
Not to return. Earth's the right place for love:
I don't know where it's likely to go better.
I'd like to go by climbing a birch tree,
And climb black branches up a snow-white trunk
*Toward* heaven, till the tree could bear no more,
But dipped its top and set me down again.
That would be good both going and coming back.
One could do worse than be a swinger of birches.

## Pea Brush

I walked down alone Sunday after church
　To the place where John has been cutting trees
To see for myself about the birch
　He said I could have to bush my peas.

The sun in the new-cut narrow gap
　Was hot enough for the first of May,
And stifling hot with the odor of sap
　From stumps still bleeding their life away.

The frogs that were peeping a thousand shrill
　Wherever the ground was low and wet,
The minute they heard my step went still
　To watch me and see what I came to get.

Birch boughs enough piled everywhere!—
　All fresh and sound from the recent ax.
Time someone came with cart and pair
　And got them off the wild flowers' backs.

They might be good for garden things
　To curl a little finger round,
The same as you seize cat's-cradle strings,
　And lift themselves up off the ground.

Small good to anything growing wild,
　They were crooking many a trillium
That had budded before the boughs were piled
　And since it was coming up had to come.

## Putting in the Seed

You come to fetch me from my work tonight
When supper's on the table, and we'll see
If I can leave off burying the white
Soft petals fallen from the apple tree
(Soft petals, yes, but not so barren quite,
Mingled with these, smooth bean and wrinkled pea;)
And go along with you ere you lose sight
Of what you came for and become like me,
Slave to a springtime passion for the earth.
How Love burns through the Putting in the Seed
On through the watching for that early birth
When, just as the soil tarnishes with weed,
The sturdy seedling with arched body comes
Shouldering its way and shedding the earth crumbs.

## A Time to Talk

When a friend calls to me from the road
And slows his horse to a meaning walk,
I don't stand still and look around
On all the hills I haven't hoed,
And shout from where I am, 'What is it?'
No, not as there is a time to talk.
I thrust my hoe in the mellow ground,
Blade-end up and five feet tall,
And plod: I go up to the stone wall
For a friendly visit.

## The Cow in Apple Time

Something inspires the only cow of late
To make no more of a wall than an open gate,
And think no more of wall-builders than fools.

Her face is flecked with pomace and she drools
A cider syrup. Having tasted fruit,
She scorns a pasture withering to the root.
She runs from tree to tree where lie and sweeten
The windfalls spiked with stubble and worm-eaten.
She leaves them bitten when she has to fly.
She bellows on a knoll against the sky.
Her udder shrivels and the milk goes dry.


## An Encounter

Once on the kind of day called 'weather breeder,'
When the heat slowly hazes and the sun
By its own power seems to be undone,
I was half boring through, half climbing through
A swamp of cedar. Choked with oil of cedar
And scurf of plants, and weary and over-heated,
And sorry I ever left the road I knew,
I paused and rested on a sort of hook
That had me by the coat as good as seated,
And since there was no other way to look,
Looked up toward heaven, and there against the blue,
Stood over me a resurrected tree,
A tree that had been down and raised again—
A barkless specter. He had halted too,
As if for fear of treading upon me.
I saw the strange position of his hands—
Up at his shoulders, dragging yellow strands
Of wire with something in it from men to men.
'You here?' I said. 'Where aren't you nowadays?
And what's the news you carry—if you know?
And tell me where you're off for—Montreal?
Me? I'm not off for anywhere at all.
Sometimes I wander out of beaten ways
Half looking for the orchid Calypso.'

## Range-Finding

The battle rent a cobweb diamond-strung
And cut a flower beside a ground bird's nest
Before it stained a single human breast.
The stricken flower bent double and so hung.
And still the bird revisited her young.
A butterfly its fall had dispossessed
A moment sought in air his flower of rest,
Then lightly stooped to it and fluttering clung.
On the bare upland pasture there had spread
O'ernight 'twixt mullein stalks a wheel of thread
And straining cables wet with silver dew.
A sudden passing bullet shook it dry.
The indwelling spider ran to greet the fly,
But finding nothing, sullenly withdrew.

## The Hill Wife

### LONELINESS

#### Her Word

One ought not to have to care
    So much as you and I
Care when the birds come round the house
    To seem to say good-by;

Or care so much when they come back
    With whatever it is they sing;
The truth being we are as much
    Too glad for the one thing

As we are too sad for the other here—
    With birds that fill their breasts
But with each other and themselves
    And their built or driven nests.

## HOUSE FEAR

Always—I tell you this they learned—
Always at night when they returned
To the lonely house from far away
To lamps unlighted and fire gone gray,
They learned to rattle the lock and key
To give whatever might chance to be
Warning and time to be off in flight:
And preferring the out- to the in-door night,
They learned to leave the house-door wide
Until they had lit the lamp inside.

## THE SMILE

### Her Word

I didn't like the way he went away.
That smile! It never came of being gay.
Still he smiled—did you see him?—I was sure!
Perhaps because we gave him only bread
And the wretch knew from that that we were poor.
Perhaps because he let us give instead
Of seizing from us as he might have seized.
Perhaps he mocked at us for being wed,
Or being very young (and he was pleased
To have a vision of us old and dead).
I wonder how far down the road he's got.
He's watching from the woods as like as not.

## THE OFT-REPEATED DREAM

She had no saying dark enough
    For the dark pine that kept
Forever trying the window-latch
    Of the room where they slept.

The tireless but ineffectual hands
    That with every futile pass
Made the great tree seem as a little bird
    Before the mystery of glass!

It never had been inside the room,
   And only one of the two
Was afraid in an oft-repeated dream
   Of what the tree might do.


### THE IMPULSE

It was too lonely for her there,
   And too wild,
And since there were but two of them,
   And no child,

And work was little in the house,
   She was free,
And followed where he furrowed field,
   Or felled tree.

She rested on a log and tossed
   The fresh chips,
With a song only to herself
   On her lips.

And once she went to break a bough
   Of black alder.
She strayed so far she scarcely heard
   When he called her—

And didn't answer—didn't speak—
   Or return.
She stood, and then she ran and hid
   In the fern.

He never found her, though he looked
   Everywhere,
And he asked at her mother's house
   Was she there.

Sudden and swift and light as that
   The ties gave,
And he learned of finalities
   Besides the grave.

## *The Bonfire*

'Oh, let's go up the hill and scare ourselves,
As reckless as the best of them tonight,
By setting fire to all the brush we piled
With pitchy hands to wait for rain or snow.
Oh, let's not wait for rain to make it safe.
The pile is ours: we dragged it bough on bough
Down dark converging paths between the pines.
Let's not care what we do with it tonight.
Divide it? No! But burn it as one pile
The way we piled it. And let's be the talk
Of people brought to windows by a light
Thrown from somewhere against their wallpaper.
Rouse them all, both the free and not so free
With saying what they'd like to do to us
For what they'd better wait till we have done.
Let's all but bring to life this old volcano,
If that is what the mountain ever was—
And scare ourselves. Let wild fire loose we will . . .'

'And scare you too?' the children said together.

'Why wouldn't it scare me to have a fire
Begin in smudge with ropy smoke and know
That still, if I repent, I may recall it,
But in a moment not: a little spurt
Of burning fatness, and then nothing but
The fire itself can put it out, and that
By burning out, and before it burns out
It will have roared first and mixed sparks with stars,
And sweeping round it with a flaming sword,
Made the dim trees stand back in wider circle—
Done so much and I know not how much more
I mean it shall not do if I can bind it.
Well if it doesn't with its draft bring on
A wind to blow in earnest from some quarter,
As once it did with me upon an April.
The breezes were so spent with winter blowing
They seemed to fail the bluebirds under them
Short of the perch their languid flight was toward

And my flame made a pinnacle to heaven
As I walked once around it in possession.
But the wind out of doors—you know the saying.
There came a gust. You used to think the trees
Made wind by fanning since you never knew
It blow but that you saw the trees in motion.
Something or someone watching made that gust.
It put the flame tip-down and dabbed the grass
Of over-winter with the least tip-touch
Your tongue gives salt or sugar in your hand.
The place it reached to blackened instantly.
The black was almost all there was by daylight,
That and the merest curl of cigarette smoke—
And a flame slender as the hepaticas,
Blood-root, and violets so soon to be now.
But the black spread like black death on the ground,
And I think the sky darkened with a cloud
Like winter and evening coming on together.
There were enough things to be thought of then.
Where the field stretches toward the north
And setting sun to Hyla brook, I gave it
To flames without twice thinking, where it verges
Upon the road, to flames too, though in fear
They might find fuel there, in withered brake,
Grass its full length, old silver goldenrod,
And alder and grape vine entanglement,
To leap the dusty deadline. For my own
I took what front there was beside. I knelt
And thrust hands in and held my face away.
Fight such a fire by rubbing not by beating.
A board is the best weapon if you have it.
I had my coat. And oh, I knew, I knew,
And said out loud, I couldn't bide the smother
And heat so close in; but the thought of all
The woods and town on fire by me, and all
The town turned out to fight for me—that held me.
I trusted the brook barrier, but feared
The road would fail; and on that side the fire
Died not without a noise of crackling wood—
Of something more than tinder-grass and weed—

That brought me to my feet to hold it back
By leaning back myself, as if the reins
Were round my neck and I was at the plow.
I won! But I'm sure no one ever spread
Another color over a tenth the space
That I spread coal-black over in the time
It took me. Neighbors coming home from town
Couldn't believe that so much black had come there
While they had backs turned, that it hadn't been there
When they had passed an hour or so before
Going the other way and they not seen it.
They looked about for someone to have done it.
But there was no one. I was somewhere wondering
Where all my weariness had gone and why
I walked so light on air in heavy shoes
In spite of a scorched Fourth-of-July feeling.
Why wouldn't I be scared remembering that?'

'If it scares you, what will it do to us?'

'Scare you. But if you shrink from being scared,
What would you say to war if it should come?
That's what for reasons I should like to know—
If you can comfort me by any answer.'

'Oh, but war's not for children—it's for men.'

'Now we are digging almost down to China.
My dears, my dears, you thought that—we all thought it.
So your mistake was ours. Haven't you heard, though,
About the ships where war has found them out
At sea, about the towns where war has come
Through opening clouds at night with droning speed
Further o'erhead than all but stars and angels,—
And children in the ships and in the towns?
Haven't you heard what we have lived to learn?
Nothing so new—something we had forgotten:
*War is for everyone, for children too.*
I wasn't going to tell you and I mustn't.
The best way is to come up hill with me
And have our fire and laugh and be afraid.'

## A Girl's Garden

A neighbor of mine in the village
    Likes to tell how one spring
When she was a girl on the farm, she did
    A childlike thing.

One day she asked her father
    To give her a garden plot
To plant and tend and reap herself,
    And he said, 'Why not?'

In casting about for a corner
    He thought of an idle bit
Of walled-off ground where a shop had stood,
    And he said, 'Just it.'

And he said, 'That ought to make you
    An ideal one-girl farm,
And give you a chance to put some strength
    On your slim-jim arm.'

It was not enough of a garden,
    Her father said, to plow;
So she had to work it all by hand,
    But she don't mind now.

She wheeled the dung in the wheelbarrow
    Along a stretch of road;
But she always ran away and left
    Her not-nice load,

And hid from anyone passing.
    And then she begged the seed.
She says she thinks she planted one
    Of all things but weed.

A hill each of potatoes,
    Radishes, lettuce, peas,
Tomatoes, beets, beans, pumpkins, corn
    And even fruit trees.

And yes, she has long mistrusted
   That a cider apple tree
In bearing there today is hers,
   Or at least may be.

Her crop was a miscellany
   When all was said and done,
A little bit of everything,
   A great deal of none.

*Now* when she sees in the village
   How village things go,
Just when it seems to come in right,
   She says, '*I* know!

'It's as when I was a farmer—'
   Oh, never by way of advice!
And she never sins by telling the tale
   To the same person twice.

## Locked Out

### As Told to a Child

When we locked up the house at night,
We always locked the flowers outside
And cut them off from window light.
The time I dreamed the door was tried
And brushed with buttons upon sleeves,
The flowers were out there with the thieves.
Yet nobody molested them!
We did find one nasturtium
Upon the steps with bitten stem.
I may have been to blame for that:
I always thought it must have been
Some flower I played with as I sat
At dusk to watch the moon down early.

## The Last Word of a Bluebird

### As Told to a Child

As I went out a Crow
In a low voice said, 'Oh,
I was looking for you.
How do you do?
I just came to tell you
To tell Lesley (will you?)
That her little Bluebird
Wanted me to bring word
That the north wind last night
That made the stars bright
And made ice on the trough
Almost made him cough
His tail feathers off.
He just had to fly!
But he sent her Good-by,
And said to be good,
And wear her red hood,
And look for skunk tracks
In the snow with an ax—
And do everything!
And perhaps in the spring
He would come back and sing.'

## 'Out, Out—'

The buzz saw snarled and rattled in the yard
And made dust and dropped stove-length sticks of wood,
Sweet-scented stuff when the breeze drew across it.
And from there those that lifted eyes could count
Five mountain ranges one behind the other
Under the sunset far into Vermont.
And the saw snarled and rattled, snarled and rattled,
As it ran light, or had to bear a load.
And nothing happened: day was all but done.
Call it a day, I wish they might have said
To please the boy by giving him the half hour
That a boy counts so much when saved from work.
His sister stood beside them in her apron
To tell them 'Supper.' At the word, the saw,
As if to prove saws knew what supper meant,
Leaped out at the boy's hand, or seemed to leap—
He must have given the hand. However it was,
Neither refused the meeting. But the hand!
The boy's first outcry was a rueful laugh,
As he swung toward them holding up the hand
Half in appeal, but half as if to keep
The life from spilling. Then the boy saw all—
Since he was old enough to know, big boy
Doing a man's work, though a child at heart—
He saw all spoiled. 'Don't let him cut my hand off—
The doctor, when he comes. Don't let him, sister!'
So. But the hand was gone already.
The doctor put him in the dark of ether.
He lay and puffed his lips out with his breath.
And then—the watcher at his pulse took fright.
No one believed. They listened at his heart.
Little—less—nothing!—and that ended it.
No more to build on there. And they, since they
Were not the one dead, turned to their affairs.

## Brown's Descent

or

### The Willy-Nilly Slide

Brown lived at such a lofty farm
    That everyone for miles could see
His lantern when he did his chores
    In winter after half-past three.

And many must have seen him make
    His wild descent from there one night,
'Cross lots, 'cross walls, 'cross everything,
    Describing rings of lantern light.

Between the house and barn the gale
    Got him by something he had on
And blew him out on the icy crust
    That cased the world, and he was gone!

Walls were all buried, trees were few:
    He saw no stay unless he stove
A hole in somewhere with his heel.
    But though repeatedly he strove

And stamped and said things to himself,
    And sometimes something seemed to yield,
He gained no foothold, but pursued
    His journey down from field to field.

Sometimes he came with arms outspread
    Like wings, revolving in the scene
Upon his longer axis, and
    With no small dignity of mien.

Faster or slower as he chanced,
    Sitting or standing as he chose,
According as he feared to risk
    His neck, or thought to spare his clothes,

He never let the lantern drop.
    And some exclaimed who saw afar
The figures he described with it,
    'I wonder what those signals are

'Brown makes at such an hour of night!
    He's celebrating something strange.
I wonder if he's sold his farm,
    Or been made Master of the Grange.'

He reeled, he lurched, he bobbed, he checked;
    He fell and made the lantern rattle
(But saved the light from going out.)
    So halfway down he fought the battle,

Incredulous of his own bad luck.
    And then becoming reconciled
To everything, he gave it up
    And came down like a coasting child.

'Well—I—be—' that was all he said,
    As standing in the river road,
He looked back up the slippery slope
    (Two miles it was) to his abode.

Sometimes as an authority
    On motor-cars, I'm asked if I
Should say our stock was petered out,
    And this is my sincere reply:

Yankees are what they always were.
    Don't think Brown ever gave up hope
Of getting home again because
    He couldn't climb that slippery slope;

Or even thought of standing there
    Until the January thaw
Should take the polish off the crust.
    He bowed with grace to natural law,

And then went round it on his feet,
   After the manner of our stock;
Not much concerned for those to whom,
   At that particular time o'clock,

It must have looked as if the course
   He steered was really straight away
From that which he was headed for—
   Not much concerned for them, I say;

No more so than became a man—
   *And* politician at odd seasons.
I've kept Brown standing in the cold
   While I invested him with reasons;

But now he snapped his eyes three times;
   Then shook his lantern, saying, 'Ile's
'Bout out!' and took the long way home
   By road, a matter of several miles.


## The Gum-Gatherer

There overtook me and drew me in
To his down-hill, early-morning stride,
And set me five miles on my road
Better than if he had had me ride,
A man with a swinging bag for load
And half the bag wound round his hand.
We talked like barking above the din
Of water we walked along beside.
And for my telling him where I'd been
And where I lived in mountain land
To be coming home the way I was,
He told me a little about himself.
He came from higher up in the pass
Where the grist of the new-beginning brooks
Is blocks split off the mountain mass—
And hopeless grist enough it looks
Ever to grind to soil for grass.

(The way it is will do for moss.)
There he had built his stolen shack.
It had to be a stolen shack
Because of the fears of fire and loss
That trouble the sleep of lumber folk:
Visions of half the world burned black
And the sun shrunken yellow in smoke.
We know who when they come to town
Bring berries under the wagon seat,
Or a basket of eggs between their feet;
What this man brought in a cotton sack
Was gum, the gum of the mountain spruce.
He showed me lumps of the scented stuff
Like uncut jewels, dull and rough.
It comes to market golden brown;
But turns to pink between the teeth.

I told him this is a pleasant life
To set your breast to the bark of trees
That all your days are dim beneath,
And reaching up with a little knife,
To loose the resin and take it down
And bring it to market when you please.

## The Line-Gang

Here come the line-gang pioneering by.
They throw a forest down less cut than broken.
They plant dead trees for living, and the dead
They string together with a living thread.
They string an instrument against the sky
Wherein words whether beaten out or spoken
Will run as hushed as when they were a thought
But in no hush they string it: they go past
With shouts afar to pull the cable taut,
To hold it hard until they make it fast,
To ease away—they have it. With a laugh,
An oath of towns that set the wild at naught
They bring the telephone and telegraph.

## *The Vanishing Red*

He is said to have been the last Red Man
In Action. And the Miller is said to have laughed—
If you like to call such a sound a laugh.
But he gave no one else a laugher's license.
For he turned suddenly grave as if to say,
'Whose business,—if I take it on myself,
Whose business—but why talk round the barn?—
When it's just that I hold with getting a thing done with.'
You can't get back and see it as he saw it.
It's too long a story to go into now.
You'd have to have been there and lived it.
Then you wouldn't have looked on it as just a matter
Of who began it between the two races.

Some guttural exclamation of surprise
The Red Man gave in poking about the mill
Over the great big thumping shuffling millstone
Disgusted the Miller physically as coming
From one who had no right to be heard from.
'Come, John,' he said, 'you want to see the wheel-pit?'

He took him down below a cramping rafter,
And showed him, through a manhole in the floor,
The water in desperate straits like frantic fish,
Salmon and sturgeon, lashing with their tails.
Then he shut down the trap door with a ring in it
That jangled even above the general noise,
And came upstairs alone—and gave that laugh,
And said something to a man with a meal-sack
That the man with the meal-sack didn't catch—then.
Oh, yes, he showed John the wheel-pit all right.

## Snow

The three stood listening to a fresh access
Of wind that caught against the house a moment,
Gulped snow, and then blew free again—the Coles
Dressed, but disheveled from some hours of sleep,
Meserve belittled in the great skin coat he wore.

Meserve was first to speak. He pointed backward
Over his shoulder with his pipe-stem, saying,
'You can just see it glancing off the roof
Making a great scroll upward toward the sky,
Long enough for recording all our names on.—
I think I'll just call up my wife and tell her
I'm here—so far—and starting on again.
I'll call her softly so that if she's wise
And gone to sleep, she needn't wake to answer.'
Three times he barely stirred the bell, then listened.
'Why, Lett, still up? Lett, I'm at Cole's. I'm late.
I called you up to say Good-night from here
Before I went to say Good-morning there.—
I thought I would.—I know, but, Lett—I know—
I could, but what's the sense? The rest won't be
So bad.—Give me an hour for it.—Ho, ho,
Three hours to here! But that was all up hill;
The rest is down.—Why no, no, not a wallow:
They kept their heads and took their time to it
Like darlings, both of them. They're in the barn.—
My dear, I'm coming just the same. I didn't
Call you to ask you to invite me home.—'
He lingered for some word she wouldn't say,
Said it at last himself, 'Good-night,' and then
Getting no answer, closed the telephone.
The three stood in the lamplight round the table
With lowered eyes a moment till he said,
'I'll just see how the horses are.'

                                    'Yes, do,'
Both the Coles said together. Mrs. Cole
Added: 'You can judge better after seeing.—

I want you here with me, Fred. Leave him here,
Brother Meserve. You know to find your way
Out through the shed.'

                'I guess I know my way,
I guess I know where I can find my name
Carved in the shed to tell me who I am
If it don't tell me where I am. I used
To play—'

       'You tend your horses and come back.
Fred Cole, you're going to let him!'

                   'Well, aren't you?
How can you help yourself?'

                 'I called him Brother.
Why did I call him that?'

                 'It's right enough.
That's all you ever heard him called round here.
He seems to have lost off his Christian name.'

'Christian enough I should call that myself.
He took no notice, did he? Well, at least
I didn't use it out of love of him,
The dear knows. I detest the thought of him
With his ten children under ten years old.
I hate his wretched little Racker Sect,
All's ever I heard of it, which isn't much.
But that's not saying—Look, Fred Cole, it's twelve.
Isn't it, now? He's been here half an hour.
He says he left the village store at nine.
Three hours to do four miles—a mile an hour
Or not much better. Why, it doesn't seem
As if a man could move that slow and move.
Try to think what he did with all that time.
And three miles more to go!'

'Don't let him go.
Stick to him, Helen. Make him answer you.
That sort of man talks straight on all his life
From the last thing he said himself, stone deaf
To anything anyone else may say.
I should have thought, though, you could make him hear
    you.'

'What is he doing out a night like this?
Why can't he stay at home?'

              'He had to preach.'

'It's no night to be out.'

                'He may be small,
He may be good, but one thing's sure, he's tough.'

'And strong of stale tobacco.'

                'He'll pull through.'

'You only say so. Not another house
Or shelter to put into from this place
To theirs. I'm going to call his wife again.'

'Wait and he may. Let's see what he will do.
Let's see if he will think of her again.
But then I doubt he's thinking of himself.
He doesn't look on it as anything.'

'He shan't go—there!'

                'It *is* a night, my dear.'

'One thing: he didn't drag God into it.'

'He don't consider it a case for God.'

'You think so, do you? You don't know the kind.
He's getting up a miracle this minute.
Privately—to himself, right now, he's thinking
He'll make a case of it if he succeeds,
But keep still if he fails.'

                    'Keep still all over.
He'll be dead—dead and buried.'

                         'Such a trouble!
Not but I've every reason not to care
What happens to him if it only takes
Some of the sanctimonious conceit
Out of one of those pious scalawags.'

'Nonsense to that! You want to see him safe.'

'You like the runt.'

                    'Don't you a little?'

                              'Well,
I don't like what he's doing, which is what
You like, and like him for.'

                         'Oh, yes you do.
You like your fun as well as anyone;
Only you women have to put these airs on
To impress men. You've got us so ashamed
Of being men we can't look at a good fight
Between two boys and not feel bound to stop it.
Let the man freeze an ear or two, I say.—
He's here. I leave him all to you. Go in
And save his life.—All right, come in, Meserve.
Sit down, sit down. How did you find the horses?'

'Fine, fine.'

       'And ready for some more? My wife here
Says it won't do. You've got to give it up.'

'Won't you to please me? Please! If I say please?
Mr. Meserve, I'll leave it to *your* wife.
What *did* your wife say on the telephone?'

Meserve seemed to heed nothing but the lamp
Or something not far from it on the table.
By straightening out and lifting a forefinger,
He pointed with his hand from where it lay
Like a white crumpled spider on his knee:
'That leaf there in your open book! It moved
Just then, I thought. It's stood erect like that,
There on the table, ever since I came,
Trying to turn itself backward or forward,
I've had my eye on it to make out which;
If forward, then it's with a friend's impatience—
You see I know—to get you on to things
It wants to see how you will take, if backward
It's from regret for something you have passed
And failed to see the good of. Never mind,
Things must expect to come in front of us
A many times—I don't say just how many—
That varies with the things—before we see them.
One of the lies would make it out that nothing
Ever presents itself before us twice.
Where would we be at last if that were so?
Our very life depends on everything's
Recurring till we answer from within.
The thousandth time may prove the charm.—That leaf!
It can't turn either way. It needs the wind's help.
But the wind didn't move it if it moved.
It moved itself. The wind's at naught in here.
It couldn't stir so sensitively poised
A thing as that. It couldn't reach the lamp
To get a puff of black smoke from the flame,
Or blow a rumple in the collie's coat.
You make a little foursquare block of air,
Quiet and light and warm, in spite of all

The illimitable dark and cold and storm,
And by so doing give these three, lamp, dog,
And book-leaf, that keep near you, their repose;
Though for all anyone can tell, repose
May be the thing you haven't, yet you give it.
So false it is that what we haven't we can't give;
So false, that what we always say is true.
I'll have to turn the leaf if no one else will.
It won't lie down. Then let it stand. Who cares?'

'I shouldn't want to hurry you, Meserve,
But if you're going—say you'll stay, you know.
But let me raise this curtain on a scene,
And show you how it's piling up against you.
You see the snow-white through the white of frost?
Ask Helen how far up the sash it's climbed
Since last we read the gauge.'

                                'It looks as if
Some pallid thing had squashed its features flat
And its eyes shut with overeagerness
To see what people found so interesting
In one another, and had gone to sleep
Of its own stupid lack of understanding,
Or broken its white neck of mushroom stuff
Short off, and died against the window-pane.'

'Brother Meserve, take care, you'll scare yourself
More than you will us with such nightmare talk.
It's you it matters to, because it's you
Who have to go out into it alone.'

'Let him talk, Helen, and perhaps he'll stay.'

'Before you drop the curtain—I'm reminded:
You recollect the boy who came out here
To breathe the air one winter—had a room
Down at the Averys'? Well, one sunny morning
After a downy storm, he passed our place

And found me banking up the house with snow.
And I was burrowing in deep for warmth,
Piling it well above the window-sills.
The snow against the window caught his eye.
"Hey, that's a pretty thought"—those were his words.
"So you can think it's six feet deep outside,
While you sit warm and read up balanced rations.
You can't get too much winter in the winter."
Those were his words. And he went home and all
But banked the daylight out of Avery's windows.
Now you and I would go to no such length.
At the same time you can't deny it makes
It not a mite worse, sitting here, we three,
Playing our fancy, to have the snowline run
So high across the pane outside. There where
There is a sort of tunnel in the frost
More like a tunnel than a hole—way down
At the far end of it you see a stir
And quiver like the frayed edge of the drift
Blown in the wind. I *like* that—I like *that*.
Well, now I leave you, people.'

                                 'Come, Meserve,
We thought you were deciding not to go—
The ways you found to say the praise of comfort
And being where you are. You want to stay.'


'I'll own it's cold for such a fall of snow.
This house is frozen brittle, all except
This room you sit in. If you think the wind
Sounds further off, it's not because it's dying;
You're further under in the snow—that's all—
And feel it less. Hear the soft bombs of dust
It bursts against us at the chimney mouth,
And at the eaves. I like it from inside
More than I shall out in it. But the horses
Are rested and it's time to say good-night,
And let you get to bed again. Good-night,
Sorry I had to break in on your sleep.'

'Lucky for you you did. Lucky for you
You had us for a halfway station
To stop at. If you were the kind of man
Paid heed to women, you'd take my advice
And for your family's sake stay where you are.
But what good is my saying it over and over?
You've done more than you had a right to think
You could do—*now*. You know the risk you take
In going on.'


              'Our snow-storms as a rule
Aren't looked on as man-killers, and although
I'd rather be the beast that sleeps the sleep
Under it all, his door sealed up and lost,
Than the man fighting it to keep above it,
Yet think of the small birds at roost and not
In nests. Shall I be counted less than they are?
Their bulk in water would be frozen rock
In no time out tonight. And yet tomorrow
They will come budding boughs from tree to tree
Flirting their wings and saying Chickadee,
As if not knowing what you meant by the word storm.'


'But why when no one wants you to go on?
Your wife—she doesn't want you to. We don't,
And you yourself don't want to. Who else is there?'


'Save us from being cornered by a woman.
Well, there's—' She told Fred afterward that in
The pause right there, she thought the dreaded word
Was coming, 'God.' But no, he only said,
'Well, there's—the storm. That says I must go on.
That wants me as a war might if it came.
Ask any man.'


            He threw her that as something
To last her till he got outside the door.
He had Cole with him to the barn to see him off.
When Cole returned he found his wife still standing

Beside the table near the open book,
Not reading it.

        'Well, what kind of a man
Do you call that?' she said.

           'He had the gift
Of words, or is it tongues, I ought to say?'

'Was ever such a man for seeing likeness?'

'Or disregarding people's civil questions—
What? We've found out in one hour more about him
Than we had seeing him pass by in the road
A thousand times. If that's the way he preaches!
You didn't think you'd keep him after all.
Oh, I'm not blaming you. He didn't leave you
Much say in the matter, and I'm just as glad
We're not in for a night of him. No sleep
If he had stayed. The least thing set him going.
It's quiet as an empty church without him.'

'But how much better off are we as it is?
We'll have to sit here till we know he's safe.'

'Yes, I suppose you'll want to, but I shouldn't.
He knows what he can do, or he wouldn't try.
Get into bed I say, and get some rest.
He won't come back, and if he telephones,
It won't be for an hour or two.'

           'Well then.
We can't be any help by sitting here
And living his fight through with him, I suppose.'

      ·   ·   ·

Cole had been telephoning in the dark.
Mrs. Cole's voice came from an inner room:
'Did she call you or you call her?'

                   'She me.
You'd better dress: you won't go back to bed.
We must have been asleep: it's three and after.'

'Had she been ringing long? I'll get my wrapper.
I want to speak to her.'

                 'All she said was,
He hadn't come and had he really started.'

'She knew he had, poor thing, two hours ago.'

'He had the shovel. He'll have made a fight.'

'Why did I ever let him leave this house!'

'Don't begin that. You did the best you could
To keep him—though perhaps you didn't quite
Conceal a wish to see him show the spunk
To disobey you. Much his wife'll thank you.'

'Fred, after all I said! You shan't make out
That it was any way but what it was.
Did she let on by any word she said
She didn't thank me?'

               'When I told her "Gone,"
"Well then," she said, and "Well then"—like a threat.
And then her voice came scraping slow: "Oh, you,
Why did you let him go?" '

               'Asked why we let him?
You let me there. I'll ask her why she let him.
She didn't dare to speak when he was here.
Their number's—twenty-one? The thing won't work.
Someone's receiver's down. The handle stumbles.
The stubborn thing, the way it jars your arm!
It's theirs. She's dropped it from her hand and gone.'

'Try speaking. Say "Hello!"'

'Hello. Hello.'

'What do you hear?'

'I hear an empty room—
You know—it sounds that way. And yes, I hear—
I think I hear a clock—and windows rattling.
No step though. If she's there she's sitting down.'

'Shout, she may hear you.'

'Shouting is no good.'

'Keep speaking then.'

'Hello. Hello. Hello.
You don't suppose—? She wouldn't go outdoors?'

'I'm half afraid that's just what she might do.'

'And leave the children?'

'Wait and call again.
You can't hear whether she has left the door
Wide open and the wind's blown out the lamp
And the fire's died and the room's dark and cold?'

'One of two things, either she's gone to bed
Or gone outdoors.'

'In which case both are lost.
Do you know what she's like? Have you ever met her?
It's strange she doesn't want to speak to us.'

'Fred, see if you can hear what I hear. Come.'

'A clock maybe.'

      'Don't you hear something else?'

'Not talking.'

    'No.'

      'Why, yes, I hear—what is it?'

'What do you say it is?'

      'A baby's crying!
Frantic it sounds, though muffled and far off.
Its mother wouldn't let it cry like that,
Not if she's there.'

      'What do you make of it?'

'There's only one thing possible to make,
That is, assuming—that she has gone out.
Of course she hasn't though.' They both sat down
Helpless. 'There's nothing we can do till morning.'

'Fred, I shan't let you think of going out.'

'Hold on.' The double bell began to chirp.
They started up. Fred took the telephone.
'Hello, Meserve. You're there, then!—And your wife?
Good! Why I asked—she didn't seem to answer.
He says she went to let him in the barn.—
We're glad. Oh, say no more about it, man.
Drop in and see us when you're passing.'

        'Well,
She has him then, though what she wants him for
I *don't* see.'

     'Possibly not for herself.
Maybe she only wants him for the children.'

'The whole to-do seems to have been for nothing.
What spoiled our night was to him just his fun.
What did he come in for?—To talk and visit?
Thought he'd just call to tell us it was snowing.
If he thinks he is going to make our house
A halfway coffee house 'twixt town and nowhere—'

'I thought you'd feel you'd been too much concerned.'

'You think you haven't been concerned yourself.'

'If you mean he was inconsiderate
To rout us out to think for him at midnight
And then take our advice no more than nothing,
Why, I agree with you. But let's forgive him.
We've had a share in one night of his life.
What'll you bet he ever calls again?'

## The Sound of the Trees

I wonder about the trees.
Why do we wish to bear
Forever the noise of these
More than another noise
So close to our dwelling place?
We suffer them by the day
Till we lose all measure of pace,
And fixity in our joys,
And acquire a listening air.
They are that that talks of going
But never gets away;
And that talks no less for knowing,
As it grows wiser and older,
That now it means to stay.
My feet tug at the floor
And my head sways to my shoulder
Sometimes when I watch trees sway,
From the window or the door.
I shall set forth for somewhere,
I shall make the reckless choice
Some day when they are in voice
And tossing so as to scare
The white clouds over them on.
I shall have less to say,
But I shall be gone.

# NEW HAMPSHIRE

## *New Hampshire*

I met a lady from the South who said
(You won't believe she said it, but she said it):
'None of my family ever worked, or had
A thing to sell.' I don't suppose the work
Much matters. You may work for all of me.
I've seen the time I've had to work myself.
The having anything to sell is what
Is the disgrace in man or state or nation.

I met a traveler from Arkansas
Who boasted of his state as beautiful
For diamonds and apples. 'Diamonds
And apples in commercial quantities?'
I asked him, on my guard. 'Oh, yes,' he answered,
Off his. The time was evening in the Pullman.
'I see the porter's made your bed,' I told him.

I met a Californian who would
Talk California—a state so blessed,
He said, in climate, none had ever died there
A natural death, and Vigilance Committees
Had had to organize to stock the graveyards
And vindicate the state's humanity.
'Just the way Stefansson runs on,' I murmured,
'About the British Arctic. That's what comes
Of being in the market with a climate.'

I met a poet from another state,
A zealot full of fluid inspiration,
Who in the name of fluid inspiration,
But in the best style of bad salesmanship,
Angrily tried to make me write a protest
(In verse I think) against the Volstead Act.

He didn't even offer me a drink
Until I asked for one to steady *him*.
This is called having an idea to sell.


It never could have happened in New Hampshire.


The only person really soiled with trade
I ever stumbled on in old New Hampshire
Was someone who had just come back ashamed
From selling things in California.
He'd built a noble mansard roof with balls
On turrets like Constantinople, deep
In woods some ten miles from a railroad station,
As if to put forever out of mind
The hope of being, as we say, received.
I found him standing at the close of day
Inside the threshold of his open barn,
Like a lone actor on a gloomy stage—
And recognized him through the iron gray
In which his face was muffled to the eyes
As an old boyhood friend, and once indeed
A drover with me on the road to Brighton.
His farm was 'grounds,' and not a farm at all;
His house among the local sheds and shanties
Rose like a factor's at a trading station.
And he was rich, and I was still a rascal.
I couldn't keep from asking impolitely,
Where had he been and what had he been doing?
How did he get so? (Rich was understood.)
In dealing in 'old rags' in San Francisco.
Oh, it was terrible as well could be.
We both of us turned over in our graves.


Just specimens is all New Hampshire has,
One each of everything as in a show-case
Which naturally she doesn't care to sell.


She had one President (pronounce him Purse,
And make the most of it for better or worse.
He's your one chance to score against the state).

She had one Daniel Webster. He was all
The Daniel Webster ever was or shall be.
She had the Dartmouth needed to produce him.

I call her old. She has one family
Whose claim is good to being settled here
Before the era of colonization,
And before that of exploration even.
John Smith remarked them as he coasted by
Dangling their legs and fishing off a wharf
At the Isles of Shoals, and satisfied himself
They weren't Red Indians, but veritable
Pre-primitives of the white race, dawn people,
Like those who furnished Adam's sons with wives;
However uninnocent they may have been
In being there so early in our history.
They'd been there then a hundred years or more.
Pity he didn't ask what they were up to
At that date with a wharf already built,
And take their name. They've since told me their name—
Today an honored one in Nottingham.
As for what they were up to more than fishing—
Suppose they weren't behaving Puritanly,
The hour had not yet struck for being good,
Mankind had not yet gone on the Sabbatical.
It became an explorer of the deep
Not to explore too deep in others' business.

Did you but know of him, New Hampshire has
One real reformer who would change the world
So it would be accepted by two classes,
Artists the minute they set up as artists,
Before, that is, they are themselves accepted,
And boys the minute they get out of college.
I can't help thinking those are tests to go by.

And she has one I don't know what to call him,
Who comes from Philadelphia every year
With a great flock of chickens of rare breeds

He wants to give the educational
Advantages of growing almost wild
Under the watchful eye of hawk and eagle—
Dorkings because they're spoken of by Chaucer,
Sussex because they're spoken of by Herrick.

She has a touch of gold. New Hampshire gold—
You may have heard of it. I had a farm
Offered me not long since up Berlin way
With a mine on it that was worked for gold;
But not gold in commercial quantities,
Just enough gold to make the engagement rings
And marriage rings of those who owned the farm.
What gold more innocent could one have asked for?
One of my children ranging after rocks
Lately brought home from Andover or Canaan
A specimen of beryl with a trace
Of radium. I know with radium
The trace would have to be the merest trace
To be below the threshold of commercial;
But trust New Hampshire not to have enough
Of radium or anything to sell.

A specimen of everything, I said.
She has one witch—old style. She lives in Colebrook.
(The only other witch I ever met
Was lately at a cut-glass dinner in Boston.
There were four candles and four people present.
The witch was young, and beautiful (new style),
And open-minded. She was free to question
Her gift for reading letters locked in boxes.
Why was it so much greater when the boxes
Were metal than it was when they were wooden?
It made the world seem so mysterious.
The S'ciety for Psychical Research
Was cognizant. Her husband was worth millions.
I think he owned some shares in Harvard College.)

New Hampshire *used* to have at Salem
A company we called the White Corpuscles,

Whose duty was at any hour of night
To rush in sheets and fools' caps where they smelled
A thing the least bit doubtfully perscented
And give someone the Skipper Ireson's Ride.

One each of everything as in a show-case.
More than enough land for a specimen
You'll say she has, but there there enters in
Something else to protect her from herself.
There quality makes up for quantity.
Not even New Hampshire farms are much for sale.
The farm I made my home on in the mountains
I had to take by force rather than buy.
I caught the owner outdoors by himself
Raking up after winter, and I said,
'I'm going to put you off this farm: I want it.'
'Where are you going to put me? In the road?'
'I'm going to put you on the farm next to it.'
'Why won't the farm next to it do for you?'
'I like this better.' It was really better.

Apples? New Hampshire has them, but unsprayed,
With no suspicion in stem-end or blossom-end
Of vitriol or arsenate of lead,
And so not good for anything but cider.
Her unpruned grapes are flung like lariats
Far up the birches out of reach of man.

A state producing precious metals, stones,
And—writing; none of these except perhaps
The precious literature in quantity
Or quality to worry the producer
About disposing of it. Do you know,
Considering the market, there are more
Poems produced than any other thing?
No wonder poets sometimes have to *seem*
So much more business-like than business men.
Their wares are so much harder to get rid of.

She's one of the two best states in the Union.
Vermont's the other. And the two have been

Yoke-fellows in the sap-yoke from of old
In many Marches. And they lie like wedges,
Thick end to thin end and thin end to thick end,
And are a figure of the way the strong
Of mind and strong of arm should fit together,
One thick where one is thin and vice versa.
New Hampshire raises the Connecticut
In a trout hatchery near Canada,
But soon divides the river with Vermont.
Both are delightful states for their absurdly
Small towns—Lost Nation, Bungey, Muddy Boo,
Poplin, Still Corners (so called not because
The place is silent all day long, nor yet
Because it boasts a whisky still—because
It set out once to be a city and still
Is only corners, cross-roads in a wood).
And I remember one whose name appeared
Between the pictures on a movie screen
Election night once in Franconia,
When everything had gone Republican
And Democrats were sore in need of comfort:
Easton goes Democratic, Wilson 4
Hughes 2. And everybody to the saddest
Laughed the loud laugh, the big laugh at the little.
New York (five million) laughs at Manchester,
Manchester (sixty or seventy thousand) laughs
At Littleton (four thousand), Littleton
Laughs at Franconia (seven hundred), and
Franconia laughs, I fear,—did laugh that night—
At Easton. What has Easton left to laugh at,
And like the actress exclaim, 'Oh, my God' at?
There's Bungey; and for Bungey there are towns,
Whole townships named but without population.

Anything I can say about New Hampshire
Will serve almost as well about Vermont,
Excepting that they differ in their mountains.
The Vermont mountains stretch extended straight;
New Hampshire mountains curl up in a coil.

I had been coming to New Hampshire mountains.
And here I am and what am I to say?
Here first my theme becomes embarrassing.
Emerson said, 'The God who made New Hampshire
Taunted the lofty land with little men.'
Another Massachusetts poet said,
'I go no more to summer in New Hampshire.
I've given up my summer place in Dublin.'
But when I asked to know what ailed New Hampshire,
She said she couldn't stand the people in it,
The little men (it's Massachusetts speaking).
And when I asked to know what ailed the people,
She said, 'Go read your own books and find out.'
I may as well confess myself the author
Of several books against the world in general.
To take them as against a special state
Or even nation's to restrict my meaning.
I'm what is called a sensibilitist,
Or otherwise an environmentalist.
I refuse to adapt myself a mite
To any change from hot to cold, from wet
To dry, from poor to rich, or back again.
I make a virtue of my suffering
From nearly everything that goes on round me.
In other words, I know wherever I am,
Being the creature of literature I am,
I shall not lack for pain to keep me awake.
Kit Marlowe taught me how to say my prayers:
'Why, this is Hell, nor am I out of it.'
Samoa, Russia, Ireland, I complain of,
No less than England, France, and Italy.
Because I wrote my novels in New Hampshire
Is no proof that I aimed them at New Hampshire.

When I left Massachusetts years ago
Between two days, the reason why I sought
New Hampshire, not Connecticut,
Rhode Island, New York, or Vermont was this:
Where I was living then, New Hampshire offered

The nearest boundary to escape across.
I hadn't an illusion in my hand-bag
About the people being better there
Than those I left behind. I thought they weren't.
I thought they couldn't be. And yet they were.
I'd sure had no such friends in Massachusetts
As Hall of Windham, Gay of Atkinson,
Bartlett of Raymond (now of Colorado),
Harris of Derry, and Lynch of Bethlehem.

The glorious bards of Massachusetts seem
To want to make New Hampshire people over.
They taunt the lofty land with little men.
I don't know what to say about the people.
For art's sake one could almost wish them worse
Rather than better. How are we to write
The Russian novel in America
As long as life goes so unterribly?
There is the pinch from which our only outcry
In literature to date is heard to come.
We get what little misery we can
Out of not having cause for misery.
It makes the guild of novel writers sick
To be expected to be Dostoievskis
On nothing worse than too much luck and comfort.
This is not sorrow, though; it's just the vapors,
And recognized as such in Russia itself
Under the new régime, and so forbidden.
If well it is with Russia, then feel free
To say so or be stood against the wall
And shot. It's Pollyanna now or death.
This, then, is the new freedom we hear tell of;
And very sensible. No state can build
A literature that shall at once be sound
And sad on a foundation of well-being.

To show the level of intelligence
Among us: it was just a Warren farmer
Whose horse had pulled him short up in the road
By me, a stranger. This is what he said,

From nothing but embarrassment and want
Of anything more sociable to say:
'You hear those hound-dogs sing on Moosilauke?
Well they remind me of the hue and cry
We've heard against the Mid-Victorians
And never rightly understood till Bryan
Retired from politics and joined the chorus.
The matter with the Mid-Victorians
Seems to have been a man named John L. Darwin.'
'Go 'long,' I said to him, he to his horse.

I knew a man who failing as a farmer
Burned down his farmhouse for the fire insurance,
And spent the proceeds on a telescope
To satisfy a life-long curiosity
About our place among the infinities.
And how was that for other-worldliness?

If I must choose which I would elevate—
The people or the already lofty mountains,
I'd elevate the already lofty mountains.
The only fault I find with old New Hampshire
Is that her mountains aren't quite high enough.
I was not always so; I've come to be so.
How, to my sorrow, how have I attained
A height from which to look down critical
On mountains? What has given me assurance
To say what height becomes New Hampshire mountains,
Or any mountains? Can it be some strength
I feel as of an earthquake in my back
To heave them higher to the morning star?
Can it be foreign travel in the Alps?
Or having seen and credited a moment
The solid molding of vast peaks of cloud
Behind the pitiful reality
Of Lincoln, Lafayette, and Liberty?
Or some such sense as says how high shall jet
The fountain in proportion to the basin?
No, none of these has raised me to my throne
Of intellectual dissatisfaction,

But the sad accident of having seen
Our actual mountains given in a map
Of early times as twice the height they are—
Ten thousand feet instead of only five—
Which shows how sad an accident may be.
Five thousand is no longer high enough.
Whereas I never had a good idea
About improving people in the world,
Here I am over-fertile in suggestion,
And cannot rest from planning day or night
How high I'd thrust the peaks in summer snow
To tap the upper sky and draw a flow
Of frosty night air on the vale below
Down from the stars to freeze the dew as starry.

The more the sensibilitist I am
The more I seem to want my mountains wild;
The way the wiry gang-boss liked the log-jam.
After he'd picked the lock and got it started,
He dodged a log that lifted like an arm
Against the sky to break his back for him,
Then came in dancing, skipping, with his life
Across the roar and chaos, and the words
We saw him say along the zigzag journey
Were doubtless as the words we heard him say
On coming nearer: 'Wasn't she an *i*-deal
Son-of-a-bitch? You bet she was an *i*-deal.'

For all her mountains fall a little short,
Her people not quite short enough for Art,
She's still New Hampshire, a most restful state.

Lately in converse with a New York alec
About the new school of the pseudo-phallic,
I found myself in a close corner where
I had to make an almost funny choice.
'Choose you which you will be—a prude, or puke,
Mewling and puking in the public arms.'
'Me for the hills where I don't have to choose.'
'But if you had to choose, which would you be?'

I wouldn't be a prude afraid of nature.
I know a man who took a double ax
And went alone against a grove of trees;
But his heart failing him, he dropped the ax
And ran for shelter quoting Matthew Arnold:
'Nature is cruel, man is sick of blood;
There's been enough shed without shedding mine.
Remember Birnam Wood! The wood's in flux!'
He had a special terror of the flux
That showed itself in dendrophobia.
The only decent tree had been to mill
And educated into boards, he said.
He knew too well for any earthly use
The line where man leaves off and nature starts,
And never over-stepped it save in dreams.
He stood on the safe side of the line talking;
Which is sheer Matthew Arnoldism,
The cult of one who owned himself 'a foiled,
Circuitous wanderer,' and 'took dejectedly
His seat upon the intellectual throne.'
Agreed in frowning on these improvised
Altars the woods are full of nowadays,
Again as in the days when Ahaz sinned
By worship under green trees in the open.
Scarcely a mile but that I come on one,
A black-cheeked stone and stick of rain-washed charcoal
Even to say the groves were God's first temples
Comes too near to Ahaz' sin for safety.
Nothing not built with hands of course is sacred.
But here is not a question of what's sacred;
Rather of what to face or run away from.
I'd hate to be a runaway from nature.
And neither would I choose to be a puke
Who cares not what he does in company,
And, when he can't do anything, falls back
On words, and tries his worst to make words speak
Louder than actions, and sometimes achieves it.
It seems a narrow choice the age insists on.
How about being a good Greek, for instance?
That course, they tell me, isn't offered this year.

'Come, but this isn't choosing—puke or prude?'
Well, if I have to choose one or the other,
I choose to be a plain New Hampshire farmer
With an income in cash of say a thousand
(From say a publisher in New York City).
It's restful to arrive at a decision,
And restful just to think about New Hampshire.
At present I am living in Vermont.


## A Star in a Stone-Boat

For Lincoln MacVeagh

Never tell me that not one star of all
That slip from heaven at night and softly fall
Has been picked up with stones to build a wall.

Some laborer found one faded and stone cold,
And saving that its weight suggested gold,
And tugged it from his first too certain hold,

He noticed nothing in it to remark.
He was not used to handling stars thrown dark
And lifeless from an interrupted arc.

He did not recognize in that smooth coal
The one thing palpable besides the soul
To penetrate the air in which we roll.

He did not see how like a flying thing
It brooded ant-eggs, and had one large wing,
One not so large for flying in a ring,

And a long Bird of Paradise's tail,
(Though these when not in use to fly and trail
It drew back in its body like a snail);

Nor know that he might move it from the spot,
The harm was done; from having been star-shot
The very nature of the soil was hot

And burning to yield flowers instead of grain,
Flowers fanned and not put out by all the rain
Poured on them by his prayers prayed in vain.

He moved it roughly with an iron bar,
He loaded an old stone-boat with the star
And not, as you might think, a flying car,

Such as even poets would admit perforce
More practical than Pegasus the horse
If it could put a star back in its course.

He dragged it through the plowed ground at a pace
But faintly reminiscent of the race
Of jostling rock in interstellar space.

It went for building stone, and I, as though
Commanded in a dream, forever go
To right the wrong that this should have been so.

Yet ask where else it could have gone as well,
I do not know—I cannot stop to tell:
He might have left it lying where it fell.

From following walls I never lift my eye
Except at night to places in the sky
Where showers of charted meteors let fly.

Some may know what they seek in school and church,
And why they seek it there; for what I search
I must go measuring stone walls, perch on perch;

Sure that though not a star of death and birth,
So not to be compared, perhaps, in worth
To such resorts of life as Mars and Earth,

Though not, I say, a star of death and sin,
It yet has poles, and only needs a spin
To show its worldly nature and begin

To chafe and shuffle in my calloused palm
And run off in strange tangents with my arm
As fish do with the line in first alarm.

Such as it is, it promises the prize
Of the one world complete in any size
That I am like to compass, fool or wise.


## The Census-Taker

I came an errand one cloud-blowing evening
To a slab-built, black-paper-covered house
Of one room and one window and one door,
The only dwelling in a waste cut over
A hundred square miles round it in the mountains:
And that not dwelt in now by men or women.
(It never had been dwelt in, though, by women,
So what is this I make a sorrow of?)
I came as census-taker to the waste
To count the people in it and found none,
None in the hundred miles, none in the house,
Where I came last with some hope, but not much
After hours' overlooking from the cliffs
An emptiness flayed to the very stone.
I found no people that dared show themselves,
None not in hiding from the outward eye.
The time was autumn, but how anyone
Could tell the time of year when every tree
That could have dropped a leaf was down itself
And nothing but the stump of it was left
Now bringing out its rings in sugar of pitch;
And every tree up stood a rotting trunk
Without a single leaf to spend on autumn,
Or branch to whistle after what was spent.

Perhaps the wind the more without the help
Of breathing trees said something of the time
Of year or day the way it swung a door
Forever off the latch, as if rude men
Passed in and slammed it shut each one behind him
For the next one to open for himself.
I counted nine I had no right to count
(But this was dreamy unofficial counting)
Before I made the tenth across the threshold.
Where was my supper? Where was anyone's?
No lamp was lit. Nothing was on the table.
The stove was cold—the stove was off the chimney—
And down by one side where it lacked a leg.
The people that had loudly passed the door
Were people to the ear but not the eye.
They were not on the table with their elbows.
They were not sleeping in the shelves of bunks.
I saw no men there and no bones of men there.
I armed myself against such bones as might be
With the pitch-blackened stub of an ax-handle
I picked up off the straw-dust covered floor.
Not bones, but the ill-fitted window rattled.
The door was still because I held it shut
While I thought what to do that could be done—
About the house—about the people not there.
This house in one year fallen to decay
Filled me with no less sorrow than the houses
Fallen to ruin in ten thousand years
Where Asia wedges Africa from Europe.
Nothing was left to do that I could see
Unless to find that there was no one there
And declare to the cliffs too far for echo,
'The place is desert and let whoso lurks
In silence, if in this he is aggrieved,
Break silence now or be forever silent.
Let him say why it should not be declared so.'
The melancholy of having to count souls
Where they grow fewer and fewer every year
Is extreme where they shrink to none at all.
It must be I want life to go on living.

## The Star-Splitter

'You know Orion always comes up sideways.
Throwing a leg up over our fence of mountains,
And rising on his hands, he looks in on me
Busy outdoors by lantern-light with something
I should have done by daylight, and indeed,
After the ground is frozen, I should have done
Before it froze, and a gust flings a handful
Of waste leaves at my smoky lantern chimney
To make fun of my way of doing things,
Or else fun of Orion's having caught me.
Has a man, I should like to ask, no rights
These forces are obliged to pay respect to?'
So Brad McLaughlin mingled reckless talk
Of heavenly stars with hugger-mugger farming,
Till having failed at hugger-mugger farming,
He burned his house down for the fire insurance
And spent the proceeds on a telescope
To satisfy a life-long curiosity
About our place among the infinities.

'What do you want with one of those blame things?'
I asked him well beforehand. 'Don't you get one!'
'Don't call it blamed; there isn't anything
More blameless in the sense of being less
A weapon in our human fight,' he said.
'I'll have one if I sell my farm to buy it.'
There where he moved the rocks to plow the ground
And plowed between the rocks he couldn't move,
Few farms changed hands; so rather than spend years
Trying to sell his farm and then not selling,
He burned his house down for the fire insurance
And bought the telescope with what it came to.
He had been heard to say by several:
'The best thing that we're put here for's to see;
The strongest thing that's given us to see with's
A telescope. Someone in every town
Seems to me owes it to the town to keep one.

In Littleton it may as well be me.'
After such loose talk it was no surprise
When he did what he did and burned his house down.

Mean laughter went about the town that day
To let him know we weren't the least imposed on,
And he could wait—we'd see to him tomorrow.
But the first thing next morning we reflected
If one by one we counted people out
For the least sin, it wouldn't take us long
To get so we had no one left to live with.
For to be social is to be forgiving.
Our thief, the one who does our stealing from us,
We don't cut off from coming to church suppers,
But what we miss we go to him and ask for.
He promptly gives it back, that is if still
Uneaten, unworn out, or undisposed of.
It wouldn't do to be too hard on Brad
About his telescope. Beyond the age
Of being given one for Christmas gift,
He had to take the best way he knew how
To find himself in one. Well, all we said was
He took a strange thing to be roguish over.
Some sympathy was wasted on the house,
A good old-timer dating back along;
But a house isn't sentient; the house
Didn't feel anything. And if it did,
Why not regard it as a sacrifice,
And an old-fashioned sacrifice by fire,
Instead of a new-fashioned one at auction?

Out of a house and so out of a farm
At one stroke (of a match), Brad had to turn
To earn a living on the Concord railroad,
As under-ticket-agent at a station
Where his job, when he wasn't selling tickets,
Was setting out up track and down, not plants
As on a farm, but planets, evening stars
That varied in their hue from red to green.

He got a good glass for six hundred dollars.
His new job gave him leisure for star-gazing.
Often he bid me come and have a look
Up the brass barrel, velvet black inside,
At a star quaking in the other end.
I recollect a night of broken clouds
And underfoot snow melted down to ice,
And melting further in the wind to mud.
Bradford and I had out the telescope.
We spread our two legs as we spread its three,
Pointed our thoughts the way we pointed it,
And standing at our leisure till the day broke,
Said some of the best things we ever said.
That telescope was christened the Star-splitter,
Because it didn't do a thing but split
A star in two or three the way you split
A globule of quicksilver in your hand
With one stroke of your finger in the middle.
It's a star-splitter if there ever was one
And ought to do some good if splitting stars
'Sa thing to be compared with splitting wood.

We've looked and looked, but after all where are we?
Do we know any better where we are,
And how it stands between the night tonight
And a man with a smoky lantern chimney?
How different from the way it ever stood?

## Maple

Her teacher's certainty it must be Mabel
Made Maple first take notice of her name.
She asked her father and he told her 'Maple—
Maple is right.'

                    'But teacher told the school
There's no such name.'

                    'Teachers don't know as much

As fathers about children, you tell teacher.
You tell her that it's M-A-P-L-E.
You ask her if she knows a maple tree.
Well, you were named after a maple tree.
Your mother named you. You and she just saw
Each other in passing in the room upstairs,
One coming this way into life, and one
Going the other out of life—you know?
So you can't have much recollection of her.
She had been having a long look at you.
She put her finger in your cheek so hard
It must have made your dimple there, and said,
"Maple." I said it too: "Yes, for her name."
She nodded. So we're sure there's no mistake.
I don't know what she wanted it to mean,
But it seems like some word she left to bid you
Be a good girl—be like a maple tree.
How like a maple tree's for us to guess.
Or for a little girl to guess sometime.
Not now—at least I shouldn't try too hard now.
By and by I will tell you all I know
About the different trees, and something, too,
About your mother that perhaps may help.'
Dangerous self-arousing words to sow.
Luckily all she wanted of her name then
Was to rebuke her teacher with it next day,
And give the teacher a scare as from her father.
Anything further had been wasted on her,
Or so he tried to think to avoid blame.
She would forget it. She all but forgot it.
What he sowed with her slept so long a sleep,
And came so near death in the dark of years,
That when it woke and came to life again
The flower was different from the parent seed.
It came back vaguely at the glass one day,
As she stood saying her name over aloud,
Striking it gently across her lowered eyes
To make it go well with the way she looked.
What was it about her name? Its strangeness lay
In having too much meaning. Other names,

As Lesley, Carol, Irma, Marjorie,
Signified nothing. Rose could have a meaning,
But hadn't as it went. (She knew a Rose.)
This difference from other names it was
Made people notice it—and notice her.
(They either noticed it, or got it wrong.)
Her problem was to find out what it asked
In dress or manner of the girl who bore it.
If she could form some notion of her mother—
What she had thought was lovely, and what good.
This was her mother's childhood home;
The house one story high in front, three stories
On the end it presented to the road.
(The arrangement made a pleasant sunny cellar.)
Her mother's bedroom was her father's yet,
Where she could watch her mother's picture fading.
Once she found for a bookmark in the Bible
A maple leaf she thought must have been laid
In wait for her there. She read every word
Of the two pages it was pressed between
As if it was her mother speaking to her.
But forgot to put the leaf back in closing
And lost the place never to read again.
She was sure, though, there had been nothing in it.

So she looked for herself, as everyone
Looks for himself, more or less outwardly.
And her self-seeking, fitful though it was,
May still have been what led her on to read,
And think a little, and get some city schooling.
She learned shorthand, whatever shorthand may
Have had to do with it—she sometimes wondered
So, till she found herself in a strange place
For the name Maple to have brought her to,
Taking dictation on a paper pad,
And in the pauses when she raised her eyes
Watching out of a nineteenth story window
An airship laboring with unship-like motion
And a vague all-disturbing roar above the river
Beyond the highest city built with hands.

Someone was saying in such natural tones
She almost wrote the words down on her knee,
'Do you know you remind me of a tree—
A maple tree?'

        'Because my name is Maple?'

'Isn't it Mabel? I thought it was Mabel.'

'No doubt you've heard the office call me Mabel.
I have to let them call me what they like.'

They were both stirred that he should have divined
Without the name her personal mystery.
It made it seem as if there must be something
She must have missed herself. So they were married,
And took the fancy home with them to live by.

They went on pilgrimage once to her father's
(The house one story high in front, three stories
On the side it presented to the road)
To see if there was not some special tree
She might have overlooked. They could find none,
Not so much as a single tree for shade,
Let alone grove of trees for sugar orchard.
She told him of the bookmark maple leaf
In the big Bible, and all she remembered
Of the place marked with it—'Wave offering,
Something about wave offering, it said.'

'You've never asked your father outright, have you?'

'I have, and been put off sometime, I think.'
(This was her faded memory of the way
Once long ago her father had put himself off.)

'Because no telling but it may have been
Something between your father and your mother
Not meant for us at all.'

        'Not meant for me?

Where would the fairness be in giving me
A name to carry for life, and never know
The secret of?'

　　　　　　　'And then it may have been
Something a father couldn't tell a daughter
As well as could a mother. And again
It may have been their one lapse into fancy
'Twould be too bad to make him sorry for
By bringing it up to him when he was too old.
Your father feels us round him with our questing,
And holds us off unnecessarily,
As if he didn't know what little thing
Might lead us on to a discovery.
It was as personal as he could be
About the way he saw it was with you
To say your mother, had she lived, would be
As far again as from being born to bearing.'

'Just one look more with what you say in mind,
And I give up'; which last look came to nothing.
But, though they now gave up the search forever,
They clung to what one had seen in the other
By inspiration. It proved there was something.
They kept their thoughts away from when the maples
Stood uniform in buckets, and the steam
Of sap and snow rolled off the sugar house.
When they made her related to the maples,
It was the tree the autumn fire ran through
And swept of leathern leaves, but left the bark
Unscorched, unblackened, even, by any smoke.
They always took their holidays in autumn.
Once they came on a maple in a glade,
Standing alone with smooth arms lifted up,
And every leaf of foliage she'd worn
Laid scarlet and pale pink about her feet.
But its age kept them from considering this one.
Twenty-five years ago at Maple's naming
It hardly could have been a two-leaved seedling
The next cow might have licked up out at pasture.

Could it have been another maple like it?
They hovered for a moment near discovery,
Figurative enough to see the symbol,
But lacking faith in anything to mean
The same at different times to different people.
Perhaps a filial diffidence partly kept them
From thinking it could be a thing so bridal.
And anyway it came too late for Maple.
She used her hands to cover up her eyes.
'We would not see the secret if we could now:
We are not looking for it any more.'

Thus had a name with meaning, given in death,
Made a girl's marriage, and ruled in her life.
No matter that the meaning was not clear.
A name with meaning could bring up a child,
Taking the child out of the parents' hands.
Better a meaningless name, I should say,
As leaving more to nature and happy chance.
Name children some names and see what you do.

## The Ax-Helve

I've known ere now an interfering branch
Of alder catch my lifted ax behind me.
But that was in the woods, to hold my hand
From striking at another alder's roots,
And that was, as I say, an alder branch.
This was a man, Baptiste, who stole one day
Behind me on the snow in my own yard
Where I was working at the chopping-block,
And cutting nothing not cut down already.
He caught my ax expertly on the rise,
When all my strength put forth was in his favor,
Held it a moment where it was, to calm me,
Then took it from me—and I let him take it.
I didn't know him well enough to know
What it was all about. There might be something

He had in mind to say to a bad neighbor
He might prefer to say to him disarmed.
But all he had to tell me in French-English
Was what he thought of—not me, but my ax,
Me only as I took my ax to heart.
It was the bad ax-helve someone had sold me—
'Made on machine,' he said, plowing the grain
With a thick thumbnail to show how it ran
Across the handle's long drawn serpentine,
Like the two strokes across a dollar sign.
'You give her one good crack, she's snap raght off.
Den where's your hax-ead flying t'rough de hair?'
Admitted; and yet, what was that to him?

'Come on my house and I put you one in
What's las' awhile—good hick'ry what's grow crooked.
De second growt' I cut myself—tough, tough!'

Something to sell? That wasn't how it sounded.

'Den when you say you come? It's cost you nothing.
Tonaght?'

              As well tonight as any night.

Beyond an over-warmth of kitchen stove
My welcome differed from no other welcome.
Baptiste knew best why I was where I was.
So long as he would leave enough unsaid,
I shouldn't mind his being overjoyed
(If overjoyed he was) at having got me
Where I must judge if what he knew about an ax
That not everybody else knew was to count
For nothing in the measure of a neighbor.
Hard if, though cast away for life with Yankees,
A Frenchman couldn't get his human rating!

Mrs. Baptiste came in and rocked a chair
That had as many motions as the world:
One back and forward, in and out of shadow,
That got her nowhere; one more gradual,

Sideways, that would have run her on the stove
In time, had she not realized her danger
And caught herself up bodily, chair and all,
And set herself back where she started from.
'She ain't spick too much Henglish—dat's too bad.'

I was afraid, in brightening first on me,
Then on Baptiste, as if she understood
What passed between us, she was only feigning.
Baptiste was anxious for her; but no more
Than for himself, so placed he couldn't hope
To keep his bargain of the morning with me
In time to keep me from suspecting him
Of really never having meant to keep it.

Needlessly soon he had his ax-helves out,
A quiverful to choose from, since he wished me
To have the best he had, or had to spare—
Not for me to ask which, when what he took
Had beauties he had to point me out at length
To insure their not being wasted on me.
He liked to have it slender as a whipstock,
Free from the least knot, equal to the strain
Of bending like a sword across the knee.
He showed me that the lines of a good helve
Were native to the grain before the knife
Expressed them, and its curves were no false curves
Put on it from without. And there its strength lay
For the hard work. He chafed its long white body
From end to end with his rough hand shut round it.
He tried it at the eye-hole in the ax-head.
'Hahn, hahn,' he mused, 'don't need much taking down.'
Baptiste knew how to make a short job long
For love of it, and yet not waste time either.

Do you know, what we talked about was knowledge?
Baptiste on his defense about the children
He kept from school, or did his best to keep—
Whatever school and children and our doubts
Of laid-on education had to do

With the curves of his ax-helves and his having
Used these unscrupulously to bring me
To see for once the inside of his house.
Was I desired in friendship, partly as someone
To leave it to, whether the right to hold
Such doubts of education should depend
Upon the education of those who held them?

But now he brushed the shavings from his knee
And stood the ax there on its horse's hoof,
Erect, but not without its waves, as when
The snake stood up for evil in the Garden,—
Top-heavy with a heaviness his short,
Thick hand made light of, steel-blue chin drawn down
And in a little—a French touch in that.
Baptiste drew back and squinted at it, pleased;
'See how she's cock her head!'


## The Grindstone

Having a wheel and four legs of its own
Has never availed the cumbersome grindstone
To get it anywhere that I can see.
These hands have helped it go, and even race;
Not all the motion, though, they ever lent,
Not all the miles it may have thought it went,
Have got it one step from the starting place.
It stands beside the same old apple tree.
The shadow of the apple tree is thin
Upon it now, its feet are fast in snow.
All other farm machinery's gone in,
And some of it on no more legs and wheel
Than the grindstone can boast to stand or go.
(I'm thinking chiefly of the wheelbarrow.)
For months it hasn't known the taste of steel,
Washed down with rusty water in a tin.
But standing outdoors hungry, in the cold,
Except in towns at night, is not a sin.

And, anyway, its standing in the yard
Under a ruinous live apple tree
Has nothing any more to do with me,
Except that I remember how of old
One summer day, all day I drove it hard,
And someone mounted on it rode it hard,
And he and I between us ground a blade.

I gave it the preliminary spin,
And poured on water (tears it might have been),
And when it almost gaily jumped and flowed,
A Father-Time-like man got on and rode,
Armed with a scythe and spectacles that glowed.
He turned on will-power to increase the load
And slow me down—and I abruptly slowed,
Like coming to a sudden railroad station.
I changed from hand to hand in desperation.
I wondered what machine of ages gone
This represented an improvement on.
For all I knew it may have sharpened spears
And arrowheads itself. Much use for years
Had gradually worn it an oblate
Spheroid that kicked and struggled in its gait,
Appearing to return me hate for hate;
(But I forgive it now as easily
As any other boyhood enemy
Whose pride has failed to get him anywhere).
I wondered who it was the man thought ground—
The one who held the wheel back or the one
Who gave his life to keep it going round?
I wondered if he really thought it fair
For him to have the say when we were done.
Such were the bitter thoughts to which I turned.

Not for myself was I so much concerned.
Oh no!—although, of course, I could have found
A better way to pass the afternoon
Than grinding discord out of a grindstone,
And beating insects at their gritty tune.
Nor was I for the man so much concerned.

Once when the grindstone almost jumped its bearing
It looked as if he might be badly thrown
And wounded on his blade. So far from caring,
I laughed inside, and only cranked the faster,
(It ran as if it wasn't greased but glued);
I'd welcome any moderate disaster
That might be calculated to postpone
What evidently nothing could conclude.
The thing that made me more and more afraid
Was that we'd ground it sharp and hadn't known.
And now were only wasting precious blade.
And when he raised it dripping once and tried
The creepy edge of it with wary touch,
And viewed it over his glasses funny-eyed,
Only disinterestedly to decide
It needed a turn more, I could have cried
Wasn't there danger of a turn too much?
Mightn't we make it worse instead of better?
I was for leaving something to the whetter.
What if it wasn't all it should be? I'd
Be satisfied if he'd be satisfied.

## Paul's Wife

To drive Paul out of any lumber camp
All that was needed was to say to him,
'How is the wife, Paul?'—and he'd disappear.
Some said it was because he had no wife,
And hated to be twitted on the subject;
Others because he'd come within a day
Or so of having one, and then been jilted;
Others because he'd had one once, a good one,
Who'd run away with someone else and left him;
And others still because he had one now
He only had to be reminded of,—
He was all duty to her in a minute:
He had to run right off to look her up,
As if to say, 'That's so, how is my wife?

I hope she isn't getting into mischief.'
No one was anxious to get rid of Paul.
He'd been the hero of the mountain camps
Ever since, just to show them, he had slipped
The bark of a whole tamarack off whole,
As clean as boys do off a willow twig
To make a willow whistle on a Sunday
In April by subsiding meadow brooks.
They seemed to ask him just to see him go,
'How is the wife, Paul?' and he always went.
He never stopped to murder anyone
Who asked the question. He just disappeared—
Nobody knew in what direction,
Although it wasn't usually long
Before they heard of him in some new camp,
The same Paul at the same old feats of logging.
The question everywhere was why should Paul
Object to being asked a civil question—
A man you could say almost anything to
Short of a fighting word. You have the answers.
And there was one more not so fair to Paul:
That Paul had married a wife not his equal.
Paul was ashamed of her. To match a hero,
She would have had to be a heroine;
Instead of which she was some half-breed squaw.
But if the story Murphy told was true,
She wasn't anything to be ashamed of.

You know Paul could do wonders. Everyone's
Heard how he thrashed the horses on a load
That wouldn't budge until they simply stretched
Their rawhide harness from the load to camp.
Paul told the boss the load would be all right,
'The sun will bring your load in'—and it did—
By shrinking the rawhide to natural length.
That's what is called a stretcher. But I guess
The one about his jumping so's to land
With both his feet at once against the ceiling,
And then land safely right side up again,
Back on the floor, is fact or pretty near fact.

Well, this is such a yarn. Paul sawed his wife
Out of a white-pine log. Murphy was there,
And, as you might say, saw the lady born.
Paul worked at anything in lumbering.
He'd been hard at it taking boards away
For—I forget—the last ambitious sawyer
To want to find out if he couldn't pile
The lumber on Paul till Paul begged for mercy.
They'd sliced the first slab off a big butt log,
And the sawyer had slammed the carriage back
To slam end on again against the saw teeth.
To judge them by the way they caught themselves
When they saw what had happened to the log,
They must have had a guilty expectation
Something was going to go with their slambanging.
Something had left a broad black streak of grease
On the new wood the whole length of the log
Except, perhaps, a foot at either end.
But when Paul put his finger in the grease,
It wasn't grease at all, but a long slot.
The log was hollow. They were sawing pine.
'First time I ever saw a hollow pine.
That comes of having Paul around the place.
Take it to hell for me,' the sawyer said.
Everyone had to have a look at it,
And tell Paul what he ought to do about it.
(They treated it as his.) 'You take a jack-knife,
And spread the opening, and you've got a dug-out
All dug to go a-fishing in.' To Paul
The hollow looked too sound and clean and empty
Ever to have housed birds or beasts or bees.
There was no entrance for them to get in by.
It looked to him like some new kind of hollow
He thought he'd *better* take his jack-knife to.
So after work that evening he came back
And let enough light into it by cutting
To see if it was empty. He made out in there
A slender length of pith, or was it pith?
It might have been the skin a snake had cast
And left stood up on end inside the tree

The hundred years the tree must have been growing.
More cutting and he had this in both hands,
And, looking from it to the pond nearby,
Paul wondered how it would respond to water.
Not a breeze stirred, but just the breath of air
He made in walking slowly to the beach
Blew it once off his hands and almost broke it.
He laid it at the edge where it could drink.
At the first drink it rustled and grew limp.
At the next drink it grew invisible.
Paul dragged the shallows for it with his fingers,
And thought it must have melted. It was gone.
And then beyond the open water, dim with midges,
Where the log drive lay pressed against the boom,
It slowly rose a person, rose a girl,
Her wet hair heavy on her like a helmet,
Who, leaning on a log looked back at Paul.
And that made Paul in turn look back
To see if it was anyone behind him
That she was looking at instead of him.
Murphy had been there watching all the time,
But from a shed where neither of them could see him.
There was a moment of suspense in birth
When the girl seemed too water-logged to live,
Before she caught her first breath with a gasp
And laughed. Then she climbed slowly to her feet,
And walked off talking to herself or Paul
Across the logs like backs of alligators,
Paul taking after her around the pond.

Next evening Murphy and some other fellows
Got drunk, and tracked the pair up Catamount,
From the bare top of which there is a view
To other hills across a kettle valley.
And there, well after dark, let Murphy tell it,
They saw Paul and his creature keeping house.
It was the only glimpse that anyone
Has had of Paul and her since Murphy saw them
Falling in love across the twilight mill-pond.
More than a mile across the wilderness

They sat together halfway up a cliff
In a small niche let into it, the girl
Brightly, as if a star played on the place,
Paul darkly, like her shadow. All the light
Was from the girl herself, though, not from a star,
As was apparent from what happened next.
All those great ruffians put their throats together,
And let out a loud yell, and threw a bottle,
As a brute tribute of respect to beauty.
Of course the bottle fell short by a mile,
But the shout reached the girl and put her light out.
She went out like a firefly, and that was all.

So there were witnesses that Paul was married,
And not to anyone to be ashamed of.
Everyone had been wrong in judging Paul.
Murphy told me Paul put on all those airs
About his wife to keep her to himself.
Paul was what's called a terrible possessor.
Owning a wife with him meant owning her.
She wasn't anybody else's business,
Either to praise her, or so much as name her,
And he'd thank people not to think of her.
Murphy's idea was that a man like Paul
Wouldn't be spoken to about a wife
In any way the world knew how to speak.


## Wild Grapes

What tree may not the fig be gathered from?
The grape may not be gathered from the birch?
It's all you know the grape, or know the birch.
As a girl gathered from the birch myself
Equally with my weight in grapes, one autumn,
I ought to know what tree the grape is fruit of.
I was born, I suppose, like anyone,
And grew to be a little boyish girl
My brother could not always leave at home.

But that beginning was wiped out in fear
The day I swung suspended with the grapes,
And was come after like Eurydice
And brought down safely from the upper regions;
And the life I live now's an extra life
I can waste as I please on whom I please.
So if you see me celebrate two birthdays,
And give myself out as two different ages,
One of them five years younger than I look—

One day my brother led me to a glade
Where a white birch he knew of stood alone,
Wearing a thin head-dress of pointed leaves,
And heavy on her heavy hair behind,
Against her neck, an ornament of grapes.
Grapes, I knew grapes from having seen them last year.
One bunch of them, and there began to be
Bunches all round me growing in white birches,
The way they grew round Leif the Lucky's German;
Mostly as much beyond my lifted hands, though,
As the moon used to seem when I was younger,
And only freely to be had for climbing.
My brother did the climbing; and at first
Threw me down grapes to miss and scatter
And have to hunt for in sweet fern and hardhack;
Which gave him some time to himself to eat,
But not so much, perhaps, as a boy needed.
So then, to make me wholly self-supporting,
He climbed still higher and bent the tree to earth
And put it in my hands to pick my own grapes.
'Here, take a tree-top, I'll get down another.
Hold on with all your might when I let go.'
I said I had the tree. It wasn't true.
The opposite was true. The tree had me.
The minute it was left with me alone
It caught me up as if I were the fish
And it the fishpole. So I was translated
To loud cries from my brother of 'Let go!
Don't you know anything, you girl? Let go!'
But I, with something of the baby grip

Acquired ancestrally in just such trees
When wilder mothers than our wildest now
Hung babies out on branches by the hands
To dry or wash or tan, I don't know which,
(You'll have to ask an evolutionist)—
I held on uncomplainingly for life.
My brother tried to make me laugh to help me.
'What are you doing up there in those grapes?
Don't be afraid. A few of them won't hurt you.
I mean, they won't pick you if you don't them.'
Much danger of my picking anything!
By that time I was pretty well reduced
To a philosophy of hang-and-let-hang.
'Now you know how it feels,' my brother said,
'To be a bunch of fox-grapes, as they call them,
That when it thinks it has escaped the fox
By growing where it shouldn't—on a birch,
Where a fox wouldn't think to look for it—
And if he looked and found it, couldn't reach it—
Just then come you and I to gather it.
Only you have the advantage of the grapes
In one way: you have one more stem to cling by,
And promise more resistance to the picker.'

One by one I lost off my hat and shoes,
And still I clung. I let my head fall back,
And shut my eyes against the sun, my ears
Against my brother's nonsense; 'Drop,' he said,
'I'll catch you in my arms. It isn't far.'
(Stated in lengths of him it might not be.)
'Drop or I'll shake the tree and shake you down.'
Grim silence on my part as I sank lower,
My small wrists stretching till they showed the banjo strings.
'Why, if she isn't serious about it!
Hold tight awhile till I think what to do.
I'll bend the tree down and let you down by it.'
I don't know much about the letting down;
But once I felt ground with my stocking feet
And the world came revolving back to me,
I know I looked long at my curled-up fingers,

Before I straightened them and brushed the bark off.
My brother said: 'Don't you weigh anything?
Try to weigh something next time, so you won't
Be run off with by birch trees into space.'

It wasn't my not weighing anything
So much as my not knowing anything—
My brother had been nearer right before.
I had not taken the first step in knowledge;
I had not learned to let go with the hands,
As still I have not learned to with the heart,
And have no wish to with the heart—nor need,
That I can see. The mind—is not the heart.
I may yet live, as I know others live,
To wish in vain to let go with the mind—
Of cares, at night, to sleep; but nothing tells me
That I need learn to let go with the heart.

## Place for a Third

Nothing to say to all those marriages!
She had made three herself to three of his.
The score was even for them, three to three.
But come to die she found she cared so much:
She thought of children in a burial row;
Three children in a burial row were sad.
One man's three women in a burial row
Somehow made her impatient with the man.
And so she said to Laban, 'You have done
A good deal right; don't do the last thing wrong.
Don't make me lie with those two other women.'

Laban said, No, he would not make her lie
With anyone but that she had a mind to,
If that was how she felt, of course, he said.
She went her way. But Laban having caught
This glimpse of lingering person in Eliza,
And anxious to make all he could of it

With something he remembered in himself,
Tried to think how he could exceed his promise,
And give good measure to the dead, though thankless.
If that was how she felt, he kept repeating.
His first thought under pressure was a grave
In a new boughten grave plot by herself,
Under he didn't care how great a stone:
He'd sell a yoke of steers to pay for it.
And weren't there special cemetery flowers,
That, once grief sets to growing, grief may rest;
The flowers will go on with grief awhile,
And no one seem neglecting or neglected?
A prudent grief will not despise such aids.
He thought of evergreen and everlasting.
And then he had a thought worth many of these.
Somewhere must be the grave of the young boy
Who married her for playmate more than helpmate,
And sometimes laughed at what it was between them.
How would she like to sleep her last with him?
Where was his grave? Did Laban know his name?

He found the grave a town or two away,
The headstone cut with *John, Beloved Husband,*
Beside it room reserved, the say a sister's,
A never-married sister's of that husband,
Whether Eliza would be welcome there.
The dead was bound to silence: ask the sister.
So Laban saw the sister, and, saying nothing
Of where Eliza wanted *not* to lie,
And who had thought to lay her with her first love,
Begged simply for the grave. The sister's face
Fell all in wrinkles of responsibility.
She wanted to do right. She'd have to think.
Laban was old and poor, yet seemed to care;
And she was old and poor—but she cared, too.
They sat. She cast one dull, old look at him,
Then turned him out to go on other errands
She said he might attend to in the village,
While she made up her mind how much she cared—

And how much Laban cared—and why he cared,
(She made shrewd eyes to see where he came in.)
She'd looked Eliza up her second time,
A widow at her second husband's grave,
And offered her a home to rest awhile
Before she went the poor man's widow's way,
Housekeeping for the next man out of wedlock.
She and Eliza had been friends through all.
Who was she to judge marriage in a world
Whose Bible's so confused in marriage counsel?
The sister had not come across this Laban;
A decent product of life's ironing-out;
She must not keep him waiting. Time would press
Between the death day and the funeral day.
So when she saw him coming in the street
She hurried her decision to be ready
To meet him with his answer at the door.
Laban had known about what it would be
From the way she had set her poor old mouth,
To do, as she had put it, what was right.

She gave it through the screen door closed between them:
'No, not with John. There wouldn't be no sense.
Eliza's had too many other men.'

Laban was forced to fall back on his plan
To buy Eliza a plot to lie alone in:
Which gives him for himself a choice of lots
When his time comes to die and settle down.


## Two Witches

### I

#### THE WITCH OF COÖS

I stayed the night for shelter at a farm
Behind the mountain, with a mother and son,
Two old-believers. They did all the talking.

MOTHER. Folks think a witch who has familiar spirits
She could call up to pass a winter evening,
But won't, should be burned at the stake or something.
Summoning spirits isn't 'Button, button,
Who's got the button,' I would have them know.

SON. Mother can make a common table rear
And kick with two legs like an army mule.

MOTHER. And when I've done it, what good have I done?
Rather than tip a table for you, let me
Tell you what Ralle the Sioux Control once told me.
He said the dead had souls, but when I asked him
How could that be—I thought the dead were souls,
He broke my trance. Don't that make you suspicious
That there's something the dead are keeping back?
Yes, there's something the dead are keeping back.

SON. You wouldn't want to tell him what we have
Up attic, mother?

MOTHER. Bones—a skeleton.

SON. But the headboard of mother's bed is pushed
Against the attic door: the door is nailed.
It's harmless. Mother hears it in the night
Halting perplexed behind the barrier
Of door and headboard. Where it wants to get
Is back into the cellar where it came from.

MOTHER. We'll never let them, will we, son! We'll never!

SON. It left the cellar forty years ago
And carried itself like a pile of dishes
Up one flight from the cellar to the kitchen,
Another from the kitchen to the bedroom,
Another from the bedroom to the attic,
Right past both father and mother, and neither stopped it.
Father had gone upstairs; mother was downstairs.
I was a baby: I don't know where I was.

MOTHER. The only fault my husband found with me—
I went to sleep before I went to bed,
Especially in winter when the bed
Might just as well be ice and the clothes snow.
The night the bones came up the cellar-stairs
Toffile had gone to bed alone and left me,
But left an open door to cool the room off
So as to sort of turn me out of it.
I was just coming to myself enough
To wonder where the cold was coming from,
When I heard Toffile upstairs in the bedroom
And thought I heard him downstairs in the cellar.
The board we had laid down to walk dry-shod on
When there was water in the cellar in spring
Struck the hard cellar bottom. And then someone
Began the stairs, two footsteps for each step,
The way a man with one leg and a crutch,
Or a little child, comes up. It wasn't Toffile:
It wasn't anyone who could be there.
The bulkhead double-doors were double-locked
And swollen tight and buried under snow.
The cellar windows were banked up with sawdust
And swollen tight and buried under snow.
It was the bones. I knew them—and good reason.
My first impulse was to get to the knob
And hold the door. But the bones didn't try
The door; they halted helpless on the landing,
Waiting for things to happen in their favor.
The faintest restless rustling ran all through them.
I never could have done the thing I did
If the wish hadn't been too strong in me
To see how they were mounted for this walk.
I had a vision of them put together
Not like a man, but like a chandelier.
So suddenly I flung the door wide on him.
A moment he stood balancing with emotion,
And all but lost himself. (A tongue of fire
Flashed out and licked along his upper teeth.
Smoke rolled inside the sockets of his eyes.)
Then he came at me with one hand outstretched,

The way he did in life once; but this time
I struck the hand off brittle on the floor,
And fell back from him on the floor myself.
The finger-pieces slid in all directions.
(Where did I see one of those pieces lately?
Hand me my button-box—it must be there.)
I sat up on the floor and shouted, 'Toffile,
It's coming up to you.' It had its choice
Of the door to the cellar or the hall.
It took the hall door for the novelty,
And set off briskly for so slow a thing,
Still going every which way in the joints, though,
So that it looked like lightning or a scribble,
From the slap I had just now given its hand.
I listened till it almost climbed the stairs
From the hall to the only finished bedroom,
Before I got up to do anything;
Then ran and shouted, 'Shut the bedroom door,
Toffile, for my sake!' 'Company?' he said,
'Don't make me get up; I'm too warm in bed.'
So lying forward weakly on the handrail
I pushed myself upstairs, and in the light
(The kitchen had been dark) I had to own
I could see nothing. 'Toffile, I don't see it.
It's with us in the room though. It's the bones.'
'What bones?' 'The cellar bones—out of the grave.'
That made him throw his bare legs out of bed
And sit up by me and take hold of me.
I wanted to put out the light and see
If I could see it, or else mow the room,
With our arms at the level of our knees,
And bring the chalk-pile down. 'I'll tell you what—
It's looking for another door to try.
The uncommonly deep snow has made him think
Of his old song, *The Wild Colonial Boy,*
He always used to sing along the tote road.
He's after an open door to get outdoors.
Let's trap him with an open door up attic.'
Toffile agreed to that, and sure enough,

Almost the moment he was given an opening,
The steps began to climb the attic stairs.
I heard them. Toffile didn't seem to hear them.
'Quick!' I slammed to the door and held the knob.
'Toffile, get nails.' I made him nail the door shut
And push the headboard of the bed against it.
Then we asked was there anything
Up attic that we'd ever want again.
The attic was less to us than the cellar.
If the bones liked the attic, let them have it.
Let them stay in the attic. When they sometimes
Come down the stairs at night and stand perplexed
Behind the door and headboard of the bed,
Brushing their chalky skull with chalky fingers,
With sounds like the dry rattling of a shutter,
That's what I sit up in the dark to say—
To no one any more since Toffile died.
Let them stay in the attic since they went there.
I promised Toffile to be cruel to them
For helping them be cruel once to him.

SON. We think they had a grave down in the cellar.

MOTHER. We know they had a grave down in the cellar.

SON. We never could find out whose bones they were.

MOTHER. Yes, we could too, son. Tell the truth for once.
They were a man's his father killed for me.
I mean a man he killed instead of me.
The least I could do was to help dig their grave.
We were about it one night in the cellar.
Son knows the story: but 'twas not for him
To tell the truth, suppose the time had come.
Son looks surprised to see me end a lie
We'd kept all these years between ourselves
So as to have it ready for outsiders.
But tonight I don't care enough to lie—
I don't remember why I ever cared.

Toffile, if he were here, I don't believe
Could tell you why he ever cared himself. . . .

She hadn't found the finger-bone she wanted
Among the buttons poured out in her lap.
I verified the name next morning: Toffile.
The rural letter box said Toffile Lajway.


II

## THE PAUPER WITCH OF GRAFTON

Now that they've got it settled whose I be,
I'm going to tell them something they won't like:
They've got it settled wrong, and I can prove it.
Flattered I must be to have two towns fighting
To make a present of me to each other.
They don't dispose me, either one of them,
To spare them any trouble. Double trouble's
Always the witch's motto anyway.
I'll double theirs for both of them—you watch me.
They'll find they've got the whole thing to do over,
That is, if facts is what they want to go by.
They set a lot (now don't they?) by a record
Of Arthur Amy's having once been up
For Hog Reeve in March Meeting here in Warren.
I could have told them any time this twelvemonth
The Arthur Amy I was married to
Couldn't have been the one they say was up
In Warren at March Meeting for the reason
He wa'n't but fifteen at the time they say.
The Arthur Amy I was married to
Voted the only times he ever voted,
Which wasn't many, in the town of Wentworth.
One of the times was when 'twas in the warrant
To see if the town wanted to take over
The tote road to our clearing where we lived.
I'll tell you who'd remember—Heman Lapish.
Their Arthur Amy was the father of mine.
So now they've dragged it through the law courts once

I guess they'd better drag it through again.
Wentworth and Warren's both good towns to live in,
Only I happen to prefer to live
In Wentworth from now on; and when all's said,
Right's right, and the temptation to do right
When I can hurt someone by doing it
Has always been too much for me, it has.
I know of some folks that'd be set up
At having in their town a noted witch:
But most would have to think of the expense
That even I would be. They ought to know
That as a witch I'd often milk a bat
And that'd be enough to last for days.
It'd make my position stronger, think,
If I was to consent to give some sign
To make it surer that I was a witch?
It wa'n't no sign, I s'pose, when Mallice Huse
Said that I took him out in his old age
And rode all over everything on him
Until I'd had him worn to skin and bones,
And if I'd left him hitched unblanketed
In front of one Town Hall, I'd left him hitched
In front of every one in Grafton County.
Some cried shame on me not to blanket him,
The poor old man. It would have been all right
If someone hadn't said to gnaw the posts
He stood beside and leave his trade mark on them,
So they could recognize them. Not a post
That they could hear tell of was scarified.
They made him keep on gnawing till he whined.
Then that same smarty someone said to look—
He'd bet Huse was a cribber and had gnawed
The crib he slept in—and as sure's you're born
They found he's gnawed the four posts of his bed,
All four of them to splinters. What did that prove?
Not that he hadn't gnawed the hitching posts
He said he had besides. Because a horse
Gnaws in the stable ain't no proof to me
He don't gnaw trees and posts and fences too.
But everybody took it for a proof.

I was a strapping girl of twenty then.
The smarty someone who spoiled everything
Was Arthur Amy. You know who he was.
That was the way he started courting me.
He never said much after we were married,
But I mistrusted he was none too proud
Of having interfered in the Huse business.
I guess he found he got more out of me
By having me a witch. Or something happened
To turn him round. He got to saying things
To undo what he'd done and make it right,
Like, 'No, she ain't come back from kiting yet.
Last night was one of her nights out. She's kiting.
She thinks when the wind makes a night of it
She might as well herself.' But he liked best
To let on he was plagued to death with me:
If anyone had seen me coming home
Over the ridgepole, 'stride of a broomstick,
As often as he had in the tail of the night,
He guessed they'd know what he had to put up with.
Well, I showed Arthur Amy signs enough
Off from the house as far as we could keep
And from barn smells you can't wash out of plowed ground
With all the rain and snow of seven years;
And I don't mean just skulls of Rogers' Rangers
On Moosilauke, but woman signs to man,
Only bewitched so I would last him longer.
Up where the trees grow short, the mosses tall,
I made him gather me wet snow berries
On slippery rocks beside a waterfall.
I made him do it for me in the dark.
And he liked everything I made him do.
I hope if he is where he sees me now
He's so far off he can't see what I've come to.
You *can* come down from everything to nothing.
All is, if I'd a-known when I was young
And full of it, that this would be the end,
It doesn't seem as if I'd had the courage
To make so free and kick up in folks' faces.
I might have, but it doesn't seem as if.

## An Empty Threat

I stay;
But it isn't as if
There wasn't always Hudson's Bay
And the fur trade,
A small skiff
And a paddle blade.

I can just see my tent pegged,
And me on the floor,
Crosslegged,
And a trapper looking in at the door
With furs to sell.

His name's Joe,
Alias John,
And between what he doesn't know
And won't tell
About where Henry Hudson's gone,
I can't say he's much help;
But we get on.

The seal yelp
On an ice cake.
It's not men by some mistake?

No,
There's not a soul
For a wind-break
Between me and the North Pole—

Except always John-Joe,
My French Indian Esquimaux,
And he's off setting traps,
In one himself perhaps.

Give a head shake
Over so much bay
Thrown away

In snow and mist
That doesn't exist,
I was going to say,
For God, man or beast's sake,
Yet does perhaps for all three.

Don't ask Joe
What it is to him.
It's sometimes dim
What it is to me,
Unless it be
It's the old captain's dark fate
Who failed to find or force a strait
In its two-thousand-mile coast;
And his crew left him where he failed,
And nothing came of all he sailed.

It's to say, 'You and I'
To such a ghost,
'You and I
Off here
With the dead race of the Great Auk!'
And, 'Better defeat almost,
If seen clear,
Than life's victories of doubt
That need endless talk talk
To make them out.'

## A Fountain, a Bottle, a Donkey's Ears and Some Books

Old Davis owned a solid mica mountain
In Dalton that would some day make his fortune.
There'd been some Boston people out to see it:
And experts said that deep down in the mountain
The mica sheets were big as plate glass windows.
He'd like to take me there and show it to me.

'I'll tell you what you show me. You remember
You said you knew the place where once, on Kinsman,
The early Mormons made a settlement
And built a stone baptismal font outdoors—
But Smith, or someone, called them off the mountain
To go West to a worse fight with the desert.
You said you'd seen the stone baptismal font.
Well, take me there.'

                    'Some day I will.'

                              'Today.'

'Huh, that old bathtub, what is that to see?
Let's talk about it.'

                    'Let's go see the place.'

'To shut you up I'll tell you what I'll do:
I'll find that fountain if it takes all summer,
And both of our united strengths, to do it.'

'You've lost it, then?'

                    'Not so but I can find it.
No doubt it's grown up some to woods around it.
The mountain may have shifted since I saw it
In eighty-five.'

                    'As long ago as that?'

'If I remember rightly, it had sprung
A leak and emptied then. And forty years
Can do a good deal to bad masonry.
You won't see any Mormon swimming in it.
But you have said it, and we're off to find it.
Old as I am, I'm going to let myself
Be dragged by you all over everywhere—'

'I thought you were a guide.'

'I am a guide,
And that's why I can't decently refuse you.'

We made a day of it out of the world,
Ascending to descend to reascend.
The old man seriously took his bearings,
And spoke his doubts in every open place.

We came out on a look-off where we faced
A cliff, and on the cliff a bottle painted,
Or stained by vegetation from above,
A likeness to surprise the thrilly tourist.

'Well, if I haven't brought you to the fountain,
At least I've brought you to the famous Bottle.'

'I won't accept the substitute. It's empty.'

'So's everything.'

'I want my fountain.'

'I guess you'd find the fountain just as empty.
And anyway this tells me where I am.'

'Hadn't you long suspected where you were?'

'You mean miles from that Mormon settlement?
Look here, you treat your guide with due respect
If you don't want to spend the night outdoors.
I vow we must be near the place from where
The two converging slides, the avalanches,
On Marshall, look like donkey's ears.
We may as well see that and save the day.'

'Don't donkey's ears suggest we shake our own?'

'For God's sake, aren't you fond of viewing nature?
You don't like nature. All you like is books.

What signify a donkey's ears and bottle,
However natural? Give you your books!
Well then, right here is where I show you books.
Come straight down off this mountain just as fast
As we can fall and keep a-bouncing on our feet.
It's hell for knees unless done hell-for-leather.'

'Be ready,' I thought, 'for almost anything.'

We struck a road I didn't recognize,
But welcomed for the chance to lave my shoes
In dust once more. We followed this a mile,
Perhaps, to where it ended at a house
I didn't know was there. It was the kind
To bring me to for broad-board paneling.
I never saw so good a house deserted.

'Excuse me if I ask you in a window
That happens to be broken,' Davis said.
'The outside doors as yet have held against us.
I want to introduce you to the people
Who used to live here. They were Robinsons.
You must have heard of Clara Robinson,
The poetess who wrote the book of verses
And had it published. It was all about
The posies on her inner window sill,
And the birds on her outer window sill,
And how she tended both, or had them tended:
She never tended anything herself.
She was "shut in" for life. She lived her whole
Life long in bed, and wrote her things in bed.
I'll show you how she had her sills extended
To entertain the birds and hold the flowers.
Our business first's up attic with her books.'

We trod uncomfortably on crunching glass
Through a house stripped of everything
Except, it seemed, the poetess's poems.
Books, I should say!—if books are what is needed.

A whole edition in a packing-case,
That, overflowing like a horn of plenty,
Or like the poetess's heart of love,
Had spilled them near the window toward the light
Where driven rain had wet and swollen them.
Enough to stock a village library—
Unfortunately all of one kind, though.
They had been brought home from some publisher
And taken thus into the family.
Boys and bad hunters had known what to do
With stone and lead to unprotected glass:
Shatter it inward on the unswept floors.
How had the tender verse escaped their outrage?
By being invisible for what it was,
Or else by some remoteness that defied them
To find out what to do to hurt a poem.
Yet oh! the tempting flatness of a book,
To send it sailing out the attic window
Till it caught wind, and, opening out its covers,
Tried to improve on sailing like a tile
By flying like a bird (silent in flight,
But all the burden of its body song),
Only to tumble like a stricken bird,
And lie in stones and bushes unretrieved.
Books were not thrown irreverently about.
They simply lay where someone now and then,
Having tried one, had dropped it at his feet
And left it lying where it fell rejected.
Here were all those the poetess's life
Had been too short to sell or give away.

'Take one,' Old Davis bade me graciously.

'Why not take two or three?'

                              'Take all you want.
Good-looking books like that.' He picked one fresh
In virgin wrapper from deep in the box,
And stroked it with a horny-handed kindness.

He read in one and I read in another,
Both either looking for or finding something.

The attic wasps went missing by like bullets.

I was soon satisfied for the time being.

All the way home I kept remembering
The small book in my pocket. It was there.
The poetess had sighed, I knew, in heaven
At having eased her heart of one more copy—
Legitimately. My demand upon her,
Though slight, was a demand. She felt the tug.
In time she would be rid of all her books.

## I Will Sing You One-O

It was long I lay
Awake that night
Wishing the tower
Would name the hour
And tell me whether
To call it day
(Though not yet light)
And give up sleep.
The snow fell deep
With the hiss of spray;
Two winds would meet,
One down one street,
One down another,
And fight in a smother
Of dust and feather.
I could not say,
But feared the cold
Had checked the pace
Of the tower clock

By tying together
Its hands of gold
Before its face.

Then came one knock!
A note unruffled
Of earthly weather,
Though strange and muffled.
The tower said, 'One!'
And then a steeple.
They spoke to themselves
And such few people
As winds might rouse
From sleeping warm
(But not unhouse).
They left the storm
That struck *en masse*
My window glass
Like a beaded fur.
In that grave One
They spoke of the sun
And moon and stars,
Saturn and Mars
And Jupiter.
Still more unfettered,
They left the named
And spoke of the lettered,
The sigmas and taus
Of constellations.
They filled their throats
With the furthest bodies
To which man sends his
Speculation,
Beyond which God is;
The cosmic motes
Of yawning lenses.
Their solemn peals
Were not their own:
They spoke for the clock
With whose vast wheels

Theirs interlock.
In that grave word
Uttered alone
The utmost star
Trembled and stirred,
Though set so far
Its whirling frenzies
Appear like standing
In one self station.
It has not ranged,
And save for the wonder
Of once expanding
To be a nova,
It has not changed
To the eye of man
On planets over
Around and under
It in creation
Since man began
To drag down man
And nation nation.

## Fragmentary Blue

Why make so much of fragmentary blue
In here and there a bird, or butterfly,
Or flower, or wearing-stone, or open eye,
When heaven presents in sheets the solid hue?

Since earth is earth, perhaps, not heaven (as yet)—
Though some savants make earth include the sky;
And blue so far above us comes so high,
It only gives our wish for blue a whet.

## Fire and Ice

Some say the world will end in fire,
Some say in ice.
From what I've tasted of desire
I hold with those who favor fire.
But if it had to perish twice,
I think I know enough of hate
To say that for destruction ice
Is also great
And would suffice.

## In a Disused Graveyard

The living come with grassy tread
To read the gravestones on the hill;
The graveyard draws the living still,
But never any more the dead.

The verses in it say and say:
'The ones who living come today
To read the stones and go away
Tomorrow dead will come to stay.'

So sure of death the marbles rhyme,
Yet can't help marking all the time
How no one dead will seem to come.
What is it men are shrinking from?

It would be easy to be clever
And tell the stones: Men hate to die
And have stopped dying now forever.
I think they would believe the lie.

## Dust of Snow

The way a crow
Shook down on me
The dust of snow
From a hemlock tree

Has given my heart
A change of mood
And saved some part
Of a day I had rued.

## To E. T.

I slumbered with your poems on my breast
Spread open as I dropped them half-read through
Like dove wings on a figure on a tomb
To see, if in a dream they brought of you,

I might not have the chance I missed in life
Through some delay, and call you to your face
First soldier, and then poet, and then both,
Who died a soldier-poet of your race.

I meant, you meant, that nothing should remain
Unsaid between us, brother, and this remained—
And one thing more that was not then to say:
The Victory for what it lost and gained.

You went to meet the shell's embrace of fire
On Vimy Ridge; and when you fell that day
The war seemed over more for you than me,
But now for me than you—the other way.

How over, though, for even me who knew
The foe thrust back unsafe beyond the Rhine,
If I was not to speak of it to you
And see you pleased once more with words of mine?

## Nothing Gold Can Stay

Nature's first green is gold,
Her hardest hue to hold.
Her early leaf's a flower;
But only so an hour.
Then leaf subsides to leaf.
So Eden sank to grief,
So dawn goes down to day.
Nothing gold can stay.


## The Runaway

Once when the snow of the year was beginning to fall,
We stopped by a mountain pasture to say, 'Whose colt?'
A little Morgan had one forefoot on the wall,
The other curled at his breast. He dipped his head
And snorted at us. And then he had to bolt.
We heard the miniature thunder where he fled,
And we saw him, or thought we saw him, dim and gray,
Like a shadow against the curtain of falling flakes.
'I think the little fellow's afraid of the snow.
He isn't winter-broken. It isn't play
With the little fellow at all. He's running away.
I doubt if even his mother could tell him, "Sakes,
It's only weather." He'd think she didn't know!
Where is his mother? He can't be out alone.'
And now he comes again with clatter of stone,
And mounts the wall again with whited eyes
And all his tail that isn't hair up straight.
He shudders his coat as if to throw off flies.
'Whoever it is that leaves him out so late,
When other creatures have gone to stall and bin,
Ought to be told to come and take him in.'

## The Aim Was Song

Before man came to blow it right
   The wind once blew itself untaught,
And did its loudest day and night
   In any rough place where it caught.

Man came to tell it what was wrong:
   It hadn't found the place to blow;
It blew too hard—the aim was song.
   And listen—how it ought to go!

He took a little in his mouth,
   And held it long enough for north
To be converted into south,
   And then by measure blew it forth.

By measure. It was word and note,
   The wind the wind had meant to be—
A little through the lips and throat.
   The aim was song—the wind could see.


## Stopping by Woods on a Snowy Evening

Whose woods these are I think I know.
His house is in the village though;
He will not see me stopping here
To watch his woods fill up with snow.

My little horse must think it queer
To stop without a farmhouse near
Between the woods and frozen lake
The darkest evening of the year.

He gives his harness bells a shake
To ask if there is some mistake.
The only other sound's the sweep
Of easy wind and downy flake.

The woods are lovely, dark and deep,
But I have promises to keep,
And miles to go before I sleep,
And miles to go before I sleep.

## For Once, Then, Something

Others taunt me with having knelt at well-curbs
Always wrong to the light, so never seeing
Deeper down in the well than where the water
Gives me back in a shining surface picture
Me myself in the summer heaven godlike
Looking out of a wreath of fern and cloud puffs.
*Once*, when trying with chin against a well-curb,
I discerned, as I thought, beyond the picture,
Through the picture, a something white, uncertain,
Something more of the depths—and then I lost it.
Water came to rebuke the too clear water.
One drop fell from a fern, and lo, a ripple
Shook whatever it was lay there at bottom,
Blurred it, blotted it out. What was that whiteness?
Truth? A pebble of quartz? For once, then, something.

## Blue-Butterfly Day

It is blue-butterfly day here in spring,
And with these sky-flakes down in flurry on flurry
There is more unmixed color on the wing
Than flowers will show for days unless they hurry.

But these are flowers that fly and all but sing:
And now from having ridden out desire
They lie closed over in the wind and cling
Where wheels have freshly sliced the April mire.

## The Onset

Always the same, when on a fated night
At last the gathered snow lets down as white
As may be in dark woods, and with a song
It shall not make again all winter long
Of hissing on the yet uncovered ground,
I almost stumble looking up and round,
As one who overtaken by the end
Gives up his errand, and lets death descend
Upon him where he is, with nothing done
To evil, no important triumph won,
More than if life had never been begun.

Yet all the precedent is on my side:
I know that winter death has never tried
The earth but it has failed: the snow may heap
In long storms an undrifted four feet deep
As measured against maple, birch, and oak,
It cannot check the peeper's silver croak;
And I shall see the snow all go down hill
In water of a slender April rill
That flashes tail through last year's withered brake
And dead weeds, like a disappearing snake.
Nothing will be left white but here a birch,
And there a clump of houses with a church.

## To Earthward

Love at the lips was touch
As sweet as I could bear;
And once that seemed too much;
I lived on air

That crossed me from sweet things,
The flow of—was it musk
From hidden grapevine springs
Down hill at dusk?

I had the swirl and ache
From sprays of honeysuckle
That when they're gathered shake
Dew on the knuckle.

I craved strong sweets, but those
Seemed strong when I was young;
The petal of the rose
It was that stung.

Now no joy but lacks salt
That is not dashed with pain
And weariness and fault;
I crave the stain

Of tears, the aftermark
Of almost too much love,
The sweet of bitter bark
And burning clove.

When stiff and sore and scarred
I take away my hand
From leaning on it hard
In grass and sand,

The hurt is not enough:
I long for weight and strength
To feel the earth as rough
To all my length.

## Good-by and Keep Cold

This saying good-by on the edge of the dark
And the cold to an orchard so young in the bark
Reminds me of all that can happen to harm
An orchard away at the end of the farm
All winter, cut off by a hill from the house.
I don't want it girdled by rabbit and mouse,

I don't want it dreamily nibbled for browse
By deer, and I don't want it budded by grouse.
(If certain it wouldn't be idle to call
I'd summon grouse, rabbit, and deer to the wall
And warn them away with a stick for a gun.)
I don't want it stirred by the heat of the sun.
(We made it secure against being, I hope,
By setting it out on a northerly slope.)
No orchard's the worse for the wintriest storm;
But one thing about it, it mustn't get warm.
'How often already you've had to be told,
Keep cold, young orchard. Good-by and keep cold.
Dread fifty above more than fifty below.'
I have to be gone for a season or so.
My business awhile is with different trees,
Less carefully nurtured, less fruitful than these,
And such as is done to their wood with an ax—
Maples and birches and tamaracks.
I wish I could promise to lie in the night
And think of an orchard's arboreal plight
When slowly (and nobody comes with a light)
Its heart sinks lower under the sod.
But something has to be left to God.

## Two Look at Two

Love and forgetting might have carried them
A little further up the mountainside
With night so near, but not much further up.
They must have halted soon in any case
With thoughts of the path back, how rough it was
With rock and washout, and unsafe in darkness;
When they were halted by a tumbled wall
With barbed-wire binding. They stood facing this,
Spending what onward impulse they still had
In one last look the way they must not go,
On up the failing path, where, if a stone
Or earthslide moved at night, it moved itself;

No footstep moved it. 'This is all,' they sighed,
'Good-night to woods.' But not so; there was more.
A doe from round a spruce stood looking at them
Across the wall, as near the wall as they.
She saw them in their field, they her in hers.
The difficulty of seeing what stood still,
Like some up-ended boulder split in two,
Was in her clouded eyes: they saw no fear there.
She seemed to think that two thus they were safe.
Then, as if they were something that, though strange,
She could not trouble her mind with too long,
She sighed and passed unscared along the wall.
'*This*, then, is all. What more is there to ask?'
But no, not yet. A snort to bid them wait.
A buck from round the spruce stood looking at them
Across the wall as near the wall as they.
This was an antlered buck of lusty nostril,
Not the same doe come back into her place.
He viewed them quizzically with jerks of head,
As if to ask, 'Why don't you make some motion?
Or give some sign of life? Because you can't.
I doubt if you're as living as you look.'
Thus till he had them almost feeling dared
To stretch a proffering hand—and a spell-breaking.
Then he too passed unscared along the wall.
Two had seen two, whichever side you spoke from.
'This *must* be all.' It was all. Still they stood,
A great wave from it going over them,
As if the earth in one unlooked-for favor
Had made them certain earth returned their love.


## Not to Keep

They sent him back to her. The letter came
Saying . . . And she could have him. And before
She could be sure there was no hidden ill
Under the formal writing, he was there,
Living. They gave him back to her alive—

How else? They are not known to send the dead—
And not disfigured visibly. His face?
His hands? She had to look, to look and ask,
'What is it, dear?' And she had given all
And still she had all—*they* had—they the lucky!
Wasn't she glad now? Everything seemed won,
And all the rest for them permissible ease.
She had to ask, 'What was it, dear?'

                         'Enough
Yet not enough. A bullet through and through,
High in the breast. Nothing but what good care
And medicine and rest, and you a week,
Can cure me of to go again.' The same
Grim giving to do over for them both.
She dared no more than ask him with her eyes
How was it with him for a second trial.
And with his eyes he asked her not to ask.
They had given him back to her, but not to keep.


## A Brook in the City

The farmhouse lingers, though averse to square
With the new city street it has to wear
A number in. But what about the brook
That held the house as in an elbow-crook?
I ask as one who knew the brook, its strength
And impulse, having dipped a finger length
And made it leap my knuckle, having tossed
A flower to try its currents where they crossed.
The meadow grass could be cemented down
From growing under pavements of a town;
The apple trees be sent to hearth-stone flame.
Is water wood to serve a brook the same?
How else dispose of an immortal force
No longer needed? Staunch it at its source
With cinder loads dumped down? The brook was thrown
Deep in a sewer dungeon under stone

In fetid darkness still to live and run—
And all for nothing it had ever done
Except forget to go in fear perhaps.
No one would know except for ancient maps
That such a brook ran water. But I wonder
If from its being kept forever under
The thoughts may not have risen that so keep
This new-built city from both work and sleep.

## The Kitchen Chimney

Builder, in building the little house,
In every way you may please yourself;
But please please me in the kitchen chimney:
Don't build me a chimney upon a shelf.

However far you must go for bricks,
Whatever they cost a-piece or a pound,
Buy me enough for a full-length chimney,
And build the chimney clear from the ground.

It's not that I'm greatly afraid of fire,
But I never heard of a house that throve
(And I know of one that didn't thrive)
Where the chimney started above the stove.

And I dread the ominous stain of tar
That there always is on the papered walls,
And the smell of fire drowned in rain
That there always is when the chimney's false.

A shelf's for a clock or vase or picture,
But I don't see why it should have to bear
A chimney that only would serve to remind me
Of castles I used to build in air.

## Looking for a Sunset Bird in Winter

The west was getting out of gold,
The breath of air had died of cold,
When shoeing home across the white,
I thought I saw a bird alight.

In summer when I passed the place
I had to stop and lift my face;
A bird with an angelic gift
Was singing in it sweet and swift.

No bird was singing in it now.
A single leaf was on a bough,
And that was all there was to see
In going twice around the tree.

From my advantage on a hill
I judged that such a crystal chill
Was only adding frost to snow
As gilt to gold that wouldn't show.

A brush had left a crooked stroke
Of what was either cloud or smoke
From north to south across the blue;
A piercing little star was through.

## A Boundless Moment

He halted in the wind, and—what was that
Far in the maples, pale, but not a ghost?
He stood there bringing March against his thought,
And yet too ready to believe the most.

'Oh, that's the Paradise-in-bloom,' I said;
And truly it was fair enough for flowers
Had we but in us to assume in March
Such white luxuriance of May for ours.

We stood a moment so in a strange world,
Myself as one his own pretense deceives;
And then I said the truth (and we moved on).
A young beech clinging to its last year's leaves.


## Evening in a Sugar Orchard

From where I lingered in a lull in March
Outside the sugar-house one night for choice,
I called the fireman with a careful voice
And bade him leave the pan and stoke the arch:
'O fireman, give the fire another stoke,
And send more sparks up chimney with the smoke.'
I thought a few might tangle, as they did,
Among bare maple boughs, and in the rare
Hill atmosphere not cease to glow,
And so be added to the moon up there.
The moon, though slight, was moon enough to show
On every tree a bucket with a lid,
And on black ground a bear-skin rug of snow.
The sparks made no attempt to be the moon.
They were content to figure in the trees
As Leo, Orion, and the Pleiades.
And that was what the boughs were full of soon.


## Gathering Leaves

Spades take up leaves
No better than spoons,
And bags full of leaves
Are light as balloons.

I make a great noise
Of rustling all day
Like rabbit and deer
Running away.

But the mountains I raise
Elude my embrace,
Flowing over my arms
And into my face.

I may load and unload
Again and again
Till I fill the whole shed,
And what have I then?

Next to nothing for weight,
And since they grew duller
From contact with earth,
Next to nothing for color.

Next to nothing for use.
But a crop is a crop,
And who's to say where
The harvest shall stop?

## The Valley's Singing Day

The sound of the closing outside door was all.
You made no sound in the grass with your footfall,
As far as you went from the door, which was not far;
But you had awakened under the morning star
The first song-bird that awakened all the rest.
He could have slept but a moment more at best.
Already determined dawn began to lay
In place across a cloud the slender ray
For prying beneath and forcing the lids of sight,
And loosing the pent-up music of over-night.
But dawn was not to begin their 'pearly-pearly'
(By which they mean the rain is pearls so early,
Before it changes to diamonds in the sun),
Neither was song that day to be self-begun.
You had begun it, and if there needed proof—
I was asleep still under the dripping roof,

My window curtain hung over the sill to wet;
But I should awake to confirm your story yet;
I should be willing to say and help you say
That once you had opened the valley's singing day.

## Misgiving

All crying, 'We will go with you, O Wind!'
The foliage follow him, leaf and stem;
But a sleep oppresses them as they go,
And they end by bidding him stay with them.

Since ever they flung abroad in spring
The leaves had promised themselves this flight,
Who now would fain seek sheltering wall,
Or thicket, or hollow place for the night.

And now they answer his summoning blast
With an ever vaguer and vaguer stir,
Or at utmost a little reluctant whirl
That drops them no further than where they were.

I only hope that when I am free
As they are free to go in quest
Of the knowledge beyond the bounds of life
It may not seem better to me to rest.

## A Hillside Thaw

To think to know the country and not know
The hillside on the day the sun lets go
Ten million silver lizards out of snow!
As often as I've seen it done before
I can't pretend to tell the way it's done.
It looks as if some magic of the sun
Lifted the rug that bred them on the floor

And the light breaking on them made them run.
But if I thought to stop the wet stampede,
And caught one silver lizard by the tail,
And put my foot on one without avail,
And threw myself wet-elbowed and wet-kneed
In front of twenty others' wriggling speed,—
In the confusion of them all aglitter,
And birds that joined in the excited fun
By doubling and redoubling song and twitter,
I have no doubt I'd end by holding none.

It takes the moon for this. The sun's a wizard
By all I tell; but so's the moon a witch.
From the high west she makes a gentle cast
And suddenly, without a jerk or twitch,
She has her spell on every single lizard.
I fancied when I looked at six o'clock
The swarm still ran and scuttled just as fast.
The moon was waiting for her chill effect.
I looked at nine: the swarm was turned to rock
In every lifelike posture of the swarm,
Transfixed on mountain slopes almost erect.
Across each other and side by side they lay.
The spell that so could hold them as they were
Was wrought through trees without a breath of storm
To make a leaf, if there had been one, stir.
It was the moon's: she held them until day,
One lizard at the end of every ray.
The thought of my attempting such a stay!

## Plowmen

A plow, they say, to plow the snow.
They cannot mean to plant it, no—
Unless in bitterness to mock
At having cultivated rock.

## On a Tree Fallen Across the Road

*(To hear us talk)*

The tree the tempest with a crash of wood
Throws down in front of us is not to bar
Our passage to our journey's end for good,
But just to ask us who we think we are

Insisting always on our own way so.
She likes to halt us in our runner tracks,
And make us get down in a foot of snow
Debating what to do without an ax.

And yet she knows obstruction is in vain:
We will not be put off the final goal
We have it hidden in us to attain,
Not though we have to seize earth by the pole

And, tired of aimless circling in one place,
Steer straight off after something into space.

## Our Singing Strength

It snowed in spring on earth so dry and warm
The flakes could find no landing place to form.
Hordes spent themselves to make it wet and cold,
And still they failed of any lasting hold.
They made no white impression on the black.
They disappeared as if earth sent them back.
Not till from separate flakes they changed at night
To almost strips and tapes of ragged white
Did grass and garden ground confess it snowed,
And all go back to winter but the road.
Next day the scene was piled and puffed and dead.
The grass lay flattened under one great tread.
Borne down until the end almost took root,
The rangey bough anticipated fruit
With snowballs cupped in every opening bud.

The road alone maintained itself in mud,
Whatever its secret was of greater heat
From inward fires or brush of passing feet.

In spring more mortal singers than belong
To any one place cover us with song.
Thrush, bluebird, blackbird, sparrow, and robin throng;
Some to go further north to Hudson's Bay,
Some that have come too far north back away,
Really a very few to build and stay.
Now was seen how these liked belated snow.
The fields had nowhere left for them to go;
They'd soon exhausted all there was in flying;
The trees they'd had enough of with once trying
And setting off their heavy powder load.
They could find nothing open but the road.
So there they let their lives be narrowed in
By thousands the bad weather made akin.
The road became a channel running flocks
Of glossy birds like ripples over rocks.
I drove them under foot in bits of flight
That kept the ground, almost disputing right
Of way with me from apathy of wing,
A talking twitter all they had to sing.
A few I must have driven to despair
Made quick asides, but having done in air
A whir among white branches great and small
As in some too much carven marble hall
Where one false wing beat would have brought down all,
Came tamely back in front of me, the Drover,
To suffer the same driven nightmare over.
One such storm in a lifetime couldn't teach them
That back behind pursuit it couldn't reach them;
None flew behind me to be left alone.

Well, something for a snowstorm to have shown
The country's singing strength thus brought together,
That though repressed and moody with the weather
Was none the less there ready to be freed
And sing the wildflowers up from root and seed.

## The Lockless Door

It went many years,
But at last came a knock,
And I thought of the door
With no lock to lock.

I blew out the light,
I tip-toed the floor,
And raised both hands
In prayer to the door.

But the knock came again.
My window was wide;
I climbed on the sill
And descended outside.

Back over the sill
I bade a 'Come in'
To whatever the knock
At the door may have been.

So at a knock
I emptied my cage
To hide in the world
And alter with age.

## The Need of Being Versed in Country Things

The house had gone to bring again
To the midnight sky a sunset glow.
Now the chimney was all of the house that stood,
Like a pistil after the petals go.

The barn opposed across the way,
That would have joined the house in flame
Had it been the will of the wind, was left
To bear forsaken the place's name.

No more it opened with all one end
For teams that came by the stony road
To drum on the floor with scurrying hoofs
And brush the mow with the summer load.

The birds that came to it through the air
At broken windows flew out and in,
Their murmur more like the sigh we sigh
From too much dwelling on what has been.

Yet for them the lilac renewed its leaf,
And the aged elm, though touched with fire;
And the dry pump flung up an awkward arm;
And the fence post carried a strand of wire.

For them there was really nothing sad.
But though they rejoiced in the nest they kept,
One had to be versed in country things
Not to believe the phoebes wept.

# WEST-RUNNING BROOK

## Spring Pools

These pools that, though in forests, still reflect
The total sky almost without defect,
And like the flowers beside them, chill and shiver,
Will like the flowers beside them soon be gone,
And yet not out by any brook or river,
But up by roots to bring dark foliage on.

The trees that have it in their pent-up buds
To darken nature and be summer woods—
Let them think twice before they use their powers
To blot out and drink up and sweep away
These flowery waters and these watery flowers
From snow that melted only yesterday.

## The Freedom of the Moon

I've tried the new moon tilted in the air
Above a hazy tree-and-farmhouse cluster
As you might try a jewel in your hair.
I've tried it fine with little breadth of luster,
Alone, or in one ornament combining
With one first-water star almost as shining.

I put it shining anywhere I please.
By walking slowly on some evening later,
I've pulled it from a crate of crooked trees,
And brought it over glossy water, greater,
And dropped it in, and seen the image wallow,
The color run, all sorts of wonder follow.

## The Rose Family

The rose is a rose,
And was always a rose.
But the theory now goes
That the apple's a rose,
And the pear is, and so's
The plum, I suppose.
The dear only knows
What will next prove a rose.
You, of course, are a rose—
But were always a rose.

## Fireflies in the Garden

Here come real stars to fill the upper skies,
And here on earth come emulating flies,
That though they never equal stars in size,
(And they were never really stars at heart)
Achieve at times a very star-like start.
Only, of course, they can't sustain the part.

## Atmosphere

### Inscription for a Garden Wall

Winds blow the open grassy places bleak;
But where this old wall burns a sunny cheek,
They eddy over it too toppling weak
To blow the earth or anything self-clear;
Moisture and color and odor thicken here.
The hours of daylight gather atmosphere.

## Devotion

The heart can think of no devotion
Greater than being shore to the ocean—
Holding the curve of one position,
Counting an endless repetition.

## On Going Unnoticed

As vain to raise a voice as a sigh
In the tumult of free leaves on high.
What are you in the shadow of trees
Engaged up there with the light and breeze?

Less than the coral-root you know
That is content with the daylight low,
And has no leaves at all of its own;
Whose spotted flowers hang meanly down.

You grasp the bark by a rugged pleat,
And look up small from the forest's feet.
The only leaf it drops goes wide,
Your name not written on either side.

You linger your little hour and are gone,
And still the woods sweep leafily on,
Not even missing the coral-root flower
You took as a trophy of the hour.

## The Cocoon

As far as I can see this autumn haze
That spreading in the evening air both ways,
Makes the new moon look anything but new,
And pours the elm-tree meadow full of blue,

Is all the smoke from one poor house alone
With but one chimney it can call its own;
So close it will not light an early light,
Keeping its life so close and out of sight
No one for hours has set a foot outdoors
So much as to take care of evening chores.
The inmates may be lonely women-folk.
I want to tell them that with all this smoke
They prudently are spinning their cocoon
And anchoring it to an earth and moon
From which no winter gale can hope to blow it,—
Spinning their own cocoon did they but know it.

## A Passing Glimpse

*To Ridgely Torrence*
*On Last Looking into His 'Hesperides'*

I often see flowers from a passing car
That are gone before I can tell what they are.

I want to get out of the train and go back
To see what they were beside the track.

I name all the flowers I am sure they weren't:
Not fireweed loving where woods have burnt—

Not bluebells gracing a tunnel mouth—
Not lupine living on sand and drouth.

Was something brushed across my mind
That no one on earth will ever find?

Heaven gives its glimpses only to those
Not in position to look too close.

## A Peck of Gold

Dust always blowing about the town,
Except when sea-fog laid it down,
And I was one of the children told
Some of the blowing dust was gold.

All the dust the wind blew high
Appeared like gold in the sunset sky,
But I was one of the children told
Some of the dust was really gold.

Such was life in the Golden Gate:
Gold dusted all we drank and ate,
And I was one of the children told,
'We all must eat our peck of gold.'


## Acceptance

When the spent sun throws up its rays on cloud
And goes down burning into the gulf below,
No voice in nature is heard to cry aloud
At what has happened. Birds, at least, must know
It is the change to darkness in the sky.
Murmuring something quiet in her breast,
One bird begins to close a faded eye;
Or overtaken too far from his nest,
Hurrying low above the grove, some waif
Swoops just in time to his remembered tree.
At most he thinks or twitters softly, 'Safe!
Now let the night be dark for all of me.
Let the night be too dark for me to see
Into the future. Let what will be, be.'

## Once by the Pacific

The shattered water made a misty din.
Great waves looked over others coming in,
And thought of doing something to the shore
That water never did to land before.
The clouds were low and hairy in the skies,
Like locks blown forward in the gleam of eyes.
You could not tell, and yet it looked as if
The shore was lucky in being backed by cliff,
The cliff in being backed by continent;
It looked as if a night of dark intent
Was coming, and not only a night, an age.
Someone had better be prepared for rage.
There would be more than ocean-water broken
Before God's last *Put out the Light* was spoken.

## Lodged

The rain to the wind said,
'You push and I'll pelt.'
They so smote the garden bed
That the flowers actually knelt,
And lay lodged—though not dead.
I know how the flowers felt.

## A Minor Bird

I have wished a bird would fly away,
And not sing by my house all day;

Have clapped my hands at him from the door
When it seemed as if I could bear no more.

The fault must partly have been in me.
The bird was not to blame for his key.

And of course there must be something wrong
In wanting to silence any song.

## Bereft

Where had I heard this wind before
Change like this to a deeper roar?
What would it take my standing there for,
Holding open a restive door,
Looking down hill to a frothy shore?
Summer was past and day was past.
Somber clouds in the west were massed.
Out in the porch's sagging floor,
Leaves got up in a coil and hissed,
Blindly struck at my knee and missed.
Something sinister in the tone
Told me my secret must be known:
Word I was in the house alone
Somehow must have gotten abroad,
Word I was in my life alone,
Word I had no one left but God.

## Tree at My Window

Tree at my window, window tree,
My sash is lowered when night comes on;
But let there never be curtain drawn
Between you and me.

Vague dream-head lifted out of the ground,
And thing next most diffuse to cloud,
Not all your light tongues talking aloud
Could be profound.

But, tree, I have seen you taken and tossed,
And if you have seen me when I slept,
You have seen me when I was taken and swept
And all but lost.

That day she put our heads together,
Fate had her imagination about her,
Your head so much concerned with outer,
Mine with inner, weather.

## The Peaceful Shepherd

If heaven were to do again,
And on the pasture bars,
I leaned to line the figures in
Between the dotted stars,

I should be tempted to forget,
I fear, the Crown of Rule,
The Scales of Trade, the Cross of Faith,
As hardly worth renewal.

For these have governed in our lives,
And see how men have warred.
The Cross, the Crown, the Scales may all
As well have been the Sword.

## The Thatch

Out alone in the winter rain,
Intent on giving and taking pain.
But never was I far out of sight
Of a certain upper-window light.
The light was what it was all about:
I would not go in till the light went out;
It would not go out till I came in.
Well, we should see which one would win,
We should see which one would be first to yield.

The world was a black invisible field.
The rain by rights was snow for cold.
The wind was another layer of mold.
But the strangest thing: in the thick old thatch,
Where summer birds had been given hatch,
Had fed in chorus, and lived to fledge,
Some still were living in hermitage.
And as I passed along the eaves,
So low I brushed the straw with my sleeves,
I flushed birds out of hole after hole,
Into the darkness. It grieved my soul,
It started a grief within a grief,
To think their case was beyond relief—
They could not go flying about in search
Of their nest again, nor find a perch.
They must brood where they fell in mulch and mire,
Trusting feathers and inward fire
Till daylight made it safe for a flyer.
My greater grief was by so much reduced
As I thought of them without nest or roost.
That was how that grief started to melt.
They tell me the cottage where we dwelt,
Its wind-torn thatch goes now unmended;
Its life of hundreds of years has ended
By letting the rain I knew outdoors
In on to the upper chamber floors.

## A Winter Eden

A winter garden in an alder swamp,
Where conies now come out to sun and romp,
As near a paradise as it can be
And not melt snow or start a dormant tree.

It lifts existence on a plane of snow
One level higher than the earth below,
One level nearer heaven overhead,
And last year's berries shining scarlet red.

It lifts a gaunt luxuriating beast
Where he can stretch and hold his highest feast
On some wild apple tree's young tender bark,
What well may prove the year's high girdle mark.

So near to paradise all pairing ends:
Here loveless birds now flock as winter friends,
Content with bud-inspecting. They presume
To say which buds are leaf and which are bloom.

A feather-hammer gives a double knock.
This Eden day is done at two o'clock.
An hour of winter day might seem too short
To make it worth life's while to wake and sport.

## The Flood

Blood has been harder to dam back than water.
Just when we think we have it impounded safe
Behind new barrier walls (and let it chafe!),
It breaks away in some new kind of slaughter.
We choose to say it is let loose by the devil;
But power of blood itself releases blood.
It goes by might of being such a flood
Held high at so unnatural a level.
It will have outlet, brave and not so brave.
Weapons of war and implements of peace
Are but the points at which it finds release.
And now it is once more the tidal wave
That when it has swept by leaves summits stained.
Oh, blood will out. It cannot be contained.

## Acquainted with the Night

I have been one acquainted with the night.
I have walked out in rain—and back in rain.
I have outwalked the furthest city light.

I have looked down the saddest city lane.
I have passed by the watchman on his beat
And dropped my eyes, unwilling to explain.

I have stood still and stopped the sound of feet
When far away an interrupted cry
Came over houses from another street,

But not to call me back or say good-by;
And further still at an unearthly height,
One luminary clock against the sky

Proclaimed the time was neither wrong nor right.
I have been one acquainted with the night.

## The Lovely Shall Be Choosers

The Voice said, 'Hurl her down!'

The Voices, 'How far down?'

'Seven levels of the world.'

'How much time have we?'

'Take twenty years.
She *would* refuse love safe with wealth and honor!
The lovely shall be choosers, shall they?
Then let them choose!'

'Then we shall let her choose?'

'Yes, let her choose.
Take up the task beyond her choosing.'

Invisible hands crowded on her shoulder
In readiness to weigh upon her.
But she stood straight still,
In broad round ear-rings, gold and jet with pearls
And broad round suchlike brooch,
Her cheeks high colored,
Proud and the pride of friends.

The Voice asked, 'You can let her choose?'

'Yes, we can let her and still triumph.'

'Do it by joys, and leave her always blameless.
Be her first joy her wedding,
That though a wedding,
Is yet—well something they know, he and she.
And after that her next joy
That though she grieves, her grief is secret:
Those friends know nothing of her grief to make it
    shameful.
Her third joy that though now they cannot help but know,
They move in pleasure too far off
To think much or much care.
Give her a child at either knee for fourth joy
To tell once and once only, for them never to forget,
How once she walked in brightness,
And make them see it in the winter firelight.
But give her friends for then she dare not tell
For their foregone incredulousness.
And be her next joy this:
Her never having deigned to tell them.
Make her among the humblest even
Seem to them less than they are.
Hopeless of being known for what she has been,
Failing of being loved for what she is,
Give her the comfort for her sixth of knowing
She fails from strangeness to a way of life

She came to from too high too late to learn.
Then send some *one* with eyes to see
And wonder at her where she is,
And words to wonder in her hearing how she came there,
But without time to linger for her story.
Be her last joy her heart's going out to this one
So that she almost speaks.
You know them—seven in all.'

'Trust us,' the Voices said.


## West-Running Brook

'Fred, where is north?'

            'North? North is there, my love.
The brook runs west.'

            'West-running Brook then call it.'
(West-running Brook men call it to this day.)
'What does it think it's doing running west
When all the other country brooks flow east
To reach the ocean? It must be the brook
Can trust itself to go by contraries
The way I can with you—and you with me—
Because we're—we're—I don't know what we are.
What are we?'

       'Young or new?'

            'We must be something.
We've said we two. Let's change that to we three.
As you and I are married to each other,
We'll both be married to the brook. We'll build
Our bridge across it, and the bridge shall be
Our arm thrown over it asleep beside it.
Look, look, it's waving to us with a wave
To let us know it hears me.'

'Why, my dear,
That wave's been standing off this jut of shore—'
(The black stream, catching on a sunken rock,
Flung backward on itself in one white wave,
And the white water rode the black forever,
Not gaining but not losing, like a bird
White feathers from the struggle of whose breast
Flecked the dark stream and flecked the darker pool
Below the point, and were at last driven wrinkled
In a white scarf against the far shore alders.)
'That wave's been standing off this jut of shore
Ever since rivers, I was going to say,
Were made in heaven. It wasn't waved to us.'

'It wasn't, yet it was. If not to you
It was to me—in an annunciation.'

'Oh, if you take it off to lady-land,
As't were the country of the Amazons
We men must see you to the confines of
And leave you there, ourselves forbid to enter,—
It is your brook! I have no more to say.'

'Yes, you have, too. Go on. You thought of something.'

'Speaking of contraries, see how the brook
In that white wave runs counter to itself.
It is from that in water we were from
Long, long before we were from any creature.
Here we, in our impatience of the steps,
Get back to the beginning of beginnings,
The stream of everything that runs away.
Some say existence like a Pirouot
And Pirouette, forever in one place,
Stands still and dances, but it runs away,
It seriously, sadly, runs away
To fill the abyss' void with emptiness.
It flows beside us in this water brook,
But it flows over us. It flows between us
To separate us for a panic moment.

It flows between us, over us, and *with* us.
And it is time, strength, tone, light, life, and love—
And even substance lapsing unsubstantial;
The universal cataract of death
That spends to nothingness—and unresisted,
Save by some strange resistance in itself,
Not just a swerving, but a throwing back,
As if regret were in it and were sacred.
It has this throwing backward on itself
So that the fall of most of it is always
Raising a little, sending up a little.
Our life runs down in sending up the clock.
The brook runs down in sending up our life.
The sun runs down in sending up the brook.
And there is something sending up the sun.
It is this backward motion toward the source,
Against the stream, that most we see ourselves in,
The tribute of the current to the source.
It is from this in nature we are from.
It is most us.'

　　　　　　　　'Today will be the day
You said so.'

　　　　　　　　'No, today will be the day
You said the brook was called West-running Brook.'

'Today will be the day of what we both said.'

## Sand Dunes

Sea waves are green and wet,
But up from where they die,
Rise others vaster yet,
And those are brown and dry.

They are the sea made land
To come at the fisher town,
And bury in solid sand
The men she could not drown.

She may know cove and cape,
But she does not know mankind
If by any change of shape,
She hopes to cut off mind.

Men left her a ship to sink:
They can leave her a hut as well;
And be but more free to think
For the one more cast-off shell.


## Canis Major

The great Overdog,
That heavenly beast
With a star in one eye,
Gives a leap in the east.

He dances upright
All the way to the west
And never once drops
On his forefeet to rest.

I'm a poor underdog,
But tonight I will bark
With the great Overdog
That romps through the dark.

## A Soldier

He is that fallen lance that lies as hurled,
That lies unlifted now, come dew, come rust,
But still lies pointed as it plowed the dust.
If we who sight along it round the world,
See nothing worthy to have been its mark,
It is because like men we look too near,
Forgetting that as fitted to the sphere,
Our missiles always make too short an arc.
They fall, they rip the grass, they intersect
The curve of earth, and striking, break their own;
They make us cringe for metal-point on stone.
But this we know, the obstacle that checked
And tripped the body, shot the spirit on
Further than target ever showed or shone.

## Immigrants

No ship of all that under sail or steam
Have gathered people to us more and more
But Pilgrim-manned the *Mayflower* in a dream
Has been her anxious convoy in to shore.

## Hannibal

Was there ever a cause too lost,
Ever a cause that was lost too long,
Or that showed with the lapse of time too vain
For the generous tears of youth and song?

## The Flower Boat

The fisherman's swapping a yarn for a yarn
Under the hand of the village barber,
And here in the angle of house and barn
His deep-sea dory has found a harbor.

At anchor she rides the sunny sod
As full to the gunnel of flowers growing
As ever she turned her home with cod
From George's bank when winds were blowing.

And I judge from that Elysian freight
That all they ask is rougher weather,
And dory and master will sail by fate
To seek for the Happy Isles together.

## The Times Table

More than halfway up the pass
Was a spring with a broken drinking glass,
And whether the farmer drank or not
His mare was sure to observe the spot
By cramping the wheel on a water-bar,
Turning her forehead with a star,
And straining her ribs for a monster sigh;
To which the farmer would make reply,
'A sigh for every so many breath,
And for every so many sigh a death.
That's what I always tell my wife
Is the multiplication table of life.'
The saying may be ever so true;
But it's just the kind of a thing that you
Nor I, nor nobody else may say,
Unless our purpose is doing harm,
And then I know of no better way
To close a road, abandon a farm,
Reduce the births of the human race,
And bring back nature in people's place.

## The Investment

Over back where they speak of life as staying
('You couldn't call it living, for it ain't'),
There was an old, old house renewed with paint,
And in it a piano loudly playing.

Out in the plowed ground in the cold a digger,
Among unearthed potatoes standing still,
Was counting winter dinners, one a hill,
With half an ear to the piano's vigor.

All that piano and new paint back there,
Was it some money suddenly come into?
Or some extravagance young love had been to?
Or old love on an impulse not to care—

Not to sink under being man and wife,
But get some color and music out of life?

## The Last Mowing

There's a place called Far-away Meadow
We never shall mow in again,
Or such is the talk at the farmhouse:
The meadow is finished with men.
Then now is the chance for the flowers
That can't stand mowers and plowers.
It must be now, though, in season
Before the not mowing brings trees on,
Before trees, seeing the opening,
March into a shadowy claim.
The trees are all I'm afraid of,
That flowers can't bloom in the shade of;
It's no more men I'm afraid of;
The meadow is done with the tame.
The place for the moment is ours

For you, oh tumultuous flowers,
To go to waste and go wild in,
All shapes and colors of flowers,
I needn't call you by name.

## The Birthplace

Here further up the mountain slope
Than there was ever any hope,
My father built, enclosed a spring,
Strung chains of wall round everything,
Subdued the growth of earth to grass,
And brought our various lives to pass.
A dozen girls and boys we were.
The mountain seemed to like the stir,
And made of us a little while—
With always something in her smile.
Today she wouldn't know our name.
(No girl's, of course, has stayed the same.)
The mountain pushed us off her knees.
And now her lap is full of trees.

## The Door in the Dark

In going from room to room in the dark,
I reached out blindly to save my face,
But neglected, however lightly, to lace
My fingers and close my arms in an arc.
A slim door got in past my guard,
And hit me a blow in the head so hard
I had my native simile jarred.
So people and things don't pair any more
With what they used to pair with before.

## Dust in the Eyes

If, as they say, some dust thrown in my eyes
Will keep my talk from getting overwise,
I'm not the one for putting off the proof.
Let it be overwhelming, off a roof
And round a corner, blizzard snow for dust,
And blind me to a standstill if it must.

## Sitting by a Bush in Broad Sunlight

When I spread out my hand here today,
I catch no more than a ray
To feel of between thumb and fingers;
No lasting effect of it lingers.

There was one time and only the one
When dust really took in the sun;
And from that one intake of fire
All creatures still warmly suspire.

And if men have watched a long time
And never seen sun-smitten slime
Again come to life and crawl off,
We must not be too ready to scoff.

God once declared he was true
And then took the veil and withdrew,
And remember how final a hush
Then descended of old on the bush.

God once spoke to people by name.
The sun once imparted its flame.
One impulse persists as our breath;
The other persists as our faith.

## *The Armful*

For every parcel I stoop down to seize,
I lose some other off my arms and knees,
And the whole pile is slipping, bottles, buns,
Extremes too hard to comprehend at once,
Yet nothing I should care to leave behind.
With all I have to hold with, hand and mind
And heart, if need be, I will do my best
To keep their building balanced at my breast.
I crouch down to prevent them as they fall;
Then sit down in the middle of them all.
I had to drop the armful in the road
And try to stack them in a better load.

## *What Fifty Said*

When I was young my teachers were the old.
I gave up fire for form till I was cold.
I suffered like a metal being cast.
I went to school to age to learn the past.

Now I am old my teachers are the young.
What can't be molded must be cracked and sprung.
I strain at lessons fit to start a suture.
I go to school to youth to learn the future.

## Riders

The surest thing there is is we are riders,
And though none too successful at it, guiders,
Through everything presented, land and tide
And now the very air, of what we ride.

What is this talked-of mystery of birth
But being mounted bareback on the earth?
We can just see the infant up astride,
His small fist buried in the bushy hide.

There is our wildest mount—a headless horse.
But though it runs unbridled off its course,
And all our blandishments would seem defied,
We have ideas yet that we haven't tried.

## On Looking Up by Chance at the Constellations

You'll wait a long, long time for anything much
To happen in heaven beyond the floats of cloud
And the Northern Lights that run like tingling nerves.
The sun and moon get crossed, but they never touch,
Nor strike out fire from each other, nor crash out loud.
The planets seem to interfere in their curves,
But nothing ever happens, no harm is done.
We may as well go patiently on with our life,
And look elsewhere than to stars and moon and sun
For the shocks and changes we need to keep us sane.
It is true the longest drouth will end in rain,
The longest peace in China will end in strife.
Still it wouldn't reward the watcher to stay awake
In hopes of seeing the calm of heaven break
On his particular time and personal sight.
That calm seems certainly safe to last tonight.

## The Bear

The bear puts both arms around the tree above her
And draws it down as if it were a lover
And its choke cherries lips to kiss good-by,
Then lets it snap back upright in the sky.
Her next step rocks a boulder on the wall
(She's making her cross-country in the fall).
Her great weight creaks the barbed-wire in its staples
As she flings over and off down through the maples,
Leaving on one wire tooth a lock of hair.
Such is the uncaged progress of the bear.
The world has room to make a bear feel free;
The universe seems cramped to you and me.
Man acts more like the poor bear in a cage
That all day fights a nervous inward rage,
His mood rejecting all his mind suggests.
He paces back and forth and never rests
The toe-nail click and shuffle of his feet,
The telescope at one end of his beat,
And at the other end the microscope,
Two instruments of nearly equal hope,
And in conjunction giving quite a spread.
Or if he rests from scientific tread,
'Tis only to sit back and sway his head
Through ninety odd degrees of arc, it seems,
Between two metaphysical extremes.
He sits back on his fundamental butt
With lifted snout and eyes (if any) shut,
(He almost looks religious but he's not),
And back and forth he sways from cheek to cheek,
At one extreme agreeing with one Greek,
At the other agreeing with another Greek
Which may be thought, but only so to speak.
A baggy figure, equally pathetic
When sedentary and when peripatetic.

## *The Egg and the Machine*

He gave the solid rail a hateful kick.
From far away there came an answering tick
And then another tick. He knew the code:
His hate had roused an engine up the road.
He wished when he had had the track alone
He had attacked it with a club or stone
And bent some rail wide open like a switch
So as to wreck the engine in the ditch.
Too late though, now, he had himself to thank.
Its click was rising to a nearer clank.
Here it came breasting like a horse in skirts.
(He stood well back for fear of scalding squirts.)
Then for a moment all there was was size
Confusion and a roar that drowned the cries
He raised against the gods in the machine.
Then once again the sandbank lay serene.
The traveler's eye picked up a turtle trail,
Between the dotted feet a streak of tail,
And followed it to where he made out vague
But certain signs of buried turtle's egg;
And probing with one finger not too rough,
He found suspicious sand, and sure enough,
The pocket of a little turtle mine.
If there was one egg in it there were nine,
Torpedo-like, with shell of gritty leather
All packed in sand to wait the trump together.
'You'd better not disturb me any more,'
He told the distance, 'I am armed for war.
The next machine that has the power to pass
Will get this plasm in its goggle glass.'

# A FURTHER RANGE

## A Lone Striker

The swinging mill bell changed its rate
To tolling like the count of fate,
And though at that the tardy ran,
One failed to make the closing gate.
There was a law of God or man
That on the one who came too late
The gate for half an hour be locked,
His time be lost, his pittance docked.
He stood rebuked and unemployed.
The straining mill began to shake.
The mill, though many, many eyed,
Had eyes inscrutably opaque;
So that he couldn't look inside
To see if some forlorn machine
Was standing idle for his sake.
(He couldn't hope its heart would break.)

And yet he thought he saw the scene:
The air was full of dust of wool.
A thousand yarns were under pull,
But pull so slow, with such a twist,
All day from spool to lesser spool,
It seldom overtaxed their strength;
They safely grew in slender length.
And if one broke by any chance,
The spinner saw it at a glance.
The spinner still was there to spin.

That's where the human still came in.
Her deft hand showed with finger rings
Among the harp-like spread of strings.

249

She caught the pieces end to end
And, with a touch that never missed,
Not so much tied as made them blend.
Man's ingenuity was good.
He saw it plainly where he stood,
Yet found it easy to resist.

He knew another place, a wood,
And in it, tall as trees, were cliffs;
And if he stood on one of these,
'Twould be among the tops of trees,
Their upper branches round him wreathing,
Their breathing mingled with his breathing.
If—if he stood! Enough of ifs!
He knew a path that wanted walking;
He knew a spring that wanted drinking;
A thought that wanted further thinking;
A love that wanted re-renewing.
Nor was this just a way of talking
To save him the expense of doing.
With him it boded action, deed.

The factory was very fine;
He wished it all the modern speed.
Yet, after all, 'twas not divine,
That is to say, 'twas not a church.
He never would assume that he'd
Be any institution's need.
But he said then and still would say
If there should ever come a day
When industry seemed like to die
Because he left it in the lurch,
Or even merely seemed to pine
For want of his approval, why,
Come get him—they knew where to search.

## Two Tramps in Mud Time

Out of the mud two strangers came
And caught me splitting wood in the yard.
And one of them put me off my aim
By hailing cheerily 'Hit them hard!'
I knew pretty well why he dropped behind
And let the other go on a way.
I knew pretty well what he had in mind:
He wanted to take my job for pay.

Good blocks of oak it was I split,
As large around as the chopping block;
And every piece I squarely hit
Fell splinterless as a cloven rock.
The blows that a life of self-control
Spares to strike for the common good
That day, giving a loose to my soul,
I spent on the unimportant wood.

The sun was warm but the wind was chill.
You know how it is with an April day
When the sun is out and the wind is still,
You're one month on in the middle of May.
But if you so much as dare to speak,
A cloud comes over the sunlit arch,
A wind comes off a frozen peak,
And you're two months back in the middle of March.

A bluebird comes tenderly up to alight
And turns to the wind to unruffle a plume
His song so pitched as not to excite
A single flower as yet to bloom.
It is snowing a flake: and he half knew
Winter was only playing possum.
Except in color he isn't blue,
But he wouldn't advise a thing to blossom.

The water for which we may have to look
In summertime with a witching-wand,
In every wheelrut's now a brook,

In every print of a hoof a pond.
Be glad of water, but don't forget
The lurking frost in the earth beneath
That will steal forth after the sun is set
And show on the water its crystal teeth.

The time when most I loved my task
These two must make me love it more
By coming with what they came to ask.
You'd think I never had felt before
The weight of an ax-head poised aloft,
The grip on earth of outspread feet,
The life of muscles rocking soft
And smooth and moist in vernal heat.

Out of the woods two hulking tramps
(From sleeping God knows where last night,
But not long since in the lumber camps).
They thought all chopping was theirs of right.
Men of the woods and lumberjacks,
They judged me by their appropriate tool.
Except as a fellow handled an ax,
They had no way of knowing a fool.

Nothing on either side was said.
They knew they had but to stay their stay
And all their logic would fill my head:
As that I had no right to play
With what was another man's work for gain.
My right might be love but theirs was need.
And where the two exist in twain
Theirs was the better right—agreed.

But yield who will to their separation,
My object in living is to unite
My avocation and my vocation
As my two eyes make one in sight.
Only where love and need are one,
And the work is play for mortal stakes,
Is the deed ever really done
For Heaven and the future's sakes.

## The White-Tailed Hornet

The white-tailed hornet lives in a balloon
That floats against the ceiling of the woodshed.
The exit he comes out at like a bullet
Is like the pupil of a pointed gun.
And having power to change his aim in flight,
He comes out more unerring than a bullet.
Verse could be written on the certainty
With which he penetrates my best defense
Of whirling hands and arms about the head
To stab me in the sneeze-nerve of a nostril.
Such is the instinct of it I allow.
Yet how about the insect certainty
That in the neighborhood of home and children
Is such an execrable judge of motives
As not to recognize in me the exception
I like to think I am in everything—
One who would never hang above a bookcase
His Japanese crepe-paper globe for trophy?
He stung me first and stung me afterward.
He rolled me off the field head over heels,
And would not listen to my explanations.

That's when I went as visitor to his house.
As visitor at my house he is better.
Hawking for flies about the kitchen door,
In at one door perhaps and out another,
Trust him then not to put you in the wrong.
He won't misunderstand your freest movements.
Let him light on your skin unless you mind
So many prickly grappling feet at once.
He's after the domesticated fly
To feed his thumping grubs as big as he is.
Here he is at his best, but even here—
I watched him where he swooped, he pounced, he struck;
But what he found he had was just a nailhead.
He struck a second time. Another nailhead.
'Those are just nailheads. Those are fastened down.'
Then disconcerted and not unannoyed,

He stooped and struck a little huckleberry
The way a player curls around a football.
'Wrong shape, wrong color, and wrong scent,' I said.
The huckleberry rolled him on his head.
At last it was a fly. He shot and missed;
And the fly circled round him in derision.
But for the fly he might have made me think
He had been at his poetry, comparing
Nailhead with fly and fly with huckleberry:
How like a fly, how very like a fly.
But the real fly he missed would never do;
The missed fly made me dangerously skeptic.

Won't this whole instinct matter bear revision?
Won't almost any theory bear revision?
To err is human, not to, animal.
Or so we pay the compliment to instinct,
Only too liberal of our compliment
That really takes away instead of gives.
Our worship, humor, conscientiousness
Went long since to the dogs under the table.
And served us right for having instituted
Downward comparisons. As long on earth
As our comparisons were stoutly upward
With gods and angels, we were men at least,
But little lower than the gods and angels.
But once comparisons were yielded downward,
Once we began to see our images
Reflected in the mud and even dust,
'Twas disillusion upon disillusion.
We were lost piecemeal to the animals,
Like people thrown out to delay the wolves.
Nothing but fallibility was left us,
And this day's work made even that seem doubtful.

## *A Blue Ribbon at Amesbury*

Such a fine pullet ought to go
All coiffured to a winter show,
And be exhibited, and win.
The answer is this one has been—

And come with all her honors home.
Her golden leg, her coral comb,
Her fluff of plumage, white as chalk,
Her style, were all the fancy's talk.

It seems as if you must have heard.
She scored an almost perfect bird.
In her we make ourselves acquainted
With one a Sewell might have painted.

Here common with the flock again,
At home in her abiding pen,
She lingers feeding at the trough,
The last to let night drive her off.

The one who gave her ankle-band,
Her keeper, empty pail in hand,
He lingers too, averse to slight
His chores for all the wintry night.

He leans against the dusty wall,
Immured almost beyond recall,
A depth past many swinging doors
And many litter-muffled floors.

He meditates the breeder's art.
He has a half a mind to start,
With her for Mother Eve, a race
That shall all living things displace.

'Tis ritual with her to lay
The full six days, then rest a day;

At which rate barring broodiness
She well may score an egg-success.

The gatherer can always tell
Her well-turned egg's brown sturdy shell,
As safe a vehicle of seed
As is vouchsafed to feathered breed.

No human specter at the feast
Can scant or hurry her the least.
She takes her time to take her fill.
She whets a sleepy sated bill.

She gropes across the pen alone
To peck herself a precious stone.
She waters at the patent fount.
And so to roost, the last to mount.

The roost is her extent of flight.
Yet once she rises to the height,
She shoulders with a wing so strong
She makes the whole flock move along.

The night is setting in to blow.
It scours the windowpane with snow,
But barely gets from them or her
For comment a complacent chirr.

The lowly pen is yet a hold
Against the dark and wind and cold
To give a prospect to a plan
And warrant prudence in a man.

## A Drumlin Woodchuck

One thing has a shelving bank,
Another a rotting plank,
To give it cozier skies
And make up for its lack of size.

My own strategic retreat
Is where two rocks almost meet,
And still more secure and snug,
A two-door burrow I dug.

With those in mind at my back
I can sit forth exposed to attack
As one who shrewdly pretends
That he and the world are friends.

All we who prefer to live
Have a little whistle we give,
And flash, at the least alarm
We dive down under the farm.

We allow some time for guile
And don't come out for a while
Either to eat or drink.
We take occasion to think.

And if after the hunt goes past
And the double-barreled blast
(Like war and pestilence
And the loss of common sense),

If I can with confidence say
That still for another day,
Or even another year,
I will be there for you, my dear,

It will be because, though small
As measured against the All,
I have been so instinctively thorough
About my crevice and burrow.

## The Gold Hesperidee

Square Matthew Hale's young grafted apple tree
Began to blossom at the age of five;
And after having entertained the bee,
And cast its flowers and all the stems but three,
It set itself to keep those three alive;
And downy wax the three began to thrive.

They had just given themselves a little twist
And turned from looking up and being kissed
To looking down and yet not being sad,
When came Square Hale with Let's see what we had;
And two was all he counted (one he missed);
But two for a beginning wasn't bad.

His little Matthew, also five years old,
Was led into the presence of the tree
And raised among the leaves and duly told,
We mustn't touch them yet, but see and see!
And what was green would by and by be gold.
Their name was called the Gold Hesperidee.

As regularly as he went to feed the pig
Or milk the cow, he visited the fruit,
The dew of night and morning on his boot.
Dearer to him than any barnyard brute,
Each swung in danger on its slender twig,
A bubble on a pipe-stem growing big.

Long since they swung as three instead of two—
One more, he thought, to take him safely through.
Three made it certain nothing Fate could do
With codlin moth or rusty parasite
Would keep him now from proving with a bite
That the name Gold Hesperidee was right.

And so he brought them to the verge of frost.
But one day when the foliage all went swish
With autumn and the fruit was rudely tossed,
He thought no special goodness could be lost

If he fulfilled at last his summer wish,
And saw them picked unbruised and in a dish,

Where they could ripen safely to the eating.
But when he came to look, no apples there
Under, or on the tree, or anywhere,
And the light-natured tree seemed not to care!
'Twas Sunday and Square Hale was dressed for meeting
The final summons into church was beating.

Just as he was without an uttered sound
At those who'd done him such a wrong as that,
Square Matthew Hale took off his Sunday hat
And ceremoniously laid it on the ground,
And leaping on it with a solemn bound,
Danced slowly on it till he trod it flat.

Then suddenly he saw the thing he did,
And looked around to see if he was seen.
This was the sin that Ahaz was forbid
(The meaning of the passage had been hid):
To look upon the tree when it was green
And worship apples. What else could it mean?

God saw him dancing in the orchard path,
But mercifully kept the passing crowd
From witnessing the fault of one so proud.
And so the story wasn't told in Gath;
In gratitude for which Square Matthew vowed
To walk a graver man restrained in wrath.

## In Time of Cloudburst

Let the downpour roil and toil!
The worst it can do to me
Is carry some garden soil
A little nearer the sea.

'Tis the world-old way of the rain
When it comes to a mountain farm
To exact for a present gain
A little of future harm.

And the harm is none too sure,
For when all that was rotted rich
Shall be in the end scoured poor,
When my garden has gone down ditch,

Some force has but to apply,
And summits shall be immersed,
The bottom of seas raised dry—
The slope of the earth reversed.

Then all I need do is run
To the other end of the slope,
And on tracts laid new to the sun,
Begin all over to hope.

Some worn old tool of my own
Will be turned up by the plow,
The wood of it changed to stone,
But as ready to wield as now.

May my application so close
To so endless a repetition
Not make me tired and morose
And resentful of man's condition.


## A Roadside Stand

The little old house was out with a little new shed
In front at the edge of the road where the traffic sped,
A roadside stand that too pathetically plead,
It would not be fair to say for a dole of bread,
But for some of the money, the cash, whose flow supports
The flower of cities from sinking and withering faint.

The polished traffic passed with a mind ahead,
Or if ever aside a moment, then out of sorts
At having the landscape marred with the artless paint
Of signs that with N turned wrong and S turned wrong
Offered for sale wild berries in wooden quarts,
Or crook-necked golden squash with silver warts,
Or beauty rest in a beautiful mountain scene.
You have the money, but if you want to be mean,
Why keep your money (this crossly), and go along.
The hurt to the scenery wouldn't be my complaint
So much as the trusting sorrow of what is unsaid:
Here far from the city we make our roadside stand
And ask for some city money to feel in hand
To try if it will not make our being expand,
And give us the life of the moving pictures' promise
That the party in power is said to be keeping from us.

It is in the news that all these pitiful kin
Are to be bought out and mercifully gathered in
To live in villages next to the theater and store
Where they won't have to think for themselves any more;
While greedy good-doers, beneficent beasts of prey,
Swarm over their lives enforcing benefits
That are calculated to soothe them out of their wits,
And by teaching them how to sleep the sleep all day,
Destroy their sleeping at night the ancient way.

Sometimes I feel myself I can hardly bear
The thought of so much childish longing in vain,
The sadness that lurks near the open window there,
That waits all day in almost open prayer
For the squeal of brakes, the sound of a stopping car,
Of all the thousand selfish cars that pass,
Just one to inquire what a farmer's prices are.
And one did stop, but only to plow up grass
In using the yard to back and turn around;
And another to ask the way to where it was bound;
And another to ask could they sell it a gallon of gas
They couldn't (this crossly): they had none, didn't it see?

No, in country money, the country scale of gain,
The requisite lift of spirit has never been found,
Or so the voice of the country seems to complain.
I can't help owning the great relief it would be
To put these people at one stroke out of their pain.
And then next day as I come back into the sane,
I wonder how I should like you to come to me
And offer to put me gently out of my pain.


## Departmental

An ant on the tablecloth
Ran into a dormant moth
Of many times his size.
He showed not the least surprise.
His business wasn't with such.
He gave it scarcely a touch,
And was off on his duty run.
Yet if he encountered one
Of the hive's enquiry squad
Whose work is to find out God
And the nature of time and space,
He would put him onto the case.
Ants are a curious race;
One crossing with hurried tread
The body of one of their dead
Isn't given a moment's arrest—
Seems not even impressed.
But he no doubt reports to any
With whom he crosses antennae,
And they no doubt report
To the higher up at court.
Then word goes forth in Formic:
'Death's come to Jerry McCormic,
Our selfless forager Jerry.
Will the special Janizary
Whose office it is to bury
The dead of the commissary

Go bring him home to his people.
Lay him in state on a sepal.
Wrap him for shroud in a petal.
Embalm him with ichor of nettle.
This is the word of your Queen.'
And presently on the scene
Appears a solemn mortician;
And taking formal position
With feelers calmly atwiddle,
Seizes the dead by the middle,
And heaving him high in air,
Carries him out of there.
No one stands round to stare.
It is nobody else's affair.

It couldn't be called ungentle.
But how thoroughly departmental.


## The Old Barn at the Bottom of the Fogs

Where's this barn's house? It never had a house,
Or joined with sheds in ring-around a dooryard.
The hunter scuffling leaves goes by at dusk,
The gun reversed that he went out with shouldered.
The harvest moon and then the hunter's moon.
Well, the moon after that came one at last
To close this outpost barn and close the season.
The fur-thing, muff-thing, rocking in and out
Across the threshold in the twilight fled him.
He took the props down used for propping open,
And set them up again for propping shut,
The wide-spread double doors two stories high.
The advantage-disadvantage of these doors
Was that tramp taking sanctuary there
Must leave them unlocked to betray his presence.
They could be locked but from the outside only.
There is a fellow on the ocean now
Or down a mine or at the mill (I met him)

Who slept there in a mow of meadow hay
One night (he told me). And the barn he meant
Was the one I meant. Our details agreed.
We said Well twice to what we had in common,
The old barn at the bottom of the fogs.
Its only windows were the crevices
All up and down it. So that waking there
Next morning to the light of day was more
Like waking in a cage of silver bars.
Its locks were props—and that reminded him.
Trust him to have his bitter politics
Against his unacquaintances the rich
Who sleep in houses of their own, though mortgaged.
Conservatives, they don't know what to save.
Consider what they treasure under glass,
Yet leave such lovely shafts outdoors to perish.
Would someone only act in time we yet
Might see them on a rack like famous oars,
Their label Prop-locks, only specimens
In chestnut now become a precious wood
As relic of a vanished race of trees—
When these go there will be none to replace them.
Yes, right I was the locks were props outside;
And it had almost given him troubled dreams
To think that though he could not lock himself in,
The cheapest tramp that came along that way
Could mischievously lock him in to stay.

## On the Heart's Beginning to Cloud the Mind

Something I saw or thought I saw
In the desert at midnight in Utah,
Looking out of my lower berth
At moonlit sky and moonlit earth.
The sky had here and there a star;
The earth had a single light afar,
A flickering, human pathetic light,
That was maintained against the night,

It seemed to me, by the people there,
With a God-forsaken brute despair.
It would flutter and fall in half an hour
Like the last petal off a flower.
But my heart was beginning to cloud my mind.
I knew a tale of a better kind.
That far light flickers because of trees.
The people can burn it as long as they please:
And when their interests in it end,
They can leave it to someone else to tend.
Come back that way a summer hence,
I should find it no more no less intense.
I pass, but scarcely pass no doubt,
When one will say, 'Let us put it out.'
The other without demur agrees.
They can keep it burning as long as they please;
They can put it out whenever they please.
One looks out last from the darkened room
At the shiny desert with spots of gloom
That might be people and are but cedar,
Have no purpose, have no leader,
Have never made the first move to assemble,
And so are nothing to make her tremble.
She can think of places that are not thus
Without indulging a 'Not for us!'
Life is not so sinister-grave.
Matter of fact has made them brave.
He is husband, she is wife.
She fears not him, they fear not life.
They know where another light has been
And more than one to theirs akin,
But earlier out for bed tonight,
So lost on me in my surface flight.

This I saw when waking late,
Going by at a railroad rate,
Looking through wreaths of engine smoke
Far into the lives of other folk.

## The Figure in the Doorway

The grade surmounted, we were riding high
Through level mountains nothing to the eye
But scrub oak, scrub oak and the lack of earth
That kept the oaks from getting any girth.
But as through the monotony we ran,
We came to where there was a living man.
His great gaunt figure filled his cabin door,
And had he fallen inward on the floor,
He must have measured to the further wall.
But we who passed were not to see him fall.
The miles and miles he lived from anywhere
Were evidently something he could bear.
He stood unshaken, and if grim and gaunt,
It was not necessarily from want.
He had the oaks for heating and for light.
He had a hen, he had a pig in sight.
He had a well, he had the rain to catch.
He had a ten-by-twenty garden patch.
Nor did he lack for common entertainment.
That I assume was what our passing train meant.
He could look at us in our diner eating,
And if so moved uncurl a hand in greeting.

## At Woodward's Gardens

A boy, presuming on his intellect,
Once showed two little monkeys in a cage
A burning-glass they could not understand
And never could be made to understand.
Words are no good: to say it was a lens
For gathering solar rays would not have helped.
But let him show them how the weapon worked.
He made the sun a pin-point on the nose
Of first one, then the other till it brought
A look of puzzled dimness to their eyes
That blinking could not seem to blink away.

They stood arms laced together at the bars,
And exchanged troubled glances over life.
One put a thoughtful hand up to his nose
As if reminded—or as if perhaps
Within a million years of an idea.
He got his purple little knuckles stung.
The already known had once more been confirmed
By psychological experiment,
And that were all the finding to announce
Had the boy not presumed too close and long.
There was a sudden flash of arm, a snatch,
And the glass was the monkeys', not the boy's.
Precipitately they retired back cage
And instituted an investigation
On their part, though without the needed insight.
They bit the glass and listened for the flavor.
They broke the handle and the binding off it.
Then none the wiser, frankly gave it up,
And having hid it in their bedding straw
Against the day of prisoners' ennui,
Came dryly forward to the bars again
To answer for themselves: Who said it mattered
What monkeys did or didn't understand?
They might not understand a burning-glass.
They might not understand the sun itself.
It's knowing what to do with things that counts.


## A Record Stride

In a Vermont bedroom closet
With a door of two broad boards
And for back wall a crumbling old chimney
(And that's what their toes are towards),

I have a pair of shoes standing,
Old rivals of sagging leather,
Who once kept surpassing each other,
But now live even together.

They listen for me in the bedroom
To ask me a thing or two
About who is too old to go walking,
With too much stress on the who.

I wet one last year at Montauk
For a hat I had to save.
The other I wet at the Cliff House
In an extra-vagant wave.

Two entirely different grandchildren
Got me into my double adventure.
But when they grow up and can read this
I hope they won't take it for censure.

I touch my tongue to the shoes now
And unless my sense is at fault,
On one I can taste Atlantic,
On the other Pacific, salt.

One foot in each great ocean
Is a record stride or stretch.
The authentic shoes it was made in
I should sell for what they would fetch.

But instead I proudly devote them
To my museum and muse;
So the thick-skins needn't act thin-skinned
About being past-active shoes.

And I ask all to try to forgive me
For being as over-elated
As if I had measured the country
And got the United States stated.

## Lost in Heaven

The clouds, the source of rain, one stormy night
Offered an opening to the source of dew;
Which I accepted with impatient sight,
Looking for my old skymarks in the blue.

But stars were scarce in that part of the sky,
And no two were of the same constellation—
No one was bright enough to identify;
So 'twas with not ungrateful consternation,

Seeing myself well lost once more, I sighed,
'Where, where in Heaven am I? But don't tell me!
Oh, opening clouds, by opening on me wide.
Let's let my heavenly lostness overwhelm me.'

## Desert Places

Snow falling and night falling fast, oh, fast
In a field I looked into going past,
And the ground almost covered smooth in snow,
But a few weeds and stubble showing last.

The woods around it have it—it is theirs.
All animals are smothered in their lairs.
I am too absent-spirited to count;
The loneliness includes me unawares.

And lonely as it is that loneliness
Will be more lonely ere it will be less—
A blanker whiteness of benighted snow
With no expression, nothing to express.

They cannot scare me with their empty spaces
Between stars—on stars where no human race is.
I have it in me so much nearer home
To scare myself with my own desert places.

## Leaves Compared with Flowers

A tree's leaves may be ever so good,
So may its bark, so may its wood;
But unless you put the right thing to its root
It never will show much flower or fruit.

But I may be one who does not care
Ever to have tree bloom or bear.
Leaves for smooth and bark for rough,
Leaves and bark may be tree enough.

Some giant trees have bloom so small
They might as well have none at all.
Late in life I have come on fern.
Now lichens are due to have their turn.

I bade men tell me which in brief,
Which is fairer, flower or leaf.
They did not have the wit to say,
Leaves by night and flowers by day.

Leaves and bark, leaves and bark,
To lean against and hear in the dark.
Petals I may have once pursued.
Leaves are all my darker mood.


## A Leaf Treader

I have been treading on leaves all day until I am autumn-
    tired.
God knows all the color and form of leaves I have trodden
    on and mired.
Perhaps I have put forth too much strength and been too
    fierce from fear.
I have safely trodden underfoot the leaves of another year.

All summer long they were overhead, more lifted up than I.
To come to their final place in earth they had to pass me by.

All summer long I thought I heard them threatening under
    their breath.
And when they came it seemed with a will to carry me with
    them to death.

They spoke to the fugitive in my heart as if it were leaf to
    leaf.
They tapped at my eyelids and touched my lips with an
    invitation to grief.
But it was no reason I had to go because they had to go.
Now up my knee to keep on top of another year of snow.


## On Taking from the Top to Broaden the Base

        Roll stones down on our head!
        You squat old pyramid,
        Your last good avalanche
        Was long since slid.

        Your top has sunk too low,
        Your base has spread too wide,
        For you to roll one stone
        Down if you tried.

        But even at the word
        A pebble hit the roof,
        Another shot through glass
        Demanding proof.

        Before their panic hands
        Were fighting for the latch,
        The mud came in one cold
        Unleavened batch.

        And none was left to prate
        Of an old mountain's case
        That still took from its top
        To broaden its base.

## They Were Welcome to Their Belief

Grief may have thought it was grief.
Care may have thought it was care.
They were welcome to their belief,
The overimportant pair.

No, it took all the snows that clung
To the low roof over his bed,
Beginning when he was young,
To induce the one snow on his head.

But whenever the roof came white
The head in the dark below
Was a shade less the color of night
A shade more the color of snow.

Grief may have thought it was grief.
Care may have thought it was care.
But neither one was the thief
Of his raven color of hair.

## The Strong Are Saying Nothing

The soil now gets a rumpling soft and damp,
And small regard to the future of any weed.
The final flat of the hoe's approval stamp
Is reserved for the bed of a few selected seed.

There is seldom more than a man to a harrowed piece.
Men work alone, their lots plowed far apart,
One stringing a chain of seed in an open crease,
And another stumbling after a halting cart.

To the fresh and black of the squares of early mold
The leafless bloom of a plum is fresh and white;

Though there's more than a doubt if the weather is not too
    cold
For the bees to come and serve its beauty aright.

Wind goes from farm to farm in wave on wave,
But carries no cry of what is hoped to be.
There may be little or much beyond the grave,
But the strong are saying nothing until they see.


## The Master Speed

No speed of wind or water rushing by
But you have speed far greater. You can climb
Back up a stream of radiance to the sky,
And back through history up the stream of time.
And you were given this swiftness, not for haste
Nor chiefly that you may go where you will,
But in the rush of everything to waste,
That you may have the power of standing still—
Off any still or moving thing you say.
Two such as you with such a master speed
Cannot be parted nor be swept away
From one another once you are agreed
That life is only life forevermore
Together wing to wing and oar to oar.


## Moon Compasses

I stole forth dimly in the dripping pause
Between two downpours to see what there was.
And a masked moon had spread down compass rays
To a cone mountain in the midnight haze,
As if the final estimate were hers,
And as it measured in her calipers,
The mountain stood exalted in its place.
So love will take between the hands a face. . . .

## *Neither Out Far Nor In Deep*

The people along the sand
All turn and look one way.
They turn their back on the land.
They look at the sea all day.

As long as it takes to pass
A ship keeps raising its hull;
The wetter ground like glass
Reflects a standing gull.

The land may vary more;
But wherever the truth may be—
The water comes ashore,
And the people look at the sea.

They cannot look out far.
They cannot look in deep.
But when was that ever a bar
To any watch they keep?

## *Voice Ways*

Some things are never clear.
But the weather is clear tonight,
Thanks to a clearing rain.
The mountains are brought up near,
The stars are brought out bright.
Your old sweet-cynical strain
Would come in like you here:
'So we won't say nothing is clear.'

## Design

I found a dimpled spider, fat and white,
On a white heal-all, holding up a moth
Like a white piece of rigid satin cloth—
Assorted characters of death and blight
Mixed ready to begin the morning right,
Like the ingredients of a witches' broth—
A snow-drop spider, a flower like a froth,
And dead wings carried like a paper kite.

What had that flower to do with being white,
The wayside blue and innocent heal-all?
What brought the kindred spider to that height,
Then steered the white moth thither in the night?
What but design of darkness to appall?—
If design govern in a thing so small.

## On a Bird Singing in Its Sleep

A bird half wakened in the lunar noon
Sang halfway through its little inborn tune.
Partly because it sang but once all night
And that from no especial bush's height;
Partly because it sang ventriloquist
And had the inspiration to desist
Almost before the prick of hostile ears,
It ventured less in peril than appears.
It could not have come down to us so far
Through the interstices of things ajar
On the long bead chain of repeated birth
To be a bird while we are men on earth
If singing out of sleep and dream that way
Had made it much more easily a prey.

## Afterflakes

In the thick of a teeming snowfall
I saw my shadow on snow.
I turned and looked back up at the sky,
Where we still look to ask the why
Of everything below.

If I shed such a darkness,
If the reason was in me,
That shadow of mine should show in form
Against the shapeless shadow of storm,
How swarthy I must be.

I turned and looked back upward.
The whole sky was blue;
And the thick flakes floating at a pause
Were but frost knots on an airy gauze,
With the sun shining through.

## Clear and Colder

Wind the season-climate mixer
In my Witches' Weather Primer
Says to make this Fall Elixir
First you let the summer simmer,
Using neither spoon nor skimmer,

Till about the right consistence.
(This like fate by stars is reckoned,
None remaining in existence
Under magnitude the second);

Then take some left-over winter
Far to north of the St. Lawrence.
Leaves to strip and branches splinter,
Bring on wind. Bring rain in torrents—
Colder than the season warrants.

Dash it with some snow for powder.
If this seems like witchcraft rather,
If this seems a witches' chowder
(All my eye and Cotton Mather!),

Wait and watch the liquor settle.
I could stand whole dayfuls of it.
Wind she brews a heady kettle.
Human beings love it—love it.
Gods above are not above it.


## Unharvested

A scent of ripeness from over a wall.
And come to leave the routine road
And look for what had made me stall,
There sure enough was an apple tree
That had eased itself of its summer load,
And of all but its trivial foliage free,
Now breathed as light as a lady's fan.
For there there had been an apple fall
As complete as the apple had given man.
The ground was one circle of solid red.

May something go always unharvested!
May much stay out of our stated plan,
Apples or something forgotten and left,
So smelling their sweetness would be no theft.

## There Are Roughly Zones

We sit indoors and talk of the cold outside.
And every gust that gathers strength and heaves
Is a threat to the house. But the house has long been tried.
We think of the tree. If it never again has leaves,
We'll know, we say, that this was the night it died.
It is very far north, we admit, to have brought the peach.
What comes over a man, is it soul or mind—
That to no limits and bounds he can stay confined?
You would say his ambition was to extend the reach
Clear to the Arctic of every living kind.
Why is his nature forever so hard to teach
That though there is no fixed line between wrong and right,
There are roughly zones whose laws must be obeyed.
There is nothing much we can do for the tree tonight,
But we can't help feeling more than a little betrayed
That the northwest wind should rise to such a height
Just when the cold went down so many below.
The tree has no leaves and may never have them again.
We must wait till some months hence in the spring to know.
But if it is destined never again to grow,
It can blame this limitless trait in the hearts of men.

## A Trial Run

I said to myself almost in prayer,
It will start hair-raising currents of air
When you give it the livid metal-sap.
It will make a homicidal roar.
It will shake its cast stone reef of floor.
It will gather speed till your nerves prepare
To hear it wreck in a thunder-clap.
But stand your ground
As they say in war.
It is cotter-pinned, it is bedded true.
Everything its parts can do
Has been thought out and accounted for.
Your least touch sets it going round,
And when to stop it rests with you.

## Not Quite Social

Some of you will be glad I did what I did,
And the rest won't want to punish me too severely
For finding a thing to do that though not forbid
Yet wasn't enjoined and wasn't expected clearly.

To punish me overcruelly wouldn't be right
For merely giving you once more gentle proof
That the city's hold on a man is no more tight
Than when its walls rose higher than any roof.

You may taunt me with not being able to flee the earth.
You have me there, but loosely as I would be held.
The way of understanding is partly mirth.
I would not be taken as ever having rebelled.

And anyone is free to condemn me to death—
If he leaves it to nature to carry out the sentence.
I shall will to the common stock of air my breath
And pay a death-tax of fairly polite repentance.

## Provide, Provide

The witch that came (the withered hag)
To wash the steps with pail and rag,
Was once the beauty Abishag,

The picture pride of Hollywood.
Too many fall from great and good
For you to doubt the likelihood.

Die early and avoid the fate.
Or if predestined to die late,
Make up your mind to die in state.

Make the whole stock exchange your own!
If need be occupy a throne,
Where nobody can call *you* crone.

Some have relied on what they knew;
Others on being simply true.
What worked for them might work for you.

No memory of having starred
Atones for later disregard,
Or keeps the end from being hard.

Better to go down dignified
With boughten friendship at your side
Than none at all. Provide, provide!

# TEN MILLS

### Precaution

I never dared be radical when young
For fear it would make me conservative when old.

### The Span of Life

The old dog barks backward without getting up.
I can remember when he was a pup.

### The Wrights' Biplane

This biplane is the shape of human flight.
Its name might better be First Motor Kite.
Its makers' name—Time cannot get that wrong,
For it was writ in heaven doubly Wright.

### Evil Tendencies Cancel

Will the blight end the chestnut?
The farmers rather guess not.
It keeps smoldering at the roots
And sending up new shoots
Till another parasite
Shall come to end the blight.

### Pertinax

Let chaos storm!
Let cloud shapes swarm!
I wait for form.

### Waspish

On glossy wires artistically bent,
He draws himself up to his full extent.
His natty wings with self-assurance perk.
His stinging quarters menacingly work.
Poor egotist, he has no way of knowing
But he's as good as anybody going.

### One Guess

He has dust in his eyes and a fan for a wing,
A leg akimbo with which he can sing,
And a mouthful of dye stuff instead of a sting.

### The Hardship of Accounting

Never ask of money spent
Where the spender thinks it went.
Nobody was ever meant
To remember or invent
What he did with every cent.

### Not All There

I turned to speak to God
About the world's despair;
But to make bad matters worse
I found God wasn't there.

God turned to speak to me
(Don't anybody laugh)
God found I wasn't there—
At least not over half.

## In Divés' Dive

It is late at night and still I am losing,
But still I am steady and unaccusing.

As long as the Declaration guards
My right to be equal in number of cards,

It is nothing to me who runs the Dive.
Let's have a look at another five.

# THE OUTLANDS

## *The Vindictives*

You like to hear about gold.
A king filled his prison room
As full as the room could hold
To the top of his reach on the wall
With every known shape of the stuff.
'Twas to buy himself off his doom.
But it wasn't ransom enough.
His captors accepted it all,
But didn't let go of the king.
They made him send out a call
To his subjects to gather them more.
And his subjects wrung all they could wring
Out of temple and palace and store.
But when there seemed no more to bring,
His captors convicted the king
Of once having started a war,
And strangled the wretch with a string.

But really that gold was not half
That a king might have hoped to compel—
Not a half, not a third, not a tithe.
The king had scarce ceased to writhe,
When hate gave a terrible laugh,
Like a manhole opened to Hell.
If gold pleased the conqueror, well,
That gold should be the one thing
The conqueror henceforth should lack.

They gave no more thought to the king.
All joined in the game of hide-gold.
They swore all the gold should go back
Deep into the earth whence it came.
Their minds ran on cranny and crack.
All joined in the maddening game.
The tale is still boastingly told

Of many a treasure by name
That vanished into the black
And put out its light for the foe.

That self-sack and self-overthrow,
That was the splendidest sack
Since the forest Germans sacked Rome
And took the gold candlesticks home.

One Inca prince on the rack,
And late in his last hour alive,
Told them in what lake to dive
To seek what they seemed so to want.
They dived and nothing was found.
He told them to dive till they drowned.
The whole fierce conquering pack
Hunted and tortured and raged.
There were suns of story and vaunt
They searched for into Brazil
Their tongues hanging out unassuaged.

But the conquered grew meek and still.
They slowly and silently aged.
They kept their secrets and died,
Maliciously satisfied.
One knew of a burial hole
In the floor of a tribal cave,
Where under deep ash and charcoal
And cracked bones, human and beast,
The midden of feast upon feast,
Was coiled in its last resting grave
The great treasure wanted the most,
The great thousand-linked gold chain,
Each link of a hundredweight,
That once between post and post
(In-leaning under the strain),
And looped ten times back and forth,
Had served as a palace gate.
Some said it had gone to the coast,
Some over the mountains east,

Some into the country north,
On the backs of a single-file host,
Commanded by one sun-priest,
And raising a dust with a train
Of flashing links in the sun.
No matter what some may say.
(The saying is never done.)
There bright in the filth it lay
Untarnished by rust and decay.
And be all plunderers curst.

'The best way to hate is the worst.
'Tis to find what the hated need,
Never mind of what actual worth,
And wipe that out of the earth.
Let them die of unsatisfied greed,
Of unsatisfied love of display,
Of unsatisfied love of the high,
Unvulgar, unsoiled, and ideal.
Let their trappings be taken away.
Let them suffer starvation and die
Of being brought down to the real.'

## The Bearer of Evil Tidings

The bearer of evil tidings,
When he was halfway there,
Remembered that evil tidings
Were a dangerous thing to bear.

So when he came to the parting
Where one road led to the throne
And one went off to the mountains
And into the wild unknown,

He took the one to the mountains.
He ran through the Vale of Cashmere,
He ran through the rhododendrons
Till he came to the land of Pamir.

And there in a precipice valley
A girl of his age he met
Took him home to her bower,
Or he might be running yet.

She taught him her tribe's religion:
How ages and ages since
A princess en route from China
To marry a Persian prince

Had been found with child; and her army
Had come to a troubled halt.
And though a god was the father
And nobody else at fault,

It had seemed discreet to remain there
And neither go on nor back.
So they stayed and declared a village
There in the land of the Yak.

And the child that came of the princess
Established a royal line,
And his mandates were given heed to
Because he was born divine.

And that was why there were people
On one Himalayan shelf;
And the bearer of evil tidings
Decided to stay there himself.

At least he had this in common
With the race he chose to adopt:
They had both of them had their reasons
For stopping where they had stopped.

As for his evil tidings,
Belshazzar's overthrow,
Why hurry to tell Belshazzar
What soon enough he would know?

## *Iris by Night*

One misty evening, one another's guide,
We two were groping down a Malvern side
The last wet fields and dripping hedges home.
There came a moment of confusing lights,
Such as according to belief in Rome
Were seen of old at Memphis on the heights
Before the fragments of a former sun
Could concentrate anew and rise as one.
Light was a paste of pigment in our eyes.
And then there was a moon and then a scene
So watery as to seem submarine;
In which we two stood saturated, drowned.
The clover-mingled rowan on the ground
Had taken all the water it could as dew,
And still the air was saturated too,
Its airy pressure turned to water weight.
Then a small rainbow like a trellis gate,
A very small moon-made prismatic bow,
Stood closely over us through which to go.
And then we were vouchsafed the miracle
That never yet to other two befell
And I alone of us have lived to tell.
A wonder! Bow and rainbow as it bent,
Instead of moving with us as we went,
(To keep the pots of gold from being found)
It lifted from its dewy pediment
Its two mote-swimming many-colored ends,
And gathered them together in a ring.
And we stood in it softly circled round
From all division time or foe can bring
In a relation of elected friends.

## Build Soil—A Political Pastoral

Why, Tityrus! But you've forgotten me.
I'm Meliboeus the potato man,
The one you had the talk with, you remember,
Here on this very campus years ago.
Hard times have struck me and I'm on the move.
I've had to give my interval farm up
For interest, and I've bought a mountain farm
For nothing down, all-out-doors of a place,
All woods and pasture only fit for sheep.
But sheep is what I'm going into next.
I'm done forever with potato crops
At thirty cents a bushel. Give me sheep.
I know wool's down to seven cents a pound.
But I don't calculate to sell my wool.
I didn't my potatoes. I consumed them.
I'll dress up in sheep's clothing and eat sheep.
The Muse takes care of you. You live by writing
Your poems on a farm and call that farming.
Oh, I don't blame you. I say take life easy.
I should myself, only I don't know how.
But have some pity on us who have to work.
Why don't you use your talents as a writer
To advertise our farms to city buyers,
Or else write something to improve food prices.
Get in a poem toward the next election.

Oh, Meliboeus, I have half a mind
To take a writing hand in politics.
Before now poetry has taken notice
Of wars, and what are wars but politics
Transformed from chronic to acute and bloody?

I may be wrong, but, Tityrus, to me
The times seem revolutionary bad.

The question is whether they've reached a depth
Of desperation that would warrant poetry's
Leaving love's alternations, joy and grief,
The weather's alternations, summer and winter,
Our age-long theme, for the uncertainty
Of judging who is a contemporary liar—
Who in particular, when all alike
Get called as much in clashes of ambition.
Life may be tragically bad, and I
Make bold to sing it so, but do I dare
Name names and tell you who by name is wicked?
Whittier's luck with Skipper Ireson awes me.
Many men's luck with Greatest Washington
(Who sat for Stuart's portrait, but who sat
Equally for the nation's Constitution).
I prefer to sing safely in the realm
Of types, composite and imagined people:
To affirm there is such a thing as evil
Personified, but ask to be excused
From saying on a jury 'Here's the guilty.'

I doubt if you're convinced the times are bad.

I keep my eye on Congress, Meliboeus.
They're in the best position of us all
To know if anything is very wrong.
I mean they could be trusted to give the alarm
If earth were thought about to change its axis,
Or a star coming to dilate the sun.
As long as lightly all their live-long sessions,
Like a yard full of school boys out at recess
Before their plays and games were organized,
They yelling mix tag, hide-and-seek, hop-scotch,
And leap frog in each other's way,—all's well.
Let newspapers profess to fear the worst!
Nothing's portentous, I am reassured.

Is socialism needed, do you think?

We have it now. For socialism is
An element in any government.

There's no such thing as socialism pure—
Except as an abstraction of the mind.
There's only democratic socialism,
Monarchic socialism—oligarchic,
The last being what they seem to have in Russia.
You often get it most in monarchy,
Least in democracy. In practice, pure,
I don't know what it would be. No one knows.
I have no doubt like all the loves when
Philosophized together into one—
One sickness of the body and the soul.
Thank God our practice holds the loves apart
Beyond embarrassing self-consciousness
Where natural friends are met, where dogs are kept,
Where women pray with priests. There is no love.
There's only love of men and women, love
Of children, love of friends, of men, of God,
Divine love, human love, parental love,
Roughly discriminated for the rough.

Poetry, itself once more, is back in love.

Pardon the analogy, my Meliboeus,
For sweeping me away. Let's see, where was I?

But don't you think more should be socialized
Than is?

What should you mean by socialized?

Made good for everyone—things like inventions—
Made so we all should get the good of them—
All, not just great exploiting businesses.

We sometimes only get the bad of them.
In your sense of the word ambition has
Been socialized—the first propensity
To be attempted. Greed may well come next.
But the worst one of all to leave uncurbed,
Unsocialized, is ingenuity:
Which for no sordid self-aggrandizement,

For nothing but its own blind satisfaction
(In this it is as much like hate as love)
Works in the dark as much against as for us.
Even while we talk some chemist at Columbia
Is stealthily contriving wool from jute
That when let loose upon the grazing world
Will put ten thousand farmers out of sheep.
Everyone asks for freedom for himself,
The man free love, the business man free trade,
The writer and talker free speech and free press.
Political ambition has been taught,
By being punished back, it is not free:
It must at some point gracefully refrain.
Greed has been taught a little abnegation
And shall be more before we're done with it.
It is just fool enough to think itself
Self-taught. But our brute snarling and lashing taught it.
None shall be as ambitious as he can.
None should be as ingenious as he could,
Not if I had my say. Bounds should be set
To ingenuity for being so cruel
In bringing change unheralded on the unready.

I elect you to put the curb on it.

Were I dictator, I'll tell you what I'd do.

What should you do?

                    I'd let things take their course
And then I'd claim the credit for the outcome.

You'd make a sort of safety-first dictator.

Don't let the things I say against myself
Betray you into taking sides against me,
Or it might get you into trouble with me.
I'm not afraid to prophesy the future,
And be judged by the outcome, Meliboeus.
Listen and I will take my dearest risk.

We're always too much out or too much in.
At present from a cosmical dilation
We're so much out that the odds are against
Our ever getting inside in again.
But inside in is where we've got to get.
My friends all know I'm interpersonal.
But long before I'm interpersonal
Away 'way down inside I'm personal.
Just so before we're international
We're national and act as nationals.
The colors are kept unmixed on the palette,
Or better on dish plates all around the room,
So the effect when they are mixed on canvas
May seem almost exclusively designed.
Some minds are so confounded intermental
They remind me of pictures on a palette:
'Look at what happened. Surely some God pinxit.
Come look at my significant mud pie.'
It's hard to tell which is the worse abhorrence
Whether it's persons pied or nations pied.
Don't let me seem to say the exchange, the encounter,
May not be the important thing at last.
It well may be. We meet—I don't say when—
But must bring to the meeting the maturest,
The longest-saved-up, raciest, localest
We have strength of reserve in us to bring.

Tityrus, sometimes I'm perplexed myself
To find the good of commerce. Why should I
Have to sell you my apples and buy yours?
It can't be just to give the robber a chance
To catch them and take toll of them in transit.
Too mean a thought to get much comfort out of.
I figure that like any bandying
Of words or toys, it ministers to health.
It very likely quickens and refines us.

To market 'tis our destiny to go.
But much as in the end we bring for sale there
There is still more we never bring or should bring;

More that should be kept back—the soil for instance
In my opinion,—though we both know poets
Who fall all over each other to bring soil
And even subsoil and hardpan to market.
To sell the hay off, let alone the soil,
Is an unpardonable sin in farming.
The moral is, make a late start to market.
Let me preach to you, will you, Meliboeus?

Preach on. I thought you were already preaching.
But preach and see if I can tell the difference.

Needless to say to you, my argument
Is not to lure the city to the country.
Let those possess the land and only those,
Who love it with a love so strong and stupid
That they may be abused and taken advantage of
And made fun of by business, law, and art;
They still hang on. That so much of the earth's
Unoccupied need not make us uneasy.
We don't pretend to complete occupancy.
The world's one globe, human society
Another softer globe that slightly flattened
Rests on the world, and clinging slowly rolls.
We have our own round shape to keep unbroken.
The world's size has no more to do with us
Than has the universe's. We are balls,
We are round from the same source of roundness.
We are both round because the mind is round,
Because all reasoning is in a circle.
At least that's why the universe is round.

If what you're preaching is a line of conduct,
Just what am I supposed to do about it?
Reason in circles?

                              No, refuse to be
Seduced back to the land by any claim
The land may seem to have on man to use it.
Let none assume to till the land but farmers.

I only speak to you as one of them.
You shall go to your run-out mountain farm,
Poor castaway of commerce, and so live
That none shall ever see you come to market—
Not for a long long time. Plant, breed, produce,
But what you raise or grow, why feed it out,
Eat it or plow it under where it stands
To build the soil. For what is more accursed
Than an impoverished soil pale and metallic?
What cries more to our kind for sympathy?
I'll make a compact with you, Meliboeus,
To match you deed for deed and plan for plan.
Friends crowd around me with their five-year plans
That Soviet Russia has made fashionable.
You come to me and I'll unfold to you
A five-year plan I call so, not because
It takes ten years or so to carry out,
Rather because it took five years at least
To think it out. Come close, let us conspire—
In self-restraint, if in restraint of trade.
You will go to your run-out mountain farm
And do what I command you. I take care
To command only what you meant to do
Anyway. That is my style of dictator.
Build soil. Turn the farm in upon itself
Until it can contain itself no more,
But sweating-full, drips wine and oil a little.
I will go to my run-out social mind
And be as unsocial with it as I can.
The thought I have, and my first impulse is
To take to market—I will turn it under.
The thought from that thought—I will turn it under.
And so on to the limit of my nature.
We are too much out, and if we won't draw in
We shall be driven in. I was brought up
A state-rights free-trade Democrat. What's that?
An inconsistency. The state shall be
Laws to itself, it seems, and yet have no
Control of what it sells or what it buys.
Suppose someone comes near me who in rate

Of speech and thinking is so much my better
I am imposed on, silenced and discouraged.
Do I submit to being supplied by him
As the more economical producer,
More wonderful, more beautiful producer?
No. I unostentatiously move off
Far enough for my thought-flow to resume.
Thought product and food product are to me
Nothing compared to the producing of them.
I sent you once a song with the refrain:

> Let me be the one
> To do what is done—

My share at least lest I be empty-idle.
Keep off each other and keep each other off.
You see the beauty of my proposal is
It needn't wait on general revolution.
I bid you to a one-man revolution—
The only revolution that is coming.
We're too unseparate out among each other—
With goods to sell and notions to impart.
A youngster comes to me with half a quatrain
To ask me if I think it worth the pains
Of working out the rest, the other half.
I am brought guaranteed young prattle poems
Made publicly in school, above suspicion
Of plagiarism and help of cheating parents.
We congregate embracing from distrust
As much as love, and too close in to strike
And be so very striking. Steal away
The song says. Steal away and stay away.
Don't join too many gangs. Join few if any.
Join the United States and join the family—
But not much in between unless a college.
Is it a bargain, Shepherd Meliboeus?

Probably, but you're far too fast and strong
For my mind to keep working in your presence.
I can tell better after I get home,
Better a month from now when cutting posts

Or mending fence it all comes back to me
What I was thinking when you interrupted
My life-train logic. I agree with you
We're too unseparate. And going home
From company means coming to our senses.

## To a Thinker

The last step taken found your heft
Decidedly upon the left.
One more would throw you on the right.
Another still—you see your plight.
You call this thinking, but it's walking.
Not even that, it's only rocking,
Or weaving like a stabled horse:
From force to matter and back to force,
From form to content and back to form,
From norm to crazy and back to norm,
From bound to free and back to bound,
From sound to sense and back to sound.
So back and forth. It almost scares
A man the way things come in pairs.
Just now you're off democracy
(With a polite regret to be),
And leaning on dictatorship;
But if you will accept the tip,
In less than no time, tongue and pen,
You'll be a democrat again.
A reasoner and good as such,
Don't let it bother you too much
If it makes you look helpless please
And a temptation to the tease.
Suppose you've no direction in you,
I don't see but you must continue
To use the gift you do possess,
And sway with reason more or less.
I own I never really warmed
To the reformer or reformed.
And yet conversion has its place
Not halfway down the scale of grace.
So if you find you must repent
From side to side in argument,
At least don't use your mind too hard,
But trust my instinct—I'm a bard.

## *A Missive Missile*

Someone in ancient Mas d'Azil
Once took a little pebble wheel
And dotted it with red for me,
And sent it to me years and years—
A million years to be precise—
Across the barrier of ice:
Two round dots and a ripple streak,
So vivid as to seem to speak.
But what imperfectly appears
Is whether the two dots were tears,
Two teardrops, one for either eye,
And the wave line a shaken sigh.
But no, the color used is red.
Not tears but drops of blood instead.
The line must be a jagged blade.
The sender must have had to die,
And wanted someone now to know
His death was sacrificial-votive.
So almost clear and yet obscure.
If only anyone were sure
A motive then was still a motive.
O you who bring this to my hand,
You are no common messenger
(Your badge of office is a spade).
It grieves me to have had you stand
So long for nothing. No reply—
There is no answer, I'm afraid,
Across the icy barrier
For my obscure petitioner.
Suppose his ghost is standing by
Importunate to give the hint
And be successfully conveyed.
How anyone can fail to see
Where perfectly in form and tint
The metaphor, the symbol lies!

Why will I not analogize?
(I do too much in some men's eyes.)
Oh, slow uncomprehending me,
Enough to make a spirit moan
Or rustle in a bush or tree.
I have the ocher-written flint,
The two dots and the ripple line.
The meaning of it is unknown,
Or else I fear entirely mine,
All modern, nothing ancient in't,
Unsatisfying to us each.
Far as we aim our signs to reach,
Far as we often make them reach,
Across the soul-from-soul abyss,
There is an aeon-limit set
Beyond which they are doomed to miss.
Two souls may be too widely met.
That sad-with-distance river beach
With mortal longing may beseech;
It cannot speak as far as this.

# A WITNESS TREE

## *Beech*

Where my imaginary line
Bends square in woods, an iron spine
And pile of real rocks have been founded.
And off this corner in the wild,
Where these are driven in and piled,
One tree, by being deeply wounded,
Has been impressed as Witness Tree
And made commit to memory
My proof of being not unbounded.
Thus truth's established and borne out,
Though circumstanced with dark and doubt—
Though by a world of doubt surrounded.

THE MOODIE FORESTER

## *Sycamore*

Zaccheus he
Did climb the tree
Our Lord to see.

THE NEW ENGLAND PRIMER

## The Silken Tent

She is as in a field a silken tent
At midday when a sunny summer breeze
Has dried the dew and all its ropes relent,
So that in guys it gently sways at ease,
And its supporting central cedar pole,
That is its pinnacle to heavenward
And signifies the sureness of the soul,
Seems to owe naught to any single cord,
But strictly held by none, is loosely bound
By countless silken ties of love and thought
To everything on earth the compass round,
And only by one's going slightly taut
In the capriciousness of summer air
Is of the slightest bondage made aware.

## All Revelation

A head thrusts in as for the view,
But where it is it thrusts in from
Or what it is it thrusts into
By that Cyb'laean avenue,
And what can of its coming come,

And whither it will be withdrawn,
And what take hence or leave behind,
These things the mind has pondered on
A moment and still asking gone.
Strange apparition of the mind!

But the impervious geode
Was entered, and its inner crust
Of crystals with a ray cathode
At every point and facet glowed
In answer to the mental thrust.

Eyes seeking the response of eyes
Bring out the stars, bring out the flowers,
Thus concentrating earth and skies
So none need be afraid of size.
All revelation has been ours.


## Happiness Makes Up in Height
## for What It Lacks in Length

Oh, stormy stormy world,
The days you were not swirled
Around with mist and cloud,
Or wrapped as in a shroud,
And the sun's brilliant ball
Was not in part or all
Obscured from mortal view—
Were days so very few
I can but wonder whence
I get the lasting sense
Of so much warmth and light.
If my mistrust is right
It may be altogether
From one day's perfect weather,
When starting clear at dawn,
The day swept clearly on
To finish clear at eve.
I verily believe
My fair impression may
Be all from that one day
No shadow crossed but ours
As through its blazing flowers
We went from house to wood
For change of solitude.

## Come In

As I came to the edge of the woods,
Thrush music—hark!
Now if it was dusk outside,
Inside it was dark.

Too dark in the woods for a bird
By sleight of wing
To better its perch for the night,
Though it still could sing.

The last of the light of the sun
That had died in the west
Still lived for one song more
In a thrush's breast.

Far in the pillared dark
Thrush music went—
Almost like a call to come in
To the dark and lament.

But no, I was out for stars:
I would not come in.
I meant not even if asked,
And I hadn't been.

## I Could Give All to Time

To Time it never seems that he is brave
To set himself against the peaks of snow
To lay them level with the running wave,
Nor is he overjoyed when they lie low,
But only grave, contemplative and grave.

What now is inland shall be ocean isle,
Then eddies playing round a sunken reef

Like the curl at the corner of a smile;
And I could share Time's lack of joy or grief
At such a planetary change of style.

I could give all to Time except—except
What I myself have held. But why declare
The things forbidden that while the Customs slept
I have crossed to Safety with? For I am There,
And what I would not part with I have kept.

## Carpe Diem

Age saw two quiet children
Go loving by at twilight,
He knew not whether homeward,
Or outward from the village,
Or (chimes were ringing) churchward.
He waited (they were strangers)
Till they were out of hearing
To bid them both be happy.
'Be happy, happy, happy,
And seize the day of pleasure.'
The age-long theme is Age's.
'Twas Age imposed on poems
Their gather-roses burden
To warn against the danger
That overtaken lovers
From being overflooded
With happiness should have it
And yet not know they have it.
But bid life seize the present?
It lives less in the present
Than in the future always,
And less in both together
Than in the past. The present
Is too much for the senses,
Too crowding, too confusing—
Too present to imagine.

## The Wind and the Rain

### I

That far-off day the leaves in flight
Were letting in the colder light.
A season-ending wind there blew
That as it did the forest strew
I leaned on with a singing trust
And let it drive me deathward too.
With breaking step I stabbed the dust,
Yet did not much to shorten stride.
I sang of death—but had I known
The many deaths one must have died
Before he came to meet his own!
Oh, should a child be left unwarned
That any song in which he mourned
Would be as if he prophesied?
It were unworthy of the tongue
To let the half of life alone
And play the good without the ill.
And yet 'twould seem that what is sung
In happy sadness by the young
Fate has no choice but to fulfill.

### II

Flowers in the desert heat
Contrive to bloom
On melted mountain water led by flume
To wet their feet.
But something in it still is incomplete.
Before I thought the wilted to exalt
With water I would see them water-bowed.
I would pick up all ocean less its salt,
And though it were as much as cloud could bear
Would load it on to cloud,
And rolling it inland on roller air,
Would empty it unsparing on the flower
That past its prime lost petals in the flood,
(Who cares but for the future of the bud?)
And all the more the mightier the shower
Would run in under it to get my share.

'Tis not enough on roots and in the mouth,
But give me water heavy on the head
In all the passion of a broken drouth.

And there is always more than should be said.

As strong is rain without as wine within,
As magical as sunlight on the skin.

I have been one no dwelling could contain
When there was rain;
But I must forth at dusk, my time of day,
To see to the unburdening of skies.
Rain was the tears adopted by my eyes
That have none left to stay.


## The Most of It

He thought he kept the universe alone;
For all the voice in answer he could wake
Was but the mocking echo of his own
From some tree-hidden cliff across the lake.
Some morning from the boulder-broken beach
He would cry out on life, that what it wants
Is not its own love back in copy speech,
But counter-love, original response.
And nothing ever came of what he cried
Unless it was the embodiment that crashed
In the cliff's talus on the other side,
And then in the far distant water splashed,
But after a time allowed for it to swim,
Instead of proving human when it neared
And someone else additional to him,
As a great buck it powerfully appeared,
Pushing the crumpled water up ahead,
And landed pouring like a waterfall,
And stumbled through the rocks with horny tread,
And forced the underbrush—and that was all.

## Never Again Would Birds' Song Be the Same

He would declare and could himself believe
That the birds there in all the garden round
From having heard the daylong voice of Eve
Had added to their own an oversound,
Her tone of meaning but without the words.
Admittedly an eloquence so soft
Could only have had an influence on birds
When call or laughter carried it aloft.
Be that as may be, she was in their song.
Moreover her voice upon their voices crossed
Had now persisted in the woods so long
That probably it never would be lost.
Never again would birds' song be the same.
And to do that to birds was why she came.

## The Subverted Flower

She drew back; he was calm:
'It is this that had the power.'
And he lashed his open palm
With the tender-headed flower.
He smiled for her to smile,
But she was either blind
Or willfully unkind.
He eyed her for a while
For a woman and a puzzle.
He flicked and flung the flower,
And another sort of smile
Caught up like finger tips
The corners of his lips
And cracked his ragged muzzle.
She was standing to the waist
In goldenrod and brake,
Her shining hair displaced.
He stretched her either arm
As if she made it ache

To clasp her—not to harm;
As if he could not spare
To touch her neck and hair.
'If this has come to us
And not to me alone—'
So she thought she heard him say;
Though with every word he spoke
His lips were sucked and blown
And the effort made him choke
Like a tiger at a bone.
She had to lean away.
She dared not stir a foot,
Lest movement should provoke
The demon of pursuit
That slumbers in a brute.
It was then her mother's call
From inside the garden wall
Made her steal a look of fear
To see if he could hear
And would pounce to end it all
Before her mother came.
She looked and saw the shame:
A hand hung like a paw,
An arm worked like a saw
As if to be persuasive,
An ingratiating laugh
That cut the snout in half,
An eye become evasive.
A girl could only see
That a flower had marred a man,
But what she could not see
Was that the flower might be
Other than base and fetid:
That the flower had done but part,
And what the flower began
Her own too meager heart
Had terribly completed.
She looked and saw the worst.
And the dog or what it was,
Obeying bestial laws,

A coward save at night,
Turned from the place and ran.
She heard him stumble first
And use his hands in flight.
She heard him bark outright.
And oh, for one so young
The bitter words she spit
Like some tenacious bit
That will not leave the tongue.
She plucked her lips for it,
And still the horror clung.
Her mother wiped the foam
From her chin, picked up her comb
And drew her backward home.


## Willful Homing

It is getting dark and time he drew to a house,
But the blizzard blinds him to any house ahead.
The storm gets down his neck in an icy souse
That sucks his breath like a wicked cat in bed.

The snow blows on him and off him, exerting force
Downward to make him sit astride a drift,
Imprint a saddle and calmly consider a course.
He peers out shrewdly into the thick and swift.

Since he means to come to a door he will come to a door,
Although so compromised of aim and rate
He may fumble wide of the knob a yard or more,
And to those concerned he may seem a little late.

## A Cloud Shadow

A breeze discovered my open book
And began to flutter the leaves to look
For a poem there used to be on Spring.
I tried to tell her 'There's no such thing!'

For whom would a poem on Spring be by?
The breeze disdained to make reply;
And a cloud shadow crossed her face
For fear I would make her miss the place.

## The Quest of the Purple-Fringed

I felt the chill of the meadow underfoot,
But the sun overhead;
And snatches of verse and song of scenes like this
I sung or said.

I skirted the margin alders for miles and miles
In a sweeping line.
The day was the day by every flower that blooms,
But I saw no sign.

Yet further I went to be before the scythe,
For the grass was high;
Till I saw the path where the slender fox had come
And gone panting by.

Then at last and following him I found—
In the very hour
When the color flushed to the petals it must have been—
The far-sought flower.

There stood the purple spires with no breath of air
Nor headlong bee
To disturb their perfect poise the livelong day
'Neath the alder tree.

I only knelt and putting the boughs aside
Looked, or at most
Counted them all to the buds in the copse's depth
That were pale as a ghost.

Then I arose and silently wandered home,
And I for one
Said that the fall might come and whirl of leaves,
For summer was done.


## The Discovery of the Madeiras

*A Rhyme of Hackluyt*

A stolen lady was coming on board,
But whether stolen from her wedded lord
Or from her own self against her will
Was not set forth in the lading bill.
A stolen lady was all it said.
She came down weakly and blindly led
To the darkening windy village slip.
She would not look at the fateful ship.
Her lover to make the ordeal swift
Had to give her the final lift
And force her farewell step off shore.
The way she clung to him the more
Seemed to argue perhaps she went
Not entirely without consent.
But with no companion of womankind
To leave the English law behind
And sail for some vague Paphian bourn
Began already to seem forlorn.

It did more distance up and down,
Their little stormy ship, than on.
Now it took a fitful run,
Now standing cracked its sail and spun;
Now stood upon its bulging prow

Till the pirate sailors made a vow
Of where they would go on pilgrimage
If God would spare them to die of age.
When the clap of two converging waves
Failed to crush their barrel staves,
Or the wind to snap their walking stick,
They laughed as if they had turned a trick.

This was no lady's time of year.
For long the lady would disappear,
And might be rolling dead below
For all the crew were let to know.
But when the ocean's worst had passed
She was carried out beside the mast,
Where all day long she lay and dozed.
Or she and her lover would sit opposed
And darkly drink each other's eyes
With faint head shakings, no more wise.
The most he asked her eyes to grant
Was that in what she does not want
A woman wants to be overruled.
Or was the instinct in him fooled?
He knew not, neither of them knew.
They could only say like any two,
'You tell me and I'll tell you.'

Sometimes with her permissive smile
He left her to her thoughts awhile
And went to lean against the rail,
And let the captain tell him a tale.
(He had to keep the captain's favor.)
The ship it seemed had been a slaver.
And once they had shipped a captive pair
Whose love was such they didn't care
Who took in them onlooker's share.
Well, when at length the fever struck
That spoils the nigger-trader's luck
The man was among the first it took.
'Throw him over alive,' they said,
'Before the thing has time to spread.

You've got to keep the quarters clean.'
But the girl fought them and made a scene.
She was a savage jungle cat
It was easy to be angry at;
Which put the thought into someone's head
Of the ocean bed for a marriage bed.
Some Tom said to Dick or Harry:
'Apparently these two ought to marry.
We get plenty funerals at sea.
How for a change would a wedding be?—
Or a combination of the two,
How would a funeral-wedding do?
It's gone so far she's probably caught
Whatever it is the nigger's got.'
They bound them naked so they faced
With a length of cordage about the waist,
Many lovers have been divorced
By having what is free enforced.
But presence of love these had in death
To kiss and drink each other's breath
Before they were hurled from the slaver's deck.
They added clasps about the neck
And went embraced to the cold and dark
To be their own marriage feast for the shark.

When after talk with other men
A man comes back to a woman again
He tells her as much of blood and dirt
As he thinks will do her not too much hurt.
'What was the pirate captain's chaff?
He laughed but he did not make you laugh.
The jest seemed his and the plaudits his.
I heard him shout "What a thing it is!"
Some standing jest between you men?
Don't tell me if you don't want to then.'
Whereat in a moment of cross unruth
He thought, 'All right if you want the truth!'
'I don't believe it! It isn't true!
It never happened! Did it, you?'
Seeing no help in wings or feet

She withdrew back in self-retreat
Till her heart almost ceased to beat.
Her spirit faded as far away
As the living ever go yet stay.
And her thought was she had had her pay.

He said to the captain, 'Give command,
And bring us to the nearest land;
And let us try an untossed place
And see if it will help her case.'
They brought her to a nameless isle.
And the ship lay in the bay for a while
Waiting to see if she would mend;
But sailed and left them in the end.
Her lover saw them sail away,
But dared not tell her all one day.
For slowly even her sense of him
And love itself were growing dim.
He no more drew the smile he sought.
The story is she died of thought.

And when her lover was left alone
He stayed long enough to carve on stone
The name of the lady with his own
To be her only marriage lines.
And carved them round with a scroll of vines.
Then he gouged a clumsy sailing trough
From a fallen tree and pushing off
Safely made the African shore;
Where he fell a prisoner to the Moor.
But the Moor strangely enough believed
The tale of the voyage he had achieved,
And sent him to the King to admire.
He came at last to his native shire.
The island he found was verified.
And the bay where his stolen lady died
Was named for him instead of her.
But so is history like to err.
And soon it is neither here nor there
Whether time's rewards are fair or unfair.

## The Gift Outright

The land was ours before we were the land's.
She was our land more than a hundred years
Before we were her people. She was ours
In Massachusetts, in Virginia,
But we were England's, still colonials,
Possessing what we still were unpossessed by,
Possessed by what we now no more possessed.
Something we were withholding made us weak
Until we found out that it was ourselves
We were withholding from our land of living,
And forthwith found salvation in surrender.
Such as we were we gave ourselves outright
(The deed of gift was many deeds of war)
To the land vaguely realizing westward,
But still unstoried, artless, unenhanced,
Such as she was, such as she would become.

## Triple Bronze

The Infinite's being so wide
Is the reason the Powers provide
For inner defense my hide.
For next defense outside

I make myself this time
Of wood or granite or lime
A wall too hard for crime
Either to breach or climb.

Then a number of us agree
On a national boundary.
And that defense makes three
Between too much and me.

## Our Hold on the Planet

We asked for rain. It didn't flash and roar.
It didn't lose its temper at our demand
And blow a gale. It didn't misunderstand
And give us more than our spokesman bargained for;
And just because we owned to a wish for rain,
Send us a flood and bid us be damned and drown.
It gently threw us a glittering shower down.
And when we had taken that into the roots of grain,
It threw us another and then another still
Till the spongy soil again was natal wet.
We may doubt the just proportion of good to ill.
There is much in nature against us. But we forget:
Take nature altogether since time began,
Including human nature, in peace and war,
And it must be a little more in favor of man,
Say a fraction of one per cent at the very least,
Or our number living wouldn't be steadily more,
Our hold on the planet wouldn't have so increased.

## To a Young Wretch

### (Boethian)

As gay for you to take your father's ax
As take his gun—rod—to go hunting—fishing.
You nick my spruce until its fiber cracks,
It gives up standing straight and goes down swishing.
You link an arm in its arm and you lean
Across the light snow homeward smelling green.

I could have bought you just as good a tree
To frizzle resin in a candle flame,
And what a saving 'twould have meant to me.
But tree by charity is not the same
As tree by enterprise and expedition.
I must not spoil your Christmas with contrition.

It is your Christmases against my woods.
But even where thus opposing interests kill,
They are to be thought of as opposing goods
Oftener than as conflicting good and ill;
Which makes the war god seem no special dunce
For always fighting on both sides at once.

And though in tinsel chain and popcorn rope,
My tree a captive in your window bay
Has lost its footing on my mountain slope
And lost the stars of heaven, may, oh, may
The symbol star it lifts against your ceiling
Help me accept its fate with Christmas feeling.

## The Lesson for Today

If this uncertain age in which we dwell
Were really as dark as I hear sages tell,
And I convinced that they were really sages,
I should not curse myself with it to hell,
But leaving not the chair I long have sat in,
I should betake me back ten thousand pages
To the world's undebatably dark ages,
And getting up my medieval Latin,
Seek converse common cause and brotherhood
(By all that's liberal—I should, I should)
With poets who could calmly take the fate
Of being born at once too early and late,
And for these reasons kept from being great.
Yet singing but Dione in the wood
And *ver aspergit terram floribus*
They slowly led old Latin verse to rhyme
And to forget the ancient lengths of time,
And so began the modern world for us.

I'd say, O Master of the Palace School,
You were not Charles' nor anybody's fool:
Tell me as pedagogue to pedagogue,

You did not know that since King Charles did rule
You had no chance but to be minor, did you?
Your light was spent perhaps as in a fog
That at once kept you burning low and hid you.
The age may very well have been to blame
For your not having won to Virgil's fame.
But no one ever heard you make the claim.
You would not think you knew enough to judge
The age when full upon you. That's my point.
We have today and I could call their name
Who know exactly what is out of joint
To make their verse and their excuses lame.
They've tried to grasp with too much social fact
Too large a situation. You and I
Would be afraid if we should comprehend
And get outside of too much bad statistics
Our muscles never could again contract:
We never could recover human shape,
But must live lives out mentally agape,
Or die of philosophical distention.
That's how we feel—and we're no special mystics.

    We can't appraise the time in which we act.
But for the folly of it, let's pretend
We know enough to know it for adverse.
One more millennium's about to end.
Let's celebrate the event, my distant friend,
In publicly disputing which is worse,
The present age or your age. You and I
As schoolmen of repute should qualify
To wage a fine scholastical contention
As to whose age deserves the lower mark,
Or should I say the higher one, for dark.
I can just hear the way you make it go:
There's always something to be sorry for,
A sordid peace or an outrageous war.
Yes, yes, of course. We have the same convention.
The groundwork of all faith is human woe.
It was well worth preliminary mention.
There's nothing but injustice to be had,

No choice is left a poet, you might add,
But how to take the curse, tragic or comic.
It was well worth preliminary mention.
But let's go on to where our cases part,
If part they do. Let me propose a start.
(We're rivals in the badness of our case,
Remember, and must keep a solemn face.)
Space ails us moderns: we are sick with space.
Its contemplation makes us out as small
As a brief epidemic of microbes
That in a good glass may be seen to crawl
The patina of this the least of globes.
But have we there the advantage after all?
You were belittled into vilest worms
God hardly tolerated with his feet;
Which comes to the same thing in different terms.
We both are the belittled human race,
One as compared with God and one with space.
I had thought ours the more profound disgrace;
But doubtless this was only my conceit.
The cloister and the observatory saint
Take comfort in about the same complaint.
So science and religion really meet.

   I can just hear you call your Palace class:
Come learn the Latin Eheu for alas.
You may not want to use it and you may.
O paladins, the lesson for today
Is how to be unhappy yet polite.
And at the summons Roland, Olivier,
And every sheepish paladin and peer,
Being already more than proved in fight,
Sits down in school to try if he can write
Like Horace in the true Horatian vein,
Yet like a Christian disciplined to bend
His mind to thinking always of the end.
Memento mori and obey the Lord.
Art and religion love the somber chord.
Earth's a hard place in which to save the soul,
And could it be brought under state control,

So automatically we all were saved,
Its separateness from Heaven could be waived;
It might as well at once be kingdom-come.
(Perhaps it will be next millennium.)

But these are universals, not confined
To any one time, place, or human kind.
We're either nothing or a God's regret.
As ever when philosophers are met,
No matter where they stoutly mean to get,
Nor what particulars they reason from,
They are philosophers, and from old habit
They end up in the universal Whole
As unoriginal as any rabbit.

One age is like another for the soul.
I'm telling you. You haven't said a thing,
Unless I put it in your mouth to say.
I'm having the whole argument my way—
But in your favor—please to tell your King—
In having granted you all ages shine
With equal darkness, yours as dark as mine.
I'm liberal. You, you aristocrat,
Won't know exactly what I mean by that.
I mean so altruistically moral
I never take my own side in a quarrel.
I'd lay my hand on his hand on his staff,
Lean back and have my confidential laugh,
And tell him I had read his Epitaph.

It sent me to the graves the other day.
The only other there was far away
Across the landscape with a watering pot
At his devotions in a special plot.
And he was there resuscitating flowers
(Make no mistake about its being bones);
But I was only there to read the stones
To see what on the whole they had to say
About how long a man may think to live,
Which is becoming my concern of late.

And very wide the choice they seemed to give;
The ages ranging all the way from hours
To months and years and many many years.
One man had lived one hundred years and eight.
But though we all may be inclined to wait
And follow some development of state,
Or see what comes of science and invention,
There is a limit to our time extension.
We all are doomed to broken-off careers,
And so's the nation, so's the total race.
The earth itself is liable to the fate
Of meaninglessly being broken off.
(And hence so many literary tears
At which my inclination is to scoff.)
I may have wept that any should have died
Or missed their chance, or not have been their best,
Or been their riches, fame, or love denied;
On me as much as any is the jest.
I take my incompleteness with the rest.
God bless himself can no one else be blessed.

I hold your doctrine of Memento Mori.
And were an epitaph to be my story
I'd have a short one ready for my own.
I would have written of me on my stone:
I had a lover's quarrel with the world.

## Time Out

It took that pause to make him realize
The mountain he was climbing had the slant
As of a book held up before his eyes
(And was a text albeit done in plant).
Dwarf cornel, gold-thread, and maianthemum,
He followingly fingered as he read,
The flowers fading on the seed to come;
But the thing was the slope it gave his head:
The same for reading as it was for thought,
So different from the hard and level stare
Of enemies defied and battles fought.
It was the obstinately gentle air
That may be clamored at by cause and sect
But it will have its moment to reflect.

## To a Moth Seen in Winter

Here's first a gloveless hand warm from my pocket,
A perch and resting place 'twixt wood and wood,
Bright-black-eyed silvery creature, brushed with brown,
The wings not folded in repose, but spread.
(Who would you be, I wonder, by those marks
If I had moths to friend as I have flowers?)
And now pray tell what lured you with false hope
To make the venture of eternity
And seek the love of kind in wintertime?
But stay and hear me out. I surely think
You make a labor of flight for one so airy,
Spending yourself too much in self-support.
Nor will you find love either nor love you.
And what I pity in you is something human,
The old incurable untimeliness,
Only begetter of all ills that are.

But go. You are right. My pity cannot help.
Go till you wet your pinions and are quenched.
You must be made more simply wise than I
To know the hand I stretch impulsively
Across the gulf of well nigh everything
May reach to you, but cannot touch your fate.
I cannot touch your life, much less can save,
Who am tasked to save my own a little while.

Circa 1900

## A Considerable Speck

### (Microscopic)

A speck that would have been beneath my sight
On any but a paper sheet so white
Set off across what I had written there.
And I had idly poised my pen in air
To stop it with a period of ink
When something strange about it made me think.
This was no dust speck by my breathing blown,
But unmistakably a living mite
With inclinations it could call its own.
It paused as with suspicion of my pen,
And then came racing wildly on again
To where my manuscript was not yet dry;
Then paused again and either drank or smelt—
With loathing, for again it turned to fly.
Plainly with an intelligence I dealt.
It seemed too tiny to have room for feet,
Yet must have had a set of them complete
To express how much it didn't want to die.
It ran with terror and with cunning crept.
It faltered: I could see it hesitate;
Then in the middle of the open sheet
Cower down in desperation to accept
Whatever I accorded it of fate.
I have none of the tenderer-than-thou

Collectivistic regimenting love
With which the modern world is being swept.
But this poor microscopic item now!
Since it was nothing I knew evil of
I let it lie there till I hope it slept.

I have a mind myself and recognize
Mind when I meet with it in any guise.
No one can know how glad I am to find
On any sheet the least display of mind.


## The Lost Follower

As I have known them passionate and fine
The gold for which they leave the golden line
Of lyric is a golden light divine,
Never the gold of darkness from a mine.

The spirit plays us strange religious pranks
To whatsoever god we owe the thanks.
No one has ever failed the poet ranks
To link a chain of money-metal banks.

The loss to song, the danger of defection
Is always in the opposite direction.
Some turn in sheer, in Shelleyan dejection
To try if one more popular election

Will give us by short cut the final stage
That poetry with all its golden rage
For beauty on the illuminated page
Has failed to bring—I mean the Golden Age.

And if this may not be (and nothing's sure),
At least to live ungolden with the poor,
Enduring what the ungolden must endure.
This has been poetry's great anti-lure.

The muse mourns one who went to his retreat
Long since in some abysmal city street,
The bride who shared the crust he broke to eat
As grave as he about the world's defeat.

With such it has proved dangerous as friend
Even in a playful moment to contend
That the millennium to which you bend
In longing is not at a progress-end

By grace of state-manipulated pelf,
Or politics of Ghibelline or Guelph,
But right beside you book-like on a shelf,
Or even better god-like in yourself.

He trusts my love too well to deign reply.
But there is in the sadness of his eye,
Something about a kingdom in the sky
(As yet unbrought to earth) he means to try.

## November

We saw leaves go to glory,
Then almost migratory
Go part way down the lane,
And then to end the story
Get beaten down and pasted
In one wild day of rain.
We heard ' 'Tis over' roaring.
A year of leaves was wasted.
Oh, we make a boast of storing,
Of saving and of keeping,
But only by ignoring
The waste of moments sleeping,
The waste of pleasure weeping,
By denying and ignoring
The waste of nations warring.

*1938*

## The Rabbit Hunter

Careless and still
The hunter lurks
With gun depressed,
Facing alone
The alder swamps
Ghastly snow-white.
And his hound works
In the offing there
Like one possessed,
And yelps delight
And sings and romps,
Bringing him on
The shadowy hare
For him to rend
And deal a death
That he nor it
(Nor I) have wit
To comprehend.

## A Loose Mountain

*(Telescopic)*

Did you stay up last night (the Magi did)
To see the star shower known as Leonid
That once a year by hand or apparatus
Is so mysteriously pelted at us?
It is but fiery puffs of dust and pebbles,
No doubt directed at our heads as rebels
In having taken artificial light
Against the ancient sovereignty of night.
A fusillade of blanks and empty flashes,
It never reaches earth except as ashes
Of which you feel no least touch on your face
Nor find in dew the slightest cloudy trace.
Nevertheless it constitutes a hint

That the loose mountain lately seen to glint
In sunlight near us in momentous swing
Is something in a Balearic sling
The heartless and enormous Outer Black
Is still withholding in the Zodiac
But from irresolution in his back
About when best to have us in our orbit,
So we won't simply take it and absorb it.

## It Is Almost the Year Two Thousand

To start the world of old
We had one age of gold
Not labored out of mines,
And some say there are signs
The second such has come,
The true Millennium,
The final golden glow
To end it. And if so
(And science ought to know)
We well may raise our heads
From weeding garden beds
And annotating books
To watch this end de luxe.

## In a Poem

The sentencing goes blithely on its way,
And takes the playfully objected rhyme
As surely as it keeps the stroke and time
In having its undeviable say.

## On Our Sympathy with the Under Dog

First under up and then again down under,
We watch a circus of revolving dogs
No senator dares in to kick asunder
Lest both should bite him in the toga-togs.

## A Question

A voice said, Look me in the stars
And tell me truly, men of earth,
If all the soul-and-body scars
Were not too much to pay for birth.

## Boeotian

I love to toy with the Platonic notion
That wisdom need not be of Athens Attic,
But well may be Laconic, even Boeotian.
At least I will not have it systematic.

## The Secret Sits

We dance round in a ring and suppose,
But the Secret sits in the middle and knows.

## An Equalizer

It is as true as Caesar's name was Kaiser
That no economist was ever wiser
(Though prodigal himself and a despiser
Of capital and calling thrift a miser).
And when we get too far apart in wealth,
'Twas his idea that for the public health,
So that the poor won't have to steal by stealth,
We now and then should take an equalizer.

## A Semi-Revolution

I advocate a semi-revolution.
The trouble with a total revolution
(Ask any reputable Rosicrucian)
Is that it brings the same class up on top.
Executives of skillful execution
Will therefore plan to go halfway and stop.
Yes, revolutions are the only salves,
But they're one thing that should be done by halves.

## Assurance

The danger not an inch outside
Behind the porthole's slab of glass
And double ring of fitted brass
I trust feels properly defied.

## An Answer

But Islands of the Blessèd, bless you, son,
I never came upon a blessèd one.

## Trespass

No, I had set no prohibiting sign,
And yes, my land was hardly fenced.
Nevertheless the land was mine:
I was being trespassed on and against.

Whoever the surly freedom took
Of such an unaccountable stay
Busying by my woods and brook
Gave me strangely restless day.

He might be opening leaves of stone,
The picture-book of the trilobite,
For which the region round was known,
And in which there was little property right.

'Twas not the value I stood to lose
In specimen crab in specimen rock,
But his ignoring what was whose
That made me look again at the clock.

Then came his little acknowledgment:
He asked for a drink at the kitchen door,
An errand he may have had to invent,
But it made my property mine once more.

## A Nature Note

Four or five whippoorwills
Have come down from their native ledge
To the open country edge
To give us a piece of their bills.

Two in June were a pair—
You'd say sufficiently loud,
But this was a family crowd,
A full-fledged family affair.

All out of time pell-mell!
I wasn't in on the joke
Unless it was coming to folk
To bid us a mock farewell.

I took note of when it occurred,
The twenty-third of September,
Their latest that I remember,
September the twenty-third.


## Of the Stones of the Place

I farm a pasture where the boulders lie
As touching as a basket full of eggs,
And though they're nothing anybody begs,
I wonder if it wouldn't signify

For me to send you one out where you live
In wind-soil to a depth of thirty feet,
And every acre good enough to eat,
As fine as flour put through a baker's sieve.

I'd ship a smooth one you could slap and chafe,
And set up like a statue in your yard,
An eolith palladium to guard
The West and keep the old tradition safe.

Carve nothing on it. You can simply say
In self-defense to quizzical inquiry:
'The portrait of the soul of my gransir Ira.
It came from where he came from anyway.'

## Not of School Age

Around bend after bend,
It was blown woods and no end.
I came to but one house
I made but the one friend.

At the one house a child was out
Who drew back at first in doubt,
But spoke to me in a gale
That blew so he had to shout.

His cheek smeared with apple sand,
A part apple in his hand,
He pointed on up the road
As one having war-command.

A parent, his gentler one,
Looked forth on her small son,
And wondered with me there
What now was being done.

His accent was not good.
But I slowly understood.
Something where I could go—
He couldn't but I could.

He was too young to go,
Not over four or so.
Well, would I please go to school,
And the big flag they had—you know

The big flag, the red—white—
And blue flag, the great sight—
He bet it was out today,
And would I see if he was right?

*1932*

## A Serious Step Lightly Taken

Between two burrs on the map
Was a hollow-headed snake.
The burrs were hills, the snake was a stream,
And the hollow head was a lake.

And the dot in *front* of a name
Was what should be a town.
And there might be a house we could buy
For only a dollar down.

With two wheels low in the ditch
We left our boiling car,
And knocked at the door of a house we found,
And there today we are.

It is turning three hundred years
On our cisatlantic shore
For family after family name.
We'll make it three hundred more

For our name farming here,
Aloof yet not aloof,
Enriching soil and increasing stock,
Repairing fence and roof;

A hundred thousand days
Of front-page paper events,
A half a dozen major wars,
And forty-five presidents.

## The Literate Farmer and the Planet Venus

*A Dated Popular-Science Medley*
*on a Mysterious Light Recently Observed in the*
*Western Sky at Evening*

My unexpected knocking at the door
Started chairs thundering on the kitchen floor,
Knives and forks ringing on the supper plates,
Voices conflicting like the candidates.
A mighty farmer flung the house door wide,
He and a lot of children came outside,
And there on an equality we stood.
That's the time knocking at a door did good.

'I stopped to compliment you on this star
You get the beauty of from where you are.
To see it so, the bright and only one
In sunset light, you'd think it was the sun
That hadn't sunk the way it should have sunk,
But right in heaven was slowly being shrunk
So small as to be virtually gone,
Yet there to watch the darkness coming on—
Like someone dead permitted to exist
Enough to see if he was greatly missed.
I didn't see the sun set. Did it set?
Will anybody swear that isn't it?
And will you give me shelter for the night?
If not, a glass of milk will be all right.'

'Traveler, I'm glad you asked about that light.
Your mind mistrusted there was something wrong,
And naturally you couldn't go along
Without inquiring if 'twas serious.
'Twas providential you applied to us,
Who were just on the subject when you came.
There is a star that's Serious by name
And nature too, but this is not the same.
This light's been going on for several years,
Although at times we think it disappears.
You'll hear all sorts of things. You'll meet with them

Will tell you it's the star of Bethlehem
Above some more religion in a manger.
But put that down to superstition, Stranger.
What's a star doing big as a baseball?
Between us two it's not a star at all.
It's a new patented electric light,
Put up on trial by that Jerseyite
So much is being now expected of,
To give developments the final shove
And turn us into the next specie folks
Are going to be, unless these monkey jokes
Of the last fifty years are all a libel,
And Darwin's proved mistaken, not the Bible.
I s'pose you have your notions on the vexed
Question of what we're turning into next.'

    'As liberals we're willing to give place
To any demonstrably better race,
No matter what the color of its skin.
(But what a human race the white has been!)
I heard a fellow in a public lecture
On Pueblo Indians and their architecture
Declare that if such Indians inherited
The cóndemned world the legacy was merited.
So far as he, the speaker, was concerned
He had his ticket bought, his passage earned,
To take the *Mayflower* back where he belonged
Before the Indian race was further wronged.
But come, enlightened as in talk you seem,
You don't believe that that first-water gleam
Is not a star?'

    'Believe it? Why, I know it.
Its actions any cloudless night will show it.
You'll see it be allowed up just so high,
Say about halfway up the western sky,
And then get slowly, slowly pulled back down.
You might not notice if you've lived in town,
As I suspect you have. A town debars
Much notice of what's going on in stars.

The idea is no doubt to make one job
Of lighting the whole night with one big blob
Of electricity in bulk the way
The sun sets the example in the day.'

'Here come more stars to character the skies,
And they in the estimation of the wise
Are more divine than any bulb or arc,
Because their purpose is to flash and spark,
But not to take away the precious dark.
We need the interruption of the night
To ease attention off when overtight,
To break our logic in too long a flight,
And ask us if our premises are right.'

'Sick talk, sick talk, sick sentimental talk!
It doesn't do you any good to walk.
I see what *you* are: can't get you excited
With hopes of getting mankind unbenighted.
Some ignorance takes rank as innocence.
Have it for all of me and have it dense.
The slave will never thank his manumitter;
Which often makes the manumitter bitter.'

'In short, you think that star a patent medicine
Put up to cure the world by Mr. Edison.'

'You said it—that's exactly what it is.
My son in Jersey says a friend of his
Knows the old man and nobody's so deep
In incandescent lamps and ending sleep.
The old man argues science cheapened speed.
A good cheap anti-dark is now the need.
Give us a good cheap twenty-four-hour day,
No part of which we'd have to waste, I say,
And who knows where we can't get! Wasting time
In sleep or slowness is the deadly crime.
He gave up sleep himself some time ago,
It puffs the face and brutalizes so.
You take the ugliness all so much dread,

Called getting out of the wrong side of bed.
That is the source perhaps of human hate,
And well may be where wars originate.
Get rid of that and there'd be left no great
Of either murder or war in any land.
You know how cunningly mankind is planned:
We have one loving and one hating hand.
The loving's made to hold each other like,
While with the hating other hand we strike.
The blow can be no stronger than the clutch,
Or soon we'd bat each other out of touch,
And the fray wouldn't last a single round.
And still it's bad enough to badly wound,
And if our getting up to start the day
On the right side of bed would end the fray,
We'd hail the remedy. But it's been tried
And found, he says, a bed has no right side.
The trouble is, with that receipt for love,
A bed's got no right side to get out of.
We can't be trusted to the sleep we take,
And simply must evolve to stay awake.
He thinks that chairs and tables will endure,
But beds—in less than fifty years he's sure
There will be no such piece of furniture.
He's surely got it in for cots and beds.
No need for us to rack our common heads
About it, though. We haven't got the mind.
It best be left to great men of his kind
Who have no other object than our good.
There's a lot yet that isn't understood.
Ain't it a caution to us not to fix
No limits to what rose in rubbing sticks
On fire to scare away the pterodix
When man first lived in caves along the creeks?'

'Marvelous world in nineteen-twenty-six.'

# STEEPLE BUSH

## *A Young Birch*

The birch begins to crack its outer sheath
Of baby green and show the white beneath,
As whosoever likes the young and slight
May well have noticed. Soon entirely white
To double day and cut in half the dark
It will stand forth, entirely white in bark,
And nothing but the top a leafy green—
The only native tree that dares to lean,
Relying on its beauty, to the air.
(Less brave perhaps than trusting are the fair.)
And someone reminiscent will recall
How once in cutting brush along the wall
He spared it from the number of the slain,
At first to be no bigger than a cane,
And then no bigger than a fishing pole,
But now at last so obvious a bole
The most efficient help you ever hired
Would know that it was there to be admired,
And zeal would not be thanked that cut it down
When you were reading books or out of town.
It was a thing of beauty and was sent
To live its life out as an ornament.

## *Something for Hope*

At the present rate it must come to pass
And that right soon that the meadow sweet
And steeple bush not good to eat
Will have crowded out the edible grass.

Then all there is to do is wait
For maple birch and spruce to push

Through meadow sweet and steeple bush
And crowd them out at a similar rate.

No plow among these rocks would pay.
So busy yourself with other things
While the trees put on their wooden rings
And with long-sleeved branches hold their sway.

Then cut down the trees when lumber grown,
And there's your pristine earth all freed
From lovely blooming but wasteful weed
And ready again for the grass to own.

A cycle we'll say of a hundred years.
Thus foresight does it and laissez faire,
A virtue in which we all may share
Unless a government interferes.

Patience and looking away ahead,
And leaving some things to take their course.
Hope may not nourish a cow or horse,
But spes alit agricolam 'tis said.


## One Step Backward Taken

Not only sands and gravels
Were once more on their travels,
But gulping muddy gallons
Great boulders off their balance
Bumped heads together dully
And started down the gully.
Whole capes caked off in slices.
I felt my standpoint shaken
In the universal crisis.
But with one step backward taken
I saved myself from going.
A world torn loose went by me.
Then the rain stopped and the blowing
And the sun came out to dry me.

## Directive

Back out of all this now too much for us,
Back in a time made simple by the loss
Of detail, burned, dissolved, and broken off
Like graveyard marble sculpture in the weather,
There is a house that is no more a house
Upon a farm that is no more a farm
And in a town that is no more a town.
The road there, if you'll let a guide direct you
Who only has at heart your getting lost,
May seem as if it should have been a quarry—
Great monolithic knees the former town
Long since gave up pretense of keeping covered.
And there's a story in a book about it:
Besides the wear of iron wagon wheels
The ledges show lines ruled southeast northwest,
The chisel work of an enormous Glacier
That braced his feet against the Arctic Pole.
You must not mind a certain coolness from him
Still said to haunt this side of Panther Mountain.
Nor need you mind the serial ordeal
Of being watched from forty cellar holes
As if by eye pairs out of forty firkins.
As for the woods' excitement over you
That sends light rustle rushes to their leaves,
Charge that to upstart inexperience.
Where were they all not twenty years ago?
They think too much of having shaded out
A few old pecker-fretted apple trees.
Make yourself up a cheering song of how
Someone's road home from work this once was,
Who may be just ahead of you on foot
Or creaking with a buggy load of grain.
The height of the adventure is the height
Of country where two village cultures faded
Into each other. Both of them are lost.
And if you're lost enough to find yourself
By now, pull in your ladder road behind you
And put a sign up CLOSED to all but me.

Then make yourself at home. The only field
Now left's no bigger than a harness gall.
First there's the children's house of make believe,
Some shattered dishes underneath a pine,
The playthings in the playhouse of the children.
Weep for what little things could make them glad.
Then for the house that is no more a house,
But only a belilaced cellar hole,
Now slowly closing like a dent in dough.
This was no playhouse but a house in earnest.
Your destination and your destiny's
A brook that was the water of the house,
Cold as a spring as yet so near its source,
Too lofty and original to rage.
(We know the valley streams that when aroused
Will leave their tatters hung on barb and thorn.)
I have kept hidden in the instep arch
Of an old cedar at the waterside
A broken drinking goblet like the Grail
Under a spell so the wrong ones can't find it,
So can't get saved, as Saint Mark says they mustn't.
(I stole the goblet from the children's playhouse.)
Here are your waters and your watering place.
Drink and be whole again beyond confusion.


## Too Anxious for Rivers

Look down the long valley and there stands a mountain
That someone has said is the end of the world.
Then what of this river that having arisen
Must find where to pour itself into and empty?
I never saw so much swift water run cloudless.
Oh, I have been often too anxious for rivers
To leave it to them to get out of their valleys.
The truth is the river flows into the canyon
Of Ceasing to Question What Doesn't Concern Us,
As sooner or later we have to cease somewhere.
No place to get lost like too far in the distance.

It may be a mercy the dark closes round us
So broodingly soon in every direction.
The world as we know is an elephant's howdah;
The elephant stands on the back of a turtle;
The turtle in turn on a rock in the ocean.
And how much longer a story has science
Before she must put out the light on the children
And tell them the rest of the story is dreaming?
'You children may dream it and tell it tomorrow.'
Time was we were molten, time was we were vapor.
What set us on fire and what set us revolving
Lucretius the Epicurean might tell us
'Twas something we knew all about to begin with
And needn't have fared into space like his master
To find 'twas the effort, the essay of love.


## An Unstamped Letter in Our Rural Letter Box

Last night your watchdog barked all night
So once you rose and lit the light.
It wasn't someone at your locks.
No, in your rural letter box
I leave this note without a stamp
To tell you it was just a tramp
Who used your pasture for a camp.
There pointed like the pip of spades
The young spruce made a suite of glades
So regular that in the dark
The place was like a city park.
There I elected to demur
Beneath a low-slung juniper
That like a blanket to my chin
Kept some dew out and some heat in,
Yet left me freely face to face
All night with universal space.
It may have been at two o'clock
That under me a point of rock
Developed in the grass and fern,

And as I woke afraid to turn
Or so much as uncross my feet,
Lest having wasted precious heat
I never should again be warmed,
The largest firedrop ever formed
From two stars' having coalesced
Went streaking molten down the west.
And then your tramp astrologer
From seeing this undoubted stir
In Heaven's firm-set firmament,
Himself had the equivalent,
Only within. Inside the brain
Two memories that long had lain,
Now quivered toward each other, lipped
Together, and together slipped;
And for a moment all was plain
That men have thought about in vain.
Please, my involuntary host,
Forgive me if I seem to boast.
'Tis possible you may have seen,
Albeit through a rusty screen,
The same sign Heaven showed your guest.
Each knows his own discernment best.
You have had your advantages.
Things must have happened to you, yes,
And have occurred to you no doubt,
If not indeed from sleeping out,
Then from the work you went about
In farming well—or pretty well.
And it is partly to compel
Myself, in forma pauperis,
To say as much I write you this.

## To an Ancient

Your claims to immortality were two.
The one you made, the other one you grew.
Sorry to have no name for you but You.

We never knew exactly where to look,
But found one in the delta of a brook,
One in a cavern where you used to cook.

Coming on such an ancient human trace
Seems as expressive of the human race
As meeting someone living face to face.

We date you by your depth in silt and dust
Your probable brute nature is discussed.
At which point we are totally nonplussed.

You made the eolith, you grew the bone,
The second more peculiarly your own,
And likely to have been enough alone.

You make me ask if I would go to time
Would I gain anything by using rhyme?
Or aren't the bones enough I live to lime?

# FIVE NOCTURNES

## I. *The Night Light*

She always had to burn a light
Beside her attic bed at night.
It gave bad dreams and broken sleep,
But helped the Lord her soul to keep.
Good gloom on her was thrown away.
It is on me by night or day,
Who have, as I suppose, ahead
The darkest of it still to dread.

## II. *Were I in Trouble*

Where I could think of no thoroughfare,
Away on the mountain up far too high,
A blinding headlight shifted glare
And began to bounce down a granite stair
Like a star fresh fallen out of the sky.
And I away in my opposite wood
Am touched by that unintimate light
And made feel less alone than I rightly should,
For traveler there could do me no good
Were I in trouble with night tonight.

### III. Bravado

Have I not walked without an upward look
Of caution under stars that very well
Might not have missed me when they shot and fell?
It was a risk I had to take—and took.

### IV. On Making Certain Anything Has Happened

I could be worse employed
Than as watcher of the void
Whose part should be to tell
What star if any fell.

Suppose some seed-pearl sun
Should be the only one;
Yet still I must report
Some cluster one star short.

I should justly hesitate
To frighten church or state
By announcing a star down
From say the Cross or Crown.

To make sure what star I missed
I should have to check on my list
Every star in sight.
It might take me all night.

## *V. In the Long Night*

I would build my house of crystal
With a solitary friend
Where the cold cracks like a pistol
And the needle stands on end.

We would pour oil on the ingle
And for want of books recite.
We would crawl out filing single
To observe the Northern Light.

If Etookashoo and Couldlooktoo
The Esquimaux should call,
There would be fish raw and cooked too
And enough drink oil for all.

As one rankly warm insider
To another I would say,
We can rest assured on eider
There will come another day.

## A Mood Apart

Once down on my knees to growing plants
I prodded the earth with a lazy tool
In time with a medley of sotto chants;
But becoming aware of some boys from school
Who had stopped outside the fence to spy,
I stopped my song and almost heart,
For any eye is an evil eye
That looks in on to a mood apart.

## The Fear of God

If you should rise from Nowhere up to Somewhere,
From being No one up to being Someone,
Be sure to keep repeating to yourself
You owe it to an arbitrary god
Whose mercy to you rather than to others
Won't bear too critical examination.
Stay unassuming. If for lack of license
To wear the uniform of who you are,
You should be tempted to make up for it
In a subordinating look or tone
Beware of coming too much to the surface,
And using for apparel what was meant
To be the curtain of the inmost soul.

## The Fear of Man

As a girl no one gallantly attends
Sets forth for home at midnight from a friend's—
She tries to make it in one catch of breath,
And this is not because she thinks of death.

The city seems intoppling from a height,
But she can trust it not to fall tonight.
(It will be taken down before it falls.)
There scarcely is a light in all its walls
Except beside a safe inside a bank
(For which assurance Mammon is to thank).
But there are little street lights she should trust
So jewel steady in the wind and dust.
Her fear is being spoken by the rude
And having her exposure misconstrued.
May I in my brief bolt across the scene
Not be misunderstood in what I mean.

## A Steeple on the House

What if it should turn out eternity
Was but the steeple on our house of life
That made our house of life a house of worship?
We do not go up there to sleep at night.
We do not go up there to live by day.
Nor need we ever go up there to live.
A spire and belfry coming on the roof
Means that a soul is coming on the flesh.

## Innate Helium

Religious faith is a most filling vapor.
It swirls occluded in us under tight
Compression to uplift us out of weight—
As in those buoyant bird bones thin as paper,
To give them still more buoyancy in flight.
Some gas like helium must be innate.

## The Courage to Be New

I hear the world reciting
The mistakes of ancient men,
The brutality and fighting
They will never have again.

Heartbroken and disabled
In body and in mind
They renew talk of the fabled
Federation of Mankind.

But they're blessed with the acumen
To suspect the human trait
Was not the *basest* human
That made them militate.

They will tell you more as soon as
You tell them what to do
With their ever breaking newness
And their courage to be new.


## Iota Subscript

Seek not in me the big I capital,
Nor yet the little dotted in me seek.
If I have in me any I at all,
'Tis the iota subscript of the Greek.

So small am I as an attention beggar.
The letter you will find me subscript to
Is neither alpha, eta, nor omega,
But upsilon which is the Greek for you.

## The Middleness of the Road

The road at the top of the rise
Seems to come to an end
And take off into the skies.
So at the distant bend

It seems to go into a wood,
The place of standing still
As long the trees have stood.
But say what Fancy will,

The mineral drops that explode
To drive my ton of car
Are limited to the road.
They deal with near and far,

But have almost nothing to do
With the absolute flight and rest
The universal blue
And local green suggest.


## Astrometaphysical

Lord, I have loved your sky,
Be it said against or for me,
Have loved it clear and high,
Or low and stormy;

Till I have reeled and stumbled
From looking up too much,
And fallen and been humbled
To wear a crutch.

My love for every Heaven
O'er which you, Lord, have lorded,
From number One to Seven
Should be rewarded.

It may not give me hope
That when I am translated
My scalp will in the cope
Be constellated.

But if that seems to tend
To my undue renown,
At least it ought to send
Me up, not down.


## Skeptic

Far star that tickles for me my sensitive plate
And fries a couple of ebon atoms white,
I don't believe I believe a thing you state.
I put no faith in the seeming facts of light.

I don't believe I believe you're the last in space,
I don't believe you're anywhere near the last,
I don't believe what makes you red in the face
Is after explosion going away so fast.

The universe may or may not be very immense.
As a matter of fact there are times when I am apt
To feel it close in tight against my sense
Like a caul in which I was born and still am wrapped.

## Two Leading Lights

I never happened to contrast
The two in the celestial cast
Whose prominence has been so vast.
The Sun is satisfied with days.
He never has in any phase
That I have heard of shone at night.
And yet he is a power of light
And could in one burst overwhelm
And dayify the darkest realm
By right of eminent domain.
He has the greatness to refrain.
The Moon for all her light and grace
Has never learned to know her place.
The notedest astronomers
Have set the dark aside for hers.
But there are many nights though clear
She doesn't bother to appear.
Some lunatic or lunar whim
Will bring her out diminished dim
To set herself beside the Sun
As Sheba came to Solomon.
It may be charitably guessed
Comparison is not her quest.
Some rumor of his wishing ring
That changes winter into spring
Has brought her merely visiting,
An irresponsible divinity
Presuming on her femininity.

## A Rogers Group

How young and unassuming
They waited in the street,
With babies in their arms
And baggage at their feet.

A trolley car they hailed
Went by with clanging gong
Before they guessed the corner
They waited on was wrong.

And no one told them so
By way of traveler's aid,
No one was so far touched
By the Rogers Group they made.

## On Being Idolized

The wave sucks back and with the last of water
It wraps a wisp of seaweed round my legs,
And with the swift rush of its sandy dregs
So undermines my barefoot stand I totter
And did I not take steps would be tipped over
Like the ideal of some mistaken lover.

## A Wish to Comply

Did I see it go by,
That Millikan mote?
Well, I said that I did.
I made a good try.
But I'm no one to quote.
If I have a defect
It's a wish to comply
And see as I'm bid.
I rather suspect
All I saw was the lid
Going over my eye.
I honestly think
All I saw was a wink.

### A Cliff Dwelling

There sandy seems the golden sky
And golden seems the sandy plain.
No habitation meets the eye
Unless in the horizon rim,
Some halfway up the limestone wall,
That spot of black is not a stain
Or shadow, but a cavern hole,
Where someone used to climb and crawl
To rest from his besetting fears.
I see the callus on his sole
The disappearing last of him
And of his race starvation slim,
Oh, years ago—ten thousand years.

### It Bids Pretty Fair

The play seems out for an almost infinite run.
Don't mind a little thing like the actors fighting.
The only thing I worry about is the sun.
We'll be all right if nothing goes wrong with the lighting.

### Beyond Words

That row of icicles along the gutter
Feels like my armory of hate;
And you, you . . . you, you utter . . .
You wait!

## A Case for Jefferson

Harrison loves my country too,
But wants it all made over new.
He's Freudian Viennese by night.
By day he's Marxian Muscovite.
It isn't because he's Russian Jew.
He's Puritan Yankee through and through.
He dotes on Saturday pork and beans.
But his mind is hardly out of his teens:
With him the love of country means
Blowing it all to smithereens
And having it all made over new.

## Lucretius versus the Lake Poets

'Nature I loved; and next to Nature, Art.'

Dean, adult education may seem silly.
What of it though? I got some willy-nilly
The other evening at your college deanery.
And grateful for it (Let's not be facetious!)
For I thought Epicurus and Lucretius
By Nature meant the Whole Goddam Machinery.
But you say that in college nomenclature
The only meaning possible for Nature
In Landor's quatrain would be Pretty Scenery.
Which makes opposing it to Art absurd
I grant you—if you're sure about the word.
God bless the Dean and make his deanship plenary.

## Haec Fabula Docet

A Blindman by the name of La Fontaine,
Relying on himself and on his cane,
Came tap-tap-tapping down the village street,
The apogee of human blind conceit.
Now just ahead of him was seen to yawn
A trench where water pipes were laying on.
The Blindman might have found it with his ferrule,
But someone over anxious at his peril
Not only warned him with a loud command,
But ran against him with a staying hand.
Enraged at what he could but think officious,
The Blindman missed him with a blow so vicious
He gave his own poor iliac a wrench
And plunged himself head foremost in the trench:
Where with a glee no less for being grim
The workmen all turned to and buried him.

### Moral

The moral is it hardly need be shown,
All those who try to go it sole alone,
Too proud to be beholden for relief,
Are absolutely sure to come to grief.

## Etherealizing

A theory if you hold it hard enough
And long enough gets rated as a creed:
Such as that flesh is something we can slough
So that the mind can be entirely freed.
Then when the arms and legs have atrophied,
And brain is all that's left of mortal stuff,
We can lie on the beach with the seaweed
And take our daily tide baths smooth and rough.

There once we lay as blobs of jellyfish
At evolution's opposite extreme.
But now as blobs of brain we'll lie and dream,
With only one vestigial creature wish:
Oh, may the tide be soon enough at high
To keep our abstract verse from being dry.


## Why Wait for Science

Sarcastic Science she would like to know,
In her complacent ministry of fear,
How we propose to get away from here
When she has made things so we have to go
Or be wiped out. Will she be asked to show
Us how by rocket we may hope to steer
To some star off there say a half light-year
Through temperature of absolute zeró?
Why wait for Science to supply the how
When any amateur can tell it now?
The way to go away should be the same
As fifty million years ago we came—
If anyone remembers how that was.
I have a theory, but it hardly does.


## Any Size We Please

No one was looking at his lonely case,
So like a half-mad outpost sentinel,
Indulging an absurd dramatic spell,
Albeit not without some shame of face,
He stretched his arms out to the dark of space
And held them absolutely parallel
In infinite appeal. Then saying, 'Hell'
He drew them in for warmth of self-embrace.
He thought if he could have his space all curved
Wrapped in around itself and self-befriended,

His science needn't get him so unnerved.
He had been too all out, too much extended.
He slapped his breast to verify his purse
And hugged himself for all his universe.


## An Importer

Mrs. Someone's been to Asia.
What she brought back would amaze ye.
Bamboos, ivories, jades, and lacquers,
Devil-scaring firecrackers,
Recipes for tea with butter,
Sacred rigmaroles to mutter,
Subterfuge for saving faces,
A developed taste in vases,
Arguments too stale to mention
'Gainst American invention;
Most of all the mass production
Destined to prove our destruction.
What are telephones, skyscrapers,
Safety razors, Sunday papers,
But the silliest evasion
Of the truths we owe an Asian?
But the best of her exhibit
Was a prayer machine from Tibet
That by brook power in the garden
Kept repeating Pardon, pardon;
And as picturesque machinery
Beat a sundial in the scenery—
The most primitive of engines
Mass producing with a vengeance.
Teach those Asians mass production?
Teach your grandmother egg suction.

## The Planners

If anything should put an end to This,
I'm thinking the unborn would never miss
What they had never had of vital bliss.
No burst of nuclear phenomenon
That put an end to what was going on
Could make much difference to the dead and gone.
Only a few of those even in whose day
It happened would have very much to say.
And anyone might ask them who were *they*.
Who *would* they be? The guild of social planners
With the intention blazoned on their banners
Of getting one more chance to change our manners?
These anyway might think it was important
That human history should not be shortened.

## No Holy Wars for Them

States strong enough to do good are but few.
Their number would seem limited to three.
Good is a thing that they the great can do,
But puny little states can only be.
And being good for these means standing by
To watch a war in nominal alliance,
And when it's over watch the world's supply
Get parceled out among the winning giants.
God, have you taken cognizance of this?
And what on this is your divine position?
That nations like the Cuban and the Swiss
Can never hope to wage a Global Mission.
No Holy Wars for them. The most the small
Can ever give us is a nuisance brawl.

## Bursting Rapture

I went to the physician to complain,
The time had been when anyone could turn
To farming for a simple way to earn;
But now 'twas there as elsewhere, any gain
Was made by getting science on the brain;
There was so much more every day to learn,
The discipline of farming was so stern,
It seemed as if I couldn't stand the strain.
But the physician's answer was 'There, there,
What you complain of all the nations share.
Their effort is a mounting ecstasy
That when it gets too exquisite to bear
Will find relief in one burst. You shall see.
That's what a certain bomb was sent to be.'

## U. S. 1946 King's X

Having invented a new Holocaust,
And been the first with it to win a war,
How they make haste to cry with fingers crossed,
King's X—no fairs to use it any more!

## The Ingenuities of Debt

These I assume were words so deeply meant
They cut themselves in stone for permanent
Like trouble in the brow above the eyes:
'Take Care to Sell Your Horse before He Dies
The Art of Life Is Passing Losses on.'
The city saying it was Ctesiphon,
Which may a little while by war and trade
Have kept from being caught with the decayed,
Infirm, worn-out, and broken on its hands,

But judging by what little of it stands,
Not even the ingenuities of debt
Could save it from its losses being met.
Sand has been thrusting in the square of door
Across the tessellation of the floor,
And only rests, a serpent on its chin,
Content with contemplating, taking in,
Till it can muster breath inside a hall
To rear against the inscription on the wall.

## The Broken Drought

The prophet of disaster ceased to shout.
Something was going right outside the hall.
A rain though stingy had begun to fall
That rather hurt his theory of the drought
And all the great convention was about.
A cheer went up that shook the mottoed wall.
He did as Shakespeare says, you may recall,
Good orators *will* do when they are out.
Yet in his heart he was unshaken sure
The drought was one no spit of rain could cure.
It was the drought of deserts. Earth would soon
Be uninhabitable as the moon.
What for that matter had it ever been?
Who advised man to come and live therein?

## To the Right Person

In the one state of ours that is a shire,
There is a District Schoolhouse I admire
As much as anything for situation.
There are few institutions standing higher
This side the Rockies in my estimation—
Two thousand feet above the ocean level.
It has two entries for coeducation.
But there's a tight shut look to either door
And to the windows of its fenestration,
As if to say mere learning was the devil
And this school wasn't keeping any more
Unless for penitents who took their seat
Upon its doorsteps as at mercy's feet
To make up for a lack of meditation.

# AN AFTERWORD

## *Choose Something Like a Star*

O Star (the fairest one in sight),
We grant your loftiness the right
To some obscurity of cloud—
It will not do to say of night,
Since dark is what brings out your light.
Some mystery becomes the proud.
But to be wholly taciturn
In your reserve is not allowed.
Say something to us we can learn
By heart and when alone repeat.
Say something! And it says, 'I burn.'
But say with what degree of heat.
Talk Fahrenheit, talk Centigrade.
Use language we can comprehend.
Tell us what elements you blend.
It gives us strangely little aid,
But does tell something in the end.
And steadfast as Keats' Eremite,
Not even stooping from its sphere,
It asks a little of us here.
It asks of us a certain height,
So when at times the mob is swayed
To carry praise or blame too far,
We may choose something like a star
To stay our minds on and be staid.

## *Closed for Good*

Much as I own I owe
The passers of the past
Because their to and fro
Has cut this road to last,
I owe them more today
Because they've gone away

And come not back with steed
And chariot to chide
My slowness with their speed
And scare me to one side.
They have found other scenes
For haste and other means.

They leave the road to me
To walk in saying naught
Perhaps but to a tree
Inaudibly in thought,
'From you the road receives
A priming coat of leaves.

'And soon for lack of sun,
The prospects are in white
It will be further done,
But with a coat so light
The shape of leaves will show
Beneath the brush of snow.'

And so on into winter
Till even I have ceased
To come as a foot printer,
And only some slight beast
So mousy or so foxy
Shall print there as my proxy.

How often is the case
I thus pay men a debt
For having left a place
And still do not forget
To pay them some sweet share
For having once been there.

## From Plane to Plane

Neither of them was better than the other.
They both were hired. And though Pike had the advantage
Of having hoed and mowed for fifty years,
Dick had of being fresh and full of college.
So if they fought about equality
It was on an equality they fought.

'Your trouble is not sticking to the subject,'
Pike said with temper. And Dick longed to say,
'Your trouble is bucolic lack of logic,'
But all he did say was, 'What *is* the subject?'

'It's whether these professions really work.
Now take the Doctor—'

                                They were giving corn
A final going over with the hoe
Before they turned from everything to hay.
The wavy upflung pennons of the corn
Were loose all round their legs—you couldn't say
How many thousand of them in an acre.
Every time Dick or Pike looked up, the Doctor
With one foot on the dashboard of his buggy
Was still in sight like someone to depend on.
Nowhere but on the Bradford Interval
By the Connecticut could anyone
Have stayed in sight so long as an example.

'Taking his own sweet time as if to show
He don't mind having lost a case,' Pike said,
And when he caught Dick looking once too often,
'Hoeing's too much like work for Dick,' he added.
'Dick wishes he could swap jobs with the Doctor.
Let's holler and ask him if he won't prescribe
For all humanity a complete rest
From all this wagery. But what's the use
Of asking any sympathy of him?

That class of people don't know what work *is*—
More than they know what courage is that claim
The moral kind's as brave as facing bullets.'

Dick told him to be fairer to the Doctor:
'He looks to me like going home successful,
Full of success, with that foot on the dashboard,
As a small self-conferred reward of virtue.
I get you when you hoe out to the river,
Then pick your hoe up, maybe shoulder it,
And take your walk of recreation back
To curry favor with the dirt some more.
Isn't it pretty much the same idea?
You said yourself you weren't avoiding work.
You'd bet you got more work done in a day,
Or at least in a lifetime, by that method.'

'I wouldn't hoe both ways for anybody!'

'And right you are. You do the way we do
In reading, don't you, Bill?—at every line end
Pick up our eyes and carry them back idle
Across the page to where we started from.
The other way of reading back and forth,
Known as boustrophedon, was found too awkward.'

Pike grunted rather grimly with misgiving
At being thus expounded to himself
And made of by a boy; then having reached
The river bank, quit work defiantly,
As if he didn't care who understood him,
And started his march back again discoursing:
'A man has got to keep his extrication.
The important thing is not to get bogged down
In what he has to do to earn a living.
What's more, I hate to keep afflicting weeds.
I like to give my enemies a truce.'

'Be careful how you use your influence.
If I decided to become a doctor,
You'd be to blame for furnishing the reasons.'

'I thought you meant to be an Indian Chief—
You said the second coming of Tecumseh.
Remember how you envied General Sherman.
William Tecumseh Sherman. Why Tecumseh?
(He tried to imitate Dick's tone of voice.)
You wished your middle name had been Tecumseh.'


'I think I'll change my mind.'

                              'You're saying that
To bother me by siding with the Doctor.
You've got no social conscience as they say,
Or you'd feel differently about the classes.
You can't claim *you're* a social visionary.'


'I'm saying it to argue his idea's
The same as your idea, only more so.
And I suspect it may be more and more so
The further up the scale of work you go.
You could do worse than boost me up to see.'


'It isn't just the same, and some day, schoolboy,
I'll show you why it isn't—not today.
Today I want to talk about the sun.
May as expected was a disappointment,
And June was not much better, cold and rainy.
The sun then had his longest day in heaven,
But no one from the feeling would have guessed
His presence was particularly there.
He only stayed to set the summer on fire,
Then fled for fear of getting stuck in lava
In case the rocks should melt and run again.
Everyone has to keep his extrication.'


'That's what the Doctor's doing, keeping his.
That's what I have to do in school, keep mine
From knowing more than I know how to think with.
You see it in yourself and in the sun;
Yet you refuse to see it in the Doctor.'

'All right, let's harmonize about the Doctor.
He may be some good in a manner of speaking.
I own he does look busy when the sun
Is in the sign of Sickness in the winter
And everybody's being sick for Christmas.
Then's when his Morgan lights out throwing snowballs
Behind her at the dashboard of his pung.'

'But Cygnus isn't in the Zodiac,'
Dick longed to say, but wasn't sure enough
Of his astronomy. (He'd have to take
A half course in it next year.) And besides,
Why give the controversy a relapse?
They were both bent on scuffling up
Alluvium so pure that when a blade
To their surprise rang once on stone all day
Each tried to be the first at getting in
A superstitious cry for farmers' luck—
A rivalry that made them both feel kinder.

And so to let Pike seem to have the palm
With grace and not too formal a surrender
Dick said, 'You've been a lesson in work wisdom
To work with, Bill. But you won't have my thanks.
I like to think the sun's like you in that—
Since you bring up the subject of the sun.
This would be my interpretation of him.
He bestows summer on us and escapes
Before our realizing what we have
To thank him for. He doesn't want our thanks.
He likes to turn his back on gratitude
And avoid being worshiped as a god.
Our worship was a thing he had too much of
In the old days in Persia and Peru.
Shall I go on or have I said enough—
To convey my respect for your position?'

'I guess so,' Pike said, innocent of Milton.
'That's where I reckon Santa Claus comes in—
To be our parents' pseudonymity

In Christmas giving, so they can escape
The thanks and let him catch it as a scapegoat.
And even he, you'll notice, dodges off
Up chimney to avoid the worst of it.
We all know his address, Mount Hecla, Iceland.
So anyone can write to him who has to;
Though they do say he doesn't open letters.
A Santa Claus was needed. And there *is* one.'

'So I have heard and do in part believe it,'
Dick said to old Pike, innocent of Shakespeare.

# A MASQUE OF REASON

*A fair oasis in the purest desert.*
*A man sits leaning back against a palm.*
*His wife lies by him looking at the sky.*

*Man*   You're not asleep?

*Wife*                                No, I can hear you. Why?

*Man*   I said the incense tree's on fire again.

*Wife*   You mean the Burning Bush?

*Man*                                The Christmas Tree.

*Wife*   I shouldn't be surprised.

*Man*                                The strangest light!

*Wife*   There's a strange light on everything today.

*Man*   The myrrh tree gives it. Smell the rosin burning?
The ornaments the Greek artificers
Made for the Emperor Alexius,
The Star of Bethlehem, the pomegranates,
The birds, seem all on fire with Paradise.
And hark, the gold enameled nightingales
Are singing. Yes, and look, the Tree is troubled.
Someone's caught in the branches.

*Wife*                                So there is.
He can't get out.

*Man*                    He's loose! He's out!

*Wife*                                It's God.
I'd know Him by Blake's picture anywhere.
Now what's He doing?

372

*Man*                               Pitching throne, I guess,
        Here by our atoll.

*Wife*                              Something Byzantine.

            (*The throne's a plywood flat, prefabricated,*
            *That God pulls lightly upright on its hinges*
            *And stands beside, supporting it in place.*)

        Perhaps for an Olympic Tournament,
        Or Court of Love.

*Man*                           More likely Royal Court—
        Or Court of Law, and this is Judgment Day.
        I trust it is. Here's where I lay aside
        My varying opinion of myself
        And come to rest in an official verdict.
        Suffer yourself to be admired, my love,
        As Waller says.

*Wife*                          Or not admired. Go over
        And speak to Him before the others come.
        Tell Him He may remember you: you're Job.

*God*   Oh, I remember well: you're Job, my Patient.
        How are you now? I trust you're quite
            recovered,
        And feel no ill effects from what I gave you.

*Job*   Gave me in truth: I like the frank admission.
        I am a name for being put upon.
        But, yes, I'm fine, except for now and then
        A reminiscent twinge of rheumatism.
        The let-up's heavenly. You perhaps will tell us
        If that is all there is to be of Heaven,
        Escape from so great pains of life on earth
        It gives a sense of let-up calculated
        To last a fellow to Eternity.

*God*   Yes, by and by. But first a larger matter.
        I've had you on my mind a thousand years

To thank you someday for the way you helped
    me
Establish once for all the principle
There's no connection man can reason out
Between his just deserts and what he gets.
Virtue may fail and wickedness succeed.
'Twas a great demonstration we put on.
I should have spoken sooner had I found
The word I wanted. You would have supposed
One who in the beginning *was* the Word
Would be in a position to command it.
I have to wait for words like anyone.
Too long I've owed you this apology
For the apparently unmeaning sorrow
You were afflicted with in those old days.
But it was of the essence of the trial
You shouldn't understand it at the time.
It had to seem unmeaning to have meaning.
And it came out all right. I have no doubt
You realize by now the part you played
To stultify the Deuteronomist
And change the tenor of religious thought.
My thanks are to you for releasing me
From moral bondage to the human race.
The only free will there at first was man's,
Who could do good or evil as he chose.
I had no choice but I must follow him
With forfeits and rewards he understood—
Unless I liked to suffer loss of worship.
I had to prosper good and punish evil.
You changed all that. You set me free to reign.
You are the Emancipator of your God,
And as such I promote you to a saint.

*Job*    You hear him, Thyatira: we're a saint.
Salvation in our case is retroactive.
We're saved, we're saved, whatever else it
    means.

*Job's Wife*    Well, after all these years!

| | |
|---|---|
| *Job* | This is my wife. |

*Job's Wife*  If You're the deity I assume You are—
(I'd know You by Blake's picture anywhere)—

*God*  The best, I'm told, I ever have had taken.

*Job's Wife*  —I have a protest I would lodge with You.
I want to ask You if it stands to reason
That women prophets should be burned as
    witches
Whereas men prophets are received with honor.

*Job*  Except in their own country, Thyatira.

*God*  You're not a witch?

*Job's Wife*                        No.

*God*                                    Have you ever been one?

*Job*  Sometimes she thinks she has and gets herself
Worked up about it. But she really hasn't—
Not in the sense of having to my knowledge
Predicted anything that came to pass.

*Job's Wife*  The witch of Endor was a friend of mine.

*God*  You wouldn't say she fared so very badly.
I noticed when she called up Samuel
His spirit had to come. Apparently
A witch was stronger than a prophet there.

*Job's Wife*  But she was burned for witchcraft.

*God*                                    That is not
Of record in my Note Book.

*Job's Wife*                                    Well, she was.
And I should like to know the reason why.

**God**   There you go asking for the very thing
We've just agreed I didn't have to give.

> (*The throne collapses. But He picks it up
> And this time locks it up and leaves it.*)

Where has she been the last half hour or so?
She wants to know why there is still injustice.
I answer flatly: That's the way it is,
And bid my will avouch it like Macbeth.
We may as well go back to the beginning
And look for justice in the case of Segub.

**Job**   Oh, Lord, let's not go *back* to anything.

**God**   Because your wife's past won't bear looking
into?
In our great moment what did you do, Madam?
What did you try to make your husband say?

**Job's Wife**   No, let's not live things over. I don't care.
I stood by Job. I may have turned on You.
Job scratched his boils and tried to think what
he
Had done or not done to or for the poor.
The test is always how we treat the poor.
It's time the poor were treated by the state
In some way not so penal as the poorhouse.
That's one thing more to put on Your agenda.
Job hadn't done a thing, poor innocent.
I told him not to scratch: it made it worse.
If I said once I said a thousand times,
Don't scratch! And when, as rotten as his skin,
His tents blew all to pieces, I picked up
Enough to build him every night a pup tent
Around him so it wouldn't touch and hurt him.
I did my wifely duty. I should tremble!
All You can seem to do is lose Your temper
When reason-hungry mortals ask for reasons.
Of course, in the abstract high singular
There isn't any universal reason;

And no one but a man would think there was.
You don't catch women trying to be Plato.
Still there must be lots of unsystematic
Stray scraps of palliative reason
It wouldn't hurt You to vouchsafe the faithful.
You thought it was agreed You needn't give
    them.
You thought to suit Yourself. I've not agreed
To anything with anyone.

*Job*                  There, there,
You go to sleep. God must await events
As well as words.

*Job's Wife*          I'm serious. God's had
Aeons of time and still it's mostly women
Get burned for prophecy, men almost never.

*Job*   God needs time just as much as you or I
To get things done. Reformers fail to see that.
She'll go to sleep. Nothing keeps her awake
But physical activity, I find.
Try to read to her and she drops right off.

*God*   She's beautiful.

*Job*            Yes, she was just remarking
She now felt younger by a thousand years
Than the day she was born.

*God*           That's about right,
I should have said. You got your age reversed
When time was found to be a space dimension
That could, like any space, be turned around in?

*Job*   Yes, both of us: we saw to that at once.
But, God, I have a question too to raise.
(My wife gets in ahead of me with hers.)
I need some help about this reason problem
Before I am too late to be got right

As to what reasons I agree to waive.
I'm apt to string along with Thyatira.
God knows—or rather, You know (God forgive
  me)
I waived the reason for my ordeal—but—
I have a question even there to ask—
In confidence. There's no one here but her,
And she's a woman: she's not interested
In general ideas and principles.

*God*   What are her interests, Job?

*Job*                 Witch-women's rights.
Humor her there or she will be confirmed
In her suspicion You're no feminist.
You have it in for women, she believes.
Kipling invokes You as Lord God of Hosts.
She'd like to know how You would take a
  prayer
That started off Lord God of Hostesses.

*God*   I'm charmed with her.

*Job*               Yes, I could see You were.
But to my question. I am much impressed
With what You say we have established.
Between us, You and I.

*God*               I make you see?
It would be too bad if Columbus-like
You failed to see the worth of your
  achievement.

*Job*   You call it mine.

*God*            We groped it out together.
Any originality it showed
I give you credit for. My forte is truth,
Or metaphysics, long the world's reproach
For standing still in one place true forever;

While science goes self-superseding on.
Look at how far we've left the current science
Of Genesis behind. The wisdom there though,
Is just as good as when I uttered it.
Still, novelty has doubtless an attraction.

*Job*   So it's important who first thinks of things?

*God*   I'm a great stickler for the author's name.
By proper names I find I do my thinking.

*Job's Wife*   God who invented earth?

*Job*                   What, still awake?

*God*   Any originality it showed
Was of the Devil. He invented Hell,
False premises that are the original
Of all originality, the sin
That felled the angels, Wolsey should have said.
As for the earth, we groped that out together,
Much as your husband Job and I together
Found out the discipline man needed most
Was to learn his submission to unreason;
And that for man's own sake as well as mine,
So he won't find it hard to take his orders
From his inferiors in intelligence
In peace and war—especially in war.

*Job*   So he won't find it hard to take his war.

*God*   You have the idea. There's not much I can tell
      you.

*Job*   All very splendid. I am flattered proud
To have been in on anything with You.
'Twas a great demonstration if You say so.
Though incidentally I sometimes wonder
Why it had had to be at my expense.

*God*   It had to be at somebody's expense.
Society can never think things out:
It has to see them acted out by actors,
Devoted actors at a sacrifice—
The ablest actors I can lay my hands on.
Is that your answer?

*Job*                No, for I have yet
To ask my question. We disparage reason.
But all the time it's what we're most concerned
   with.
There's will as motor and there's will as brakes.
Reason is, I suppose, the steering gear.
The will as brakes can't stop the will as motor
For very long. We're plainly made to go.
We're going anyway and may as well
Have some say as to where we're headed for;
Just as we will be talking anyway
And may as well throw in a little sense.
Let's do so now. Because I let You off
From telling me Your reason, don't assume
I thought You had none. Somewhere back
I knew You had one. But this isn't it
You're giving me. You say we groped this out.
But if You will forgive me the irreverence,
It sounds to me as if You thought it out,
And took Your time to it. It seems to me
An afterthought, a long long afterthought.
I'd give more for one least beforehand reason
Than all the justifying ex-post-facto
Excuses trumped up by You for theologists.
The front of being answerable to no one
I'm with You in maintaining to the public.
But, Lord, we showed them what. The audience
Has all gone home to bed. The play's played
   out.
Come, after all these years—to satisfy me.
I'm curious. And I'm a grown-up man:
I'm not a child for You to put me off
And tantalize me with another 'Oh, because.'

You'd be the last to want me to believe
All Your effects were merely lucky blunders.
That would be unbelief and atheism.
The artist in me cries out for design.
Such devilish ingenuity of torture
Did seem unlike You, and I tried to think
The reason might have been some other
    person's.
But there is nothing You are not behind.
I did not ask then, but it seems as if
Now after all these years You might indulge
    me.
Why did You hurt me so? I am reduced
To asking flatly for the reason—outright.

*God*   I'd tell you, Job—

*Job*                All right, don't tell me then
If you don't want to. I don't want to know.
But what is all this secrecy about?
I fail to see what fun, what satisfaction
A God can find in laughing at how badly
Men fumble at the possibilities
When left to guess forever for themselves.
The chances are when there's so much pretense
Of metaphysical profundity
The obscurity's a fraud to cover nothing.
I've come to think no so-called hidden value's
Worth going after. Get down into things
It will be found there's no more given there
Than on the surface. If there ever was,
The crypt was long since rifled by the Greeks.
We don't know where we are, or who we are.
We don't know one another; don't know You;
Don't know what time it is. We don't know,
    don't we?
Who says we don't? Who got up these
    misgivings?
Oh, we know well enough to go ahead with.
I mean we seem to know enough to act on.

It comes down to a doubt about the wisdom
Of having children—after having had them,
So there is nothing we can do about it
But warn the children they perhaps should have
    none.
You could end this by simply coming out
And saying plainly and unequivocally
Whether there's any part of man immortal.
Yet You don't speak. Let fools bemuse
    themselves
By being baffled for the sake of being.
I'm sick of the whole artificial puzzle.

*Job's Wife*    You won't get any answers out of God.

*God*    My kingdom, what an outbreak!

*Job's Wife*                                   Job is right.
Your kingdom, yes, Your kingdom come on
    earth.
Pray tell me what does that mean. Anything?
Perhaps that earth is going to crack someday
Like a big egg and hatch a heaven out
Of all the dead and buried from their graves.
One simple little statement from the throne
Would put an end to such fantastic nonsense;
And, too, take care of twenty of the four
And twenty freedoms on the party docket.
Or is it only four? My extra twenty
Are freedoms from the need of asking
    questions.
(I hope You know the game called twenty
    questions.)
For instance, is there such a thing as Progress?
Job says there's no such thing as Earth's
    becoming
An easier place for man to save his soul in.
Except as a hard place to save his soul in,
A trial ground where he can try himself

And find out whether he is any good,
It would be meaningless. It might as well
Be Heaven at once and have it over with.

*God*   Two pitching on like this tend to confuse me.
One at a time, please. I will answer Job first.
I'm going to tell Job why I tortured him
And trust it won't be adding to the torture.
I was just showing off to the Devil, Job,
As is set forth in chapters One and Two.
(*Job takes a few steps pacing.*) Do you mind?
(*God eyes him anxiously.*)

*Job*              No. No, I mustn't.
'Twas human of You. I expected more
Than I could understand and what I get
Is almost less than I can understand.
But I don't mind. Let's leave it as it stood.
The point was it was none of my concern.
I stick to that. But talk about confusion!
How is that for a mix-up, Thyatira?
Yet I suppose what seems to us confusion
Is not confusion, but the form of forms,
The serpent's tail stuck down the serpent's
   throat,
Which is the symbol of eternity
And also of the way all things come round,
Or of how rays return upon themselves,
To quote the greatest Western poem yet.
Though I hold rays deteriorate to nothing,
First white, then red, then ultra red, then
   out.

*God*   Job, you must understand my provocation.
The tempter comes to me and I am tempted.
I'd had about enough of his derision
Of what I valued most in human nature.
He thinks he's smart. He thinks he can
   convince me

It is no different with my followers
From what it is with his. Both serve for pay.
Disinterestedness never did exist
And if it did, it wouldn't be a virtue.
Neither would fairness. You have heard the
    doctrine.
It's on the increase. He could count on no one:
That was his look out. I could count on you.
I wanted him forced to acknowledge so much.
I gave you over to him, but with safeguards.
I took care of you. And before you died
I trust I made it clear I took your side
Against your comforters in their contention
You must be wicked to deserve such pain.
That's Browning and sheer Chapel Non-
    conformism.

*Job*    God, please, enough for now. I'm in no mood
For more excuses.

*God*               What I mean to say:
Your comforters were wrong.

*Job*                    Oh, that committee!

*God*    I saw you had no fondness for committees.
Next time you find yourself pressed on to one
For the revision of the Book of Prayer
Put that in if it isn't in already:
Deliver us from committees. 'Twill remind me.
I would do anything for you in reason.

*Job*    Yes, yes.

*God*        You don't seem satisfied.

*Job*                        I am.

*God*    You're pensive.

| | |
|---|---|
| *Job* | Oh, I'm thinking of the Devil.<br>You must remember he was in on this.<br>We can't leave him out. |
| *God* | No. No, we don't need to.<br>We're too well off. |
| *Job* | Someday we three should have<br>A good old get-together celebration. |
| *God* | Why not right now? |
| *Job* | We can't without the Devil. |
| *God* | The Devil's never very far away.<br>He too is pretty circumambient.<br>He has but to appear. He'll come for me,<br>Precipitated from the desert air.<br>Show yourself, son. I'll get back on my throne<br>For this I think. I find it always best<br>To be upon my dignity with him. |

> (*The Devil enters like a sapphire wasp*
> *That flickers mica wings. He lifts a hand*
> *To brush away a disrespectful smile.*
> *Job's wife sits up.*)

| | |
|---|---|
| *Job's Wife* | Well, if we aren't all here.<br>Including me, the only Dramatis<br>Personae needed to enact the problem. |
| *Job* | We've waked her up. |
| *Job's Wife* | I haven't been asleep.<br>I've heard what you were saying—every word. |
| *Job* | What did we say? |
| *Job's Wife* | You said the Devil's in it. |

*Job*    She always claims she hasn't been asleep.
And what else did we say?

*Job's Wife*                Well, what led up—
Something about— (*The three men laugh.*)
—The Devil's being God's best inspiration.

*Job*    Good, pretty good.

*Job's Wife*             Wait till I get my Kodak.
Would you two please draw in a little closer?
No—no, that's not a smile there. That's a grin.
Satan, what ails you? Where's the famous
    tongue,
Thou onetime Prince of Conversationists?
This is polite society you're in
Where good and bad are mingled
    everywhichway,
And ears are lent to any sophistry
Just as if nothing mattered but our manners.
You look as if you either hoped or feared
You were more guilty of mischief than you are.
Nothing has been brought out that for my part
I'm not prepared for or that Job himself
Won't find a formula for taking care of.

*Satan*    Like the one Milton found to fool himself
About his blindness.

*Job's Wife*           Oh, he speaks! He *can* speak!
That strain again! Give me excess of it!
As dulcet as a pagan temple gong!
He's twitting us. Oh, by the way, you haven't
By any chance a Lady Apple on you?
I saw a boxful in the Christmas market.
How I should prize one personally from you.

*God*    Don't *you* twit. He's unhappy. Church neglect
And figurative use have pretty well
Reduced him to a shadow of himself.

*Job's Wife*    *That* explains why he's so diaphanous
        And easy to see through. But where's he off to?
        I thought there were to be festivities
        Of some kind. We could have charades.

    *God*    He has his business he must be about.
        Job mentioned him and so I brought him in
        More to give his reality its due
        Than anything.

*Job's Wife*                      He's very real to me
        And always will be. Please don't go. Stay, stay
        But to the evensong and having played
        Together we will go with you along.
        There are who won't have had enough of you
        If you go now. Look how he takes no steps!
        He isn't really going, yet he's leaving.

    *Job*    (*Who has been standing dazed with new ideas*)
        He's on that tendency that like the Gulf
          Stream,
        Only of sand not water, runs through here.
        It has a rate distinctly different
        From the surrounding desert; just today
        I stumbled over it and got tripped up.

*Job's Wife*    Oh, yes, that tendency! Oh, do come off it.
        Don't let it carry you away. I hate
        A tendency. The minute you get on one
        It seems to start right off accelerating.
        Here, take my hand.

                    (*He takes it and alights*
             *In three quick steps as off an escalator.*
             *The tendency, a long, long narrow strip*
             *Of middle-aisle church carpet, sisal hemp,*
             *Is worked by hands invisible off stage.*)

        I want you in my group beside the throne—
        Must have you. There, that's just the right
          arrangement.

Now someone can light up the Burning Bush
And turn the gold enameled artificial birds on.
I recognize them. Greek artificers
Devised them for Alexius Comnenus.
They won't show in the picture. That's too bad.
Neither will I show. That's too bad moreover.
Now if you three have settled anything
You'd as well smile as frown on the occasion.

(*Here endeth chapter forty-three of Job.*)

# A MASQUE OF MERCY

*A bookstore late at night. The Keeper's wife*
*Pulls down the window curtain on the door*
*And locks the door. One customer, locked in,*
*Stays talking with the Keeper at a show case.*
*The Keeper's wife has hardly turned away*
*Before the door's so violently tried*
*It makes her move as if to reinforce it.*

Jesse Bel  You can't come in! (*Knock, knock*) The store is
   closed!

Paul  Late, late, too late, you cannot enter now.

Jesse Bel  We can't be always selling people things.
   He doesn't go.

Keeper        You needn't be so stern.
  Open enough to find out who it is.

Jesse Bel  Keeper, you come and see. Or you come,
   Paul.
  Our second second-childhood case tonight.
  Where do these senile runaways escape from?
  Wretchedness in a stranger frightens me
  More than it touches me.

Paul         You may come in.

Fugitive  (*Entering hatless in a whirl of snow*)
  God's after me!

Jesse Bel       You mean the Devil is.

Fugitive  No, God.

Jesse Bel      I never heard of such a thing.

389

*Fugitive*   Haven't you heard of Thompson's Hound of
              Heaven?

*Paul*       'I fled Him, down the nights and down the
                 days;
              I fled Him, down the arches of the years.'

*Keeper*     This is a bookstore—not a sanctuary.

*Jesse Bel*  I thought you just now said it was a gift shop.

*Keeper*     Don't you be bitter about it. I'm not bitter.

*Fugitive*   Well, I could use a book.

*Keeper*                            What book?

*Fugitive*                                      A Bible.

*Keeper*     To find out how to get away from God?
              Which is what people use it for too often—
              And why we wouldn't have one in the store.
              We don't believe the common man should
                 read it.
              Let him seek his religion in the Church.

*Jesse Bel*  Keeper, be still. Pay no attention to him.
              He's being a religious snob for fun.
              The name his mother gave him is to blame
              For Keeper's levity: My Brother's Keeper.
              She didn't do it to him to be quaint,
              But out of politics. She told me so.
              She was left over from the Brook Farm
                 venture.

*Keeper*     Why is God after you?—to save your soul?

*Fugitive*   No, make me prophesy.

| | |
|---|---|
| *Jesse Bel* | And—you—just—won't? |

*Fugitive*   Haven't you noticed anything (hear that!)
Since I came in?

*Keeper*                  Hear what? That army truck?

*Fugitive*   Look, I don't need the Bible to consult.
I just thought if you had a copy handy,
I could point out my sort of passport in it.
There is a story you may have forgotten
About a whale.

*Keeper*             Oh, you mean Moby Dick
By Rockwell Kent that everybody's reading.
Trust me to help you find the book you
    want.

*Jesse Bel*   Keeper, be still. He knows what book he
    wants.
He said the Bible.

*Fugitive*             I should hate to scare you
With the suspicion at this hour of night
That I might be a confidence impostor.
I'm Jonas Dove—if that is any help.

*Paul*   Which is the same as saying Jonah, Jonah—
Ah, Jonah, Jonah—twice—reproachfully.

*Fugitive*   Spare me the setting of my fate to music.
How did you know that way to break my
    heart?
Who are you?

*Paul*            Who are you?

*Jonah*              I think you know,
You seem so ready at translating names.

Unless I'm much mistaken in myself
This is the seventh time I have been sent
To prophesy against the city evil.

*Keeper*　What have you got against the city?

*Jonah*　　　　　　　　　　　　*He* knows.
We have enough against it, haven't we?
Cursed be the era that congested it.

*Keeper*　Come, come, you talk like an agrarian.
The city is all right. To live in one
Is to be civilized, stay up and read
Or sing and dance all night and see sunrise
By waiting up instead of getting up.
The country's only useful as a place
To rest at times from being civilized.
You take us two, we're losers in this store,
So losers in the city, but we're game:
We don't go back on grapes we couldn't
　　reach.
We blame ourselves. We're good sports, aren't
　　we, Bel?

*Jesse Bel*　I'm not a sport and don't pretend I am one.
It's only fair to Keeper to inform you
His favorite reading is seed catalogues.
When he gets too agrarian for me
I take to drink—at least I take *a* drink.

(*She has her own glass in a vacant chair*)

*Paul*　She'll take to drink and see how we like that.

*Keeper*　Bel is a solitary social drinker.
She doesn't mind not offering a drink
To anyone around when she is drinking.

*Jesse Bel*　We're poor—that's why. My man can't earn a
　　living.

*Keeper*    Is it just any city you're against?

*Jonah*    Yes, but New York will do as an example.

*Keeper*    Well, you're as good as in New York this
        minute—
    Or bad as in New York.

*Jonah*                      I know I am.
    That was where my engagement was to speak
    This very night. I had the hall all hired,
    The audience assembled. There I was
    Behind the scenes ordained and advertised
    To prophesy, and full of prophecy,
    Yet could not bring myself to say a word.
    I left light shining on an empty stage
    And fled to you. But you receive me not.

*Keeper*    Yes, we do, too, with sympathy, my friend.
    Your righteous indignation fizzled out,
    Or else you were afraid of being mobbed
    If what you had to say was disagreeable.

*Jesse Bel*    Your courage failed. The saddest thing in life
    Is that the best thing in it should be courage.
    Them is my sentiments, and, Mr. Flood,
    Since you propose it, I believe I will.

*Jonah*    Please, someone understand.

*Paul*                    I understand.

*Jonah*    These others don't.

*Paul*                You don't yourself entirely.

*Jonah*    What don't I understand? It's easy enough.
    I'm in the Bible, all done out in story.
    I've lost my faith in God to carry out

The threats He makes against the city evil.
I can't trust God to be unmerciful.

*Keeper*    You've lost your faith in God? How wicked of
you.

*Jesse Bel*  You naughty kitten, you shall have no pie.

*Paul*    Keeper's the kind of Unitarian
Who having by elimination got
From many gods to Three and Three to One,
Thinks why not taper off to none at all,
Except as father putative to sort of
Legitimize the brotherhood of man,
So we can hang together in a strike.

*Keeper*    Now we are hearing from the Exegete.
You don't know Paul: he's in the Bible too.
He is the fellow who theologized
Christ almost out of Christianity.
Look out for him.

*Paul*                           'Look out for me' is right.
I'm going to tell you something, Jonas Dove.
I'm going to take the nonsense out of you
And give you rest, poor Wandering Jew.

*Jonah*                                   I'm not
The Wandering Jew—I'm who I say I am,
A prophet with the Bible for credentials.

*Paul*    I never said you weren't. I recognized you.
You are the universal fugitive,
Escapist as we say, though you are not
Running away from Him you think you are
But from His mercy-justice contradiction.
Mercy and justice are a contradiction.
But here's where your evasion has an end.
I have to tell you something that will spoil
Indulgence in your form of melancholy

Once and for all. I'm going to make you see
How relatively little justice matters.

*Jonah*   I see what you are up to: robbing me
Of my incentive—canceling my mission.

*Paul*   I am empowered to excuse you from it.

*Jonah*   You! Who are you? I asked you once before.

*Jesse Bel*   He is our analyst.

*Jonah*                      Your analyst?

*Keeper*   Who keeps our bookstore annals.

*Jesse Bel*                          Stop it, Keeper.
An analyst's the latest thing in doctors.
He's mine. That's what he is (you asked)—my
  doctor.
I'm sick.

*Jonah*          Of what?

*Jesse Bel*                      Oh, everything, I guess.
The doctors say the trouble with me is
I'm not in love. I didn't love the doctor
I had before. That's why I changed to Paul—
To try another.

*Paul*                      Jesse Bel's a girl
Whose cure will lie in getting her idea
Of the word love corrected. She got off
To a bad start it seems in the wrong school
Of therapy.

*Jesse Bel*                  I don't love Paul—as yet.

*Jonah*   How about loving God?

| | |
|---|---|
| *Jesse Bel* | You make me shrug. |
| | And I don't love you either, do I, Keeper? |

| | |
|---|---|
| *Keeper* | Don't lay your hand on me to say it, |
| | shameless. |
| | Let me alone. |

| | |
|---|---|
| *Jesse Bel* | I'm sick. Joe's sick. The world's sick. |
| | I'll take to drink—at least I'll take *a* drink. |

| | |
|---|---|
| *Jonah* | My name's not Joe. I don't like what she says. |
| | It's Greenwich Village cocktail party talk— |
| | Big-city talk. I'm getting out of here. |
| | I'm—bound—away. (*He quotes it to the tune*) |

| | |
|---|---|
| *Paul* | Oh, no, you're not. You're staying here |
| | tonight. |
| | You locked the door, Bel. Let me have the |
| | key. |

(*He goes and takes it from the door himself*)

| | |
|---|---|
| *Jonah* | Then I'm a prisoner? |

| | |
|---|---|
| *Paul* | You are tonight. |
| | We take it you were sent in here for help. |
| | And help you're going to get. |

| | |
|---|---|
| *Jonah* | I'll break your door down. |
| | Always the same when I set out in flight. |
| | I take the first boat. God puts up a storm |
| | That someone in the crew connects with me. |
| | The sailors throw me overboard for luck, |
| | *Or* as you might say throw me to the whale— |
| | For me to disagree with him and get spit out |
| | Right back in the same trouble I was in. |
| | You're modern; so the whale you throw me to |
| | Will be some soulless lunatic asylum— |
| | For me to disagree with any science |
| | There may be there and get spit out again. |

| | |
|---|---|
| *Jesse Bel* | You poor, poor swallowable little man. |

*Paul*  If you would take the hands out of your hair
And calm yourself. Be sane! I hereby hold
Your forearms in the figure of a cross
The way it rested two points on the ground
At every station but the final one.

*Jonah*  What good is that?

*Paul*                    I'll make you see what good.

*Jonah*  I *am* sick as she says. Nothing exhausts me
Like working myself up to prophesy
And then not prophesying. (*He sits down*)

*Jesse Bel*  Can you interpret dreams? I dreamed last
                night
Someone took curved nail scissors and snipped
                off
My eyelids so I couldn't shut my eyes
To anything that happened any more.

*Jonah*  She's had some loss she can't accept from
                God—
Is that it? Some Utopian belief—
Or child, and this is motherly resentment?

*Jesse Bel*  You look so sleepless. If he'd promise us
To go straight home. We wouldn't keep him,
                would we?
Where are you staying—anywhere in town?

*Jonah*  Under the bandstand in Suburban Park.

*Jesse Bel*  Why, what a story. At this time of year
There's not a footprint to it in the snow.

*Paul*  Jonah, I'm glad, not sad to hear you say
You can't trust God to be unmerciful.
There you have the beginning of all wisdom.

*Keeper*    One minute, may I, Paul?—before we leave
            Religion for these philosophic matters.
            That's the right style of coat for prophecy
            You're sporting there. I'll bet you're good at
                it.
            Shall it be told we had a prophet captive
            And let him get off without prophesying?
            Let's have some prophecy. What form of ruin
            (For ruin I assume was what it was)
            Had you in mind to visit on the city,
            Rebellion, pestilence, invasion?

*Jonah*                                      Earthquake
            Was what I thought of.

*Keeper*                             Have you any grounds,
            Or undergrounds, for confidence in
                earthquake?

*Jonah*     It's good geology—the Funday Fault,
            A fracture in the rocks beneath New York
            That only needs a finger touch from God
            To spring it like a deadfall and the fault
            In nature would wipe out all human fault.
            (*He stops to listen*) That's a mighty storm,
            And we are shaken. But it isn't earthquake.
            Another possibility I thought of—

            (*He stops to listen and his unspoken thought,
            Projected from the lantern of his eyes,
            Is thrown in script as at Belshazzar's feast
            On the blank curtain on the outer door*)

            —Was Babel: everyone developing
            A language of his own to write his book in,
            And one to cap the climax by combining
            All language in a one-man tongue-confusion.

            (*He starts to speak, but stops again to listen.
            The writing on the screen must change too fast
            For any but the rapidest eye readers*)

Suspicion of the income-tax returns,
A question who was getting the most out
Of business, might increase into a madness.
The mob might hold a man up in the streets
And tear his clothes off to examine him
To find if there were pockets in his skin
As in a smuggler's at the diamond fields,
Where he was hoarding more than they
     enjoyed.

*Paul*    We can all see what's passing in your mind.
(I won't have Keeper calling it religion.)
It's a hard case. It's got so prophecy
Is a disease of your imagination.
You're so lost in the virtuosity
Of getting up good ruins, you've forgotten
What the sins are men ought to perish for.

*Jonah*    You wrong me.

*Keeper*                    Well then, name a single sin.

*Jonah*    Another possibility I thought of—

*Jesse Bel*    There he goes off into another trance.

*Keeper*    You stick to earthquake, you have something
     there—
Something we'll know we're getting when we
     get it.

*Paul*    (*Taking a walk off down the store distressed*)
Keeper, I'll turn on you if you keep on.

*Keeper*    If I were in your place though, Mr. Prophet,
I'd *want* to be more certain I was called
Before I undertook so delicate
A mission as to have to tell New York
'Twas in for an old-fashioned shaking down
Like the one Joshua gave Jericho.

You wouldn't want the night clubs laughing at
    you.

*Jesse Bel*    Or THE NEW YORKER.

*Keeper*                       When was the last time
You heard from God—I mean had orders
    from Him?

*Jonah*    I'm hearing from Him now, did you but
    notice.
Don't any of you hear a sound?

*Keeper*                         The storm!
Merely the windows rattling in the storm.
Trucks going by to war. A war is on.

*Jonah*    That is no window. That's a show case
    rattling.
That is your antiques rattling on a shelf.

*Jesse Bel*    You're doing it.

*Jonah*                   I'm not. How could I be?

*Jesse Bel*    You're doing something to our minds.

*Jonah*                       I'm not.
Don't *you* feel something?

*Paul*                     Leave me out of this.

(*He leans away in tolerant distaste*)

*Jonah*    And here come all your Great Books tumbling
    down!
You see the Lord God is a jealous God!
He wrote one book. Let there be no more
    written.
How are their volumes fallen!

*Keeper*                                    Only one!

*Jonah*    Hold on there. Leave that open where it lies.
           Be careful not to lose the place. Be careful.
           Please let me have it.

*Jesse Bel*                              Read us what it says.

*Jonah*    Look, will you look! God can't put words in
               my mouth.
           My tongue's my own as True Thomas used to
               say.

*Keeper*   So you've been Bohning up on Thomism too.

*Jonah*    Someone else read it.

*Keeper*                           No, you read it to us.
           And if it's prophecy, we'll see what happens.

*Jonah*    Nothing would happen. That's the thing of it.
           God comes on me to doom a city for Him.
           But oh, no, not for Jonah. I refuse
           To be the bearer of an empty threat.
           He may be God, but me, I'm only human:
           I shrink from being publicly let down.

*Jesse Bel*  Is this the love of God you preached to me?

*Jonah*    There's not the least lack of the love of God
           In what I say. Don't be so silly, woman.
           His very weakness for mankind's endearing.
           I love and fear Him. Yes, but I fear for Him.
           I don't see how it can be to His interest
           This modern tendency I find in Him
           To take the punishment out of all failure
           To be strong, careful, thrifty, diligent,
           Anything we once thought we had to be.

*Keeper*　You know what lets us off from being careful?
　　　　The thing that did what you consider mischief,
　　　　That ushered in this modern lenience
　　　　Was the discovery of fire insurance.
　　　　The future state is springing even now
　　　　From the discovery that loss from failure
　　　　By being spread out over everybody
　　　　Can be made negligible.

*Paul*　　　　　　　　　　　　What's your book?
　　　What's this?

*Jonah*　　　　　　　Don't lose the place.

*Paul*　　　　　　　　　　　　Old Dana Lyle
　　　Who reconciled the Pentateuch with science.

*Jonah*　Where shall I start in? Where my eyes fell first?
　　　　It seems to be a chapter head in meter.

*Jesse Bel*　It's too big for him. Help him hold it up.

*Jonah*　Someone else read it.

*Keeper*　　　　　　　　　　No, you asked for it.

*Jesse Bel*　Come on, or we'll begin to be afraid.

*Jonah*　Well, but remember this is unofficial.
　　　　'The city's grotesque iron skeletons
　　　　Would knock their drunken penthouse heads together
　　　　And cake their concrete dirt off in the streets.'
　　　　Then further down it seems to start from where
　　　　The city is admittedly an evil:
　　　　'O city on insecure rock pedestal,
　　　　So knowing—and yet needing to be told
　　　　The thought that added cubits to your height

Would better have been taken to your depth.'
(*A whole shelf cascades down*) Here come some
   more.
The folly crashes and the dust goes up.

(*When the dust settles it should be apparent
Something has altered in the outer door*)

Jesse Bel   Mercy, for mercy's sake!

Keeper                          Bel wants some mercy.
Kneel to your doctor. He dispenses mercy.
You're working it, old man. Don't be
   discouraged.

Jonah   This isn't it. I haven't prophesied.
This is God at me in my skulking place
Trying to flush me out. That's all it is.

Keeper   It's nothing but the Lending Library.
All secondhand. Don't get excited, folks,
The one indecency's to make a fuss
About our own or anybody's end.

Jonah   It's nothing I brought on by words of mine.

Keeper   You know there may have been a small
   temblor.
If so, it will be in tomorrow's paper.

Paul   Now if we've had enough of sacrilege,
We can go back to where we started from.
Let me repeat: I'm glad to hear you say
You can't trust God to be unmerciful.
What would you have God if not merciful?

Jonah   Just, I would have Him just before all else,
To see that the fair fight is really fair.
Then he could enter on the stricken field
After the fight's so definitely done

There can be no disputing who has won—
Then he could enter on the stricken field
As Red Cross Ambulance Commander in
   Chief
To ease the more extremely wounded out
And mend the others up to go again.

Paul   I thought as much. You have it all arranged,
Only to see it shattered every day.
You should be an authority on Mercy.
That book of yours in the Old Testament
Is the first place in literature I think
Where Mercy is explicitly the subject.
I say you should be proud of having beaten
The Gospels to it. After doing Justice justice,
Milton's pentameters go on to say,
But Mercy first and last shall brightest shine,
Not only last, but first, you will observe;
Which spoils your figure of the ambulance.

Keeper   Paul only means you make too much of
   justice.
There's some such thing and no one will deny
   it—
Enough to bait the trap of the ideal
From which there can be no escape for us
But by our biting off our adolescence
And leaving it behind us in the trap.

Jonah   Listen, ye! It's the proletariat!
A revolution's coming down the street!
Lights out, I say, so's to escape attention.

(*He snaps one bulb off. Paul snaps on another*)

Jesse Bel   You needn't shout like that, you wretched
   man.
There's nothing coming on us, is there, Paul?
We've had about enough of these sensations.
It's a coincidence, but we were on

The subject of the workers' revolution
When you came in. We're revolutionists.
Or Keeper is a revolutionist.
Paul almost had poor Keeper in a corner
Where he would have to quit his politics
Or be a Christian. Paul, I wish you'd say
That over. I shall have to retail it
To some of Keeper's friends that come in
    here,
A bunch of smalltime revolutionaries.
Paul makes it come out so they look like
    Christians.
How they'll like that. Paul said con-
    servatives—
You say it, Paul.

*Paul*                    You mean about success,
And how by its own logic it concentrates
All wealth and power in too few hands?
The rich in seeing nothing but injustice
In their impoverishment by revolution
Are right. But 'twas intentional injustice.
It was their justice being mercy-crossed.
The revolution Keeper's bringing on
Is nothing but an outbreak of mass mercy,
Too long pent up in rigorous convention—
A holy impulse towards redistribution.
To set out to homogenize mankind
So that the cream could never rise again
Required someone who laughingly could play
With the idea of justice in the courts,
Could mock at riches in the right it claims
To count on justice to be merely just.
But we are talking over Jonah's head,
Or clear off what we know his interests are.
Still not so far off come to think of it.
There is some justice even as Keeper says.
The thing that really counts though is the
    form
Of outrage—violence—that breaks across it.

The very sleep we sleep is an example.
So that because we're always starting fresh
The best minds are the best at premises.
And the most sacred thing of all's abruption.
And if you've got to see your justice crossed
(And you've got to) which will you prefer
To see it, evil-crossed or mercy-crossed?

Keeper   We poets offer you another: star-crossed.
Of star-crossed, mercy-crossed, or evil-crossed
I choose the star-crossed as a star-crossed
   lover.

Jonah   I think my trouble's with the crisises
Where mercy-crossed to me seemed evil-
   crossed.

Keeper   Good for you, Jonah. That's what I've been
   saying.
For instance, when to purify the Itzas
They took my love and threw her down a
   well.

Jesse Bel   If it is me in my last incarnation
He's thinking of, it wasn't down a well
But in a butt of malmsey I was drowned.

Jonah   Why do you call yourself a star-crossed lover?

Keeper   Not everything I say is said in scorn.
Some people want you not to understand
   them,
But I want you to understand me wrong.

Jonah   I noticed how he just now made you out
A revolutionary—which of course you can't
   be.

Keeper   Or not at least the ordinary kind.
No revolution I brought on would aim
At anything but change of personnel.

The Andrew Jackson slogan of Vae Victis
Or 'Turn the rascals out' would do for me.

Paul   Don't you be made feel small by all this
      posing.
    Both of them caught it from Bel's favorite
      poet
    Who in his favorite pose as poet thinker
    (His was the doctrine of the Seven Poses)
    Once charged the Nazarene with having
      brought
    A darkness out of Asia that had crossed
    Old Attic grace and Spartan discipline
    With violence. The Greeks were hardly
      strangers
    To the idea of violence. It flourished
    Persisting from old Chaos in their myth
    To embroil the very gods about their spheres
    Of influence. It's been a commonplace
    Ever since Alexander Greeced the world.
    'Twere nothing new if that were all Christ
      brought.
    Christ came to introduce a break with logic
    That made all other outrage seem as child's
      play:
    The Mercy on the Sin against the Sermon.
    Strange no one ever thought of it before Him.
    'Twas lovely and its origin was love.

Keeper   We know what's coming now.

Paul                    You say it, Keeper,
    If you have learned your lesson. Don't be
      bashful.

Keeper   Paul's constant theme. The Sermon on the
      Mount
    Is just a frame-up to insure the failure
    Of all of us, so all of us will be
    Thrown prostrate at the Mercy Seat for Mercy.

*Jesse Bel*    Yes, Paul, you do say things like that
            sometimes.

    *Paul*    You all have read the Sermon on the Mount.
            I ask you all to read it once again.

            (*They put their hands together like a book
            And hold it up nearsightedly to read*)

*Keeper and
Jesse Bel*    We're reading it.

    *Paul*              Well, now you've got it read,
            What do you make of it?

*Jesse Bel*                 The same old nothing.

  *Keeper*    A beautiful impossibility.

    *Paul*    Keeper, I'm glad you think it beautiful.

  *Keeper*    An irresistible impossibility.
            A lofty beauty no one can live up to
            Yet no one turn from trying to live up to.

    *Paul*    Yes, spoken so we can't live up to it
            Yet so we'll have to weep because we can't.
            Mercy is only to the undeserving.
            But such we all are made in the sight of God.

             'Oh, what is a king here,
             And what is a boor?
             Here all starve together.
             All dwarfed and poor.'

            Here we all fail together, dwarfed and poor.
            Failure is failure, but success is failure.
            There is no better way of having it.
            An end you can't by any means achieve
            And yet can't turn your back on or ignore,

That is the mystery you must accept.
Do you accept it, Master Jonas Dove?

*Jonah*   What do you say to it, My Brother's Keeper?

*Keeper*  I say I'd rather be lost in the woods
Than found in church.

*Jonah*                         That doesn't help me much.

*Keeper*  Our disagreement when we disagree, Paul,
Lies in our different approach to Christ,
Yours more through Rome, mine more
    through Palestine.
But let's be serious about Paul's offer.
His irresistible impossibility,
His lofty beauty no one can live up to
Yet no one turn away from or ignore—
I simply turn away from it.

*Paul*                          You Pagan!

*Keeper*  Yes, call me Pagan, Paul, as if you meant it.
I won't deceive myself about success
By making failure out of equal value.
Any equality they may exhibit's
In making fools of people equally.

*Paul*   But you—what is your answer, Jonas Dove?

*Jonah*  You ask if I see yonder shining gate,
And I reply I almost think I do,
Beyond this great door you have locked
    against me,
Beyond the storm, beyond the universe.

*Paul*   Yes, Pilgrim now instead of runaway,
Your fugitive escape become a quest.

*Keeper*   Don't let him make you see too bright a gate
Or you will come to with a foolish feeling.
When a great tide of argument sweeps in
My small fresh water spring gets drowned of
  course.
But when the brine goes back as go it must
I can count on my source to spring again
Not even brackish from its salt experience.
No true source can be poisoned.

*Jonah*                                Then that's all.
You've finished. I'm dismissed. I want to run
Toward what you make me see beyond the
  world.
Unlock the door for me.

*Keeper*                                Not that way out.

*Jonah*   I'm all turned round.

*Paul*                          There is your way prepared.

*Jonah*   That's not my door.

*Keeper*                        No, that's another door.
Your exit door's become a cellar door.

(*The door here opens darkly of itself*)

*Jonah*   You mean I'm being sent down in the cellar?

*Paul*   You must make your descent like everyone.

*Keeper*   Go if you're going.

*Jonah*                          Who is sending me?
Whose cellar is it, yours or the apostle's?

*Keeper*   It is the cellar to my store. What ho, down
  there!

My dungeoneers, come fetch us.—No one
  answers.
There's not much we can do till Martin gets
  here.—
Don't let me scare you. I was only teasing.
It is the cellar to my store, but not my cellar.
Jesse has given Paul the rent of it
To base his campaign on to save the world.

*Jesse Bel*   Something's the matter everyone admits.
On the off-chance it may be lack of faith
I have contributed the empty cellar
To Paul to see what he can do with it
To bring faith back. I'm only languidly
Inclined to hope for much. Still what we
  need
Is something to believe in, don't we, Paul?

*Keeper*   By something to believe in Jesse means
Something to be fanatical about
So as to justify the orthodox
In saving heretics by slaying them,
Not on the battlefield, but down in cellars.
That way's been tried too many times for me.
I'd like to see the world tried once without it.

*Jesse Bel*   The world seems crying out for a Messiah.

*Keeper*   Haven't you heard the news? We already have
  one,
And of the Messianic race, Karl Marx.

*Jesse Bel*   Light, bring a light!

*Keeper*           Awh, there's no lack of light, you—
A light that falls diffused over my shoulder
And is reflected from the printed page
And bed of world-flowers so as not to
  blind me.

If even the face of man's too bright a light
To look at long directly (like the sun),
Then how much more the face of truth
   must be.
We were not given eyes or intellect
For all the light at once the source of light—
For wisdom that can have no counterwisdom.
In our subscription to the sentiment
Of one God we provide He shall be one
Who can be many Gods to many men,
His church on earth a Roman Pantheon;
Which is our greatest hope of rest from war.
Live and let live, believe and let believe.
'Twas said the lesser gods were only traits
Of the one awful God. Just so the saints
Are God's white light refracted into colors.

*Jesse Bel*   Let's change the subject, boys, I'm getting
      nervous.

*Keeper*   Nervous is all the great things ever made you.
      But to repeat and get it through your head:
      We have all the belief that's good for us.
      Too much all-fired belief and we'd be back
      Down burning skeptics in the cellar furnace
      Like Shadrach, Meshach, and Abednego.

*Jonah*   What's all this talk of slaying down in cellars—
      So sinister? You spoke to someone down
        there.

*Keeper*   My friends and stokers, Jeffers and O'Neill.
      They fail me. Now I'm teasing you again.
      There's no one down there getting tortured
        save
      A penitent perhaps self-thrown on Mercy.

*Jonah*   I heard a deep groan—maybe out of him.
      What's really down there?

Paul                              Just an oubliette,
Where you must lie in self-forgetfulness
On the wet flags before a crucifix
I have had painted on the cellar wall
By a religious Aztec Indian.

Jonah    Then it's not lethal—to get rid of me?
Have they been down?

Paul                              Not in the proper spirit.
These two are stubborn children as you see.
Their case is not so simple. You are good.

Jonah    I am your convert. Tell me what I think.
My trouble has been with my sense of justice.
And you say justice doesn't really matter.

Paul    Does it to you as greatly as it did?

Jonah    I own the need of it had somewhat faded
Even before I came in here tonight.

Paul    Well then!

Jonah                        And that's what I'm to meditate?

Paul    Meditate nothing. Learn to contemplate.
Contemplate glory. There will be a light.
Contemplate Truth until it burns your eyes
     out.

Jonah    I don't see any staircase.

Keeper                              There are stairs.

Paul    Some lingering objection holds you back.

Jonah    If what you say is true, if winning ranks
The same with God as losing, how explain
Our making all this effort mortals make?

*Keeper*   Good for you, Jonah. That's what I've been
            saying.

*Jonah*   You'll tell me sometime. All you say has
           greatness.
           Yet your friend here can't be quite
           disregarded.

*Keeper*   I say we keep him till we wring some more
            Naïveness about Justice out of him,
            As once the Pharaoh did it out of Sekhti
            By having him whipped every day afresh
            For clamoring for justice at the gate
            Until the scribes had taken down a bookful
            For distribution to his bureaucrats.

*Jonah*   I'm going now. But don't you push me off.

*Keeper*   I was supporting you for fear you'd faint
            From disillusionment. You've had to take it.

            (*Jonah steps on the threshold as the door
            Slams in his face. The blow and the repulse
            Crumple him on the floor. Keeper and Paul
            Kneel by him. Bel stands up beside her chair
            As if to come, but Keeper waves her off*)

*Jonah*   I think I may have got God wrong entirely.

*Keeper*   All of us get each other pretty wrong.

*Jesse Bel*   Now we have done it, Paul. What did he say?

*Jonah*   I should have warned you, though my sense
           of justice
           Was about all there ever was to me.
           When that fades I fade—every time I fade.
           Mercy on me for having thought I knew.

*Jesse Bel*   What did he say? I can't hear what he says.

| | |
|---|---|
| *Paul* | Mercy on him for having asked for justice. |

*Keeper*    Die saying that, old-fashioned sapient,
You poor old sape, if I may coin the slang.
We like you, don't we, Paul? (*Paul takes his
   wrist*)

*Jesse Bel*  (*Still standing off*) We've all grown fond of
you.

*Paul*    We've all grown fond of you. (*Paul says it
   louder,
But Jonah gives no sign of having heard*)

*Keeper*    Who said too late you cannot enter now?

*Jesse Bel*  He was rejected for his reservations!

*Keeper*    (*Still on his knees he sits back on his heels*)
But one thing more before the curtain falls.
(*The curtain starts to fall*) Please hold the
   curtain—
All Paul means, and I wish the dead could
   hear me,
All you mean, Paul, I think—

*Jesse Bel*                              Will you stand there
And let that tell you what you think like that?

*Paul*    Suffer a friend to try to word you better.

*Jesse Bel*  Oh, there's to be a funeral oration.
And we're an orator. Get up. Stand up
For what you think your doctor thinks, why
   don't you?
Don't wear your pants out preaching on your
   knees.
Save them to say your prayers on.—What's the
   matter?

Keeper        (*He doesn't rise, but looks at her a moment*)
              Lady, at such a time, and in the Presence!
              I won't presume to tell Bel where to go.
              But if this prophet's mantle fell on me
              I should dare say she would be taken care of.
              We send our wicked enemies to Hell,
              Our wicked friends we send to Purgatory.
              But Bel gets some things right—and she was
                  right—

Jesse Bel     (*She startles at the sudden note of kindness*)
              I *am* right then?

Keeper                              In glorifying courage.
              Courage is of the heart by derivation,
              And great it is. But fear is of the soul.
              And I'm afraid. (*The bulb lights sicken down.
              The cellar door swings wide and slams again*)

Paul          The fear that you're afraid with is the fear
              Of God's decision lastly on your deeds.
              That is the Fear of God whereof 'tis written.

Keeper        But not the fear of punishment for sin
              (I have to sin to prove it isn't that).
              I'm no more governed by the fear of Hell
              Than by the fear of the asylum, jail, or
                  poorhouse,
              The basic three the state is founded on.
              But I'm too much afraid of God to claim
              I have been fighting on the angels' side.
              That is for Him and not for me to say.
              For me to say it would be irreligious.
              (Sometimes I think you are too sure you have
                  been.)
              And I can see that the uncertainty
              In which we act is a severity,
              A cruelty, amounting to injustice
              That nothing but God's mercy can assuage.

I can see that, if that is what you mean.
Give me a hand up, if we are agreed.

*Paul*    Yes, there you have it at the root of things.
We have to stay afraid deep in our souls
Our sacrifice, the best we have to offer,
And not our worst nor second best, our best,
Our very best, our lives laid down like
    Jonah's,
Our lives laid down in war and peace, may not
Be found acceptable in Heaven's sight.
And that they may be is the only prayer
Worth praying. May my sacrifice
Be found acceptable in Heaven's sight.

*Keeper*    Let the lost millions pray it in the dark!
My failure is no different from Jonah's.
We both have lacked the courage in the heart
To overcome the fear within the soul
And go ahead to any accomplishment.
Courage is what it takes and takes the more of
Because the deeper fear is so eternal.
And if I say we lift him from the floor
And lay him where you ordered him to lie
Before the cross, it is from fellow feeling,
As if I asked for one more chance myself
To learn to say (*He moves to Jonah's feet*)
Nothing can make injustice just but mercy.

*Curtain*

# IN THE CLEARING

*"And wait to watch the water clear, I may."*

*But God's own descent*
*Into flesh was meant*
*As a demonstration*
*That the supreme merit*
*Lay in risking spirit*
*In substantiation.*
*Spirit enters flesh*
*And for all it's worth*
*Charges into earth*
*In birth after birth*
*Ever fresh and fresh.*
*We may take the view*
*That its derring-do*
*Thought of in the large*
*Is one mighty charge*
*On our human part*
*Of the soul's ethereal*
*Into the material.*

# Contents

## QUANDARY

## Pod of the Milkweed

Calling all butterflies of every race
From source unknown but from no special place
They ever will return to all their lives,
Because unlike the bees they have no hives,
The milkweed brings up to my very door
The theme of wanton waste in peace and war
As it has never been to me before.
And so it seems a flower's coming out
That should if not be talked then sung about.
The countless wings that from the infinite
Make such a noiseless tumult over it
Do no doubt with their color compensate
For what the drab weed lacks of the ornate.
For drab it is its fondest must admit.
And yes, although it is a flower that flows
With milk and honey, it is bitter milk,
As anyone who ever broke its stem
And dared to taste the wound a little knows.
It tastes as if it might be opiate.
But whatsoever else it may secrete,
Its flowers' distilled honey is so sweet
It makes the butterflies intemperate.
There is no slumber in its juice for them.
One knocks another off from where he clings.
They knock the dyestuff off each other's wings—
With thirst on hunger to the point of lust.
They raise in their intemperance a cloud
Of mingled butterfly and flower dust
That hangs perceptibly above the scene.
In being sweet to these ephemerals
The sober weed has managed to contrive
In our three hundred days and sixty five
One day too sweet for beings to survive.
Many shall come away as struggle worn
And spent and dusted off of their regalia
To which at daybreak they were freshly born
As after one-of-them's proverbial failure

425

From having beaten all day long in vain
Against the wrong side of a window pane.

But waste was of the essence of the scheme.
And all the good they did for man or god
To all those flowers they passionately trod
Was leave as their posterity one pod
With an inheritance of restless dream.
He hangs on upside down with talon feet
In an inquisitive position odd
As any Guatemalan parakeet.
Something eludes him. Is it food to eat?
Or some dim secret of the good of waste?
He almost has it in his talon clutch.
Where have those flowers and butterflies all gone
That science may have staked the future on?
He seems to say the reason why so much
Should come to nothing must be fairly faced.*

*And shall be in due course.


## Away!

Now I out walking
The world desert,
And my shoe and my stocking
Do me no hurt.

I leave behind
Good friends in town.
Let them get well-wined
And go lie down.

Don't think I leave
For the outer dark
Like Adam and Eve
Put out of the Park.

Forget the myth.
There is no one I
Am put out with
Or put out by.

Unless I'm wrong
I but obey
The urge of a song:
I'm—bound—away!

And I may return
If dissatisfied
With what I learn
From having died.

## A Cabin in the Clearing

for Alfred Edwards

MIST

I don't believe the sleepers in this house
Know where they are.

SMOKE

They've been here long enough
To push the woods back from around the house
And part them in the middle with a path.

MIST

And still I doubt if they know where they are.
And I begin to fear they never will.
All they maintain the path for is the comfort
Of visiting with the equally bewildered.
Nearer in plight their neighbors are than distance.

SMOKE

I am the guardian wraith of starlit smoke
That leans out this and that way from their chimney.
I will not have their happiness despaired of.

MIST

No one—not I—would give them up for lost
Simply because they don't know where they are.
I am the damper counterpart of smoke
That gives off from a garden ground at night
But lifts no higher than a garden grows.
I cotton to their landscape. That's who I am.
I am no further from their fate than you are.

SMOKE

They must by now have learned the native tongue.
Why don't they ask the Red Man where they are?

MIST

They often do, and none the wiser for it.
So do they also ask philosophers
Who come to look in on them from the pulpit.
They will ask anyone there is to ask—
In the fond faith accumulated fact
Will of itself take fire and light the world up.
Learning has been a part of their religion.

SMOKE

If the day ever comes when they know who
They are, they may know better where they are.
But who they are is too much to believe—
Either for them or the onlooking world.
They are too sudden to be credible.

MIST

Listen, they murmur talking in the dark
On what should be their daylong theme continued.
Putting the lamp out has not put their thought out.
Let us pretend the dewdrops from the eaves
Are you and I eavesdropping on their unrest—
A mist and smoke eavesdropping on a haze—
And see if we can tell the bass from the soprano.

*Than smoke and mist who better would appraise*
*The kindred spirit of an inner haze.*

## Closed for Good

They come not back with steed
And chariot to chide
My slowness with their speed
And scare me to one side.
They have found other scenes
For haste and other means.

They leave the road to me
To walk in saying naught
Perhaps but to a tree
Inaudibly in thought,
"From you the road receives
A priming coat of leaves.

"And soon for lack of sun,
The prospects are in white
It will be further done,
But with a coat so light
The shape of leaves will show
Beneath the spread of snow."

And so on into winter
Till even I have ceased
To come as a foot printer,
And only some slight beast
So mousy or so foxy
Shall print there as my proxy.

## *America Is Hard to See*

Columbus may have worked the wind
A new and better way to Ind
And also proved the world a ball,
But how about the wherewithal?
Not just for scientific news
Had the Queen backed him to a cruise.

Remember he had made the test
Finding the East by sailing West.
But had he found it? Here he was
Without one trinket from Ormuz
To save the Queen from family censure
For her investment in his venture.

There had been something strangely wrong
With every coast he tried along.
He could imagine nothing barrener.
The trouble was with him the mariner.
He wasn't off a mere degree;
His reckoning was off a sea.

And to intensify the drama
Another mariner, Da Gama,
Came just then sailing into port
From the same general resort,
And with the gold in hand to show for
His claim it was another Ophir.

Had but Columbus known enough
He might have boldly made the bluff
That better than Da Gama's gold
He had been given to behold
The race's future trial place,
A fresh start for the human race.

He might have fooled Valladolid.
I was deceived by what he did.
If I had had my chance when young
I should have had Columbus sung

As a god who had given us
A more than Moses' exodus.

But all he did was spread the room
Of our enacting out the doom
Of being in each other's way,
And so put off the weary day
When we would have to put our mind
On how to crowd but still be kind.

For these none too apparent gains
He got no more than dungeon chains
And such small posthumous renown
(A country named for him, a town,
A holiday) as where he is
He may not recognize for his.

They say his flagship's unlaid ghost
Still probes and dents our rocky coast
With animus approaching hate,
And for not turning out a strait,
He has cursed every river mouth
From fifty North to fifty South.

Some day our navy, I predict,
Will take in tow this derelict
And lock him through Culebra Cut,
His eyes as good (or bad) as shut
To all the modern works of man
And all we call American.

America is hard to see.
Less partial witnesses than he
In book on book have testified
They could not see it from outside—
Or inside either for that matter.
We know the literary chatter.

Columbus, as I say, will miss
All he owes to the artifice
Of tractor-plow and motor-drill.
To naught but his own force of will,

Or at most some Andean quake,
Will he ascribe this lucky break.

High purpose makes the hero rude;
He will not stop for gratitude.
But let him show his haughty stern
To what was never his concern
Except as it denied him way
To fortune-hunting in Cathay.

He will be starting pretty late.
He'll find that Asiatic state
Is about tired of being looted
While having its beliefs disputed.
His can be no such easy raid
As Cortez on the Aztecs made.

## One More Brevity

I opened the door so my last look
Should be taken outside a house and book.
Before I gave up seeing and slept
I said I would see how Sirius kept
His watch-dog eye on what remained
To be gone into if not explained.
But scarcely was my door ajar,
When past the leg I thrust for bar
Slipped in to be my problem guest,
Not a heavenly dog made manifest,
But an earthly dog of the carriage breed;
Who, having failed of the modern speed,
Now asked asylum—and I was stirred
To be the one so dog-preferred.
He dumped himself like a bag of bones,
He sighed himself a couple of groans,
And head to tail then firmly curled
Like swearing off on the traffic world.
I set him water, I set him food.

He rolled an eye with gratitude
(Or merely manners it may have been),
But never so much as lifted chin.
His hard tail loudly smacked the floor
As if beseeching me, "Please, no more,
I can't explain—tonight at least."
His brow was perceptibly trouble-creased.
So I spoke in terms of adoption thus:
"Gustie, old boy, Dalmatian Gus,
You're right, there's nothing to discuss.
Don't try to tell me what's on your mind,
The sorrow of having been left behind,
Or the sorrow of having run away.
All that can wait for the light of day.
Meanwhile feel obligation-free.
Nobody has to confide in me."
'Twas too one-sided a dialogue,
And I wasn't sure I was talking dog.
I broke off baffled. But all the same
In fancy, I ratified his name,
Gustie, Dalmatian Gus, that is,
And started shaping my life to his,
Finding him in his right supplies
And sharing his miles of exercise.

Next morning the minute I was about
He was at the door to be let out
With an air that said, "I have paid my call.
You mustn't feel hurt if now I'm all
For getting back somewhere or further on."
I opened the door and he was gone.
I was to taste in little the grief
That comes of dogs' lives being so brief,
Only a fraction of ours at most.
He might have been the dream of a ghost
In spite of the way his tail had smacked
My floor so hard and matter-of-fact.
And things have been going so strangely since
I wouldn't be too hard to convince,
I might even claim, he was Sirius

(Think of presuming to call him Gus)
The star itself, Heaven's greatest star,
Not a meteorite, but an avatar,
Who had made an overnight descent
To show by deeds he didn't resent
My having depended on him so long,
And yet done nothing about it in song.*
A symbol was all he could hope to convey,
An intimation, a shot of ray,
A meaning I was supposed to seek,
And finding, wasn't disposed to speak.

*But see "The Great Overdog" and "Choose Something Like a Star," in which latter the star could hardly have been a planet since fixity is of the essence of the piece.


## Escapist—Never

He is no fugitive—escaped, escaping.
No one has seen him stumble looking back.
His fear is not behind him but beside him
On either hand to make his course perhaps
A crooked straightness yet no less a straightness.
He runs face forward. He is a pursuer.
He seeks a seeker who in his turn seeks
Another still, lost far into the distance.
Any who seek him seek in him the seeker.
His life is a pursuit of a pursuit forever.
It is the future that creates his present.
All is an interminable chain of longing.

# For John F. Kennedy His Inauguration

### Gift Outright of "The Gift Outright"
## With Some Preliminary History in Rhyme

Summoning artists to participate
In the august occasions of the state
Seems something artists ought to celebrate.
Today is for my cause a day of days.
And his be poetry's old-fashioned praise
Who was the first to think of such a thing.
This verse that in acknowledgment I bring
Goes back to the beginning of the end
Of what had been for centuries the trend;
A turning point in modern history.
Colonial had been the thing to be
As long as the great issue was to see
What country'd be the one to dominate
By character, by tongue, by native trait,
The new world Christopher Columbus found.
The French, the Spanish, and the Dutch were downed
And counted out. Heroic deeds were done.
Elizabeth the First and England won.
Now came on a new order of the ages
That in the Latin of our founding sages
(Is it not written on the dollar bill
We carry in our purse and pocket still?)
God nodded his approval of as good.
So much those heroes knew and understood,
I mean the great four, Washington,
John Adams, Jefferson, and Madison,—
So much they knew as consecrated seers
They must have seen ahead what now appears,
They would bring empires down about our ears
And by the example of our Declaration
Make everybody want to be a nation.
And this is no aristocratic joke
At the expense of negligible folk.

We see how seriously the races swarm
In their attempts at sovereignty and form.
They are our wards we think to some extent
For the time being and with their consent,
To teach them how Democracy is meant.
"New order of the ages" did we say?
If it looks none too orderly today,
'Tis a confusion it was ours to start
So in it have to take courageous part.
No one of honest feeling would approve
A ruler who pretended not to love
A turbulence he had the better of.
Everyone knows the glory of the twain
Who gave America the aeroplane
To ride the whirlwind and the hurricane.
Some poor fool has been saying in his heart
Glory is out of date in life and art.
Our venture in revolution and outlawry
Has justified itself in freedom's story
Right down to now in glory upon glory.
Come fresh from an election like the last,
The greatest vote a people ever cast,
So close yet sure to be abided by,
It is no miracle our mood is high.
Courage is in the air in bracing whiffs
Better than all the stalemate an's and ifs.
There was the book of profile tales declaring
For the emboldened politicians daring
To break with followers when in the wrong,
A healthy independence of the throng,
A democratic form of right divine
To rule first answerable to high design.
here is a call to life a little sterner,
And braver for the earner, learner, yearner.
Less criticism of the field and court
And more preoccupation with the sport.
It makes the prophet in us all presage
The glory of a next Augustan age
Of a power leading from its strength and pride,
Of young ambition eager to be tried,

Firm in our free beliefs without dismay,
In any game the nations want to play.
A golden age of poetry and power
Of which this noonday's the beginning hour.


## "THE GIFT OUTRIGHT"

The land was ours before we were the land's.
She was our land more than a hundred years
Before we were her people. She was ours
In Massachusetts, in Virginia,
But we were England's, still colonials,
Possessing what we still were unpossessed by,
Possessed by what we now no more possessed.
Something we were withholding made us weak
Until we found out that it was ourselves
We were withholding from our land of living,
And forthwith found salvation in surrender.
Such as we were we gave ourselves outright
(The deed of gift was many deeds of war)
To the land vaguely realizing westward,
But still unstoried, artless, unenhanced,
Such as she was, such as she would become.

## *Accidentally on Purpose*

The Universe is but the Thing of things,
The things but balls all going round in rings.
Some of them mighty huge, some mighty tiny,
All of them radiant and mighty shiny.

They mean to tell us all was rolling blind
Till accidentally it hit on mind
In an albino monkey in a jungle
And even then it had to grope and bungle,

Till Darwin came to earth upon a year
To show the evolution how to steer.
They mean to tell us, though, the Omnibus
Had no real purpose till it got to us.

Never believe it. At the very worst
It must have had the purpose from the first
To produce purpose as the fitter bred:
We were just purpose coming to a head.

Whose purpose was it? His or Hers or Its?
Let's leave that to the scientific wits.
Grant me intention, purpose, and design—
That's near enough for me to the Divine.

And yet for all this help of head and brain
How happily instinctive we remain,
Our best guide upward further to the light,
Passionate preference such as love at sight.

## A Never Naught Song

There was never naught,
There was always thought.
But when noticed first
It was fairly burst
Into having weight.
It was in a state
Of atomic One.
Matter was begun—
And in fact complete,
One and yet discrete
To conflict and pair.
Everything was there
Every single thing
Waiting was to bring,
Clear from hydrogen
All the way to men.
It is all the tree
It will ever be,
Bole and branch and root
Cunningly minute.
And this gist of all
Is so infra-small
As to blind our eyes
To its every guise
And so render nil
The whole Yggdrasil.
Out of coming-in
Into having been!
So the picture's caught
Almost next to naught
But the force of thought.

## *Version*

Once there was an Archer
And there was a minute
When He shot a shaft
On a New Departure.
Then He must have laughed:
Comedy was in it.
For the game He hunted
Was the non-existence,
And His shaft got blunted
On its non-resistance.


## *A Concept Self-Conceived*

The latest creed that has to be believed
And entered in our childish catechism
Is that the All's a concept self-conceived,
Which is no more than good old Pantheism.

Great is the reassurance of recall.
Why go on further with confusing voice
To say God's either All or over all?
The rule is, never give a child a choice.

———————

Forgive, O Lord, my little jokes on Thee
And I'll forgive Thy great big one on me.

# Kitty Hawk

*Back there in 1953 with the Huntington Cairnses*
*(A Skylark for Them in Three-Beat Phrases)*

## PART ONE

### PORTENTS, PRESENTIMENTS, AND PREMONITIONS

Kitty Hawk, O Kitty,
There was once a song,
Who knows but a great
Emblematic ditty,
I might well have sung
When I came here young
Out and down along
Past Elizabeth City
Sixty years ago.
I was, to be sure,
Out of sorts with Fate,
Wandering to and fro
In the earth alone,
You might think too poor-
Spirited to care
Who I was or where
I was being blown
Faster than my tread—
Like the crumpled, better
Left-unwritten letter
I had read and thrown.
Oh, but not to boast,
Ever since Nag's Head
Had my heart been great,
Not to claim elate,
With a need the gale
Filled me with to shout
Summary riposte
To the dreary wail
There's no knowing what
Love is all about.

Poets know a lot.
Never did I fail
Of an answer back
To the zodiac
When in heartless chorus
Aries and Taurus,
Gemini and Cancer
Mocked me for an answer.
It was on my tongue
To have up and sung
The initial flight
I can see now might—
Should have been my own—
Into the unknown,
Into the sublime
Off these sands of Time
Time had seen amass
From his hourglass.
Once I told the Master,
Later when we met,
I'd been here one night
As a young Alastor
When the scene was set
For some kind of flight
Long before he flew it.
Just supposing I—
I had beat him to it.
What did men mean by
THE original?
Why was it so very,
Very necessary
To be first of all?
How about the lie
That he wasn't first?
I was glad he laughed.
There was such a lie
Money and maneuver
Fostered over long
Until Herbert Hoover
Raised this tower shaft

To undo the wrong.
Of all crimes the worst
Is to steal the glory
From the great and brave,
Even more accursed
Than to rob the grave.
But the sorry story
Has been long redressed.
And as for my jest
I had any claim
To the runway's fame
Had I only sung,
That is all my tongue.
I can't make it seem
More than that my theme
Might have been a dream
Of dark Hatteras
Or sad Roanoke,
One more fond alas
For the seed of folk
Sowed in vain by Raleigh,
Raleigh of the cloak,
And some other folly.

Getting too befriended,
As so often, ended
Any melancholy
Götterdämmerung
That I might have sung.
I fell in among
Some kind of committee
From Elizabeth City,
Each and every one
Loaded with a gun
Or a demijohn.
(Need a body ask
If it was a flask?)
Out to kill a duck
Or perhaps a swan
Over Currituck.

This was not their day
Anything to slay
Unless one another.
But their lack of luck
Made them no less gay
No, nor less polite.
They included me
Like a little brother
In their revelry—
All concern to take
Care my innocence
Should at all events
Tenderly be kept
For good gracious' sake.
And if they were gentle
They were sentimental.
One drank to his mother
While another wept.
Something made it sad
For me to break loose
From the need they had
To make themselves glad
They were of no use.
Manners made it hard,
But that night I stole
Off on the unbounded
Beaches where the whole
Of the Atlantic pounded.
There I next fell in
With a lone coast guard
On midnight patrol,
Who as of a sect
Asked about my soul
And where-all I'd been.
Apropos of sin,
Did I recollect
How the wreckers wrecked
Theodosia Burr
Off this very shore?
'Twas to punish her,

But her father more—
We don't know what for:
There was no confession.
Things they think she wore
Still sometimes occur
In someone's possession
Here at Kitty Hawk.
We can have no notion
Of the strange devotion
Burr had for his daughter:
He was too devoted.
So it was in talk
We prolonged the walk,
On one side the ocean,
And on one a water
Of the inner sound;
"And the moon was full,"
As the poet said
And I aptly quoted.
And its being full
And right overhead,
Small but strong and round,
By its tidal pull
Made all being full.
Kitty Hawk, O Kitty,
Here it was again
In the selfsame day,
I at odds with men
Came upon their pity,
Equally profound
For a son astray
And a daughter drowned.

## PART TWO

When the chance went by
For my Muse to fly
From this Runway Beach
As a figure of speech
In a flight of words,

Little I imagined
Men would treat this sky
Some day to a pageant
Like a thousand birds.
Neither you nor I
Ever thought to fly.
Oh, but fly we did,
Literally fly.
That's because though mere
Lilliputians we're
What Catullus called
Somewhat (aliquid).
Mind you, we are mind.
We are not the kind
To stay too confined.
After having crawled
Round the place on foot
And done yeoman share
Of just staying put,
We arose from there
And we scaled a plane
So the stilly air
Almost pulled our hair
Like a hurricane.

Then I saw it all.

Pulpiteers will censure
Our instinctive venture
Into what they call
The material
When we took that fall
From the apple tree.
But God's own descent
Into flesh was meant
As a demonstration
That the supreme merit
Lay in risking spirit
In substantiation.
Westerners inherit

A design for living
Deeper into matter—
Not without due patter
Of a great misgiving.
All the science zest
To materialize
By on-penetration
Into earth and skies
(Don't forget the latter
Is but further matter)
Has been West Northwest.
If it was not wise,
Tell me why the East
Seemingly has ceased
From its long stagnation
In mere meditation.
What is all the fuss
To catch up with us?
Can it be to flatter
Us with emulation?

Spirit enters flesh
And for all it's worth
Charges into earth
In birth after birth
Ever fresh and fresh.
We may take the view
That its derring-do
Thought of in the large
Was one mighty charge
On our human part
Of the soul's ethereal
Into the material.
In a running start
As it were from scratch
On a certain slab
Of (we'll say) basalt
In or near Moab
With intent to vault
In a vaulting match,

Never mind with whom—
(No one, I presume,
But ourselves—mankind,
In a love and hate
Rivalry combined.)
'Twas a radio
Voice that said, "Get set
In the alphabet,
That is A B C,
Which some day should be
Rhymed with 1 2 3
On a college gate."
Then the radio
Region voice said, "Go,
Go you on to know
More than you can sing.
Have no hallowing fears
Anything's forbidden
Just because it's hidden.
Trespass and encroach
On successive spheres
Without self-reproach."
Then for years and years
And for miles and miles
'Cross the Aegean Isles,
Athens Rome France Britain,
Always West Northwest,
As have I not written,
Till the so-long kept
Purpose was expressed
In the leap we leapt.
And the radio
Cried, "The Leap—The Leap!"
It belonged to US,
Not our friends the Russ,
To have run the event
To its full extent
And have won the crown,
Or let's say the cup,

On which with a date
Is the inscription though,
"Nothing can go up
But it must come down."
Earth is still our fate.
The uplifted sight
We enjoyed at night
When instead of sheep
We were counting stars,
Not to go to sleep,
But to stay awake
For good gracious' sake,
Naming stars to boot
To avoid mistake,
Jupiter and Mars,
Just like Pullman cars,
'Twas no vain pursuit.
Some have preached and taught
All there was to thought
Was to master Nature
By some nomenclature.
But if not a law
'Twas an end foregone
Anything we saw
And thus fastened on
With an epithet
We would see to yet—
We would want to touch
Not to mention clutch.

### TALK ALOFT

Someone says the Lord
Says our reaching toward
Is its own reward.
One would like to know
Where God says it though.

We don't like that much.

Let's see where we are.
What's that sulphur blur
Off there in the fog?
Go consult the log.
It's some kind of town,
But it's not New York.
We're not very far
Out from where we were.
It's still Kitty Hawk.

We'd have got as far
Even at a walk.

Don't you crash me down.
Though our kiting ships
Prove but flying chips
From the science shop
And when motors stop
They may have to drop
Short of anywhere,
Though our leap in air
Prove as vain a hop
As the hop from grass
Of a grasshopper,
Don't discount our powers;
We have made a pass
At the infinite,
Made it, as it were,
Rationally ours,
To the most remote
Swirl of neon-lit
Particle afloat.
Ours was to reclaim
What had long been faced
As a fact of waste
And was waste in name.

That's how we became
Though an earth so small,
Justly known to fame

As the Capital
Of the universe.
We make no pretension
Of projecting ray
We can call our own
From this ball of stone,
None I don't reject
As too new to mention.
All we do's reflect
From our rocks, and yes,
From our brains no less.
And the better part
Is the ray we dart
From this head and heart,
The *mens animi.*

Till we came to be
There was not a trace
Of a thinking race
Anywhere in space.
We know of no world
Being whirled and whirled
Round and round the rink
Of a single sun
(So as not to sink),
Not a single one
That has thought to think.

## THE HOLINESS OF WHOLENESS

Pilot, though at best your
Flight is but a gesture,
And your rise and swoop,
But a loop the loop,
Lands on someone hard
In his own backyard
From no higher heaven
Than a bolt of levin,
I don't say retard.
Keep on elevating.

But while meditating
What we can't or can
Let's keep starring man
In the royal role.
It will not be his
Ever to create
One least germ or coal.
Those two things we can't.
But the comfort is
In the covenant
We may get control
If not of the whole
Of at least some part
Where not too immense,
So by craft or art
We can give the part
Wholeness in a sense.
The becoming fear
That becomes us best
Is lest habit ridden
In the kitchen midden
Of our dump of earning
And our dump of learning
We come nowhere near
Getting thought expressed.

### THE MIXTURE MECHANIC

This wide flight we wave
At the stars or moon
Means that we approve
Of them on the move.
Ours is to behave
Like a kitchen spoon
Of a size Titanic
To keep all things stirred
In a blend mechanic
Saying That's the tune,
That's the pretty kettle!
Matter mustn't curd,

Separate and settle.
Action is the word.

Nature's never quite
Sure she hasn't erred
In her vague design
Till on some fine night
We two come in flight
Like a king and queen
And by right divine,
Waving scepter-baton,
Undertake to tell her
What in being stellar
She's supposed to mean.

God of the machine,
Peregrine machine,
Some still think is Satan,
Unto you the thanks
For this token flight,
Thanks to you and thanks
To the brothers Wright
Once considered cranks
Like Darius Green
In their home town, Dayton.

## Auspex

Once in a California Sierra
I was swooped down upon when I was small
And measured, but not taken after all
By a great eagle bird in all its terror.

Such auspices are very hard to read.
My parents when I ran to them averred
I was rejected by the royal bird
As one who would not make a Ganymede.

Not find a barkeep unto Jove in me?
I have remained resentful to this day
When any but myself presumed to say
That there was anything I couldn't be.

## The Draft Horse

With a lantern that wouldn't burn
In too frail a buggy we drove
Behind too heavy a horse
Through a pitch-dark limitless grove.

And a man came out of the trees
And took our horse by the head
And reaching back to his ribs
Deliberately stabbed him dead.

The ponderous beast went down
With a crack of a broken shaft.
And the night drew through the trees
In one long invidious draft.

The most unquestioning pair
That ever accepted fate
And the least disposed to ascribe
Any more than we had to to hate,

We assumed that the man himself
Or someone he had to obey
Wanted us to get down
And walk the rest of the way.

## Ends

Loud talk in the overlighted house
That made us stumble past.
Oh, there had once been night the first,
But this was night the last.

Of all the things he might have said,
Sincere or insincere,
He never said she wasn't young,
And hadn't been his dear.

Oh, some as soon would throw it all
As throw a part away.
And some will say all sorts of things,
But some mean what they say.

## Peril of Hope

It is right in there
Betwixt and between
The orchard bare
And the orchard green,

When the orchard's right
In a flowery burst
Of all that's white,
That we fear the worst.

For there's not a clime
But at any cost
Will take that time
For a night of frost.

## Questioning Faces

The winter owl banked just in time to pass
And save herself from breaking window glass.
And her wings straining suddenly aspread
Caught color from the last of evening red
In a display of underdown and quill
To glassed-in children at the window sill.


## Does No One at All
## Ever Feel This Way in the Least?

O ocean sea for all your being vast,
Your separation of us from the Old
That should have made the New World newly great
Would only disappoint us at the last
If it should not do anything foretold
To make us different in a single trait.

This though we took the Indian name for maize
And changed it to the English name for wheat.
It seemed to comfort us to call it corn.
And so with homesickness in many ways
We sought however crudely to defeat
Our chance of being people newly born.

And now, O sea, you're lost by aeroplane.
Our sailors ride a bullet for a boat.
Our coverage of distance is so facile
It makes us to have had a sea in vain.
Our moat around us is no more a moat,
Our continent no more a moated castle.

Grind shells, O futile sea, grind empty shells
For all the use you are along the strand.
I cannot hold you innocent of fault.

Spring water in our mountain bosom swells
To pour fresh rivers on you from the land
Till you have lost the savor of your salt.*

I pick a dead shell up from where the kelp
Lies in a windrow, brittle dry and black,
And holding it far forward for a symbol
I cry "Do work for women—all the help
I ask of you. Grind this I throw you back
Into a lady's finger ring or thimble."

The ocean had been spoken to before.†
But if it had no thought of paying heed
To taunt of mine I knew a place to go
Where I need listen to its rote no more,
Nor taste its salt, nor smell its fish and weed,
Nor be reminded of them in a blow—

So far inland the very name of ocean
Goes mentionless except in baby-school
When teacher's own experiences fail her
And she can only give the class a notion
Of what it is by calling it a pool
And telling them how Sinbad was a sailor.

*At this writing it seems pretty well accepted that any rivers added can only make the sea saltier.
†By King Canute and Lord Byron among others.

## The Bad Island—Easter

(Perhaps so called because it may have risen once)

That primitive head
So ambitiously vast
Yet so rude in its art
Is as easily read
For the woes of the past

As a clinical chart.
For one thing alone,
The success of the lip
So scornfully curled
Has that tonnage of stone
Been brought in a ship
Half way round the world.

They were days on that stone.
They gave it the wedge
Till it flaked from the ledge.
Then they gave it a face.
Then with tackle unknown
They stood it in place
On a cliff for a throne.
They gave it a face
Of what was it? Scorn
Of themselves as a race
For having been born?
And then having first
Been cajoled and coerced
Into being be-ruled?
By what stratagem
Was their cynical throng
So cozened and fooled
And jollied along?
Were they told they were free
And persuaded to see
Something in it for them?
Well they flourished and waxed
By executive guile,
By fraud and by force,
Or so for a while;
Until overtaxed
In nerve and resource
They started to wane.
They emptied the aisle
Except for a few
That can but be described
As a vile residue,

And a garrulous too.
They were punished and bribed;
All was in vain,
Nothing would do.
Some mistake had been made
No book can explain,
Some change in the law
That nobody saw
Except as a gain.
But one thing is sure
Whatever kultur
They were made to parade,
What heights of altrur-
ian thought to attain,
Not a trace of it's left
But the gospel of sharing,
And that has decayed
Into a belief
In being a thief
And persisting in theft
With cynical daring.


## Our Doom to Bloom

"Shine, perishing republic."
ROBINSON JEFFERS


Cumaean Sibyl, charming Ogress,
What are the simple facts of Progress
That I may trade on with reliance
In consultation with my clients?
The Sibyl said, "Go back to Rome
And tell your clientele at home
That if it's not a mere illusion
All there is to it is diffusion—
Of coats, oats, votes, to all mankind.
In the Surviving Book we find
That liberal, or conservative,

The state's one function is to give.
The bud must bloom till blowsy blown
Its petals loosen and are strown;
And that's a fate it can't evade
Unless 'twould rather wilt than fade."


## The Objection to Being Stepped On

At the end of the row
I stepped on the toe
Of an unemployed hoe.
It rose in offence
And struck me a blow
In the seat of my sense.
It wasn't to blame
But I called it a name.
And I must say it dealt
Me a blow that I felt
Like malice prepense.
You may call me a fool,
But *was* there a rule
The weapon should be
Turned into a tool?
And what do we see?
The first tool I step on
Turned into a weapon.


## A-Wishing Well

A poet would a-wishing go,
And he wished love were thus and so.
"If but it were" he said, said he,
"And one thing more that may not be,
This world were good enough for me."
I quote him with respect verbatim.

Some quaint dissatisfaction ate him.
I would give anything to learn
The one thing more of his concern.
But listen to me register
The one thing more I wish there were.
As a confirmed astronomer
I'm always for a better sky.
(I don't care how the world gets by.)
I'm tempted to let go restraint
Like splashing phosphorescent paint,
And fill the sky as full of moons
As circus day of toy balloons.
That ought to make the Sunday Press.
But that's not like me. On much less
And much much easier to get
From childhood has my heart been set.
Some planets, the unblinking four,
Are seen to juggle moons galore.
A lot would be a lot of fun.
But all I ask's an extra one.
Let's get my incantation right:
"I wish I may I wish I might"
Give earth another satellite.
Where would we get another? Come,
Don't you know where new moons are from?
When clever people ask me where
I get a poem, I despair.
I'm apt to tell them in New York
I think I get it via stork
From some extinct old chimney pot.
Believe the Arcadians or not,
They claim they recollect the morn
When unto Earth her first was born.
It cost the Earth as fierce a pang
As Keats (or was it Milton?) sang
It cost her for Enormous Caf.
It came near splitting her in half.
'Twas torn from her Pacific side.
All the sea water in one tide

And all the air rushed to the spot.
Believe the Arcadians or not,
They saved themselves by hanging on
To a plant called the silphion,
Which has for its great attribute
It can't be pulled up by the root.
Men's legs and bodies in the gale
Streamed out like pennants swallow-tail.
Most of them let go and were gone.
But there was this phenomenon:
Some of them gave way at the wrist
Before they gave way at the fist.
In branches of the silphion
Is sometimes found a skeleton
Of desperately clutching hand
Science has failed to understand.
One has been lately all the talk
In the museum of Antioch.
That's how it was from the Pacific.
It needn't be quite so terrific
To get another from the Atlantic.
It needn't be quite so gigantic
As coming from a lesser ocean.
Good liberals will object my notion
Is too hard on the human race.
That's something I'm prepared to face.
It merely would entail the purge
That the just pausing Demiurge
Asks of himself once in so often
So the firm firmament won't soften.
I am assured at any rate
Man's practically inexterminate.
Someday I must go into that.
There's always been an Ararat
Where someone someone else begat
To start the world all over at.

## *How Hard It Is to Keep from Being King When It's in You and in the Situation*

The King said to his son: "Enough of this!
The Kingdom's yours to finish as you please.
I'm getting out tonight. Here, take the crown."

But the Prince drew away his hand in time
To avoid what he wasn't sure he wanted.
So the crown fell and the crown jewels scattered.
And the Prince answered, picking up the pieces,
"Sire, I've been looking on and I don't like
The looks of empire here. I'm leaving with you."

So the two making good their abdication
Fled from the palace in the guise of men.
But they had not walked far into the night
Before they sat down weary on a bank
Of dusty weeds to take a drink of stars.
And eyeing one he only wished were his,
Rigel, Bellatrix, or else Betelgeuse,
The ex-King said, "Yon star's indifference
Fills me with fear I'll be left to my fate:
I needn't think I have escaped my duty,
For hard it is to keep from being King
When it's in you and in the situation.
Witness how hard it was for Julius Caesar.
He couldn't keep himself from being King.
He had to be stopped by the sword of Brutus.
Only less hard was it for Washington.
My crown shall overtake me, you will see,
It will come rolling after us like a hoop."

"Lets' not get superstitious, Sire," the Prince said.
"We should have brought the crown along to pawn."
"You're right," the ex-King said, "we'll need some money.
How would it be for you to take your father
To the slave auction in some market place
And sell him into slavery? My price

Should be enough to set you up in business—
Or making verse if that is what you're bent on.
Don't let your father tell you what to be."

The ex-King stood up in the market place
And tried to look ten thousand dollars' worth.
To the first buyer coming by who asked
What good he was he boldly said, "I'll tell you:
I know the *Quint*essence of many things.
I know the *Quint*essence of food, I know
The *Quint*essence of jewels, and I know
The *Quint*essence of horses, men, and women."

The eunuch laughed: "Well, that's a lot to know.
And here's a lot of money. Who's the taker?
This larrikin? All right. You come along.
You're off to Xanadu to help the cook.
I'll try you in the kitchen first on food
Since you put food first in your repertory.
It seems you call quint*ess*ence *quint*essence."

"I'm a Rhodes scholar—that's the reason why.
I was at college in the Isle of Rhodes."

The slave served his novitiate dish-washing.
He got his first chance to prepare a meal
One day when the chief cook was sick at heart.
(The cook was temperamental like the King)
And the meal made the banqueters exclaim
And the Great King inquire whose work it was.

"A man's out there who claims he knows the secret,
Not of food only but of everything,
Jewels and horses, women, wine, and song."
The King said grandly, "Even as we are fed
See that our slave is also. He's in favor.
Take notice, Haman, he's in favor with us."

There came to court a merchant selling pearls,
A smaller pearl he asked a thousand for,

A larger one he asked five hundred for.
The King sat favoring one pearl for its bigness,
And then the other for its costliness
(He seems to have felt limited to one),
Till the ambassadors from Punt or somewhere
Shuffled their feet as if to hint respectfully,
"The choice is not between two pearls, O King,
But between peace and war as we conceive it.
We are impatient for your royal answer."
No estimating how far the entente
Might have deteriorated had not someone
Thought of the kitchen slave and had him in
To put an end to the King's vacillation.

And the slave said, "The small one's worth the price,
But the big one is worthless. Break it open.
My head for it—you'll find the big one hollow.
Permit me"—and he crushed it under his heel
And showed them it contained a live teredo.

"But tell us how you knew," Darius cried.

"Oh, from my knowledge of its *quint*essence.
I told you I knew the *quint*essence of jewels.
But anybody could have guessed in this case,
From the pearl's having its own native warmth,
Like flesh, there must be something living in it."

"Feed him another feast of recognition."

And so it went with triumph after triumph
Till on a day the King, being sick at heart
(The King was temperamental like his cook,
But nobody had noticed the connection),
Sent for the ex-King in a private matter.
"You say you know the inwardness of men
As well as of your hundred other things.
Dare to speak out and tell me about myself.
What ails me? Tell me. Why am I unhappy?"

"You're not where you belong. You're not a King
Of royal blood. Your father was a cook."

"You die for that."

                    "No, you go ask your mother."

His mother didn't like the way he put it,
"But yes," she said, "some day I'll tell you, dear.
You have a right to know your pedigree.
You're well descended on your mother's side,
Which is unusual. So many kings
Have married beggar maids from off the streets.
Your mother's folks—"

                    He stayed to hear no more,
But hastened back to reassure his slave
That if he had him slain it wouldn't be
For having lied but having told the truth.
"At least you ought to die for wizardry.
But let me into it and I will spare you.
How did you know the secret of my birth?"

"If you had been a king of royal blood,
You'd have rewarded me for all I've done
By making me your minister-vizier,
Or giving me a nobleman's estate.
But all you thought of giving me was food.
I picked you out a horse called Safety Third
By Safety Second out of Safety First,
Guaranteed to come safely off with you
From all the fights you had a mind to lose.
You could lose battles, you could lose whole wars,
You could lose Asia, Africa, and Europe,
No one could get you: you would come through smiling.
You lost your army at Mosul. What happened?
You came companionless, but you came home.
Is it not true? And what was my reward?
This time an all-night banquet, to be sure,

But still food, food. Your one idea was food.
None but a cook's son could be so food-minded.
I knew your father must have been a cook.
I'll bet you anything that's all as King
You think of for your people—feeding them."

But the King said, "Haven't I read somewhere
There is no act more kingly than to give?"

"Yes, but give character and not just food.
A King must give his people character."

"They can't have character unless they're fed."

"You're hopeless" said the slave.

                                    "I guess I am;
I am abject before you," said Darius.
"You know so much, go on, instruct me further.
Tell me some rule for ruling people wisely,
In case I should decide to reign some more.
How shall I give a people character?"

"Make them as happy as is good for them.
But that's a hard one, for I have to add:
Not without consultation with their wishes;
Which is the crevice that lets Progress in.
If we could only stop the Progress somewhere,
At a good point for pliant permanence,
Where Madison attempted to arrest it.
But no, a woman has to be her age,
A nation has to take its natural course
Of Progress round and round in circles
From King to Mob to King to Mob to King
Until the eddy of it eddies out."

"So much for Progress," said Darius meekly.
"Another word that bothers me is Freedom.

You're good at maxims. Say me one on Freedom.
What has it got to do with character?
My satrap Tissaphernes has no end
Of trouble with it in his Grecian cities
Along the Aegean coast. That's all they talk of."

"Behold my son in rags here with his lyre,"
The ex-King said. "We're in this thing together.
He is the one who took the money for me
When I was sold—and small reproach to him.
He's a good boy. 'Twas at my instigation.
I looked on it as a Carnegie grant
For him to make a poet of himself on
If such a thing is possible with money.
Unluckily it wasn't money enough
To be a test. It didn't last him out.
And he may have to turn to something else
To earn a living. I don't interfere.
I want him to be anything he has to.
He has been begging through the Seven Cities
Where Homer begged. He'll tell you about Freedom.
He writes free verse, I'm told, and he is thought
To be the author of the Seven Freedoms,
Free Will, Trade, Verse, Thought, Love, Speech, Coinage.
(You ought to see the coins done in Cos.)
His name is Omar. I as a Rhodes Scholar
Pronounce it Homer with a Cockney rough.
Freedom is slavery some poets tell us.
Enslave yourself to the right leader's truth,
Christ's or Karl Marx', and it will set you free.
Don't listen to their play of paradoxes.
The only certain freedom's in departure.
My son and I have tasted it and know.
We feel it in the moment we depart
As fly the atomic smithereens to nothing.
The problem for the King is just how strict
The lack of liberty, the squeeze of law
And discipline should be in school and state
To insure a jet departure of our going
Like a pip shot from 'twixt our pinching fingers."

"All this facility disheartens me.
Pardon my interruption; I'm unhappy.
I guess I'll have the headsman execute me
And press your father into being King."

"Don't let him fool you: he's a King already.
But though almost all-wise, he makes mistakes.
I'm not a free-verse singer. He was wrong there.
I claim to be no better than I am.
I write real verse in numbers, as they say.
I'm talking not free verse but blank verse now.
Regular verse springs from the strain of rhythm
Upon a metre, strict or loose iambic.
From that strain comes the expression *strains of music*.
The tune is not that metre, not that rhythm,
But a resultant that arises from them.
Tell them Iamb, Jehovah said, and meant it.
Free verse leaves out the metre and makes up
For the deficiency by church intoning.
Free verse so called is really cherished prose,
Prose made of, given an air by church intoning.
It has its beauty, only I don't write it.
And possibly my not writing it should stop me
From holding forth on Freedom like a Whitman—
A Sandburg. But permit me in conclusion:
Tell Tissaphernes not to mind the Greeks.
The freedom they seek is by politics,
Forever voting and haranguing for it.
The reason artists show so little interest
In public freedom is because the freedom
They've come to feel the need of is a kind
No one can give them—they can scarce attain—
The freedom of their own material;
So, never at a loss in simile,
They can command the exact affinity
Of anything they are confronted with.
This perfect moment of unbafflement,
When no man's name and no noun's adjective
But summons out of nowhere like a jinni.
We know not what we owe this moment to.

It may be wine, but much more likely love—
Possibly just well-being in the body,
Or respite from the thought of rivalry.
It's what my father must mean by departure,
Freedom to flash off into wild connections.
Once to have known it nothing else will do.
Our days all pass awaiting its return.
You must have read the famous valentine
Pericles sent Aspasia in absentia:

*For God himself the height of feeling free*
*Must have been his success in simile*
*When at sight of you he thought of me.*


Let's see, where are we? Oh, we're in transition,
Changing an old King for another old one.
What an exciting age it is we live in—
With all this talk about the hope of youth
And nothing made of youth. Consider me,
How totally ignored I seem to be.
No one is nominating me for King.
The headsman has Darius by the belt
To lead him off the Asiatic way
Into oblivion without a lawyer.
But that is as Darius seems to want it.
No fathoming the Asiatic mind.
And father's in for what we ran away from.
And superstition wins. He blames the stars,
Aldebaran, Capella, Sirius,
(As I remember they were summer stars
The night we ran away from Ctesiphon)
For looking on and not participating.
(Why are we so resentful of detachment?)
But don't tell me it wasn't his display
Of more than royal attributes betrayed him.
How hard it is to keep from being king
When it's in you and in the situation.
And that is half the trouble with the world
(Or more than half I'm half inclined to say)."

## Lines Written in Dejection
## on the Eve of Great Success

I once had a cow that jumped over the moon,
Not on to the moon but over.
I don't know what made her so lunar a loon;
All she'd been having was clover.

That was back in the days of my godmother Goose.
But though we are goosier now,
And all tanked up with mineral juice,
We haven't caught up with my cow.

### POSTSCRIPT

But if over the moon I had wanted to go
And had caught my cow by the tail,
I'll bet she'd have made a melodious low
And put her foot in the pail;

Than which there is no indignity worse.
A cow did that once to a fellow
Who rose from the milking stool with a curse
And cried, "I'll larn you to bellow."

He couldn't lay hands on a pitchfork to hit her
Or give her a stab of the tine,
So he leapt on her hairy back and bit her
Clear into her marrow spine.

No doubt she would have preferred the fork.
She let out a howl of rage
That was heard as far away as New York
And made the papers' front page.

He answered her back, "Well, who begun it?"
That's what at the end of a war
We always say—not who won it,
Or what it was foughten for.

## The Milky Way Is a Cowpath

On wings too stiff to flap
We started to exult
In having left the map
On journey the penult.

But since we got nowhere,
Like small boys we got mad
And let go at the air
With everything we had.

Incorrigible Quid-nuncs,
We *would* see what would come
Of pelting heaven with chunks
Of crude uranium.

At last in self-collapse
We owned up to our wife
The Milky Way perhaps
Was woman's way of life.

Our un-outwitted spouse
Replied she had as soon
Believe it was the cow's
That overshot the moon.

The parabolic curve
Of her celestial track
As any might observe
Might never bring her back.

The famous foster nurse
Of man and womankind
Had for the universe
Left trivia behind;

And gone right on astray
Through let-down pasture bars

Along the Milky Way
A-foraging on stars,

Perennial as flowers,
To where as some allege
This universe of ours
Has got a razor edge;

And if she don't take care
She'll get her gullet cut,
But that is no affair
Of anybody's but—

The author of these words
Whose lifelong unconcern
Has been with flocks and herds
For what they didn't earn.

## Some Science Fiction

The chance is the remotest
Of its going much longer unnoticed
That I'm not keeping pace
With the headlong human race.

And some of them may mind
My staying back behind
To take life at a walk
In philosophic talk;

Though as yet they only smile
At how slow I do a mile,
With tolerant reproach
For me as an Old Slow Coach.

But I know them what they are:
As they get more nuclear

And more bigoted in reliance
On the gospel of modern science,

For them my loitering around
At less than the speed of sound
Or even the speed of light
Won't seem unheretical quite.

They may end by banishing me
To the penal colony
They are thinking of pretty soon
Establishing on the moon.

With a can of condensed air
I could go almost anywhere,
Or rather submit to be sent
As a noble experiment.

They should try one wastrel first
On a landscape so accursed
To see how long they should wait
Before they make it a state.

\*

## ENVOI TO HYDE THE CASTAWAY
## OF CROW ISLAND

I made this you to beguile
With some optimism for Christmas
On your isle that would be an isle
But isn't because it's an isthmus.

## Quandary

Never have I been sad or glad
That there was such a thing as bad.
There had to be, I understood,
For there to have been any good.
It was by having been contrasted
That good and bad so long had lasted.
That's why discrimination reigns.
That's why we need a lot of brains
If only to discriminate
'Twixt what to love and what to hate.
To quote the oracle of Delphi,
Love thou thy neighbor as thyself, aye,
And hate him as thyself thou hatest.
There quandary is at its greatest.
We learned from the forbidden fruit
For brains there is no substitute.
"Unless it's sweetbreads," you suggest
With innuendo I detest.
You drive me to confess in ink:
Once I was fool enough to think
That brains and sweetbreads were the same,
Till I was caught and put to shame,
First by a butcher, then a cook,
Then by a scientific book.
But 'twas by making sweetbreads do
I passed with such a high I.Q.

## A Reflex

Hear my rigmarole.
Science stuck a pole
Down a likely hole
And he got it bit.
Science gave a stab
And he got a grab.
That was what he got.
"Ah," he said, "Qui vive,
Who goes there, and what
ARE we to believe?
That there is an It?"

## In a Glass of Cider

It seemed I was a mite of sediment
That waited for the bottom to ferment
So I could catch a bubble in ascent.
I rode up on one till the bubble burst
And when that left me to sink back reversed
I was no worse off than I was at first.
I'd catch another bubble if I waited.
The thing was to get now and then elated.

## From Iron

### Tools and Weapons

To Ahmed S. Bokhari

Nature within her inmost self divides
To trouble men with having to take sides.

Four-room shack aspiring high
With an arm of scrawny mast
For the visions in the sky
That go blindly pouring past.
In the ear and in the eye
What you get is what to buy.
Hope you're satisfied to last.

But outer Space,
At least this far,
For all the fuss
Of the popul*ace*,
Stays more popu*lar*
Than popul*ous*.

## On Being Chosen Poet of Vermont

Breathes there a bard who isn't moved
When he finds his verse is understood
And not entirely disapproved
By his country and his neighborhood?

We vainly wrestle with the blind belief
That aught we cherish
Can ever quite pass out of utter grief
And wholly perish.

---

It takes all sorts of in and outdoor schooling
To get adapted to my kind of fooling.

---

In winter in the woods alone
Against the trees I go.
I mark a maple for my own
And lay the maple low.

At four o'clock I shoulder axe
And in the afterglow
I link a line of shadowy tracks
Across the tinted snow.

I see for Nature no defeat
In one tree's overthrow
Or for myself in my retreat
For yet another blow.

UNCOLLECTED POEMS

# Contents

## La Noche Triste

TENOCHTITLAN.

Changed is the scene: the peace
And regal splendor which
Once that city knew are gone,
And war now reigns upon
That throng, who but
A week ago were all
Intent on joy supreme.
Cries of the wounded break
The stillness of the night,
Or challenge of the guard.
The Spaniard many days
Besieged within the place,
Where kings did rule of old,
Now pressed by hunger by
The all-relentless foe,
Looks for some channel of
Escape. The night is dark;
Black clouds obscure the sky—
A dead calm lies o'er all.
The heart of one is firm,
His mind is constant still,
To all, his word is law.
Cortes his plan hath made,
The time hath come. Each one
His chosen place now takes,
There waits the signal, that
Will start the long retreat.

THE FLIGHT.

Anon the cry comes down the line,
The portals wide are swung,
A long dark line moves out the gate,
And now the flight's begun.

Aye, cautiously it moves at first,
As ship steered o'er the reef,
Looking for danger all unseen,
But which may bring to grief.

Straight for the causeway now they make,
The bridge is borne before,
'Tis ta'en and placed across the flood,
And all go trooping o'er.

Yet e'er the other side is reached,
Wafted along the wind,
The rolling of the snake-skin drum
Comes floating from behind.

And scarcely has its rolling ceased,
Than out upon the lake,
Where all was silence just before,
A conch the calm doth break.

What terror to each heart it bears,
That sound of ill portent,
Each gunner to escape now looks,
On safety all are bent.

Forward they press in wild despair,
On to the next canal,
Held on all sides by foe and sea,
Like deer within corral.

Now surging this way, now in that,
The mass sways to and fro,
The infidel around it sweeps—
Slowly the night doth go.

A war cry soundeth through the night,
The 'tzin! the 'tzin! is there,
His plume nods wildly o'er the scene,
Oh, Spaniard, now beware!

With gaping jaws the cannon stands,
Points it among the horde;
The valiant Leon waits beside,
Ready with match and sword.

The 'tzin quick springeth to his side,
His mace he hurls on high,
It crasheth through the Spanish steel,
And Leon prone doth lie.

Falling, he died beneath his gun,—
He died at duty's call,
And many falling on that night,
Dying, so died they all.

The faithful guarders at the bridge,
Have worked with might and main,
Nor can they move it from its place,
Swollen by damp of rain.

On through the darkness comes the cry,
The cry that all is lost;
Then e'en Cortes takes up the shout,
And o'er the host 'tis tossed.

Some place their safety in the stream,
But sink beneath the tide,
E'en others crossing on the dead,
Thus reach the other side.

Surrounded and alone he sits,
Upon his faithful steed;
Here Alvarado clears a space,
But none might share the deed—

For darkness of that murky night
Hides deeds of brightest fame,
Which in the ages yet to come,
Would light the hero's name.

His faithful charger now hath fall'n,
Pierced to the very heart.
Quick steps he back, his war cry shouts,
Then onward doth he dart.

Runs he, and leaping high in air,
Fixed does he seem a space,
One instant and the deed is done,
He standeth face to face—

With those who on the other side
Their safety now have found.
The thirst for vengeance satisfied,
The Aztec wheels around.

So, as the sun climbs up the sky,
And shoots his dawning rays,
The foe, as parted by his dart,
Each go their sep'rate ways.

Upon the ground the dead men lie,
Trampled midst gold and gore,
The Aztec toward his temple goes,
For now the fight is o'er.

Follow we not the Spaniard more,
Wending o'er hill and plain,
Suffice to say he reached the coast,
Lost Fortune to regain.

The flame shines brightest e'er goes out,
Thus with the Aztec throne,
On that dark night before the end,
So o'er the fight it shone.

The Montezumas are no more,
Gone is their regal throne,
And freemen live, and rule, and die,
Where they have ruled alone.

1890

## Song of the Wave

"Rolling, rolling, o'er the deep,
Sunken treasures neath me sleep
As I shoreward slowly sweep.

Onward peacefully I roll,
Ever thoughtless of the goal,
Sea-bells round me chime and toll.

There is peace above, below,
Far beneath me sea-weeds grow,
Tiny fish glide to and fro,

Now in sunlight, now in shade,
Lost within some ocean glade
By the restless waters made.

Pushing onward as before,
Now descry the distant shore,
Hear the breakers sullen roar;

Quicken then my rolling pace,
With glad heart I join the race
O'er the white-capp'd glittering space,

Thinking naught of woe or grief,
Dancing, prancing, like a leaf,
Caring not for cliff or reef.

Lo! black cliffs above me loom,
Casting o'er me awful gloom,
And fortell my coming doom.

O! that I might reach the land,
Reach and lave the sunny sand,
But these rocks on every hand—

Seem my joyous course to stay,
Rise and bar my happy way,
Shutting out the sun's bright ray.

I must now my proud crest lower
And the wild sea roam no more."
Hark! the crash and mighty roar,
Then the wave's short life is o'er.

1890

## A Dream of Julius Cæsar

A dreamy day; a gentle western breeze
That murmurs softly 'midst the sylvan shades;
Above, the fleecy clouds glide slowly on
To sink from view; within the forest's depth,
A thrush's drowsy note starts echoes through
The vistas of the over-hanging trees.
All nature seems to weave a circle of
Enchantment round the mind, and give full sway
To flitting thoughts and dreams of bygone years.
Thus, as the summer afternoon wears on,
In Nature's cradle lulled to calm repose,
I watch the shifting of a purling rill,
As visions of a busy throng, of life,
Of passing days that come not back again,
Rush in confusion through my weary brain;
Till rumblings wafted o'er the distant hills,
Proclaim a timely warning to the one
Who, wandering far from shelter and from home,
Forgets that space exists, that still he lives:—
But, wrapped in Nature's all entrancing shroud,
Is lured to seek her wildest inmost realms.
The dying cadences are tossed from vale
To vale, but fall unheeded on my ear.
Anon, the winds burst on the silent scene,

And cause the leaves to dance and sing for joy.
Then clouds with bosoms darker than the night,
Rise up along the whole horizon's brink,
And all the sky is flecked with hurrying forms.
Thus, ever as the storm comes on, led by
The heralds of its wrathful power, between
The foremost rifts, like ladders long, by which
From earth to heaven the woodland nymphs may pass
Beyond the clouds, bright rays of light stretch down
Upon each grove and mead.
      So, far and wide
A charm of magic breathes its spell around:
For at my feet a far upreaching ladder rests,
And as I gaze, a form, scarce seen at first,
Glides down; a moment, and before me stands,
With stately mien and noble wreathéd brow,
His toga streaming to the western wind,
The restless fire still gleaming in those eyes,
Just as before the Roman Senate, years
Agone, he stood and ruled a people with
His mighty will, Cæsar, first conqueror of
The Roman World. Within his hand the bolt
Of Jove gleams forth with frequent flash. Clasping
The toga's waving folds, a gem of ray
Most pure, that nigh outshines the sun, rests like
The dew of heaven. I gaze in awe, a space;
Then, with majestic mien, he points me toward
A bridge, an ancient moss-grown trunk that fell
In some fierce storm to join the brook's green banks,
And speaks: "Be gone! from Jupiter I come
To rule with storm and darkness o'er the world,"
Then with uplifted arm: "Look up, behold
My might, my legions. Conquest still is the
One passion of this fiery breast. Speak they
Farewell to all this scene of quietude
And peace; ere from this hand I launch the fire
Of Jove, and pierce the darkness with its gleam;
Ere yonder cohorts with resistless march
Spread terror in the air and vanquish light."

He speaks and vanishes from sight. The roar
Of chariot wheels breaks on my ear. The fight
Is on, for blood in torrents falls around,
Not crimson, but a lighter hue, such as
The fairy hosts of silvery light might shed.

1891

## Our Camp

### in the Autumn Woods

In a haunt in the depths of the forest,
    Enshrined by a lonely wood lake,
With the trees bending over its waters
    Where moon-crested ripples break,—

Where far down the long arching vistas,
    The moon-beams all peacefully lie,
And the night wind that steals through the tree-tops,
    Moans softly and lingers by:—

Here, oft in the midnight above me,
    I watch a lone, hemlock-wreathed star;
Till over the sands of the silence,
    Wave music comes swelling afar.

My mind is born on by the singing,
    A rudderless craft on the deep;
And 'tis left by the ebbing waters,
    To strand on the sands of sleep.

1891

## Clear and Colder

*Boston Common*

As I went down through the common,
  It was bright with the light of day,
For the wind and rain had swept the leaves
  And the shadow of summer away.
The walks were all fresh-blacked with rain
  As I went briskly down:—
I felt my own quick step begin
  The pace of the winter town.

As I went down through the common,
  The sky was wild and pale;
I saw one tree with a jib of leaves
  In the stress of the aftergale;
But the others rattled naked poles
  As I went briskly down.
I felt my own quick step begin
  The pace of the winter town.

As I went down through the common
  In the crisp October dawn,
Benches were wet and stuck with leaves
  And the idle ones were gone.
The folk abroad raced on with me
  As I went briskly down.
I felt my own quick step begin
  The pace of the winter town.

As I went down through the common,
  Then felt I first delight
Of the city's thronging winter days
  And dazzling winter night,
Of the life and revelry to be—
  As I went briskly down.
I felt my own quick step begin
  The pace of the winter town.

1891

## The Sachem of the Clouds

*(A Thanksgiving Legend)*

When the sedge upon the meadows crosses, falls and
 interweaves,
Spent, the brook lies wrapt in silence on its bed of autumn
 leaves;
When the barren fields are moaning, where the Autumn
 winds rush by,
And the leaves start up in eddies and are whirled athwart
 the sky;

On the lonely hillside, darkened by the over-hurrying
 clouds,
Ghostly, stand the withered corn-rows, in their waving
 moonlight shrouds,
Like the band of those departed, murmuring with discontent,
Come again to tell their sadness, hid in vengeance as they
 went.

Then the traveler, wending downward from the mountain's
 fading height,
Deep among the woody marshes, stretching back within the
 night,
Sees a hermit, grey and feeble, dwarfed beside a giant oak,
Sees the sachem of the storm-cloud, clad about with
 wreaths of smoke,

Piling high his pyre of hemlocks, weaving spell and crossing
 limb,
Till a hazy phosphorescence plays around the circle's rim;
All night long, 'mid incantations, hears the wizard's voice
 arise,
On the bleak wind wildly mingled with the forest's eerie cries.

And when far the flames up-reaching, lurid, gleam upon
 the vale,
Then the wizard's muttered croaking rises to a piercing wail:
"Come, O come, with storm, come darkness! Speed my
 clouds on Winter's breath.

All my race is gone before me, all my race is low in death!
Ever, as I ruled a people, shall this smoke arise in cloud;
Ever shall it freight the tempest for the ocean of the proud.
'Thanks!' I hear their cities thanking that my race is low in
     death,
Come, O come, with storm, come darkness! Speed my
     clouds on Winter's breath!"

Thus his voice keeps ringing, ringing, till appears the dreary
     dawn,
And the traveler, looking backward, sees the ashes on the
     lawn,
Sees the smoke crowd to the hilltops, torn away, and
     hurried south,
Hears a shrieking answer speeded from the Winter's snowy
     mouth.

                                                    1891


## Parting

### To —— ——

I dreamed the setting sun would rise no more.
My spirit fled; nor sought an aimless sun
Whirled madly on through pathless space, and free
Amid a world of worlds enthralled. Ah no!
But deep within a silent solitude
It lingered on. The twilight waned; across
The hills and dark'ning sky the west wind stole,
And broad-cast spread the sun-path gathered gold,
Undying memories of the hopeless dead.
The dew of sadness fell, and far into
The coming night of storm and calm I gazed.
Oh, sadness, who may tell what joy is thine?
A whisper breathed: "What lies unvoiced on earth
Is heaven sung." And gloom crept softly down
With longing deep as everlasting night.

                                                    1891

## Down the Brook

I leave the meadow for the brook,
        Speed, speed, my icy carriers,
    Away, away, the black ice lies,
And where I glide, on either side
        The woody midnight's rise—
            Speed, speed, speed on ye tarriers.
The ice-fields fall—a distant boom—
On, on, from gloom to deeper gloom—
            Speed, speed, let darkness follow.
Alone, alone, the breezes moan
Gives steel to steel; I wheel and reel
            On rippled ice and hollow.
The ice once more is smooth, before
    I swerve from brook to river,
        And as I dash, the musk-rat's plash
Comes from the hazy, fleeing shore,
    Where first the moonbeams quiver.

## and Back

The moon is up, and I am weary.
Beyond, the lane-like brook lies dreary;
Hours fleet, I stumble on o'er crusted snow;
With reeds the ice is bearded as I go.
Afar I wend, and I am weary,—
The clouded moon is dim and bleary.

1891

## The Traitor

Sea-bird of the battle surf,
      Lorna is dead.
Black on Colla's castled hill
      Ruin is spread.
Weep for Lorna who rode forth
With his king against the North.

Lorna came again at morn,
      Riding from war.
Messenger of battle won,
      Tidings he bore:—
"Quenchless was the charge he made,
Low the insurgent walls were laid."

And while revelry was rife
      Through Colla's halls,
Then the lonely warder saw,
      Pacing the walls,
Eastward in the morning's greys,
Serried spears in the sunrise blaze.

By an altar in a vault—
      Night dripping dew—
Lorna's muffled cry arose;
      Bat-like it flew:—
"Sacrifice for victory!
Priest and victim find in me!"

Sea-bird of the battle surf,
      Lorna is dead.
Black on Colla's castled hill
      Ruin is spread.
Royal seal upon the tomb
Where he sleeps in endless gloom.

1892

## Class Hymn

There is a nook among the alders
Still sleeping to the cat-bird's "Hush";
　Below, a long stone-bridge is bending
Above a runnel's silent rush.

　A dreamer hither often wanders
And gathers many a snow-white stone;
　He weighs them, poised upon his fingers,
Divining each one's silvery tone.

　He drops them! When the stream makes music,
Fair visions with its vault-voice swell:
　And so, for us, the future rises,
As thought-stones stir our heart's "Farewell!"

1892

## Twilight

Why am I first in thy so sad regard,
O twilight gazing from I know not where?
I fear myself as one more than I guessed!
Am I instead of one so very fair?—
That thou art sorrowful and I oppressed?

High in the isolating air,
Over the inattentive moon,
Two birds sail on great wings,
　　　And vanish soon.
(And they leave the north sky bare!)

The far-felt solitudes that harbor night,
Wake to the singing of the wood-bird's fright.

By invocation, O wide silentness,
Thy spirit and my spirit pass in air!
They are unmemoried consciousness,
        Nor great nor less!
And thou art here and I am everywhere!

1894

## Summering

I would arise and in a dream go on—
Not very far, not very far—and then
Lie down amid the sunny grass again,
And fall asleep till night-time or next dawn.

In sleepy self-sufficiency I'd turn;
I'd seek new comfort and be hard to please—
Far in a meadow by an isle of trees,
All summer long amid the grass and fern.

Forests would have to be all round about,
And the mead silent, and the grasses deep,
Else I might not gain such a tireless sleep!
I could not slumber if the wains were out!

1894

## The Falls

'Tis a steep wood of rocks,
With the fern grown everywhere;
But with no birds—not a wing!
And the falls come down there.

Even an Indian trail
Would swerve to a haunt so fair!
One used to—there were the ferns
And the falls came down there.

1894

## An Unhistoric Spot

Ah passionate is rest when to the earth
I yield in full length contact of sweet pain!
Here just within the bars in the chill grass,
And the great shadow of a fruitless tree,
I at once sleep and am awake in joy.
And when I sit half-conscious on the slope,
And lean upon one grass-wrought hand and gaze,
The lone thrush gurgles nectar in his throat,
On some green spire, adjusting his furled wings,
The local cricket quavers to the wind,
And every one that passes looks at me.

1894

## The Birds Do Thus

I slept all day.
    The birds do thus
That sing a while
    At eve for us.

To have you soon
    I gave away—
Well satisfied
    To give—a day.

Life's not so short
    I care to keep
The unhappy days;
    I choose to sleep.

1896

## A Summer's Garden

I made a garden just to keep about me
The birds and things I love, all summer long.
I doubt not they'd live well enough without me;
How would I live without them—their sweet song?

I made a garden and had my own flowers—
All that I cared to pick and more too, there.
Most of them died and fell in scented showers
Upon the beds, and colored the warm air.

Mine was not such a garden as I'd thought of—
A deep wild garden that no hand has trimmed
In many years—a tangle that is wrought of
Old fashioned flowers 'neath old trees, barren limbed

But so my flowers brought the insects winging,
The butterflies, the neighbors' murmuring bees,
And birds one must not cage or they cease singing,
I asked no more, well satisfied with these.

My garden my fair garden! I saw wither
Flower, leaf, and branch, and from the maple bough
Leaves race across the bare beds none knows whither.
The lives I entertained where are they now?

1896

## Cæsar's Lost Transport Ships

Some fell away to westward with the wind,
And one full darkly figured on the sun
At sunset; but the fight on Briton's beach
Got us a shelter under Dover cliff,
And all night long a voice made wild lament
Circling the confines of the restless camp;
So that we had sad thoughts of those at sea.

There would no messenger come back from them!
Each one alone went leaping down the world
With no sail set, deserted on the deck,
And in the hull a tremor of low speech.
And overhead the petrel wafted wide.

1891–97

## Greece

They say: "Let there be no more war!"
  And straightway, at the word,
Along the Mediterranean shore,
  The call to arms is heard.

Greece could not let her glory fade!
  Although peace be in sight,
The race the Persian wars arrayed
  Must fight one more good fight.

Greece! rise triumphant. Long ago
  It was you proved to men,
A few may countless hosts o'erthrow:
  Now prove it once again!

1897

## Warning

The days will come when you will cease to know,
 The heart will cease to tell you; sadder yet,
Tho you say o'er and o'er what once you knew,
 You will forget, you will forget.

There is no memory for what is true,
 The heart once silent. Well may you regret,
Cry out upon it, that you have known all
 But to forget, but to forget.

Blame no one but yourself for this, lost soul!
 I feared it would be so that day we met
Long since, and you were changed. And I said then,
 He will forget, he will forget.

1895–Sept. 1897

## God's Garden

God made a beauteous garden
 With lovely flowers strown,
But one straight, narrow pathway
 That was not overgrown.
And to this beauteous garden
 He brought mankind to live,
And said: "To you, my children,
 These lovely flowers I give.
Prune ye my vines and fig trees,
 With care my flowerets tend,
But keep the pathway open,
 Your home is at the end."

Then came another master,
 Who did not love mankind,
And planted on the pathway
 Gold flowers for them to find.

And mankind saw the bright flowers,
   That, glitt'ring in the sun,
Quite hid the thorns of av'rice
   That poison blood and bone;
And far off many wandered,
   And when life's night came on,
They still were seeking gold flowers,
   Lost, helpless and alone.

O, cease to heed the glamour
   That blinds your foolish eyes,
Look upward to the glitter
   Of stars in God's clear skies.
Their ways are pure and harmless
   And will not lead astray,
But aid your erring footsteps
   To keep the narrow way.
And when the sun shines brightly
   Tend flowers that God has given
And keep the pathway open
   That leads you on to heaven.

1898

## The Rubaiyat of Carl Burell

There was a young fellow, begad,
Who hadn't, but wished that he had—
   God only knows what,
   But he blasphemed a lot
And showed he was generally mad.

There was a young man from Vermont,
Who voted for Bryan and Want
   And argued demented,
   But now he's repented,
So be easy on him and Vermont.

There was a young poet who tried
Making boxes when preoccupied;
   One day he made one
   And when he got done,
He had nailed himself on the inside.

There was a man went for to harma
Quiet but human old farmer:
   Now he wishes he'd known
   To let folks alone,
For this is the doctrine of Karma.

There was a young man moribund, who
Met with a fate few or none do
   He went out one day
   In his usual way
And was eaten alive by a sun-dew.

1898

———————

The reason of my perfect ease
In the society of trees
Is that their cruel struggles pass
Too far below my social class
For me to share them or be made
For what I am and love afraid.

ca. 1890s

### Evensong

Came the wind last
When the dew was strown?
  Someone has passed,
   That the stars are down:
Out of the sunset,
   Into the twilight,
Someone has passed,
   That the stars are down.

ca. 1890s

### Despair

I am like a dead diver after all's
Done, still held fast in the weeds' snare below,
Where in the gloom his limbs begin to glow
Swaying at his moorings as the roiled bottom falls.
There was a moment when with vainest calls
He drank the water, saying, 'Oh let me go—
*God* let me go,'—for then he could not know
As in the sun's warm light on earth and walls.

I am like a dead diver in this place.
I was alive here too one desperate space,
And near prayer in the one whom I invoked.
I tore the muscles from my limbs and choked.
My sudden struggle may have dragged down some
White lily from the air—and now the fishes come.

ca. 1890s

## Old Age

My old uncle is long and narrow.
And when he starts to rise
After his after-dinner nap
I think to myself
He may do it this once more
But this is the last time.
He lets one leg slip off the lounge
And fall to the floor.
But still he lies
And looks to God through the ceiling.
The next thing is to get to his outside elbow
And so to a sitting posture
And so to his feet.
I avert my eyes for him till he does it.
Once I said from the heart,
"What is it, Uncle?—
Pain or just weakness?
Can't we do anything for it?"
He said "It's Specific Gravity"
"Do you mean by that that it's grave?"
"No, not as bad as that yet, child,
But it's the Grave coming on."
Then I knew he didn't mean Seriousness
When he said Gravity.
Old age may not be kittenish
But it is not necessarily serious.

1903

## A Winter's Night

Oh, little cot beside the wood,
Whose windows twain are dark with sleep,
Thine icicles along the eves
The moon shall keep, the moon shall keep.

The rounded snow upon thy roof,
The snows about thee many deep,
Far better than the midday sun,
The moon shall keep, the moon shall keep.

1905

## Love Being All One

Could I forget thee, I should forget
(Love being all one) to stand at gaze
Sometimes descending by winding ways
And say of the earth, How very fair!
I should forget to forget dull care.

Could I forget thee, I should forget
(Love being all one) the pride of youth
That would not abate one tittle of truth—
Such things as are reckoned or rendered vain.
I should forget to forget my gain.

Could I forget thee, I should forget
(Love being all one) the thing afar
We may face like a faintly illuming star
But were never destined to run to, sweet.
I should forget to forget defeat.

1905

## Midsummer Birds

Could there be aught more hushed
Than their quietest of wings,
It is their treble voices now
As they drop from the sacred bough
Intent on distant things.

Could there be aught more safe
Than the hush in which they flit,
It is the little driven nest
That leans out high o'er every quest
With its darkness of the pit.

In the warm field to which
They dip, blue-winged, all day,
The tree about the fruit it feeds,
The grass about its little seeds,
Is not more still than they.

1905

## The Mill City

It was in a drear city by a stream,
And all its denizens were sad to me,—
I could not fathom what their life could be—
Their passage in the morning like a dream
In the arc-light's unnatural bluish beam,
Then back, at night, like drowned men from the sea,
Up from the mills and river hurriedly,
In weeds of labor, to the shriek of steam.

Yet I supposed that they had all one hope
With me (there is but one.) I would go out,
When happier ones drew in for fear of doubt,
Breasting their current, resolute to cope
With what thoughts they compelled who thronged
     the street,
Less to the sound of voices than of feet.

1905

## What Thing a Bird Would Love

As I was faring home
The slow hill-climbing way
A lonely bird sang once
And seemed to bid me stay.

I paused to rest and turned,
And if I had not turned,
I had not seen the west
Behind me, how it burned.

So when he sang again
As I resumed the slope,
My heart regarded him—
I turned again with hope.

The sunset!—and beneath
The valley ebon dark
And featureless, wherein
A lamp was but a spark.

But that he would not cease,
But still would call and call
When I must go was proof
The sunset was not all.

I left him to the waste
And gathering stars above,
In doubt if I could know
What thing a bird would love.

1905

## When the Speed Comes

When the speed comes a-creeping overhead
And belts begin to snap and shafts to creak,
And the sound dies away of them that speak,
And on the glassy floor the tapping tread;
When dusty globes on all a pallor shed,
And breaths of many wheels are on the cheek;
Unwilling is the flesh, the spirit weak,
All effort like arising from the dead.

But the task ne'er could wait the mood to come;
The music of the iron is a law:
And as upon the heavy spools that pay
Their slow white thread, so ruthlessly the hum
Of countless whirling spindles seems to draw
Upon the soul, still sore from yesterday.

1906

## The Later Minstrel

Remember some departed day,
    When bathed in autumn gold,
You wished for some sweet song, and sighed
    For minstrel days of old.

And that same golden autumn day,
    Perhaps the fates would bring
At eve, one knocking at your heart,
    With perfect songs to sing.

You knew that never bard on earth,
    Did wander wide as he—
Who sang the long, long thoughts of Youth,
    The Secret of the Sea.

You knew not when he might not come,
    But while he made delays,
You wronged the wisdom that you had,
    And sighed for vanished days.

Song's times and seasons are its own,
    Its ways past finding out,
But more and more it fills the earth,
    And triumphs over doubt.

1907

## The Lost Faith

We shrine our fathers as their wars recede
With the heroic dead that died of old,
We shall strew flowers for them year after year;
They shall have flowers themselves more than they need!
But for the cause that was to them so dear,
Where shall it be so much as justly told
What that cause was?—which, as they lie in mould,
In our hearts dies as cold.
Have we for that no flowers, no mournful rhythm,
The soldiers' dream, that when they died, died with them?

No less a dream than of one law of love,
One equal people under God above!
But fallen to be a word of easy scorn,
See if it dies not—if it is not dead!
Who in our latter wisdom so unread
As not to know
Dark life too well for such a dream of morn,
What child so uninured to literal woe?
The Californian, by the western sea
Exults, and by the Gulf they laugh,
Saying, 'How can all men be free,
How equal, when God made them wheat and chaff?'
They mock, that, in these recreant hearts of ours,
There should no fingering answer be,
And where it sprung the dream at last should fade
That did defy their powers.

Too strange it seems to men of the dull throng
That such belief can have been soldier's shroud
More glorious than his battle colors proud.
Yet how they do them wrong!
'Twere not enough to reckon the men brave,
'Twere not enough to reckon the men strong,
Not with the men themselves,—far more they crave
One tribute to the meaning of their strife,
To which they gave youth, life.

It was the dream that woke them in the north,
And led the young men forth,
And pitched against the embittered foe their tent;
And fought their fight for them on many a field,
Their sword, their shield,
The still small voice that like a clarion pealed;
Strong as a dream and deathless as a dream,
As it did seem,
(Though destined to go down the way they went.)

The dream that, as it sent them on that way,
Gave Love the strength to stay
In these brave hills apart—
It, and naught else, for many a fireside heart!

Oh, such a dream as cannot have lost worth
Forever, for an unredeemed earth.
I cannot make it wholly dead to men.
Not late, but soon, it must return again—
In blood mayhap, with maddening fife and drum,
And reaping souls—I care not, so it come!
All beautiful and human as it was,
It could be terrible in its own cause;
As when it swept the skirts of Malvern Hill
And when it crouched in wait as deadly still
On Gettysburg's low height,
As the oncoming foe were swift and shrill.
Men knew us not until that wavering fight!
And keep not now the thought that moved in us!
How earthly death came ever near to touch

A dream so deathless, we to forget it thus,
I do not know; we saw it fade from sight,
Not while we slept, but while we strove too much
For things that were not beautiful and bright.

But fair it seems in passing as still day
In fainter gold behind the golden stars,
Or mists on water that the morning ray,
Without a seeming zephyr, moves away;
And truer in comparison of truth,
Than all the hopes the years abate from youth;
Truer than aught recovered from the vast
By souls that could not slumber, but must climb
The starlight in far suns to dwell a time—
So true in passing, if it must be past.

1907

## *Genealogical*

It was my grandfather's grandfather's grandfather's
Great-great-grandfather or thereabouts I think—
One cannot be too precise in a matter like this.
He was hanged the story goes. Yet not for grief
Have I vowed a pilgrimage to the place where he lies
Under a notable bowlder in Eliot, Maine,
But for pride if for aught at this distance of time.
Yearly a chosen few of his many descendants
At solemn dinner assembled tell over the story
Of how in his greatness of heart he aspired
To wipe out the whole of an Indian tribe to order,
As in those extravagant days they wasted the woods
With fire to clear the land for tillage.
It seems he was rather pointedly *not* instructed
To proceed in the matter with any particular
Regard to the laws of civilized warfare.
He wasted no precious time in casting about
For means he could call his own. He simply seized
Upon any unprotected idea that came to hand.
I will not set up the claim for my progenitor
That he was an artist in murder or anything else,

Or that any of his descendants would have been
Without the infusion of warmer blood from somewhere.
Were it imperative to distinguish between statesman and
    artist
I should say that the first believes that the end justifies the
    means
The second that the means justify the end.
The Major (for such was his title) *virumque cano*
Was one of your thoroughgoing jobbers
Who held that the end and means justify each other.
He knew that the Indians were usually in a state of not
    having
Eaten for several days and hungry accordingly.
So he invited them to a barbecue (if that isn't an
    anachronism)
And then as they feasted he fell upon them with slaughter
And all that he didn't slay he bound and sold
Into slavery where Philip the Chief's son went.
And then well satisfied with the day's work
He doubtless called the place something and claimed the
    victory.
All that detracted from the glory of his achievement
Was the escape of a few of the devoted tribesmen
Either by running away or staying away
An awkward remnant that would have lain, methinks,
Even upon my somewhat sophisticated conscience
Given to the sympathetic fallacy of attributing to savages
The feelings of human beings,
More heavily than those who were slain.
He good sleeper and eater serenely forgot them.
But here again he just missed greatness as a captain.
For these waylaid him one Sunday on his way home
From the proper church completely edified
And slew him in turn with great barbarity
And left him outspread for filial burial.
His sons with dignity dug him a decent grave
And duly laid him to rest.
But the Redskins, not quite sure they had done enough
To satisfy the eternal vengeances,
Returned and had him out of the ground and hanged him up.

And so he was hanged!
The indefatigable sons cut him down and buried him again,
And this time to secure him against further disturbance,
With the help of their neighbors at a sort of burying bee
They rolled a stone upon him that once it was sunk in place
Not strong men enough could come at together to lift it.
And there he lies in glory the ancestor of a good many of us.
And I think he explains my lifelong liking for Indians.

1908

## The Parlor Joke

You won't hear unless I tell you
How the few to turn a penny
Built complete a modern city
Where there shouldn't have been any,
And then conspired to fill it
With the miserable many.

They drew on Ellis Island.
They had but to raise a hand
To let the living deluge
On the basin of the land.
They did it just like nothing
In smiling self-command.

If you asked them *their* opinion,
They declared the job as good
As when, to fill the sluices,
They turned the river flood;
Only then they dealt with water
And now with human blood.

Then the few withdrew in order
To their villas on the hill,
Where they watched from easy couches
The uneasy city fill.
"If it *isn't* good," they ventured,
"At least it isn't ill."

But with child and wife to think of,
They weren't taking any chance.
So they fortified their windows
With a screen of potted plants,
And armed themselves from somewhere
With a manner and a glance.

You know how a bog of sphagnum
Beginning with a scum
Will climb the side of a mountain,
So the poor began to come,
Climbing the hillside suburb
From the alley and the slum.

As their tenements crept nearer,
It pleased the rich to assume,
In humorous self-pity,
The mockery of gloom
Because the poor insisted
On wanting all the room.

And there it might have ended
In a feeble parlor joke,
Where a gentle retribution
Overtook the gentlefolk;
But that some beheld a vision:
Out of stench and steam and smoke,

Out of vapor of sweat and breathing,
They saw materialize
Above the darkened city
Where the murmur never dies,
A shape that had to cower
Not to knock against the skies.

They could see it through a curtain,
They could see it through a wall,
A lambent swaying presence
In wind and rain and all,
With its arms abroad in heaven
Like a scarecrow in a shawl.

There were some who thought they heard it
When it seemed to try to talk
But missed articulation
With a little hollow squawk,
Up indistinct in the zenith,
Like the note of the evening hawk.

Of things about the future
Its hollow chest was full,
Something about rebellion
And blood a dye for wool,
And how you may pull the world down
If you know the prop to pull.

What to say to the wisdom
That could tempt a nation's fate
By invoking such a spirit
To reduce the labor-rate!
Some people don't mind trouble
If it's trouble up-to-date.

1910


## My Giving

I ask no merrier Christmas
Than the hungry bereft and cold shall know
    That night.
This is all I can give so that none shall want—
My heart and soul to share their depth of woe.
I will not bribe their misery not to haunt
My merrymaking by proffer of boon
That should only mock the grief that is rightly theirs.
Here I shall sit, the fire out, and croon
All the dismal and joy-forsaken airs,
Sole alone, and thirsty with them that thirst,
Hungry with them that hunger and are accurst.
No storm that night can be too untamed for me;
If it is woe on earth, woe let it be!

Am I a child that I should refuse to see?
What could I plead asking them to be glad
      That night?
      My right?
Nay it is theirs that I with them should be sad
      That night.

                             1911

## On the Sale of My Farm

Well-away and be it so,
To the stranger let them go.
Even cheerfully I yield
Pasture or chard, mowing-field,
Yea and wish him all the gain
I required of them in vain.
Yea and I can yield him house,
Barn, and shed, with rat and mouse
To dispute possession of.
These I can unlearn to love.
Since I cannot help it? Good!
Only be it understood,
It shall be no trespassing
If I come again some spring
In the grey disguise of years,
Seeking ache of memory here.

                             1911

## Pussy-willow Time

That every footprint's now a pool,
And every rut a river cool,
Are things light vernal hearts make nought of;
For mud time's pussy-willow time
When tender-hearted bluebirds chime,
And unborn violets first are thought of.

                             1911

## Pursuit of the Word

What, shall there be word single to express
Two Cinderella slippers on the hearth,
Two birds of the air the fowler brings to earth,
Two vowel sounds that haply coalesce,
Two such divinities as came to bless
The white swan-mother, Leda, at a birth,
Two prettiest souls that make of pain and mirth,
Presence and absence, one long life-caress?

Yet none that leaves the vision less than double
Which through bare boughs I saw this April night,
And weds in utterance what was really one,
Venus and new Moon, water-drop and bubble,
Equally hanging at an hour's height
Over the blackened hills that hid the sun?

1911

## The Rain Bath

Do you remember how in camp one day
We boys awoke with shouts of joy to hear
A fresh young gale in the forest plunge and rear
And thrash our sylvan roof with boughs in play?
Suddenly with a jolt some cloud gave way.
Down came a flood, instilling frolic fear.
It reached our bed from the open window near
And brought us standing up from where we lay.

We laughed at that. We flung the house door wide,
Then waited till the rapid sky once more
Turned darkest with the irrepressive tide,
And then, when ripping leaves the wild downpour
Was dashed to mist along the steps and path,
We ran forth naked to the morning bath.

1911

## New Grief

Where two had walked awhile, now only one
One only wandered, like a holy nun,
Down pebbly aisles of summer shadow cool
That slowly brought her,
All dreamy, to the lily-padded pool
And leaping water.

And the mist slowly veered to her unblown,
And breathing through a many colored zone,
Swept her a little while with vague concern
That might have spoken
And asked her word perchance of love's return.
She gave no token,

No token either when it did depart.
Ah, love dies hardly in the broken heart,
And wrestles dumbly with the blind belief
That naught we cherish
Can ever quite pass into utter grief,
Or wholly perish.

1911

## Winter Winds

At twelve o'clock tonight,
When every house is dark,
Who ride the roads alone?
The winds of winter. Hark!

The moon is clear above,
The earth is hard below;
And with a little dust
They drive a little snow.

They make the maples roar,
The withered flowers hiss,
Along the way they go
On such a night as this.

The winds usurp the earth,
And even safely housed,
Folk must cling fast to sleep
Not to be oft aroused.

1911

## In England

Alone in rain I sat today
On top of a gate beside the way,
And a bird came near with muted bill,
And a watery breeze kept blowing chill
From over the hill behind me.

I could not tell what in me stirred
To hill and gate and rain and bird,
Till lifting hair and bathing brow
The watery breeze came fresher now
From over the hill to remind me.

The bird was the kind that follows a ship,
The rain was salt upon my lip,
The hill was an undergoing wave,
And the gate on which I balanced brave
Was a great ship's iron railing.

For the breeze was a watery English breeze
Always fresh from one of the seas,
And the country life the English lead
In beachen wood and clover mead
Is never far from sailing.

1912

## Good Relief

Shall we, then, wish as many as possible
As merry Christmases as possible
And charge the limitation up to thought?
No, be the Christmas card with which we greet:
A Merry Christmas to the World in Full.
And as for happiness not being bought—
Remember how two babes were on the street—
And so were many fathers out on strike,
The vainest of their many strikes in vain,
And lost already as at heart they knew.
But the two babes had stopped alone to look
At Christmas toys behind a window pane,
And play at having anything they chose.
And when I lowered level with the two
And asked them what they saw so much to like,
One confidentially and raptly took
His finger from his mouth and pointed, "Those!"
A little locomotive with a train.
And where he wet the window pane it froze.
What good did it do anyone but him—
His brother at his side, perhaps, and me?
And think of all the world compared with three!
But why like the poor fathers on the curb
Must we be always partizan and grim?
No state has found a perfect cure for grief
In law or gospel or in root or herb.
'Twas in this very city thoroughfare
I heard a doctor of the Kickapoo
By torch light from a cart-tail once declare:
The most that any root or herb can do
In suffering is give you Good Relief.

1912

## In Equal Sacrifice

Thus of old the Douglas did:
He left his land as he was bid
With the royal heart of Robert the Bruce
In a golden case with a golden lid,

To carry the same to the Holy Land;
By which we see and understand
That that was the place to carry a heart
At loyalty and love's command,

And that was the case to carry it in.
The Douglas had not far to win
Before he came to the land of Spain,
Where long a holy war had been

Against the too-victorious Moor;
And there his courage could not endure
Not to strike a blow for God
Before he made his errand sure.

And ever it was intended so,
That a man for God should strike a blow,
No matter the heart he has in charge
For the Holy Land where hearts should go.

But when in battle the foe were met,
The Douglas found him sore beset,
With only strength of the fighting arm
For one more battle passage yet—

And that as vain to save the day
As bring his body safe away—
Only a signal deed to do
And a last sounding word to say.

The heart he wore in a golden chain
He swung and flung forth into the plain,
And followed it crying 'Heart or death!'
And fighting over it perished fain.

So may another do of right,
Give a heart to the hopeless fight,
The more of right the more he loves;
So may another redouble might

For a few swift gleams of the angry brand,
Scorning greatly not to demand
In equal sacrifice with his
The heart he bore to the Holy Land.

1890s–1913

## Asking for Roses

A house that lacks, seemingly, mistress and master,
  With doors that none but the wind ever closes,
Its floor all littered with glass and with plaster;
  It stands in a garden of old-fashioned roses.

I pass by that way in the gloaming with Mary;
  'I wonder,' I say, 'who the owner of those is.'
'Oh, no one you know,' she answers me airy,
  'But one we must ask if we want any roses.'

So we must join hands in the dew coming coldly
  There in the hush of the wood that reposes,
And turn and go up to the open door boldly,
  And knock to the echoes as beggars for roses.

'Pray, are you within there, Mistress Who-were-you?'
  'Tis Mary that speaks and our errand discloses.
'Pray, are you within there? Bestir you, bestir you!
  'Tis summer again; there's two come for roses.

'A word with you, that of the singer recalling—
    Old Herrick: a saying that every maid knows is
A flower unplucked is but left to the falling,
    And nothing is gained by not gathering roses.'

We do not loosen our hands' intertwining
    (Not caring so very much what she supposes),
There when she comes on us mistily shining
    And grants us by silence the boon of her roses.

                                                    1913


## Spoils of the Dead

Two fairies it was
    On a still summer day
Came forth in the woods
    With the flowers to play.

The flowers they plucked
    They cast on the ground
For others, and those
    For still others they found.

Flower-guided it was
    That they came as they ran
On something that lay
    In the shape of a man.

The snow must have made
    The feathery bed
When this one fell
    On the sleep of the dead.

But the snow was gone
    A long time ago,
And the body he wore
    Nigh gone with the snow.

The fairies drew near
  And keenly espied
A ring on his hand
  And a chain at his side.

They knelt in the leaves
  And eerily played
With the glittering things,
  And were not afraid.

And when they went home
  To hide in their burrow,
They took them along
  To play with to-morrow.

When *you* came on death,
  Did you not come flower-guided
Like the elves in the wood?
  I remember that I did.

But I recognised death
  With sorrow and dread,
And I hated and hate
  The spoils of the dead.

1913

## Poets Are Born Not Made

My nose is out of joint
For my father-in-letters—
My father mind you—
Has been brought to bed of another poet,
And I am not nine months old.
It is twins this time
And they came into the world prodigiously united in
    wedlock.
(Don't try to visualize this.)

Already they have written their first poems in vers libre
And sold it within twenty-four hours.
My father-in-letters was the affluent American buyer—
There was no one to bid against him.
The merit of the poems is the new convention
That definitely locates an emotion in the belly,
Instead of scientifically in the viscera at large,
Or mid-Victorianly in the heart.
It voices a desire to grin
With the grin of a beast more scared than frightened
    For why?
Because it is a cinch that twins so well born
    will be able to sell almost anything they write.

1913

———————

I am a Mede and Persian
In my acceptance of harsh laws laid down for me
When you said I could not read
When you said I looked old
When you said I was slow of wit
I knew that you only meant
That you could read
That you looked young
That you were nimble of wit
But I took your words at their face value
I accepted your words like an encyclical letter
It did not matter
At worst they were good medicine
I made my stand elsewhere

I did not ask you to unsay them.
I was willing to take anything you said from you
If I might be permitted to hug the illusion
That you liked my poetry
And liked it for the right reason.

You reviewed me,
And I was not sure—
I was afraid it was not artistically done.
I decided I couldn't use it to impress my friends
Much less my enemies.
But in as much it was praise I was grateful
For praise I do love.

I suspected though that in praising me
You were not concerned so much with my desert
As with your power
That you praised me arbitrarily
And took credit to yourself
In demonstrating that you could thrust anything upon the
     world
Were it never so humble
And bid your will avouch it

And here we come close to what I demanded of you
   I did not want the money that you were disbursing
   among your favorites
   for two American editors.
                         Not that.
All I asked was that you should hold to one thing
That you considered me a poet.
That was why I clung to you
   As one clings to a group of insincere friends
   For fear they shall turn their thoughts against him the
     moment he is out of hearing.
The truth is I was afraid of you

                                        1913

## Flower Guidance

As I went from flower to flower
(I have told you how)
I have told you what I found
Dead not growing on the ground.
Look upon me now.

If you would not find yourself
In an evil hour
Too far on a fatal track
Clasp your hands behind your back.
Never pick a flower.

1912–15

———————

Nothing ever so sincere
That unless it's out of sheer
Mischief and a little queer
It won't prove a bore to hear.

1913–14

———————

                    Franconia, October
Dear Stark Young:

Winter has beaten Summer in fight
And shaken the Summer state.
He has come to her capital city of Trees
To find but an open gate,

None to resist him; Summer herself
Gone from her windy towers,
First having hurried away her birds
And hidden away her flowers.

He has set her desert citadel
In one autumnal blaze,
Whereover the crows like something charred
Rise and fall in the haze.

So has he served her Summer pride
And punished a royal fault.
And he has appointed a day to sow
Her ruined city with salt.

Faithfully<br>R.F.

1916

## On Talk of Peace at This Time

France. France, I know not what is in my heart.
But God forbid that I should be more brave
As watcher from a quiet place apart
Than you are fighting in an open grave.
I will not ask more of you than you ask
O Bravest, of yourself. But shall I less?
You know the depth of your appointed task
Whether you still can bear its bloodiness.
Not mine to say you shall not think of peace.
Not mine, not mine: I almost know your pain.
But I will not believe that you will cease,
Nor will I bid you cease, from being slain
Till everything that might have been distorted
Is made secure for us and Hell is thwarted.

1916

## One Favored Acorn

More than a million seed
Most of which must fail
And go for squirrel feed.

Some had got themselves hurled
On the equinoctial gale
Far out into the world.

Some when the wind was still
Had fallen plummet direct
(But may have bounced down hill).

In a hollow some lay in a heap
Not knowing what to expect
Two or three acorns deep.

Already at one extreme
By autumn dampness' aid
Some were showing a toothlike gleam

What might have been a fuse
To some small devil grenade
Fat-loaded ready to use.

All that mast must perish
Unless I should intervene
And pick one up to cherish.

I might plant one in a yard
To alter a village scene
And be of long regard.

But whether with faithfully shut
Or intelligently open eyes
I wished I could choose a nut

That would be most appreciative
And would feel the most surprise
At being allowed to live.

late 1910s?

## Forest Flowers

Some flowers take station close to where we stay,
And some draw up on either side the way
To watch us, horse and foot, go trooping by,
And take our dust when summer winds are dry.
With neither of these the forest flowers belong,
Whose love for us perhaps is no less strong
Because they will that whoso touches stem
Of theirs must leave the world and come to them.

1911–17

## The Seven Arts

In the Dawn of Creation that morning
I remember I gave you fair warning
The Arts are but Six!
You add Politics
And the Seven will all die a-Bourneing.

1917

---

For Allan
Who wanted to see how I wrote a poem.

Among these mountains, do you know,
I have a farm, and on it grow
A thousand lovely Christmas trees.
I'd like to send you one of these,
But it's against the laws.
A man may give a little boy
A book, a useful knife, a toy,
Or even a rhyme like this by me
(I write it just like this you see).
But nobody may give a tree
Excepting Santa Claus.

1917

### Fish-Leap Fall

From further in the hills there came
A river to our kitchen door
To be the water of the house
And keep a snow-white kitchen floor.

The fall we made the river take
To catch the water in a dish
(It wasn't deep enough to dip)
Was good for us, but not for fish.

For when the trout came up in spring
And found a plunging wall to pass,
It meant, unless they met it right,
They glanced and landed in the grass.

I recollect one fingerling
That came ashore to dance it out;
And if he didn't like the death,
He'd better not have been a trout.

I found him faded in the heat.
But there was one I found in time
And put back in the water where
He wouldn't have the fall to climb.

1919

## On the Inflation of the Currency
### 1919

The pain of seeing ten cents turned to five!
We clutch with both hands fiercely at the part
We think we feel it in—the head, the heart.
Is someone cutting us in two alive?

Is someone at us cutting us in half?
We cast a dangerous look from where we lie
Up to the enthroned kings of earth and sky.
They know what's best for them too well to laugh.

1919

## A Correction

When we told you minus twenty
Here this morning, that seemed plenty.
We were trying to be modest
(Said he spitting in the sawdust),
And moreover did our guessing
By the kitchen stove while dressing.
Come to dress and make a sortie,
What we found was minus forty.

1920

———

Oh thou that spinnest the wheel
Give speed
Give such speed
That in going from point A
To point B
I may not have had time to forget A
Before I arrive at B
And there may result comparison
And metaphor
From the presence in the mind
Of two images at the same instant practically.

—

Oh thou that spinnest the wheel,
Give heed!
Those long curves of the road to left and right
That I have hitherto experienced with the eye
And the eye only—
They are too long-drawn for me to feel swayed to
Till my rate of travel shall have risen to a mile a minute.
Swiften me
That I may feel them like a dancer
In the sinews of my back and neck.

1925

## The Pans

The voice on Patmos speaking bade me "Shut your eyes!"
I shut them once for all and lo am blind.
"Hold out your hand, it said, for the surprise."
I held it out relaxed and stood resigned.

"A penny for your thoughts." Not overmuch.
The less the better from the Greeks, I said.
I waited cringing for the coming touch.
For fear the penny might be molten lead.

And when it came I flinched, I drew away.
And clang! clang-clang! clang-clang! down through the
    night.
It was a trust. The great scales of assay.
I was to have been Justice on a height,

Was to have had the gift of being just.
The scale-pans crashed and clanged. It was a trust.

ca. 1926

## The Cow's in the Corn

### A One-Act Irish Play in Rhyme

A kitchen. Afternoon. Through all O'Toole
Behind an open paper reads Home Rule.
His wife irons clothes. She bears the family load.
A shout is heard from someone on the road.

*Mrs. O'Toole.*
Johnny, hear that? The cow is in the corn!

*Mr. O'Toole.*
I hear you say it.

*Mrs. O'Toole.*
Well then if you do
Why don't you go and drive her in the barn?

*Mr. O'Toole.*
I'm waiting; give me time.

*Mrs. O'Toole.*
Waiting, says you!
Waiting for what, God keep you always poor!
The cow is in the corn, I say again.

*Mr. O'Toole.*

Whose corn's she in?

*Mrs. O'Toole.*
Our own, you may be sure.

*Mr. O'Toole.*
Go drive her into someone else's then!

She lifts her flat iron at him. To escape her
He slightly elevates the open paper.
The cow's heard mooing through the window (right).
For curtain let the scene stay on till night.

1918–27

## The Middletown Murder

Jack hitched into his sky blue bob
And drove away to the lumber job.

A week was what he had aimed to stay,
And here he was back inside of a day.

Kate came to the door to ask him why.
"To give you another kiss goodbye."

The gun he took to the woods for meat
Came out from under his blanket seat.

Kate tried to laugh at him. "You go long,
And don't be silly. Is something wrong?"

They stood and looked at each other hard,
Kate plainly blocking the door on guard.

Suddenly Jack began to shout:
"I know who's in there. So come on out!"

If someone extra was there with Kate,
He wasn't to be brought out by hate.

(Some people are best brought out by love.
The others you have to drag or shove.)

Then suddenly something frightened Jack,
And sent him shouting around in back.

"Hey, no you don't you goddam snide,
None of your tricks on me," he cried.

Kate cut across the house inside,
Leaving the door of the kitchen wide.

Now three of them choked the door emerging;
You couldn't tell which was pulling or urging.

"In a killer's choice like this of three,
There's some can't tell which it should be;
But I'll soon show you it won't be me.

"You have been my friend; you have eaten my salt;
But this was eating my sugar, Walt.

"The joke's on me for trusting a whore.
Wouldn't it make a rifle roar?

"To pro-long life and humor Kate
I'll give you a start as far as the gate."

He looked at a button along his gun,
But kept from shooting and told him, "Run!"

The first shot fired was over Walt's head.
He still was running; he wasn't dead.

The second shot went by one arm,
The third by the other, and did no harm.

The fourth, and next to the last, was low.
Walt felt it under him ploughing snow.

He thought, "I'm running in luck to-day,
I'm getting away—I'm getting away."

Just what to Jack would be meat and drink
To have the galloping bastard think.

All four misses were only art.
The fifth shot fired went through the heart.

The fifth was the bullet that stained his shirt,
And dove him into the snow and dirt.

We call that "bounding a man all round
Before locating his principal town."

"Now, back to your keeping house," Jack said.
"I guess you'd better go make the bed.

"No first you'd better put up your hair.
After that's done we'll see what's fair."

He pulled her in and shut the door,
And wouldn't let her look out any more.

Kate didn't know what the law would say
To a man for killing a man that way.

She hated to be the death of two.
But what was a woman going to do?

Be ready for when the sheriff came,
And say Jack wasn't the one to blame?

The least you could always do was lie
To hurry the day of trouble by;

And it wouldn't be long before you were glad
Of the worst young day you ever had,

It was so much better than any old.
But my, the sheriff would probably scold.

All the sheriff said was, "Cousin Kate,
You're the prettiest black haired girl in the state."

(The township numbered a couple of dozen,
And most of them called each other cousin.)

"I suppose you were born to have your fun,
But in doing to these two what you've done,

"If you wanted to get the good one jailed,
The bad one murdered, you haven't failed.

"I'll do it as gently as I can,
But cousin, I've come to take your man.

"Let it be a lesson to you for life:
Next time you marry, be a wife."

Someone lying stiff in the road
Like a cordwood stick from a farmer's load.

And over him like a frightened dunce
A guide post pointed all ways at once.

No curious crowd had gathered yet,
But a rural letter-box choir quartette

That stood in drift at the crossroads corner.
They had human names like Stark and Warner.

But more like ghouls than men they stood,
As much as singing that bad was good.

1928

Lowes took the obvious position
That all of art is recognition
And I agreed. But the perfection
Of recognition is detection
That's why Lowes reads detective stories
And why in scholarship he glories
A poet need make no apology
Because his works are one anthology
Of other poets' best creations
Let him be nothing but quotations
(That's not as cynic as it sounds)
The game is one like Hare and Hounds
To entertain the critic pack
The poet has to leave a track
Of torn up scraps of prior poets.

1930

## Trouble Rhyming

It sort of put my spirits in the      whole
When my Scotch friend from the adjoining      sweet
Came bursting in on us with "Greet, oh      greet!
Someone's been locked in a Chicago      goal (tr?)
Not just for robbing Croesus of his      roll,
But for inditing verse in rhymes and      feet.
No wonder Truslow Adams says we're      neat;
But if we're cattle we are not the      soul—
There's others capable of such a      sleep,
As the French say in English, or fox      pass,
As we might say in French, but ah, it's      know
Excuse for us that others sin as      deep.
A man, and not a pusil, not      alas,
I take my share of shame for Chica      go.

1930

Dear Louis:

The telescope has come and I am charmed.
I don't see how on earth I ever farmed
A day without a tool so all important.
I have to tell you though (perhaps I oughtn't)
That come to get the barrel up and pointed
I can't see Hoover as the Lord's annointed;
I can't see E. A. Robinson's last book—
As yet—I'll have to have another look.
At first I couldn't even see the moon.
And that not just because there wasn't one;
There was, according to the almanac.
One whole night I was pretty well set back.
Perhaps the object glass demanded dusting
Or the small lenses needed readjusting.
Perhaps as in the picture I'm inclosing
Some question of the day was interposing
Between me sinful and my hope of heaven.
But never mind, I didn't blaspheme even.
I had one of the two things Shakespeare wanted most.
Write on my tombstone for post-mortem boast:
I had—I had the other fellow's scope.
I need nobody else's art, I hope.

Yours ever<br>R.F.

1931

A man is as tall as his height
Plus the height of his home town.
I know a Denverite
Who, measured from sea to crown,
Is one mile five-foot-ten,
And he swings a commensurate pen.

1932

## The Offer

I narrow eyes and double night;
But still the flakes in bullet flight
More pointedly than ever smite.
What would they more than have me blink?
What is it? What am I to think—
That hard and dry to hard and dry
They may have said for years?
Am I, are they, or both to melt?
If I supply the sorrow felt,
Will they supply the tears?

1932

## Let Congress See To It

Wainwrights and Wheelwrights from old we've had.
Now comes a Wright to whom we need but add
An honorary Wing to make him Wingwright.
That would not only say right: it would sing right.

1932

## A Restoration

In the dark moment on the Eastern Stairs,
I had one of my characteristic scares.
On feeling in my soul I missed my name.
(I'd swear I had it on me when I came.)
'Twas when the gods began to brag of theirs.
Without my name in this place, I could see
I should be no one—simply nobodee.
Incontinently I became outpourous:
"O Ra Rah Rah, Osiris and O Horus,
Oh let my name be given back to me!"
"You're sure you didn't lose it through a hole,"

Osire suggested. "N'Osire it was stole."
A female voice piped up "What's all the crisis?
Is something missing?" I replied "Aye, Aye-sis
My name is missing. Someone's picked my soul."
On the last Staircase, my but what a row.
Someone to calm me asked me with a bow
Was this nym I was after just my pseudo.
I only shouted louder "No, my Kudo.
I want my name back and I want it now."
The Ra Rah Rah King summoned Robert Hillyer
"Do something to abate this clamor will yer?
Find and restore this fellow's Kudonym."
And Robert did it, glory be to him.
Oh what a friend to have for my familiar.

1932

———

A little kingdom
Where there had been
The brief glory
Of discipline.

The king in his palace
Knew of dangers.
There was a rumor
Of northern strangers,

Mere homeless pirates,
And yet a host,
Working nearer
Along the coast.

He meant to be ready.
He built a fort.
He kept arms burnished
In martial sport.

But he made it unlawful
To name the name
Of war and slaughter
Until it came.

He wanted his people
To love and increase
And be peaceful minded
In time of peace.

ca. 1932

## Winter Ownership

Who is it gathering snow on lash and lip
    In the dead of the year to the muffled evening goes?
Some owner asserting winter ownership.
    He may be incidentally counting snows,

And has to be out in the snows for the snows to count.
    Full fifty firsts he has kept on nights like this
(To walk a level and yet in courage mount).
    A spill of snow goes down with a sandy hiss

Through a withered-leaf-clad oak. A sudden flight
    Of tiniest birds goes by like a charge of shot,
As if recalled by the storm-made-early night
    From berry and seed to a southern aim forgot.

No danger of his forgetting his aim or quest.
    The muffled evening gives a long-drawn sigh,
So charged with both possessing and being possessed
    He can scarcely resist the impulse to make reply.

Is there some assurance he comes to the woods to beg?
    Why doesn't he enter the woods and say what it is?
The feel of the solid meadow up his leg
    Is enough assurance that what is his is his.

And the snow may have depth to reduce his step to a plod,
    But he somehow gathers the speed to realize
The contour curves of the forest rod by rod
    Along the way it rests its hidden size.

He is content to let it go at a pass—
    As turning dust to dew or brow and lip,
He cuts steps darkly down to the very grass,
    Caressing contour, asserting ownership.

1934

---

I only go
When I'm the show.

1935

## Pride of Ancestry

The Deacon's wife was a bit desirish
And liked her sex relations wild
So she lay with one of the shanty Irish
And he begot the Deacon's child.

The Deacon himself was a man of money
And upright life and a bosom shirt;
Which made her infidelity funny
And gave her pleasure in doing him dirt.

And yet for all her romantic sneakin
Out the back door and over the wall
How was she sure the child of the Deacon
Wasn't the Deacon's after all?

Don't question a story of high eugenics.
She lived with the Deacon and bedded with him
But she no doubt restricted his calesthenics
To the sterile arc of her lunar rhythm.

And she only had to reverse the trick
And let the Irishman turn her turtle
When by his faith as a Catholic
A woman was almost sure to be fertile.

Her portrait hangs in the family gallery
And a family of nobodies likes to think
That their descent from such a calorie
Accounts for their genius and love of drink.

1934–37

———————

Dear Leonard Bacon:

   I don't know whether you are in this world or in the Old
But I wanted to tell you before what is between us gets too
    cold
How much moral satisfaction not to say pleasure I took in
    your punishing rhymes.
I can see you feel pretty much as I do about these pro-
    vocative times.
Neither of us would be driven to drink by them nor to
    suicide
But that we find them rather too diverting from our
    preferred pursuits cannot be denied.
Still we wouldn't have missed them, would we, by any of
    the close calls we have ever had?
For my part I have got more out of the last four years
    perhaps than out of any previous Olympiad.
The only exception to our almost absolute unanimity
Is the way you ride the Methodists to an extremity.
As a good Congregationalist out of Peace Dale, I take it
    you are willing to interpose the Episcopalian

Between our Puritan institutions and the none too
     sympathetic Catholic alien.
But after using the Episcopalian in their way you have him
     on your hands unless you are foxy
Enough to bring in Methodism to render him harmless to
     our Orthodoxy.
Set an Anglican to catch a Roman and a Chapel-goer to
     catch an Anglican
And I don't see how the good old world can ever again be
     stolen from the honest man.
I'd say we called a meeting and organized a party to pro-
     mote our politics
But I know myself too well; I have had that idea before and
     it never sticks.
There may be a show-down coming, but if there is, we'll
     just have to wait for the day
Before we go to Abercrombie and Fitch's to outfit for the
     fray.
I rely on the large number of our kind there must be in a
     country like this that don't easily get worked up and
     excited.
They can stand no end of being left out of account and
     slighted
They even enjoy looking unimpressive
To the truculent and aggressive.
But there's a concentrated something in them away at the
     core
That I'd advise anybody to look out for if it ever comes to a
     war.
No there's nothing that we can do for the present except
     write poems and farm
And meet in some quiet place like Franconia for a talk next
     summer—that couldn't do any harm.
Don't think I got this trick of rhyme without much obvious
     metre from Ogden Nash, dod rot it.
No I got it from the Sweet Singer of Michigan where he is
     honest enough to acknowledge he got it.

                              Ever yours
                              Robert Frost

                                     1937

———

Unless I call it a pewter tray
Of precious jewels with which to play
A life-long game of solitaire,
I haven't found yet the thing to say
To Connick's stained glass wonder gift.
And still it isn't exactly fair
To call it a game of solitaire;
Since not permitted to move a stone
I must ask the help of the light of day
In order to make the colors shift,
And that's not playing it quite alone.

1937

———

To prayer I think I go,
I go to prayer—
Along a darkened corridor of woe
And down a stair
In every step of which I am abased.
I wear a halter-rope about the waist.
I bear a candle end put out with haste.
For such as I there is reserved a crypt
That from its stony arches having dripped
Has stony pavement in a slime of mould.
There I will throw me down an unconsoled
And utter loss,
And spread out in the figure of a cross.—
Oh, if religion's not to be my fate
I must be spoken to and told
Before too late!

1921, 1942

## Traces

These woods have been loved in and wept in.
It is not supposed to be known
That of two that came loving together
But one came weeping alone.

Yet the conifers sigh to the warblers
That lisp in their lofty tops
And their bark sheds tears everlasting
Of silvery rosin drops.

1940s

## Let's Not Think

The east wind had its say
But now the west replying
Makes another kind of day
With used-up clouds sent flying
And rain-fresh nature drying.

The little pools of rain
That seem made for reflection
The wind lets these remain,
But in blurred imperfection
To keep them from reflection.

O wind, if you object
That it's against the rules,
Henceforth we won't reflect,
I promise for the pools,
The shallow little fools.

1940s

Dear Louis:

I'd rather there had been no war at all
Than have you cross with me because of it.
I know what's wrong: the war is more or less
About the Jews and as such you believe
I ought to want to take some part in it.
You ought to know—I shouldn't have to tell you—
The army wouldn't have me at the front.
And hero at the rear I will not be—
I mean by going berserker at home
Like a post warden bashing in a door
To put a light out some fool family
Has treasonably left burning in a blackout
To go off on a round of night-club parties.
I couldn't bring myself Tyrtaeus like
To sing and cheer the young men into dangers
I can't get hurt in. I am too untried
A soldier to preach soldiering to others.
And then please recollect I'm not a writer.
I'm good at most things as I ever was
I can't deny (you may deny it for me).
But I was never any good at routine writing.
I always hate in filling out a form
To call myself a writer. It would sound
Pretentious now to call myself a farmer,
But when it was a modest claim to make
I liked to make it. I'm a lecturer
And teacher now on income tax returns,
Though lecturer's another parlous word.
I could no more have taken pen to Hitler
Than taken gun (but for a different reason).
There may have been subconscious guile at work
To save my soul from the embarrassment
Of a position where with praise of us (US)
I had to mingle propaganda praise
Of a grotesque assortment of allies.
False friendships I accept for what they're worth
And what I may get out of them in peace and war,
But always with a minimum of talk

And not for long. I'm bad at politics.
I was born blind to faults in those I love,
But I refuse to blind myself on purpose
To the faults of my mere confederates.
Great are the communistic Soviets!
If nothing more were asked of me to say
I could pass muster with the State Department.
Hull may be right about their being good
As well as great. He may be also right
About their interests lying close enough
To ours for us to help them run the world.
I'm waiting to see where their interests lie.
I hope they will be good to lesser breeds.
I hope John Bull and we two other Bullies
Can get together for the post-war good
Of all the small fry nations, Finland Poland
Roumania Greece Belgium and France,
Yes and our own poor South Americans.*
Hull's a nice man, though, and to hear him talk
Diminishes my doubts to unimportance.
You have to recollect as Lesley says
In District of Columbia dialect
I'm not a big shot. None of you down there
Would think of me for any liquidation
(Dread word!) or purge the Sandburg-Browder bloc
May have in mind. You told me so yourself.
Nothing I do can matter. I make verse.
In rhyme and meter. You and Kay indulge me
Once in so often I get round to feel
For what support I have in being useless.
Well you know whom I have to count on most.
Guy is a word of slang vicissitudes.
But good guy ought to mean a good guy wire
That stays the smokestack upright in its place.
Four wires it seems are a security.
Well I have had Kay Lesley you and Larry,
Exactly four, the sacred New Deal number—
Four terms four freedoms and four Bully nations.
That's if you stretch a point and bring in China.

*I hope we make the little brats be good.

One of *my* four you'll notice is a Jew—
No credit claimed for either him or me.
The best part of my friendship for your race
Is that I thought of it as lost in ours,
And the long time it's taken me to see
It was in part at least a race apart.
And even the part that is a race apart
I sympathize with. Give them back I say
All Palestine. No race without a country
Can be a nation. I take sides with all
Who want a platform they can call their own
To speak their language from—a platform country.
I'll tell Great Britain to be kind to them.
But see Great Britain: plead your cause in London—
If such your cause is. Talk is our ally.
Don't bother me: I have no pull with Arabs.
I am no Lawrence of Arabia.
I am so sick of all the vexing questions
This war has raised about our duty to resist
With force of armament on our allies
Being as just as we expect to be
To small fry nations and minorities,
I wouldn't much care if we never had
Another war. I vow I wouldn't care.
By way of bidding politics farewell,
And speaking of great nations, look at us (US)
The mighty upstart, full of upstart people
Or Shoe-string Starters as I like to call them.
Where have we come from in these hundred years
Up to a place beside the mightiest?
By what traits—virtues and propensities?
All the democracy in me demands
Is that I get surprised at where men come from.
I am not unsusceptible to stories
Of princes of democracy like Lee
And the two Roosevelts who were never forced
To pay their way through school by mowing lawns.
I get as much surprise as I require
In seeing any good come out of Groton.
But as I read the lives I find most pleasure

In those who have come up from being
Clerks, printer's devils, railroad section hands,
Mill hands coal miners elevator boys.
About the extent of my democracy's
A sort of mystical delight
In staying innocent or ignorant
Of the conditions that produce a man.
I like a world where nobody dare say
Or bet his fiat money out of what
Advantages or disadvantages
The hero may not come. A year ago
I thought I had us in the formula
That our democracy was a diffusion
Of quality, such quality for instance
As may sit back with feet crossed on the mantel
Thumbs in the armholes of its vest to doubt
The value of its own prosperity.
Think of how many commoners attain
To the superiority that says
As Solomon the king said Vanity
Of Vanities all all is Vanity;
And in one generation without waiting
The way the Adams family had to wait
For the third to produce a Henry Adams.
You may remember out from my back door
We have a bolt hole the choke cherries choke,
And a path through a patch of bracken snares
To open pasture where the view is free
Across the near horizon of black spruce
To a far off horizon of dim mountains—
Your Adirondacs which to us are you.
They fold you in but we in thought unfold you.
We leave your veil of distance undisturbed
For fear of being charged with lèse-romance,
But fold on fold we lay the ridges back
Till by your house beside the headlong brook
Among the spiring flowers you stand disclosed
In a companionship that loses nothing
By being left in part at least to fancy.
I have an album full of pictures of you

Looking expert as you step up to flowers,
Delphinium, to take their quality.
Or go against a painting on the wall,
Or pick out themes on a piano for us,
Or listen to a poem. Once is all
You have to listen to get every word.
No one can look so aquiline-expert.

Aw come on off your cosmic politics.
Not having heard from you for very long
Sets us to going over what a friend
How many kinds of friend I've had in you—
She who should be the great authority
Says no one else I know knows who I am
As well as you. That in itself would put
My debt to you so far beyond my power
To pay I can but turn up now and then
And by acknowledging the debt renew it.
I trust the explanations given you here
You only—no one else—will satisfy you
I am entitled to a day of grace.
I'll pay a first instalment pretty soon
I promise you. Hold on! Here's one right now,
An idea for one more anthology.
You say no more anthology, you're wrong.
I know the very name to call your next.
I'll tell you more about it when I see you
I'd take a hand in it if you would let me.

1944


## Ten Thirty A.M.

How much rain can down pour
To make the shingles roar
The drain pipe metal ring
And yet not change a thing
Inside the house or me
In any least degree

ca. 1944

Were that star shining there by name
As vast as men of science claim
All I could say would be the star
Would surely have to be as far
As men of science also claim
To shine with such a tiny flame
Prove A by B then B by A
Things prove each other in a way—

1945

## A Bed in the Barn

He said we could take his pipe away
To make him safe to sleep in the hay.
And here were his matches—tramp polite.
He said he wanted to do things right.
Which started him off on a rigmarole
Of self respect to shame the soul,
Much too noble a hard luck yarn
To pay for an unmade bed in the barn.

I thought how lucky the one who stays
Where other people can tell his praise,
Such as it is however brief:
That he isn't a firebug or thief.
For you're sadly apt to overdo
Your praise when wholly left to you.

1944–47

## Pares Continuas Fututiones

Says our Harvard Neo Malthushian
"We can't keep the poor from futution;
But by up to date feeding
We can keep them from breeding."
Which seems a licentious conclusion!

1951

## Waste or Cod Fish Eggs

Some Harvard boys when they were rudely faced
By science with the awful fact of waste
It takes a million eggs to hatch one cod
Their totem symbol just gave up their god
And suicided with a lightning rod.

early 1950s?

## Wanton Waste

Sweet if you wonder at the expense of seed
When such a little would suffice to breed,
Take glass some night for your most distant look
And realize the wanton waste it took
Of the sidereal principle in space
To bring to birth the puny human race.

early 1950s

## Sym-ball-ism

The symbol of the number ten—
The naught for girls, the one for men—
Defines how many times does one
In mathematics or in fun
Go as you might say into zero.
You ask the heroine and hero.

1957

———

Her husband gave her a ring
To keep her a virtuous thing.
But the fellow to whom I'm referring
He gave her an earring for erring.
He also gave her a necklace
For being so sinfully reckless.

1957

## The Prophet

They say the truth will make you free.
My truth will bind you slave to me—
Which may be what you want to be.

1936, 1959

## Marx and Engels

Them two panacea guys
Getting economics wise,
Did mankind homogenize
So the cream no more could rise.
Am I simply telling lies?
No, they did it in a dream,
On which Stalin rose supreme.
And who said *he* wasn't cream?
Very very very few
At the time of his debut.
Maybe none but me and you.

1955–59

---

For travelers going sidereal
The danger they say is bacterial.
I don't know the pattern
On Mars or on Saturn
But on Venus it must be venereal.

1955–61

---

The purpose of the universal plan
Admits of little purposes in man.

1955–61

### The Prophets Really Prophesy as Mystics
### The Commentators Merely by Statistics

With what unbroken spirit naïve science
Keeps hurling our Promethean defiance
From this atomic ball of rotting rock
At the Divine Safe's combination lock.

In our defiance we are still defied.
But have not I, as prophet, prophesied:
Sick of our circling round and round the sun
Something about the trouble will be done.

Now that we've found the secret out of weight,
So we can cancel it however great,
Ah, what avail our lofty engineers
If we can't take the planet by the ears,

Or by the poles or simply by the scruff,
And saying simply we have had enough
Of routine and monotony on earth,
Where nothing's going on but death and birth

And man's of such a limited longevity,
Now in the confidence of new-found levity
(Our gravity has been our major curse)
We'll cast off hawser for the universe

Taking along the whole race for a ride
(Have I not prophesied and prophesied?)
All voting *viva voce* where to go,
The noisier because they hardly know

Whether to seek a scientific sky
Or wait and go to Heaven when they die,
In other words to wager their reliance
On plain religion or religious science.

They need to crash the puzzle of their lot
As Alexander crashed the Gordian knot,
Or as we crashed the barrier of sound
To beat the very world's speed going round.

Yet what a charming earnest world it is,
So modest we can hardly hear it whizz,
Spinning as well as running on a course
It seems too bad to steer it off by force.

1962

# PLAYS

*A Way Out*
*In an Art Factory*
*The Guardeen*

# A Way Out

*Scene: A bachelor's kitchen bedroom in a farmhouse with a table spread for supper.*

*Someone rattles the door-latch from outside. Asa Gorrill, in loose slippers, shuffles directly to the door and unbolts it. A stranger opens the door for himself and walks in.*

STRANGER (*After a survey*): Huh! So this is what it's like. Seems to me you lock up early. What you afraid of?

ASA (*In a piping drawl*): 'Fraid of nothing, because I ain't got nothing—nothing't anybody wants.

STRANGER: I want some of your supper.

ASA: Have it and welcome if it tempts your appetite. You see what it is.

STRANGER (*After looking*): What is it?

ASA: Well, it's some scrapings of potatoes and string beans from other meals I was warming over. They've got kind of mixed together.

STRANGER: Should think so. What else you got in the house? What you got in here?

ASA: That door's closed with nails. You can't get in there. This is all the room I live in. Here's the cupboard, if you're looking for it. It's bare.

STRANGER: (*He knocks over a chair as he goes about.*) Got any bread?

ASA (*Trembling*): I don't know what you mean by coming into a person's house as if you owned it. I never was subject to anything like it. If I had some bread, you don't go the right way about to get any.

STRANGER: Cut that. I'm here for business. You're supposed to be poor then?

ASA (*With dignity*): I am poor.

STRANGER: Sure there's nothing hidden in the mattress—or in that nailed-up room? Oh, I haven't come to kill you for it. I shan't kill you anyway till I have something to go on. You needn't be scared till you're hurt. I only meant your being poor was part of the job if anybody was going to undertake it.

ASA: See here, it's time you told me what your business is in my house or go out. I don't understand a word you say. I ain't been subject to anything like it all these years since Orin died.

STRANGER: Aw, don't whine to me about it. I've heard of you and your brother keeping old-maid's hall over here in this neck of the woods, patching each other's trousers and doing up each other's back hair. Look ahere, old boy, I ain't going to be a mite harder on you than I have to be for my own good. I was passing this way and in trouble and I just thought I'd look in on you and look you over as a possible way out.

ASA: As to that I don't know. I don't know what I might or mightn't do to help a person that didn't come at me wrong and spoke me civil. I think you can't pass this way very often—who does for the matter of that? I don't remember of ever seeing you before. You know me though?

STRANGER: Better than you know me. I only just came to the shoeshop down at the Falls last winter. But I've heard of you times enough. As a matter of fact I wasn't exactly passing: your reputation brought me somewhat off my road. You popped into my head like an idea.

ASA: I'm going to give you some tea before it gets cold and have some myself to steady me. Another time see to it you make a civiler beginning with anybody you're expecting favors of . . . You take it without milk? Brother and I ain't had no cow since the barn burned down in '98. Brother Orin died the year after that.

STRANGER: For God's sake what do you live on—nothing but potato mash?

ASA: There again! Criticising! I don't see what there is in that to make you take it the way you do. Where does it pinch you? Shall I give you some?

STRANGER (*Pausing as he walks back and forth in perplexity*): Mash! Don't. Is it pretty generally known you live on potato mash?

ASA: Generally known—

STRANGER: I mean, would it excite suspicion if you gave it up and took to eating mince pie, damn it?

ASA: Excite—

STRANGER: Do you ever have bread?

ASA: When I bake, when I happen to have flour in the house.

STRANGER: Where do you get money to buy flour?

ASA: I sell eggs.

STRANGER: Oh, eggs are at the bottom of it. Nothing unless eggs. God, it's worse than I thought, worse than I bargained for after twenty dollars a week and nobody to take care of but myself. But there's one thing I noticed there: you do go into the village shopping now and then when the hens are laying— when there are eggs. It's not just as if you never bought a thing, nor spoke to a soul.

ASA: You ain't pitying me, be you, mister?

STRANGER: Pitying you! No, I'm pitying myself. You like it all and I shan't. Sit down and let me tell you. I can see you haven't heard. As you see me here, I'm—well I'm in no position to waste pity on anybody else, or think of anybody else and I'm not going to. You can bank on that. I'm running away from a murder I'm accused of having committed.

(*Asa drops his face into his hands on the table and groans*)

STRANGER: And I've turned in here to you for help.

ASA: Oh, I can't have anything to do with this. I never have had no trouble and I ain't a-going to begin now. I'm a peaceable man.

STRANGER: I wasn't intending to give you much choice in the business.

ASA: Oh, but you won't drag me into your crime. After all I've done to keep out of things!

STRANGER: It just shows you—

ASA: You want me to hide you here. Think of it!

STRANGER: I haven't quite decided what I want you to do yet. All is, I've done the deed, they're out after me, I've been zigzagging 'cross country (not daring to use the trains) for three days and now I've hit on you as my only salvation. And I'm going to use you one way or another; so you might as well pick your head up off the table and be a man about it— not a wet dishrag. The cuss of it is I was seen at least once today, walked right out of the woods onto a team full of women and hadn't sense enough to keep to the road as if nothing was up, but dodged back into the woods where I came from. That'll tell 'em I haven't got far off. I've got to think quick, but not too quick. No use losing my head.

ASA: I don't see that there's so very much to think of except a hiding place. I'll hide you for tonight. If I must, I must.

STRANGER: Yes, you must, old boy, or I might kill you. It wouldn't amount to another crime to kill a half man like you. Throw you in extra and call it one crime. Does anyone know for certain you're not a woman in man's clothing anyway? . . . But it's not so simple. Tonight's not all I have to consider. There's other nights coming. Where will I be tomorrow night and the night after that? I'll leave it to you if it's not a puzzler.

ASA: Just as fur as you can get from here, I should think.

STRANGER: I don't know that you know, but it's the fashion now-a-days to hide just as near the scene of the crime as you can stay.

ASA: Oh, dear, you don't mean you're thinking of fastening onto me for good and living the rest of your nat'ral life in any concealment I can give you.

STRANGER: Maybe, maybe. I'm out of a good job in the cutting room, anyway. I can't go back there, can I? I'm willing to let you advise me up to any reasonable point. I was thinking how it would be to be you if worst came to worst as it may yet. We might agree to be you turn and turn about, one of us lying up in hiding while the other was out stretching his legs and satisfying the hanker to see folks. The danger there, is that there would be always an extra one around to be discovered. And there are a lot of dangers. It would never do. I should have to trust you too much not to give me away. And we might quarrel as to who had the lion's share of the time out. And then appearing in turn might be almost as risky as side by side. People might be led to see differences that they could only explain on the assumption that you were two instead of one.

ASA: If you're expecting followers, the less noise we make talking the better. What's to hender their being all round the house now and looking in the window? That curtain's no more than a piece of cotton sheet. You can see right through it when the balance of light is on this side from the fire. (*He tucks the sheet in at the edges and corners.*) But say, it comes to me if you could tell me you didn't do this murder—then I shouldn't be doing anything wrong.

STRANGER: I did it fast enough.

ASA: How—how—how—. Don't tell me though. I'd best not hear. Do you mean by the cutting room the place where you done it?

STRANGER: Queer codger, aren't you?

ASA: Guess I am.

STRANGER: Say, I've been getting it through my head you must have been the one meant by that hermit article in one of the Boston papers here awhile back—before I came to the Falls. Recollect anyone's calling on you with a pencil and a piece of paper held out in front of him so-fashion? Or did he write you up from a safe distance the way Whoses did the North Pole? Great talk he put in your mouth about hermiting —if you were the one. Let's see, what did he say was the matter with you?—crossed in love?

ASA: You've heard that, most like.

STRANGER: I've heard something.

ASA: No it was Orin that was crossed in love in a manner of speaking. He was promised to a gal who kept him waiting more than fifteen years and then married someone else because she wouldn't come to live in this house till he divided the property with me or bought me out and got rid of me. Orin stood by me; so I stood by him.

STRANGER: You haven't got any real prejudices in favor of this way of living then? I mean you didn't take it up as a man goes into the Methodist Church in preference to the Baptist or the Orthodox?

ASA: Dunno's I did.

STRANGER: What I'm trying to get at is how you look at things—if you look at them.

ASA: As f'r instance?

STRANGER: Well what do you say about women when they come up in conversation? Supposed to hate 'em?

ASA: I so seldom have occasion to speak of 'em.

STRANGER: Then what do you do when you see 'em? Run? Same as I did today from that carriage-load of 'em.

ASA: Don't know's I run exactly. I'd a leetle rather not meet 'em face to face.

STRANGER: All right, we've got that then. Think the world's a bad place and all that nonsense?

ASA: Sholy it ain't any better'n it ought to be, what with all the killing and the murdering and the whatnot. Now is it? Come.

STRANGER: I was reading where a man living on a farm back like this had a queer religion about inhaling from your own shoes when you took them off to go to bed so's to get back the strength lost by settling in the daytime. And there was something about not having the cow calf when the sun was "in his legs." "Awlmanick" expression—"in his legs." Ain't that right? You see I'm up on some of this already. There were three cities the man could see throwing light on the sky at night, which, being a God-fearing man, he called "the cities of the plain." According to him they kept getting brighter and brighter attempting like to turn night into day in the face of nature. You could judge how the Lord took it from the way the thunder storms kept increasing in number and destructiveness owing to the attraction of the electricity and the wiring. Stood to reason. Anyway the old man expected nothing but that some night the Lord would fetch up a storm that would wipe out those cities in a blue blaze.

ASA: Wasn't it awful!

STRANGER: It hasn't happened yet. I suppose you've a notion or two like that. But *you* wouldn't know it if you had.

ASA: I don't hold with no such doctrine as that of inhaling from your own shoes, certain.

STRANGER: Ever been heard to say you like the innocent woods and fields and flowers like a poem in print?

ASA: Dunno's I have.

STRANGER: I guess it's just a case of plain damn fool; which ought not to be hard to give an imitation of. I supposed people that lived alone had to have something to say for themselves. But that's what comes of my being all bothered up with literary reading. You haven't got ideas enough to make a hermit's life interesting. And the reporter lied when he said you had. I'll bet he never came nearer than five miles of you. Afraid you'd spoil the story if he came too near. But what gets me is what you say to people in self-defense, the ministers for instance, when they tell you you've no right to keep yourself to yourself the way you do. How do you fend 'em off?

ASA: It's so long since I was bothered by anybody I've most forgotten.

STRANGER: I bet you have.

ASA: Orin knew how to send 'em about their business.

STRANGER: Orin by the side of you must have been some-one . . . I guess if I can get the outside appearances right—Oh, one thing more: Neighbor with anyone?

ASA: No, as you may say, no.

STRANGER: Write any letters?—And your handwriting! I'll be sure to forget something in all this rush. Got a pencil? Here's a stub. On that paste-board box cover. Anywhere. Just your name. Write it two or three times—will you?—as long as it don't cost any more. What—what's that? Asie Gorrill. So it was: seems to me I remember it was Asie. (*After a considering pause, he goes to the window, draws aside the curtain and looks out.*) Those your pine woods?

ASA: It ain't right, mister, examining into me further and further. You ain't got time to plague me so—not if you're going to save your own skin—not if you're what you are by your own telling.

STRANGER: Never you mind me. You're rich, you old ski-vins. You own all that timber, and you won't touch it. Pre-tending to be poor! You're just as two-faced as the next man. I knew I could get something against you to work me up if I tried hard enough. Who are you saving the woods for? Any heirs? Me?

ASA: What does that mean?

STRANGER: It means I ought to kill you and skip the coun-try with it under my arm.

ASA: I shouldn't think you'd feel (*he gulps aloud*) as much like joking as you appear to. Hee, hee.

STRANGER: Asie, I believe you're a bad lot and entitled to no more consideration than any other grown-up man. . . . About my age, though. About my build. All I'd have to do is cave in a little, slump—let my mouth and eyes hang open. Say, push the table back and walk up and down the way you've seen me doing. Them's orders. I'm not inviting you. Do it! . . . I'll thank you for what you have on your feet—slippers is it? How do I know they aren't some I made? Make you a present of my shoes.

ASA: Oh, I shan't need 'em. I mostly go barefoot anyway. I only slipped these on to haul wood.

STRANGER: Oh, wood. How do you haul wood? Wheelbarrow?

ASA: No, I drag it in, in poles two at a time, one under each arm. I take what's died standing—

STRANGER (*Going to a bed-post*): What's all this? Extra togs? Jumper? (*Comparing it with what Asa has on.*) Overalls? (*Comparing.*) Watch me! (*Putting on jumper and overalls.*) Light a light, why don't you?

ASA: Oh, I don't allow myself no lamp! I'll throw the stove door open. I can put on some more wood. It's about my bedtime anyway.

STRANGER: I'm putting you to bed tonight. I'm going to let you stay up later than usual on account of company. Now watch me. (*He takes a turn up and down the room. Asa stumbles getting out of his way.*) No trouble about the thin voice. (*He speaks more or less in Asa's piping drawl from here on.*) Now I want you should let me show you something that'll amuse and maybe bother you. I'm going to mix us up like your potato and stringbeans, and then see if even you can tell us apart. The way I propose to do is to take both your hands like this and then whirl round and round with you till we're both so dizzy we'll fall down when we let go. Don't you resist or holler! I ain't agoing to hurt ye—*yet*. Only I've got to get up some sort of excitement to make it easier for both of us. And then when we're down, I want you should wait till you can see straight before you speak and try to tell which is which and which is t'other. Wait some time.

ASA: Let go of me. I know what you be; you're a crazy man from a madhouse.

STRANGER: You'd best humor me then. (*He lifts Asa's hands still higher and stands looking at him. The fire burns brighter and lights them unevenly.*) Old boy!

ASA: What is it?

STRANGER: I'm thinking—

ASA: What?

STRANGER: Old boy, are you happy?

ASA: Oh!

STRANGER: Are you happy? Have you anything to live for? Lord, didn't you ever ask yourself a question like that—with so much time on your hands? I ought not to expect it of you. It will take me to do this thing right when I come into office. Oh, well.

ASA (*Looking wildly behind him toward the door*): I wouldn't have believed it.

STRANGER: What was I telling you! It just shows that if you won't go to life, why life will come to you. I should think a man in your position would have to think such thoughts. I know I should. And you would if you'd ever read so much as a Sunday paper to set you going on them. But I mustn't be any longer with you. Come! One, two, three, swing! Swing, damn you! Don't hold back. Faster! . . . Faster!

(*Asa moans as he circles. The Stranger moans too. The slippers fly off his feet. After some time they break apart and go to the floor where they lie both moaning.*)

FIRST TO SPEAK: I know. I ain't lost track. It's you that done the crime!

SECOND (*Screaming*): It's not! (*He half rises and falls back.*)

FIRST: It is! And I'm not afraid of you any more. You've got to go. God will give me strength to wrastle with a rascal.

(*The Second snarls, throws himself backward, and faints. The First strikes him a blow with his fist on the head and drags him across the floor and out of the house. The room is left empty for some time. . . .*

(*A loud knock. Another. The door is thrown open. Heads appear in the doorway.*)

A VOICE: Gone to bed, Asie? His fire's lit. He can't be far off. Here he is now. (*The Hermit pushes in past them breathless and faces them from the table.*) We're after a man, Asie. You haven't seen him?

ASA: Ain't I though? He's been and gone.

A VOICE: How long since? Which way?

ASA: Not five minutes. Through the woods. He was dragging me off to kill when he heard you coming and run. I was going to follow, but I gave it up and came back. What's he been up to?

A VOICE: You're no good, Asie.

ANOTHER VOICE: What had you done to him to get him against you?

ASA: You'd better hurry. (*He beats the table with his fist.*)

A VOICE: Someone had better be not too far off so as to take care of Asie.

(*They confer, gradually closing the door. The minute they are gone, the Hermit snatches the socks off his feet and throws them into the fire. He picks up the pair of shoes on the floor and sends them the same way. He bolts the door softly. He stands listening.*)

SOMEONE (*Later, as if repassing, sings out*): Good-night, Asie!

THE HERMIT (*Getting into bed so as to answer with his face in the pillow*): Good-night.

*Curtain.*

# In an Art Factory

*A barn-like studio badly lighted through large dirty windows by a street lamp that throws a ripple pattern on the walls. Little is visible in the room but three shrouded figures in a row. A door opens after the rattling of a key in the lock and Tony enters from a dark stair case leading Blanche by the hand. He throws down a match he has burnt out and lights another.*

TONY: Stand where you are till I find the gas. There's a jet here—or was the last I knew. (*He burns out another match searching the wall before he finds it.*)

BLANCHE (*as the gas leaps into a noisy blue column*): Oh that won't do.

TONY: No that's no improvement. The cap's gone. The place is never used at night. (*He quiets the gas by lowering it.*)

BLANCHE: It's cold Tony.

TONY: Shut the door then.

BLANCHE: I'm afraid to—and shut the street out. It's warmer outside than in. (*She shuts it.*)

TONY (*turns on the radiator and gets no response*): No good. The heat's not kept up. I believe not a soul sleeps in this building now except old Krail and he don't count. You know Krail. Of course you know Krail. I forgot. You posed for his Mary with the Body of Christ.

BLANCHE: Tony! (*She goes to a chair against the wall under the gas jet.*)

TONY: And you had to hold old Peaseley across your lap so as to make his ribs prominent. And Peaseley chewed as well as smoked.

BLANCHE: I hated it.

TONY: Oh, we all know about that. But Peaseley didn't hate it. And it almost made you religious for a while. You went to Mass every day to get into the spirit of it.

BLANCHE: I had to find some way to take it. But I hated it.

TONY: And damn it, I hate it still. Damn it.

BLANCHE: It seems to me you hate pretty much everything tonight.

TONY: You're right there. Anyway I hate the ways art is produced. (*He walks back and forth as if he were kept by the bars of a cage from getting at her.*)

BLANCHE: Then what are you dragging me all round town for to wind up in this place at this hour of night?

TONY: To give you a good time though I can't have one myself. It's my nature to think of the happiness of others.

BLANCHE: Then take me home.

TONY: Just a moment Blanche. (*He goes to the middle one of the three shrouded figures and uncovers it.*)

BLANCHE: Look here, Tony, what's the matter with you. (*She turns him toward her by force.*) I'm not going to have any more of it.

TONY: Nothing's the matter with me.

BLANCHE: Are you cross at me for what I said about models deserving all the credit?

TONY: Credit! What the hell do you suppose I care who gets the credit?

BLANCHE: Tony what's the matter?

TONY: I've got half a mind to tell you.

BLANCHE: Tell me.

TONY: You look pretty enough to understand it. But it's a hard thing.

BLANCHE: Tell me.

TONY: No I'm going to let you think it out for yourself. You may never—and for that matter I may never.

BLANCHE: Take me home.

TONY: Not till I look my last at my What's 'er-name—before she ceases to be mine—before Campbell comes to take her over. Not till I look my last at her and tell her what I think of her.

BLANCHE: You won't see much in this light.

TONY: (*He fills and lights his pipe thoughtfully in front of the figure.*) Blanche, I want you to see it too—what I see—before it's wiped out. Come here girl. (*She obeys.*) The Campbell is coming hurrah, hurrah. The Campbell is coming—tomorrow. He will don his apron. He will stand in front of her like a surgeon with his scalpel. He will put forth a hand toward the clay. Touch touch touch, and she will be Campbellized. She will be nationalized. She will be commercialized. She will be made to be worth so much that if she were broken in shipment on the railroad Campbell would ask and get ten times the damages obtained for loss of life. Which is better than Pygmalion. She will be sentimentalized. She will be lost. Tonight she is mine. I made her. She is lovely.

BLANCHE: She is Evelyn Dace I suppose. Make love to her. I don't care. She's flattered out of recognition.

TONY: In a way she is flattered. She is changed. I should hope so. She is made truer than Evelyn—not prettier.

BLANCHE: Oh I've been through all that. The tricks of you men to prove you owe us nothing.

TONY: My dear we owe you everything, but not even in one work do we owe all of it to any one of you.

BLANCHE: If she's so lovely, why don't you carry her off in your arms and exhibit her as your own?

TONY: And sell her and get married on the proceeds.

BLANCHE: Or go to Paris for a new stock of ideas.

TONY: But do I want to sell her. Isn't she too—something?

BLANCHE: Beautiful—say it.

TONY: Beautiful if you understand what I mean by the word. Beauty is truth, you may say. But beauty is just beauty too. There is the beauty of truth and the beauty of beauty.

BLANCHE: I wonder which I have.

TONY: The latter is a kind of specialized beauty that we find isolated where any fool can see it in youth and health and models—

BLANCHE: Thanks.

TONY: —in jewelry and fashion and in Campbell's sculpture. Oh Campbell knows what he wants all right—and gets it. He stands for a certain sort of thing we have to admit.

BLANCHE: I thought he was your business agent—nothing more—who took your soul to market. You did the work and he sold it.

TONY: I have so far fallen in with the boys' studio talk as to say that. But I lied. I don't believe it. I didn't believe it when I said it. Nothing goes out of here that is not hopelessly Campbell's, which is what I can't forgive him. After all I could part with anything I do in the ordinary way of sale. I'm not a fool, am I? To make things for him to buy is one thing. But to make things for him to alienate! I never felt it as I do tonight. I'm sick I guess.

BLANCHE: I should think Campbell might have some mercy on you.

TONY: I suppose he thinks he has. He pays us ten dollars a day. We are in less danger of coming to want than most young artists in this town. He calls this place his Genius Asylum or the Unknown Artists' Home.

BLANCHE: Tony if you will let me say it, a man's proudest privilege is to go to Hell in his own way. You are a fatted slave.

TONY: I know I ought to strike out for myself. She ought to be the last. I wonder if she will be. I shall have to do something or shut my mouth, shan't I?

BLANCHE: Is she the best thing you have ever done Tony?

TONY: Look Blanche. (*He turns desperately to the gas.*) I know. (*He fetches from a corner a heap of newspapers which he proceeds to roll and crumple.*)

BLANCHE: What are you going to do? Set her on fire? Touch her off?

TONY: (*He lights a roll of paper at the gas as a torch and lifts it close to the wet clay figure over their heads.*) She is so good—that I shall never go as far again.

BLANCHE: What is it about her? What has someone else been doing here? (*She lifts another shroud.*)

TONY: A dead thing. Don't lift the face cloth. Come back. (*He lights another torch from the first before he drops it on the floor and puts it out with his foot.*)

BLANCHE: I like her Tony. What do you call her? Is she a goddess?

TONY: No. Manhood reaches its height in immortal gods; womanhood reaches its depth in mortal maids. Gods are better than men but women are better than goddesses. That's why the gods couldn't let women alone. She's you.

BLANCHE: And a lot of other women.

TONY: Aw Blanche don't spoil everything. If women are mixed in our minds we're sorry. And this is all you where it counts.

BLANCHE (*avidly*): What will Campbell do to her?

TONY: He won't have to do much with his devilish cunning. It will be as simple as touching for the King's evil. One stroke will make it whol-ly his. But I wonder if I can tell where his hand will light. On that lip to correct it—you see where I mean—there. Yes I am sure there—I wince so at the thought of it. And on the eyelids to make them more alike. Oh I don't know. Where I have deviated the least bit for frailty, he will bring me back to perfection. In general he will take you out of it. (*He drops the torch without lighting another.*)

BLANCHE: Can't we prevent him.

TONY: We can't run away with it. It's too cumbrous. We should be noticed by the police.

BLANCHE: I will go to Campbell tomorrow and throwing myself at his feet so he won't think I am throwing myself at his head memorialize him as follows: Please Mr. Campbell!

TONY: I've been near enough to asking him to spare me before this. He doesn't see what there would be to spare.

BLANCHE: You'd think a great man could see.

TONY: Campbell can see only the beautiful—where I see the—well the defective, the tragic.

BLANCHE: You know what some say.

TONY: What do some say?

BLANCHE: Well Langford says Italy is full of the kind of craftsmen Campbell hires, all of them better craftsmen than Michael Angelo ever thought of being and for all they themselves know better artists.

TONY: You're striking the wrong note, Blanchie. I know what Langford says: only an artist can tell the difference between an artist and a craftsman: a craftsman never can. And Langford's right of course.

BLANCHE: But that makes it very funny—you see what I mean?

TONY: No.

BLANCHE: It puts the certainty of the artist against the certainty of the craftsman. How can you be certain which certainty is certain?

TONY: (*He looks at her a long while.*) You can.

BLANCHE: And that's all, haha?

TONY: That's all. (*He is absorbed in the figure.*) I'll tell you how you can tell I am a real artist and not just a craftsman if you need to know in your profession, whatever it is Blanchie.

You can tell in the same way Solomon found out who was the real parent—by threatening the child. I feel for this as if it were my own flesh and blood. Levine here and Robson can stand by and see anything done to their work. You can't cut them to the quick in such outwork any more than if you took a pair of scissors to their hair. But you can me. You'd better not tell me what to do to a thing to make it right, much less undertake to do it yourself. To hell with your criticism, yours or anyone else's, Blanchie. I make a thing and you take it or leave it. That's all the intercourse there is between you and me Blanchie. No I am right about my not being a craftsman and you are wrong. I can tell by the way I behave you are wrong. I wouldn't go by my thoughts and feelings. I go by the way I behave.

BLANCHE: Nonsense you know I know you're an artist dear. I refuse to be separated off like this. (*He sidesteps her advance toward him.*)

TONY: You pretty damn near separate yourself off. No the more I think of it the surer I am you're wrong.

BLANCHE: Stop it.

TONY: I'm willing to entertain a reasonable doubt for what it is worth to please anyone but in the end—

BLANCHE: Stop!

TONY: What makes you cross is I don't doubt myself enough to satisfy the maternal comforter in you.

BLANCHE: Yes you do too Tony. Didn't I tell you not two blocks up the street not to come on me with any of your doubts. The doubts are yours, not mine. No sir, I'm in on your ground floor. I believed in you before you believed in yourself.

TONY: Well then what are we talking about.

BLANCHE: I don't know Tony. I guess we've both lost the connection, haven't we?

TONY: No we haven't either lost the connection. You were saying—

BLANCHE: No I wasn't.

TONY: —that my work—

BLANCHE: —was as different from Claussen's work— (*She lifts a cloth.*)

TONY: Drop it. I forbid you to lift the cerements. Let's leave those idols out of it. Idols is all they are. That's a definition of their kind of work, idolatry—mechanical repetition of old art forms like the heathen—rote repetition of beauty forms. But speaking of where art comes from: Campbell thinks it's from him. You posies think it's from you merely because you pose for it—and I—well I think the newspapers do the whole goddam business. They make the artist and his art out of whole cloth with their write-ups and reproductions in their art sections on Sunday. (*He uses the callipers on her and the figure to verify proportions.*)

BLANCHE: We posies. You said yourself this was all me.

TONY (*with a gesture of concession*): You be my Beatrice— my Ann Rutledge. Though you'd have to be lost or dead for that.

BLANCHE: You'll find me easier to kill than love.

TONY: Ah sentimentahl!

BLANCHE: There goes one of your sweet dagoisms Tony that still clings to you and that I love you for. You don't say the word as we say it. And you don't mean what we mean. Call Campbell a crimeenahl just once for me in this dark room.

TONY: He is a crimeenahl to run an art factory.

BLANCHE: Ah seeneestair Tony!

TONY: But I tell you you are wrong about my not being the sole creator of any—creature. It is an axiom that no two people can give birth to the same child.

BLANCHE: Why I thought that was just the number it took to.

TONY: Mothers. I mean mothers. No two mothers. Listen to me seriously now. I'm going to have this out with you.

BLANCHE: There's nothing to have out.

TONY: You have given yourself away in this night's talk as one who doesn't know the right thing to say to an artist. That is the definition of one of the public—a person that doesn't know the right thing to say to an artist. The only person who ever said the right thing about any art of mine—I put the words into his mouth to say it with. Sometimes I put the wrong things in out of perversity to flagellate myself. Listen to anybody from the head of General Electric to the head of General Motors talking about art. Did you read what one of them said at the Big University Commencement about Shakespeare. He said a great man like Shakespeare would naturally in our time have come to the top as an industrial leader instead of a poet. He said that thanks to the party in power the country was now rich enough to go in for a few spiritual values. Spiritual values.

BLANCHE: I saw that. He was dedicating a bird tower in Florida. Some words ought to be copyrighted so the wrong people can't take them in vain. I agree with you.

TONY: My but I hate to hear real estate agents use the word beauty.

BLANCHE: We'll have to stop them by law, the way we stopped their drinking.

TONY: Every word they say is an offence to the muses or at least the graces. The goddam awkward squad.

BLANCHE: There you go off the track again. It's not so much their awkwardness you mind is it? It's their facility with words that cost them nothing. They have their own things to keep to but they want to reach over and take up ours too.

TONY: The definition of the USA is a place where—

BLANCHE: It seems to me you are pretty full of your definitions tonight. What's needed is a definition of you.

TONY: You supply it. You can't.

BLANCHE: I know one thing. I know what's the matter with you better than you do yourself.

TONY: What is the matter with me do you suppose.

BLANCHE: You thought it was Campbell's larcenous touch.

TONY: I say this and I say that on trial. I've got to find something or somebody to blame for my misery.

BLANCHE: What will you give me to tell you what's the matter? But you wouldn't believe it from me.

TONY: Out of the mouths of ba-thing beauties.

BLANCHE: Give me two guesses.

TONY: Why two?

BLANCHE: Because it's more than one thing. In the first place you are suffering a reaction at the end of just having loved your creature too much. You are away down low in exhausted love.

TONY: Guess again.

BLANCHE: In the second place, you are too feminine. This is the breaking down in you of the feminine barriers against being put to use. You are coarsening as a woman has to coarsen to stand a husband. You are being born some more. We only get born part way into the world the first time. Every little while we have to get born further in. And it's supposed to hurt.

TONY: It sounds like something you have been working up in that short story so much is expected of. How's it coming?

BLANCHE: It's coming.

TONY: Making copy of me as I am of you. Fair exchange. What? But if you will take the critical suggestion Blanchie, you are no fairer in my sight for your literary ambitions. I hope they come to nothing for your sake. But how did you know all that stuff.

BLANCHE: You said it.

TONY: When?

BLANCHE: Tonight and other times. Just now.

TONY: I didn't.

BLANCHE: You as good as said it—when you said your malady was a kind of fastidiousness. You don't remember, you say so many things. It's my place to watch till you say the right thing, then put my arms around you and hold you to it. And do you know I don't believe you hate Campbell because he actually changes your figures so very much.

TONY: It's an absolute fiction I've got up that he changes them at all. He almost never touches them at all. Why lie about it? Why make a myth? That's right! stop me.

BLANCHE: Anyway you mind his words more than his touch I've noticed. His expropriating words.

TONY: My God when he begins to apply words to it. But it won't do to say that his hands are nothing. It doesn't have to be much to be everything.

BLANCHE: The way he takes it takes it away from you.

TONY: Yes and he's just the beginning of a long line of alienations. I see what you mean. An artist wants a public, the more public the better. But he lives in resentment toward their ways of mistaking him. He resists coarsening to them. I'll take your word for it. I guess so.

BLANCHE: It's your word for it. And it makes it all right now that you understand it, doesn't it? (*She tries to hold him from tossing about.*)

TONY: My God I don't know. (*He lifts a crooked arm as if to signal.*)

BLANCHE: Tony what is it?

TONY: I'm undergoing my change. (*As he flings her off. They are indistinct in the gaslight when no torch is burning.*)

BLANCHE: Towards me? No!

TONY: Like a snake sloughing its skin—or a werewolf back into a man. (*He stumbles to one knee.*)

BLANCHE: Tony!

TONY: It hurts terribly somewhere.

BLANCHE: I'm good to you Tony.

TONY: There isn't anyone alive enough like me to be good to me.

BLANCHE: Tony I'm afraid of you. (*As she gets between him and the door.*) What did you bring me here for?

TONY: Not to do anything to you.

BLANCHE: Tony shake yourself. I'd shake you—

TONY: What's there to do that I haven't done—except kill you or—make you watch me kill myself— There, it's past. I shall never be lonely again. I'm abated for life. I'm down to ordinary. My difference will never bother me again. Only (*half weeping*) someone's got to find the right thing to say about my work—the right thing to do—pretty soon or I shan't be able to stand the suspense. It was terrible though.

BLANCHE: Where was it?

TONY: Not in the heart—that's sure. Nor in the head. (*Tries his head.*) I don't know where it was. It was in this arm.

BLANCHE: I said the wrong things to you?

TONY: I don't know.

BLANCHE: But it's better?

TONY: I think. It was anger fury—crescendo. Did I take it out on you? (*He rises to her as she comes back to him and lets her half enfold him though he refuses to be distracted entirely from looking at the statue.*) It wasn't against you.

BLANCHE: I know.

TONY (*after a long silence*): I don't think it's spent yet.

BLANCHE: You feel it terribly.

TONY: Just getting it through your head Blanchie.

BLANCHE: There, there. (*He leaves her violently to light another torch.*) Darling I don't see but that you'll have to give this one up and resolve that it shan't happen again. We'll keep everything you do after this for ourselves. No one shall lay a finger on it or apply a word to it.

TONY: I can't stand it I tell you. At least I can be beforehand—with Campbell can't I—if murder has got to be done?

BLANCHE: But I thought we decided it wasn't Campbell.

TONY: No we didn't, did we?

BLANCHE: I thought we did. Tony wait a minute.

TONY: I'm a champeen transmogrifyer myself just while you're going round the corner. Let's have more light. (*He lights another paper torch.*) You hold it. Higher. I'm the man what advertises beauty soap and beauty surgery. I correct the bats wing ear and the rolling nose. Consultation free. What shall I make of her. Tell me before I do anything I shall be sorry for. Shall I put race on her as you writers put adjectives on your nouns. Shall I put Irish on her as his friends put it on George Moore's prose.

BLANCHE: Tony stop, you dago.

TONY: Her father and mother were Irish and she was Irish too.

BLANCHE: You've done it. You've done it.

TONY: You speak as if I couldn't restore Jerusalem in a day at day's wages. Nothing is irreparable. (*She drops the torch.*) Look out for your dress. Light another. (*He lights it for her.*) Hold it till I have done. I am the Roman father that slew his daughter before he would see her violated by his prince. (*He snatches the pipe from his pocket and drives it into the mouth of the statue. He strikes the torch from Blanche's hand.*) Come. All out! (*They run for the door but Tony turns back to put out the gas. Blanche shrieks as she stumbles down stairs with a clatter of heels. After having gone out and closed the door Tony bursts in again, lunges at the statue and over it goes with a tremendous thud of wet clay. He cries:*) Murder (*starts to run out but turns back panting at the door as if there might be more to charge and overthrow*).

# The Guardeen

FIVE SCENES

Characters

Henry Dow, a countryman over sixty given to eloquence
Richard Scott, a graduate student given to eloquence
Professor Titcombe, Richard's debunking teacher, not many
    years older than Richard
Lida Robie, daughter of the lumber camp; of about
    Richard's age
Charles Robie, Lida's brother
Socrates Robie, their father left off stage
Tug and Guinea, lumberjacks
A few other lumbermen

## Scene I

*The room contains for furniture one table against the wall,*
*a trunk and a small box on end. It has a very broad unpainted*
*wainscot. The time is late afternoon. Enter Henry Dow, a small*
*wiry countryman of sixty, and Richard Scott, a city boy, pushing*
*and jamming an overstuffed bed tick ahead of them through a*
*door in the rear.*

HENRY DOW: Steady by jerks. Both of us pushing so lumps
it up. You climb in over it and pull. (*Richard does. Henry Dow*
*comes falling forward into the room with the mattress.*) Let
down of it and take our time. You're blowed. But as you were
saying son, it would have been some better if you could have
got here earlier.

PROF. TITCOMBE (*entering with blankets and a basket of pro-*
*visions*): Don't let him scare you Richard.

HENRY DOW: Nothing to give you confidence in a new
place like a chance to look round a little before you go to
bed. I meant to have told you when you wrote about taking
the house. But I let Tom Titcombe answer you seeing it was
him that sort of brought us together. He used to be your
teacher as I understand it.

RICHARD: Is now somewhat—shouldn't you say, Professor?

PROF. TITCOMBE: I don't know what I am to you any more Richard, since you rose to be my equalitarian equal in the pursuit of happiness for all mankind.

RICHARD: Easy does it with the imperatives, teacher, if you don't want to keep me awake all night. Them's tocsin words you utter.

HENRY DOW: You aiming to keep the boy company his first night ain't ye?

PROF. TITCOMBE: No Richard'll be all right Henry. I must be getting along home to my supper.

RICHARD (*eloquently*): Before you go and before I forget it I must tell you my new definition of Democracy. It's just one more form of government the upper class thought it could concede to the lower classes and still keep on top of them.

PROF. TITCOMBE: Richard you're as radical as a bag of beets and carrots. You're my first choice for new youth leader of the permanently unemployed in the coming revolution.

RICHARD (*as Prof. Titcombe goes out*): Careful what you say if you don't intend to be understood.

HENRY DOW: I ain't heard a thing and if I had I wouldn't tell on ye.

PROF. TITCOMBE (*returning*): And last of all here's a great big cake my wife made for you to experiment on and settle it once for all how long you can keep a cake and yet eat it. I leave you to Henry. Let nothing you dismay. Your work's cut out for you. Remember all is grist to the mills of science. All that's expected of you is great results. And if anything goes wrong don't holler because we're too many miles off to hear you. Be as courageous as I have always found you outrageous. Good bye.

HENRY DOW: Now nothing's going to hurt you here. I don't want to infer there is. But all the same it's only reasonable you should want to know what you're in for. Wild stretch of country here on the mountingside. Hardly a year we don't see a bear or a wild cat. Where was you thinking you'd locate your bed?

RICHARD: In the back corner there, wouldn't you?

HENRY DOW: It's you that's got to lie in it. Still if it was me, seems as if I should want it on the side here against the other-room door; where it would be as good as a lock to you.

RICHARD: Let's have it there then. But you needn't try to scare me because you'll find I simply don't scare.

HENRY DOW: Pshaw, I wouldn't try any tomfoolishness on ye. Only I didn't want harm should come to you through neglect of mine. I don't mind telling you part of my object in letting you in here cheap was to get you to take care of the—well, I was going to say of the house.

RICHARD (*dropping an end of the mattress*): Take care of the house?

HENRY DOW: Yes. Now I don't mean anything underhanded. I mean I chose you sooner than anybody else because, well, because from what I could make out I thought you wouldn't burn the house down—that's all. I mean you wouldn't have a lot of roisterous companions in to drink with you. I take it you ain't much of a drinking man.

RICHARD: I don't drink much.

HENRY DOW: There! I knew my confidence in you wa'n't misplaced. Not cider? 'Cause if you do I can offer you a little. I got some hardening in the cellar right under us. (*He stomps sharply.*) Just coming of age—like you, if you ain't too important to be joked with on such short acquaintance.

RICHARD (*drawing away as Henry Dow tries to slap him on the shoulder*): I won't drink, thank you. (*After standing puzzled for a moment*) Isn't this too full? (*He climbs onto the mattress.*)

HENRY DOW: I had you stuff it so a'puppose, so it couldn't be said you didn't get your money's worth for twenty-five cents. I want to tell you about that there bed. You can't expect to get much sleep out of it the first few nights. It may take three or four nights to break in. Anyway you work it, it's bound to settle down more under the heft of your body than of your legs; which will tend to make you lie with your feet in the air. The secret of the damn thing is to turn it end for end regular every day till you get it level as a board.

RICHARD (*as he stretches his length on it*): And hard as a board.

HENRY DOW: But by that time you'll be so hard too you won't notice.

RICHARD: How would it be to put my trunk on it in the day time?

HENRY DOW: Nooo! I shouldn't want to do that! You won't get the good of the springiness of the hay. The trunk will get it all. What's into the thing to make it so tarnation heavy?

RICHARD: Books, Mr. Dow.

HENRY DOW: Which explains your looking so pickéd. Now listen: when I brought you here to take care of anything of mine, I didn't intend for an instant you wa'n't to look out for yourself too—especially this being your first experience camping out—as I take it. I hope and trust you haven't come without a weepon of some description.

RICHARD: As it happens I did bring a small gun, though I shouldn't have thought I needed to. It should be here somewhere if it didn't get left out in the packing. Why? (*After some rummaging he brings it out of the trunk and lays it on the floor.*)

HENRY DOW: Sho, you don't call that a gun! That's a watch-charm. Is the barrel bored clean through? Or is it a dummy?

RICHARD: I shouldn't look down it. It's loaded I think.

HENRY DOW: Kind of a bee sting affair. I meant to have warned ye. But as I say, it's you I'm thinking of.

RICHARD: What's all the anxiety?

HENRY DOW: Just that I want you to be careful of yourself away off on the side of the mounting out of call of doctors and all. I'm appointing you the guardeen—well of yourself first and foremost. You must be your own guardeen now. You will have no reliance but yourself in what's to come.

RICHARD: Hell, Mr Dow what's the matter? Has Shucks Titcombe been putting you up to something?

HENRY DOW: Nothing's the matter. Only that revoliver is about as practical as you be. Hear anything?

RICHARD: I thought I heard a horse and wagon.

HENRY DOW: Must be my horse down there pawing.

RICHARD: No—

LIDA (*appearing in the doorway*): Henry Dow, your daughter wanted me to bring word you're wanted at home. (*She turns to go.*)

HENRY DOW: Where—

LIDA: I saw her in the blacksmith's shop in Robinstown.

HENRY DOW: Well, I'm agoing home tomorrow. Thank *you* for bringing word.

LIDA: I brought it. (*She turns to go.*)

HENRY DOW: Hold on there sister. Which way'd you come from—up or down. I bet you came from up. Somebody sent you to get rid of me. Some of their tricks. You're too late. Look at this I've got in to take my place when I can't be on duty. Miss Lida Robie—Mr

RICHARD (*drifting a step or two forward*): Richard Scott.

HENRY DOW: Now will you folks own up beat?

LIDA: Huh!

HENRY DOW: Look him over, do: so you can tell 'em if he ain't a good one for the job. He's a college athalete.

LIDA: Henry Dow, you're a fool. (*She goes.*)

HENRY DOW: I've got her mad by not believing her about my datter.

RICHARD (*going to the door*): Who is she? Why she's headed up the mountain. I thought this house was the end of everything. Who is she? Where's she going. (*He shouts*) Say!

HENRY DOW: Hoigh! Don't you go calling after that girl!—not if you don't want the whole gang of them about your ears. She's going up the mounting where she came from. That girl lives up there.

RICHARD: I was given to understand I was the last person on the road. Shucks Titcombe said you said after me the road turned into a squirrel track and ran up a tree.

HENRY DOW: I was coming to that tactful by degrees. I might just as well begin right now and tell you where you are so you can't say you ain't been cautioned. This house is exactly four measured miles up the mounting. Back down a mile is the Avery place where I'm supposed to be staying when I'm off by myself on a vacation from my datters. But it seems my datter wants me, does she. She begretches me every minute I spend in the neighborhood of a barrel of cider. I'm a old-fashioned drinker young man. I drink hard when I drink. But I defy the face of man to say I ever let liquor interfere with business. I brought up a considerable family right into this little house you're in and I did well by 'em. And yet it's as much as ever I can get away for so much as a week at a time to get back here for old sake's sake without being sent after the way you seen. It's a shame to me before folks. I shan't put up with everything and you wouldn't have me (*almost weeping*).

RICHARD: You were going to tell me about the girl.

HENRY DOW: The gal's all right. It's the gang she belongs with which she ought to be ashamed of but she ain't. I'll say that for her: she's got spunk about standing by her father and brother.

RICHARD: You mean her family's bad.

HENRY DOW: Family! It ain't a family. It's a gang of left-overs from a lumber job that run out a good while back.

RICHARD: Are they dishonest?

HENRY DOW: I ought not to say because I don't know. But the town has it that a foot-pedlar with safety pins clim up among them by mistake and nothing was ever seen of him again but the safety pins all over the gang's clothes in the place of buttons, there being not enough women in the camp to sew things on.

RICHARD: Cut-throats, hey?

HENRY DOW: I don't say it's every bit true, mind ye. It won't do for you to say so if you believe it.

RICHARD: I begin to see the game. Shucks Titcombe needn't think he can bring me in here for a criminal investigation. You've had some row with these people I suspect.

HENRY DOW: They don't love me. But that's got nothing to do with you. I'll say one thing though: it might not do any harm for you to be heard letting of that pistol off for practice now and then to impress them. It wouldn't skeer them as I knows on, but it might tend to make them respect you for a grown-up man.

RICHARD: You mean fire at a target?

HENRY DOW: In your spare time. And another thing that might help: if you should fall into conversation with them (which I hope and trust you won't) you could relate to them any heroic actions you may have done in Boston. No matter if you exaggerated within reason. I don't infer I look for them to come at you in a body. Did you think you heard anything?

RICHARD: Your horse probably.

HENRY DOW: You may expect to hear some of them round now and then. They're considerable night prowlers from not being overworked in the daytime.

RICHARD: That girl is the only woman among them?

HENRY DOW: Her brother Charles looks after her. Father owns the saw mill.

RICHARD: Does she work?

HENRY DOW: She can use the cant dogs like a man. Folks say she chews.

RICHARD: But she doesn't chew.

HENRY DOW: She would if she took it into her head to.

RICHARD: But that isn't saying she does. You don't say she does.

HENRY DOW: I don't know's I ought to say she does when she don't.

RICHARD: I should say not. Been to school any?

HENRY DOW: Some. I suppose you wouldn't look at 'em unless they was eddicated.

RICHARD: I wasn't thinking of that. I was trying to make out what her life would be like in such surroundings.

HENRY DOW: You won't have a glass of cider with me before I go? You won't mind if I have one more seeing as how I won't be up this way for some time maybe—if I can manage to keep away. (*He lights Richard's brand new lantern and descends into the cellar with it by a door in the room. Richard is left thoughtfully toying with the revolver.*)

RICHARD (*as he sits down on the trunk*): Oh, Mr Dow. Mr Dow, are you still there? Oh, nothing. I was just beginning to wonder what had become of you. Take your time. It's your cider.—Now what? Have you hurt yourself? Stand where you are till I bring you a match then.

HENRY DOW (*emerging from the cellar with the lantern out*): Guess you thought I'd gone to sleep on my back with my mouth to the spigot like a babe in arms. I just did that thing one time and my lying all night on the wet cellar bottom brought on an attack of the Civil War rumatiz I contracted into my system at the battle of Saratogie. The trouble with me is, I'm too ambitious. I'd rather drink the hull of that cider myself in one go than have that gang get one drop of it. But you got to delegate things. I found that out. I can't drink all the cider and I can't stay and watch over it; which is what I been leading up to gradual and where you come in. It's took time to reach the point where I could hereby in the absence of witnesses appoint you guardeen for better or worse of all the cider herein under. Do you accept the trust?

RICHARD: I'll fool you by pulling out tomorrow. Don't you and Shucks Titcombe think you're smart?

HENRY DOW: Tom Titcombe wasn't in on this, honest!—Your mind's excited by the strangeness and full of imaginings. The Bible says, Quit ye like men. I say don't quit like anybody. Don't quit at all. Don't be a quitter. Rev. Haines says I and the Bible mean the same.

RICHARD (*helping him out the door*): You'd better go.

HENRY DOW (*retarding*): To Hell had I?

RICHARD: I didn't say that. You better go home to your daughter.

(*The curtain goes down as Richard alone very slowly and listeningly takes off one shoe.*)

## Scene II

*A cloudy moonlight night outside Richard's cottage, which presents two darkened windows with a door between. (The cottage stands well back in the far left hand corner of the scene.) Two stealthy figures are moving about on hands and knees. One withdraws to a distance (right front corner) by a pointed boulder and calls off the other with violent gestures, but without speaking. He picks up and sets down an empty galvanized iron bucket. Both stand looking at the house.*

GUINEA: He's in there all right. He's tore up a sheet for curtains.

TUG: I'll bet he's gone off. Didn't I see him going down to Avery's along about supper time?

GUINEA: He must have come back. Didn't I hear him still firing as late as nine o'clock?

TUG: Go 'way! In the dark?

GUINEA: In the dark.

TUG: By crimes! He wasn't firing when I came up from Benton.

GUINEA: Must have let up for a while to cool his battery. He's in there all right.

TUG: Well, I'll find out whether he's in there or not. You stay back. (*He creeps up to the house and scratches the clapboards across the grain of the wood with a rock. There is no answering sound, but presently the square of a window fills with light and Tug retreats.*)

GUINEA: I told ye.

TUG: Damn smart job Henry Dow thinks he's put up on us, don't he?

GUINEA: I wish we'd left the spigots all on the last time we was down and drawed off every last drop of his cider onto the cellar bottom.

TUG: Wish something sensible while you're wishing. I wish we'd got a barrelful out the way I recommended. Look out. (*They both duck at the muffled sound of a shot fired in the house and run behind the boulder where they crowd each other for shelter.*) Listen, will you! What does the infant think he's doing?

GUINEA: The war is over!—No! More yet. At least he isn't firing at us. We needn't have gone down like we was shot till we *was* shot.

TUG: What is he firing at?

GUINEA: Target. Hear it ring. Some old stove lid he's set up.

TUG: He couldn't hit a object of that size as often as that running.

GUINEA: Then it's a stove door—from the rusty junk down there where there was the school house once.

TUG: Do'ye know what I think? He's practicing for something—a command in the army maybe. And his shooting hasn't nothing to do with us.

GUINEA: Who said it had?

TUG: Goes at it any time of the day or night he happens to be awake or think of it.—He's done ain't he, for the time being?

GUINEA: If I thought he'd run out of ammunition I'd rush the house and take him alive.

TUG: What good would he be to you if you had him?

GUINEA: Never jedge a boy of his age by appearances Tug.

TUG: I'm going to tickle the house some more. The way to do is to keep him awake till he has to go somewhere else for a night's rest. (*He creeps up and rasps the house with a stone as before. Richard resumes firing. Tug retreats.*) Some of them shots ain't hitting your stove lid or whatever it is. Blaze away, child, if it's a comfort to ye. Some of the noises of the night you can explain away and those you can't explain you can keep your courage up to by whistling with bullets.

GUINEA: *Now* it's over.

TUG: Bet he's fainted in a smother of blue smoke with the window tight shut's 'tis. Don't give him a moment's let up now we've got him going. Finish the job tonight. Much'll you bet he don't strike for home come morning? Tickle the house some more. (*He creeps up and scratches as before but this time without results. He retires.*) What do you make of it Guinea? Lost his interest?

GUINEA: Maybe he's gone to sleep on the thery we're a hedgehog making a meal off the sharp corners of the house.

TUG: What would an Algerine like him know about hedge-hogs. You ought to have heard Lida describe him.

GUINEA: I heard her.

TUG: She said she seen him first. He's hers. What do you say if we go up and hit the house one in the side and see how he'll account for that?

GUINEA: Take care of yourself Tug. I'm suspicious he's spying on us from somewhere.

TUG: Time enough to look for danger when he puts the light out. He can't see us from inside the way it is. You do something. I'm doing all the work. Go up on the side there and hit it a saunker. I'll take the blame if anything happens to you—or if the house falls down.

GUINEA: Well. (*He creeps up and strikes the house a blow that makes the windows rattle. He comes back laughing.*)

TUG: Shu-tup. He'll hear you and it'll be all off. You can't expect him to be serious unless we are. (*Richard resumes firing.*) As *you say*, he's there all right. He still lives. Pop! Pop! But I expect him out among us any minute if only to breathe. He's bound to gas himself out sooner or later. (*A pane of glass goes crash in the window.*) Wow! (*They duck.*) Why, it positively ain't safe to come down here for cider any more.

GUINEA: Now what'll he do? Pick up the pieces?

TUG: Look out! Where you going with your big feet? (*As Guinea backs into the empty pail and goes down over it with an outrageous clatter. Tug lies down beside him. They suppress laughter.*) What'll he say to a rattle-de-bang like that?

GUINEA: His spent bullet hit the moon—after breaking the window.

TUG: Pa Robie's coming home. Tell by the way the democrat creaks under his tonnage. (*An owl hoots.*) Listen; it's Charles. It's reinforcements in the nick of time. Saved! (*He answers the owl hoot with a crow caw.*)

CHARLES: Get your cider and come home why don't you?

TUG: 'Tain't a question of getting cider so much as it is of getting satisfaction.

GUINEA: Henry Dow has filled the house with Massachusetts State Melitie.

CHARLES: Pa told you not to touch the cider unless you could do it without disturbing anyone.

GUINEA: Without disturbing anyone! Is Pa down there?

TUG: I guess we better let up on him for tonight.

GUINEA: I was about to propose shouting some awful word like Boo in the hole in the window.

CHARLES (*leaving*): Come along.

GUINEA: We got to say good night to the kid.

TUG: Down, down! Drop down! He's looking. (*Richard's head comes between the curtain and the window.*) Don't move. (*Richard withdraws.*)

GUINEA: Will you look? Lie tight.

(*Richard appears in the doorway in night clothes. He carries a lantern in one hand and his revolver in the other. For a moment he stares blindly. Then he steps out gingerly on bare feet and makes a stately progress once around the house and back to the door. His strides are long but deliberate enough to suggest some control. [The house is far enough back so that a puppet about half life size would best be used for Richard in this scene.]*)

TUG: Ghosts! I wish Charles could have seen that.

GUINEA: Not after anybody in particular though. That's the regular Boston way I take it of overcoming imaginary fears.

TUG: He went in that door faster than he came out.

GUINEA: And he sounded a little sudden on the lock when he got in. Still he done very well. There, he feels better. He's blowed the light out. He thinks he can sleep.

(*Tug and Guinea get up from the ground and brush themselves. Tug holds high the empty pail and pretends to drink from it. Guinea crowding for his share says:* "Leave some for someone else." *They rough each other off the stage as the curtain falls.*)

## Scene III

*Richard sits sunning late in the forenoon in the open door of the cottage. His hair is combed wet but there is nothing else of morning freshness in his appearance. He hangs his head dully between the elbows on his knees and yawns. He rubs his eyes.*

*Presently as if to throw off heaviness he makes an impatient gesture and stretches lengthily for something indoors till nothing but his feet show on the threshold. It proves to be the revolver with barrel broken and a rag drawn halfway through it. He works cleaning it. He looks through it at the light; then loads it with cartridges from a pocket and lets it hang apathetically in his hand at his side. He levels it once to follow a bird in flight but does not fire. At last he rises and fetching from round the house a large dark empty bottle sets it on the outcrop of granite in the dooryard and stands back to take aim. But the expected shot doesn't come. He withdraws his trigger finger and wriggles it under inspection. He looks forlornly round the mountain.*

LIDA (*unseen, in a tigerish voice*): Here!—

RICHARD (*turning halfway with a ridiculous limp and going down on the revolver side almost to the ground*): Now what have I done?

LIDA (*appearing and dropping her voice*): You! (*They look at each other a moment.*) What do you think you're trying to do? (*Richard looks at the bottle then at the revolver.*) You came within an inch of my head, careless. (*Richard helplessly uses one arm to indicate the direction of the rock, the other to indicate the direction of the road, and shakes his head to indicate the great difference.*) Can't help it. You almost had me.

RICHARD: Bullet must have glanced. As a matter of fact I don't—

LIDA: It did something.

RICHARD: As a matter of fact I don't believe I fired, did I? And anyway I hope you didn't mind very much if I did.

LIDA: Mind very much!

RICHARD: Because you don't look as if you did.

LIDA (*with a laugh*): The nerve!—Say my brother is coming down here to talk to you. Don't you two fight. I just ran ahead to warn you. (*She goes round the end of the house.*)

RICHARD: Which side do you think (*He discovers her absence.*) I ought to fire from? (*He fires in a daze two or three times. The bottle stands intact. In a daze he walks over and taking it by the neck breaks it across the rock.*) Break damn you!

CHARLES (*coming from behind*): That the way it's done? Can't you hit them. (*Charles keeps stooping nervously and pulling and biting spears of June grass.*)

RICHARD: Yes but I'm going stale.

CHARLES: I wondered if you were trying to see how near you could come without hitting. I told my dad I didn't think you were firing to kill. Some of the boys heard you last night and they didn't think you were firing to kill. But what's all the firing about if it's any of my business?

RICHARD: Well, you see, Mr Dow—

CHARLES: Oh Hen Dow hey? Hen Dow been talking about us?

RICHARD: He said your father had a sawmill up back.

CHARLES: Tell you to look out for us?

RICHARD: No—not—

CHARLES: Hard crowd, hey? Well I'll tell you something about Henry Dow, and that is he don't know anything about us. What's more he's a liar. Say put up that toy and shake. You don't need it. Don't you see any object Henry might have in filling you up with lies against us? Well, if you don't, you will.

RICHARD: Maybe you take my steady firing as a reflection on your lumber gang. I didn't mean it so.

CHARLES: Wouldn't care if you did. (*He sits on his heels.*)

RICHARD: That your sister just now here giving me a piece of her mind.

CHARLES: Yes I guess so. Lida been here? Hen Dow been saying anything about Lida?

RICHARD: Nothing but the best.

CHARLES: She hates him.

(*Suddenly a shrill but husky steam whistle sets up call on call in the near distance. Charles gets to his feet.*)

RICHARD: What is it?

CHARLES: Blest if I don't believe she's set the mountain on fire again.

RICHARD: You don't mean to tell me that lovely girl—

CHARLES (*taking one look at Richard and shouting with a laugh*): The saw mill—the saw mill—you—

RICHARD: Excuse me.

CHARLES: You poor crazy! What's Hen Dow been doing to you. Or is it Tom Titcombe?

RICHARD: Is it a forest fire?

CHARLES: That calls me.

RICHARD: Shall I come too? Could I help?

CHARLES: It'll whistle more when it gets up more steam if it's serious. But I better go. (*Exit*)

(*Richard leans into the house to get rid of the revolver. He turns to find Lida waiting for him at the door side.*)

RICHARD: Oh, you back? You didn't go? You been listening to your brother and me?

LIDA: I got out of the way so I wouldn't have to listen unless you two got noisy. We've got a fire at the mill.

RICHARD: Your brother said so. Aren't you worried about it?

LIDA: It isn't the first one I ever had to worry about. It'll be all right. Let them that set the fire put it out.—Say, I don't know what Charles told you but what I want you to tell me is: Did you know you were brought here to guard Hen Dow's cider?

RICHARD: You want me to be honest with you? I'll tell you exactly what I came for or was brought for by Professor Titcombe. It was to make a social study of you.

LIDA: A what kind of a study of me?

RICHARD: A social study.

LIDA: A social study?

RICHARD: Yes a study that's made of the underprivileged because it would be too hard to make it of the privileged. I need it for a thesis in college and to help Professor Titcombe out with his book. If you want to make a social study of the rich you have to do it in a court of law under the Sherman Act.

LIDA: Why didn't Tom Titcombe make the study for himself. He knows a lot about us to start with. He's a relative of ours.

RICHARD: No! That's something he never told me.

LIDA: Well he is. He's a second cousin of mine once removed. I heard father figure it out.

RICHARD: Well I'll be damned by these teachers.

LIDA: Social study of me! How do you propose to do it?

RICHARD: I certainly can't do it if you refuse to be social. Aw, come on, be social. Sit down and stay a while as long as you aren't going to the fire. Let me ask you some routine questions.

LIDA: Now what are you getting at?

RICHARD: I only mean let's talk. You and I! Let's forget every single human being but us two. Henry Dow is nothing to me. Neither is Shucks Titcombe. Shucks is what we call him in college from it's being his favorite word to debunk everything fine a fellow was brought up to believe. One got me here to protect his cider from you, the other got me here to make a social study of you. I'm here by two mistakes. Don't hold them against me.

LIDA: Two mistakes are better than one to take the conceit out of you.

RICHARD: Excuse me for mentioning it. But have you noticed the big smoke. Though I say it that for my own interest shouldn't, that's getting to be quite a fire you've got up there.

LIDA: Oh bother the fire.

RICHARD: No, let's not bother the fire if it doesn't bother you. Come on then—sit down—and let's talk.

LIDA (*as she sits*): Talk about what?

RICHARD: Let's not talk if you don't feel like it. Let's just sit here serenely since you don't care about the fire. No, I'll tell you what, instead of my looking into you, I'll give you a good look into me. I'm interested in politics. I have a great idea: (*eloquently*) I want practically everyone of both sexes to be politicians and run for office. I want to see many many more offices but of course twice as many candidates as offices so people can run against each other in pairs.

LIDA: Isn't that the way it is now?

RICHARD: Good girl! There's nothing so very new yet. You're right. But wait, I haven't started. (*eloquently*) Never before has any provision been made for the candidates that get defeated. I want to see all candidates sufficiently insured by the government so that those defeated, they and their families, can live without privation and temptation till the next election. As it is now, good men have to run the risk not only of not getting into office but also of being thrown out of office, often at very awkward times of life. The Outs constitute the greatest of Have-nots in our society and are its chief menace because they can't keep from lying and cheating to get into or back into office. That is to say I advocate unemployed politicians' insurance. I hold bona fide candidates out of office ought to be paid say half as much as those in office. Did you ever think of that?

LIDA: *No.* It sounds to me like poetry—the way you say it.

RICHARD: Do you like poetry? Did you—do you go to school? You look young enough to be still going.

LIDA: I teach school. That is I substituted part of last year over in Bethlehem.

RICHARD: There seems to be a complete misunderstanding here. But no matter so long as you and I are friends. For something to do together suppose you let me read you some poetry this summer.

LIDA: You mean you'll make me some poetry? I have something I wanted to get a poem written about if I could get just the right person to handle it. It's about my father.

RICHARD: You mean a tribute for his birthday or something. I'm sorry, I never wrote important things like that and besides I haven't written any verse at all lately since I got to worrying about the Haves and Have-nots. If you would care to hear (*eloquently*), I go the whole length in my expropriativeness—

LIDA: If I had a pencil I could give you just what I wanted said.

RICHARD: My dear child poems aren't written like that.

LIDA: Oh yes they are, my dear child. I knew someone who had a bereavement poem written to be put into *The Caledonian*. The space paid for of course. You see my father is something special.

RICHARD: Oh?

LIDA: He's like Solomon only different. Solomon waited till he had got possession of everything before he turned against worldly goods and started to cry vanity of vanities. My father didn't wait to get property. He saw through it beforehand. I think he is greater than Solomon. His first name is Socrates.

RICHARD: Listen to her. The whole philosophy of riffraff rabbledom in one pretty little head. My, I'd like to write your poem if I hadn't lost the art. You ought to write it. There's the greatest possible mistake been made here. (*He moves over and lays a hand on hers.*)

LIDA: Don't laugh at me.

RICHARD: Not for the world. I used to think democracy meant giving everybody a college education free. I was full of sympathetic ambition for everyone. And along come you and take the strength all out of me. You ought to be called Delila instead of Lila.

LIDA: My name is Lida.

RICHARD: From this day forth it shall be called Lila with or without the aristocratic prefix De. But don't feel too responsible for my reformation. You only recall me to my truer self. Naturally it is the unworthy poor I side with rather than the worthy poor. I'm so indulgent of reasonable badness I begin to think I missed my calling in not becoming a jailor. I can conceive of becoming very fond of criminals.

LIDA: You're not old enough to have missed anything by very much.

RICHARD: How old do you think I am?

LIDA: Plainly not old enough to keep from being taken advantage of by Henry Dow and not only by him but by your own teacher.

RICHARD: One planted me here to be guardeen over his cider, the other to look into you.

LIDA: And you never suspected a thing. You need a guardeen over yourself.

RICHARD: Haven't I got one?—you—now? You help me get even with those two.—You aren't leaving me? Have you decided you must go to the fire?

LIDA: There comes the professor's car.

RICHARD: I should like it if you kissed me goodbye.

LIDA: He'd see us.

RICHARD: And then it would be statistics than which—

LIDA (*hastily*): I believe in your plan to insure political candidates. Is it what some people think?

RICHARD: Nobody but me so far. And now you. Isn't it a big idea? (*eloquently*) I've got a whole lot of big ideas for you to come round and believe in when you can find time. One about confusion to bugs by spraying plants with each other's juices and— (*He follows her saying Goodbye while Professor Tit-combe stands waiting. The car has been heard but has been left unseen at the foot of the yard.*)

PROF. TITCOMBE (*with a confidential nod in the direction of the departed girl*): How goes it. We heard there was a big fire on the mountain so I came over to see if you were all right. You seem to be in one respect.

RICHARD: Oughtn't we to do something about the Robies' fire?

PROF. TITCOMBE: It is a big one even for them I should say. But they hate to have any fuss made over their fires. Listen! What's all that? (*Confused shouts are heard in the distance. Lida comes running back.*)

RICHARD: What is it?

LIDA: Can't you hear what they're saying?

RICHARD AND PROF. TITCOMBE (*together in answer to a loud cry of* Back): We are back.

LIDA: It means something's going to blow up. There's going to be an explosion.

RICHARD: Dynamite?

LIDA: I guess the boiler.

PROF. TITCOMBE: When?

LIDA: Anytime between now and Christmas. But the sooner the better for nerves. I hope to the Lord everybody's in a safe shelter. (*She lays a hand on Richard's arm.*)

CHARLES (*entering*): Oh you're here, Sis.

LIDA: Yes. Why?

CHARLES: I just wanted to locate you.

LIDA: Where's Pa?

CHARLES: I left him sitting in fresh pitch on a pine stump. He's all right.

RICHARD: You people may think you know each other. But watch me give you an introduction to each other that will make you feel like strangers. Professor Titcombe, these are Lida and Charles Robie of the hard-cider drinking community you neglected to tell me were to be my nearest neighbors on the mountain. Miss Lida, Charles, this is Professor Titcombe, the most important thing about whom is that he is down on the country.

LIDA: The country or the nation.

RICHARD: I guess both come to think of it. Girl how you do make a man think. But particularly the country as in the expression country Jakes for Rubes. He hates all Jakes Rubes Hicks and Hayseeds, really because they don't vote with the city proletariat; but he pretends it's because they are degenerate. Tell Charles and Lida that story of yours about Henry Dow. Lida's like me: she can bear to hear anything but good about Henry Dow. The Doctor's motto is you've got to get down to the low down if you're going to get anywhere in sociology.

PROF. TITCOMBE: No my motto is you can't afford to be intolerant of any one you can put in a book. Well, the story is more about Henry's twelve children than it is about Henry. It seems Henry had mumps the bad way when he was a young man, but that didn't prevent his wife's having a family of twelve children to help him run the farm. They were of twelve different nationalities each according with the nationality of the hired man they had in the house in the year of it. I've had my attention called to some of them still living in these parts. One looks Irish, one Dutch, one Kanuck and one even nigger.

RICHARD: It's a good story but pshaw—I mean shucks, there's nothing to it, is there Charles?

CHARLES: I'm afraid there is.

PROF. TITCOMBE: That sobers you.

RICHARD: But you don't believe it do you Lida?

LIDA: I never heard it denied.

RICHARD: Which proves it true of course. Shucks again. There must be some natural way to explain it. I begin to think outrageous fiction is what these people blackguard each other with. Hate inspires them to imaginative slander. You ought to have heard the story Henry told me about safety-pins and cannibalism in your camp.

LIDA AND CHARLES: In our camp!

PROF. TITCOMBE: Tell me! Richard means it's a kind of poetry—what pastoral poetry has sunk to in New Hampshire. There speaks the ex-poet in Richard.

RICHARD: On the other hand—

PROF. TITCOMBE: Other hand than what?

RICHARD: Other than Henry Dow. Have you stopped to consider that Lida's father is known as old Soc to distinguish him from the Old Soak Henry Dow.

PROF. TITCOMBE: I know his name is Socrates—Socrates Robie. But what's that to make you so contentious?

RICHARD: And he's a philosopher. Perhaps bearing the name has made him a conscious philosopher.

PROF. TITCOMBE: For the mind's sake!

RICHARD: Honestly. I leave it to Lida.

LIDA: I didn't quite say he was a philosopher. A sage was more what I meant.

RICHARD: But speaking of scandal, let me tell you the best piece of it I have picked up since I came. I have it on pretty good authority that you and Miss Lida (please bow to each other again) are cousins.

PROF. TITCOMBE: Pretty authority and pretty good too. For Heaven's sake, I must have told you I was related to Henry Dow anyway.

RICHARD: No.

PROF. TITCOMBE: I'm related to every single person in this town by breeding and inbreeding: which is why I felt so qualified for getting at them for a Middletown case history.

RICHARD: And you're not ashamed of them for being poor, just curious to find out what being poor has done to their mentality?

PROF. TITCOMBE: Aren't you? You seem excited about it.

RICHARD: Not to make copy of it any more.

PROF. TITCOMBE: Then you wouldn't approve of that other story of mine about the fellow who had both arms round a girl taking notes on her with a pad and pencil behind her back?

RICHARD: It rings nastier than ever on the forty-eleventh hearing.

PROF. TITCOMBE: Young man! Miss Lida I appeal to you. Help! Charles what has your sister been doing to Richard to make him so disagreeable. He thinks he's the only one who sees good in the poor. If you think you can prove we all ought to pattern our lives after Tug Blaisdell and Guinea Whatshis-name, for God's sake get ordained and go to it.

RICHARD: Say, Teacher, Charles and Lida aren't really in on this. They don't follow you. Neither do I any more. You have sure lost a follower in me, and that's a tragic pity, for followers are all you teach school for.

LIDA (*who has been half turned away looking at the smoke*): Yes I am too following you. I've been listening to every word. I know what Richard's put out about. He thinks you and Henry Dow have conspired to make a fool of him.

PROF. TITCOMBE: I thought there was something being kept back. Henry Dow and I conspired—Hell let's leave this till we can talk it over with dignity.—Here's Henry Dow now. Let's ask him if we have conspired—

HENRY DOW: Yes there's a fire. The mill's burning.

RICHARD: So I've been told before.

HENRY DOW: The boiler's going to bust.

LIDA: Aren't you glad?

PROF. TITCOMBE: What are we all standing round with embarrassment for. Are we waiting for someone to speak or something to happen. Oh that damn boiler I suppose. I forgot. Why doesn't it roar as per schedule? Would it help if one of us counted. One, two, three, go! It pays no attention to *me*. You don't mind if I take it no more momentously than you seem to Cousin Lida. Let's all count together. Now! One—two—three. (*He does it alone. No one joins in.*) Pshaw I guess the curtain may as well go down. You can't keep an audience waiting forever for a climax. Let's have our catastrophe in the next scene. (*He is fussing for a match as the curtain goes down.*) It would be strange if half the world on fire I couldn't get a light.

## Scene IV

*Richard on a low box is reading a book on the table with his head close to the window.*

CHARLES (*in the doorway*): Hoigh Dick.

RICHARD: Come in. (*He rises.*)

LIDA (*in the doorway*): Want to see company? Busy?

RICHARD: Oh you're both here. Come in.

CHARLES: Everybody's here. (*Everybody breaks into talk outside.*) Will the house hold us?

RICHARD: It will have to or be stretched. Pile in everybody. Lida, you have the box—box seat for yours. (*Five or six lumbermen fill the middle of the floor waiting to be disposed of.*) You fellows—I shall have to offer you a seat on the floor against the wall.

CHARLES: Seat and back of a chair without the legs.

TUG: Pa Robie sends regrets. He's in mourning for his saw mill. Says he never goes out to parties anymore anyway.

RICHARD: (*He is the last one seated. He takes his ankles in his hands with embarrassment.*) Where did you all drop down from? I didn't hear a thing.

TUG: Maybe you weren't listening the way you were a while back.

GUINEA (*throwing his hat at Tug*): Shut!

TUG (*after another silence of embarrassment*): For Godsake somebody say something.

CHARLES: You say it, Tug.

TUG: I wish I was sure of drinking half the cider I'm asetting over. (*All applaud by shuffling.*)

RICHARD (*rising from the floor and going to sit on the table next to Lida*): Cider! Sure! Where are my manners? Who'll get it? I'm no good at this sort of thing. Who knows where it is? I shouldn't want to mistake the barrel and give you vinegar.

GUINEA: Tug can find it in the dark. Tug was down here for some the other night, but you wouldn't let him have any.

RICHARD: Nobody asked me for any cider.

GUINEA: Tug was hinting around for more than an hour.

RICHARD: Hinting? (*All laugh. Richard looks awkward from not being in on the joke. Lida moves from the box to sit by him against rather than on the table. She speaks to Richard and he tosses his head. They talk a little to each other during what follows.*)

CHARLES: Well Tug.

TUG: Can I have the bucket? It's needed by the bucketful, hey Guinea?

RICHARD: Take it. Throw the water outdoors. Do you need a light?

TUG (*descending into the cellar*): Match'll do.

RICHARD: I'm afraid I haven't cups enough to go round.

(*After a moment's hesitation all with one motion draw large cups of tin and china from their pockets and bring them down on the floor with a bang.*)

RICHARD (*throwing his head back again with pleasure*): You didn't bring one, Charles. I've got one or two extra.

CHARLES: (*Getting on his knees on the floor to receive the bucket from Tug. He dips with his own cup and pours from it for all.*) Now you roughnecks knock your cups together for luck or this drink may not agree with you.

RICHARD: All we lack is Henry Dow for good fellowship.

LIDA: And Tom Titcombe.

ALL: Looking *at* you on the table. *Looking* at you. (*They knock their cups together till they spill in generous libation.*)

HENRY DOW (*in the open door*): Well, I swan!

ALL: Henry, Henry, Henry!

HENRY DOW: (*He makes his way slowly like a sleepwalker into the middle of the room. His eyes run round the company on the floor.*) What have you done with the guardeen? (*He stops in front of the two on the table.*) Well, I swan! It'll larn me not to put my trust in a thing like you again. Overpowered ye I suppose they must of. Or the girl overpowered ye. Leastways they got the cider. I might ha' knowed.

RICHARD: This is my company, Mr Dow. I'm entertaining them.

HENRY DOW: On my liquor. I swan some more. Gone over to the enemy have ye?—and let them in on me in the face of all I warned ye? What did I get you in here for?

LIDA: You must have hinted, Henry. Richard Scott doesn't know how to take a hint.

GUINEA: Not in this country. He may in Boston. (*Applause.*) He ain't at home here yet.

TUG: You hinting old son-of-a-gun, Henry!

HENRY DOW: Didn't I tell you these people was a pack of thieves to be looked out for?—well you may not be thieves, but I know one thing, I never could keep a barrel of cider within a mile of where you was.

RICHARD: You mustn't insult my friends, Mr Dow.

HENRY DOW: It beats the barnyard what a week's growth will do for a crittur like you. You *have* come on.

TUG: A lot has happened sence you was last here, Henry.

CHARLES: Dick helped us put the fire out.

HENRY DOW: Which fire?

CHARLES: The big one—the last one.

TUG: He lost a coat in that calamity.

GUINEA: Tried to beat the fire out with his coat and only catched his coat on fire.

HENRY DOW: That all he accomplished? Didn't save no lives but his own did he? Boiler blowed up on you at last didn't she? Now what'll you do?

CHARLES: Haul to the lake maybe.

HENRY DOW: I was thinking there wouldn't be much to keep you in these parts now the mill was gone.

LIDA: Don't you be in a hurry to get rid of us Henry Dow. We may go to farming again.

HENRY DOW: Say them two ain't married already be they? This ain't a wedding I've blundered in on?

LIDA: Henry Dow! Charles!

HENRY DOW: Ain't you any of you going to offer me a drink of my own cider?

GUINEA (*imitating his whine*): —that I'm so precious fond of.

TUG: You're too late, Henry. Stand back please. We've drunk so much already we'll surely want this second bucket for ourselves.

GUINEA: And the cellar's closed for the night per order of the *See*lectmen. Couldn't open it for the Secretary of Prohibition.

LIDA: He's not to have a drop Charles unless he asks Richard.

TUG: You might not find any in the cellar if you was to look. I can't for the life of me remember turning off the spigot when I drored what I did. By this time the whole barrelful has most likely soaked into the floor. You couldn't lap it up.

GUINEA: And serve you right for endangering Richard's life here for the sake of saving a little drink. If it had been anybody but us there's no telling how dead the boy would have been by now.

TUG: It was a low down dirty trick, Henry.

HENRY DOW: You let me down there. Get out of my way.

(*Several stand up and surround him.*)

HENRY DOW (*querulously*): I'm dry!

GUINEA: You needn't cry about it.

LIDA: Drink water, Henry.

TUG: That's it, drink water, Henry. You can't begin too young.

CHARLES: All up and escort Henry to the spring for a drink of water.

HENRY DOW: Water your grandmother. (*To Richard on the table:*) You you dratted young—

RICHARD: Honestly Mr Dow you didn't make me understand I was to keep the cider all for you. You couldn't have told me in so many words. And as you say yourself, your daughter doesn't—

HENRY DOW: You leave my datter out of it.

CHARLES: Come Henry, your good nature won't let you refuse when it's our treat—when it's on us.

HENRY DOW: You keep hands off me Tug Blaisdell, or I'll have the law on ye. You too Guinea.

TUG: You got to come! There ain't no use hanging back.

LIDA: It's water or nothing for you, Henry Dow. I've got some say in this. I almost forgot. Your daughter made me a free gift of every bunged barrel in the cellar and wasn't gracious enough to accept thanks for it; so it's mine.

MINGLED VOICES: When was this? Why didn't you tell us? Your daughter said we could have it Henry.

LIDA: No, she said I could.

TUG: She meant us.

LIDA: No, for I was particular to ask her. I said do you mean me when you say me? It's mine and I give it to Dick—

CHARLES: Dick's it is.

RICHARD: I accept it.

LIDA: —on one condition that Dick doesn't give a drop of it to Henry Dow.

RICHARD: Tonight.

LIDA: Nor for a long time to come.

CHARLES: You see how helpless we are Henry?

TUG: Water for yours.

HENRY DOW: Hands off. I'll go myself out of this house. I won't be dragged. And I won't be ducked. What do you want me to do?

ALL (*harshly*): Drink water.

CHARLES (*last of the crowd conducting Henry Dow out the door*): Coming, Lida? See that they don't overdo it?

LIDA: No, we'll stay here.

RICHARD: I'm afraid they'll hurt him.

LIDA: What's that to us? Charles will take care of him.

(*They swing their feet in silence a moment.*)

LIDA: What are you going to give me for all that cider?

RICHARD: Does it include the vinegar?

LIDA: No I don't suppose that's mine to give. Why?

RICHARD: I couldn't be expected to give you anything very sweet for vinegar.

LIDA: You. Now it's your turn to ask what I want you to give.

RICHARD: What would you?

LIDA: I thought you said you might write me a poem.

RICHARD: All I said was I wished I hadn't got interested in politics so I *could* write you one.

LIDA: Then if you won't give me a poem for the cider, I'll take your revolver. It's a lady's revolver anyway I believe. You won't need it any more with me to protect you.

RICHARD (*bringing it from the trunk to lay in her lap*): What will you do with it?

LIDA: Keep it away from you to make you less of a terror to the neighborhood.

RICHARD: Are *you* afraid of me?

LIDA: Were you trying to scare me with your talk about the vinegar? I'm no more afraid of you than I am of this. Don't you love the smell of burnt powder in a gun muzzle?

CHARLES: Lida—it's me. Don't mind. I've come back for a cup for Henry. He won't kneel at the spring and he won't be stood on his head, he swears he won't. He stands as stiff as a ramrod. He agrees to drink water if we'll let him have it in a cup. He's begging us not to make him drink it raw though. Haven't you got some ginger or red pepper to put in it to give it a flavor?

RICHARD: Pepper, but don't use it. Don't be too hard on him.

CHARLES: You needn't be so tender of his feelings. He says he has it in for you all right.

RICHARD: Then maybe I ought not to have parted with the revolver.

CHARLES: Hello! Is it loaded?

LIDA: Richard has given it to me to keep. I've disarmed him.

CHARLES: Be careful. I'll be back in a moment when I get rid of Henry and the crowd. We don't want them. I'll set these things outside (*pail and cups*) where the boys can gratify their further cravings.

RICHARD: *Lida*—Charles, let Henry have cider.

CHARLES (*after considering with his back turned*): I'll tell you what. I'll take some in the cup and not let him see it. Then I'll pretend to dip up water from the spring. He'll have his mouth set for water. See if he don't gag and spit the cider out and maybe tip the cup over. Then he'll be sorry.

LIDA: We don't care what you do to make a fool of him. Go long!

CHARLES: You come too and see the circus.

LIDA: Shall we? (*Richard takes her hand but the curtain goes down on her still unpersuaded.*)

## Scene V

*Lida and Richard arrive as Henry Dow breaks from the crowd and runs gagging toward them.*

LIDA AND RICHARD: What's the matter?

HENRY DOW: Cider—give me cider! Lemme by. Something to wash the taste of water out of my mouth.

CHARLES: Overdose of water he thinks. Taken by surprise at the taste of the stuff. Forgotten how his own spring tasted. Shoot him down, Lida, if he tries to get by you. He's desperate. (*Several surround him to seize him.*)

HENRY DOW (*picking up a great stone*): Come between a man and his natural cider would you?

A DRUNKEN VOICE: Where's Richard's professor? Let's initiate him while our hand's in.

RICHARD: Hold on. Let me tell you, Henry. It was cider you just had and choked over. Don't you take any stock in these fellows. They've given you cider—do you hear me?—cider. And you didn't like it when you didn't know what it was. Nobody likes the rotten apple taste of the stuff. People just pretend. I've tasted it.

HENRY DOW (*violently fighting and leaping about*): You've tasted it! It's pasture-ized milk you must be talking about, young feller.

GUINEA: Leave him loose. He'll hurt himself struggling.

TUG (*shouting after Henry Dow as he disappears toward the house*): You needn't pretend to be so drownded by a mouthful of water, Henry. The best of us has to use the stuff *once* a year to wash our outsides with.

PROF. TITCOMBE (*who has arrived during this talk*): Shows we don't like anything except for its reputation—what, Richard?

SAME DRUNKEN VOICE: Nother country heard from. (*harshly*) What's the professor laughing at?

(*Charles having gathered Guinea, Tug and a couple of others in conference, leads them round behind Titcombe and then suddenly forward against him with a rush that bumps him into the middle of the ring. Titcombe swings at them with a laugh and they fall back.*)

CHARLES: Give him room, fellers. Tom Titcombe I have a word to say to you. You stand accused of having written a literary book about us.

PROF. TITCOMBE: No such thing: I haven't written a book about you.

CHARLES: But you're writing one now and that's what you're round here for listening to gossip and luring this innocent young dustyrhodes scholar to help you rake up stories about us. Don't try to squirm out of it. We have it on pretty good authority.

PROF. TITCOMBE: Pretty authority is not necessarily good authority.

CHARLES: We'll leave her out of it. Answer me this: Have you or have you not got it down in writing that one of our folks is a fire bug? Who do you mean is a fire bug?

PROF. TITCOMBE: I haven't named a name.

CHARLES: You better be careful. Didn't you say down in the store the day of the big fire when the boiler blew up, Let them that set the fire put it out. Don't you know that spells arson?

PROF. TITCOMBE: Oh come, you're getting serious, Charles Robie. You know very well I could have meant all of you with your damned old saw mill. You were always setting fire with it.

CHARLES: Well you didn't help put it out and you kept Dick here from helping us. Put that in your book and smoke it— or burn it for all of us. And put what's going to happen next into your book if you have the patience to wait for it. The worse it is the better for your book, hey?

RICHARD: That's right, teacher. The low down is the only subject matter of your social sciences.

CHARLES: Tug just skip down to the back of my car and fetch me the piece of old rope that's there.—Don't you try to run away! And don't be unduly scared. This is no lynching bee. Lord no, that would be too extreme a penalty for writing a book. This is all in fun, though it may incidentally improve your mind. If you have fun with us you can't object to our having our fun with you. Guinea, tell him about the game you learned out west in the cattle country.

GUINEA: It's called Side o' Beef. It's the way they train for putting out prairie fires—grass fires. We'll show you.

PROF. TITCOMBE: Cider Beef? (*Everyone laughs as in school at the error of their superior.*)

GUINEA: You must have cider on the brain. There's been a lot of liquor drunk on all hands today. Side *of* Beef I said. They chop a carcass of fresh beef in two the long way from head to tail right down the spine—so. (*He shows it on Titcombe.*) That leaves one front leg and one hind leg for handles to drag half of it along by, bloody side down along the rim of any grass fire they want to smother out. But sho, they don't need to kill any beef crittur. They can do it just as well with a live man in his clothes.

TUG: *Sho* yes. (*He is just back with the rope.*) They don't need no beef crittur.

PROF. TITCOMBE (*to Richard*): Traitor! Did you get this up?

TUG: Don't you make no false move.

CHARLES: The idea is to use a man when there is no cow to spare. The custom on our Fourth of July field days has grown up to use a volunteer for the sacrifice—or two volunteers so there can be a competition—a race.

RICHARD: I don't know a thing about it. Honestly. You needn't think I'm mixed up in it.

CHARLES: It's just us having our fun with you in return for your fun with us. You best just relax and get the experience.

RICHARD: It'll give you the best license in the world for your book.

CHARLES: We shan't hurt you.

GUINEA: Ready? (*He means to light the grass.*)

CHARLES: No you fool. Mr Titcombe, we've got to ask you to lie down on your side till we can tie your hands together and your feet together.

PROF. TITCOMBE: I'll be goddamned if you will.

RICHARD (*advancing with Lida*): I begin to see. Lida says it's just a neat trick like putting a lighted match in your mouth.

LIDA: Or putting out a candle with your bare finger.

RICHARD: It's a country lark. Don't spoil sport.

PROF. TITCOMBE (*weakening*): Traitor!

HENRY DOW (*loudly from back as he comes prancing from the cellar*): I trusted him and you trusted him, and look at what we get. Healthy guardeen you are.

RICHARD: I'm the guardeen of these people's good name. You make too much fuss, teacher. As Lida says, it's in the interests of science. It's some folk ways for the great book.

HENRY DOW (*still prancing round with high knee action*): You owe it to your admirers, Professor, not to let them do this to you. They're aiming to drag your dignity in the dirt.

GUINEA (*pushing Henry off*): You keep out of this Henry Dow.

HENRY DOW: The Professor's been drinking or he never would submit.

GUINEA: Henry can't bear to see anyone made a fool of except by him.

HENRY DOW (*dancing like a satyr and flapping his arms like a rooster*): Hoigh!—Hoigh!

PROF. TITCOMBE : I'd be more than human and a liberal if I didn't mark you off for this in college Richard Scott. (*He lies down on his side.*) I'm coerced.

CHARLES: Nothing will suffer but your flossy overalls a little. But what's a professor doing in the unchristened clothes of a working man all summer.

(*They tie his hands together and his feet together leaving a short length of rope at each end to drag him by. Tug takes one end, Charles the other.*)

CHARLES: Now if the incendiary suspect will stand forth confessed.

GUINEA: Here. I heard what you said about me, Professor.

CHARLES: It is customary to make an instructive moral speech at the beginning of these ceremonies. Fools like Richard will try to beat a fire out with coats or green boughs and so only fan and spread the fire. The wise rub it out with a board on edge or with a side of beef or as here with the body of a man in his clothes. His old clothes or his brand-new overalls. The secret of success is to get the right speed—not too fast and not too slow. Too fast lets the fire pass under the man. Too slow burns the man. When I say Fire, Guinea you may touch off the grass right here. Fire! (*The dry June grass blazes lightly at once.*) Let it run! (*The crowd retreat.*) The side toward the house, Tug. We must keep Henry's house from burning.

HENRY DOW: You burn my house down and you'll pay for it out of your poor allowance you banjing paupers. The Professor's not himself I claim. Hoigh!

CHARLES: Lida—someone hold Henry. The excitement will kill him. One—two—three, go, Tug.

(*The fire is left to burn itself out toward the front. Charles and Tug wipe it out with Prof. Titcombe in the rear. Richard and Lida try to control Henry Dow as he leaps spasmodically along beside Prof. Titcombe.*)

CHARLES: The hero of our play is Professor Titcombe the fire extinguisher. We wish we had had him in time for the fire that burned the mill down. Let him arise in his bonds and receive the applause of the audience.

LIDA (*pushing between her brother and Prof. Titcombe as he gets up and drawing Richard with her*): Richard Scott says it isn't fair to call Professor Titcombe a fire extinguisher. For this one small fire that he has put out, he has kindled countless other fires of revolt in the breasts of his students.

HENRY DOW (*brushing Prof. Titcombe off*): Did it singe ye?

# LECTURES, ESSAYS,
# STORIES, AND LETTERS

# Contents

# Petra and Its Surroundings

ON THE SUMMIT of Mt. Hor, nestles a shrine beneath which, the Arabians say, lie the bones of the priest, Aaron. It is a place of the wildest grandeur—one worthy the last resting place of the Israelitish orator, overlooking as it does the mountain fastnesses of the warlike sons of Esau, through whose country the Jews strove so long in vain to force a passage.

Mountains rise on every hand; to the north, to the west as far as the great desert, and south and east as far as the eye can reach.

From Mt. Hor the view is one of magnificent sameness; but not until the cliffs have towered above, not until the storm has crowded its overwhelming torrents down the ravines, can the grand sublimity of the situation be felt. In its unstability, the region is like an ice-floe. Everything is constantly changing; mountains are torn away in storm, and mountains totter and threaten in calm.

But the centre of all, once the busy capital of a thriving nation, now the "City of Tombs," the capital of ruin and decay, is in the sublimest situation of the wilderness. To reach it a detour must be made to the south and east to the city's ancient entrance, now called the Sik, which led up to the old mart.

From the confusing accounts of many travelers, one might suppose that Petra was a city, honey-combed with tombs, rising perpendicularly from the plain to the height of a thousand feet; but Petra of the Edomites, Jews, Greeks and Romans, is in a far wilder and romantic location. It lies couched down among the peaks south of Mt. Hor. To it the Sik winds down between mighty red cliffs that tower seven hundred feet above, closing in here and there where the rocks have cracked and slid forward, leaving nothing but a streaking of blue where the cliffs seem to meet.

It is summer; a dim light falls down into the chasm. The torrent bed that follows the gorge is parched and almost buried in tamarisk and thickets of oleanders in full bloom. The cliffs are festooned with pale fern; ivy climbs everywhere;

and the searching roots of the fig-tree cling to the ravine's walls.

As one wanders on over the few chariot-worn flags which once completely paved the way, how strange must be the feeling, as the mind reverts to the cave dwellers whose homes are now mere black squares upon the red crags, and then comes down to the time of the Roman, and sees the chariot hurrying down its last stadia after a weary mountain and desert journey, starting with its echo the eagle from his aerie in the crags above.

How dreary must seem this present desolation of which the Hebrew prophet so often prophesied.

Here the way narrows again, and over it sweeps a great arch, perhaps the city gate, perhaps triumphal.

The Sik winds on, its sides excavated, and marked with Semitic and Latin inscriptions. Suddenly it widens, turns, and there stand a row of pink columns. It is this strange mixture of decay and preservation,—for these columns which front a Roman structure, or rather excavation, are nearly perfect, while but one other building in the city is standing—barbarism and debased civilization, that give Petra its great, strange wildness.

When the road unexpectedly fronts the old theatre, a new characteristic of the city is presented. The seats are of stone alternately red and purple. We have noticed the pink of the columns; the mountains in the distance are white.

The colors around are almost countless; there are maroon, scarlet, yellow, purple, pale rose, blue, grey, and many mixtures, for one traveler compares certain cliffs to mahogany, another, the same cliffs to watered silk.

So varied are the hues of the city that one wonders that the natives did not call it the Rainbow City instead of the "Red City."

Beyond the theatre, which is said to be like that of Tusculum, the road widens, and the city proper spreads out deep in among the mountains. The open ground, whose small rolling hills are covered with ruined foundations, is walled for the most part by sheer precipices, falling for hundreds of feet into the city.

What little is known of the history of Petra is of the wildest interest. Never has there been a stronghold as impregnable. What a place for romance where everything is as vague as a rainbow half faded in mid-air. In our society novels the imagination displayed is as it were a flying squirrel's flight from a tree-top downward; here it might take its flight as a bird from a fountain of youth.

In the city there are traces of four distinct races. For hundreds of years the Edomites held the city, *in* which they were never really conquered. The Jews were sculptors at the time of their conquest, but their chisel was the sword, and they carved naught but destruction. The Pharos, under Rome, made Petra their capital, and by them were built the pillars in the pass and the one building that still stands in the city. Since those days the Mohammedans have built shrines in the cliff niches and on the summits to which the stone-cut stairways lead.

To-day, all is ruin but the tombs that honey-comb the cliffs, and the city is a city of the dead.

Lawrence, Massachusetts,
*High School Bulletin*, December 1891

# A Monument to After-Thought Unveiled

A TRIBUTE to the living? We are away beneath the sombre pines, amid a solitude that dreams to the ceaseless monotone of the west wind, the blue sky looking sleepily between the slowly bending boughs, and to, its veil of morning mist, up-lifted by the morning breeze, white as pure thought, the monument of monuments.

From sun-beat dizzy marts, from grassy lawns, from surging summer trees, rise countless marble columns, wrought as noiselessly as if from snow, and all by the one hand here honored alone in loneliness.

Well might this marble be a shrine, this grove, a temple whence devotees might seek the world again, and fame!

The God—but wait, that carven silence kneeling at its base, whence it tapers away into the boughs above, writes, and this is what she writes:—

There are men—that poet who has left us uniting the battered harp the sea storm cast for him upon the shore, was one of these—who go to death with such grey grandeur that we look back upon their past for some strange sorrow, such as does not fall to others, even though we know sorrow to be the same through all time. They seem like Merlins looking ages from their deep calm eyes. With what awe we stand before the mystery of their persons. Such lives are the growth of the after-thought of the soul—the serene rest after toil, in questioning and answering whence and why misfortune is.

This nobility distinguishes personality only in the degree of its development, and the broader future, will give to every soul the opportunity to come into the possession of this, its divine right. Then, when no man's life is a strife from day to day, from year to year, with poverty, will it be an attribute commonality of the world.

Aggressive life is two-fold: theory, practice; thought, action: and concretely, poetry, statesmanship; philosophy, socialism—infinitely.

Not in the strife of action, is the leader made, nor in the face of crisis, but when all is over, when the mind is swift with keen regret, in the long after-thought. The after-thought of one action is the forethought of the next.

It is when alone, in converse with their own thoughts so much that they live their conventionalities, forgetful of the world's, that men form those habits called the heroism of genius, and lead the progress of the race. This, the supreme rise of the individual—not a conflict of consciousness, an effort to oppose, but bland forgetfulness, a life from self for the world—is the aim of existence.

All this is doubly so of the theoretical. In it the after-thought of long nights beneath the universe, of soul stirrings, of the act of thought itself, is more clearly a part of the next action—its expression. Events influence the first class, the limits of language alone the second.

The poet's insight is his after-thought. It is of varied heart-beats and converse with nature. And the grandest of his ideas come when the last line is written.

Life is an after-thought: how wonderful shall be the world? that is the after-thought of life.

But look again, all this is mere shadow sheen upon the white marble. The one word there is: After-thought.

Now this dark pool beneath the trees is still. There is a white finger on its lips. Let ripples whisper here no more.

And now a last after-thought.

To those who fix today a point through which from earlier years they draw a line of life projected far into the future, this hour is of a deep significance. But there is no change here, and he who thinks to rest will rest as in a winter storm, to die.

Unbounded full ambition for the greatest heights yet un-attained is not too noble for one human mind. Who or what can bound our aspirations? Will courage fail before a thousand unfavorable comparisons? There is a space of time when me-teor and rain drop falling side by side may touch the yielding earth with equal force. The lighter outspeeding weight may seem in a space to strike with greater force. But who at last can tell which has the greater influence on the world, the one that bore, as scientists have said, plant life or that which makes it live.

Strength and all the personality that we can crowd upon the world are ours to give in obligation. Let hope be limitless for all and let each follow hope as best he may.

To all old school associations here we show our purposed way in one bell-toned Farewell!

Lawrence, Massachusetts,
*High School Bulletin*, June 1892

# The Question of a Feather

### How an Editor Got Out
### of the Frying Pan Into the Fire

THE EDITOR sat at his desk. He had been writing about hens all day, and he hadn't heard a hen since he left home in the suburbs in the morning, and he was tired of it. Perhaps the nearest live hens were in the death coops of the Faneuil Hall market. It was a hot day, and he had opened the window for air, but had let in only street noise and the smell of a livery stable. He was at his letters, and his brain reeled at the steady recurrence of the roup letter and the lice letter, and he was on the verge of things unimaginable when there came a fresh clear call from the fields.

It was just another letter, but the quaintness of it:—"You see many poultry places in a year," it ran, "but perhaps have not happened to see—we thought you might be interested to see—a place of which it could be truthfully said, as of ours, that it was the result of following your instructions to the letter. Sister Martha has read your paper ever since we began to keep hens, and gives you all the credit for what we have made of our Minorcas. You have been our only teacher, and we want you to be the judge whether it has been to our advantage. We learn that you pass near us every day on your way to and from the city. Would it be overmuch to ask that you turn aside sometime to visit us?"

Here was precisely what the editor had always feared—that someone would follow his instructions to the letter, and therefore it had been part of his instructions that they should do no such thing. Before everything he had advised the use of judgment in keeping hens. So that if sister Martha had followed his instructions to the letter, be it upon her own head. He was sorry about her Minorcas. He wondered what sister Martha had managed to make of them—Leghorns or only scrubs. Still, he did not feel that he was to blame, and if he was, what was sister Martha going to do about it?

He smiled at his fancies, and as he did so looked at the clock. "I doubt if 'tis as bad as that," he said, "but just to

639

see how bad it is, or how amusing, why not knock off now, and look in on them this afternoon when I'm in need of the recreation? I never have seen a place of which it could be truthfully said that it was all my doing, and while I am not sure that I shall derive much pleasure from seeing one, I had much rather see it myself than have anyone else see it."

As he found his coat and hat, he tried to picture to himself sister Martha, the poultry woman, his constant reader. He thought he knew the type—"Old maid," he said, "and the one that wrote the letter, too. Innocent, credulous kind, or under the circumstances I shouldn't trust myself to their tender mercies in a lonely suburb toward supper time. Now if it was a man that wanted to confront me with his failure to make money in hens—but why speculate when I shall soon know."

On the electric cars he referred to the letter again, once for the address, and once to refresh his memory of the contents. He considered himself as having one of the good times incident to his calling. He liked nothing better than visiting a poultry farm, and visiting this one had a spice of real adventure.

"So here we are," he said at last, referring once more to the letter in front of a little vine clad cottage. The surroundings were almost rural. In the near distance lingered a dark clump of tall timber; there were fields and gardens and orchards. But here and there you saw a house going up, and you heard the sound of boards unloading, and of nails driven home. The city streets were there, too, though it was plain that the house he sought had been there before the streets, for it was set down without reference to their direction, like some mirage through which you might expect to see the more substantial objects behind it.

He satisfied himself from the safe side of the fence before it was too late to retreat had he cared to, that everything about the place was as it should be. The fruit trees were thrifty; the hen houses were right, and the yards were right, and, unless he was mistaken, the hens in them approximated Minorcas—Black Minorcas.

He thought as it was near feeding time he might catch someone out of doors, in which case he would make an informal yard call, and get home to an early supper and long evening. And sure enough, as he stood irresolute who should click the latch of the hen house door but sister Martha herself, (as her looks told him), in her hand, for a subject of conversation, a pailful of eggs.

"And so these are the Minorcas?" he said. "They lay well. How many do you keep?" He had been within a thought of saying, "So this is sister Martha," but had fortunately suppressed that as perhaps too much for a beginning. "I'm the editor of *Hendom*," he made haste to add at the sight of the lady's consternation.

"Oh, oh, Mr. Fulton. Won't—well, sister Martha—won't you come into the—" she appeared from her movements to break off in doubt as between house and hen house. She decided for the former. "Sister Martha will want to see you first. Won't you come into the house?"

So there was some mistake, and this was not sister Martha. Well, if it was not it ought to be, and he did not cease to assert her claims to the name until presently in the house he was confronted by the superior claims of the other.

His visit made the ladies sit up very straight. In their embarrassment they let slip precious moments without a word. As much to help them as to make himself at home, the editor conceived and executed a pleasantry.

"To which of you after myself, always after myself, am I to give most credit for the pailful of eggs I have just seen?" But while serving to compose nerves, it had rather a sobering effect than the reverse. It was the author of the letter that spoke, "Sister Martha wouldn't be able to do much, you know, and so the work out of doors falls to me; but she is the one that is interested in showing and such things."

The editor, of course, had not known, but now he guessed. Sister Martha was an invalid, and the extent of her share in the hen business was looking at the hens through the window. It was only a sisterly fiction that made her chief poultryman.

The editor was properly subdued by the intelligence. Only after a prolonged pause did he attempt to give a more cheerful turn to the conversation by venturing to suggest that the subject of showing had been mentioned.

"Yes," said the author of the letter, "we have not shown yet, but if we are prospered in our stock this year, we intended to go to Boston in the winter, and perhaps New York, and that reminds me—Martha, that feather; you are just in time, Mr. Fulton, to help us with that feather on the leg of, I think, our best pullet."

"Pull it?"

"Yes, pullet."

"Help you pull it, I mean."

"Tell us whether it is right to pull it," she answered, flushed and serious.

His call to see the hens had degenerated into a call on sister Martha, which was more than he bargained for, and now he found himself confronted with a very nice question of ethics that up to this time in his life he had always managed to avoid. The question of pulling feathers was one to which he had always thrown his columns open for discussion—freely, but you could ask anyone if he had ever joined in the discussion. He was above suspecting that he had fallen into a trap set by his enemies, but he liked the situation none the better. Perhaps he was unreasonably shy of old maids disposed to follow his instructions to the letter.

He was thinking, thinking, and Martha, seeing his difficulty, came to his rescue. "Perhaps Mr. Fulton doesn't care to take it upon his conscience to decide for us in such a matter. It is too much to ask him."

The editor laughed uneasily at her penetration. "Oh, don't consider me," he said gallantly, "anything I can do to help you." But he was none the less inclined to temporize. "How comes a feather on the leg of a Minorca?" he asked.

"I know, and she from one of our best matings."

"Bring her in," said Martha.

The bird was brought, and sat cowering on the center table, unmistakably a picture pullet.

"Isn't it a shame?" sighed Helen.

"I am afraid it is the temptation that is the shame," said Martha. "We have had pullets before spoiled by a single defect, and have not felt as now. It is because the fault is so remediable. And people ought to face their own temptations, and not ask others to face them for them."

"But temptation implies wrong, and we only asked Mr. Fulton to tell us if it is wrong."

"We know it is wrong."

The editor was grateful to sister Martha for letting him out. "Really," he said, "I wish you wouldn't ask me to decide for you. But I shouldn't worry; 'tis a long time before the shows; the pullet may shed the feather."

"But if she doesn't?" said Helen, who was inconsolable.

"She may develop defects less remediable than a leg feather."

"Oh, but she won't," persisted Helen. "She is well along now, and you know how it is with the Mediterraneans."

He looked closer for the feather. He wondered if they would thank him for pulling it by stealth. What prevented him from pulling it, and so ending their perplexity, he did not know, unless it was the fear of lowering himself in the estimation of two very respectful ladies.

"Well," he said, "I don't see but that you will have to give up the idea of showing her."

The sisters were glum. His visit had done them no good. He was disappointed. He reached for the knob of the door.

"I must be going, and I haven't seen your place at all. Perhaps some other time."

But one thing and another prevented his repeating the visit. He often thought of the two, however, and once alluded to them indirectly in an article on "Women and Poultry." And at the Boston show he looked among the Minorcas for the outcome of their moral struggle. There was their pullet, disqualified. If those goody goodies hadn't compromised by frankly showing her with the offending feather intact. Who but two old maids would have thought of that way out of it?

*Farm-Poultry*, July 15, 1903

# The Original and Only

"You want to hear about our hen," said the practical poultryman, "the original and only—the hen that diverted us from the fancy, and laid the foundation for our present profitable egg business.

"Well, I bought her for her shape and color, and for nothing else, with no thought of the eggs in her—they might be solid gold for all I cared. She was a prize bird, but that wasn't what I bought her for. I bought her because she suited me. I had the mate to her, as cocky a cockerel as you ever saw, raised right on this place, and as I was going into the fancy for keeps, I paid twelve good dollars for that hen. It was a genuine plunge for a conservative farmer. I was five years younger than I am now, but I did just right. I'd do the same thing again today. She was a good beginning. She'd have been the making of us if we'd staid in the fancy, only she didn't let us stay.

"I remember well the day I got her home here. It was early in December, but cold as January. She was given the run of the barn for the time being, along with another bird I had picked up at the show, until I could make up the pen they were going into. The barn was no place for her in such weather, but she hadn't been there an hour when that boy of mine comes into the house and reports, 'That hen's laid another egg.'

" 'Which one,' says I.

" 'The one that laid in the box in the cars on the way—'tis the same egg.'

"I got to know that egg before long as well as my own name. It was a light glossy brown, flecked with pink. I can show you a specimen that we keep blown as a trophy.

"I said to myself, 'That's a pretty good hen not to let anything interfere with her plans like that. I wonder if it would stop her laying to pluck her.' I vow I don't believe it would, though come to think of it, I can't say that she ever laid in the molt, and that's about the same thing as being plucked by nature. But I never asked her to lay in the molt. She laid hard enough anyway to scare a man. I was always afraid she couldn't keep the pace, or something would go wrong, and finally it did. She got to making eggs faster than she could lay them. They came so fast that they crowded each other and broke, and she died of sort of an internal custard, so to speak. But I'm getting ahead.

"Along at first we didn't know which hen she was. I said to the boy, 'You make it a point to find out which hen is doing this.' He said he couldn't tell them apart. I told him to lift them off the nest and get the numbers on their leg bands. We didn't have any trap nests on the place then. The boy was our first trap nest. He deserves some of the credit for what followed.

"It turned out that No. 5 was the layer—the prize bird, the one that cost twelve dollars. I paid for her show points and got her eggs thrown in, but her eggs alone were worth the money. Not that she laid enough to bring that much in the market, though there's no telling what she might have done if she'd lived long enough; but they were worth it for what they taught me. For one thing, they taught me the importance of the egg of the best bred hen, which is something I doubt if one in a thousand thinks of in buying, and it wouldn't do one much good if he did think of it. It was the contrast between her egg and that of the other hen, I suppose, that brought it home to me. The other hen laid about once a week, and when she did lay it was a dead white, gritty, thin shelled egg, just misshapen enough at the pick to be unhatchable. She was money thrown away, though she wasn't bad looking.

"Of course at first all I saw in No. 5's eggs was fancy chickens. I was glad she laid good eggs, and laid often, because it meant chickens, and lots of them. But one day the boy said something that set me thinking. 'It seems to me,' he said, 'that that No. 5 lays three days and rests one.'

" 'Are you sure of that?' I said.

" 'No, I'm not sure.'

" 'Well, don't say anything you aren't sure of. Make sure. There's a calendar; you can keep score for her on that.'

"So a fire insurance calendar on the wall was our first egg record book.

"The boy was right; she did lay three days out of four; when the days got longer, four out of five. I said to myself: 'If there are other hens like that there must be others still altogether *unlike* that to pull down the average, because we think we're doing well at this season if we get half as many eggs as we have hens. It looks as if there must be some hens that only lay one day a week to offset the work of those that lay every day but one. 'Tis plain that a poultryman is as much in need of a weeder as a market gardener, and what's the trap nest but a weeder?'

"Suddenly I saw the trap nest in a new light. Before that it had been associated in my mind with big egg stories and line breeding for eggs. But it has no necessary connection with either. One needn't abuse his trap nests to make his hens too prolific for the stamina of the stock, if such a thing is possible; neither need he lie about their findings, neither need he tell the truth about them if the truth was so remarkable as to look like a lie. He could keep his mouth shut in that case. There may be such a thing as a 300-egg hen, but I'm not going to be the fellow to say so—not at this stage of the game. If you watch you'll see how careful I am not to be too definite about No. 5's laying. I am satisfied to claim for her about 200. It was more than that. But you don't catch me saying whether it was one more or a hundred more.

"I don't know whether I should have made a success of the fancy or not, and probably never shall know, because right at this point I was diverted from it for good and all. The trap nest as a weeder appealed to me as a sure thing. I felt that the fancy was considerably chancy. Fanciers are born, not made, and I wasn't sure that I felt particularly born, and as the ministers say that's the test, if you don't feel as if you are called you aren't called. There were already a lot of good men in the fancy who easily made the birds it would probably be cheaper for me to buy. And as far as I knew, the ranks of those who were tending strictly to the trap nests were mighty slim.

"You see what one hen can do. We knew that she laid 200 eggs—call it that. We didn't have to take anyone's word for it. It don't satisfy you, but it satisfied us. It gave us faith to go ahead. It gave us a sound basis to figure on, which is the hardest thing in this world to get. We have housed about 400 hens for years, and they laid for us upwards of 125 eggs a year; if they could be converted into 200-egg hens, by selection or otherwise, it would mean a clear gain of $ 1.50 per head with very little extra trouble. It would just double profits at what it costs us to feed, and what we get for eggs at wholesale.

"You may form some idea of what No. 5 may have been for shape and size and constitution from the general appearance of our flock today, for they are all her offspring in the fifth and sixth generations. They were not bred exclusively to lay. They were bred for everything that No. 5 was, and that was a good deal. But we are not afraid to say that we believe in eggs—we believe in the 200-egg hen. I am not prepared to say just how common she is, but probably not over-common. Two hundred eggs should be enough to entitle a hen to the name of the new hen, for of course we are not to have the new everything else without the new hen, and the new hen must distinguish herself from the old hen and the old pullet by marked superiority as a layer. She is not to crow or sport sickle feathers or talk politics. She must succeed without going out of her sphere.

"I'm going to observe the same caution about making claims for our 400 as I did for No. 5. We haven't got them all up to the 200 mark yet, not by any manner of means, and we've got some above it. It would surprise you to see the average—if you could believe it. They do very well—very. Of course 400 hens are not many. Now neighbor Davis over here is a real poultry man. He has something like a thousand in a three story building with no dirt on the floors except what the hens supply. We can't compare with him. But I sometimes think neighbor Davis isn't as fat as he used to be, and he talks too much of Belgian hares and squabs and ginseng for a man that's satisfied with hens."

*Farm-Poultry*, September 1, 1903

# The Cockerel Buying Habit

THE OLD GENTLEMAN took his corncob out of his mouth, and leaning toward me lowered his voice almost to a whisper: "What's your opinion of inbreeding, anyway?" he said.

"I'm a safe man to talk it over with," I laughed. "What's your opinion? There's no law against it, is there?"

"Law of nature," he suggested.

"I'd risk it."

"You're not afraid of it then?"

"Pshaw!"

He rolled his eyes on me with unfeigned admiration of my recklessness; but he shook his head.

"I snum I don't know," he reflected. "It's attended with awful consequences in the human family. You know how it's supposed to be when cousins marry. You can hear some awful stories against it."

"You can hear just as many the other way, and more authentic."

"Did ever I tell you how George Hill bred Cochins in till he got them that squat and fluffy and Cochiny they were a sight for sore eyes? But come to set their eggs one year there wasn't a single one fertile."

"I believe you have told me, but I don't think he proved anything. So many considerations enter into a case of the kind."

"Yes, of course it might have been something else. And maybe it's all prejudice on my part, but I snum I don't know. Don't seem as if anything'd ever make me feel about it as you do."

We had been on the point of considering his hens when the conversation took this serious turn. They were running at large, but as it was near feeding time a number had gathered around us as we talked. Our thoughts went back to them.

"Well, there they are, *such* as they are," said the old gentleman with a sweep of the hand. "It's as much as a year or two since you've seen them, I guess."

"What's the matter with those? They're a nice looking lot," I protested.

"If you don't see it, I'm not going to tell you."

All hens in a flock look pretty much alike at first glance, and it is hard to pick out individual characteristics. But I had to say something.

"Perhaps you mean they vary somewhat in size. You have some very white birds."

"I mean they're of all sorts and kinds. I've got some very white birds, and I've got some not so white. I've got some big ones, and I've got some all fired runts. The fact is they come every which way. I haven't anything like a strain."

As I looked I became convinced that there was something to what he said.

He sat down on his heels and pointed with his pipe stem. "There that one facing this way—tail to tail with that other one—she's eating now."

"Yes, I see her."

"Well, she's what I call a pretty middling fair bird—good full breast, and nice spread of tail. There may be a couple of others something like her in the flock—not exactly like—not on your life—but something like. I know where they come from. I know them as much as anything by a certain defect they all have—a hollow comb—worse in the males than in the females, of course—or more noticeable. They keep showing up since I bought a cockerel of So and so a few years back. Then take that one over there—alone—walking. She's likely to have a few stubs on her legs, though you can't see them from here. That's the tendency of the strain she comes from. But even if she hadn't feathered legs, and the other hadn't a bad comb, and both of them were all that they ought to be, they wouldn't be any more alike than the animals in a happy family at the circus."

I listened to this confession in silence.

As the old gentleman recovered his feet he shied a chip at another specimen. "And that one takes after what you may call 'im's strain. And there's another—I can tell you who breeds them like that—oh—now I know that as well as I know my own name—he lives out there in Milledge—never mind, it will come to me. You see I've got them all and some besides, especially the some besides, the combinations that are neither this, that, nor the other, all right here together where I can study and compare them. But of course I could do that at the shows, couldn't I?"

"Not so much at your leisure," I consoled him.

"No, no, you're right there. I've had a chance to improve myself a lot. And no one can accuse me of having bred in. I could leave it to a jury of summer boarders if it looked as if I had bred in, couldn't I? And now what? At the age of sixty the indications are that I'm about ready to begin over again— dress the lot and begin over again. And I call myself a breeder? So much for the cockerel buying habit. And the question before the house is, another time shall I breed in?"

"Chance it—why don't you chance it?"

"That's what I asked you for—would you advise me to? I guess you don't think I could have come out any worse than I have, anyway."

"You don't think so yourself, do you? Come."

"Don't seem as if I could have, does it? But I snum I don't know."

*Farm-Poultry*, February 1, 1904

# Dalkins' Little Indulgence

## A Christmas Story

IT IS NO MATTER how much Dalkins paid for the bird; the point is that the man who sold it to him somehow got the impression that he did not pay enough—that he would have paid more. He could not have denied that Dalkins paid him all he asked. So that he had himself to blame if it was not enough. But he got to talking as if he had been cheated—and badly cheated. He enlarged upon the bird until he said he shouldn't wonder if Dalkins would get a cool fifty for it. He groomed it, so to speak, as he thought of it. He made it a little whiter than white, a little more symmetrical than symmetry.

As a matter of fact it was the kind of bird that is worth what one can get for it. It transcended scoring, as it was better than any score reputable judges are willing to sign. It was a bird framed by nature for comparison judging.

If the man who sold it to Dalkins made the mistake of parting with it for a cent less than fifty dollars, he deserved sympathy, but he was the only one who could see that Dalkins deserved blame. He showed himself a poor loser. He talked early and late to all comers about his misfortune that was another man's fault. But almost all comers had been in the same fix themselves, and knew how to make allowances. They did not believe too heartily in the pricelessness of his bird—a suspicion of which made him but talk the more.

The wonderful part of this story is that this fellow had picked the bird up away over back in Peacham, Vt., for one dollar and fifty cents. These figures I am willing to vouch for. In that case he did fairly well if he got a five for it. Mind you, I don't say what he got. At the time I heard various rumors. This part of the story must remain shrouded in mystery—men are such liars. I vouch for nothing that you cannot safely believe.

Though he was far enough away from this man and his troubles, the facts here stated somehow or other reached Dalkins. He had come by the bird through an agent of his who had spotted it by the merest accident from his carriage in passing. He had not been too curious about its history and antecedents at the outset; with him the bird in the hand was the thing. But a certain letter aroused his interest. It was anonymous, doubtless from someone in no way concerned, but bent on mischief making, and informed him that the remarkable bird had been raised by the writer's next door neighbor, and had been started on its career for one dollar and fifty cents. He questioned his agent about it. The agent had heard some such tale. Evidently gossip had been buzzing in the hill town of Peacham. He had heard also that the bird was of the Dalkins strain direct. That was calculated to please Dalkins. He wondered if they couldn't find out who raised it. He would have liked the poor benighted fellow who would part with such a jewel for one fifty to know by its fruits what a thing the Dalkins strain was.

"He didn't suspect what he was doing," he said.

"It isn't likely," said the agent.

"And the fellow who sold him to you?"

"He had some idea, because he's kicking himself for having sold it. I have seen him since. He is talking at a great rate."

"The bird has made some stir already, then; that's what they call the fatal gift of beauty, isn't it?"

The agent was duly embarrassed. Dalkins was thinking.

"Say," he said at last, "I want you to find that original owner and bring him to the New York show on me. And bring the other fellow, too—both of them. I guess I'm good for it. Tell them 'tis a Christmas notion of mine—the show is near enough to Christmas for that. It'll make it easier for you. We'll show them a thing or two, and we'll show the kicker that he only knows a little bit more than the other fellow. And I think I'll show you something. Not a word of this to anyone outside, and not too many words to them. Just say 'tis my treat—consolation treat. 'Tis an order."

Dalkins' agent found the original owner away over in Peacham one bitter cold morning a day or two after Christmas. Peacham is a New England street town, that is to say, it consists of but one street, which runs north and south along a sharp ridge that looks like the back of a razor backed world. The railroad, when it was built, missed it by about eight miles on the right, and that seemed to send it into a decline—such a close call, no doubt. Many of its fine old houses are going to ruin, and there is never a new one to take their place. The age and size of its shade trees suggested that it might do very well in summer; but on such a day in winter it made the agent fairly groan at the patience of the people who could abide there. He inquired at the postoffice store for his man, and was sent to the woods for him. He came upon him snaking out logs in a grove recently laid waste, as seriously at work as if he had entirely given up seeing Santa Claus that year. He laid before him his invitation, and while not persuading him on the spot to accept it, succeeded in making him regard it as worth considering. At any rate, he carried him away in triumph from his toil like a Cincinnatus, a Putnam, or a Parker. He left his ox team standing in a brush pile in the care of his fellow workmen.

Before he left he had dinner with him, and it was all arranged. The fellow was a little sheepish at first, as one accused of deliberately circulating counterfeit money—only in this case it would have been a counterfeit bird. He suspected that his punishment was going to take the form of a practical joke. But he decided he was equal to it if only it wasn't to cost him anything, and the return ticket the agent laid down for him set at rest his fears on that score.

The agent had less trouble with the other fellow—Durgin, if the name must out. He considered the invitation his due. "Aw yes," he yawped, "he knew how it all was. Nobody probably intended to do him. It was business, just business. Only he thought," etc. Of course he wasn't a fool. He knew a good bird when he saw one. Only sometimes his mind didn't work quick enough, etc. Yes, he'd be glad to meet Mr. Dalkins. He bore no grudge. He wasn't that kind. Only he thought, etc. The main thing was that he accepted the ticket.

Scene, the New York show. Mr. Dalkins is doing the honors. When I say doing, I mean doing. He never let those two importations of his out of his sight for three days, and he never gave them a restful half hour. And it was not all inside the Garden. But let us draw a veil over anything that was irrelevant to the show proper. What have I to do with the Rialto and the Bowery? Suffice it to say that he gave two simple souls the time of their lives, and beat them out in his own enjoyment of it, in spite of the fact that it was on him and it came high.

The grand finale Mr. Dalkins had all prearranged, and he looked forward to it with the anticipation of a boy. No one had an inkling of what was coming, unless it was his agent to whom he once said in an aside: "The bird, *the* bird, was sold, I suppose you didn't know, before anything was placed, but he's not to change hands till the last day of the show. I want you to be there when he does."

And once he had said to the second in line of possession, "So it sticks in your crop that you should have had fifty for your trade. Well, we won't let that spectre intrude on our festivities. Time enough for discussion afterward. There's always a way to settle such matters between gentlemen."

But the victim, though disliking the tone of banter in this, smelt not a rat. He and the original owner came to the final catastrophe as unprepared as the babe new born. They were so absorbed in the pleasure of the hour that it never occurred to either that he might be destined in the mind of the master to point a moral or adorn a tale. When it suited Dalkins' sense of dramatic fitness, they were led like lambs to the slaughter.

He towed the brace of them round to a certain much be-ribboned coop in the last hours of the show. He had made it a point to take them there several times a day during their stay to punctuate their experiences and keep them from forgetting to whom they were indebted for their popularity. He had never said much in the feathery presence. He found it more impressive to look in silence. His charges divided their hushed regard between him and the bird, awed by the thought of what great things might be passing in the mind of such a man at such a moment.

Now he led them there for the last time. Tomorrow it was good bye. The tumult and the crowing would die away. He told them that they must have a last look at the prize they had let slip through their fingers. Might it be a lesson to them!

As it happened they found someone there before them. He showed himself more than usually interested, and they hung back until he should have completed his scrutiny. Upon lifting his head from the note book he employed, he recognized Dalkins. He had been about to move off. He stood still. There may have been a momentary gleam of fun in his eye. It passed unnoticed.

"Splendid," he said, with an indicative wave of the hand, "I want him."

"I thought of you, Wilson, when I put him in here. Isn't he what you were looking for in the fall? I thought you would want him."

"I do. Your price?"

Dalkins made a movement with his fingers as if he despaired of having enough to give the sign. He ended by holding up, side by side, and far forward, one finger on each hand.

The agent, Durgin, and the original owner, turned pale. The first thought he was insane, the second that he was making a fake sale, the third that he hadn't been so far wrong in his estimate of the bird. To these three the two fingers meant two dollars.

"Shade it," said Mr. Wilson.

"Will you give me a dollar fifty?" laughed Dalkins.

"What are a few dollars here or there when it is a question of such a bird?" said Wilson as he went down for his wad.

"This is the payee." Dalkins obtruded the original owner.

"His bird, is it?"

"In a way, yes. He raised it up back here a few hundred miles, and I don't consider that he was ever honestly separated from it." This with a withering eye to Durgin.

"It wasn't stolen?"

"It comes to that. He was induced to sell it for one dollar and fifty cents."

For a moment Wilson hesitated and drew back, but it was only a moment. He looked at the bird again. "Well," he said, "I'm not supposed to know that. A bargain's a bargain."

At the moment of being thrust into prominence by the collar, the original owner, somewhat taken by surprise, had mechanically turned up a hand. Now Dalkins seized upon this and held it as in a vice, while Wilson heaped bills upon it till the count should have been lost, though it wasn't. The sum total was two hundred dollars. All the time Durgin had been opening wider and wider at the mouth.

"If I let go," said Dalkins to the original owner, "can I trust you to put that money where it belongs, and not bother me with arguments? Remember it is Christmas, or was a week or so since."

The original owner smiled weakly, but made no remonstrance.

"Where do I come in?" piped up poor Durgin.

"For a good time, and a valuable lesson," snapped Dalkins. "If there's anything else you want but can't seem to lay your hands on, just take it out in kicking."

Then Dalkins gently but forcibly closed the original's fingers over the paper in his hand, and headed him down the aisle. Durgin followed with a rattling in his throat that suggested roup, but merely indicated the impulse to speak without the ability.

Everybody followed, the little procession attracting considerable attention in the hall. It was thought someone had been arrested by a plain clothes man for stealing ribbons from the cages. The original had almost lost consciousness of what was going on around him. He heard as in a dream amid the uproar of roosters, that sounded like a dying yell that wouldn't die, the voice of Dalkins saying, "Go tell that up in the hills, and make them stop breeding mongrel stock."

*Farm-Poultry*, December 15, 1905

# Children's Stories

## Schneider and the Woodchuck

ONE DAY Schneider chased a woodchuck down his hole and began digging after him like everything.

But the woodchuck had two holes and he came up out of the other one and sat up and said, "I see your tail, Schneider, I see your tail!"

Schneider ran over and chased him down that hole and began digging there.

Then the woodchuck came up out of the first hole and sat up and called again, "I see your tail, Schneider, I see your tail!"

Schneider was so mad that he gave up and went home.

The woodchuck laughed and said, "Goodbye Schneider. Come again."

Schneider said, "Oh stop talking—woodchucks can't talk."

And the woodchuck said, "Neither can dogs."

That's so: they can't.

## Schneider and the Little Bird

SCHNEIDER was asleep on the piazza and he felt something pull his hair and he jumped up and looked but he couldn't see anything. So he lay down again and went to sleep and pretty soon he felt it again. He went right in the house and asked Lesley if she did it. Lesley said no, and Schneider couldn't understand. The next time he lay down he only went to sleep with one eye—this one—no I guess it was this one.

In a minute he saw a little bird fly out of the woodpecker tree right at him.

It was so near when he jumped up that it got scared and lit on his nose. "Ouch!" it said. "Cold!" It flew up into the woodbine.

"What do you want?" Schneider said.

"Hair for a nest."

"Why don't you use your own feathers?—you're full of them."

And the bird said, "Do you mean full like a pillow?"

## The Wise Men

CAROL kissed us all goodbye and climbed up into the nut tree, going quickly round and round the trunk where the branches were best until he was out of sight. He was out of hearing too before any of us thought to ask him when he would be back, so there was nothing to do but wait and see. He was so long gone with no sign of him, not a falling twig or nut, that we began to wonder, especially as it grew dark. We were afraid that he would not risk climbing down by starlight and we would have to stay under the tree all night.

That was the way it turned out. We took turns watching for him and morning came and there was no Carol. The night was perfectly quiet and the leaves were still in the whole great tree and each of us as he sat alone listened intently for any sound of the little boy. We thought he might have shouted to us some word of what was keeping him. But he seemed to have forgotten us.

It was the same all day for the tree seemed as deserted as if it hadn't held so much as a bird's nest. We let everything else go on the farm, the cow unmilked, the weeds unhoed while we stood and talked about the strange thing that had happened to us. The day passed and another night.

But toward evening the next day there was the cry, "Here he comes!" Margy had seen him or seen the nails of his boot-heels feeling for a footing away among the branches. How strange he looked! He looked changed. First we all ran forward: then we all ran back—three steps. He had touched ground and now he turned toward us blinking—an old grey man. His beard was long and white and pointed and his hat was long and red and pointed and all covered with stars and new moons. He wore a long cloak clear to his feet and carried a big book under his arm. He turned three times round and round as if he wished to make himself dizzy but it was only to get his bearings. Then without a look to show that he knew we were there he walked straight past us up the little hill into the sweet ferns and tramp tramping away into the woods. Well!

We hadn't said a word. We hadn't moved until he was gone. Now we started chattering. Irma said he was as small as Carol, but too old. Lesley said, "To get as old as that he would first have to grow to the size of a man and that might take five years if he eat well and then he would first have to shrink back to his own size and that would take five hundred years because it takes longer to grow small than it does to grow large."

Margy was for going after him.

Lesley said, "The way he's headed he'll come out in the village if he goes far enough and doesn't climb another tree; and the people will bring him back to us—if they can tell who he is—that's so—they can't can they?"

Suddenly Margy and Irma cried out at the same time, "Here he comes again!" and "Here comes another!" We didn't know which was right.

This one was exactly like the other, beard hat cloak book and all. He went through the same movements turning slowly three times to get his bearings and then set out for the ferns and the wood in the footsteps of the other. But we were not so surprised as before. We got our voices and managed to speak. We even tried to stop him by putting ourselves in his way though we didn't dare to lay hands on him he was so queer. He brushed past us and out of sight.

We all gathered under the tree to look up for the appearance of another one. As we were standing so along came Smith and pulled up his horse to talk about the weather. But you may imagine that we didn't want him there when another of those old men might come down at any minute and then what would people think of our farm? So we tried not to encourage him to talk, answering him only with yes or no and not saying anything new ourselves. We got rid of him just in time. If he had looked back as he drove away he might have seen as it was, but I think he was a little cross at our bad manners. It was the third of the old men and exactly like the other two. I am sure you would have found the number of stars and new moons on the hats of all three precisely the same. He left us like the others.

The question was, Were they Carol? How could they be? It was a great puzzle.

But not for long, for hardly had we lifted our eyes to the tree again when we saw the real Carol coming down in the same clothes he went up in. He came to the ground with a thud.

"Have you seen my cap down here?" he said.

"No but we saw three old men," we said.

"It ought to have come down. I dropped it. Are you sure you didn't see it?"

"No but we saw three old men," we said.

"Oh those fellows."

"Who were they?"

"Three old know-it-alls I got acquainted with up there. How long have I been gone? Say it's the strangest thing about that hat. I dropped it for you so you'd know I was all right. It must have been day before yesterday. I don't want to lose that. I'll tell you about the old men some other time. Let's hunt for the hat."

"No tell us now. What were they doing in our Nut Tree?"

"Trying to find out how high the sky is. When I arrived on top there they sat in a ring looking up in the sky with their hats sticking out behind and their beards in front. Each had a book open in his lap and his finger marking a place on a page. I said hello to them but they were too solemn to notice anything like that, so I tried again with a question.

" 'What are you doing?'

"Every one looked suddenly at me as if I was new, rounding his eyes terribly and opening his mouth. Then they looked at each other. No one spoke.

" 'What are you doing?' I said again.

" 'Trying to find out something!' They answered in one voice and tipped their heads back again.

" 'What?' No answer.

" 'I should think such old men as you would know every-thing,' I said to tease them.

" 'We do we do we do. Everything but just one thing and

if you had not come and interrupted us we'd have known that in a few minutes.'

" 'What is it?'

" 'How high the sky is.'

" 'Oh, I'll give you something you can tell me if you know everything. What's it going to do tomorrow?'

"They all tipped up their faces again.

" 'What's it going to do tomorrow if you know everything? That's what I'm up here to find out.'

" 'We don't want to talk to you,' they mumbled without taking their eyes off the sky.

"But I stuck to it. 'Tell me what it's going to do tomorrow?' That was too much for one of them; I don't know which one for there was no way of telling them apart. He slapped his book shut, got up and went down the tree.

"So I bothered the other two for a while without getting a word out of them though I could tell by the shaking of the little tassle away out on the end of their hats that they were disturbed; until one after the other they left me in a rage. Then I came down. But the funniest thing is about that cap."

1900–1908

# The Pinkerton Academy
# English Curriculum

## ENGLISH.

The general aim of the course in English is twofold: to bring our students under the *influence* of the great books, and to teach them the *satisfaction* of superior speech.

### English I.

Reading:—Treasure Island, Robinson Crusoe (not in class), Horatius at the Bridge, Sohrab and Rustum, selections from Odyssey, selections from Arabian Nights, ten short stories (in class). Expression in oral reading rather than intelligent comment is made the test of appreciation.

Composition:—Fifty themes, written and oral; given direction by assignment of subjects. Criticism addressed to subject matter equally with form.

Rhetoric:—Talks on the subject, what it is (with copious illustrations from the experience of the teacher) and where to be found.

Memorizing:—Twenty poems from the Golden Treasury; basis of subsequent study of the history of English literature.

### English II.

Reading:—Pilgrim's Progress, Ivanhoe, thirty short stories (not in class), As You Like It, Ancient Mariner, Gareth and Lynette, Passing of Arthur, selections from Hanson's Composition (in class). Discussion proceeds more and more without the goad of the direct question.

Composition:—Fifty themes.

Rhetoric:—Talks chiefly on the technicalities of writing.

Memorizing:—Twenty poems learned from dictation. These form the basis for subsequent talks on literary art.

### English III.

Reading:—Silas Marner, Tale of Two Cities, House of Seven Gables, Kenilworth (not in class), Julius Caesar, selections from Walden (in class); some voluntary work in Scott, Dickens and Hawthorne, or Shakespeare, Marlowe, and

662

Sheridan, or the lyrics of Wordsworth, Browning, Tennyson and Kipling.

Composition:—Thirty themes. Woolley's Handbook is used in theme correcting.

*English IV.*

Reading:—College requirements. Especially in this year a point is made of re-reading a great many selections remembered with pleasure from previous years.

Composition:—Thirty themes.

Memorizing:—Lines from Milton.

Parts of such books as the following have been read from the desk to one class and another this year: Jonson's Silent Woman, Clemens' Yankee in King Arthur's Court, Gilbert's Bab Ballads, Goldsmith's She Stoops to Conquer, Maeterlinck's Blue Bird.

Pinkerton Academy *Catalogue,*
1910–11

# To John T. Bartlett

The Bungs
Beaks
Bucks

Dear John:—                                    Fourth-of-July. 1913

   Those initials you quote from T. P.'s belong to a fellow named Buckley and the explanation of Buckley is this that he has recently issued a book with David Nutt, but at his own expense, whereas in my case David Nutt assumed the risks. *And* those other people Buckley reviewed are his personal friends or friends of his friends or if not that simply examples of the kind of wrong horse most fools put their money on. You will be sorry to hear me say so but they are not even craftsmen. Of course there are two ways of using that word the good and the bad one. To be on the safe side it is best to call such dubs mechanics. To be perfectly frank with you I am one of the most notable craftsmen of my time. That will transpire presently. I am possibly the only person going who works on any but a worn out theory* of versification. You see the great successes in recent poetry have been made on the assumption that the music of words was a matter of harmonised vowels and consonants. Both Swinburne and Tennyson aimed largely at effects in assonation. But they were on the wrong track or at any rate on a short track. They went the length of it. Any one else who goes that way must go after them. And that's where most are going. I alone of English writers have consciously set myself to make music out of what I may call the sound of sense. Now it is possible to have sense without the sound of sense (as in much prose that is supposed to pass muster but makes very dull reading) and the sound of sense without sense (as in Alice in Wonderland which makes anything but dull reading). The best place to get the abstract sound of sense is from voices behind a door that cuts off the words. Ask yourself how these sentences would sound without the words in which they are embodied:

*Principle I had better say.

You mean to tell me you can't read?
I said no such thing.
Well read then.
You're not my teacher.

———————

He says it's too late
Oh, say!
Damn an Ingersoll watch anyway.

———————

One-two-three—go!
No good! Come back—come back.
Haslam go down there and make those kids get out
   of the track.

Those sounds are summoned by the audile imagination and they must be positive, strong, and definitely and unmistakeably indicated by the context. The reader must be at no loss to give his voice the posture proper to the sentence. The simple declarative sentence used in making a plain statement is one sound. But Lord love ye it mustn't be worked to death. It is against the law of nature that whole poems should be written in it. If they are written they won't be read. The sound of sense, then. You get that. It is the abstract vitality of our speech. It is pure sound—pure form. One who concerns himself with it more than the subject is an artist. But remember we are still talking merely of the raw material of poetry. An ear and an appetite for these sounds of sense is the first qualification of a writer, be it of prose or verse. But if one is to be a poet he must learn to get cadences by skillfully breaking the sounds of sense with all their irregularity of accent across the regular beat of the metre. Verse in which there is nothing but the beat of the metre furnished by the accents of the pollysyllabic words we call doggerel. Verse is not that. Neither is it the sound of sense alone. It is a resultant from those two. There are only two or three metres that are worth anything. We depend for variety on the infinite play of accents in the sound of sense. The high possibility of emotional expression all lies in this mingling of sense-sound and word-accent. A curious thing. And all this has its bearing on your prose me boy. Never if you can help it write down a sentence in which the voice will not know how to posture *specially*.

That letter head shows how far we have come since we left Pink. Editorial correspondent of the Montreal Star sounds to me. Gad, we get little mail from you.

Affectionately
R. F.

Maybe you'll keep this discourse on the sound of sense till I can say more on it.

# To John T. Bartlett

Dear John                                    The Bung Hole, Still
    Never you let that silly business of remembering me to my
Derry friends put any strain on your feeling for me. I keep
not hearing from you; and I begin to be afraid I have asked
you to do more than you could do or wanted to do. Very
likely you didn't like the idea of stirring 'em up in our old
haunts. I don't know that I blame you. It was just my impulse.
You are quite free to beg off in the matter. I trust it is no
worse than that. It occurs to me as possible that you may have
tried to deliver the article on Birch Street and got a snub for
your pains. It would have been through no fault of yours, but
you may have been uncomfortable about it all this time. The
whole thing is of no importance—utterly. I ought not to give
way to thoughts of revenge in the first place. Still there were
a few people in Derry who vexed me and one or two who did
more than that and I am human enough to want to make
them squirm a little before I forgive them.
    You are about all I saved from the years I spent in Derry,
you and Margaret, and the three children born to us on the
farm, and the first book that was mostly written on the farm
before I attended school at Pinkerton. I really care not a fig
either way for or against any one else I fell in with in my
teaching days. I don't want you to grow cold in letter writing.
You are to act always on the assumption that we are going to
get together again across the meridians. Of course we are. I
always think if you would take measures to strike up a cor-
respondence for one of these London papers you would
sooner or later land here among the literary people, and with
better prospects of staying than I have because you know how
to make money. Think it over. I am reminded of you every
time I see a special article from British Columbia.
    You mustn't take me too seriously if I now proceed to brag
a bit about my exploits as a poet. There is one qualifying fact
always to bear in mind: there is a kind of success called "of
esteem" and it butters no parsnips. It means a success with

the critical few who are supposed to know. But really to arrive where I can stand on my legs as a poet and nothing else I must get outside that circle to the general reader who buys books in their thousands. I may not be able to do that. I believe in doing it—dont you doubt me there. I want to be a poet for all sorts and kinds. I could never make a merit of being caviare to the crowd the way my quasi-friend Pound does. I want to reach out, and would if it were a thing I could do by taking thought. So much by way of depreciation before I begin. Now for it, a little of it.

I suppose I arrived in a sense the other day when Laurence Binyon asked me to lunch with Robert Bridges the Laureate. It meant this much: Binyon had decided that my book was one of the few and he was good enough to want me to have my chance with the Chief. So I took it. That is the best sounding thing I have to tell. I don't know that it pleased me any more than to find Trevelyan, a man who is known as a patron of art, with my book in his pocket. He had bought it on the recommendation of somebody who is supposed to know all about poetry. I am sure that it pleased me less than the friendly attentions I have had from Wilfrid Gibson and Lascelles Abercrombie. These fellows you can know if you can get hold of either Q's Oxford Book of Victorian Verse or The Georgian Anthology. They are something more than my casual acquaintances. If or when we can get rid of this house I am going down into Gloucester to live near them. The second book is what has drawn them to me. Some of the manuscript has been passed around and they have seen it.

I think that's all except that Mrs. Nutt in her devotion to my cause has already announced the second book without waiting for me to say the word. So the anxiety of finding a publisher is off my mind. As the boys say here, It is success enough if your first book does well enough to get you a publisher for the second. The book should be out in February. You shall have some of it before then if you write me a decent letter and give me your new address. Gone out of the rabbit business, hey? Ain't working the land? Easier to write about it? Think I don't understand?

You and Margaret ought to see how few pieces of furniture

we keep house with. It is cosy enough, but it would be a lesson to you in plain living. I would give anything if you could drop in on us.

Affectionately
Rob

c. November 5, 1913

# To Sidney Cox

The Bungalow
Beaconsfield
Bucks

Dear Cox                                          Jan 19 1914

Absolve me of trying to make you think of me as hobnob-
bing with the great over here and I am ready to begin my
*very* short talks based on Quiller-Couch. I'm far from impor-
tant enough for the likes of the Poet Laureate to have sought
me out. I'm simply going to tell you about him because I
happen to have eaten at the same table with him by an acci-
dent. I was visiting Lawrence Binyon (see anthology) when
Bridges turned up. I have a right to tell you how the king
looked to the cat that looked at him.

He's a fine old boy with the highest opinion—of his poetry
you thought I was going to say—perhaps of his poetry, but
much more particularly of his opinions. He rides two hobbies
tandem, his theory that syllables in English have fixed quantity
that cannot be disregarded in reading verse, and his theory
that with forty or fifty or sixty characters he can capture and
hold for all time the sounds of speech. One theory is as bad
as the other and I think owing to much the same fallacy. The
living part of a poem is the intonation entangled somehow in
the syntax idiom and meaning of a sentence. It is only there
for those who have heard it previously in conversation. It is
not for us in any Greek or Latin poem because our ears have
not been filled with the tones of Greek and Roman talk. It is
the most volatile and at the same time important part of
poetry. It goes and the language becomes a dead language the
poetry dead poetry. With it go the accents the stresses the
delays that are not the property of vowels and syllables but
that are shifted at will with the sense. Vowels have length there
is no denying. But the accent of sense supercedes all other
accent overrides and sweeps it away. I will find you the word
"come" variously used in various passages as a whole, half,
third, fourth, fifth, and sixth note. It is as long as the sense
makes it. When men no longer know the intonations on which

we string our words they will fall back on what I may call the absolute length of our syllables which is the length we would give them in passages that meant nothing. The psychologist can actually measure this with a what-do-you-call-it. English poetry would then be read as Latin poetry is now read and as of course Latin poetry was never read by Romans. Bridges would like it read so now for the sake of scientific exactness. Because our poetry must sometime be as dead as our language must Bridges would like it treated as if it were dead already.

I say you cant read a single good sentence with the salt in it unless you have previously heard it spoken. Neither can you with the help of all the characters and diacritical marks pronounce a single word unless you have previously heard it actually pronounced. Words exist in the mouth not in books. You can't fix them and you don't want to fix them. You want them to adapt their sounds to persons and places and times. You want them to change and be different. I shall be sorry when everybody is so public-schooled that nobody will dare to say Haow for What. It pleases me to contemplate the word Sosieti that the reformers sport on their door plate in a street in London. The two i's are bad enough. But the o is what I love. Which o is that if we must be exact.

Bridges wants to fix the vocables here and now because he sees signs of their deteriorating. He thinks they exist in print for people. He thinks they are of the eye. Foolish old man is all I say. How much better that he should write good poetry if he hasn't passed his time. He has been a real poet, though you never would judge it from a thing in the Dec Poetry and Drama in which he takes the unsentimental view of teachers that they cram us with dead dry stuff like the dead flies on the window sill.

You will have to import your own books I'm afraid, unless Sherman French & Co of Boston would get them for you. Books and postage in the awful quantity you mention would cost you four American dollars. You mustn't get one book more than you honestly feel that you can dispose of. No silly promises are binding.

Yours
R Frost

Make you a present of all the words I have misspelled in this letter. They'll do you good if they correct a little your tendency to think as a teacher that everything must be correct.

# To John T. Bartlett

Bung Beak Buck
Eng
22 Feb '14

Dear John:

I consent not to guess, but I insist on knowing. And I don't intend to wait too many "moons of Marriage" either.

I feel as if I were losing track of you you write so seldom and so meagrely not to say mysteriously. The facts of your case as I have them at date are these: Some thing is going to happen to you in not more than nine months that you refuse to tell me about till it happens.

You have lost a lot of money by Alex Paton, but you expect to get 250 dollars out of him. I shall feel better when I hear that you have it.

You are still earning something a week from The Sun and something a week from several other papers. At least you haven't told me that you aren't.

I'm not supposed to know it if you are not writing for an agricultural paper or two and one monthly magazine.

You have friends in that bad country, one of them a highly educated journalist who knows so much more about poetry than you that you let him tell you what is good poetry and what isn't.

The District of Columbia is bad country in every way, physically socially and financially.

You dont mind making me tremble a little (as much as you can) for your security away off there at your age and with a wife to support.

You are dissatisfied with journalism as she is in Vanc. (I wonder if the Editor of The World that Marie Dowd whipped isnt dissatisfied with it too? Was he someone you wanted whipped?)

You dont like your own stuff. You are tired of it. It seems to you to come the same way all the time as it naturally would on the same monotonous subjects.

You are fairly well, though not perfectly free from asthma. You would probably be as sick as you used to be if you weren't so much happier than you used to be. I wonder if you think it would kill you to go back to New England. It wouldn't break your heart anyway, would it?

Some of these informations I am indebted to Margaret for. I think I have set down all I know or am warranted in inferring.

I dont mind your being tired of your own stuff. Isis got tired of the millions of men and sought the millions of the gods but in the end she got tired of the millions of the gods and sought the millions of the spirit. Much virtue in getting tired of your work if you are free enough in body or mind either to go away from it or to convert it into something different or better.

I set a good deal of store by the magazine work you are doing or going to do. That is your way out of bondage. You can—must write better for a magazine than there is any inducement to do for a daily.

My notion is that your work is coming on. Your style tightens up. What you will have to guard against is the lingo of the newspaper, words that nobody but a journalist uses, and worse still, phrases. John Cournos who learned his trade on the Philadelphia Record, where he went by the nickname of Gorky, has come over here to write short stories. He is thirty. His worst enemy is going to be his habit of saying cuticle for skin.

I really liked what you wrote about me. Your sentences go their distance straight and sure and they relay each other well. You always had ideas and apprehended ideas. You mustnt lose that merit. You must find some way to show people that you have initiative and judgement. You must "get up" new things as new even as a brand new department for some paper.

But as I was about to say, I am sure your style improves. Let me see some of the more important things you do. I'll traverse them line by line with a pencil if you will let me. Some of my criticism may be wrong but it will stir you up. It won't hurt you and you won't let it offend you.

You can know and you are going to know as much about poetry and any other form of literature as anybody. You know a good deal more now than you think you do, as would soon transpire if you and I were where we could protract talk.

I want to write down here two or three cardinal principles that I wish you would think over and turn over now and again till we *can* protract talk.

I give you a new definition of a sentence:

A sentence is a sound in itself on which other sounds called words may be strung.

You may string words together without a sentence-sound to string them on just as you may tie clothes together by the sleeves and stretch them without a clothes line between two trees, but—it is bad for the clothes.

The number of words you may string on one sentence-sound is not fixed but there is always danger of over loading.

The sentence-sounds are very definite entities. (This is no literary mysticism I am preaching.) They are as definite as words. It is not impossible that they could be collected in a book though I don't at present see on what system they would be catalogued.

They are apprehended by the ear. They are gathered by the ear from the vernacular and brought into books. Many of them are already familiar to us in books. I think no writer invents them. The most original writer only catches them fresh from talk, where they grow spontaneously.

A man is all a writer if *all* his words are strung on definite recognizable sentence-sounds. The voice of the imagination, the speaking voice must know certainly how to behave how to posture in every sentence he offers.

A man is a marked writer if his words are largely strung on the more striking sentence sounds.

A word about recognition: In literature it is our business to give people the thing that will make them say, "Oh yes I know what you mean." It is never to tell them something they don't know, but something they know and hadn't thought of saying. It must be something they recognize.

A Patch of Old Snow

In the corner of the wall where the bushes haven't been trimmed, there is a patch of old snow like a blow-away newspaper that has come to rest there. And it is dirty as with the print and news of a day I have forgotten, if I ever read it.

Now that is no good except for what I may call certain points of recognition in it: patch of old snow in a corner of the wall,—you know what that is. You know what a blow-away newspaper is. You know the curious dirt on old snow and last of all you know how easily you forget what you read in papers.

Now for the sentence sounds. We will look for the marked ones because they are easiest to discuss. The first sentence sound will do but it is merely ordinary and bookish: it is entirely subordinate in interest to the meaning of the words strung on it. But half the effectiveness of the second sentence is in the very special tone with which you must say news of a day I have forgotten—if I ever read it. You must be able to say Oh yes one knows how that goes. (There is some adjective to describe the intonation or cadence, but I won't hunt for it.)

One of the least successful of the poems in my book is almost saved by a final striking sentence-sound (Asking for Roses.)

> Not caring so very much *what* she supposes.

Take My November Guest. Did you know at once how we say such sentences as these when we talk?

> She thinks I have no eye for these.

> ———

> Not yesterday I learned etc.

> ———

> But it were vain to tell her so

> ———

Get away from the sing-song. You must hear and recognize in the last line the sentence sound that supports, No use in telling him so.

Lets have some examples pell-mell in prose and verse because I dont want you to think I am setting up as an authority on verse alone.

> My father used to say—
> You're a liar!
> If a hen and a half lay an egg and a half etc.
> A long long time ago—
> Put it there, old man! (Offering your hand)
> I aint a going hurt you, so you neednt be scared.

Suppose Henry Horne says something offensive to a young lady named Rita when her brother Charles is by to protect her. Can you hear the two different tones in which she says their respective names. "Henry Horne! Charles!" I can hear it better than I can say it. And by oral practice I get further and further away from it.

> Never you say a thing like that to a man!
> And such they are and such they will be found
> Well I swan!
> Unless I'm greatly mistaken—
> Hence with denial vain and coy excuse
> A soldier and afraid! (afeared)
> Come, child, come home.
> The thing for me to do is to get right out of here
> while I am able.
> No fool like an old fool.

It is so and not otherwise that we get the variety that makes it fun to write and read. *The ear does it.* The ear is the only true writer and the only true reader. I have known people who could read without hearing the sentence sounds and they were the fastest readers. Eye readers we call them. They can get the meaning by glances. But they are bad readers because they miss the best part of what a good writer puts into his work.

Remember that the sentence sound often says more than the words. It may even as in irony convey a meaning opposite to the words.

I wouldnt be writing all this if I didn't think it the most important thing I know. I write it partly for my own benefit, to clarify my ideas for an essay or two I am going to write some fine day (not far distant.)

To judge a poem or piece of prose you go the same way to work—apply the one test—greatest test. You listen for the sentence sounds. If you find some of those not bookish, caught fresh from the mouths of people, some of them striking, all of them definite and recognizable so recognizable that with a little trouble you can place them and even name them you know you have found a writer.

Before I ring off you may want to hear the facts in the case of us.

We are still in Beaconsfield but trying hard to get rid of our house six months before our lease is out in order to get away into Gloucester with Wilfrid Gibson and Lasselles Abercrombie (see Victorian anthology for both of them).

Book II, North of Boston, should be out now. The publisher is dilatory. I shall have another book done (out and out plays this time) before she gets Book II out. This is rough on me because I feel that now is the time to strike while there is a certain interest in me for what I have done.

I expect to be roasted more for Book III than for Book II—if for no other reason, because the fact is out that I am an American. That nasty review by Alford in the magazine I sent shows you how they feel toward us here. He begins by saying he cant get hold of enough books to find out whether we have any literature or not and then he proceeds to say we have none. I am sure he will lay for me somewhere. And there are others who have me marked.

J. C. Smith (editor of an edition of Shakes. and several other classics for the Oxford library) will give an evening to a new American poet named Me before an Edinburgh literary society in March.

Poetry (Chicago) printed in Feb the thing I call The Code. Did I send it to you? If I didn't, you may want to look it up. It may be in the library.

No money comes in of course yet. I won't make much from poetry—I suppose you know that. I talk about prose but as long as I can put off writing pot boilers I shall. It seems to me as I look at it now I had much rather farm than write for money.

We plan to go home in September of 1915. I dont know where I shall settle. You may be coming back to New England some time. Somehow we must plan to be together.

The children all keep well but as they have found the schools impossible here they come pretty heavily on Elinor. She has not been at all well this year. I may have to give up my wilder schemes and turn to money making for the family. Not that I am ever asked to. On the contrary.

I wonder if there is anything more you are as anxious to hear as I am anxious to hear more about you.

Our love to you both. And may God amend my spelling.

Affectionately<br>Rob.

# *To John Cournos*

Little Iddens
Ledington
Ledbury
July 8 1914

Dear Cournos:

Thanks for your good news. I have just read Hueffer's article and I like every word of it. What more could anyone ask for a while?

My versification seems to bother people more than I should have expected—I suppose because I have been so long accustomed to thinking of it in my own private way. It is as simple as this: there are the very regular preestablished accent and measure of blank verse; and there are the very irregular accent and measure of speaking intonation. I am never more pleased than when I can get these into strained relation. I like to drag and break the intonation across the metre as waves first comb and then break stumbling on the shingle. That's all, but it's no mere figure of speech, though one can make figures enough about it.

I am down here farming on my own for economy this summer, where I should be glad to see you if you ever range so far. I shall be in London from the 20th on for a few days and will look you up then if I may.

You mustnt say such things about New York to a poor cuss who may have to go back there to live some time.

Sincerely yours
Robert Frost.

# To Sidney Cox

Ryton Dymock Gloucestershire
England
Dear Cox                                    Dec 1914

I am glad you are going into it with me and one or two others. Thomas thinks he will write a book on what my definition of the sentence means for literary criticism. If I didn't drop into poetry every time I sat down to write I should be tempted to do a book on what it means for education. It may take some time to make people see—they are so accustomed to look at the sentence as a grammatical cluster of words. The question is where to begin the assault on their prejudice. For my part I have about decided to begin by demonstrating by examples that the sentence as a sound in itself apart from the word sounds is no mere figure of speech. I shall show the sentence sound saying all that the sentence conveys with little or no help from the meaning of the words. I shall show the sentence sound opposing the sense of the words as in irony. And so till I establish the distinction between the grammatical sentence and the vital sentence. The grammatical sentence is merely accessory to the other and chiefly valuable as furnishing a clue to the other. You recognize the sentence sound in this: *You*, you—! It is so strong that if you hear it as I do you have to pronounce the two you's differently. Just so many sentence sounds belong to man as just so many vocal runs belong to one kind of bird. We come into the world with them and create none of them. What we feel as creation is only selection and grouping. We summon them from Heaven knows where under excitement with the audile imagination. And unless we are in an imaginative mood it is no use trying to make them, they will not rise. We can only write the dreary kind of grammatical prose known as professorial. Because that is to be seen at its worst in translations especially from the classics, Thomas thinks he will take up the theme apropos of Somebodys scholarly translation of Horace or Catullus some day when such a book comes his way for review.

I throw all this out as it comes to me to show you where we are at present. Use anything you please. I am only too glad

681

of your help. We will shake the old unity-emphasis-and-coherence Rhetoric to its foundations.

A word more. We value the seeing eye already. Time we said something about the hearing ear—the ear that calls up vivid sentence forms.

We write of things we see and we write in accents we hear. Thus we gather both our material and our technique with the imagination from life: and our technique becomes as much material as material itself.

All sorts of things must occur to you. Blaze away at them. But expect to have to be patient. There are a lot of completely educated people in the world and of course they will resent being asked to learn anything new.

You aren't influenced by that Beauty is Truth claptrap. In poetry and under emotion every word used is "moved" a little or much—moved from its old place, heightened, made, made new. See what Keats did to the word "alien" in the ode. But as he made it special in that place he made it his—and his only in that place. He could never have used it again with just that turn. It takes the little one horse poets to do that. I am probably the only Am poet who haven't used it after him. No if I want to deal with the word I must sink back to its common usage at Castle Garden. I want the unmade words to work with not the familiar made ones that everybody exclaims Poetry! at. Of course the great fight of any poet is against the people who want him to write in a special language that has gradually separated from spoken language by this "making" process. His pleasure must always be to make his own words as he goes and never to depend for effect on words already made even if they be his own.

Enough of that. I don't blame your good friend. Nor do I blame the poor educated girl who thought the little book was difficult. The "contents" notes were a piece of fooling on my part. They were not necessary and not very good.

I'd like to thank specially the fellow who picked out Mowing. I guess there is no doubt that is the best poem in Book I. We all think so over here. Thank Hatch for me too. Don't forget.

And thank yourself for all you are doing for me. I need it in this game.

I should like a good talk or three with you. On the war if you chose. On anything. You are going to do a lot all round I know. Your opinions are worth listening to because you mean to put them into action—if for no other reason. But there is no other reason as important. What a man will put into effect at any cost of time money life or lives is what is sacred and what counts. As I get older I dont want to hear about much else.

I have nearly written myself tired for tonight.

Write often and keep my courage up.

Yours ever<br>R. F.

Get rid of that Mr. on my name next letter or take the consequences.

# To William Braithwaite

Littleton N.H.
R.F.D. No 5
March 22

Dear Mr. Braithwaite:

I've got as far as finding you the copy of Book I I promised you. Perhaps as a busy man you wont resent my telling you what to read in it if you are going to read at all. It is the list I always give to friends I wish the minimum of suffering: pages 1, 2, 4, 7, 9, 14, 20, 22, 23, 25, 26, 34, 41, 42 (once printed in The Transcript) 45, 46 (8–18 line—first poetry I ever wrote that I could call my own—year 1892) and 49. Don't read those unless you have to, but don't read the others on any account.

The book is an expression of my life for the ten years from eighteen on when I thought I greatly preferred stocks and stones to people. The poems were written as I lived the life quite at the mercy of myself and not always happy. The arrangement in a book came much later when I could look back on the past with something like understanding.

I kept farm, so to speak for nearly ten years, but less as a farmer than as a fugitive from the world that seemed to me to "disallow" me. It was all instinctive, but I can see now that I went away to save myself and fix myself before I measured my strength against all creation. I was never really out of the world for good and all. I liked people even when I believed I detested them.

It would seem absurd to say it (and you mustn't quote me as saying it) but I suppose the fact is that my conscious interest in people was at first no more than an almost technical interest in their speech—in what I used to call their sentence sounds—the sound of sense. Whatever these sounds are or aren't (they are certainly not of the vowels and consonants of words nor even of the words themselves but something the words are chiefly a kind of notation for indicating and fastening to the printed page) whatever they are, I say, I began to hang on them very young. I was under twenty when I deliberately put it to myself one night after good conversation that there are moments when we actually touch in talk what the best writing can only come near. The curse of our book language is not so much that it keeps forever to the same set phrases (though Heaven knows those are bad enough) but that it sounds forever with the same reading tones. We must go out into the vernacular for tones that havent been brought to book. We must write with the ear on the speaking voice. We must imagine the speaking voice.

I say all this biographically to lead up to Book II (North of Boston). There came a day about ten years ago when I made the discovery that though sequestered I wasnt living without reference to other people. Right on top of that I made the discovery in doing The Death of the Hired Man that I was interested in neighbors for more than merely their tones of speech—and always had been. I remember about when I began to suspect myself of liking their gossip for its own sake. I justified myself by the example of Napoleon as recently I have had to justify myself in seasickness by the example of Nelson.

I like the actuality of gossip, the intimacy of it. Say what you will effects of actuality and intimacy are the greatest aim an artist can have. The sense of intimacy gives the thrill of sincerity. A story must always release a meaning more readily to those who read than life itself as it goes ever releases meaning. Meaning is a great consideration. But a story must never seem to be told primarily for meaning. Anything, an inspired irrelevancy even to make it sound as if told the way it is chiefly because it happened that way.

I have run on unpardonably. I couldn't write a whole biography; so I just had to plunge into the middle of things. I have pretty well jumbled the story of how I see my own development and some of my theories of art. You are not going to use anything directly, I take it. You will be sure to veil what is too personal. This isn't quite the same as an interview. I have met you and now we are getting further in getting acquainted.

Ask me for anything I don't think to supply for your newspaper article. Probably you want a few dates and data.

I was born in San Francisco forty years ago. My father was an editor out there. He died when I was young.

I went to the public schools in Lawrence Mass. I was married there.

My farm was in Derry, New Hampshire.

I taught literature at Pinkerton Academy, Derry, and psychology at the Normal School, Plymouth for the five years before I went to England.

In England I saw a good deal of two or three literary circles in London for a year or two and then went down into Gloucestershire and Herefordshire for another year. I never saw *New* England as clearly as when I was in Old England.

Just to show you that the interest in my work over there was partly on the technical side or where the material shades off into the technical I enclose a circular my English publisher got out. The quotation from The Nation was used by The Listener in the Transcript (July 8).

No more of this.

May I hope really to see something of you when I am in Boston again? I'd like to have a talk about poetry by ourselves alone.

Sincerely yours
Robert Frost.

1915

# "The Imagining Ear"

MR. BROWNE has alluded to the seeing eye. I want to call your attention to the function of the imagining ear. Your attention is too often called to the poet with extraordinarily vivid sight, and with the faculty of choosing exceptionally telling words for the sight. But equally valuable, even for schoolboy themes, is the use of the ear for material for compositions. When you listen to a speaker, you hear words, to be sure, —but you also hear tones. The problem is to note them, to imagine them again, and to get them down in writing. But few of you probably ever thought of the possibility or of the necessity of doing this. You are generally told to distinguish simple, compound, and complex sentences,—long and short, —periodic and loose,—to varying sentence structure, etc. "Not all sentences are short, like those of Emerson, the writer of the best American prose. You must vary your sentences, like Stevenson, etc." All this is missing the vital element. I always had a dream of getting away from it, when I was teaching school,—and, in my own writing and teaching, of bringing in the *living* sounds of speech. For it is a fundamental fact that certain forms depend on the sound;—e.g., note the various tones of irony, acquiescence, doubt, etc. in the farmer's "I guess so." And the great problem is, can you get these tones down on paper? How *do* you tell the tone? By the context, by the animating spirit of the living voice. And how many tones do you think there are flying round? Hundreds of them—hundreds never brought to book. Compare T. E. Brown's *To a Blackbird*: "O blackbird, what a boy you are" Compare W. B. Yeats's "Who dreamed that beauty passes like a dream"

I went to church, once (loud laughter)—this will sound funnier when I tell you that the only thing I remember is the long line of "Nows" that I counted. The repetition grew tiresome. I knew just when to expect a 'Now', and I knew beforehand just what the tone was going to be. There is no objection to repetition of the right kind,—only to the mechanical repetition of the tone. It is all right to repeat, if there is something for the voice to do. The vital thing, then, to consider in all composition, in prose or verse, is the ACTION of the voice,—sound-posturing, gesture. Get the *stuff* of life into the technique of your writing. That's the only escape from dry rhetoric.

When I began to teach, and long after I began to write, I didn't know what the matter was with me and my writing and with other people's writing. I recall distinctly the joy with which I had the first satisfaction of getting an expression adequate for my thought. I was so delighted that I had to cry. It was the second stanza of the little poem on the Butterfly, written in my eighteenth year. And the Sound in the mouths of men I found to be the basis of all effective expression, —not merely words or phrases, but sentences,—living things flying round,—the vital parts of speech. And my poems are to be read in the appreciative tones of this live speech. For example, there are five tones in this first stanza,

### The Pasture

| | |
|---|---|
| I'm going out to clean the pasture spring; | (light, informing tone) |
| I'll only stop to rake the leaves away | ("only" tone— reservation) |
| (And wait to watch the water clear, I may): | (supplementary, possibility) |
| I sha'n't be gone long.—You come too. | (free tone, assuring) |
| | (after thought, inviting) |
| | "Rather well for me"— |

I'm going out to fetch the little calf
That's standing by the mother. It's so young,
It totters when she licks it with her tongue.
I sha'n't be gone long.—You come too.

(Similar,
free, persua-
sive, assur-
ing, and in-
viting tones
in second
stanza)

(Similar demonstration in "Mending Wall". . . .) Just see and hear the two farmers across the old wall in the spring, picking up stones, and placing them back in their places on the wall. Note the tone, challenging and threatening, at

"We have to use a spell to make them balance:
" 'Stay where you are until our backs are turned!' "

Playful note at "Oh, just another kind of outdoor game"—
Idiomatic balance, "He is all pine and I am apple orchard."
Incredulity of the other's dictum: "Good fences make good neighbors." and "But here there are no cows." Shaking his head as he says, "Before I built a wall" etc.—Can't you see him? and hear him?

So, my advice to you boys in all your composition work is: "Gather your sentences by ear, and reimagine them in your writing." . . .

From notes of George H. Browne,
Browne and Nichols School Lecture,
May 10, 1915

# To Walter Pritchard Eaton

Franconia N.H.
Sept 18 1915

My dear Eaton:

Of course if you refuse to come within talking distance I must just do as I have to do and write you a letter (with map of the surrounding country.) Mind you it is not altogether from laziness that I prefer talking to letter writing. Let it not go unsaid that once I enjoyed letter writing as much as anybody. And I intend some day to have back my pleasure in it— or you may protest me the baby of a girl. All that is required of me is to deal summarily with a few people like N. H. Dole and I shall be free to. (I hope Dole isn't a particular friend of yours. Poole is, I suppose!)

It was nice of Howells to do what you say wasnt it? Long long ago my mother was a little schoolma'am in Columbus Ohio when he was there and I have heard her speak of meeting him once or twice in society when Columbus society was gay in the sixties. He has always stood for something to me away off and high up. So that I felt that I had rounded some sort of a circle when he did what you say.

You don't mention my having had a whole article to myself in The Atlantic as among my signal honors: from which I infer that you don't like the article. I wonder why. Others seem to ignore it on purpose. I wonder what's the matter.

I was grateful to both Howells and Garnett for making so little difficulty of my blank verse. I have nothing in common with the free-verse people. There is no more distressing mistake than to assume that I have. (Some of the western reviewers have been assuming it) I am really not so very novel—take it from me. I am only interesting to myself for having ventured to try to make poetry out of tones that if you can judge from the practice of other poets are not usually regarded as poetical. You can get enough of those sentence tones that suggest grandeur and sweetness everywhere in poetry. What bothers people in my blank verse is that I have tried to see what I could do with boasting tones and quizzical tones and shrugging tones (for there are such) and forty eleven other tones. All I care a cent for is to catch sentence tones that havent been brought to book. I dont say to make them, mind you, but to catch them. No one makes them or adds to them. They are always there—living in the cave of the mouth. They are real cave things: they were before words were. And they are as definitely things as any image of sight. The most creative imagination is only their summoner. But summoning them is not all. They are only lovely when thrown and drawn and displayed across spaces of the footed line. Everyone knows that except a free-verster. It is the conventional thing. It may not be in the text-books but everyone knows it though he may have lost sight of it in an age of mere diction and word-hunting. Now Tennyson—

I bore you stiff.

You speak of going to New York. Would I find you for a talk somewhere there near the first of October. What you say about coming to Stockbridge is very tempting. But I can't be away from home this fall or winter except on business. Business takes me to New York this time—pressing business with my publishers. But if we could find a corner to lunch together in——

Always yours
Robert Frost

# To Louis Untermeyer

Dear Louis:

You gave us a good part of our good Christmas. We are a bejeweled family.

And speaking of families, how like the family affairs we flatter ourselves we only find in country villages was that shop of yours I had a glimpse of in the middle of the greatest city in the world where everybody seemed to know everybody else if everybody wasn't quite related to everybody else. I should be jealous of you for having such an institution in a modern city where it doesn't belong according to all our theories, if I wasn't so fond of seeing our theories knocked into cocked hats. What I like about Bergson and Fabre is that they have bothered our evolutionism so much with the cases of instinct they have brought up. You get more credit for thinking if you restate formulae or cite cases that fall in easily under formulae, but all the fun is outside saying things that suggest formulae that won't formulate—that almost but don't quite formulate. I should like to be so subtle at this game as to seem to the casual person altogether obvious. The casual person would assume that I meant nothing or else I came near enough meaning something he was familiar with to mean it for all practical purposes. Well well well.

R.

I have never known you better than you are in A Side Street. It is the solid stuff, especially from "I see them there" on to the end. You are so clever you have to be careful about not cheating yourself about your rhyme words. You can make yourself think they are not there just for the rhyme when they really are. Lowell perishes of just that self-deception. Your rhymes justify this time very well. Excuse this troubling thought. A Side Street is a lovely thing.

Address me at Amherst next.

R.

January 1, 1917

# To Régis Michaud

SOME twenty-two lines in "Monadnoc" beginning "Now in sordid weeds they sleep" (I dont need to copy them out for such an Emersonian as you, Michaud) meant almost more to me than anything else on the art of writing when I was a youngster; and that not just on the art of writing colloquial verse but on the art of writing any kind of verse or prose. I suffer from the way people abuse the word colloquial. All writing, I dont care how exalted, how lyrical, or how seemingly far removed from the dramatic, must be as colloquial as this passage from "Monadnoc" comes to. I am as sure that the colloquial is the root of every good poem as I am that the national is the root of all thought and art. It may shoot up as high as you please and flourish as widely abroad in the air, if only the roots are what and where they should be. One half of individuality is locality: and I was about venturing to say the other half was colloquiality. The beauty of the high thinking in Emerson's Uriel and Give All to Love is that it is well within the colloquial as I use the word. And so also is all the lyric in Palgrave's Treasury for that matter, no matter at what level of sentiment it is pitched. Consider Herrick's To Daffodils. But sometime more of this when we can sit down together.

Inscription in *North of Boston*,
c. January 1918

# The Unmade Word

## or Fetching and Far-Fetching

THERE ARE two ways of taking notes: when a man is speaking to you and after he has spoken to you. I never could take notes while a man was talking; but I have known men who have taken notes that way successfully. I am going to talk to you this morning, briefly, and I want you to try to take the thing in as a whole; then write it up for me afterward as a reporter would write an account for his paper—with no glowing introduction, but just the mere, honest, straightforward report of what I say to you.

I am going to call the thing by a name, two names in fact. You needn't pay much attention to them at first, and I will repeat them at the end when perhaps you will understand them better. I will call it first "the unmade word," or second, "Fetching and Far-fetching." You won't know much about either: I couldn't give you those names as theme subjects. Probably you don't know what I mean; I shouldn't have to talk to you if you did.

There are two kinds of language: the spoken language and the written language—our everyday speech which we call the vernacular; and a more literary, sophisticated, artificial, elegant language that belongs to books. We often hear it said that a man talks like a book in this second way. We object to anybody's talking in this literary, artificial English; we don't object to anybody's writing in it; we rather expect people to write in a literary, somewhat artificial style. I, myself, could get along very well without this bookish language altogether. I agree with the poet who visited this country not long ago when he said that all our literature has got to come down, sooner or later, to the talk of everyday life. William Butler Yeats says that all our words, phrases, and idioms to be effective must be in the manner of everyday speech.

We've got to come down to this speech of everyday, to begin with—the hard everyday word of the street, business, trades, work in summer—to begin with; but there is some sort of obligation laid on us, to lift the words of every day, to give them a metaphorical turn. No, you don't want to use that term—give the words a poetic touch. I'll show you what I mean by an example: take for example the word "lemon," that's a good practical word with no literary associations—a word that you use with the grocer and in the kitchen; it has no literary associations at all; "Peach" is another one; but you boys have taken these two words and given them a poetic twist, a poetic movement—you have not left the peach on the tree or in the basket; you couldn't let the lemon alone, you had to move it. What is the need in you of moving words? Take the word "pill" (laughter)—have you let that alone? A person is a pill, a baseball is a pill. You sometimes move even phrases. In baseball you have the phrase, "put one over on him." I suppose I know the origin of that phrase, though it's not one of my invention. Doesn't it mean "pitch one by him that he doesn't hit at at all." Isn't that what it means? Correct me if I'm wrong. "Get his goat" has been explained to me, but I didn't like the explanation. I don't know the origin of that phrase. Now the rest of the world—ladies that never saw a baseball game in their lives, who couldn't trace to their origin any of these phrases—are now using these words and phrases as a matter of everyday speech. Poetry and literature are plumb full, chock full of words and phrases like "lemon, peach, pill, and put one over on him."

But are such expressions allowable in writing? No. When a man sits down with pen and paper to write, he declares his purpose of being original, instead of taking these second-hand words and phrases. I am sick of people who use only these ready-made words and phrases. I like better a boy who invents them for himself—who takes a word or phrase from where it lies and moves it to another place. Did you ever get one up? Are you contented to use the same old words all the time or do you ever get up a new one? Now "fetching" a word or name from its place is what your textbooks call using words figuratively—metaphor, simile, analogy, or allegory—equivalent to using the word "like"; "like a peach"; he isn't a lemon, but "like a lemon." The other day someone said the snow was "mealy." I liked the word. It sounded fresh; but it was an old one that I had heard in the country, and it had lost some of its goodness from use. The other day I heard a new morning salutation; instead of "how d'y'do, how are things coming?"—a new one anyway—a man came into a train and said, "Are you satisfied?" Ever hear that? Is that a going one? At any rate the man had an inspiration and got a new one that pleased me—as if they had had a little quarrel and one wanted to know if the other was satisfied. He had "fetched" the phrase from its regular place to a new and effective place, and got away with it.

He didn't try to be original; but I know people who like that sort of thing so well that they are forever "fetching" words and phrases too far. They overdo it. Well, I don't see why a fellow shouldn't overdo it, at the beginning—it's freshening his language. "How d'y, how do you do, how are you?"—we are tired of those expressions, they need freshening. Now, there are two ways of freshening your language. First by "fetching" words out of their places, and second by going to a thesaurus [a commotion]. You don't know what a thesaurus is? Well, it's a dictionary of synonyms—ministers use 'em, poor men! After they've preached a long time in one place they begin to suspect that their parishioners are getting a little tired of their vocabulary, so they freshen their sermons out of a dictionary. But what I have chiefly in mind is a figurative fetching of fresh words to your use. The word lies in our everyday speech, practical, hard, and unliterary; and that's the way I like the word—there's where my fun with it begins. I don't care for the word already made figurative. I haven't done anything to it. I don't see what more can be done to it. Mr. Browne doesn't object to my poking a little fun at him. He tells me that yesterday morning, inspired by the brilliant effect of the ice encased trees, reflecting the morning in prismatic colors, he strove to add a new word to your vocabulary by quoting the opening sentence of Emerson's famous Divinity School Address: "In this *refulgent* summer it has been a luxury to draw the breath of life." Of course, anybody would sit up and take notice when a speaker began like that. Undoubtedly there's a freshness there in the use of that word that amounts to brilliance; but you ought not to use the word in just that way. Emerson made it his own; let it alone.

But do the same thing with *your* new words. Compare the use of the word "alien," a practical, everyday word with whose meaning you are familiar—a common word until a great poet, Keats, used it in his "Ode to the Nightingale"

> "The self-same song that found a path
> Through the sad heart of Ruth, when, sick for home,
> She stood in tears amid the alien corn"

That use of "alien" fascinated poets as "peach" and "lemon" fascinate you boys. All poets are now using "alien." I've heard of "alien bean." The idea now is, use it anywhere where you want to be poetic, as you use "peach, lemon, pill," etc., when you want to sound like a boy—slangy, fresh. . . .

Now I'm going to read you, at Mr. Browne's request, one of my poems, and I'd like to point out to you one or two of these words that I "fetched"—and I'd like you to consider where I got them, where I fetched them to, and whether I fetched them too far. In this poem on "The Birches," I'm trying to give you the effect of a similar ice storm; the birch twigs encased in ice:

> "Often you must have seen them
> Loaded with ice a sunny winter morning
> After a rain. They click upon themselves
> As the breeze rises, and turn many-colored
> As the stir cracks and crazes their enamel."

There are other words in the poem I like, but where do you think I got that word "crazes"? [no answer] Mr. Frost went to the blackboard, and drew the pattern of crackly china, like the Dedham pottery.

> "Such heaps of broken glass to sweep away
> You'd think the inner dome of heaven had fallen."

I wonder if you think I fetched that word dome too far? It's not so good as the other, in spite of the "broken glass," but I like it. . . .

Browne and Nichols School Lecture,<br>March 13, 1918

# Address to the Amherst Alumni Council

I OUGHT to say at first perhaps that the Language and Literature Group is probably about as it was when you were in College. We do not change much. It is about as it was, I know, where I went to college—the language at one end—I take it that the two words are significant—the language at one end, and the literature at the other. Language for scholarship, we will say, and literature for art. At the one end we still have in our work here the men who are interested in books as scientists, as scholars; and at the other end men who are interested in books for what they were intended by the author; that is to say—I mean that [laughter] I myself have that feeling for all books that I would refuse to put them to any use that the author did not intend them for.

There is not very much for me to describe. I would just like to give you the spirit of the thing as I understand it. You know I have been a great deal worried lately, what with all this Bolshevism, and syndicalism, and anarchism, and socialism—I have been a great deal worried about an ancient institution, namely, poverty. [Laughter.] I have heard some people say they were going to abolish poverty, just as they might say, "Let us go up and abolish the Amherst House" because they don't like the looks of it; it is ugly. Now, poverty would be, perhaps, a good thing to lose. I don't know; I have my doubts about it, as a writer, as a person sympathetic with young aspirations. You see, poverty has always kept up in the world as a kind of institution of refuge, a kind of life which is suited to young genius, to young aspiration before it makes good its promise. The young scholar, the young poet, the young painter, the young inventor, the young musician has always found a Latin Quarter where he could decently live in a garret, or a Barbizon where he could decently live in a cottage; and go half hungry, and get along somehow, and wear old clothes until he got the thing done and could show it to the world. Let poverty be abolished and where will the young poet, the young scholar, the young painter go then? I only see one place left for him to go and that is to college. [Laughter.] The only place left for him where his inclinations will have a chance is here at College.

You remember when teachers began to talk against rote memory. The day of reason came in and they began to say, "Let us have a college where people think for themselves." I say, yes, that is all right. Let us have a college where people think for themselves; but it is more important that we have a college where they make projects for themselves; where the believing and the desiring part of their nature has a chance. I like to think of a college as something like that—a place where something in it has a chance; I don't expect to make painters or musicians in my class; I don't make them; I hope I give them a chance; I hope I give the desiring part of their nature a chance. I value the college in this as it resembles the institution of poverty. It is calling an awful power to humble functions perhaps. It may seem so to you.

What is a department where inclination has its chance, where the will has its chance? Why, it is something like what Mr. Meiklejohn has described. It is where wills are pushing their way. At its best it is a confluence of wills, rather than a conflict of wills, young wills and older wills driving toward the same thing. It is as much made from below by the student as from above by the teacher.

It is hard for me not to have my own department particularly in mind in all this. Here we are a department of what I might call not philosophical ease but reminiscent ease, where everything that a man has ever done or read comes home to be a memory and a meaning and a phrase; where it comes home to be an expression; where it comes home to be either good talk or good writing. Such a department as that has to be conducted in its own special way. Like the rest of the College, it must, first of all, be for the man of inclination, who knows his likes and dislikes, and wants to cultivate his likes and dislikes. I should wish to conduct it always so that those who will, may, and those who won't, must. [Laughter.] I should want some sort of whip hand for those who won't, but I should like to be gentle enough and unassuming enough simply to stand aside to let the man who will have his chance. There was nothing I hated so much when I was young as to be told or commanded to do something I was about to do anyway. [Laughter.]

In my work with the boys in writing I like to stand aside entirely. The only whip I use on those with the will is the whip that the mother of George III used on him, "Be a king, George; be a king." I like to say to them "Oh, be a writer, be a writer; or oh, be a reader." If they come to me and say, "Help me to be a reader, tell me how to be a reader," I say, "That is too hard a thing to tell you. Read." I mean to be satisfied to have them readers; but I am always forgetting and telling them to be writers. Of course, the department must have two objects, must it not? One, to make the American writer who won't be very numerous; and the other, to make the American audience who ought to be very numerous; whoever he is. The other departments in my group have nearly as much to do with that, I take it, as mine—making the great American audience and making the great American writer.

*Proceedings of the Alumni Council . . .*
*November 7–9, 1919,* 1920

# Some Definitions

"SOMETIMES I have my doubts of words altogether, and I ask myself what is the place of them. They are worse than nothing unless they do something; unless they amount to deeds, as in ultimatums or battle-cries. They must be flat and final like the show-down in poker, from which there is no appeal. My definition of poetry (if I were forced to give one) would be this: words that have become deeds."

"All poetry is a reproduction of the tones of actual speech."

"There are two types of realists: the one who offers a good deal of dirt with his potato to show that it is a real one, and the one who is satisfied with the potato brushed clean. I'm inclined to be the second kind. To me, the thing that art does for life is to clean it, to strip it to form."

"A poem begins with a lump in the throat; a home-sickness or a love-sickness. It is a reaching-out toward expression; an effort to find fulfilment. A complete poem is one where an emotion has found its thought and the thought has found the words."

*Robert Frost: The Man and His Work,*
1923

# To Louis Untermeyer

Dear old Louis:

Since last I saw you I have come to the conclusion that style in prose or verse is that which indicates how the writer takes himself and what he is saying. Let the sound of Stevenson go through your mind empty and you will realize that he never took himself other than as an amusement. Do the same with Swinburne and you will see that he took himself as a wonder. Many sensitive natures have plainly shown by their style that they took themselves lightly in self-defense. They are the ironists. Some fair to good writers have no style and so leave us ignorant of how they take themselves. But that is the one important thing to know: because on it depends our likes and dislikes. A novelist seems to be the only kind of writer who can make a name without a style: which is only one more reason for not bothering with the novel. I am not satisfied to let it go at the aphorism that the style is the man. The man's ideas would be some element then of his style. So would his deeds. But I would narrow the definition. His deeds are his deeds; his ideas are his ideas. His style is the way he carries himself toward his ideas and deeds. Mind you if he is downspirited it will be all he can do to have the ideas without the carriage. The style is out of his superfluity. It is the mind skating circles round itself as it moves forward. Emerson had one of the noblest least egotistical of styles. By comparison with it Thoreau's was conceited, Whitmans bumptious. Carlyle's way of taking himself simply infuriates me. Longfellow took himself with the gentlest twinkle. I don't suppose you know his miracle play in The Golden Legend, Birds of Killingworth, Simon Danz, or Othere.

I own any form of humor shows fear and inferiority. Irony is simply a kind of guardedness. So is a twinkle. It keeps the reader from criticism. Whittier when he shows any style at all is probably a greater person than Longfellow as he is lifted priestlike above consideration of the scornful. Belief is better than anything else and it is best when rapt above paying its respects to anybody's doubts whatsoever. At bottom the world isnt a joke. We only joke about it to avoid an issue with someone; to let someone know that we know he's there with his questions: to disarm him by seeming to have heard and done justice to his side of the standing argument. Humor is the most engaging cowardice. With it myself I have been able to hold some of my enemy in play far out of gunshot.

There are people like John Gould Fletcher I would fain not have let in on myself; if I could have held them off all my life with smiles they could take as they pleased. But John G. pushed through my defenses. Let me tell you what happened. It was amusing. You might like to pass it along to Huebsch: you know him so well. You could quote this part of my letter word for word. Three months ago John Gould Fletcher wrote me saying "I learn you have a book out. I wish you would use your influence with Henry Holt & Co to help me get a book out. I am sending them a manuscript." I spoke to Lincoln MacVeagh in the matter. He said he wouldn't publish John Gould Fletcher's book for two simple reasons: first because it wouldnt sell and second because he hated the kind of thing Fletcher wrote. I said I wouldnt ask him to publish it to get me a good review or save me from a bad one. Obviously he might have published Fletcher's book and charged it up to advertising mine. Maurice Firuski knew about this and made haste to tell me the minute it was out that I had got the bad review in The Freeman. No doubt I deserved it on two counts that we neednt go into. But I can't excuse Fletcher his bad taste—worthy of Washington politics or New York business. Have I not written in New Hampshire that it's no wonder poets some times have to *seem* so much more businesslike than businessmen? It is because they are so much less sensitive from having overused their sensibilities. Men who have to feel for a living would unavoidably become altogether unfeeling except professionally. And The Freeman's part in it interests me. It just shows how hard it is for an American publication, however lofty its pretensions, to keep from lending itself to blackmail and corruption. Probably The Freeman is having the most superior editorials on the state of affairs in Washington. There endeth all that might concern the editors and publisher of The Freeman.

We havent given up the idea of getting to France and England this summer. Amherst goes sadly, I'm afraid I have to admit. I'd like to look at it receding from the deck of an outward bound ship. The trouble seems to be the usual one in this world, to stop being crazy without falling stupid. But you know me Al. I'm always on the point of jumping overboard because the ship is unseaworthy. Take my advice and never jump unless the ship is actually sinking or on fire. All ships are relatively unseaworthy.

You did not err. The story in The Bookman was Lesley's. But be more truthful than common. You never recognized it from any family resemblance. You had many clues to help you: the knowledge that Lesley was writing under an assumed name, the personal note on her devotion to stone-breaking in Vermont and the name Leslie. You mustn't tell her any more that she repeats her father. The charge is dangerous to her further development. She has been held back long enough by our discretion and her own. It's time she let out in prose and verse. The bookstore she has contemplated is going to be a mistake if she is driven to it by our coolness to her in her art. I havent wanted to do anything to excite her to creation. Anyone of mine who writes prose or verse shall be a self-starter. But neither do I want to hold her from it too much or too long. I know you'll sympathise with me in this as much as in anything I have at heart. I thought her story all poetry. I hadnt seen it before it was in print.

I wish I could see you and hear all about what you are getting done. And I hope Jean likes her voice better and better. One reason for our wanting to get over is to see you both off your native heath. It would be fun meeting there where we never met before, maybe a foretaste of our meeting in heaven by accident at a soirée of Mrs God's. Mrs Olds, the new Presidents wife, gives lots of soirées and dinners—if that's all that's needed.

Affectionately
Robert.—

March 10, 1924

# Preface to
## 'Memoirs of the
## Notorious Stephen Burroughs'

PELHAM, MASSACHUSETTS, may never have produced any-thing else; it had a large part in producing the *Memoirs of the Notorious Stephen Burroughs*—this good book; or at least in starting the author on the criminal career of which it is a rec-ord. I like setting up the claim for Pelham, because I once lived there or thereabouts. But it is the kind of town I should have wanted to magnify anyway, whether I had lived in it or not, just one high old street along a ridge, not much to begin with and every year beautifully less. The railroads have worked modern magic against it from away off in the valleys and the woods have pressed in upon it till now there is nothing left but the church where Burroughs preached his unsanctified sermons, a few houses (among them, possibly, the one where he preached the funeral sermon that began his undoing), and here and there a good mowing field of about the size of a tea-tray in the sky.

I was back there the other day looking for Burroughs, and I saw three great ghosts instead of one, Burroughs, the rogue, Glazier Wheeler, the coiner, and Daniel Shays, the rebel, a shining company. Such places always have all their great men at once, as if they were neither born nor self-made, but created each other. I suppose I saw the three as they must have gotten together to talk subversion of an evening at the Leanders'. Poor old Shays! He was so scared by his own rebellion that once he started running away from it, he never stopped till he got to Sandgate, Vermont,—if you can imagine how far out of the world that is—at any rate it was then outside of the United States. Burroughs should have told us more about his Pelham friends, and especially about Glazier Wheeler, who on his serious side was concerned with the transmutation of metals and may have been a necromancer.

I was anxious to ask Burroughs if he wouldn't agree with me that his own chief distinction was hypocrisy. Many will be satisfied to see in him just another specimen of the knowing

rascal. I choose to take it that he is here raised up again as an
example to us of the naïve hypocrite.

We assume that by virtue of being bad we are at least safe
from being hypocrites. But are we any such thing? We bad
people I should say had appearances to keep up no less dan-
gerously than the good. The good must at all costs seem
good; that is the weakness of their position. But the bad must
seem amiable and engaging. They must often have to pass for
large-hearted when it is nothing but a strain on the heart that
makes the heart secretly sick. That is one curse that is laid on
them; and another is that in every out-and-out clash with the
righteous they must try to make themselves out more right
than the righteous. You can see what that would lead to. No,
I am afraid hypocrisy is as increasing to evil as it is diminishing
to good.

I was not a church-goer at the time when Burroughs was
preaching in Pelham, and there may have been circumstances
in aggravation that he does not set down, but, let him tell it,
I see little in the story to count against him. If the sermons
were sound and the preacher able, it couldn't have mattered
much that they were stolen and he not ordained. Technically,
he was an impostor, and I suppose I am too inclined to be
lenient with irregularity in both school and church. But I re-
member that Melchizedek was not a Levite and men have
taught in colleges with no degree beyond a bachelor's. And
take Burroughs' first serious lapse in attempting to pass coun-
terfeit money in Springfield. Crime couldn't be made more
excusable. Just one little dollar at a drugstore in the interests
of scientific experiment and to save the tears of a lovely lady.
I suspect he was not frank with us about what brought him
sneaking back to Pelham after he was driven out with pitch-
forks. The friendship of the Leanders, was it? And equally that
of Mr. and Mrs. Leander? And not at all the poetic young
dream of easy money? The sweet hypocrite, we must never let
him drop.

And couldn't he write, couldn't he state things? In his life-
time, he made the only two revolts from Puritanism anyone
has yet thought of, one backwards into Paganism and the
other, let us say, sideways into the Catholic Church. In making

the first, he put the case for Paganism almost as well as Milton puts it in the mouth of the sorcerer Comus: "We that are of purer fire." How well he argues against holding anyone locked up in a jail in a free country, and in favor of free coining in a free country!

I should like to have heard his reasons for winding up in the Catholic Church. I can conceive of their being honest. Probably he was tired of his uncharted freedom out of jail and wanted to be moral and a Puritan again as when a child, but this time under a cover where he couldn't be made fun of by the intellectuals. The course might commend itself to the modern Puritan (what there is left of the modern Puritan).

Let me tell the reader where he must put this book if he will please me and why there. On the same shelf with Benjamin Franklin and Jonathan Edwards (grandfather of Aaron Burr). Franklin will be a reminder of what we have been as a young nation in some respects, Edwards in others. Burroughs comes in reassuringly when there is question of our not unprincipled wickedness, whether we have had enough of it for salt. The world knows we are criminal enough. We commit our share of blind and inarticulate murder, for instance. But sophisticated wickedness, the kind that knows its grounds and can twinkle, could we have been expected to have produced so fine a flower in a pioneer state? The answer is that we had it and had it early in Stephen Burroughs (not to mention Aaron Burr). It is not just a recent publisher's importation from Europe.

Could anything recent be more teasing to our proper prejudices than the way Burroughs mixed the ingredients when he ran off on his travels? He went not like a fool with no thought for the future and nothing to his name but the horse between his legs. He took with him a pocketful of sermons stolen from his father, in one fell act combining prudence, a respect for religion (as property) and a respect for his father (as a preacher). *He* knew how to put the reverse on a ball so that when it was going it was also coming. It argues a sophisticated taste in the society around him that he should have found friends such as the Leanders to enjoy his jokes with him.

A book that I for one should be sorry to have missed. I have to thank my friend W. R. Brown for bringing it to my attention.

South Shaftsbury, Vermont
1924

# Introduction to
## 'The Arts Anthology: Dartmouth Verse'

No one given to looking under-ground in spring can have failed to notice how a bean starts its growth from the seed. Now the manner of a poet's germination is less like that of a bean in the ground than of a waterspout at sea. He has to begin as a cloud of all the other poets he ever read. That can't be helped. And first the cloud reaches down toward the water from above and then the water reaches up toward the cloud from below and finally cloud and water join together to roll as one pillar between heaven and earth. The base of water he picks up from below is of course all the life he ever lived outside of books.

These, then, are the three figures of the waterspout and the first is about as far as the poet doomed to die young in everyone of us usually gets. He brings something down from Dowson, Yeats, Morris, Masefield, or the Imagists (often a long way down), but lifts little or nothing up. If he were absolutely certain to do as doomed and die young, he would hardly be worth getting excited over in college or elsewhere. But you can't be too careful about whom you will ignore in this world. Cases have been known of his refusing at the last minute to abdicate the breast in favor of the practical and living on to write lyric like Landor till ninety.

Right in this book he will be found surviving into the second figure of the waterspout, and, by several poems and many scattered lines, even into the third figure. "The Heritage," "Sonnet," "I Have Built a Vessel," and "The Wanderer," good as they are of their kind—accomplished and all that—are of the first figure and frankly derivative. They are meant to do credit to anyone's reading. But "The Letter," "The Village Daily," "For a Salvationist," and best of all, "The Ski Jumper," at least get up the salt water. Their realism represents an advance. They show acceptance of the fact that the way to better is often through worse. In such a poem as "Underneath Sleep" the pillar revolves pretty much unbroken.

We are here getting a long way with poetry, considering all there is against it in school and college. The poet, as everyone knows, must strike his individual note sometime between the ages of fifteen and twenty-five. He may hold it a long time, or a short time, but it is then he must strike it or never. School and college have been conducted with the almost express purpose of keeping him busy with something else till the danger of his ever creating anything is past. Their motto has been, the muses find some mischief still for idle hands to do. No one is asking to see poetry regularized in courses and directed by coaches like sociology and football. It must remain a theft to retain its savor. But it does seem as if it could be a little more connived at than it is. I for one should be in favor of the colleges setting the expectation of poetry forward a few years (the way the clocks are set forward in May), so as to get the young poets started earlier in the morning before the freshness dries off. Just setting the expectation of poetry forward might be all that was needed to give us our proportioned number of poets to Congressmen.

June 1925

# Tribute to Percy MacKaye

PERCY MACKAYE has spent precious time trying to make the world an easier place to write poetry in. Everybody knows how he has spread himself over the country, as with two very large wings, to get his fellow poets all fellowships at the universities. That is but an incident in the general campaign he is forever on, to hasten the day when our national life, the raw material of poetry, having become less and less raw, shall at last cease to be raw at all, and poetry shall almost write itself without the intervention of the artist.

It is angelic of him to wish all poets a livelihood and a beauty of life that shall be poetry, without being worked up into poetry. That is why many think of him as an angel before they think of him as a poet. He is none the less a poet, one of the truest. He has come his way through three distinct periods of poetry, always Percy MacKaye, with no undue perturbations in his nature from what was going on around him.

I don't know how much he is read today, whether more or less than he has been in the past, but I am sure it is less than he will be in the future.—May he be read at least twice as much in the last fifty years of his life as he was in the first fifty!

*Percy MacKaye: a Symposium on His Fiftieth Birthday, 1925,* 1928

# The Poetry of Amy Lowell

IT IS ABSURD to think that the only way to tell if a poem is lasting is to wait and see if it lasts. The right reader of a good poem can tell the moment it strikes him that he has taken an immortal wound—that he will never get over it. That is to say, permanence in poetry as in love is perceived instantly. It hasn't to await the test of time. The proof of a poem is not that we have never forgotten it, but that we knew at sight that we never could forget it. There was a barb to it and a toxin that we owned to at once. How often I have heard it in the voice and seen it in the eyes of this generation that Amy Lowell had lodged poetry with them to stay.

The most exciting movement in nature is not progress, advance, but expansion and contraction, the opening and shutting of the eye, the hand, the heart, the mind. We throw our arms wide with a gesture of religion to the universe; we close them around a person. We explore and adventure for a while and then we draw in to consolidate our gains. The breathless swing is between subject matter and form. Amy Lowell was distinguished in a period of dilation when poetry, in the effort to include a larger material, stretched itself almost to the breaking of the verse. Little ones with no more apparatus than a teacup looked on with alarm. She helped make it stirring times for a decade to those immediately concerned with art and to many not so immediately.

The water in our eyes from her poetry is not warm with any suspicion of tears; it is water flung cold, bright and many-colored from flowers gathered in her formal garden in the morning. Her Imagism lay chiefly in images to the eye. She flung flowers and everything there. Her poetry was forever a clear resonant calling off of things seen.

*The Christian Science Monitor*,
May 16, 1925

# Preface to
## 'A Way Out'

EVERYTHING written is as good as it is dramatic. It need not declare itself in form, but it is drama or nothing. A least lyric alone may have a hard time, but it can make a beginning, and lyric will be piled on lyric till all are easily heard as sung or spoken by a person in a scene—in character, in a setting. By whom, where and when is the question. By a dreamer of the better world out in a storm in autumn; by a lover under a window at night. It is the same with the essay. It may manage alone or it may take unto itself other essays for help, but it must make itself heard as by Stevenson on an island, or Lamb in London.

A dramatic necessity goes deep into the nature of the sentence. Sentences are not different enough to hold the attention unless they are dramatic. No ingenuity of varying structure will do. All that can save them is the speaking tone of voice somehow entangled in the words and fastened to the page for the ear of the imagination. That is all that can save poetry from sing-song, all that can save prose from itself.

I have always come as near the dramatic as I could this side of actually writing a play. Here for once I have written a play without (as I should like to believe) having gone very far from where I have spent my life.

*A Way Out*, 1929

# To Sidney Cox

Dear Sidney:

I may want to write you two or three letters as I think over all you came up here with yesterday—and I may not. One thing I will write about at once that I didnt quite bring myself to talk about face to face. It reaches me from many directions sometimes with the kind of smile I don't care for and some-times with an out-and-out sneer that I am too much with you in the class room. I am sure you have used me to your own hurt at Dartmouth. I'd just like to see what leaving me en-tirely out of it for a year or two would do—not severely alone and out of it but just gently and unobtrusively out of it, so that no one would notice the omission till some day toward the end of the two years someone uncommonly observing should wake up and exclaim "Let's see! Whats become of Frost in this course?" I doubt if our friends, wives, children, or even ourselves are to be looked on as resources in class-room work. Offhand you might think it was an advantage in teaching contemporary literature to be personally acquainted with me. On the contrary it is a great disadvantage in my way of looking at it. It keeps you from talking about me as mod-estly as you could talk about Mrs William Rose Benet for in-stance. Everybody knows something has to be kept back for pressure and to anybody puzzled to know what I should sug-gest that for a beginning it might as well be his friends, wife, children, and self. That would be the part of *mature* wisdom. Poetry is measured in more senses than one: it is measured feet but more important still it is a measured amount of all we could say an we would. We shall be judged finally by the delicacy of our feeling of where to stop short. The right peo-ple know, and we artists should know better than they know. There is no greater fallacy going than that art is expression—an undertaking to tell all to the last scrapings of the brain pan. I neednt qualify as a specialist in botany and astronomy for a license to invoke flowers and stars in my poetry. I needn't have scraped those subjects to the point of exhaustiveness. God forbids that I should have to be an authority on anything even the psyche before I can set up for an artist. A little of anything goes a long way in art. Im never so desperate for material that I have to trench on the confidential for one thing, nor on the private for another nor on the personal, nor in general on the sacred. A little in the fist to manipulate is all I ask. My object is true form—is was and always will be—form true to any chance bit of true life. Almost any bit will do. I dont naturally trust any other object. I fight to be allowed to sit cross-legged on the old flint pile and flake a lump into an artifact. Or if I dont actually fight myself, the soldiers of my tribe do for me to keep the unsympathetic off me and give me elbow room. The best hour I ever had in the class room was good only for the shape it took. I like an encounter to shape up, unify however roughly. There is such a thing as random talk, but it is to be valued as a scouting expedition for coinable gold. I may say this partly to save myself from being misunderstood; I say it partly too to help you what I can toward your next advance in thought if not in office. You'll find yourself most effective in things people find out by accident you might have said but didnt say. Those are the things that make people take a good reestimating look at you. You have to refrain from saying many things to get credit for refraining from a few. There is a discouraging waste there as everywhere else in life. But never mind: there is a sense of strength gained in not caring. You feel so much in in having something to yourself. You have added to the mass of your private in reserve. You are more alluring to your friends and baffling to your foes.

Ever yours you know,<br>Robert Frost.

c. September 19, 1929

# To Kimball Flaccus

My dear Flaccus:

The book has come and I have read your poems first. They are good. They have loveliness—they surely have that. They are carried high. What you long for is in them. You wish the world better than it is, more poetical. You are that kind of poet. I would rate as the other kind. I wouldnt give a cent to see the world, the United States or even New York made better. I want them left just as they are for me to make poetical on paper. I dont ask anything done to them that I dont do to them myself. I'm a mere selfish artist most of the time. I have no quarrel with the material. The grief will be simply if I can't transmute it into poems. I dont want the world made safer for poetry or easier. To hell with it. That is its own look-out. Let it stew in its own materialism. No, not to Hell with it. Let it hold its position while I do it in art. My whole anxiety is for myself as a performer. Am I any good? That's what I'd like to know and all I need to know. I wonder which kind of poet is more numerous, your kind or my kind. There should have been a question in the census-taking to determine. Not that it should bother us. We can be friends across the difference. You'll have me watching you. We must meet again and have a talk about poetry and nothing but poetry. The great length of this letter is the measure of my thanks for the book.

Always yours friendly,<br>Robert Frost

Amherst Mass
October 26 1930

# Education by Poetry

## A Meditative Monologue

I AM going to urge nothing in my talk. I am not an advocate. I am going to consider a matter, and commit a description. And I am going to describe other colleges than Amherst. Or, rather say all that is good can be taken as about Amherst; all that is bad will be about other colleges.

I know whole colleges where all American poetry is barred—whole colleges. I know whole colleges where all contemporary poetry is barred.

I once heard of a minister who turned his daughter—his poetry-writing daughter—out on the street to earn a living, because he said there should be no more books written; God wrote one book, and that was enough. (My friend George Russell, "Æ," has read no literature, he protests, since just before Chaucer.)

That all seems sufficiently safe, and you can say one thing for it. It takes the onus off the poetry of having to be used to teach children anything. It comes pretty hard on poetry, I sometimes think,—what it has to bear in the teaching process.

Then I know whole colleges where, though they let in older poetry, they manage to bar all that is poetical in it by treating it as something other than poetry. It is not so hard to do that. Their reason I have often hunted for. It may be that these people act from a kind of modesty. Who are professors that they should attempt to deal with a thing as high and as fine as poetry? Who are *they*? There is a certain manly modesty in that.

That is the best general way of settling the problem; treat all poetry as if it were something else than poetry, as if it were syntax, language, science. Then you can even come down into the American and into the contemporary without any special risk.

There is another reason they have, and that is that they are, first and foremost in life, markers. They have the marking problem to consider. Now, I stand here a teacher of many years' experience and I have never complained of having had to mark. I had rather mark anyone for anything—for his looks, carriage, his ideas, his correctness, his exactness, anything you please,—I would rather give him a mark in terms of letters, A, B, C, D, than have to use adjectives on him. We are all being marked by each other all the time, classified, ranked, put in our place, and I see no escape from that. I am no sentimentalist. You have got to mark, and you have got to mark, first of all, for accuracy, for correctness. But if I am going to give a mark, that is the least part of my marking. The hard part is the part beyond that, the part where the adventure begins.

One other way to rid the curriculum of the poetry nuisance has been considered. More merciful than the others it would neither abolish nor denature the poetry, but only turn it out to disport itself, with the plays and games—in no wise discredited, though given no credit for. Anyone who liked to teach poetically could take his subject, whether English, Latin, Greek or French, out into the nowhere along with the poetry. One side of a sharp line would be left to the rigorous and righteous; the other side would be assigned to the flowery where they would know what could be expected of them. Grade marks where more easily given, of course, in the courses concentrating on correctness and exactness as the only forms of honesty recognized by plain people; a general indefinite mark of $X$ in the courses that scatter brains over taste and opinion. On inquiry I have found no teacher willing to take position on either side of the line, either among the rigors or among the flowers. No one is willing to admit that his discipline is not partly in exactness. No one is willing to admit that his discipline is not partly in taste and enthusiasm.

How shall a man go through college without having been marked for taste and judgment? What will become of him? What will his end be? He will have to take continuation courses for college graduates. He will have to go to night schools. They are having night schools now, you know, for college graduates. Why? Because they have not been educated enough to find their way around in contemporary literature. They don't know what they may safely like in the libraries and galleries. They don't know how to judge an editorial when they see one. They don't know how to judge a political cam-

paign. They don't know when they are being fooled by a met-
aphor, an analogy, a parable. And metaphor is, of course, what
we are talking about. Education by poetry is education by
metaphor.

Suppose we stop short of imagination, initiative, enthusi-
asm, inspiration and originality—dread words. Suppose we
don't mark in such things at all. There are still two minimal
things, that we have got to take care of, taste and judgment.
Americans are supposed to have more judgment than taste,
but taste is there to be dealt with. That is what poetry, the
only art in the colleges of arts, is there for. I for my part would
not be afraid to go in for enthusiasm. There is the enthusiasm
like a blinding light, or the enthusiasm of the deafening shout,
the crude enthusiasm that you get uneducated by poetry, out-
side of poetry. It is exemplified in what I might call "sunset
raving." You look westward toward the sunset, or if you get
up early enough, eastward toward the sunrise, and you rave.
It is oh's and ah's with you and no more.

But the enthusiasm I mean is taken through the prism of
the intellect and spread on the screen in a color, all the way
from hyperbole at one end—or overstatement, at one end—
to understatement at the other end. It is a long strip of dark
lines and many colors. Such enthusiasm is one object of all
teaching in poetry. I heard wonderful things said about Virgil
yesterday, and many of them seemed to me crude enthusiasm,
more like a deafening shout, many of them. But one speech
had range, something of overstatement, something of state-
ment, and something of understatement. It had all the colors
of an enthusiasm passed through an idea.

I would be willing to throw away everything else but that:
enthusiasm tamed by metaphor. Let me rest the case there.
Enthusiasm tamed to metaphor, tamed to that much of it. I
do not think anybody ever knows the discreet use of meta-
phor, his own and other people's, the discreet handling of
metaphor, unless he has been properly educated in poetry.

Poetry begins in trivial metaphors, pretty metaphors,
"grace" metaphors, and goes on to the profoundest thinking
that we have. Poetry provides the one permissible way of say-
ing one thing and meaning another. People say, "Why don't
you say what you mean?" We never do that, do we, being all

of us too much poets. We like to talk in parables and in hints and in indirections—whether from diffidence or some other instinct.

I have wanted in late years to go further and further in making metaphor the whole of thinking. I find someone now and then to agree with me that all thinking, except mathematical thinking, is metaphorical, or all thinking except scientific thinking. The mathematical might be difficult for me to bring in, but the scientific is easy enough.

Once on a time all the Greeks were busy telling each other what the All was—or was like unto. All was three elements, air, earth, and water (we once thought it was ninety elements; now we think it is only one). All was substance, said another. All was change, said a third. But best and most fruitful was Pythagoras' comparison of the universe with number. Number of what? Number of feet, pounds, and seconds was the answer, and we had science and all that has followed in science. The metaphor has held and held, breaking down only when it came to the spiritual and psychological or the out of the way places of the physical.

The other day we had a visitor here, a noted scientist, whose latest word to the world has been that the more accurately you know where a thing is, the less accurately you are able to state how fast it is moving. You can see why that would be so, without going back to Zeno's problem of the arrow's flight. In carrying numbers into the realm of space and at the same time into the realm of time you are mixing metaphors, that is all, and you are in trouble. They won't mix. The two don't go together.

Let's take two or three more of the metaphors now in use to live by. I have just spoken of one of the new ones, a charming mixed metaphor right in the realm of higher mathematics and higher physics: that the more accurately you state where a thing is, the less accurately you will be able to tell how fast it is moving. And, of course, everything is moving. Everything is an event now. Another metaphor. A thing, they say, is an event. Do you believe it is? Not quite. I believe it is almost an event. But I like the comparison of a thing with an event.

I notice another from the same quarter. "In the neighborhood of matter space is something like curved." Isn't that a good one! It seems to me that that is simply and utterly charming—to say that space is something like curved in the neighborhood of matter. "Something like."

Another amusing one is from—what is the book?—I can't say it now; but here is the metaphor. Its aim is to restore you to your ideas of free will. It wants to give you back your freedom of will. All right, here it is on a platter. You know that you can't tell by name what persons in a certain class will be dead ten years after graduation, but you can tell actuarially how many will be dead. Now, just so this scientist says of the particles of matter flying at a screen, striking a screen; you can't tell what individual particles will come, but you can say in general that a certain number will strike in a given time. It shows, you see, that the individual particles can come freely. I asked Bohr about that particularly, and he said, "Yes, it is so. It can come when it wills and as it wills; and the action of the individual particle is unpredictable. But it is not so of the action of the mass. There you can predict." He says, "That gives the individual atom its freedom, but the mass its necessity."

Another metaphor that has interested us in our time and has done all our thinking for us is the metaphor of evolution. Never mind going into the Latin word. The metaphor is simply the metaphor of the growing plant or of the growing thing. And somebody very brilliantly, quite a while ago, said that the whole universe, the whole of everything, was like unto a growing thing. That is all. I know the metaphor will break down at some point, but it has not failed everywhere. It is a very brilliant metaphor, I acknowledge, though I myself get too tired of the kind of essay that talks about the evolution of candy, we will say, or the evolution of elevators—the evolution of this, that, and the other. Everything is evolution. I emancipate myself by simply saying that I didn't get up the metaphor and so am not much interested in it.

What I am pointing out is that unless you are at home in the metaphor, unless you have had your proper poetical education in the metaphor, you are not safe anywhere. Because you are not at ease with figurative values: you don't know the metaphor in its strength and its weakness. You don't know how far you may expect to ride it and when it may break down with you. You are not safe in science; you are not safe in history. In history, for instance—to show that is the same in history as elsewhere—I heard somebody say yesterday that Aeneas was to be likened unto (those words, "likened unto"!) George Washington. He was that type of national hero, the middle-class man, not thinking of being a hero at all, bent on building the future, bent on his children, his descendants. A good metaphor, as far as it goes, and you must know how far. And then he added that Odysseus should be likened unto Theodore Roosevelt. I don't think that is so good. Someone visiting Gibbon at the point of death said he was the same Gibbon as of old, still at his parallels.

Take the way we have been led into our present position morally, the world over. It is by a sort of metaphorical gradient. There is a kind of thinking—to speak metaphorically—there is a kind of thinking you might say was endemic in the brothel. It is always there. And every now and then in some mysterious way it becomes epidemic in the world. And how does it do so? By using all the good words that virtue has invented to maintain virtue. It uses honesty, first,—frankness, sincerity—those words; picks them up, uses them. "In the name of honesty, let us see what we are." You know. And then it picks up the word joy. "Let us in the name of joy, which is the enemy of our ancestors, the Puritans . . . Let us in the name of joy, which is the enemy of the kill-joy Puritan . . ." You see. "Let us," and so on. And then, "In the name of health . . ." Health is another good word. And that is the metaphor Freudianism trades on, mental health. And the first thing we know, it has us all in up to the top knot. I suppose we may blame the artists a good deal, because they are great people to spread by metaphor. The stage too—the stage is always a good intermediary between the two worlds, the under and the upper,—if I may say so without personal prejudice to the stage.

In all this I have only been saying that the devil can quote Scripture, which simply means that the good words you have lying around the devil can use for his purposes as well as anybody else. Never mind about my morality. I am not here to urge anything. I don't care whether the world is good or bad—not on any particular day.

Let me ask you to watch a metaphor breaking down here before you.

Somebody said to me a little while ago, "It is easy enough for me to think of the universe as a machine, as a mechanism."

I said, "You mean the universe is like a machine?"

He said, "No. I think it is one . . . Well, it is like . . ."

"I think you mean the universe is like a machine."

"All right. Let it go at that."

I asked him, "Did you ever see a machine without a pedal for the foot, or a lever for the hand, or a button for the finger?"

He said, "No—no."

I said, "All right. Is the universe like that?"

And he said, "No. I mean it is like a machine, only . . ."

". . . it is different from a machine," I said.

He wanted to go just that far with that metaphor and no further. And so do we all. All metaphor breaks down somewhere. That is the beauty of it. It is touch and go with the metaphor, and until you have lived with it long enough you don't know when it is going. You don't know how much you can get out of it and when it will cease to yield. It is a very living thing. It is as life itself.

I have heard this ever since I can remember, and ever since I have taught: the teacher must teach the pupil to think. I saw a teacher once going around in a great school and snapping pupils' heads with thumb and finger and saying, "Think." That was when thinking was becoming the fashion. The fashion hasn't yet quite gone out.

We still ask boys in college to think, as in the nineties, but we seldom tell them what thinking means; we seldom tell them it is just putting this and that together; it is just saying one thing in terms of another. To tell them is to set their feet on the first rung of a ladder the top of which sticks through the sky.

Greatest of all attempts to say one thing in terms of another is the philosophical attempt to say matter in terms of spirit, or spirit in terms of matter, to make the final unity. That is the greatest attempt that ever failed. We stop just short there. But it is the height of poetry, the height of all thinking, the height of all poetic thinking, that attempt to say matter in terms of spirit and spirit in terms of matter. It is wrong to call anybody a materialist simply because he tries to say spirit in terms of matter, as if that were a sin. Materialism is not the attempt to say all in terms of matter. The only materialist—be he poet, teacher, scientist, politician, or statesman—is the man who gets lost in his material without a gathering metaphor to throw it into shape and order. He is the lost soul.

We ask people to think, and we don't show them what thinking is. Somebody says we don't need to show them how to think; bye and bye they will think. We will give them the forms of sentences and, if they have any ideas, then they will know how to write them. But that is preposterous. All there is to writing is having ideas. To learn to write is to learn to have ideas.

The first little metaphor . . . Take some of the trivial ones. I would rather have trivial ones of my own to live by than the big ones of other people.

I remember a boy saying, "He is the kind of person that wounds with his shield." That may be a slender one, of course. It goes a good way in character description. It has poetic grace. "He is the kind that wounds with his shield."

The shield reminds me—just to linger a minute—the shield reminds me of the inverted shield spoken of in one of the books of the "Odyssey," the book that tells about the longest swim on record. I forget how long it lasted—several days, was it?—but at last as Odysseus came near the coast of Phaeacia, he saw it on the horizon "like an inverted shield."

There is a better metaphor in the same book. In the end Odysseus comes ashore and crawls up the beach to spend the night under a double olive tree, and it says, as in a lonely farmhouse where it is hard to get fire—I am not quoting exactly—where it is hard to start the fire again if it goes out, they cover the seeds of fire with ashes to preserve it for the night, so Odysseus covered himself with the leaves around him and went to sleep. There you have something that gives you character, something of Odysseus himself. "Seeds of fire." So Odysseus covered the seeds of fire in himself. You get the greatness of his nature.

But these are slighter metaphors than the ones we live by. They have their charm, their passing charm. They are as it were the first steps toward the great thoughts, grave thoughts, thoughts lasting to the end.

The metaphor whose manage we are best taught in poetry —that is all there is of thinking. It may not seem far for the mind to go but it is the mind's furthest. The richest accumulation of the ages is the noble metaphors we have rolled up.

I want to add one thing more that the experience of poetry is to anyone who comes close to poetry. There are two ways of coming close to poetry. One is by writing poetry. And some people think I want people to write poetry, but I don't; that is, I don't necessarily. I only want people to write poetry if they want to write poetry. I have never encouraged anybody to write poetry that did not want to write it, and I have not always encouraged those who did want to write it. That ought to be one's own funeral. It is a hard, hard life, as they say.

(I have just been to a city in the West, a city full of poets, a city they have made safe for poets. The whole city is so lovely that you do not have to write it up to make it poetry; it is ready-made for you. But, I don't know—the poetry written in that city might not seem like poetry if read outside of the city. It would be like the jokes made when you were drunk; you have to get drunk again to appreciate them.)

But as I say, there is another way to come close to poetry, fortunately, and that is in the reading of it, not as linguistics, not as history, not as anything but poetry. It is one of the hard things for a teacher to know how close a man has come in reading poetry. How do I know whether a man has come close to Keats in reading Keats? It is hard for me to know. I have lived with some boys a whole year over some of the poets and I have not felt sure whether they have come near what it was all about. One remark sometimes told me. One remark was their mark for the year; had to be—it was all I got that told me what I wanted to know. And that is enough, if it was the right remark, if it came close enough. I think a man might make twenty fool remarks if he made one good one some time in the year. His mark would depend on that good remark.

The closeness—everything depends on the closeness with which you come, and you ought to be marked for the closeness, for nothing else. And that will have to be estimated by chance remarks, not by question and answer. It is only by accident that you know some day how near a person has come.

The person who gets close enough to poetry, he is going to know more about the word *belief* than anybody else knows, even in religion nowadays. There are two or three places where we know belief outside of religion. One of them is at the age of fifteen to twenty, in our self-belief. A young man knows more about himself than he is able to prove to anyone. He has no knowledge that anybody else will accept as knowledge. In his foreknowledge he has something that is going to believe itself into fulfilment, into acceptance.

There is another belief like that, the belief in someone else, a relationship of two that is going to be believed into fulfilment. That is what we are talking about in our novels, the belief of love. And the disillusionment that the novels are full of is simply the disillusionment from disappointment in that belief. That belief can fail, of course.

Then there is a literary belief. Every time a poem is written, every time a short story is written, it is written not by cunning, but by belief. The beauty, the something, the little charm of the thing to be, is more felt than known. There is a common jest, one that always annoys me, on the writers, that they write the last end first, and then work up to it; that they lay a train toward one sentence that they think is pretty nice and have all fixed up to set like a trap to close with. No, it should not be that way at all. No one who has ever come close to the arts has failed to see the difference between things written that way, with cunning and device, and the kind that are believed into existence, that begin in something more felt than known. This you can realize quite as well—not quite as well, perhaps, but nearly as well—in reading as you can in writing. I would undertake to separate short stories on that principle; stories that have been believed into existence and stories that have been cunningly devised. And I could separate the poems still more easily.

Now I think—I happen to think—that those three beliefs that I speak of, the self-belief, the love-belief, and the art-belief, are all closely related to the God-belief, that the belief in God is a relationship you enter into with Him to bring about the future.

There is national belief like that, too. One feels it. I have been where I came near getting up and walking out on the people who thought that they had to talk against nations, against nationalism, in order to curry favor with international-ism. Their metaphors are all mixed up. They think that be-cause a Frenchman and an American and an Englishman can all sit down on the same platform and receive honors together, it must be that there is no such thing as nations. That kind of bad thinking springs from a source we all know. I should want to say to anyone like that: "Look! First I want to be a person. And I want you to be a person, and then we can be as interpersonal as you please. We can pull each other's noses—do all sorts of things. But, first of all, you have got to have the personality. First of all, you have got to have the nations and then they can be as international as they please with each other."

I should like to use another metaphor on them. I want my palette, if I am a painter, I want my palette on my thumb or on my chair, all clean, pure, separate colors. Then I will do the mixing on the canvas. The canvas is where the work of art is, where we make the conquest. But we want the nations all separate, pure, distinct, things as separate as we can make them; and then in our thoughts, in our arts, and so on, we can do what we please about it.

But I go back. There are four beliefs that I know more about from having lived with poetry. One is the personal be-lief, which is a knowledge that you don't want to tell other people about because you cannot prove that you know. You are saying nothing about it till you see. The love belief, just the same, has that same shyness. It knows it cannot tell; only the outcome can tell. And the national belief we enter into socially with each other, all together, party of the first part, party of the second part, we enter into that to bring the future of the country. We cannot tell some people what it is we be-lieve, partly, because they are too stupid to understand and partly because we are too proudly vague to explain. And any-way it has got to be fulfilled, and we are not talking until we know more, until we have something to show. And then the literary one in every work of art, not of cunning and craft, mind you, but of real art; that believing the thing into existence, saying as you go more than you even hoped you were going to be able to say, and coming with surprise to an end that you foreknew only with some sort of emotion. And then finally the relationship we enter into with God to believe the future in—to believe the hereafter in.

Amherst Alumni Council Address,
November 15, 1930

# *To Sidney Cox*

Amherst

Honestly Sidney

You are getting out of hand. I'm afraid you aren't going to let yourself be unduly influenced by me any more.

I grow surer I don't want to search the poet's mind too seriously. I might enjoy threatening to for the fun of it just as I might to frisk his person. I have written to keep the over curious out of the secret places of my mind both in my verse and in my letters to such as you. A subject has to be held clear outside of me with struts and as it were set up for an object. A subject must be an object. There's no use in laboring this further years. My objection to your larger book about me was that it came thrusting in where I did not want you. The idea is the thing with me. It would seem soft for instance to look in my life for the sentiments in the Death of the Hired Man. There's nothing to it believe me. I should fool you if you took me so. I'll tell you my notion of the contract you thought you had with me. The objective idea is all I ever cared about. Most of my ideas occur in verse. But I have always had some turning up in talk that I feared I might never use because I was too lazy to write prose. I think they have been mostly educational ideas connected with my teaching, actually lessons. That's where I hoped you would come in. I thought if it didnt take you too much from your own affairs you might be willing to gather them for us both. But I never reckoned with the personalities. I keep to a minimum of such stuff in any poets life and works. Art and wisdom with the body heat out of it. You speak of Shirley. He is two or three great poems—one very great. He projected, he got, them out of his system and I will not carry them back into his system either at the place they came out of or at some other place. I state this in the extreme. But relatively I mean what I say. To be too subjective with what an artist has managed to make objective is to come on him presumptuously and render ungraceful what he in pain of his life had faith he had made graceful.

Leave us look at the Gilchrist book. I am curious to see where it touches me.

Ever yours
RF.

c. April 19, 1932

# On "Birches"

(OLD KNOWER): The tide of evil rises. Your Ark is sailing and you make me a last-minute allowance of a single plant on board for seed. (It would have to be two if animals, or there would be no seed.) Well, let it be a tree—Birches. Don't ask me why at a time of doom and confusion like this. My reasons might be forced and unreal. But if I must defend my choice, I will say I took it for its vocality and its ulteriority.

*Fifty Poets: An American
Auto-Anthology*, 1933

# To Wilbert Snow

Dear Bill

For me especially The Hungry Shark, January Thaw, Wave Music and so on through the lyrics and sonnets. It need not bother you that those against anything or anybody such as an Indian Pioneer, the Ballad of Jonathan Coe, The Evangelist, Heritage and The Flood are less to my taste. Your attitude of political agitator has to be allowed for. You wouldn't be you if you suspected as I suspect that there is really nothing the matter with anybody. We are a sad lot, rather than a bad lot. My mind goes back to how true Turgeneff holds the balance between protagonists and antagonists in the death of Bazarov in Fathers and Sons. He is perfect in his non-partizanship. I never quite like to hear a wife turned on against her husband or vice versa. They know too much about each other and they are not disinterested. They lack, what they should lack, detachment. Maybe it bothers me as a breach of manners. But if manners count so much with me, then why don't I answer people's letters or properly acknowledge their books. I'll tell you in a minute. But first I want to finish with you where we are. The Evangelist reminds me not too painfully of Sinclair Lewis and a song we used to sing fifty years ago:

> "Oh my God I'm feeling blue
> For I'm six months overdue"

Only in this case

> "It was from a grey haired drummer
> Who was round here all last summer."

As George Meredith says we girls are not so much betrayed by evangelists and drummers however; "We are betrayed by what is false within."

But here I go quarreling with your tenets when it wasn't more than a week ago I was saying in public that in verse as in trapeze performance is all. And that's why nothing around college absolutely nothing, is as near poetry and the arts in general as the sports of the stadium. The Greeks agreed with me, or they wouldn't have had drama and games at the same time and place.

And all through the book you satisfy me with your performance. You are a going poet and no mistake. I'm happy to be of your audience and proud to be remembered with a complimentary ticket now and then.

Which brings me back to why I didn't acknowledge your fine book as soon as I got it. Well I got it for last Christmas, didn't I? I thought it would be a good idea if I gave you a letter of thanks for next Christmas. Honestly! And I should have carried out the idea, if I could have stood the strain of being misjudged by you a whole year and liable to one of your narrow condemnations.

Dust to dust and salt of blood back to salt of sea. I may be tempted to steal that some day. But if I do steal it it won't be unknowingly: the source is too deeply stamped in my memory.

Love to you all<br>R. F.

c. May 16, 1933

# To Lesley Frost Francis

Dear Lesley:

The difficulty of a job like that is to keep it from getting out of your mind for a single instant that you are speaking for Us the Frost Family and not just for yourself. In the last year or two owing to a nasty slap I got from an American follower of Eliots, I confess I have several times forgotten my dignity in speaking in public of Eliot. I mean I have shown a hostility I should like to think in my pride unworthy of my position. I could wish you would do better for us. For the most part describe rather than judge, or seem to judge only in a occasional ironical shading or lightly and unvenomously toward the end. Present them nearly as they would present themselves. Remember you are my daughter you are speaking in Cambridge and Eliots sister Mrs Sheffield the wife of my instructor in English at Harvard may very well be in your audience. Show no animus. Be judicial. Don't take anybody *alive* too seriously.

Let me tell you a few things about the new Movement you may or may not have taken in amid all the talk you have had to listen to.

Ezra Pound was the Prime Mover in the Movement and must always have the credit for whats in it. He was just branching off from the regular poets when we arrived in England. His Δώρια (Doria) had won second prize in a contest where Rupert Brooke's Dust had won first. Δώρια was a more or less conscious departure. The coming in second made it very conscious.

One of the first things Pound thought of was that rhyme and meter made you use too many words and even subsidiary ideas for the sake of coming out even. He and his friends Flint H. D. and Aldington used to play a game of rewriting each others poems to see if they couldnt reduce the number of words. Pound once wrote to me that John Gould Fletcher failed as a free verse writer because he failed to understand the purpose of free verse, which was, namely, to be less free, not more free, with the verbiage.

Pound began to talk very early about rhythm alone without meter.

I assume you'll find in Reed his latest descendant a full statement of the doctrine of Inner Form, that is to say the form the subject itself takes if left to itself without any considerations of outer form. Everything else is to have two compulsions, an inner and an outer, a spiritual and a social, an individual and a racial. I want to be good, but that is not enough the state says I have got to be good. Everything has not only formity but conformity. Everything but poetry according to the Pound-Eliot-Richards-Reed school of art. For my part I should be as satisfied to play tennis with the net down as to write verse with no verse form set to stay me. I suppose I could display my energy, agility and intense nature as well in either case. That's me. Remember you are speaking for them and do them justice. But whatever you do, do Pound justice as the great original.

He was the first Imagist too—although I believe our friend T. E. Hulme coined the name. An Imagist is simply one who insists on clearer sharper less muddled half realized images (chiefly eye images) than the common run of small poets. Thats certainly good as far as it goes. Strange with all their modernity and psychology they didnt have more to say about ear images and other images—even kinesthetic.

Pounds tightness naturally tended to stripping poetry of connective tissue. Never mind connections—they'll take care of themselves—if only you make your poetic points. The method gives a very ancient Old-Testament flavor to expression.

The same aspiration toward brevity and undersaying rather than oversaying has led to the poetry of intimation implication insinuation and innuendo as an object in itself. All poetry has always said something and implied the rest. Well then why have it say anything? Why not have it imply everything? Harte Crane has gone to great lengths here. There is some excuse for their extravagances. It is true much poetry is simply flat from being said too fully outright. I suppose Gertrude Stein has come in confluently to encourage the intimators or innuendots. A little of her is fun, but goes a long way. I read that negroes were chosen to sing her opera because they have less need than white men to know what they are talking about. That is a thing that can be reported without malice. "The bailey beareth away the bell" poem is taken as justification of poetry by elipsis hiatus and hint. It's a fine poem beyond cavil. I wish somebody could write more like it. Gerard Manley Hopkins' obscurities and awkwardnesses are some more of their Bible. Hopkins is well enough. His friend Robert Bridges judged his limitations very fairly. His poem about All Pied Things good as it is disappoints me by not keeping, short as it is, wholly to pied things. I'm sending you this long poem by Perse as a further instance. I read the Proem in Chapel one morning with success. I had to practice up a way to perform it. Most of the boys laughed but some there were who pretended to be subconscious of what it was about. On the same principle a child of two three and four gets legitimate pleasure out of hearing Miltons Paradise Lost read aloud. If the child's legitimate he does. We've got to keep control of our mysteries. Above all things no vindictiveness.

From Pound down to Eliot they have striven for distinction by a show of learning, Pound in old French Eliot in forty languages. They quote and you try to see if you can place the quotation. Pound really has great though inaccurate learning. Eliot has even greater. Maurice Hewlett leaned on Pound for medieval facts. Yates has leaned on him for facts and more than facts. Pound has taught Yates his later style of expression. Not many realize this. There's a significant reference to Pound in the preface to Yeates last book.

Last we come to who means the most, Pound or Eliot. Eliot has written in the throes of getting religion and foreswearing a world gone bad with war. That seems deep. But I dont know. Waste Lands—your great grand mother on the grand mother on your mothers side! I doubt if anything was laid waste by war that was not laid waste by peace before.

Claim every thing for America. Pound Eliot and Stein are all American though expatriate.

Affectionately<br>Papa

You'll notice Eliot translates this

> This Song is what I read the boys
> Auden is their latest recruit

Notice in Eliots Ash Wednesday how he misquotes Shakespeare's "Desiring this mans art and that man's scope"

Why does he do it if on purpose? Is he improving on Shakespeare or merely giving him an interesting twist up to date? Ash Wednesday is supposed to be deeply religious—last phase before going to Rome.

Send it back

1934

# To 'Books We Like'

1 THE ODYSSEY chooses itself, the first in time and rank of all romances. Palmer's translation is by all odds the best. As Lawrence in a preface to his own translation describes the author of the original, he is evidently a man much more like Palmer than like Lawrence. I can permit myself but one translation out of ten books.

2 *Robinson Crusoe* is never quite out of my mind. I never tire of being shown how the limited can make snug in the limitless.

3 *Walden* has something of the same fascination. Crusoe was cast away; Thoreau was self-cast away. Both found themselves sufficient. No prose writer has ever been more fortunate in subject than these two. I prefer my essay in narrative form. In Walden I get it and always near the height of poetry.

4 Poe's *Tales.* Here is every kind of entertainment the short story can afford, the supernatural, the horrific, pseudo-scientific, ingenious, and detective. (Every kind I should perhaps say but the character.)

5 *The Oxford Book of English Verse* and

6 Untermeyer's *Modern American and British Poetry* pretty well cover between them the poetry of our race. I am permitting myself two and one half numbers of actual verse in the ten—twenty-five per cent. That doesn't seem for the moment an undue proportion.

7 *The Last of the Mohicans* supplies us once for all with our way of thinking of the American Indian.

8 *The Prisoner of Zenda*—surely one of the very best of our modern best-sellers.

9 *The Jungle Book* (1st). I shall read it again as often as I can find a new child to listen to me.

10 Emerson's *Essays and Poems*—the rapture of idealism either way you have it, in prose or in verse and in brief.

Key West
December 18 1934

*Books We Like*, Massachusetts
Library Association, 1936

# Letter to
## 'The Amherst Student'

IT IS very, very kind of the STUDENT to be showing sympathy with me for my age. But sixty is only a pretty good age. It is not advanced enough. The great thing is to be advanced. Now ninety would be really well along and something to be given credit for.

But speaking of ages, you will often hear it said that the age of the world we live in is particularly bad. I am impatient of such talk. We have no way of knowing that this age is one of the worst in the world's history. Arnold claimed the honor for the age before this. Wordsworth claimed it for the last but one. And so on back through literature. I say they claimed the honor for their ages. They claimed it rather for themselves. It is immodest of a man to think of himself as going down before the worst forces ever mobilized by God.

All ages of the world are bad—a great deal worse anyway than Heaven. If they weren't the world might just as well be Heaven at once and have it over with. One can safely say after from six to thirty thousand years of experience that the evident design is a situation here in which it will always be about equally hard to save your soul. Whatever progress may be taken to mean, it can't mean making the world any easier a place in which to save your soul—or if you dislike hearing your soul mentioned in open meeting, say your decency, your integrity.

Ages may vary a little. One may be a little worse than another. But it is not possible to get outside the age you are in to judge it exactly. Indeed it is as dangerous to try to get outside of anything as large as an age as it would be to engorge a donkey. Witness the many who in the attempt have suffered a dilation from which the tissues and the muscles of the mind have never been able to recover natural shape. They can't pick up anything delicate or small any more. They can't use a pen. They have to use a typewriter. And they gape in agony. They can write huge shapeless novels, huge gobs of raw sincerity bellowing with pain and that's all that they can write.

Fortunately we don't need to know how bad the age is. There is something we can always be doing without reference to how good or how bad the age is. There is at least so much good in the world that it admits of form and the making of form. And not only admits of it, but calls for it. We people are thrust forward out of the suggestions of form in the rolling clouds of nature. In us nature reaches its height of form and through us exceeds itself. When in doubt there is always form for us to go on with. Anyone who has achieved the least form to be sure of it, is lost to the larger excruciations. I think it must stroke faith the right way. The artist, the poet might be expected to be the most aware of such assurance. But it is really everybody's sanity to feel it and live by it. Fortunately, too, no forms are more engrossing, gratifying, comforting, staying than those lesser ones we throw off, like vortex rings of smoke, all our individual enterprise and needing nobody's cooperation; a basket, a letter, a garden, a room, an idea, a picture, a poem. For these we haven't to get a team together before we can play.

The background is hugeness and confusion shading away from where we stand into black and utter chaos; and against the background any small man-made figure of order and concentration. What pleasanter than that this should be so? Unless we are novelists or economists we don't worry about this confusion; we look out on it with an instrument or tackle it to reduce it. It is partly because we are afraid it might prove too much for us and our blend of democratic-republican-socialist-communist-anarchist party. But it is more because we like it, we were born to it, born used to it and have practical reasons for wanting it there. To me any little form I assert upon it is velvet, as the saying is, and to be considered for how much more it is than nothing. If I were a Platonist I should have to consider it, I suppose, for how much less it is than everything.

*The Amherst Student*, March 25, 1935

# Introduction to
# E. A. Robinson's 'King Jasper'

IT MAY come to the notice of posterity (and then again it may
not) that this, our age, ran wild in the quest of new ways to
be new. The one old way to be new no longer served. Science
put it into our heads that there must be new ways to be new.
Those tried were largely by subtraction—elimination. Poetry,
for example, was tried without punctuation. It was tried with-
out capital letters. It was tried without metric frame on which
to measure the rhythm. It was tried without any images but
those to the eye; and a loud general intoning had to be kept
up to cover the total loss of specific images to the ear, those
dramatic tones of voice which had hitherto constituted the
better half of poetry. It was tried without content under the
trade name of poesie pure. It was tried without phrase, epi-
gram, coherence, logic and consistency. It was tried without
ability. I took the confession of one who had had deliberately
to unlearn what he knew. He made a back-pedalling move-
ment of his hands to illustrate the process. It was tried pre-
mature like the delicacy of unborn calf in Asia. It was tried
without feeling or sentiment like murder for small pay in the
underworld. These many things was it tried without, and what
had we left? Still something. The limits of poetry had been
sorely strained, but the hope was that the idea had been some-
what brought out.

Robinson stayed content with the old-fashioned way to be
new. I remember bringing the subject up with him. How does
a man come on his difference, and how does he feel about it
when he first finds it out? At first it may well frighten him, as
his difference with the Church frightened Martin Luther.
There is such a thing as being too willing to be different. And
what shall we say to people who are not only willing but anx-
ious? What assurance have they that their difference is not
insane, eccentric, abortive, unintelligible? Two fears should
follow us through life. There is the fear that we shan't prove
worthy in the eyes of someone who knows us at least as well
as we know ourselves. That is the fear of God. And there is

the fear of Man—the fear that men won't understand us and we shall be cut off from them.

We began in infancy by establishing correspondence of eyes with eyes. We recognized that they were the same feature and we could do the same things with them. We went on to the visible motion of the lips—smile answered smile; then cautiously, by trial and error, to compare the invisible muscles of the mouth and throat. They were the same and could make the same sounds. We were still together. So far, so good. From here on the wonder grows. It has been said that recognition in art is all. Better say correspondence is all. Mind must convince mind that it can uncurl and wave the same filaments of subtlety, soul convince soul that it can give off the same shimmers of eternity. At no point would anyone but a brute fool want to break off this correspondence. It is all there is to satisfaction; and it is salutary to live in the fear of its being broken off.

The latest proposed experiment of the experimentalists is to use poetry as a vehicle of grievances against the un-Utopian state. As I say, most of their experiments have been by subtraction. This would be by addition of an ingredient that latter-day poetry has lacked. A distinction must be made between griefs and grievances. Grievances are probably more useful than griefs. I read in a sort of Sunday School leaflet from Moscow that the grievances of Chekhov against the sordidness and dullness of his home-town society have done away with the sordidness and dullness of home-town society all over Russia. They were celebrating the event. The grievances of the great Russians of the last century have given Russia a revolution. The grievances of their great followers in America may well give us, if not a revolution, at least some palliative pensions. We must suffer them to put life at its ugliest and forbid them not as we value our reputation for liberality.

I had it from one of the youngest lately: "Whereas we once thought literature should be without content, we now know it should be charged full of propaganda." Wrong twice, I told him. Wrong twice and of theory prepense. But he returned to his position after a moment out for reassembly: "Surely art can be considered good only as it prompts to action." How soon, I asked him. But there is danger of undue levity in teasing the young. The experiment is evidently started. Grievances are certainly a power and are going to be turned on. We must be very tender of our dreamers. They may seem like picketers or members of the committee on rules for the moment. We shan't mind what they seem, if only they produce real poems.

But for me, I don't like grievances. I find I gently let them alone wherever published. What I like is griefs and I like them Robinsonianly profound. I suppose there is no use in asking, but I should think we might be indulged to the extent of having grievances restricted to prose if prose will accept the imposition, and leaving poetry free to go its way in tears.

Robinson was a prince of heartachers amid countless achers of another part. The sincerity he wrought in was all sad. He asserted the sacred right of poetry to lean its breast to a thorn and sing its dolefullest. Let weasels suck eggs. I know better where to look for melancholy. A few superficial irritable grievances, perhaps, as was only human, but these are forgotten in the depth of griefs to which he plunged us.

Grievances are a form of impatience. Griefs are a form of patience. We may be required by law to throw away patience as we have been required to surrender gold; since by throwing away patience and joining the impatient in one last rush on the citadel of evil, the hope is we may end the need of patience. There will be nothing left to be patient about. The day of perfection waits on unanimous social action. Two or three more good national elections should do the business. It has been similarly urged on us to give up courage, make cowardice a virtue, and see if that won't end war, and the need of courage. Desert religion for science, clean out the holes and corners of the residual unknown, and there will be no more need of religion. (Religion is merely consolation for what we don't know.) But suppose there was some mistake; and the evil stood siege, the war didn't end, and something remained unknowable. Our having disarmed would make our case worse than it had ever been before. Nothing in the latest advices from Wall Street, the League of Nations, or the Vatican inclines me to give up my holdings in patient grief.

There were Robinson and I, it was years ago, and the place (near Boston Common) was the Place, as we liked afterward to call it, of Bitters, because it was with bitters, though without bitterness, we could sit there and look out on the welter of dissatisfaction and experiment in the world around us. It was too long ago to remember who said what, but the sense of the meeting was, we didn't care how arrant a reformer or experimentalist a man was if he gave us real poems. For ourselves, we would hate to be read for any theory upon which we might be supposed to write. We doubted any poem could persist for any theory upon which it might have been written. Take the theory that poetry in our language could be treated as quantitative, for example. Poems had been written in spite of it. And poems are all that matter. The utmost of ambition is to lodge a few poems where they will be hard to get rid of, to lodge a few irreducible bits where Robinson lodged more than his share.

For forty years it was phrase on phrase on phrase with Robinson and everyone the closest delineation of something that *is* something. Any poet, to resemble him in the least, would have to resemble him in that grazing closeness to the spiritual realities. If books of verse were to be indexed by lines first in importance instead of lines first in position, many of Robinson's poems would be represented several times over. This should be seen to. The only possible objection is that it could not be done by any mere hireling of the moment, but would have to be the work of someone who had taken his impressions freely before he had any notion of their use. A particular poem's being represented several times would only increase the chance of its being located.

The first poet I ever sat down with to talk about poetry was Ezra Pound. It was in London in 1913. The first poet we talked about, to the best of my recollection, was Edwin Arlington Robinson. I was fresh from America and having read *The Town Down the River*. Beginning at that book I have slowly spread my reading of Robinson twenty years backward and forward, about equally in both directions.

I remember the pleasure with which Pound and I laughed over the fourth "thought" in

> Miniver thought and thought and thought
> And thought about it.

Three "thoughts" would have been "adequate" as the critical praise-word then was. There would have been nothing to complain of if it had been left at three. The fourth made the intolerable touch of poetry. With the fourth the fun began. I was taken out on the strength of our community of opinion here to be rewarded with an introduction to Miss May Sinclair, who had qualified as the patron authority on young and new poets by the sympathy she had shown them in *The Divine Fire*.

There is more to it than the number of the "thoughts." There is the way the last one turns up by surprise round the corner, the way the shape of the stanza is played with, the easy way the obstacle of verse is turned to advantage. The mischief is in it.

> One pauses half afraid
> To say for certain that he played—

a man as sorrowful as Robinson. His death was sad to those who knew him, but nowhere near as sad as the lifetime of poetry to which he attuned our ears. Nevertheless, I say his much-admired restraint lies wholly in his never having let grief go further than it could in play. So far shall grief go, so far shall philosophy go, so far shall confidences go, and no further. Taste may set the limit. Humor is a surer dependence.

> Once a man was there all night
> Expecting something every minute.

I know what the man wanted of Old King Cole. He wanted the heart out of his mystery. He was the friend who stands at the end of a poem ready in waiting to catch you by both hands with enthusiasm and drag you off your balance over the last punctuation mark into more than you meant to say. "I understand the poem all right, but please tell me what is behind it." Such presumption needs to be twinkled at and baffled. The answer must be, "If I had wanted you to know, I should have told you in the poem."

We early have Robinson's word for it:

> The games we play
> To fill the frittered minutes of a day
> Good glasses are to read the spirit through.

He speaks somewhere of Crabbe's stubborn skill. His own was a happy skill. His theme was unhappiness itself, but his skill was as happy as it was playful. There is that comforting thought for those who suffered to see him suffer. Let it be said at the risk of offending the humorless in poetry's train (for there are a few such): his art was more than playful; it was humorous.

The style is the man. Rather say the style is the way the man takes himself; and to be at all charming or even bearable, the way is almost rigidly prescribed. If it is with outer seriousness, it must be with inner humor. If it is with outer humor, it must be with inner seriousness. Neither one alone without the other under it will do. Robinson was thinking as much in his sonnet on Tom Hood. One ordeal of Mark Twain was the constant fear that his occluded seriousness would be overlooked. That betrayed him into his two or three books of out-and-out seriousness.

Miniver Cheevy was long ago. The glint I mean has kept coming to the surface of the fabric all down the years. Yesterday in conversation, I was using "The Mill." Robinson could make lyric talk like drama. What imagination for speech in "John Gorham"! He is at his height between quotation marks.

> The miller's wife had waited long.
> The tea was cold, the fire was dead.
> And there might yet be nothing wrong
> In how he went and what he said.
> "There are no millers any more,"
> Was all that she had heard him say.

"There are no millers any more." It might be an edict of the New Deal against processors (as we now dignify them). But no, it is of wider application. It is a sinister jest at the expense of all investors of life or capital. The market shifts and leaves them with a car-barn full of dead trolley cars. At twenty I commit myself to a life of religion. Now, if religion should go out of fashion in twenty-five years, there would I be, forty-five years old, unfitted for anything else and too old to learn anything else. It seems immoral to have to bet on such high things as lives of art, business, or the church. But in effect, we have no alternative. None but an all-wise and all-powerful government could take the responsibility of keeping us out of gambling or of insuring us against loss once we were in.

The guarded pathos of "Mr. Flood's Party" is what makes it merciless. We are to bear in mind the number of moons listening. Two, as on the planet Mars. No less. No more ("No more, sir, that's enough"). One moon (albeit a moon, no sun) would have laid grief too bare. More than two would have dissipated grief entirely and would have amounted to dissipation. The emotion had to be held at a point.

> He set the jug down slowly at his feet
> With trembling care, knowing that most things break,
> And only when assured that on firm earth
> It stood, as the uncertain lives of men
> Assuredly did not—

There twice it gleams. Nor is it lost even where it is perhaps lost sight of in the dazzle of all those golden girls at the end of "The Sheaves." Granted a few fair days in a world where not all days are fair.

> "Well, Mr. Flood, we have the harvest moon
> Again, and we may not have many more.
> The bird is on the wing, the poet says
> And you and I have said it here before.
> Drink to the bird."

Poetry transcends itself in the playfulness of the toast.

Robinson has gone to his place in American literature and left his human place among us vacant. We mourn, but with the qualification that after all, his life was a revel in the felicities of language. And not just to no purpose. None could deplore,

> The inscrutable profusion of the Lord
> Who shaped as one of us a thing

so sad and at the same time so happy in achievement. Not for me to search his sadness to its source. He knew how to forbid encroachment. And there is solid satisfaction in a sadness that is not just a fishing for ministration and consolation. Give us immedicable woes—woes that nothing can be done for—woes flat and final. And then to play. The play's the thing. Play's the thing. All virtue in "as if."

> As if the last of days
> Were fading and all wars were done.

As if they were. As if, as if!

1935

# Introduction to
## Sarah Cleghorn's 'Threescore'

Security, security! We run in all directions for security in the game of Pussy-wants-a-corner. I find security chiefly in proper names—the thought of certain people, I mean people I can be certain of at their posts or postoffices. I am like Childe Roland on his way to the Dark Tower: I need someone pleasant to think of. They that are against us should be more than they that are for us by all present-day accounts.

> "May be true what I have heard:
> Earth's a howling wilderness
> Truculent with force and fraud."

It will not do to underestimate the relative strength of the enemy. But neither will it do to overestimate it. That, I take it, is one lesson of Grant's greatness as a general. It is necessary to keep in mind in a campaign just whom we can muster in an emergency. We in Vermont are taken care of on the north by three great ladies up the valley, three verities who can be depended on to hold Vermont true to its winter self against all summer comers. And one of these is wise and a novelist, one is mystic and an essayist, and the third is saintly and a poet. This book is about them all, but principally (and charmingly and naturally) about the poet. It is her own story of her life told with a beautiful unconsciousness of its beauty.

Saint, poet—*and* reformer. There is more high explosive for righteousness in the least little line of Sarah Cleghorn's poem about the children working in the mill where they could look out the window at their grown-up employers playing golf than in all the prose of our radical bound-boys pressed together under a weight of several atmospheres of revolution. The reformer has to be taken with the rest of it. And why not? Some of us have developed a habit of saying we can't stand a reformer. But we don't mean it except where the reformer is at the same time a raw convert to the latest scheme for saving the soul or the state. The last we heard of him may have been two or three fashions ago as one of the ultra-arty insisting that

749

we join him in his minor vices at his wild parties. Now he turns up at our door to ask without ceremony—You don't mean to say you don't love God or you don't mean to say you don't love humanity.—Don't you believe public confession is good for the soul?—Don't you believe so-and-so died a martyr to the cause of humanity?—Let me recall you to your better self.—Have you given anything any thought?

I don't know what makes this so nettling unless it is that it ignores so superciliously the strain we may have been under for years trying to decide between God and the Devil, between the rich and the poor (the greed of one and the greed of the other), between keeping still about our troubles and enlarging on them to the doctor and—oh, between endless other things in pairs ordained to everlasting opposition. No, it is not the reformer we object to. Nor is it yet the convert. The convert has his defense. It is the rawness, the egotism, the gross greed to take spiritual advantage of us. We have all had attempts on our self-respect of the kind, and we cringe at the memory. I have had four, one of them lately that would afford one scene in a comedy. But a reformer who has all her life long pursued the even tenor of her aspiration, is no one to resent. On the contrary she is one for me to claim friendship with and, if permitted, kindred spirit with. Pride enters into it, as may be seen.

Just after the great Democratic victory of 1932 I made occasion to bring the election into conversation with a Negress who had come to our door soliciting alms for a school for Negroes in the deep south.

"My people don't very much like the Democrats in power again," she said.

"Surely you aren't afraid of them anymore!"

"I wouldn't just say we weren't afraid of them. You wouldn't think there was much they could do. But there's small things an outsider wouldn't notice."

She was a poor creature, poorly clothed, but she touched her wrists with a pretty pathos for this:

"Here a shackle, there a shackle, and before we know it we're back in slavery."

"Not while Sarah Cleghorn lives in Manchester, Vermont," I answered. Then I went on to explain that Sarah Cleghorn was an abolitionist as of 1861. One of her best poems was about a Negress who personally conducted troop on troop of runaway slaves northward. Many lightly argue that since we have tolerated wage slavery and child labor, we might as well have tolerated Negro slavery. She reasons the other way round: that since we have abolished Negro slavery we are bound in logic to abolish all other slavery. She is the complete abolitionist. She has it in for race prejudice and many another ignobleness besides. Some time I intend to ask her if she isn't bent on having the world perfect at last.

Did I know her?

"Yes, very well," I said with effect.

I have just come indoors from boasting among the egrets of the Everglades of Florida that I was acquainted with the lady up north who by writing to the papers (see page 110) had done more than anyone else to get them free of the terrible yearly Minoan tax on the flower of their youth and beauty. I don't know what impression I made in this case. The egret standing nearest me in the water simply lifted stiffly and withdrew further into the Everglades, as unresponsive as a bank clerk with whom I should have attempted to establish credit. The fact remains that I do know one or two people who have done measurable good. And I think I have a right to speak of them when the chance offers.

You get some notion of Sarah Cleghorn's range of beneficence—all the way from pure black to snow white—which may sound dangerously like being an extremist—and typically a New Englander. But you have only to read to find out that she was not born a New Englander nor of wholly New England stock.

We can't all be judges. There must always be a thousand *ex parte* lawyers for one judge, sitting out impartial till sides have all but wiped each other out in encounter and judgment has all but pronounced itself. A philosopher may worry about a tendency that, if run out to its logical conclusion, might ruin all; but he worries only till he can make out in the confusion the particular counter tendency that is going to collide with it to the cancellation of both. Formidable equations often resolve into no more information than that nothing equals nothing. It is a common question: What has become of the

alarming old tendency to come to grief from each one's mind-
ing his own business? Oh, if I remember rightly, that bumped
head on into the tendency to come to grief from minding
each other's business. The philosopher values himself on the
inconsistencies he can contain by main force. They are two
ends of a strut that keeps his mind from collapsing. He may
take too much satisfaction in having once more remarked the
two-endedness of things. To a saint and a reformer like Sarah
Cleghorn the great importance is not to get hold of both
ends, but of the right end. She has to be partisan and even a
trifle grim. I heard a clergyman say she is the kind we need
most of to get the world forward. Well, here we have her, her
whole story from the first dawning on her in childhood of the
need of goodness and mercy.

1936

# To Louis Untermeyer

Dear Louis

Away back early in September I swore off on letter-writing till I should get well entirely. But I begin to think if I wait till then I shall wait forever. So here I am writing again though from bed.

Don't imagine I haven't been up all this time. I have been up and down. At one stroke I cut out all duties away from Amherst. I left Harvard to the English and I left the American Academy to Billy Phelps. I dropped all the pay engagements. From that moment I was a different man. It dawned on me that all this I had been imperceptibly getting deeper and deeper into wasn't the life of my choice and liking. What a relief to have the spell broken by Herpes Zoster Agonistes! None of my friends would back me to backing down. They probably couldn't bear to see me with my bravery off. It would disillusion them. They left it to God, and God saved me with a charge of bird-shot in my right bump of ideality where all could see my incapacitation. I was in great agony of countenance when I was with you at Bread Loaf, but my stigmata hadn't yet shown on the surface. When it did come out I thought it smallpox and as such something I had better keep still about if I didn't want to start a panic. It was quite a malady. I had hardly noticed it before. That was because it was others misfortune and none of my own, I suppose. I don't mean it is humanity not to feel the suffering of others. The last election would confute me if I did. I judged that half the people that voted for his Rosiness were those glad to be on the receiving end of his benevolence and half were those over glad to be on the giving end. The national mood is humanitarian. Nobly so—I wouldn't take it away from them. I am content to let it go at one philosophical observation: isn't it a poetical strangeness that while the world was going full blast on the Darwinian metaphors of evolution, survival values and the Devil take the hindmost, a polemical Jew in exile was working up the metaphor of the State's being like a family to displace them from mind and give us a new figure to live by?

Marx had the strength not to be overawed by the metaphor in vogue. Life is like battle. But so is it also like shelter. Apparently we are now going to die fighting to make it a secure shelter. The model is the family at its best. At the height of the Darwinian metaphor, writers like Shaw and Butler were found to go the length of saying even the family within was strife, and perhaps the worst strife of all. We are all toadies to the fashionable metaphor of the hour. Great is he who imposes the metaphor. From each according to his ability to each according to his need. Except ye become as little children under a good father and mother! I'm not going to let the shift from one metaphor to another worry me. You'll notice the shift has to be made rather abruptly. There are no logical steps from one to the other. There is no logical connection.

Which makes me think of Larry and Joseph. I hope you and Esther and they are all together for Thanksgiving wherever you are, and that you will temper the wind of experience to them for a long time and not let them hear too much, see too much, do too much, or have too much done to them. What we don't know won't hurt us. I know too much for my age, if I may take myself for an example. I can tell you offhand the difference between a Communist and a Fascist and even between a Nazi and a Fascist. Much discrimination has made me mad at people I don't side with.

There's more to write but it must wait till I am stronger.

Ever yours

Rob't

November 25, 1936

# What Became of New England?

FRIENDS, graduating class of 1937 and New England—once removed, perhaps, as Western Reserve; twice removed, from Wisconsin; four times removed, like me, from California—but New England:

I never gave up willingly any love I've had. The poets I cared for when I was young I still care for, alongside of poets I liked later. Finding a new doesn't turn me against an old. I stand on the defensive . . . against anyone who would take it away from me. I stand on the defensive lately a good deal for New England. . . .

People say to me, "What has become of New England?" Twenty years ago I published a little book that seemed to have something to do with New England. It got praise in a way that cost me some pain. It was described as a book about a decadent and lost society.

A distinguished critic (I could name him—he is visiting in this country now) has said: "The Catholic peasantry of Europe renews itself through the ages. The Protestants, the Puritan peasantry of New England, has dried up and blown away in three hundred years." The first mistake, of course, was the word peasantry. The rest we will consider.

Only the other day I picked up a book about Mexico and there was an analogy between the races that had displaced other races in Mexico and the same thing in New England. "A sharper, shrewder, a more virile population has crowded out the Yankees." Someone had been visiting for a summer there.

You have been reading, probably, a very beautiful book called "The Flowering of New England," by a friend of mine. I have only one regret, and that is that there is in the end of it a slight suggestion of the Spengler history—indication of decline. . . . Van Wyck Brooks' next book is going to be called "Indian Summer." (I suppose we'll be even farther down by then.) . . .

What was New England? It was the first little nation that bade fair to be an English speaking nation on this continent.

. . . In the first hundred years it had pushed off from England—it had drawn off and been pushed off to a certain extent—into almost a nation with its capital at Boston. . . . Ships, etc. . . . People in Virginia remarked the rapid development of the little nation there. . . . There was Boston, there was much beautiful architecture, art. They want to rob the Puritans of art. . . . They didn't mind a play if it was in a book—Cotton Mather had one of the first folios of Shakespeare—and you could *read* a play in Boston. There were ten silversmiths in Boston before there was a single lawyer. People forget all those things.

I should say another thing about New England that we have lost. It was the port of entry of our freedom. We call some of the men who came there by the name of rebels. New England was all that. And what has become of it that these people should pity us about or taunt us with?

I don't know how much of a fight you make to hang onto what's yours. You're younger than I by a good many years, and I suppose the older one is the harder he hangs onto what he's built into his life. When the meaning goes out of anything, as happens, forms crumble, formulae . . . But the whole function of poetry is the renewal of words, is the making of words mean again what they meant. Let me take one or two illustrations, in politics and religion. I heard as I marched in today, ahead of me in the line, two words in the center—I don't know what the rest was. The two words were "divine right." Words with an ancient history, words with a great history, words that too many people too easily give up. They've been laughed out of their meaning. But before I'd give them up I'd . . . In government we have two things: we have the ruler and the ruled. We have two answers. . . . Its first answerability is to itself. Its second is the consent of the ruled. Consent? How can there be consent without some guidance to consent to? We've had rulers in this country who had nothing within themselves to which to consent to—one with ear to ground, attempting to find out what people would consent to.

In 1897 I was sitting in a class in college when I heard a man spend quite the part of an hour making fun of the expression that we were all free and equal. So easy to dismiss. Let's have a look at it. All men were created free and equally funny. Before you laugh too much at that, take another look at it. Four hundred years ago the only people who were funny were yokels. . . . Now, today, even kings are funny. We've come a long way.

We hear today about the conquest of fear, and we speak lightly of that old thing, a God-fearing man. Fear? Banish fear from your mind. What kind of a God is it that you should fear? . . . One might forget God in a lull of faith. One might forget God, and talk about the highest in himself. . . . I can't imagine any honest man without the fear of finding himself unworthy in the sight of someone who knows him at least as well as he knows himself. It might be God; it might be someone else; it might be something you didn't care to call by name.

I don't give up New England too easily. I don't give up these words that I've cared for, these phrases; I long to renew them; I seek to renew them. . . .

Another one—a jealous God. . . . In Greenwich Village I've heard two words dismissed—fear and jealousy, and that makes all the excitement in Greenwich Village. What is jealousy? It's the claim of the object on the lover. The claim is that the lover should be true to the object; the claim of God that you should be true to Him, and so true to yourself. . . . The word still lives for me.

New England now . . . What's become of it? It's not necessarily to be found in a literature to be restricted to New England. The little nation that was and was to be gave itself, as Virginia gave herself, westward, into the great nation that she saw coming, and so gave help to America. And so any of us are not New Englanders particularly; any writers we were, any statesmen we were, were to be Americans, United States statesmen, United States writers.

And the thing New England gave most to America was the thing I am talking about: a stubborn clinging to meaning; to purify words until they meant again what they should mean. Puritanism had that meaning entirely: a purifying of words and a renewal of words and a renewal of meaning. That's what brought them to America and that's what kept them believing in the reality of . . . They saw there was a meaning that was not elusive.

You can get out a theory that meanings go out of things, you can call it disillusionment. You can get disillusionment of a phrase such as fearing God and equality. And then you can form a religion like George Santayana. He lets you see that there is nothing but illusion, and it can be just as well one kind as another. There is illusion that you are unconscious of, and there is illusion that you become conscious of later. . . . But you should go right on anyway because there's no proof, all is illusion. You grow to be a sad person. . . .

Some people pity a person who loses his hero. . . . Who suffers the worst, the person who loses his hero, or the lost hero? . . . You must seek your reality forever in things you care for. . . . Witchcraft was an illusion, wasn't it, and so is all this industrialism, and so is the New Deal. . . . You can make it all illusion with a little help of Santayana. He says right out in his philosophy that there are two kinds of illusion, two kinds of madness: one is normal madness, and the other is abnormal madness.

Let's take one more: prayer. I'll tell you one of the poems which comes out of the eighteenth century, and ought by rights to be dead by this time:

> Strong is the lion—like a coal
> His eyeball,—like a bastion's mole
>   His chest against the foes:
> Strong the gier-eagle on his sail;
> Strong against tide th' enormous whale
>   Emerges as he goes.
>
> But stronger still, in earth and air,
> And in the sea, the man of prayer,
>   And far beneath the tide:
> And in the seat to faith assign'd,
> Where ask is have, where seek is find
>   Where knock is open wide.

Oberlin College Commencement Address,
June 8, 1937

# Poverty and Poetry

I GAVE OUT a subject, but it never reached you; so I am free to talk about what I please or not talk at all—or read to you. I shall read chiefly.

There's a little matter that has been on my mind. I am often more or less tacitly on the defensive about what I might call "my people." That doesn't mean Americans—I never defend America from foreigners. But when I speak of my people, I sort of mean a class, the ordinary folks I belong to. I have written about them entirely in one whole book: I called it *A Book of People*. But I found as I went around, seeing colleges more than anything else, that one and another spoke or implied something about my people that I didn't care for. I went a long way once to see one or two of my little things acted as if they were plays. They are very short plays, too short to act, but they have something of the dramatic in them. All the actors were cultivated people and they thought the way to represent my three people on the stage was to have them hop a little as if they were going over clods. And one of the actors who acted in the thing—I did not know what to say to him afterwards. I was full of too much to say, and I thought perhaps I would put it this way:

"They are much the same as we are. As a matter of fact," I said—I didn't know just how to make him understand—"as a matter of fact, both of them had been to college."

I don't think he would ever hop for them again. I was a little angry with him, but that was what I had to say to him, because there are people who don't go to college and who don't hop clods.

I spent all that part of my life, over twenty years of it, with just country neighbors around me. Some of them had been educated and some of them hadn't. They were all much the same. I was brought up in a family who had just come to the industrial city of Lawrence, Massachusetts. My grandfather was an overseer in the Pacific Mills. They had just come to the city from Kingston, New Hampshire, up by Exeter.

The other day I was reading a book called *A Proletarian Journey* by a boy named Fred Beal. His family ran into more poverty in Lawrence than I ran into. I ran into some: I don't know how to measure poverty (I'm not boasting). His people went right down and he went to work at fourteen years of age in two of the same mills that I worked in. He talks of himself as a proletarian; he went *radical*. It is a very interesting book to me because he names overseers and men at the mill—and all people I knew. He was twenty years after me. We had memories of the farm and the country that I went back to. I walked out of it all one day.

He uses the word *proletarian* for himself and a great man in Lawrence. The great man was named Wood, of the Wood's Mills—a great figure against Bill Haywood, his antagonist in the big Lawrence strike of 1910–1911, I think. Now Wood was really a proletarian in my use of the word. As the swear-word is, he was really a son of a sea-cook—I mean it literally—a son of a Portuguese sea-cook. He grew up in New Bedford—and rose to be the head of all the woollen mills; the Woollen Association, or whatever they call it.

Then he had the tragedy, after patronizing the poor and doing everything he could for his employees—even giving them escalators in the mills. He got a great strike on his hands and came out very badly in it. He lost the affection of his people and committed suicide afterwards. He was the genuine proletarian, because he came up from nowhere.

Now Fred Beal, who calls himself the same thing, is a Beal and a Hay of New Hampshire. Right away that's something a little different; he never knew the peasant life of Europe. He also counts himself a kin of Hannibal Hamlin, who was Vice-President with Lincoln in his first administration—that is another thing. For no matter how educated or poor a man is, a certain level up there in Vermont and New Hampshire stays about the same. We people just sort of fountain up, jet up out of it.

When I meet very wealthy people, I have to face them. I remember facing once a small group, not a thousand miles from Philadelphia. I did it for a charity-working friend of mine. She told me that the girls I must speak to must be gone for: they were worth at least a million apiece, and I could be rough on them. I knew they were all helping her in her charity work, so you can see my state of mind. I felt cross to be there. I took for my text,

"Let not man bring together what God hath set asunder."

Let the rich keep away from the poor for all of me, as the slang is. Well, that's just the way I feel.

I suppose I take that position as an artist. "You wrote about the poor," they said. I never measured that; I wouldn't have done it if I knew anything was going to be made of it. I didn't do it to get rid of the poor because I need them in my business.

What is the position of poetry toward the poor? I think, if you look back all through the years, you will find that—maybe falsely, hypocritically—poetry has praised poverty. It may be hypocritical because wealth is sour grapes—there is a good deal of that. I've sometimes thought that England was a very convenient place to be an artist in, because you have a whole class there who is poorer than any class here, for an artist to retire into in his poor years. Cabbage, bread, cheese, and tea without milk—he can have that. He can lose himself to his relatives and have that. I am not saying that poverty shouldn't be abolished. I do not know anything about it.

But what *is* the relation of poverty and poetry? I know once in self-defense I did come near to swearing. It says in the Bible, you think—I don't—it says in the Bible that you always have the poor with you. That isn't what it says. It says, "For Christ's sake, forget the poor some of the time." There are many beautiful things in the world besides poverty. I have praised poverty and spoken of its beauty and its use for the arts, but there are other things. I'm not here to dwell with too much emphasis on poverty. I just bring up the little question of the relationship and make a few suggestions, because I run the risk of reading about people—I wouldn't dare say whether they were rich or poor people.

I saw this summer one of the poorest spots in Vermont. I saw an old, old lady who couldn't seem to go on relief because she owned a little house. She hadn't much object in selling the house, because it wouldn't bring much. When she did sell it, she had to give all the money to pay her debts. But even then she couldn't go on relief because they had the record of her having sold a house. They thought she sold it on purpose to go on relief—a very corrupt happening in this impure world. A strange situation: she has a hired man and he is about half her age. And he goes out and earns their living as her hired man. She gives him part of what he earns.

And then I'll just tell you of a charitable act of my own. I don't often do charitable acts; only once in a great while. I went over there just as winter was coming on. The hired man had got hold of an old schoolhouse, long deserted, and had moved it onto an old cellar-hole by an old well. And they were starting to live there. The house was like a hen standing up in the nest; it hadn't settled down on its foundations. It looked kind of cold and windy, and I said:

"You'd better get the wall up under there."

The lady said:

"He is doing it just as fast as he can find the means."

And I said:

"He could raise the means, I guess you know," fidgeting a little, "and I wouldn't take it out in work right away."

He hung his head, and she said:

"James likes to know where he stands."

Of course you know as far as pity is concerned, there's nothing in it. It touches you a little, I suppose, in the middle, like amusement—there's a not unmixed feeling that people have about it. That's the last of a village once quite distinguished. I won't say any more for fear you'll run across it some day. All I say about it is that we're in danger, in our way of thinking that mercy comes first in the world. It comes in, but it comes in second. The thing you are most interested in is justice; all you ask for is justice in the struggle.

I had a boy come to me with poetry the other day. Who is a poor thing? He comes to me with talk about mercy on earth—everything has now gone merciful; kinder times ahead. I let him talk and have it all his own way. That's all right. Finally he came out with the poetry he'd brought. I said:

"You've come for mercy?"

He looked at me for a second, and said:

"No, sir, I just want fairness."

You see, they really have more spunk than you think. I said:

"I thought so."

After I treated him with fairness—and he came out, as it happened, very poorly in my estimation—then I might in mercy carry him home to his mother. It's there, of course. It's part of everything. But there's so much confusion about who is a poor thing, nowadays, that I can't help saying there's not much of that sort of thing around my poor people.

Now suppose I read you a few things. Suppose I begin with that very poem about me and the mills in Lawrence. This one is called, "The Lone Striker." It is all right to be a striker, but not a lone striker. You might think that I might get in right with my radical friends, but the trouble with me is that I was a lone striker; if I called it a "collectivist striker," that would be another matter. This was the way it was to me, not a very serious thing. It is odd that the first part of Fred Beal's book is almost the same as this, though I wrote it several years ago:

[He reads, "A Lone Striker."]

The next poem is one of the little plays: "The Death of the Hired Man." Some day, in the middle of it all, I shall write another kind of poem like this—and I'm afraid that it will be a little less innocent, a little more argumentative and authoritative. When I wrote the "Book of People," *North of Boston*, it was in innocence of heart—no implications. These are sad times, in a way.

[He reads, "The Death of the Hired Man."]

The thing about that, the danger, is that you shall make the man too hard. That spoils it. That's the error the people made: they made the man too hard. And all our thinking turns on that.

I was thinking about the hired man's relations. That's so common all over the United States, I suppose. We stopped in a town called Vict'ry—you say it that way, Vict'ry—not Victory. It was hardly inhabited in its best days; it is pretty near empty now. I remember an old man years ago speaking of it as "the jumping-off place." We stopped there this summer to ask the way, to ask whether the road went through. It looked as if it stopped. A man stepped up to the car with a kind of bright interest—as if he didn't see much society. He turned out to be a very pleasant man. Intelligent. He said that years before, the place had been the center of everything; that he

had once kept a little store and mill there. He was in hopes
that something would make business come back there—the
pulp business or something like that. I asked him his name
and he told me. I said:

"That's an old Vermont name."

"No, sir, it belongs in N' Yawk State."

And I said:

"Well, we have a distinguished judge in Washington, of
that name."

He said:

"Oh yes, he's my first cousin."

You never know when you're talking to one of those. He
wasn't so much to look at, but he knew just as much about
things as you and I. It's a perpetual marvel to me. All I want
to point out is that you can't generalize about things, you can
not go around saying things carelessly.

You take the poor women's clubs. All my sophisticated
friends make fun of them. I don't suppose women's clubs
know how poor they are in the estimation of some of my
friends. They think just about the same of women's clubs
as they think of Rotary Clubs—I'm betraying them to you.
When I get with that kind of people, I feel like telling them
about what happened to me in "Terre Hut." (That's what
the conductor called it. I'm always picking on dialect,
though I never use it.) Well, I went to Terre Hut. Once on
a time I knew only the poor farmers in New Hampshire;
lately I've got sort of travelled. Before I read to the club
there, I was asked what I'd like to see before sentence was
pronounced on me by the women's club. I said I'd like to
see Eugene Debs. (I thought that would blast them. They
were all bankers' wives and such.) They looked at each other
rather regretfully:

"Why, you must see him. But you know, he's very ill."

I said:

"I wouldn't want to disturb him. My idea was to disturb
you."

And they said:

"Disturb *us?*"

I said:

"I supposed he was an enemy of society."

And they said:

"Why, I suppose so."

And I said:

"I suppose he ruined your city."

They said:

"Well, he has done a good deal of harm. But he's such a nice person. We've just been singing carols to him."

There you are again—just as much blended generosity and largesse as you want to see anywhere—in Terre Hut, in the poor Middle West. One of my friends jokes, "East is East and West is West, but the Middle West is terrible." There's no argument to it. You just can't generalize.

Coming down on the train, a boy just about to get his doctor's degree at Yale told me:

"Anthologies are the worst thing in the world. You don't want to read anthologies, do you?"

I said:

"I've heard that a good many times. I don't want to contradict your teachers."

Poor thing. If anthologies are bad, so is all criticism, for anthologies are just a form of criticism. There's no better way for you to approach Shakespeare's sonnets than through reading the selections Palgrave made of them and the selections Quiller-Couch made of them. It's the example without too many words. Maybe the anthologies are bad; on the other hand, they are good, too. Maybe the poor are unfortunate, but on the other hand, they may be fortunate.

Let me read a poem to you. Here's my last book and it has got a good deal more of the times in it than anything I ever wrote before. And there's a little bit in this one called, "A Drumlin Woodchuck." You see, I had a funny time this year about this book. One well known paper called me a "counter-revolutionary" for writing it. I didn't know who wrote that. But I was called a "counter-revolutionary" with frills—there were some other words with it. In New York, I stood up and said:

"I wish I could think the man who called me that was in this audience. I would like to call him a 'bargain-counter revolutionary.'"

I didn't mean any harm; I just meant a little harm. I had

word afterward that he knew what I meant. Some go-be-
tween, some semi-radical was in the audience. And I'd better
look out, because he had a sense of humor, and got the point
about the bargain-counter revolutionary. I'd better look out,
I'd get a firecracker. I told his friend I had a sense of humor,
too: I knew what a firecracker meant. We forgot about it in
the family and along about a holiday a box arrived. I never
get things in boxes. I didn't think much about it, though. I
started to open it, when I noticed that my name was printed
by hand. Some people write that way, artists do, you know.
Then I noticed up in the corner there was no name. It came
from nobody, nowhere. I said to my wife:

"Don't you think we'd better give this back to the
postman?"

She said:

"Well, we don't want the whole town to know about it."

So I said:

"I guess we'll take the paper off carefully, so that the jack-
in-the-box won't jump out if he's in there."

I took the paper off very carefully. There was a cigar-box.
And strangely enough, the seal was broken. There was a very
large tack holding it shut. I didn't like the looks of that tack.
I said:

"Well, I'm in for it now and might as well see it through.
Let's go out in the yard with it. The house might be
destroyed."

(We counter-revolutionaries believe in property.) We went
out. I tied a large stone securely to it so that it would have
some weight. Then I stood off, facing a great big tree of ours,
and hurled the thing at the tree—and scattered cigars all over
the yard! So whatever's coming to me hasn't come to me yet.

[He reads, "A Drumlin Woodchuck."]

I'm tempted to read a sort of philosophical poem, in clos-
ing. It's called, "Two Tramps In Mud Time." Few back roads
are left now; mud time is going by. We used to be shut in by
mud longer than by snow. All the old pleasures of mud time
are nearly gone. When we first went to another farm, we
helped get somebody out of the mud. But this is in memory
of those good days.

[He reads, "Two Tramps in Mud Time."]

That last part is what I wanted to read to you. It has nothing to do with the times. It is a very general thing: getting your need and your love together in everything. I don't say we do it. Somebody was nice enough to say,

"Of course, what you mean by that is heaven."

That is saving your soul some way; we all barely scramble into that. It's just that we don't quite do it; we almost do it. That's just the object of everything. To get your love and your need together.

Haverford College Address,
October 25, 1937

# The Poet's Next of Kin in College

Don't think for a minute that I think it matters much whether a poet has any kin or friends in a college. I suppose that a poet should lead a dog's life for a long, long time; that he should be late in knowing too well that he is a poet. But when it is all over and his diploma rolls away, he looks back sometimes, I suppose, and wonders who was nearest him and who was kindest to him.

Of course the kindest to him will always be the English department, if we are to speak by departments. It was not always so. The English department grows sentimental with age: it is often overly kind. And poets are often spoiled for facing editors, by this over-kindness. The teachers look on themselves as paid to like young writers: they have to like so many per year. Editors are paid to hate new writers. There is quite a gulf to bridge from teachers who love you to editors who hate you. The editors especially hate poetry, because they don't know where to put it. That is one practical reason. Sometimes I get a letter, a kind letter, from an editor who knows me and wants to do something for poetry. He says, have I a long thing that nobody else will take? That shows what they think about each other.

The English department may be the poet's best and surest friend. But I am talking about kin. Who is nearest the poet in age and occupation? He looks around the English department and sees all kinds of teachers. One you might call the keeper of the texts. That means, of course, very little to a writer. Then there is the person who lectures on literature as representative. That is, he is interested in poetry as it represents its age. If it is a dull age, it should be dull poetry; if it is a rotten age, then it should be rotten poetry; if it is an inscrutable age, it should be inscrutable poetry. That is another concern, I think, that does not matter to the poet at all. He should not be bothered. Then, of course, there is just the general critical approach. That is very dangerous, for the poet—it puts too many words around poetry. For him, the anthology is the best form of criticism to meddle with. It is pure example. I was told, when I was young, let the anthologies alone. You might as well say, let all opinion in poetry alone, for the anthology is the best of all opinionation. It is a good form of criticism, just because it is pure example. But the critical approach is dangerous. It is not the spirit, quite, of the young poet.

Let's leave that department and look at the socio-economic department. That is to blame for the vitiation of much of our poetry today. A poet's main interest is in doing something well. That department's interest is in doing people good, doing the world good. A poet must always prefer to do something well to doing people good. He is lost if he is interested in doing people good. Leave that to the socio-economic department—while it lasts.

Now let us look briefly at science. That might be nearer than most: pure science, because it is nothing if it is not achievement, if it is not creative. Even with young men, it expects something on the ball, something of originality. But science is antagonistic to the English department and has done it much harm. It has introduced scientific methods of criticism. I said to a literary-scientific-research man, recently:

"I suppose poetry is the least of all things given to quotation."

"On the contrary," he replied, after a moment's thought. "It is one texture of quotations. You write it out of all of the books you have ever read, and it is my place to come after you and trace it to its source!"

I didn't write anything for six months after that. It drove me into what I might call deceptions. That's the intrusion of the scientific into the artistic.

I myself, since forty, have had a great leaning toward the philosophy department—but you know that's just letting all my prejudices out. My admiration for philosophy. I'll tell you why. I think that young people have insight. They have a flash here and a flash there. It is like the stars coming out in the sky in the early evening. They have flashes of light. They have that sort of thing which belongs to youth. It is later in the dark of life that you see forms, constellations. And it is the constellations that are philosophy. It is like forcing a too early mathematics on a child, to bring him to philosophy too

young. We have system and we have plan all too soon now.
You know too well and have convictions too well by the time
you are forty. The flashing is done, the coming out of the
stars. It is all constellations—night.

You see, I have said that the growth of a poet is through
flashes. Sight and insight makes poetry, and that belongs to
the beginning poet—the poet coming out. I suppose that
poets die into philosophy as they grow older—if they don't
die the other way. They die into wisdom. Maybe it is a good
way to die.

I will tell you a story, to bring you to the point. One of my
great friends was a college president, now gone. He came to
me years ago with a boyish interest in poetry, a naïve interest.
And this is the way he had come to it. He had looked on
poetry as performance. He was a Welshman. His father had
made pottery (and poetry) in America, at Utica, New York.
His earliest recollection of poetry was sitting with his father,
at the close of a prize contest and hearing the prizes awarded
for poetry. The judge was an old Welshman, brought over
from Wales, to deliver the prizes. The first prize was awarded
for a certain poem and the old judge said, "Will the writer of
it stand." My friend's father stood up. That was his first en-
counter with poetry. Performance. Bravo! Victory!

He went afterward to play baseball on a country ball team
one summer, and was picked up by some college boys and
taken to their college and educated free. I think I am right in
saying that he pitched all four years on his college team and
only lost two games in four years. From there he went to the
Boston Nationals and after one year of some pitching blos-
somed out into the greatest pitcher in the country. For one
year. And then he said to himself: "This ends early—can't last
many years—and there is always poetry, which is akin. I'm
going back to that." So he went back to college and got some
more degrees—and ended up a college president. He came to
me in that spirit entirely.

Now don't imagine I don't know all the problems of ath-
letics. But I never look around on athletics in college with
anything but an affectionate spirit. Take a boy who is intel-
lectual, who spends his time worrying over the athletes about

him. He will never write poetry. If he tries, he will never write anything but criticism. He'll be like a variable approaching its limit: never quite getting there. Poetry is a young thing, as we all know. Most of the poets have struck their notes be-tween the ages of fifteen and twenty-five. That is just the time when you are in college and graduate school. It is in those ten years that you will strike your note or never. And it is very like athletic prowess in that respect. They are very close together.

When I see young men doing so wonderfully well in ath-letics, I don't feel angry at them. I feel jealous of them. I wish that some of my boys in writing would do the same thing. I wish they would stop grouching at the athletes—leave them alone and do something as well in the arts. Remember, you can't excuse yourself on the grounds of age. Sight and insight. You must have form—performance. The thing itself is inde-scribable, but it is felt like athletic form. To have form, feel form in sports—and by analogy feel form in verse. One works and waits for form in both. As I said, the person who spends his time criticizing the play around him will never write poetry. He will write criticism—for the *New Republic*!

When one looks back over his own poetry, his only criticism is whether he had form or not. Did he worry it out or pour it out? You can't go back to a tennis game and play it over—except with alibis. You can go back over a poem and touch it up—but never unless you are in the same form again. Yet the great pleasure in writing poetry is in having been carried off. It is as if you stood astride of the subject that lay on the ground, and they cut the cord, and the subject gets up under you and you ride it. You adjust yourself to the motion of the thing itself. That is the poem.

So many ways I have tried to say what I feel. Keeping the thing in motion is sometimes like walking a rolling barrel. Again, a small poem is like the five or six balls a pitcher pitches to a given batter. There is a little system—a little set of pitched balls; a little set of sentences. You make the little set and the coming off is it—long or short. When Poe said that all poems were short, he meant that a long poem was just full of little runs—you could take them out; you could tell where it happened. I've boasted I could tell whether it happened in the morning or midnight—with morning calmness or midnight intoxication! It's different, of course, if a poem is just penned to bother. I can understand that kind, even—if I will be bothered. But all I ask is to be smitten.

Princeton University Address,
October 26, 1937

# To Robert P. T. Coffin

Dear Coffin,               24 February 1938   Gainesville

It is my bad luck I am away off down here where I can't help you help me. I suppose you have nothing to call you even part way in this direction till you come to Baltimore for your lectures. I would venture some way into the cold but I mustn't come so far as to seem inconsistent to those with whom I have used the cold as an excuse to stay away from their platforms and dinner tables. A lot would come out in talk once you got me started with what you happened to re-member of that Poetry Society affair. I'm terrible about my lectures. In my anxiety to keep them as long as possible from becoming part of my literary life, I leave them rolling round in my head like clouds rolling round in the sky. Watch them long enough and you'll see one near-form change into an-other near-form. Though I am sure they are hardly permiss-able on the platform, I continue to bring them there with no more apology than to a parlor or class room. Their chief value to me is for what I pick up from them when I cut across them with a poem under emotion. They have been my inner world of raw material and my instinct has been to keep them raw. That can't long retain their state however. The day approaches when they will lose their fluidity and in spite of my stirring spoon become crystal. Then one kind of fun will be over and I shall have to find another to take its place (tennis most likely or hoeing). I thought I was about ready to let them set when I accepted the Harvard invitation to deliver them in writing after delivering them by word of mouth. Something in me still fights off the written prose. The nearest I ever came to getting myself down in prose was in the preface to Robinson's *King Jasper*. That is so much me that you might suspect the application to him of being forced. It was really no such thing. We two were close akin up to a certain point of thinking. He would have trusted me to go a good way in speaking for him particularly on the art of poetry. We only parted company over the badness of the world. He was cast in the mold of sadness. I am neither optimist nor pessimist. I never voted either ticket.

If there is a universal unfitness and unconformity as of a but-
toning so started that every button on the vest is in the wrong
button hole and the one empty button hole at the top and
the one naked button at the bottom so far apart they have no
hope of getting together, I don't care to decide whether God
did this for the fun of it or for the devil of it. (The two ex-
pressions come to practically the same thing anyway.) Then
again I am not the Platonist Robinson was. By Platonist I
mean one who believes what we have here is an imperfect
copy of what is in heaven. The woman you have is an imper-
fect copy of some woman in heaven or in someone else's bed.
Many of the world's greatest—maybe all of them—have been
ranged on that romantic side. I am philosophically opposed
to having one Iseult for my vocation and another for my
avocation; as you may have inferred from a poem called Two
Tramps in Mud Time. You see where that lands me on the
subject of Dante's Beatrice. Mea culpa. Let me not sound the
least bit smug. I define a difference with proper humility. A
truly gallant Plantonist will remain a bachelor as Robinson did
from unwillingness to reduce any woman to the condition of
being used without being idealized.

But you didn't ask me to distinguish between myself and
Robinson. I fell accidentally into a footnote to the *King Jasper*
preface in self defence. What you asked for is any recollection
I have of my recent talks. I may be able to bring some of
them back in detail—give me time. What in the world did I
say in New York. Was my subject "Neither or Both." Do you
want to show me the notes you made? Is there time? I'm
going to hurry this off tonight for a beginning and then if
you say so try to tell you a little more. One of my subjects at
Harvard was Does Wisdom Matter. I mean in art. Does it
matter for instance that I am so temperamentally wrong about
Beatrice. You can hear more if it is worth your while. Another
subject was The Renewal of Words. Molly Colum had been
saying the world was old, people were jaded and the languages
worn out. My whole lecture was an answer to her defeatism,
though I took good care not to name her—and don't you
name her. Poetry is the renewal of words forever and ever.
Poetry is that by which we live forever and ever unjaded. Po-
etry is that by which the world is never old. Even the poetry

of trade names gives the lie to the unoriginal who would drag us down in their own powerlessness to originate. Heavy they are but not so heavy that we can't rise under them and throw them off.

Well well well ——

Sincerely yours
Robert Frost

# The Figure a Poem Makes

ABSTRACTION is an old story with the philosophers, but it has been like a new toy in the hands of the artists of our day. Why can't we have any one quality of poetry we choose by itself? We can have in thought. Then it will go hard if we can't in practice. Our lives for it.

Granted no one but a humanist much cares how sound a poem is if it is only *a* sound. The sound is the gold in the ore. Then we will have the sound out alone and dispense with the inessential. We do till we make the discovery that the object in writing poetry is to make all poems sound as different as possible from each other, and the resources for that of vowels, consonants, punctuation, syntax, words, sentences, meter are not enough. We need the help of context—meaning—subject matter. That is the greatest help towards variety. All that can be done with words is soon told. So also with meters—particularly in our language where there are virtually but two, strict iambic and loose iambic. The ancients with many were still poor if they depended on meters for all tune. It is painful to watch our sprung-rhythmists straining at the point of omitting one short from a foot for relief from monotony. The possibilities for tune from the dramatic tones of meaning struck across the rigidity of a limited meter are endless. And we are back in poetry as merely one more art of having something to say, sound or unsound. Probably better if sound, because deeper and from wider experience.

Then there is this wildness whereof it is spoken. Granted again that it has an equal claim with sound to being a poem's better half. If it is a wild tune, it is a poem. Our problem then is, as modern abstractionists, to have the wildness pure; to be wild with nothing to be wild about. We bring up as aberrationists, giving way to undirected associations and kicking ourselves from one chance suggestion to another in all directions as of a hot afternoon in the life of a grasshopper. Theme alone can steady us down. Just as the first mystery was how a poem could have a tune in such a straightness as meter, so the second mystery is how a poem can have wildness and at the same time a subject that shall be fulfilled.

It should be of the pleasure of a poem itself to tell how it can. The figure a poem makes. It begins in delight and ends in wisdom. The figure is the same as for love. No one can really hold that the ecstasy should be static and stand still in one place. It begins in delight, it inclines to the impulse, it assumes direction with the first line laid down, it runs a course of lucky events, and ends in a clarification of life—not necessarily a great clarification, such as sects and cults are founded on, but in a momentary stay against confusion. It has denouement. It has an outcome that though unforeseen was predestined from the first image of the original mood—and indeed from the very mood. It is but a trick poem and no poem at all if the best of it was thought of first and saved for the last. It finds its own name as it goes and discovers the best waiting for it in some final phrase at once wise and sad—the happy-sad blend of the drinking song.

No tears in the writer, no tears in the reader. No surprise for the writer, no surprise for the reader. For me the initial delight is in the surprise of remembering something I didn't know I knew. I am in a place, in a situation, as if I had materialized from cloud or risen out of the ground. There is a glad recognition of the long lost and the rest follows. Step by step the wonder of unexpected supply keeps growing. The impressions most useful to my purpose seem always those I was unaware of and so made no note of at the time when taken, and the conclusion is come to that like giants we are always hurling experience ahead of us to pave the future with against the day when we may want to strike a line of purpose across it for somewhere. The line will have the more charm for not being mechanically straight. We enjoy the straight crookedness of a good walking stick. Modern instruments of precision are being used to make things crooked as if by eye and hand in the old days.

I tell how there may be a better wildness of logic than of inconsequence. But the logic is backward, in retrospect, after the act. It must be more felt than seen ahead like prophecy. It must be a revelation, or a series of revelations, as much for the poet as for the reader. For it to be that there must have been the greatest freedom of the material to move about in it and to establish relations in it regardless of time and space,

previous relation, and everything but affinity. We prate of free-
dom. We call our schools free because we are not free to stay
away from them till we are sixteen years of age. I have given
up my democratic prejudices and now willingly set the lower
classes free to be completely taken care of by the upper classes.
Political freedom is nothing to me. I bestow it right and left.
All I would keep for myself is the freedom of my material—
the condition of body and mind now and then to summons
aptly from the vast chaos of all I have lived through.

Scholars and artists thrown together are often annoyed at
the puzzle of where they differ. Both work from knowledge;
but I suspect they differ most importantly in the way their
knowledge is come by. Scholars get theirs with conscientious
thoroughness along projected lines of logic; poets theirs cav-
alierly and as it happens in and out of books. They stick to
nothing deliberately, but let what will stick to them like burrs
where they walk in the fields. No acquirement is on assign-
ment, or even self-assignment. Knowledge of the second kind
is much more available in the wild free ways of wit and art. A
school boy may be defined as one who can tell you what he
knows in the order in which he learned it. The artist must
value himself as he snatches a thing from some previous order
in time and space into a new order with not so much as a
ligature clinging to it of the old place where it was organic.

More than once I should have lost my soul to radicalism if
it had been the originality it was mistaken for by its young
converts. Originality and initiative are what I ask for my coun-
try. For myself the originality need be no more than the fresh-
ness of a poem run in the way I have described: from delight
to wisdom. The figure is the same as for love. Like a piece of
ice on a hot stove the poem must ride on its own melting. A
poem may be worked over once it is in being, but may not
be worried into being. Its most precious quality will remain
its having run itself and carried away the poet with it. Read it
a hundred times: it will forever keep its freshness as a metal
keeps its fragrance. It can never lose its sense of a meaning
that once unfolded by surprise as it went.

*Boston, January 11, 1939.*

Preface to *Collected Poems*, 1939

# Remarks on Receiving the Gold Medal

"HAVE YOU ever thought about rewards," I was asked lately in a tone of fear for me that I might not have thought at my age. I don't know what I was supposed to think unless it was that the greatest reward of all was self-esteem. Saints like John Bunyan are all right in jail if they are sure of their truth and sincerity. But so also are many criminals. The great trouble is to be sure. A stuffed shirt is the opposite of a criminal. He cares not what he thinks of himself so long as the world continues to think well of him. The sensible and healthy live somewhere between self-approval and the approval of society. They make their adjustment without too much talk of compromise.

Still, an artist, however well he may fare within and without, must often feel he has to rely too heavily on self-appraisal for comfort. For twenty years the world neglected him; then for twenty years it entreated him kindly. He has to take the responsibility of deciding when the world was wrong. He can't help wishing there was some third more disinterested party such as God or Time to give absolute judgement.

> O Time whose verdicts mock our own
> The only righteous judge art thou.

The scientist seems to have the advantage of him in a court of larger appeal. A planet is perturbed in its orbit. The scientist stakes his reputation on the perturber's being found at a certain point in the sky at a certain time of night. All telescopes are turned that way, and sure enough, there the perturber is as bright as a button. The scientist knows he is good without being told. He has a mind and he has instruments, the extensions of mind that fit closely into the nature of the Universe. It is the same when an engineer has plotted two shafts to meet under the middle of a mountain and make a tunnel. The shafts approach each other; the workmen in one can hear the pick axes of the workmen in the other. A sudden gleam of pick ax breaks through. A human face shows in the face of the rock. The engineer is justified of his figures. He knows he has a mind. It has fitted into the nature of the Universe.

I should be sorry to concede the artist had no such recourse to tests of certainty at all. His hope must be that his work will prove to have fitted into the nature of people. Beyond my belief in myself, beyond another's critical opinion of me, lies this. I should like to have it that your medal is a token of my having fitted not into the nature of the Universe but in some small way at least into the nature of Americans—into their affections is perhaps what I mean. I trust you will be willing to indulge me here and let me have it so for the occasion. But whatever the medal may or may not symbolize I take it as a very great honor.

National Institute of Arts and Letters Address,
January 18, 1939

# The Doctrine of Excursions

You who are as much concerned as I for the future of Bread Loaf will agree with me that once in so often it should be redefined if it is to be kept from degenerating into a mere summer resort for routine education in English or worse still for the encouragement of vain ambition in literature. We go there not for correction or improvement. No writer has ever been corrected into importance. Nor do we go to find a publisher or get help in finding a publisher. Bringing manuscript to Bread Loaf is in itself publication.

A writer can live by writing to himself alone for days and years. Sooner or later to go on he must be read. It may well be that in appealing to the public he has but added to his own responsibility; for now besides judging himself he must judge his judges. For long the public received him not. Then the public received him. When were the public right? Why when the final authority is his should he be bothered with any other? The answer is an article in the doctrine of excursions. All we know is that the crowning mercy for an author is publication in some form or other.

Undeniably the best form is a book with a reputable house at the expense of the house. The next best is a book with a reputable house at the expense of the author. Those two constitute publication in the first and second degrees. But there are several humbler degrees, among them the Bread Loaf Conference. It must not be forgotten that much good poetry has never risen above the second degree and some has undoubtedly come out in newspapers that pay nothing for contributions. Publication in book form like this anthology of ours was not contemplated in the original scheme of Bread Loaf and is not of the essence of the institution. It has simply been added unto us as a reward for modesty.

Bread Loaf is to be regarded then as a place in Vermont where a writer can try his effect on readers. There as out in the world he must brave the rigors of specific criticism. He will get enough and perhaps more than enough of good set praise and blame. He will help wear out the words "like" and "dislike." He will hear too many things compared to the disadvantage of all of them. A handkerchief is worse than a knife because it can be cut by a knife; a knife is worse than a stone because it can be blunted by a stone; a stone is worse than a handkerchief because it can be covered by a handkerchief; and we have been round the silly circle. All this is as it has to be where the end is a referee's decision. There is nothing so satisfactory in literature as the knock-out in prize-fighting.

But more than out in the world a writer has a chance at Bread Loaf of getting beyond this cavil and getting his proof of something better than approval in signs—looks, tones, manners. Many words are often but one small sign. There is the possibility of his winning through to the affections of the affectionate.

Beyond self-esteem and the critical opinion of others the scientist has a third proof I have envied for the artist. From the perturbation of a planet in its orbit he predicts exactly where in the sky and at what time of night another planet will be discovered. All telescopes point that way and there the new planet is. The scientist is justified of his figures. He knows he is good. He has fitted into the nature of the universe. A topical play of the eighties had in it a scene from the digging of the Hoosac Tunnel. The engineer had triangulated over the mountain and driven in shafts from opposite sides to meet each other under the middle of the mountain. It was the eleventh hour of the enterprise. There stood the engineer among the workmen in one shaft waiting to hear the workmen in the other. A gleam of pick ax broke through; a human face appeared in the face of the rock. The engineer was justified of his figures. He knew he was an engineer. He had fitted into the nature of the universe.

I should like to believe the poet gets an equivalent assurance in the affections of the affectionate. He has fitted into the nature of mankind. He is justified of his numbers. He has accrued friends who will even cheat for him a little and refuse to see his faults if they are not so glaring as to show through eyelids. And friends are everything. For what have we wings if not to seek friends at an elevation?

Preface to *Bread Loaf Anthology*, 1939

# Preface to Poems in
## 'This Is My Best'

IT WOULD be hard to gather biography from poems of mine except as they were all written by the same person, out of the same general region north of Boston, and out of the same books, a few Greek and Latin, practically no others in any other tongue than our own. This was as it happened. To show that there was no rule about place laid down, I may point to two or three poems reminiscent of my ten years as a child in San Francisco and a few others actually written in California at the time of the Olympic games. More than a few were written in Beaconsfield and in Ryton, England, where I farmed, or rather gardened in a very small way from 1912 to 1915. My first two books were published in England by the Scotch and English, to whom I am under obligations for life for my start in life. This too was as it happened. I had on hand when I visited England the material of those two books and more than half of another. I had had poems in American magazines but not many, and my relative unsuccess with magazines had kept the idea of a book from ever entering my head. It was perhaps the boldness of my adventure among entire strangers that stirred me up to try appealing from the editors of magazines to the publishers of books.

I have made this selection much as I made the one from my first book, *A Boy's Will*, and my second book, *North of Boston*, looking backward over the accumulation of years to see how many poems I could find towards some one meaning it might seem absurd to have had in advance, but it would be all right to accept from fate after the fact. The interest, the pastime, was to learn if there had been any divinity shaping my ends and I had been building better than I knew. In other words could anything of larger design, even the roughest, any broken or dotted continuity, or any fragment of a figure be discerned among the apparently random lesser designs of the several poems. I had given up convictions when young from despair of learning how they were had. Nevertheless I might not have been without them. They might be turned up out of the heap by assortment. And if not convictions, then perhaps native prejudices and inclinations. I took thirty poems for *A Boy's Will* to plot a curved line of flight away from people and so back to people. For *North of Boston* I took group enough to show the people and to show that I had forgiven them for being people. The group here given brings out my inclination to country occupations. It began with a farm in the back yard in San Francisco. This is no prejudice against the city. I am fond of several great cities. It is merely an inclination to country things. My favorite implements (after the pen) are the axe and the scythe, both of which besides being tools of peace have also been weapons of war. The Hungarian peasantry under Kossuth carried the scythe into battle in their attempt at independence from Austria, and the axle of an ancient war chariot was prolonged into a scythe at either end. In three of the poems I celebrate the axe, in one the scythe.

Ripton, Vt.
July 26, 1942

*This Is My Best*, 1942

# Preface to
## 'The Death of the Hired Man'

IN ASKING ME to preface my poem, Mr. Burnett's idea is no doubt to have me bring it up to date by connecting it with some such thing as National Labor Relations. I am always glad to give my poems every extraneous help possible. The employee here depicted is no longer numerous enough to be dealt with statistically by the Departments of Economics and Sociology. Nevertheless I should like to flatter myself that it is at least partly for his sake that the revolution is being brought on. In conclusion I beg to protest that it was with no such thoughts as these that the poem was written. By the way, it's in blank verse, not free verse.

October 1942

# The Constant Symbol

THERE SEEMS to be some such folk saying as that easy to understand is contemptible, hard to understand irritating. The implication is that just easy enough, just hard enough, right in the middle, is what literary criticism ought to foster. A glance backward over the past convinces me otherwise. The *Iliad*, *Odyssey*, and *Aeneid* are easy. The *Purgatorio* is said to be hard. The Song of Songs *is* hard. There have been works lately to surpass all records for hardness. Some knotted riddles tell that may be worth our trouble. But hard or easy seems to me of slight use as a test either way.

Texture is surely something. A good piece of weaving takes rank with a picture as decoration for the wall of a studio, though it must be admitted to verge on the arty. There is a time of apprenticeship to texture when it shouldn't matter if the stuff is never made up into anything. There may be scraps of repeated form all over it. But form as a whole! Don't be shocking! The title of his first book was *Fragments*. The artist has to grow up and coarsen a little before he looks on texture as not an end in itself.

And there are many other things I have found myself saying about poetry, but the chiefest of these is that it is metaphor, saying one thing and meaning another, saying one thing in terms of another, the pleasure of ulteriority. Poetry is simply made of metaphor. So also is philosophy—and science, too, for that matter, if it will take the soft impeachment from a friend. Every poem is a new metaphor inside or it is nothing. And there is a sense in which all poems are the same old metaphor always.

Every single poem written regular is a symbol small or great of the way the will has to pitch into commitments deeper and deeper to a rounded conclusion and then be judged for whether any original intention it had has been strongly spent or weakly lost; be it in art, politics, school, church, business, love, or marriage—in a piece of work or in a career. Strongly spent is synonymous with kept.

We may speak after sentence, resenting judgment. How can the world know anything so intimate as what we were intending to do? The answer is the world presumes to know. The ruling passion in man is not as Viennese as is claimed. It is rather a gregarious instinct to keep together by minding each other's business. Grex rather than sex. We *must* be preserved from becoming egregious. The beauty of socialism is that it will end the individuality that is always crying out mind your own business. Terence's answer would be all human business is my business. No more invisible means of support, no more invisible motives, no more invisible anything. The ultimate commitment is giving in to it that an outsider may see what we were up to sooner and better than we ourselves. The bard has said in effect, Unto these forms did I commend the spirit. It may take him a year after the act to confess he only betrayed the spirit with a rhymester's cleverness and to forgive his enemies the critics for not having listened to his oaths and protestations to the contrary. Had he anything to be true to? Was he true to it? Did he use good words? You couldn't tell unless you made out what idea they were supposed to be good for. Every poem is an epitome of the great predicament; a figure of the will braving alien entanglements.

Take the President in the White House. A study of the success of his intention might have to go clear back to when as a young politician, youthfully step-careless, he made choice between the two parties of our system. He may have stood for a moment wishing he knew of a third party nearer the ideal; but only for a moment, since he was practical. And in fact he may have been so little impressed with the importance of his choice that he left his first commitment to be made for him by his friends and relatives. It was only a small commitment anyway, like a kiss. He can scarcely remember how much credit he deserved personally for the decision it took. Calculation is usually no part in the first step in any walk. And behold him now a statesman so multifariously closed in on with obligations and answerabilities that sometimes he loses his august temper. He might as well have got himself into a sestina royal.

Or he may be a religious nature who lightly gets committed to a nameable church through an older friend in plays and games at the Y.M.C.A. The next he knows he is in a theological school and next in the pulpit of a Sunday wrestling with the angel for a blessing on his self-defensive interpretation of the Creed. What of his original intention now? At least he has had the advantage of having it more in his heart than in his head; so that he should have made shift to assert it without being chargeable with compromise. He could go a long way before he had to declare anything he could be held to. He began with freedom to squander. He has to acknowledge himself in a tighter and tighter place. But his courage asked for it. It would have been the same if he had gone to the North Pole or climbed Everest. All that concerns *us* is whether his story is one of conformance or performance.

There's an indulgent smile I get for the recklessness of the unnecessary commitment I made when I came to the first line in the second stanza of a poem in my book called "Stopping By Woods on a Snowy Evening." I was riding too high to care what trouble I incurred. And it was all right so long as I didn't suffer deflection.

The poet goes in like a rope skipper to make the most of his opportunities. If he trips himself he stops the rope. He is of our stock and has been brought up by ear to choice of two metres, strict iambic and loose iambic (not to count varieties of the latter). He may have any length of line up to six feet. He may use an assortment of line lengths for any shape of stanza, like Herrick in "To Daffodils." Not that he is running wild. His intention is of course a particular mood that won't be satisfied with anything less than its own fulfillment. But it is not yet a thought concerned with what becomes it. One thing to know it by: it shrinks shyly from anticipatory expression. Tell love beforehand and, as Blake says, it loses flow without filling the mould; the cast will be a reject. The freshness of a poem belongs absolutely to its not having been thought out and then set to verse as the verse in turn might be set to music. A poem is the emotion of having a thought while the reader waits a little anxiously for the success of dawn. The only discipline to begin with is the inner mood that at worst may give the poet a false start or two like the almost microscopic filament of cotton that goes before the blunt thread-end and must be picked up first by the eye of the needle. He must be entranced to the exact premonition. No mystery is meant. When familiar friends approach each other in the street both are apt to have this experience in feeling before knowing the pleasantry they will inflict on each other in passing.

Probably there is something between the mood and the vocal imagination (images of the voice speaking) that determines a man's first commitment to metre and length of line.

Suppose him to have written down "When in disgrace with Fortune and men's eyes." He has uttered about as much he has to live up to in the theme as in the form. Odd how the two advance into the open *pari passu*. He has given out that he will descend into Hades, but he has confided in no one how far before he will turn back, or whether he will turn back at all, and by what jutting points of rock he will pick his way. He may proceed as in blank verse. Two lines more, however, and he has let himself in for rhyme, three more and he has set himself a stanza. Up to this point his discipline has been the self-discipline whereof it is written in so great praise. The harsher discipline from without is now well begun. He who knows not both knows neither. His worldly commitments are now three or four deep. Between us, he was no doubt bent on the sonnet in the first place from habit, and what's the use in pretending he was a freer agent than he had any ambition to be. He had made most of his commitments all in one plunge. The only suspense he asks us to share with him is in the theme. He goes down, for instance, to a depth that must surprise him as much as it does us. But he doesn't even have the say of how long his piece will be. Any worry is as to whether he will outlast or last out the fourteen lines—have to cramp or stretch to come out even—have enough bread for the butter or butter for the bread. As a matter of fact, he gets through in twelve lines and doesn't know quite what to do with the last two.

Things like that and worse are the reason the sonnet is so suspect a form and has driven so many to free verse and even to the novel. Many a quatrain is salvaged from a sonnet that went agley. Dobson confesses frankly to having changed from one form to another after starting: "I intended an Ode, And it turned to a Sonnet." But he reverses the usual order of being driven from the harder down to the easier. And he has a better excuse for weakness of will than most, namely, Rose.

Jeremiah, it seems, has had his sincerity questioned because the anguish of his lamentations was tamable to the form of twenty-two stanzas for the twenty-two letters of the alphabet. The Hebrew alphabet has been kept to the twenty-two letters it came out of Egypt with, so the number twenty-two means as much form as ever.

But there they go again with the old doubt about law and order. (The communist looks forward to a day of order without law, bless his merciful heart.) To the right person it must seem naïve to distrust form as such. The very words of the dictionary are a restriction to make the best of or stay out of and be silent. Coining new words isn't encouraged. We play the words as we find them. We make them do. Form in language is such a disjected lot of old broken pieces it seems almost as non-existent as the spirit till the two embrace in the sky. They are not to be thought of as encountering in rivalry but in creation. No judgment on either alone counts. We see what Whitman's extravagance may have meant when he said the body was the soul.

Here is where it all comes out. The mind is a baby giant who, more provident in the cradle than he knows, has hurled his paths in life all round ahead of him like playthings given— data so-called. They are vocabulary, grammar, prosody, and diary, and it will be too bad if he can't find stepping stones of them for his feet wherever he wants to go. The way will be zigzag, but it will be a straight crookedness like the walking stick he cuts himself in the bushes for an emblem. He will be judged as he does or doesn't let this zig or that zag project him off out of his general direction.

Teacher or student or investigator whose chance on these defenseless lines may seize, your pardon if for once I point you out what ordinarily you would point me out. To some it will seem strange that I should have written my verse regular all this time without knowing till yesterday that it was from fascination with this constant symbol I celebrate. To the right person it will seem lucky; since in finding out too much too soon there is danger of arrest. Does anyone believe I would have committed myself to the treason-reason-season rhyme-set in my "Reluctance" if I had been blasé enough to know that these three words about exhausted the possibilities? No rhyming dictionary for me to make me face the facts of rhyme. I may say the strain of rhyming is less since I came to see words as phrase-ends to countless phrases just as the syllables *ly*, *ing*, and *ation* are word-ends to countless words. Leave something to learn still later. We'd have lost most of our innocence by forty anyway even if we never went to school a day.

## TO THE RIGHT PERSON

### *Fourteen Lines*

In the one state of ours that is a shire
There is a District Schoolhouse I admire—
As much as anything for situation.
There are few institutions standing higher
This side the Rockies in my estimation—
Two thousand feet above the ocean level.
It has two entries for co-education.
But there's a tight-shut look to either door
And to the windows of its fenestration
As if to say mere knowledge was the devil,
And this school wasn't keeping any more,
Unless for penitents who took their seat
Upon its doorsteps as at Mercy's feet
To make up for a lack of meditation.

*Atlantic Monthly*, October 1946

# "Sermon" at
# Rockdale Avenue Temple

I HAVE come here as a sort of exchange preacher with Rabbi Reichert. He has preached twice or three times in our little church in Ripton, Vermont. This is the second time I have stood in this pulpit, the first time to speak: in the name of friendship and in the name of more than friendship—affection.

Rabbi Reichert told me that his text was to have been, "They shall not come before the Lord empty," with the reference, I suppose, to the Horn of Plenty, the Cornucopia, pouring out something. And so I'm asked to offer some little thing, poured out carelessly as that is poured out. *That* doesn't quite remind me of Vermont. There are too many things there we can't raise in Vermont. But it's a little like Vermont. At this time of the year we have some of *that*.

I have had two or three strange religious experiences lately that I'm going to tell you a little about. A very ancient Latin poet, Roman poet, named Ennius, said that courage was not the greatest of all virtues. Sometimes I almost think it is the greatest of all virtues. He said it was only the second greatest of virtues, courage, bravery. The greatest of virtues was wisdom. It was rarer, he said, than courage. Many bad men have been brave, he says in Latin. Many bad men have been brave—we know that. It is hard for us to pay tribute to them when they are too bad, you know, though very brave. Sometimes when you forget that they have that second-best virtue, your detestation shouldn't go so far as to forget that they were at least brave. But wisdom is better than bravery.

Now religion always seems to me to come round to something beyond wisdom. It's a straining of the spirit forward to a wisdom beyond wisdom. Many men have the kind of wisdom that will do well enough in the day's work, you know, living along, fighting battles, going to wars, beating each other, striving with each other, in war or in peace—sufficient wisdom. They take their own side, naturally, and do well enough. But if they have religious natures they constantly, inside, they constantly tremble a little with the fear of God.

And the fear of God always has meant the fear that one's wisdom, one's own wisdom, one's own human wisdom is not quite acceptable in His sight. Always I hear that word "acceptable"—"acceptable" about offerings like *that*, like offerings of mine. Always the fear that it may not quite be acceptable. That, I take it, is the fear of God, and is with every religious nature, always.

One of the experiences was with a man from India, living in this country, and living by success in this country, a successful man—detesting us. His wisdom, at variance with our wisdom, always. I shook hands with him. We're friends in a way, we could be friends for all our differences. Why? Because I know, and perhaps he does—I hope he does—that something beyond our wisdom is still to be thought of, something over us, that may set my wisdom and his wisdom at naught.

I have often been struck with that: the clash in the world of wisdoms, on the worldly plane, on the plane where I live mostly and where you live mostly.

A little while ago I visited with friends in Cambridge, Massachusetts. The lady of the house was from the Deep South. I knew all about her. She was from Mississippi. She was married to a well-known, a very well-known, reformer, advanced thinker. She's a reformer herself. With us was a man whose father's picture hung on the wall—small picture—in officer's uniform.

I didn't know much about it, but I said: "What was he?"

The son said: "He was a commander in the Union army of negro troops."

It is death to be caught—hanging to be caught—in command of negro troops, you may know. That's far away now. We didn't weep or anything. He got through it apparently. He didn't get hanged.

Then here was this lady from the Deep South, the reformer, friend of people high up in these new movements in the world. I said to her: "Now I've got you two where I want you. I'm going to find out which side God was on in the Civil War." I said: "The lady speaks first, courtesy." The lady from the Deep South, mind you, whose father had been an officer—he'd been a fighting Bishop, been fighting on the Southern side as a Bishop—you know some did.

I said: "Which side was God on in the Civil War?"

We were making a little light of wisdom, you know, so she just spoke right up and said: "My father was a Methodist Bishop, Southern, and a Bishop ought to know, and he thought God was on the Southern side."

And I said: "That settles it!"

I didn't give the other man a chance! But that was, you see, the way. All of us know better than that. But anyway all of us knew that beyond the wisdom that clashed there—the two wisdoms that clashed there—was something of God.

I heard another man to the point of irritation the other day, I heard a man talking about being on the side of the angels. He knew he was on their side, and you could tell he knew it. He was preaching—the same position I'm in. He *knew* he was on the side of the angels all the time, over and over again. I said to him afterwards: "It seems to me it might be for God to say whether you are on His side or not." That's what we mean by our humility and our modesty.

We don't quite know! We do the best we can with what we know, and then there is something we come to church about, something we pray about. Prayer is all about that!

The blessing you ask for is for God to give you some sort of sense that perhaps you are acceptable in His sight.

Now I have on the worldly plane—I'm very sure of America, the United States. But I sat the other night with a pleasant young man who said he didn't see America. He'd been educated here, had a doctor's degree, recently acquired, and I asked him about what he had been doing in history and things, economics, sociology. And the outcome of it all was that he didn't quite see America. That's all right—his wisdom against my wisdom. He's pretty unsure, and I'm fairly sure. But beyond both of us is this wisdom beyond wisdom.

It says here—it would be *my* text—connected with another religious experience, I might call it "The Irreligious Experience," almost—it says here: "And none can say unto Thee, 'What doest Thou?'" Nobody can say to God: "What are you doing? What do you think you're doing?" That's our modesty. That's our humility. That's our prayer. To accept us—

So we're below His wisdom. Of course we're below His wisdom. That's His mercy. I'm pretty sure of America. This young man unsure of America.

Another little experience out of the war. Someone, an aunt, was sent to tell me of the death of a young doctor in Bataan. She was an able and self-assured woman of sixty. She knew all about what God ought to do. And she kept repeating as she told me the dreadful news of the young man's death, "the young doctor"—that seemed to be something special to her—she kept saying *that*, as if doctors were the only good people—she kept saying, "I resent it! I resent it!", as much as to say, "What are you doing, God? What do you think you're doing, killing boys like that?"

Irreligious. Worse than atheism. We're sure—sure enough —have to be—day by day—to go on living. We have to be. But always the humility and the modesty that ventures not to say to God: "What are you doing now? What do you think you're doing?"

Amen

Rockdale Avenue Temple,
Cincinnati, Ohio, October 10, 1946

# Speaking of Loyalty

CHARLIE COLE and I, and George Whicher, are just back from having inaugurated the first president of a brand new college. The extenuating circumstance is that it is a seedling from Amherst College. The chief event of the occasion for me was the history of the founding of Amherst College as told by Charlie Cole, and the analogy he drew between the shoe-string start of this new college on a mountain in Vermont and the shoe-string start of Amherst College a hundred and so many years ago. My ear is always cocked for anything democratic these days, and the most democratic thing I know about America is shoe-string starts.

I don't know whether or not they have them in other countries to compare with ours, but they move me—whether of an enterprise or of an individual, of a person—these shoe-string starts. I read the obituaries in the *Times* and the *Tribune* for the stories of them.

At the same place, Marlboro College, our national friend—our Vermont lady of the manor—Dorothy Canfield Fisher made an attempt to define democracy in other terms. She would have it that Vermont, anyway, had always had a classless society, whether Massachusetts had or not, or New Hampshire had or not. And her proof of it was that the wife of the first governor of Vermont, Governor Chittenden, always cooked the meal before she sat down at the table with the guests from New Haven and Boston to eat it. And Dorothy Canfield insisted that was still the Vermont way of life. I'm only a bastard Vermonter, and so I don't know. (I had that from Reed Powell once. He told me I was only a bastard Vermonter. I'm really a Californian.)

I'm here in a sort of grand bath of loyalties. And I'd like to say a little bit in connection with this—the founding of this new college. There someone is starting a new thing to be loyal to. And the one starting it, the president we inaugurated, was of the class, I think, of 1917, Walter Hendricks. He was a Bond Prize winner. I sat on the platform here in 1917 when his oration won the Bond Prize, an oration on "Adventures in

Education," and right there he set out to establish something new to be loyal to.

You often wonder about that. There are talkers abroad who confuse the word loyalty, make confusion with the word loyalty. They use Emerson and they use Josiah Royce to prove that you can be as loyal as Benedict Arnold or Aaron Burr, we'll say, and still be a loyal person. Loyal to something else, that's all they mean. The leading article in the *Harper's Magazine* a month or two ago was written to prove that. I heard a speech like that here many years ago confusing the loyalties. There is loyalty to chemistry, loyalty to physics, loyalty to geography, loyalty to history, and just incidentally, there might be loyalty to Amherst College and, more incidentally still, loyalty to the United States of America. The only hitch is that the United States is in a stronger position than chemistry, physics, or history to compel loyalty.

Most confusing of all there is loyalty to the next thing ahead of you.

> Heartily know
> When half-gods go,
> The gods arrive.

Emerson was the original heretic—the villain of the piece. But you have to ask yourself (without any help from semantics), "What is the meaning of loyalty to the common ordinary person, to me, for instance?"

I had a questionnaire the other day from an editor. He asked, "What in your opinion is the present state of middle-brow literature in America?" That was new slang to me. I'd got behind a little bit, being off in the country. I hadn't heard of "middle-brow" before. What he meant to say was, "You old skeezix, what's the present state of your own middle-brow stuff?" There was something invidious, I am sure, in that. But right away I thought of a way to use it, not here but in verse, in writing. You make it like this:

> High-brow, low brow,
> Middle-brow, and no brow.

There is a refrain for the next poem.

> High-brow, low brow,
> Middle-brow, and no brow.

Now what is the middle-brow attitude toward loyalty? There's the high-brow attitude—that is the one I speak of— Josiah Royce's and Ralph Waldo Emerson's. That is loyalty, not to your attachment, but to your attractions. The next one is your concern—let's see what comes next—who's the next lady?

> Heartily know
> When half-gods go,
> The quarter-gods arrive.

Emerson says the gods arrive, the whole gods, but you see we don't know that for sure. The loyalty as he defines it could be the loyalty of a quisling. That's loyalty too, to the next thing. But what's my own poor middle-brow, or low-brow notion of loyalty—not no brow, I won't grant that? . . . By the way, I've got a poem I'm going to write about that some day. It begins something like this. It's about the girl Hanno—I don't want to entertain you with too much scholarship, but about the girl Hanno and his sailors captured on the coast of Africa, down the Gold Coast, outside the Gates. It's one of those old Polybius stories. And the poem should begin like this:

> She had no brow but a mind of her own,
> She wanted the sailors to let her alone;
> She didn't like sailors, she didn't like men,
> So they had to shut her up in a pen.

And so on, offhand. They found her so incorrigible, or whatever you call it, that they got sick of it in the end. She scratched and bit, I suppose; so they skinned her alive and took her skin back to Carthage and hung it up to Astarte.

Well, to my loyalty question again. When someone asked a mother what service her son had been in, she answered proudly, "In the Intelligentsia." That's the high-brow of it. Nobody can escape it—it's everywhere. I was looking up "potatoes" in the *Columbia Encyclopedia*—I don't know whether you know the great book—but I was looking up "potato" and I stumbled onto "poetry." You know I write verse? I had never read about poetry before, and so I stopped and read about it. And this is what I read. (The same high-brow stuff. I wonder who wrote it. I should like to catch him before I cool off. He put it like this as if to embarrass me in particular.) He said: "Poetry is largely a matter of rhythm and diction; meaning is not essential, and by many is considered detrimental." I quote from memory.

Well, when Dorothy Canfield talked about a classless society in Vermont, you and I know how to shade it—into more or less classless. But there are these classes apparently, anyway: high-brow, low-brow, middle-brow, and no brow. And my view, whatever it is—I suppose it's somewhere between middle and low—about loyalty is just the plain one of her pride in Vermont. It pleases me, for instance, that Vermont after litigation for a hundred years has established it that New Hampshire has no right to tax the wharves of the seaports (or should we say riverports?) on the Merrimack River, on her side of the river. It took over a hundred years of litigation to establish that, and even now the line between the two states has to be re-perambulated every seven years so as to keep the feeling open. That's the national feeling for you! That's the patriotism! That's the loyalty on both sides of the river.

A very high official in California, almost the highest, I guess the highest, said to me as a renegade native son—he said, "Why did you leave California?" I told him, "I went out very young. I was carried out screaming." That made it all right. I was on the spot, but I got out all right.

And right here and now I am looking at somebody who is watching me, too. He's from Dartmouth. And he's wondering how I straighten all this out with Dartmouth when I get back there. I remember once, one of the first times I appeared here, years ago, back in 1916 it was, that one of the faculty members, my fellows-to-be, said to me, "From Dartmouth!" he said. "I never saw a Dartmouth man yet who didn't deserve to be shot." We began like that. I was in that transition stage—it's one of the problems of life—that transition between one loyalty and another, between an attraction and an attachment.

How do you get from an attachment to follow an attraction? It ought to be painful to you, it ought to be, if you're any good. It ought not to be easy. You ought not to do it cheerfully, lightly, the way Emerson talked of doing it. He didn't do it in practice. I know people who do it in practice, however, on his advice. The loyalty I'm speaking of—I don't know whether I'm permitted here to deal with it in written words of my own—I've written a great deal about it; once away back when I was very young in a stanza I'll venture to say to you.

> Ah, when to the heart of man
>     Was it ever less than a treason
> To go with the drift of things,
>     To yield with a grace to reason,
> To bow and accept the end
>     Of a love or a season?

Even a season—that pain of the end of summer—is in it for me, the person, the place, friendship, parting is such sweet sorrow, and so on. One of the poems I'll say has to do with the breaking off, with the cost of breaking off with one attachment to form another. And then I'll say a couple of short ones just to wind up and say goodbye.

[Mr. Frost then recited "The Gift Outright", which he called "a history of the United States in a dozen lines of blank verse."]

And that, I take it, is the whole thing. Lately I've been thinking more and more about it. All there is is belonging and belongings; belonging and having belongings. You belong and I belong. The sincerity of their belonging is all I have to measure people by. I hate to take great names in vain, but I am tempted to call some men quislings that perhaps some of you would not like to hear me call quislings. Men in great places. I can't quite take them. My namesake anyway, Robert Lee, never came up to Washington to curry favor with those that had licked him. He sawed wood. That was the only thing for him to do when beaten.

You have to ask yourself in the end, how far will you go when it comes to changing your allegiance.

[In conclusion Mr. Frost recited "One Step Backward Taken", remarking: "So many of my poems have Amherst memories. This one remembers the time of the big flood, when I set out to come to see Mr. Pease inaugurated here and didn't get here." Next "Departmental": "I wrote this in entire detachment. . . . And you can't go looking into it with a Freudian eye for anything that's eating me. It's about an ant, A-N-T, that I met in Florida." And finally "A Considerable Speck": "This one has some of my animosities in it—buried, you know. Somebody said I didn't have to talk politics, they shone out of me."]

Amherst College Alumni luncheon,
June 19, 1948

# A Romantic Chasm

HAVING a book in London is not quite the same thing to-day as it was in 1913 when I had my first book there or anywhere—half a lifetime and two wars ago. To be sure by 1913 I had already had it from Kipling that I was hopelessly hedged from the elder earth with alien speech. But hearing then I heard not. I was young and heedless. My vitality shed discouragement as the well-oiled feathers of a healthy duck shed wetness. And to be merely hedged off was no great matter. What was a hedge to the poacher in my blood of a shiny night in the season of the year? It took an American, a friend, Henry L. Mencken, to rouse me to a sense of national differences. My pedantry would be poor and my desert small with the educated if I could pretend to look unscared into the gulf his great book has made to yawn between the American and English languages.

I wish Edward Thomas (that poet) were here to ponder gulfs in general with me as in the days when he and I tired the sun down with talking on the footpaths and stiles of Leddington and Ryton. I should like to ask him if it isn't true that the world is in parts and the separation of the parts as important as the connection of the parts. Isn't the great demand for good spacing? But now I do not know the number of his mansion to write him so much as a letter of inquiry. The mansions so many would probably be numberless. Then I must leave it to Jack Haines in Gloucester to tell me frankly if the gulf in word or idiom has been seriously widening since the night when to illustrate our talk about the internationality of ferns, he boosted me up a small cliff to see by matchlight a spleenwort he knew of there.

The Dea knows (as we still say in New England) I would go to any length short of idolatry to keep Great Britain within speaking, or at least shouting, distance of America in the trying times seen ahead. I might not care to go for a hero myself, but I could perhaps persuade some Mark Curtius of our race to leap into the gulf in the forum for me and close it as much as it was thought needful. Anyway I might be tempted to enlist with the forlorn hope who would sacrifice all the words in both languages except a very limited few we could agree on as meaning the same in both; only with the proviso that I should be drawn on the committee for vocabulary where I could hold out for certain favorites for my own use, such as quackery for remedies too unorthodox, boustrophedon for a more scientific eye-reading (if science is really in earnest about advancing the humanities), ornery for the old-fashioned colonial pronunciation of ordinary with only one accent. And there are other good words I should have to consult Ivor Brown about before giving them up. Sursanure for instance for the way my wounds heal after cruel criticism.

It is beyond idealism of mine to think of closing the gulf so tight as to embarrass the beneficiaries of it on either verge. The Mother Country will hardly deny having profited in several ways by American independence in business and government. May she profit more. For me I should hate to miss the chance for exotic charm my distance overseas might lend me. Charm may be too strong a word. Suppose American had got as far away from English as present day English is from Chaucerian, or at least Elizabethan; obviously my verse by being in American would automatically, without mental expense on my part, be raised to the rank of having to be annotated. It might be advertised as with glossary. It might be studied.

I should surely hesitate to squeeze the Atlantic out from between the two continents lest it should raise the tide too high for ports in the Pacific to adjust their wharves to the change.

But I mustn't talk myself entirely out of respect for the gulf. I don't doubt its awesome reality. Still I begin to wonder if it is anything more than a "romantic chasm" of poetry and slang.

If that is a question, Phoebus replied (and touched my trembling ears), I can support you in your wild Coleridgian surmise. The estrangement in language is pretty much due to the very word-shift by metaphor you do your best to take part in daily so as to hold your closest friend off where you can "entertain her always as a stranger"—with the freshness of a stranger. It often looks dangerously like aberration into a new dialect. But it is mostly back and forth in the same place like the jumping of a grasshopper whose day's work gets him nowhere. And even when it is a word-drift, which is a chain of word-shifts all in one direction, it is nothing but that an average ingenuity with figures of speech can be counted on to keep up with, or in half a jiffy overtake. You are both free peoples so used to your freedom that you are not interested in talking too much about what you are free from. Your pride is in what you dare to take liberties with, be it word, friend, or institution. In the beginning was the word, to be sure, very sure, and a solid basic comfort it remains in situ, but the fun only begins with the spirited when you treat the word as a point of many departures. There is risk in the play. But if some of the company get lost in the excitement, charge it up to proving the truth of chapter and verse in the Gospel according to Saint Mark, although the oracle speaking is Delphic. Remember the future of the world may depend on your keeping in practice with each other's quips and figures.

Preface to British Edition of
*A Masque of Reason*, 1948

# Preface to Poems in 'The World's Best'

IT WOULD BE a very false pose for me to pretend to know what I have done best. Any choice I made would mean little or nothing an hour after I had made it. Every new moon I could get up something entirely new. By the time my friend Whit Burnett had completed all the anthologies he could think of, I should have been in them with nearly everything I ever wrote. After all, what I have published represents a pretty strict essential selection as it is in my seven or eight books. But if I may be permitted to put forward a few that I have lately been looking fondly back over as deserving more attention than they get, let me seize the chance to name these.

*The World's Best*, 1950

# Poetry and School

WHY POETRY is in school more than it seems to be outside in the world, the children haven't been told. They must wonder.

The authorities that keep poetry in school may be divided into two kinds, those with a conscientious concern for it and those with a real weakness for it. They are easily told apart.

School is founded on the invention of letters and numbers. The inscription over every school door should be the rhyme A B C and One Two Three. The rest of education is apprenticeship and for me doesn't belong in school.

The chief reason for going to school is to get the impression fixed for life that there is a book side to everything.

We go to college to be given one more chance to learn to read in case we haven't learned in High School. Once we have learned to read the rest can be trusted to add itself unto us.

The way to read a poem in prose or verse is in the light of all the other poems ever written. We may begin anywhere. We *duff* into our first. We read that imperfectly (thoroughness with it would be fatal), but the better to read the second. We read the second the better to read the third, the third the better to read the fourth, the fourth the better to read the fifth, the fifth the better to read the first again, or the second if it so happens. For poems are not meant to be read in course any more than they are to be made a study of. I once made a resolve never to put any book to any use it wasn't intended for by its author. Improvement will not be a progression but a widening circulation. Our instinct is to settle down like a revolving dog and make ourselves at home among the poems, completely at our ease as to how they should be taken. The same people will be apt to take poems right as know how to take a hint when there is one and not to take a hint when none is intended. Theirs is the ultimate refinement.

We write in school chiefly because to try our hand at writing should make us better readers.

Almost everyone should almost have experienced the fact that a poem is an idea caught fresh in the act of dawning.

Also that felicity can't be fussed into existence.

Also that there is such a thing as having a moment. And that the great thing is to know a moment when you have one.

Also to know what Catullus means by *mens animi.*

Also to know that poetry and prose too regarded as poetry is the renewal of words.

Emotion emoves a word from its base for the moment by metaphor, but often in the long run even on to a new base. The institution, the form, the word, have regularly or irregularly to be renewed from the root of the spirit. That is the creed of the true radical.

Emotions must be dammed back and harnessed by discipline to the wit mill, not just turned loose in exclamations. No force will express far that isn't shut in by discipline at all the pores to jet at one outlet only. Emotion has been known to ooze off.

Better readers, yes, and better writers too, if possible. Certainly not worse writers as many are made by being kept forever at it with the language (not to say jargon) of criticism and appreciation. The evil days will come soon enough, and we shall have no pleasure in them, when we shall have dried up into nothing but abstractions. The best educated person is one who has been matured at just the proper rate. Seasoned but not kiln dried. The starch thickening has to be stirred in with slow care. The arteries will harden fast enough without being helped. Too many recent poems have been actually done in the language of evaluation. They are too critical in spirit to admit of further criticism.

And this constant saying what amounts to no more than variations on the theme of "I don't like this and I do like that" tends to aesthetic Puritanism. "For goodness' sake," said one teacher to a class, "write for a change about what you are neither for nor against." When one bold boy asked if there could be any such thing, he was told he had flunked the course.

The escape is to action in words: to stories, plays, scenes, episodes, and incidents.

Practice of an art is more salutary than talk about it. There is nothing more composing than composition.

We were enjoined of old to learn to write now while young so that if we ever had anything to say later we would know how to say it. All there is to learning to write or talk is learning how to have something to say.

Our object is to say something that *is* something. One teacher once said that it was something at once valid and sensational with the accent on both. Classmates punish us for failure better than the teachers by very dead silence or exchanging glances at our expense.

One of the dangers of college to anyone who wants to stay a human reader (that is to say a humanist) is that he will become a specialist and lose his sensitive fear of landing on the lovely too hard. (With beak and talon.)

Another danger nowadays to sensitiveness is getting inured to translations. The rarity of a poem well brought over from one language into another should be a warning. Some translation of course in course for utility. But never enough to get broken to it. For self assurance there should always be a lingering unhappiness in reading translations.

The last place along the line where books are safely read as they are going to be out in the world in polite society is usually in so-called Freshman English. There pupils are still treated as if not all of them were going to turn out scholars.

The best reader of all is one who will read, can read, no faster than he can hear the lines and sentences in his mind's ear as if aloud. Frequenting poetry has slowed him down by its metric or measured pace.

The eye reader is a barbarian. So also is the writer for the eye reader, who needn't care how badly he writes since he doesn't care how badly he is read.

It is one thing to think the text and be totally absorbed in it. There is however an ascendancy in the mood to spare that can also think ABOUT the text. From the induced parallel current in the mind over and above the text the notes are drawn that we so much resent other people's giving us because we want the fun of having them for ourselves.

A B C is letters. One Two Three is numbers—mathematica. What marks verse off from prose is that it talks letters in numbers. Numbers is a nickname for poetry. Poetry plays the rhythms of dramatic speech on the grid of meter. A good map carries its own scale of miles.

For my pleasure I had as soon write free verse as play tennis with the net down.

*Atlantic Monthly*, June 1951

# On the Poems of Hervey Allen

THE COURSE of true poetry is from more ethereal than substantial to more substantial than ethereal. What begins lyric may be counted on if not broken off by death or business to end epic. By pure poetry some would seem to mean poetry purely not substantial at all. That's an extravagance of theory. But where has there ever been any such thing with success? It may have been tried for the purpose of sinning with originality. The result if any would be of scientific rather than esthetic interest. Such notion relegates to the realm where in the cyclotron nothing is perceptibly becoming something. That would be funny if it wasn't wicked. The surest thing we know is that the scale of soul is not quadruple, none, some, more, most, but eternally triple, merely some, more, most. Nothing can be done with nothing. Nothing but weight can put on weightiness. The most diaphanous wings carry a burden of pollen from flower to flower. No song without a burden.

What begins as lyric may be counted on if not broken off by death or business to end as epic. The principle was never better exemplified than in the fine poems of Hervey Allen and through the years to a book heard round the world it was translated from admiration into so many languages. The book was a novel in prose but only a poet could have written it and its very name rang with poetry. Unquestionably it is best regarded as just one more poem on top of all his others, longer than all the rest put together, an epic that had come in the disguise of prose to get past our modern prejudice against the epic. Hervey Allen would have wanted it taken as part and parcel of his life in poetry. He would live to regret it in the Elysian fields if it wasn't.

Unfinished preface to
an unpublished collection, 1951 (?)

# "Reading Poems at Tufts"

PROFESSOR CHARLES FAY invited me to read the Phi Beta Kappa poem at Tufts thirty seven years ago and so began this career for me of reading poetry in public and looking to colleges for critical and financial support. I read him three poems at the time and have been reading poems at Tufts ever since. He was the one in those days as Professors John Holmes and Harold Blanchard are the special ones at Tufts today willing to risk the live bard on undergraduates. What the idea was or is nobody has yet told: possibly to test the judgement the young are supposed to have acquired from the long harsh study of the dead-sure reputations of the past; or simply to entertain them at an intellectual level, though for no credit toward a degree—to give them as it were a gay flyer in the insecurities of the moment. We should all owe Tufts much for pioneering thus somewhat out of bounds.

*The Tufts Weekly,* October 11, 1952

# The Hear-Say Ballad

"AN ORDINARY SONG or ballad that is the delight of the common people cannot fail to please all such readers as are not unqualified for the entertainment by their affectation or their ignorance."

Thus Addison with his challenge two hundred odd years ago and it might be Mrs. Flanders speaking today. We are defied not to love ballads on pain of being thought what Addison says. Balladry belongs to the none too literate and its spirit, and probably the spirit of all poetry, is safest in the keeping of the none too literate—people who know it by heart where it can weather and season properly. Ballads lead their life in the mouths and ears of men by hear-say like bluebirds and flickers in the nest holes of hollow trees. But that's no reason specimens shouldn't be brought in and brought to book now and then for sport and scholarship. We have a right to satisfy our curiosity as to what variants they may have been running wild into while our backs were turned. We can't touch their existence as a breed either to increase or destroy them. Nothing we do can. Trout have to be killed carefully so as not to exterminate them; have even to be fished out and multiplied artificially in captivity for restocking their own brooks. Ballads are different. Child hunted them, Mrs. Flanders hunts them; and they have the vitality to stay game at large, not to say gamey. You won't see the ballads of this book going back from here in print to alter the versions of the singers they were found on. No patronage of ours will smile them out of using "fee" for a rhyme word, "lily-white hands" for beauty, and lords and ladies for goodness knows what away off here three thousand miles across the ocean and after three hundred years of democracy. Their singers ought in consistency to be equally excited over the coronation and the inauguration that are in conjunction this graceful year of nineteen hundred and fifty-three.

One word more to speed the launching enterprise.

The voice and ear are left at a loss what to do with the ballad till supplied with the tune it was written to go with. That might be the definition of a true ballad to distinguish it

from a true poem. A ballad does not or should not supply its
own way of being uttered. For tune it depends on the music
of music—a good set score. Unsung it stays half lacking—as
Mrs. Flanders knows full well. She has been at the same pains
to recruit singers to sing the ballads for her on the stage as
to collect the ballads. It is always interesting to watch how
lowly the thing may lapse and still be poetry for the right
people. It may flaw in metre, syntax, logic and sense. It may
seem to be going to pieces, breaking up, but it is only as the
voice breaks with emotion.

Preface to Ballads Migrant in<br>New England, 1953

# The Prerequisites

SOME SIXTY YEARS AGO a young reader ran into serious trouble with the blind last stanza of a poem otherwise perfectly intelligible. The interest today might be in what he then did about it. He simply left it to shift for itself. He might see to it if he ever saw it again. He guessed he was no more anxious to understand the poem than the poem was to be understood.

He might have gone to college for help. But he had just left college to improve his mind if he had any. Or he might have gone to Asia. The whole poem smacked of Asia. He suspected a whole religion behind it different from the one he was brought up to. But as he was no traveler except on foot he must have gone by way of the Bering Strait when frozen over and that might have taken him an epoch from East to West as it had the Indians from West to East.

The poem was called "Brahma" and he was lilting along on such lines as the following in easy recognition:

> They reckon ill who leave me out
> When me they fly I am the wings.
> I am the doubter and the doubt
> And I the hymn the Brahmin sings.

which was all very pretty. For Brahma he naturally read God— not the God of the Old Testament nor of the New either, but near enough. Though no special liberal he valued himself on his tolerance of heresy in great thinkers. He could always lend himself to an unsound idea for the duration of the piece and had been even heard to wish people would cling to their heresies long enough for him to go and tell on them.

Success in taking figures of speech is as intoxicating as success in making figures of speech. It had to be just when he was flushed with having held his own with the poem so far and was thinking "good easy man" "What a good boy am I" that the disaster happened. The words were still Brahma's:

> The strong gods pine for my abode
> And pine in vain the sacred seven
> But thou meek lover of the good
> Find me and turn thy back on Heaven.

814

There he blacked out as if he had bumped his head and he only came to dazed. I remember his anger in asking if anybody had a right to talk like that. But he wasn't as put out as he let on to be. He didn't go back on poetry for more than the particular poem or on that for more than the time being. His subconscious intention was to return on it by stealth some day if only it would stay in print till he was ready for it. All was he didn't want the wrong kind of help. The heart sinks when robbed of the chance to see for itself what a poem is all about. Any immediate preface is like cramming the night before an examination. Too late, too late! Any footnote while the poem is going is too late. Any subsequent explanation is as dispiriting as the explanation of a joke. Being taught poems reduces them to the rank of mere information. He was sure the Muse would thank him for reserving a few of her best for being achieved on the spur of the moment.

Approach to the poem must be from afar off, even generations off. He should close in on it on converging lines from many directions like the divisions of an army upon a battlefield.

A poem is best read in the light of all the other poems ever written. We read A the better to read B (we have to start somewhere; we may get very little out of A). We read B the better to read C, C the better to read D, D the better to go back and get something more out of A. Progress is not the aim, but circulation. The thing is to get among the poems where they hold each other apart in their places as the stars do.

And if he stubbornly stayed away from college and Asia (he hated to be caught at his age grooming his brains in public) perhaps in time college and Asia, even the Taj Mahal, might come to him with the prerequisites to that poem and to much else not yet clear.

Well, it so happened. For the story has a happy ending. Not fifty years later when the poem turned up again he found himself in a position to deal with all but two lines of it. He was not quite satisfied that the reference to "strong gods," plural, was fair poetry practice. Were these Titans or Yidags or, perish the thought, Olympians?—Oh no! not Olympians. But he now saw through the "meek lover of the good" who sounded so deceptively Christian. His meekness must have meant the perfect detachment from ambition and desire that can alone rescue us from the round of existence. And the "me" worth turning "thy back on Heaven" for must of course be Nirvana—the only nothing that is something. He had grown very fastidious about not calling the round of existence a wheel. He was a confirmed symbolist.

Preface to *Aforesaid*, 1954

# To the Poets of Japan

THIS IS LOOKING towards you across 3000 miles of land and twice as many of water all in one flight unless I put down in San Francisco to make a fresh start from the city I was born in. Poetry is what makes you think of me and poetry is what makes me think of you. We aspire towards each other in the arts. But our aim is not soon to be lost in each other. We must always remember that a poet exists only by his difference from any other poet. He can be nobody's repetition. Our differences must be maintained even at the risk of their sometimes becoming acute and sanguinary. I do not change my little watch for every big clock it doesn't agree with. We must be brave but before all else brave about our differences to see them through to some real achievement. I have been slow to learn but it has not taken me all these eighty years to find out. An instinct told me long ago that I had to be national before I was international. I must be personal before I can hope to be interestingly interpersonal. There must first be definite nations for the world sentiment to flourish between. You may be more international than I am. I wish I were international enough to be speaking in Japanese the friendship some of you have made me feel by your writing. And I wish I could read in the original the Japanese poetry I have admired even as it was in translation.

1954

# On Taking Poetry

I'VE BEEN THINKING about a good many things lately because I've been at a good many places. I have to say something wherever I go. I get into a good deal. What's been on my mind mostly of late is something that comes round, I suppose, to how people take a poem—how they take anything written—how they take a poem particularly.

I suppose a poem is a kind of fooling. I've just been reading in a sermon by a great Unitarian friend of mine about "the foolishness of God"! The foolishness of God. God's foolish, you know, and God's fooling. And I've just been reading about the last days of Einstein, the old man, by somebody who knows his science and who knew his philosophy because he was a great philosopher among great scientists. And the thing about him was that every few minutes it was a burst of laughter about something philosophical or something—God, relativity, or something about Newton. He got a great laugh over his little quarrel with Newton. He once said something in print, something we've seen: "Forgive me, Newton. Forgive me, Newton." Of course, if the height of everything is fooling—God's foolishness—then poetry mounts somewhere into a kind of fooling. It's something hard to get. It's what you spend a good deal of education on—just getting it right.

I thought if I came up again some evening, I'd like to talk about Puritanism—in Greek, Roman, Early Roman, New England, and Later Roman—and right out of the head, not out of my books. I'm one of these people who read some. You can see how little I depend on books for anything I do. They are in such disorder that they're very fresh to me whenever I happen on one that I've been looking for. [*Laughter*] *A Pleasant Night:* I haven't seen that for twenty years. I'll have to get that down and read it. But I can't get a talk out of it. I'll just have to come up and talk off the cuff, as they say, about Puritanism and the greatest poem that it produced: *Comus.* You thought I was going to say something else, I see. Shall I say that Puritanism didn't repent, you know? It relented a little and became Unitarianism. I've found it relenting. [*Laughter*] I'll come up and talk about that.

But this thing that I've brought up before here. I've quoted it, I think, in a couple of places, and it's always coming into my head: that these things are said in parable so the wrong people can't understand them and so get saved. It says that twice in the New Testament. It seems very harsh and un-democratic, doesn't it? Sounds esoteric. And one of my good friends went forth from my saying that to say that I was es-oteric—that my thinking was esoteric. But not at all. Because it also says in the New Testament that except you become as little children, you know. That meant that so professors won't understand it. It's so simple and so foolish that only little children can understand it. We try too hard—we strike too hard—that's the danger of it. Now take God's foolishness as the question. And you've got to be in an awfully easy mental state. That's the thing you acquire through the years of poetry—from *Mother Goose* on—easy does it. And you've got to know that it's being played with—it's said—as I say: I can say and you can take it a good deal your own way—that's for conversation. You don't have to contradict it. But make it a rule almost. I was saying that over at Dartmouth: make it a rule, almost, never to contradict anybody. Just say: "Let them have their say and then take it your way."

That comes to this question of who has a right to do what he pleases with my poetry—the right kind of people that can take it their way. There's a good deal of sway in it. There's a certain deftness, definiteness, but it sways at its anchor. It swings at its anchor tow. And of course that's the fun of it. Of course, now I go through a good deal about that, and there's a common laugh you can get among students about the right of teachers to go on with a poem and carry it their way a little. It can be wrong; it can be utterly wrong. This matter of getting it right and wrong. That's what you grow up in, getting it right and wrong, in and out, trial and error with it—in this spirit of the thing. And there's such a thing as throwing dust in the eye, you know—a person can write so that he's insulting. He is just throwing dust in the eyes. And that's again just going a little over the edge about this play, this fooling. To tease people is all right but to insult them is going too far. It's always one of my concerns.

I'll start saying some of my poems. I thought as I came in

that I ought to bring somebody else's poems. I'll bring Shelley or Milton or somebody, you know. Forever me, you know, and it's just because people want to hear the way I say them. They probably know how to say them better than I do. They just want to know out of curiosity how I say them. [*Laughter*] That's all they want, some association with it.

You see, one of the great things about it all, the depth of it all, is where if you were reading aloud—it has to be something rather new. I've been a reader aloud all of my life, probably. I was at home. I was the one that did the reading aloud. And I've read in school, and then I've got to reading this way, more and more. Done a good deal of it. And the question, when reading a new thing at home or sitting around with anyone, is where do I have to hide it when I am having almost too hard a time with my emotions. Where do I let on? I never let on; I try to hide it—but it will move me almost to breaking in the voice. Well, it's never anything ever sad—never! It's a strange thing. You can kill all the babies you want to and it won't make me cry. And it isn't about bombs and things; nothing like that. It's always magnanimity—the heroism of magnanimity. See. Always that I can hardly keep my voice right about. Always. My own poetry of course is too much accustomed with me now. It's always something about the largeness, something about the greatness of spirit.

I have just been thinking about Einstein a little. Just saw a very pretty thing about him that almost moved me to tears. I couldn't read it to you—probably couldn't—without pretending I was not seeing the page or the light wasn't right or something like that. But it was about this. There was a book, and there are a lot of professors in this country—noted liberals—who threatened a publisher. If he didn't stop printing it, they wouldn't buy his textbooks any more. And they were noted liberals. One was a noted Red, you'd almost call him. He used to go to Moscow and come back and say they were the only people who knew how to treat a great man like him right. [*Laughter*] But he was supposed to be of the free modern world, and he led this attack on Macmillan's. He was one of the kind of people who talk about burning books. They wanted to burn that book, and old Einstein just happened to speak of it casually, you know, and he didn't name the book, but you could tell what it was from the description of it. He didn't name the publishing house. He didn't name the suppressors. He just said what a charmingly crazy book it was. I've got some on the shelf of my library. Just as charming as Ignatius Donnelly's *Lost Atlantis*. That's another wonderful book. And the books about Shakespeare who didn't write Shakespeare. What's all this severity about back over these years? The old man Einstein made a laugh about it—that crazy book. How charming! And terrible—with passion, he said: "How terrible suppressing any book!" That's too much for me. Well, I'll leave that. But you can almost judge yourself by how deep you go into things. It's what you call compassion. But I think this is more than compassion—this magnanimity.

*Compassion* is almost as tiresome a word critically used nowadays, as threadbare a word, as the word *escape*. "Why do children look at television?" I was reading. Why do they look at it? A scientific person in the psychology department of one of the great colleges has found out that children of the upper middle class (which doesn't exist, of course) look at movies more if they've been too much disciplined. See. This is a complicated thing. And children of the lower middle class (that doesn't exist), they look at movies a little more than children of the upper middle class, but they look at it the same whether they've been overdisciplined or not. [*Laughter*] This is what you call holy smoke. [*Laughter*] Of course the word *escape* I came on this way made me think of it. The whole question was one of escape. I talked about that in the old days. It is a long time since I've talked about escape and made it out that life was a pursuit of a pursuit of a pursuit of a pursuit. You know, one person pursuing something else and he pursuing something else, and this modern psychological idea seems to be that everybody is escaping from something or somebody. So you're an escape from an escape from an escape from an escape until you get to hell. [*Laughter*] But this word *compassion—escape*—are rather tiresome critical words. I remember saying to a professor friend of mine fifty years ago nearly—no, forty; no, thirty—that I was sick of that word then and I don't want to hear it any more, and he said, "You're going to have to." And I have.

Well, take one of my poems to begin with, a little poem. And I'm not going to dwell on what I've been saying except for one or two poems. Suppose I say: this is what I was talking about—our Revolutionary War, you know. Was it an escape or a pursuit? Pursuit of nationality—as simple as could be. Not an escape at all. One person understood it one way, one another. Tom Paine understood it as the beginning of a world revolution. That's wrong. It wasn't that; it was a pursuit of nationality. Wanting to be, feeling that we were, something. Tom Paine was one of the first to see that—speak of the continent as something; something with the meaning of the land and it all. This one of mine is about the Revolutionary War. [*Reads "The Gift Outright"*]

That's a whole story of just that—the realization that we've got to belong to what belonged to us. That's all. We had a big part of it. It's as simple a statement as that. Interesting in it, too, that it's a pursuit, you know, artless, unstoried, vaguely realizing westward but still unstoried, artless, unenhanced—all to be storied and enhanced. See. A vague aspiration as much as anything that made it. Not an escape from anything. Pursuit, pursuit. And that was in the nature of the best people in it. See. Just that thing. Leave that there.

Now let's take another one. There's nothing very dubious about that one. Not much play that you can make with it in the sense of that I spoke of first. I'll say this little one. I've got to say old ones, familiar ones, to some of you, for what I've heard people make of it. [*Reads "Stopping by Woods"*]

Now, you see, the first thing about that is to take it right between the eyes just as it is, and that's the ability to do that: to take it right between the eyes like a little blow and not, you know, take it in neuter sort of. And then, you know, the next thing is your inclinations with it. I never read anything, in Latin, say, without a constant expectation of meaning that I'm either getting justified in or corrected. See. Confirmed in or corrected. I've got that going on all the time or else I'd be a dead translator. I've got to have something that's a little aggressive to it, but that's so with a poem. Right away you begin to take it your way. And you can almost say in a poem that you see in it the place where it begins to be ulterior, you know, where it goes a little with you, carries you on somewhere. And if you're very strong about it—of course, it may not be the same day. I know that's the way with me. I hear a talk like this from somebody else, see, and I may not be able to hold my own with it—not then. I think to myself that when this is over I'll get going again. [*Laughter*] My own stream-of-consciousness will get going again. I'll be all right. I'll be all right on Monday after hearing it on Sunday. Many a time I thought that. This is putting it all over but I'm still there, you know. I'll resume my thread, and no matter what's said to me I want to be sure if I differ with it a little that I know what it is that I'm differing with.

Now this little thing you see very simply as I wrote it—night, evening, snowstorm, woods, dark, late, snow falling among the alders, and trees, and with a little poetic exaggeration, you know (to see the woods fill up with snow). Did they fill up? How high? See. You want to know. Don't ask me. [*Laughter*] And I've been asked such things, you know. [*Laughter*] I've had people say—somebody who ought to know better—quote me as saying in that poem, "the coldest evening of the year." See. Now that's getting a thermometer into it. [*Laughter*] And "The darkest evening of the year" 's better—more poetical some way. Never mind why. I don't know. More foolish. That's where the foolishness comes in. Got to be a little foolish or a good deal foolish. But then it goes on and says "The woods are lovely, dark and deep," and then if I were reading it for somebody else I'd begin to wonder what he's up to. See. Not what he means but what he's up to.

> The woods are lovely, dark and deep.
> But I have promises to keep,
> And miles to go before I sleep.

There are so many things that have happened, too, that way. People have come to me to ask me what were the promises, and I've joined in on that. Let them have their say, and I took it my way. I remember telling one committee that came to me about that from a college—committee of students—and I said, promises may be divided into two kinds: those that I myself make for myself and those that my ancestors made for me, known as the social contract. [*Laughter*] Now did I think of that when I wrote it? You know better. I've just got to say something. Just take it. [*Laughter*] They take it their way and I take it my way. But this is the thing I finally said about it— partly in self-defense; I said: What does it say there? "The woods are lovely, dark and deep." That's just as I might be getting along. That's all. That's the nicest way out of it—if you've got to get out of it.

Now take another old one and then I'll drop this. What's the moral of it? The aesthetic moral is: to go any poem one better, not one worse, and you just don't chew it, take it all to pieces; just get another poetic something going—one step more poetic anywhere. "We that are of purer fire." You know that I'll come up to talk about it. "We that are of purer fire." The best statement of the great rout of Comus—of the anti-Puritans—the Episcopalians—is the ultimate. We sit up all night and that's the gayer way. I seem to shock 'em. Shock 'em gently. Wait until you hear me on the subject. Come up and I'll really shock you, going away back to the Greeks— Attis and all that sort of thing.

Then this one. It's about walls that Doc Cook has been telling about. It's about a spring occupation in my day. When I was farming seriously we had to set the wall up every year. You don't do that any more. You run a strand of barbed wire along it and let it go at that. We used to set the wall up. If you see a wall well set up you know it's owned by a lawyer in New York [*laughter*]—not a real farmer. This is just about that spring occupation, but of course all sorts of things have been done with it and I've done something with it myself in self-defense. I've gone it one better—more than once in different ways for the Ned of it—just for the foolishness of it. [*Reads "Mending Wall"*]

Now, you can see the first person that ever spoke to me about it was at that time becoming the president of Rollins College—making Rollins College over—and he took both my hands to tell me I had written a true international poem. And just to tease him I said: "How do you get that?" You know. I said I thought I'd been fair to both sides—both national. "Oh, no," he said, "I could see what side you were on." And I said: "The more I say I the more I always mean somebody else." [*Laughter*] That's objectivity, I told him. That's the way we talked about it, kidding. That's where the great fooling comes in. But my latest way out of it is to say: I've got a man there; he's both a wall builder and a wall toppler. He makes boundaries and he breaks boundaries. That's man. And all human life is cellular, outside or inside. In my body every seven years I'm made out of different cells and all my cell walls have been changed. I'm cellular within and life outside is cellular. Even the Communists have cells. [*Laughter*] That's where I've arrived at that.

Now we go away from those things. That's what's going on it. I'm always distressed when I find somebody being ugly about it, outraging the poem, going some way, especially if it's on some theory I can see their applying to everything. See, this is a loose thing, just as my library is. I don't want it in order. I'm not organized that way. And this is a free and loose thing—the association—the beauties of the association are always something you didn't know you were going to have. If you're going to think of something, study them out, grind them, nothing much to it. When it gets so that something doesn't come into my head that I never thought of before, you know, in connection with the emergency of the moment—the emergency of reading or talking, something I never thought of them—when I get that way I'm done. I don't want to go any more.

You sit listening to a lecture in class, and you always ought to be unhappy if it's just being put all over you. Ought to be some unhappiness in it—just that sort of mood of I'll know what to do with it before tomorrow, you know, if it crosses me up. I talked about that over at Dartmouth, about just the one little item I might mention. I remember when I was very young. I didn't go into the details when I was young; my mother, I suppose, was getting somewhat distressed about evolution—not very much—she was a very faithful Christian and very assured about all that and a kind of a Presbyterian-Unitarian-Swedenborgian. [*Laughter*] And she was all right. But still it bothered her a little about evolution and it was supposed to bother me, but I got old enough to say to her one day: I don't see that this makes any difference at all. I don't know how old—in high school, it was. I said I didn't see that it made any difference at all. "Your idea was that God made man out of mud; the new idea is that God made man out of prepared mud." [*Laughter*] You've still got God, you see—nothing very disturbing about it. You've got to have something to say to it—that's all—to the Sphinx. That's what the Sphinx is there for. And you don't have to do it with presence of mind. And it's nice when you do—when you can sass it right back. Some of us are slower than others. I always want something a long, long time. For instance, about the tendency to smear: what are you going to say to smear? I don't think I ever heard the word until '32 or somewhere near that. I wasn't used to the thought of smearing. And now it's regular. So that I'm out when I ever hear anything about anybody on our side or the other side or any side; I think, "I wonder how much is smear in that," and again I'm saved from it to tears by somebody's largeness that takes that out of it, you know, gets you back to what is partly so, you know. And I've just been going through it lately, always going through it—it's the day's news to me always—somebody straightening something out that way and doing it for myself.

All right, now I've got to read to you a little and I'm superstitious to this extent. Religion is one thing, you know, and superstition is another. I always like to read out of my latest book a little, and that doesn't give you much hope because my latest book is just made out of my old books. [*Laughter*] But I made the selections. Let's see what I've got here. I'm going to read you one—nice light tonight, thanks be. This is called "Directive." And I'll do it slow and you take it straight. But it's all full of dangers, sideways, off, and all that, you know. [*Reads "Directive"*]

Here's another little curious one beside that I see here: "To an Ancient"—ancient, ancient. [*Reads "To an Ancient"*] That's an archaeological one. Doesn't get quoted enough. Then here's one more, familiar again. [*Reads "Desert Places"*]

You see, I prefer in reading the poems ordinarily a great deal better not to go on with them into anything beyond. But that's somebody else's business. I did that just for the fun of it.

Now something else for a change. See what I've got in this little book here. [*Reads "Reluctance"*] That's one of the early ones.

And another early one that I want to read to you. This is one I think I handed in in English A at Harvard. [*Laughter*] It's called "The Tuft of Flowers." And it's about this subject—another one that you get awfully tired of—the subject of togetherness. There's a word been coined—togetherness. And it turns up everywhere nowadays. As if everybody hadn't thought about that. Some people say, "You know why that crowd's in a crowd? Because they're lonely." The question of loneliness: Oppenheimer seems to think he's the only person who was ever lonely because he had deep thoughts. One thing I couldn't stand. This is what I was thinking about in the nineties. This is what I might be thinking about now if I were out helping in the haying. "I went to turn . . . before the sun." And I might just say that in the old days we mowed by hand a great deal—more than we do now. We do some of that now. There was always a boy or somebody—some fellow around like me—to toss the grass, open it up, let the sun at it. The mowing was apt to be done in the dew of the morning for better mowing, but it left the grass wet and had to be scattered. We called it—the word for it was "turning" the grass. I went to turn the grass once more. [*Reads "The Tuft of Flowers"*]

See. I said it both ways in the middle nineties—early in my life. I got over with that, but I get into trouble about it today. Some people think I don't believe in togetherliness. I don't like the word. Terrible about that. But then, one of the interesting things again is I keep running onto this idea of what's your pose. See. What's your pose? Who do you think you are? See. Now there's a nice way of saying that: who the hell do you think you are? [*Laughter*] That's a nicer way to say it. That just means you know you aren't so much. But when you say, what is your pose? Yeats says somewhere you have a choice of one of seven poses. Only seven poses possible—which is yours? Are you putting on airs as a don or a teacher, you know, or are you putting on airs as what—as a farmer, or as a common man, see? That's one of the horrible ones. And that kind of stuff. And what would you do if you got a choice of poses and you were afraid you weren't keeping out of the seven? What would you do? The only thing I can see is, do nothing. Commit suicide or something. Get out of it. Isn't it terrible to think that that's all it is? And I said that there. "Nor yet to draw . . . not for us . . . to flourish." These words are all in it for me, my life. Leave something to flourish, "not for us/Nor yet to draw one thought of ours to him." No self-consciousness about it. "But from sheer morning gladness at the brim." See. That's the height of it all. That's clear out of the posing: "sheer morning gladness at the brim." Butterfly and I lit upon as a poem, you know, too: "butterfly and I had lit upon, / Nevertheless, a message from the dawn." Just as if I had seen that all about poetry then; that I had thought about it all. I hadn't. Seeing it there, you know about it before you know it. Let me see what time we're getting to.

I ought to read you one of the character ones, should I? This little book—I'm not used to. Here's another. Let me see just a minute. Suppose I do "Paul's Wife." It's a lumber-camp one. And you might be interested to hear that I wrote a book called *North of Boston* and I liked the name so well—the luck of the name. I got it out of the advertisements in the *Boston Globe* years and years ago. It came back to me far from the *Boston Globe*. I was away off in England, and all of a sudden I just remembered that constantly in the advertisements that I used to read with interest—and still do—this phrase "north of Boston" popped into my head—just the name. And I got a dozen poems together—a dozen or fifteen, I think it was—that hadn't been written toward that name and hadn't been written toward any particular ideas. They had been scattered among lyrics. They were blank-verse things scattered through twenty years. Then, all of a sudden, I put them together with some little dim notion of their belonging together—swept them together. They're not organic. Then I got that name on them. Just as I didn't write that toward any name or toward any idea—I refused to go on and do some more of the same kind at the time. I was asked to go on and urged to go on, by friends and by publishers, but I refused to have anything to do with it. Then I forgot myself entirely about it and now, lately, looking back I see I did it. I went on scattering some more around. And so now I'm going to have for my literary pleasure—I'm going to have a book called "North of Boston" and subtitled "Twice Over," and then put fifteen-fifteen, like two baskets, you know, on each side of the donkey. This is one of those. I went on. I never thought about it. Little more than fifteen. But I think I'll try to balance it—just have them equal weight. That'll give me a little chance to select.

One of the important ones in it is that "Directive" that I read you and also the one called "The Witch of Coös" that's too long to go into tonight. And then several—quite a number—like this. [*Reads "Paul's Wife"*]

Now, one or two little ones. I brought this little book up, and it's so much smaller print than my other ones that it's bothered me a little. I hadn't looked at it very closely. It's nice print but it's real small for my eyes. [*Reads "Acquainted with the Night"*]

You know, so many things are packed into one little place like that. "One luminary clock against the sky . . . right." That's out of years when I remember a friend of mine who constantly said from reading Henry Adams and people like that—constantly said—"the times are not right." "The times are not right." No times are right. No times are otherwise than right. They're all bad. All bad; all bad.

Let's see if I can think of something else. [*Reads "Choose Something Like a Star"*]

I've got another new one here—a new book—very small one for a cent. Never been on the market. And I guess I'll read that and one little lyric. This one's about a dog. It's called "One More Brevity." [*Reads "One More Brevity"*]

That's that. Then I'll say one of the old ones Doc Cook asked me to say. [*Reads "Come In"*]

Bread Loaf English School Address,
June 30, 1955

# "Caveat Poeta"

CAVEAT POETA. I don't know where a poet could better mew his youth than in the academic world as long as he keeps one leg out of the grave. Caveat poeta. Let him look out for himself. Much goes on in college that is against the spirit. But so does it go on everywhere. The English departments may lean a little too far on the side of treating us all as if we were going to wind up as scholars like our teachers. The last place after high school where we were allowed to read books like men and women of the world was in the courses of Freshman English known at Harvard and some other places as English A. The authorities give themselves away in their attitude towards this. They are sure of the good their thoroughness is doing young scholars in prospect and sure they are not doing harm to the young business men in prospect. They can at least impose a respect for scholarship on the business men that will last them after graduation to keep contributing to the college fund for the rest of their lives. We have to admit that there aren't enough poets and other artists around to be worth much consideration. Such as there are, as I say, let them look out for themselves. Caveat poeta. He has less to fear perhaps if what he is out for is writing epics.

What I have been speaking of is partly the danger of too much analysis. I am glad to learn of the teachers' regret that their students come short in the initiative of discussion and question. My own personal regret is for their lack of initiative in getting up notions to surprise, shock, and amuse me. I mean rigmaroles and frame-ups that have some ingenuity of structure as in Meccano. They often show best in their own student publications provided they have no faculty adviser responsible for their deviations or effronteries.

One can't help a feeling, I suppose, of what is conventionally expected of him in school, on the stage, or in a book. The conventions have to be locked horns with somewhere. It may as well be in school as anywhere. We are the luckier given some choice where. It is hard to tell at this distance of time how much I was governed in writing by any demand there was or wasn't for my sort of thing. I don't know how much longer I might or might not have been able to do without readers.

I catch at the suggestion from someone that my encounter with the conventions may have always been with ironical detachment whether from school, from the stage, from the arts, from politics, or from life itself. One of the conventions of politics in America, for instance, is that we should belong with something almost like patriotism to one party or another. No one can accuse me of not having been ironical enough in my attachment to and my detachment from the Democratic party. It is the same with education for another example. I guess my open secret is that in the wrestling ring the hold with reality should be as much mine as my opponent's. I want, I am expecting everything and everybody in on me and my art, but as much as possible with a force tempered to my terms. There is always the chance it will be on their terms more than on mine and then I shall go down writing.

1955 (?)

# A Perfect Day—A Day of Prowess

AMERICANS would rather watch a game than play a game. Statement true or false? Why, as to these thousands here today to watch the game and not play it, probably not one man-jack but has himself played the game in his athletic years and got himself so full of bodily memories of the experience (what we farmers used to call kinesthetic images) that he can hardly sit still. We didn't burst into cheers immediately, but an exclamation swept the crowd as if we felt it all over in our muscles when Boyer at third made the two impossible catches, one a stab at a grounder and the other a leap at a line drive that may have saved the day for the National League. We all winced with fellow feeling when Berra got the foul tip on the ungloved fingers of his throwing hand.

As for the ladies present, they are here as next friends to the men, but even they have many of them pitching arms and batting eyes. Many of them would prefer a league ball to a pumpkin. You wouldn't want to catch them with bare hands. I mustn't count it against them that I envision one in the outfield at a picnic with her arms spread wide open for a fly ball as for a descending man-angel. Luckily it didn't hit her in the mouth which was open too, or it might have hurt her beauty. It missed her entirely.

How do I know all this and with what authority do I speak? Have I not been written up as a pitcher in *The New Yorker* by the poet, Raymond Holden?—though the last full game I pitched in was on the grounds of Rockingham Park in Salem, New Hampshire, before it was turned into a race track. If I have shone at all in the all-star games at Breadloaf in Vermont it has been as a relief pitcher with a soft ball I despise like a picture window. Moreover I once took an honorary degree at Williams College along with a very famous pitcher, Ed Lewis, who will be remembered and found in the record to have led the National League in pitching quite a long time ago. His degree was not for pitching. Neither was mine. His was for presiding with credit over the University of New Hampshire and the Massachusetts College of Agriculture. He let me into the secret of how he could make a ball behave when his arm was just right. It may sound superstitious to the uninitiated, but he could push a cushion of air up ahead of it for it to slide off from any way it pleased. My great friendship for him probably accounts for my having made a trivial 10¢ bet on the National League today. He was a Welshman from Utica who, from having attended eisteddfods at Utica with his father, a bard, had like another Welsh friend of mine, Edward Thomas, in England, come to look on a poem as a performance one had to win. Chicago was my first favorite team because Chicago seemed the nearest city in the league to my original home town, San Francisco. I have conquered that prejudice. But I mean to see if the captain of it, Anson my boyhood hero, is in the Hall of Fame at Cooperstown where he belongs.

May I add to my self-citation that one of my unfulfilled promises on earth was to my fellow in art, Alfred Kreymborg, of an epic poem some day about a ball batted so hard by Babe Ruth that it never came back, but got to going round and round the world like a satellite. I got up the idea long before any artificial moon was thought of by the scientists. I meant to begin something like this:

> It was nothing to nothing at the end of the tenth
> And the prospects good it would last to the nth.

It needs a lot of work on it before it can take rank with *Casey at the Bat.*

In other words, some baseball is the fate of us all. For my part I am never more at home in America than at a baseball game like this in Clark Griffith's gem of a field, gem small, in beautiful weather in the capital of the country and my side winning. Here Walter Johnson flourished, who once threw a silver dollar across the Potomac (where not too wide) in emulation of George Washington, and here Gabby Street caught the bullet-like ball dropped from the top of George Washington's monument. It is the time and the place. And I have with me as consultant the well-known symbolist, Howard Schmitt of Buffalo, to mind my baseball slang and interpret the incidentals. The first player comes to the bat, Temple of the Redlegs, swinging two bats as he comes, the meaning of which or moral of which, I find on application to my consultant, is that we must always arrange to have just been doing something beforehand a good deal harder than what we are just going to do.

But when I asked him a moment later what it symbolized when a ball got batted into the stands and the people instead of dodging in terror fought each other fiercely to get and keep it and were allowed to keep it, Howard bade me hold on; there seemed to be a misunderstanding between us. When he accepted the job it was orally; he didn't mean to represent himself as a symbolist in the high-brow or middle-brow sense of the word, that is as a collegiate expounder of the double entendre for college classes; he was a common ordinary cymbalist in a local band somewhere out on the far end of the Eeryie Canal. We were both honest men. He didn't want to be taken for a real professor any more than I wanted to be taken for a real sport. His utmost wish was to contribute to the general noise when home runs were made. He knew they would be the most popular hits of the day. And they were—four of them from exactly the four they were expected from, Musial, Williams, Mays and Mantle. The crowd went wild four times. Howard's story would have been more plausible if he had brought his cymbals with him. I saw I would have to take care of the significances myself. This comes of not having got it in writing. The moral is always get it in writing.

Time was when I saw nobody on the field but the players. If I saw the umpire at all it was as an enemy for not taking my side. I may never have wanted to see bottles thrown at him so that he had to be taken out by the police. Still I often regarded him with the angry disfavor that the Democratic Party showed the Supreme Court in the '30s and other parties have shown it in other crises in our history. But now grown psychological, shading 100, I saw him as a figure of justice, who stood forth alone to be judged as a judge by people and players with whom he wouldn't last a week if suspected of the least lack of fairness or the least lack of faith in the possibility of fairness. I was touched by his loneliness and glad it was relieved a little by his being five in number, five in one so to speak, *e pluribus unum*. I have it from high up in the judiciary that some justices see in him an example to pattern after. Right there in front of me for reassurance is the umpire brought up perhaps in the neighborhood of Boston who can yet be depended upon not to take sides today for or against the American League the Boston Red Sox belong to. Let me celebrate the umpire for any influence for the better he may have on the Supreme Court. The justices suffer the same predicaments with him. I saw one batter linger perceptibly to say something to the umpire for calling him out on a third strike. I didn't hear what the batter said. One of the hardest things to accept as just is a called third strike.

It has been a day of prowess in spite of its being a little on the picnic side and possibly not as desperately fought as it might be in a World Series. Prowess, prowess, in about equal strength for both sides. Each team made 11 hits, two home runs and not a single error. The day was perfect, the scene perfect, the play perfect. Prowess of course comes first, the ability to perform with success in games, in the arts and, come right down to it, in battle. The nearest of kin to the artists in college where we all become bachelors of arts are their fellow performers in baseball, football and tennis. That's why I am so particular college athletics should be kept from corruption. They are close to the soul of culture. At any rate the Greeks thought so. Justice is a close second to prowess. When displayed toward each other by antagonists in war and peace, it is known as the nobility of noble natures. And I mustn't forget courage, for there is neither prowess nor justice without it. My fourth, if it is important enough in comparison to be worth bringing in, is knowledge, the mere information we can't get too much of and can't ever get enough of, we complain, before going into action.

As I say, I never feel more at home in America than at a ball game be it in park or in sandlot. Beyond this I know not. And dare not.

*Sports Illustrated*, July 23, 1956

# Maturity No Object

MATURITY is no object except perhaps in education where you might think from all the talk the aim and end of everything was to get sophisticated before educated. Shakespeare says it is the right virtue of the medlar to be rotten before it is ripe. Overdevelop the social conscience and make us all social meddlers. But I digress before I begin. My theme is not education, but poetry and how young one has to be or stay to make it. And it is not schools in general I reflect on, only bad schools which something should be done about before they get much larger. My excuse is that school and poetry come so near being one thing. Poetry has been a great concern of school all down the ages. A large part of reading in school always has been and still is poetry; and it is but an extension from the metaphors of poetry out into all thinking, scientific and philosophic. In fact the poet and scholar have so much in common and live together so naturally that it is easy to make too much of a mystery about where they part company. Their material seems the same—perhaps differs a little in being differently come by and differently held in play. Thoroughness is the danger of the scholar, dredging to the dregs. He works on assignment and self-assignment with some sense of the value of what he is getting when he is getting it. He is perhaps too avid of knowledge. The poet's instinct is to shun or shed more knowledge than he can swing or sing. His most available knowledge is acquired unconsciously. Something warns him dogged determination however profound can only result in doggerel. His danger is rhyming trivia. His depth is the lightsome blue depth of the air.

But I suppose the special distinction I was going to invest the poet with, that is making no object of maturity, was a mistake. It certainly belongs as much to the composer, the musician, the general, and I'm told the mathematician and the scientist. And it probably belongs to the scholar. Be that as it may, all poets I have ever heard of struck their note long before forty, the deadline for contributions to this book. The statistics are all in favor of their being as good and lyric as they will ever be. They may have ceased to be poets by the time appreciation catches up with them as Matthew Arnold complains somewhere. (I don't have to say exactly where because I'm not a scholar.) I have personal reasons to trust that they may go phasing on into being as good poets in their later mental ages. For my country's sake I might wish one or two of them an old age of epic writing. A good epic would grace our history. Landor has set an example in prolonging the lyric out of all bounds.

Maturity will come. We mature. But the point is that it is at best irrelevant. Young poetry is the breath of parted lips. For the spirit to survive, the mouth must find how to firm and not harden. I saw it in two faces in the same drawing room—one youth in Greek sculpture, the other manhood in modern painting. They were both noble. The man was no better than the boy nor worse because he was older. The poets of this group, many of them my friends and already known to many of us, need live to write no better, need only wait to be better known for what they have written.

The reader is more on trial here than they are. He is given his chance to see if he can tell all by himself without critical instruction the difference between the poets who wrote because they thought it would be a good idea to write and those who couldn't help writing out of a strong weakness for the Muse, as for an elopement with her. There should be some way to tell that just as there is to tell the excitement of the morning from the autointoxication of midnight. Any distinction between maturity and immaturity is not worth making unless as a precaution. If school is going to proclaim a policy of maturing boys and girls ultimately it might become necessary for us to stay away from school or at least play hooky a good deal to season slowly out of doors rather than in an oven or in a tanning vat. And that seems too bad; for so many of us like school and want to go there.

As I often say a thousand, two thousand, colleges, town and gown together in the little town they make, give us the best audiences for poetry poetry ever had in all this world. I am in on the ambition that this book will get to them—heart and mind.

Introduction to
*New Poets of England and America*, 1957

# Preface to
## 'A Swinger of Birches,'
### by Sidney Cox

THIS OUGHT to be a good book. Everybody who has seen it in manuscript says it is. The author probably knew me better than he knew himself and consequently contrariwise he very likely portrayed himself in it more than me. I trust it is in my favor. I know he would mean it to be. I don't read about myself well or easily. But I am always happier to hear that I am liked faults and all than that I am disliked. I had to tell Sidney once that I didn't believe it did me the least good to be told of the enemies he had had to defend me from. I have stolen look enough over the edge of the book to see that what went on between us is brought out much as in our correspondence. My letters to him I might mention are on deposit in the Dartmouth College library. I wish I had kept some of the great letters he wrote me but I am no curator of letters or anything else. He was at his best in his free letters. Yes, and of course in his teaching. A great teacher. He was all sincerity and frankness. He once wrote an article for the *New Republic* about *my* sincerity. I know that because it was in the title. We differed more in taste perhaps than in thinking. But we stood up to each other to support each other as two playing cards may be made to in building. I am a great equalitarian: I try to spend most of my time with my equals. He seemed worried at first lest it should appear I didn't seek him as much as he sought me. He respected me very highly. And he was more serious about such things than I. Not that he lacked a sense of humor. He liked a good story, and I am sure he would have enjoyed my version of our first encounter. It began one evening in 1911 when we met as strangers looking on at a school dance at Plymouth, New Hampshire, where we were both teachers, he in one school, I in another. I didn't know who he was except that he looked very teasably young. He didn't know who I was except, it seems, that I looked too old. By saying something flippant about the theme papers he had to hurry away to correct I angered him to the point of his inquiring behind my back if it was because of alcohol I had got no further up in the world at my age. I was thirty-seven. I was just teaching psychology in the Plymouth Normal School. He disdained to speak to me on the street for a while afterwards. But his seriousness piqued the mischief in me and I set myself to take him. He came round all right, but it wasn't the last time he had to make allowances for me. He worked at it devotedly. He must have been about half my age then. He was all of two thirds my age when he died. He was catching up. He was cut off before he came all the way through with himself. But he had made up his mind to much. My heart was in his literary success and I have hopes this is it.

*A Swinger of Birches*, 1957

# *To the Poets of Korea*

KOREA is much on our mind nowadays with its national sorrows. It did me good to meet your poetess Youn-Sook Moh and hear from her in person in her own excellent English that in spite of everything you still have poets and poetry to support you and cheer you on. Poetry and the other arts are for me what a country chiefly lives by. They mark national characters better than anything else. And they bring peoples together in spirit the more apparently that they separate them in language. The language barrier has so much to do with individuality and originality that we wouldn't want to see it removed. We must content ourselves with seeing it more or less got over by interpretation and translation. We must remember that one may be national without being poetical, but one can't be poetical without being national. Youn-Sook Moh's visit made me wish I had as much Korean to read your poetry as she had English to read ours. Bless you in the name of whatever Muse of poetry may preside over your works in Korea.

*Korea Times*, March 21, 1957

## "What Worries You Most About America Today?"

WORRIES is a hard word for me. I am interested in strengthening the high schools of America, bringing them up. A little thing I want is named chairs in the high schools. Once you got it, you would be in it for life. This would enrich the position of the high-school teacher. Their position is not dignified enough. The first chair, I'd have for mathematics. The other chair could be of the school's choosing. Instead of spraying money all over the colleges, I'd like to see something done for high-school teachers.

Esquire magazine, February 1958

# Merrill Moore

IT WAS a life overflowing with poetic sympathy, whether in or out of form. His professional treatments seemed on the principle of poetry toward all. He may have written too many of what it amused him to call sonnets. And then again he may not. Louis Untermeyer was saying the other day he may prevail by sheer force of numbers; and numbers is after all the old-fashioned name for poetry. It can't be expected that the hundred thousand pieces he tossed off and never looked back at will be taken without discrimination. Louis Untermeyer made a beginning on the formidable task. Already he and such admirers as John Crowe Ransom, Dudley Fitts, William Carlos Williams, and Theodore Morrison have penetrated to seeing the trees in the woods. He was one of John Ransom's remarkable children at Vanderbilt University.

Serious physician and serious artist, he had no notion of being taken lightly; still there was something of the rogue there that was a part of his great charm. He seldom more than cracked a smile. The first time he ever called me in on a case, and in fact the first time I ever met him, was thirty years ago after a big party at the St. Botolph Club. He had hardly asked me if like a country swain he might see me home before he asked if he might use me for a visit at that hour of night at the house of a lady patient. It would do her a world of good to talk literary with me in particular at that hour of night. Anything once I said. He briefed me: she was a case of wanting to try one more doctor to see if she couldn't be cured of not knowing how to write. It sounded hopeless. Wouldn't he just have to tell that girl to be good? As a last resort he might. I think he would rather tell her to be brave than good. Besides poetry he dispensed courage. Like the boys that go aloft to crash the sound barrier he was a rebuke to the stupid give-it-ups who are willing to have it that heroism is out of date.

On a visit to Sanibel Island he had the bright idea of shovelling up from the beach with his own hands a ton or two of sea shells and shipping them North for his patients to sort out. I wish you could hear the disc recording of his speech about the therapeutic value of this exercise in beauty. Possibly he thought it would do us the same kind of good to sort out the poems he left. Anyway I know he wouldn't mind my saying so.

No praise would mean anything to him that forgot he was a poet. Poetry was his rapture. He could hardly say it without singing it. I remember an evening out for a ride with him weaving through the traffic when he recited all of "L'Allegro" and "Il Penseroso" and to round them off with almost the same gentle sweetness and delight "The Ballad of the Revenge." On another evening he sang me somebody's setting of Omar. On another still in a cabaret he sang me and everybody present a long, long ballad of the World War (something he had picked up as Colonel in our army in China) to the ukulele accompaniment of a handsome Italian South Sea islander from South Boston. The South Sea islander might have sung it himself but for the laws of Petrillo. Merrill carried it off like a troubadour.

I looked for him once at Squantum. He was out swimming in the ocean somewhere between here and Europe. I might have to wait for him an hour or two. He was a great swimmer. He struck out boldly the same in the water as in poetry. As I have said he dispensed courage as well as poetry. He was a soldier poet, a true Tyrtaeus.

*Harvard Medical Alumni Bulletin,*
February 1958

# The Case of
# The United States of America
# versus Ezra Pound

I AM HERE to register my admiration for a government that can rouse in conscience to a case like this. Relief seems in sight for many of us besides the Ezra Pound in question and his faithful wife. He has countless admirers the world over who will rejoice in the news that he has hopes of freedom. I append a page or so of what they have been saying lately about him and his predicament. I myself speak as much in the general interest as in his. And I feel authorized to speak very specially for my friends, Archibald MacLeish, Ernest Hemingway and T. S. Eliot. None of us can bear the disgrace of our letting Ezra Pound come to his end where he is. It would leave too woeful a story in American literature. He went very wrong-headed in his egotism, but he insists it was from patriotism—love of America. He has never admitted that he went over to the enemy any more than the writers at home who have despaired of the Republic. I hate such nonsense and can only listen to it as an evidence of mental disorder. But mental disorder is what we are considering. I rest the case on Dr. Overholser's pronouncement that Ezra Pound is not too dangerous to go free in his wife's care, and too insane ever to be tried—a very nice discrimination.

Mr. Thurman Arnold admirably put this problem of a sick man being held too long in prison to see if he won't get well enough to be tried for a prison offense. There is probably legal precedent to help toward a solution of the problem. But I should think it would have to be reached more by magnanimity than by logic and it is chiefly on magnanimity I am counting. I can see how the Department of Justice would hesitate in the matter from fear of looking more just to a great poet than it would be to a mere nobody. The bigger the Department the longer it might have to take thinking things through.

Read in court by Thurman Arnold,
April 18, 1958

# On Being Appointed Consultant to the Library of Congress

WHAT would be said of me if I didn't hasten to acknowledge any notice taken of poetry by the government of the United States. One reason for my not hesitating is that poetry is my cause and so is the government of the United States. Another reason if needed would be more personal and selfish. I am far from insensible of the honor of being appointed as a poet to an office in the capital of the country among the rulers of the country. I have always thought and always said I should have liked nothing better than to be sent to Washington by my neighbors at home. I have envied with admiration the lives of fine senators like Flanders and Aiken from the state I vote in, but since there was no hope of my being elected like them by backers behind I can content myself with being selected from in front and a way may be found for my taking some small part in what I like to call politics. My father was seriously ambitious to represent California in Congress but he died young and never got nearer Washington than with a small book on the life of General Rosecrans in the Library to which I am becoming consultant. The inclination I myself own I had towards affairs of state will be amply and handsomely satisfied by the small token job I am to have down there. I promise.

I was not brought up to the distrust of politics that so many scholars and artists seem to suffer from. Neither was I to distrust of big business for that matter. Nor of small business either. Long before my luck changed I went on record as willing to accept the trial by market everything must come to.

I never believed in our being stand-offish with statesmen or letting them be stand-offish with us any more than we can help. Some of them are much more able than cultivated. A pathetic uneasiness often shows itself in their hurry to turn us over to their womenfolk to deal with. We are much more sympathetic with them however than they are with us. And we understand them better than they understand us. We know what's good for them better than they know what's good for us. And we're supposed to have language and should be willing to use it with them. I never shared the common artistic prejudice against politics that tends to make artists too arty. I'm no Platonist to agree with Plato that the philosopher should be king. Neither do I agree with him that the poet should be suppressed. The poet would make a better king than the philosopher. Anyway poetry has had something to do with the magnificence of great government. But I mustn't slur philosophy. I wasn't brought up to distrust philosophy or politics either. I look on enterprise as all one. In a great period there should be great statesmen, great soldiers, great artists, and great men of business. The whole nation seems full of one great undertaking. We have had two such times when we were flushed with spirit.

The Capital should be a place where all the ambitions should be thrown together in emulation and rivalry. I am only saying what should be, not what is. Give us an inch and we'll take an ell. There came a day when it occurred to someone that labor should be represented in Washington. My small toehold is in danger of rousing the proletariat to feeling the need of a Secretary of Poetry. My office will be merely that of consultant to everybody in general. I suppose even a statesman might consult me about what to do next.

May 1958 (?)

# The Way There

It would be the footpath way. "Jog on, jog on, the footpath way and merrily hent the stile-a." The measured way, so many feet to the mile-a; so many feet to the line, seldom less than two or more than five in our language. Footbeats for the metre and heartbeats for the rhythm. The unevenness of the heartbeats will keep the footbeats from jogging dogged to the point of doggerel. You may not realize it, but it is the way you have all come thus far from the days of your Godmother Goose through books and nature, gathering bits and scraps of real magic that however flowery still clung to you like burrs thrown on your clothes in holiday foolery. You don't have to worry about clinging to such trophies. They will cling to you.

Sometimes it is a whole poem if short enough that takes possession of you. A little girl I heard of got so possessed of one of the poems in this book that she must hurry home and recite it to her mother. When her mother said, "Why, my dear, I knew that poem before you were born," the little girl came back with, "Then why didn't you tell me?" But perhaps it is parts of poems that season into most meaning for us. They will come lilting to mind unexpectedly in the most remote situations. We must remember that poetry is said to have been invented as an aid to memory. It might be described as the most unforgettable experience man can have of words. No painting can do the source of light. No poem even can describe itself. And here I am trying to define poetry in prose.

I could almost wish the stile of my quotation was spelled with a "y" so that I could use it for the airs and graces of poetry. The way there may be as airily as a bird's from tree to tree or as a squirrel's, or anyway a flying squirrel's, without touching the ground. It may be as airily airy as the course I have taken through this book with an inner logic I don't have to account for from the poem "Birches" to the poem "Wild Grapes." The first birches were trees I swung near the district school I went to in Salem, New Hampshire. The birch of "Wild Grapes" was one a girl swung in when she didn't weigh enough to bring it to earth. She told me about it eighty years later and asked me to write a poem about it for girls to match

847

the other birch poem that she claimed was written for boys. She clenched her hands in memory of the pain of having had to hang on in the tree too long. I had to write the poem for her because she was the first editor ever to publish me. Her name was Susan Hayes Ward. The poem was the first thing in prose or verse I ever wrote to order. She was my first publisher unless I count the Senior in the Lawrence High School who published three years earlier in our high school paper the first thing in prose or verse I ever wrote at all. And his name was Ernest Jewell.

The way there may be from tree to tree as in this book. Some day in another book, it may be from Nicasio to Ripton "if it comes in my mind just right."

Unpublished preface, summer 1958

# Preface to an Expanded
## 'North of Boston'

*North of Boston* (I want it to say) was not written as a book nor towards a book. It was written as scattered poems in a form suggested by the eclogues of Virgil. Beginning with one about Julius Caesar in the year I was reading about Aenius and Meliboeus, luckily (I consider it) in no vain attempt to Anglicize Virgil's versification, dactylic hexameter. It gathered itself together in retrospect and found a name for itself in the real estate advertising of the *Boston Globe*. It was written along with all sorts of briefer things in rhyme. It was what was left after these had gone through the sieve. Its public acceptance seemed to call for a sequel. At the time nothing seemed further from my mind. I even scouted the idea when it was proposed to me. But it turned out in the natural course of events that I was to write a second *North of Boston* and even a third as unintentionally as I had written the first. Only recently it has occurred to me that they may as well be added to the first under the same head in summing up. Some of them are a little nearer one act plays than eclogues but they seem to have something in common that I don't want to seek a better name for. I like its being locative.

Unpublished manuscript, 1958 (?)

# Dorothy Canfield

DOROTHY CANFIELD was the great lady of Vermont just as
someone else we all admire might be called the great lady
of the United States. But there was more to it than just that.
It was as a great story teller with a book called "Hillsboro
People" that I was introduced to her by her publisher,
Alfred Harcourt, who was then my publisher too. There was
nothing she was happier in than story telling in prose and
speech unless it was doing good to everybody and anybody.
She came from all directions from as far West as Kansas and
from as far East as France. She was brought up by a no-
madic mother who pursued the practice of art in Paris and
New York. I believe she won her doctorate in old French
at Columbia University. But everything that ever happened
or occurred to her converged as into a napkin ring and
came out wide on the other side of it Vermontly. I don't
know whether she realized it or not, but even the Basques
she lived with and wrote about read to me like Vermonters.
The people of her witchcraft story among the Basques
might well be Ethan Allen's Green Mountain boys.

Her benefactions weren't restricted to Vermont (I con-
sider her work with the Book of the Month Club one of
them). But of course they were most intimately felt there all
up and down the state. She made it a welfare state. I re-
member her remarking that the Puritan word Common-
wealth meant exactly the same thing. Her great good nature
kept her from thinking too hard about doctrines, though
she was plainly proud of a Vermont ancestry, Episcopalian,
among the other sects non-conformist that came up from
Connecticut and Rhode Island to settle the state.

Alfred Harcourt brought our families together from a no-
tion he had that the White Mountains we lived in were
neighborly to the Green Mountains she lived in. Many are
our family obligations to her. She is often in our thoughts.
Only the other day my granddaughter fresh from college
asked me about her young resolution to devote her life
to doing good. I used a parable to make it out better to

do well. She was unconvinced. Hers was the last word: "Wouldn't it be enough of an ideal to do good well—like Dorothy Canfield?"

*Dorothy Canfield Fisher:*
*In Memorium, 1958*

# "Books That Have Meant the Most"

THE BOOKS that have meant the most to me in my lifetime:

1—The Old Testament.

2—"The Odyssey," by Homer.

3—"The Poems of Catullus."

4—"The Decline and Fall of the Roman Empire," by Edward Gibbon.

5—"Incidents of Travel in Yucatan," by John L. Stevens.

*Chicago Tribune,* November 30, 1958

# Conversations on the Craft of Poetry

WITHERS: Mr. Frost, I once heard you say that for a poem to stick it must have a dramatic accent.

FROST: If it doesn't, it will not stay in anybody's head. It won't be *catchy*. . . .

Catchiness has a lot to do with it, all of it, all the way up from the ballads you hear on the street to the lines in Shakespeare that stay with you without your trying to remember them. I just say catchy. They stick on you like burrs thrown on you in holiday foolery. You don't have to try to remember them. It's from the way they're said, you know, an archness or something.

WARREN: Well, I'm sure you're right about the dramatic quality being the basic quality of good poetry. That would bring up the relation of meter and rhythm to the dramatic moment—moment by moment—in a poem, wouldn't it?

FROST: That's right.

WARREN: I'd like to hear you say it in your way, how meter enters into this picture—the dramatic quality.

FROST: The meter seems to be the basis of—the waves and the beat of the heart seems to be basic in all making of poetry in all languages—some sort of meter.

WARREN: The strain of the rhythm against the meter. Is that itself just a dramatic fact that permeates a poem?

FROST: From those two things rises what we call this tune that's different from the tune of the other kind of music. It's a music of itself. And when people say that this will easily turn into—be set to music, I think it's bad writing. It ought to fight being set to music if it's got expression in it.

BROOKS: Yes, there's something resistant and unique in it; you can't just turn it into something else. This is to overstate the matter, but I do want to get it clear, if I can for myself: Would you say that even though the meter is based on the human pulse or some kind of basic rhythm in our natures, still for the poet it's something to be played over against—it's something to be fought with, to be tussled with? It's not directly expressive—ta-DA, ta-DA, ta-DA, ta-DA, ta-DA.

FROST: No, it's doggerel when you do that. You see, and

how you save it from doggerel is having enough dramatic meaning in it for the other thing to break the doggerel. And it mustn't break *with* it.

I said years ago that it reminds me of a donkey and a donkey cart; for some of the time the cart is on the tugs and some of the time on the hold-backs. You see it's that way all the time. The one's doing that and the other—the one's holding the thing back and the other's pushing it forward—and so on, back and forward. . . . I puzzled over it many years and tried to make people see what I meant. They use the word "rhythm" about a lot of free verse; and gee, what's the good of the rhythm unless it is on something that trips it—that it ruffles? You know, it's got to ruffle the meter.

BROOKS: Isn't this the fault of—to name the name of a man who did write some very fine poems, I think: Vachel Lindsay depends too much on just the doggerel—the stamp of the. . . .

FROST: Singsong, yes. And you know when he had something else, he thought he ought to put a note about it in the margin. Did you notice that?

BROOKS: Yes, to tell you how to read it.

FROST: "Say this in a golden tone," he says. You ought not to have to say that in the margin.

BROOKS: No, no. It's built in.

FROST: That ought to be in the meaning. This is why you have to have a meaning, 'cause you don't know what to do with anything if you don't have a meaning. It makes you act up; you've got to act up.

"What sayest thou, old barrelful of lies?" Chaucer says. What d'you say, "old barrelful of lies"? And you can hear it talk just the same today—and all of it. That's why it exists. It's beautiful, anywhere you look into Chaucer:

> Since I from love escaped am so fat,
> I never think to have been in his prison lean;
> Since I am free, I count him not a bean.

This is Chaucer talking too. It's just the same now. I hear the country people talking, England and here, with these same ways of acting up. Put it that way—call it "acting up."

You act up when you talk. Some do more than others. Some

little children do: some just seem to be rather straight line, but some switch their whole body when they talk—switch their skirts. *Expressiveness* comes over them. Words aren't enough.

And of course all before words came the expressiveness—groans and murmurs and things like that emerging into words. And some few of these linger, like "um-hnm" and "unh-unh" and "mmm" and all our groans. By myself sometimes I groan at something already done that I'd like to avert.

WARREN: From a groan to a sonnet's a straight line.

FROST: Yes, that's right.

WARREN: You are distinguishing, then, the meaning in the most limited sense from the over-all, felt meaning of the whole thing. Is that it?

FROST: That's your whole guide, the over-all meaning.

WARREN: That's your guide and your end product.

FROST: Yes, your end product. And also, you know, one of the funny things is that this *mood* you're writing in foretells the end product. See, it begins sort of that way and a way of talking that foretells the end product. There's a logic of that sort of thing.

Somebody said to be a master writer you don't have to wait for your moods. That'd be like Browning as he got older. You get to be a virtuoso, and you aren't a poet any more. He'd lost his moods somewhere. He'd got to be a master. We don't want to be masters.

WARREN: In other words you don't want even to be master—is that right?—of the particular poem. Before you start you're moving from mood to the exploration of the mood, is that it?

BROOKS: Poem is a discovery. . . .

FROST: Yes, that's right. You're on a little voyage of discovery. And there's a logic in it. You're going to come out somewhere with great certainty. And you can tell whether you've lost it on the way. And you throw the poem away—if you lose it.

WARREN: Yes.

FROST: Down the years, looking back over it all. And you see, a good many who think they're writing free verse are really writing old-fashioned iambic. A good deal of Whitman's like that, and a lot of Masters is like that: he just never got away from blank verse—the sound of blank verse.

And so there are places where this thing takes place that I'm talking about—there's both the meter and the expressiveness on it—and so we get a poem.

Ezra Pound used to say that you've got to get all the meter out of it—extirpate the meter. If you do, maybe you've got true free verse, and I don't want any of it!

WARREN: Well, you can go at it another way: I guess it's Winters who said that behind all good free verse—I may be misinterpreting him, but I think that's what he says—behind all good free verse there's a shadow of formal verse.

FROST: That's right. And if we hadn't had the years of formal verse, this stuff wouldn't be any good, you know. The shadow is there; that's what gives it any charm it has. You see, I'm hard on free verse a little—too hard, I know.

BROOKS: Would you be hard, Mr. Frost, also, on the business of the beatniks and chanting poetry to jazz? Is that letting too much of music—of the wrong side of music come in?

FROST: Yes, absolutely. Death! Hang 'em all!

This fellow that's going to talk with me (A. P. Herbert from London) tomorrow, they've told me what his prejudices are, you know, to see if they couldn't rouse me to say something to him. He's in favor of hanging delinquent children. That's the funniest prejudice. And he'd be in favor of exterminating the free-verse writers, I'm pretty sure. I'm not as bad as that.

Let's put it this way, that prose and verse are alike in having high poetic possibilities of ideas, and free verse is anywhere you want to be between those two things, prose and verse. I like to say, guardedly, that I could define poetry this way: It is that which is lost out of both prose and verse in translation. That means something in the way the words are curved and all that—the way the words are taken, the way you take the words.

WARREN: The best-order notion: the old Coleridgean best-order notion.

FROST: Yes, I'm pretty extreme about it.

You know, I've given offense by saying that I'd as soon write free verse as play tennis with the net down. I want something there—the other thing—something to hold and something for me to put a strain on; and I'd be lost in the air with just cutting loose—unless I'm in my other mood of making it prose right out, you know, and I don't write much of that. But that's another thing. . . .

BROOKS: Speaking of tune, Yeats said that he started a poem with a little tune in his head.

FROST: Yeats said a good many things, and I've talked with him about that. He said that nothing he hated more than having his poems set to music. It stole the show. It wasn't the tune he heard in his ear. And what this other thing is. . . . If he meant a tune, it doesn't seem to go with that, does it?

Burns without any doubt had old music—old songs—in his head that he wrote from. But I don't think that of Yeats; I don't know what he meant by that. But if he meant a tune. . . . I have a tune, but it's a tune of the blend of these two things. Something rises—it's neither one of these things. It's neither the meter nor the rhythm; it's a tune arising from the stress on those—same as your fingers on the strings, you know. The twang!

WARREN: The twang.

FROST: The twang of one on the other. And I don't know what he meant. I think he must have meant what we mean: from a result of something beginning to rise from it right away when you're playing one on the other; that's what he carried. There must be a oneness as you're doing it. You aren't putting two things together—laying them together. It isn't synthetic like that; no.

BROOKS: No, it's growing a plant, not building a wall.

WARREN: Growing in terms of this dominating mood—is that right?—that you referred to as a germ of the poem?

FROST: Yes.

WARREN: The tune is the mood groping for its logic, is that it? Something like that?

FROST: That's right; that's right, yes. I'm glad that we feel that way together. Yes, you know that, when I begin a poem I don't know—I don't want a poem that I can tell was written toward a good ending—one sentence, you know. That's trickery. You've got to be the happy discoverer of your ends.

BROOKS: That's a very fine way of phrasing it, "the happy discoverer of your end." Because otherwise it is contrived. You can see it coming a mile off.

FROST: A mile away.

I've often said that another definition of poetry is dawn—that it's something dawning on you while you're writing it. It comes off if it really dawns when the light comes at the end. And the feeling of dawn—the freshness of dawn—that you didn't think this all out and write it in prose first and then translate it into verse. That's abhorrent! . . .

One of the things that I notice with myself is that I can't make certain word sounds go together, sometimes; they won't say. This has got something to do with the way one vowel runs into another, the way one syllable runs into another. And then I never know—I don't like to reason about that too much. I don't understand it, but I've changed lines because there was something about them that my ear refused. And I suppose it has something to do with this vowels and consonants.

You know what I've thought sometimes: that the mouth and throat are like this, that it's certain sounds are here, and you can't go right from this one to that one; you've got to go like this. The mouth's got to be doing that inside. I don't know.

But gee, you know, I don't want any science of it. It's got to be—not trial and error. You don't correct it if you're going well—if you're felicitous—if you're having a happy day.

Well, we've come a good way. And it's fun. I don't often sit with somebody to talk about it this way. Sometimes from the platform I say some of these things, you know. And I used to do it more than I do it now. I had a notion I had to tell the public how to read lines. Then I decided no; that's in them anyway. They all had Mother Goose and everything. Don't you see that you throw them back on their Mother Goose? And then all with the play of ideas in it; how deep the Mother Goose is, you see:

> Pussy cat, pussy cat, where have you been?
> I've been to London to see the Coronation!

To pervert a little:

> Pussy cat, pussy cat, what did you see there?
> I saw nothing but what I might have seen just
>     as well by staying right here in Nashville!
> I saw a mouse run under a chair.

And that's very deep. But it's so pretty the way it's set off, you know, and nobody need see it at all unless they're any discerning. "I saw a mouse run under a chair." That's meant a lot to me, that has, all my life.

WARREN: That's a good one.

FROST: That's what makes regionalists, you see. You could stay right at home and see it all.

You know another thing I think belongs to poetry is fresh observation, don't you? All the time, little insights. They say "nothing new," but there is all the time. For instance, I was saying about women the other day—they were plaguing me to leave some boys I wanted to talk to; they thought I was getting tired or something. Finally I turned on them, and I said, "A woman would rather take care of you than listen to you think."

WARREN: That's a mark of a good woman.

FROST: And then I softened that to them by saying, "That's why we like you, my dears. You see, because we know that what we think doesn't amount to much anyway, we men." You see, that was a fresh observation.

WARREN: Well, the mere observation of just the facts of the world is a constant refresher for poetry. It's a waking up of yourself when you get the least little turn of an observation of the way a leaf or a light is, or something.

FROST: Little insights into a character and a little observation of something growing. You know how it does, something with life.

Recorded conversation with Cleanth Brooks,
Robert Penn Warren, and Kenny Withers, 1959

# On Emerson

ALL THAT ADMIRATION for me I am glad of. I am here out of admiration for Emerson and Thoreau. Naturally on the proud occasion I should like to make myself as much of an Emersonian as I can. Let me see if I can't go a long way. You may be interested to know that I have right here in my pocket a little first edition of Emerson's poetry. His very first was published in England just as was mine. His book was given me on account of that connection by Fred Melcher, who takes so much pleasure in bringing books and things together like that.

I suppose I have always thought I'd like to name in verse some day my four greatest Americans: George Washington, the general and statesman; Thomas Jefferson, the political thinker; Abraham Lincoln, the martyr and savior; and fourth, Ralph Waldo Emerson, the poet. I take these names because they are going around the world. They are not just local. Emerson's name has gone as a poetic philosopher or as a philosophical poet, my favorite kind of both.

I have friends it bothers when I am accused of being Emersonian, that is, a cheerful Monist, for whom evil does not exist, or if it does exist, needn't last forever. Emerson quotes Burns as speaking to the Devil as if he could mend his ways. A melancholy dualism is the only soundness. The question is is soundness of the essence.

My own unsoundness has a strange history. My mother was a Presbyterian. We were here on my father's side for three hundred years but my mother was fresh a Presbyterian from Scotland. The smart thing when she was young was to be reading Emerson and Poe as it is today to be reading St. John Perse or T. S. Eliot. Reading Emerson turned her into a Unitarian. That was about the time I came into the world; so I suppose I started a sort of Presbyterian-Unitarian. I was transitional. Reading on into Emerson, that is into "Representative Men" until she got to Swedenborg, the Mystic, made her a Swedenborgian. I was brought up in all three of these religions, I suppose. I don't know whether I was baptized in them all. But as you see it was pretty much under the auspices of

Emerson. It was all very Emersonian. Phrases of his began to
come to me early. In that essay on the mystic he makes Swe-
denborg say that in the highest heaven nothing is arrived at
by dispute. Everybody votes in heaven but everybody votes
the same way as in Russia today. It is only in the second-
highest heaven that things get parliamentary; we get the two-
party system or the hydra-headed as in France.

Some of my first thinking about my own language was cer-
tainly Emersonian. "Cut these sentences and they bleed," he
says. I am not submissive enough to want to be a follower,
but he had me there. I never got over that. He came pretty
near making me an anti-vocabularian with the passage in
"Monadnock" about our ancient speech. He blended praise
and dispraise of the country people of New Hampshire. As an
abolitionist he was against their politics. Forty per cent of
them were states rights Democrats in sympathy with the
South. They were really pretty bad, my own relatives included.

> "The God who made New Hampshire
> Taunted the lofty land
> With little men;—"

And if I may be further reminiscent parenthetically, my friend
Amy Lowell hadn't much use for them either. "I have left
New Hampshire," she told me. Why in the world? She
couldn't stand the people. What's the matter with the people?
"Read your own books and find out." They really differ from
other New Englanders, or did in the days of Franklin Pierce.

But now to return to the speech that was his admiration
and mine in a burst of poetry in "Monadnock":

> "Yet wouldst thou learn our ancient speech
> These the masters that can teach.
> Fourscore or a hundred words
> All their vocal muse affords.
> Yet they turn them in a fashion
> Past the statesman's art and passion.
> Rude poets of the tavern hearth
> Squandering your unquoted mirth,
> That keeps the ground and never soars,
> While Jake retorts and Reuben roars.

Scoff of yeoman, strong and stark,
Goes like bullet to the mark,
And the solid curse and jeer
Never balk the waiting ear."

Fourscore or a hundred is seven hundred less than my friend Ivor Richards' basic eight hundred. I used to climb on board a load of shooks (boxes that haven't been set up) just for the pleasure I had in the driver's good use of his hundred word limit. This at the risk of liking it so much as to lose myself in mere picturesqueness. I was always in favor of the solid curse as one of the most beautiful of figures. We were warned against it in school for its sameness. It depends for variety on the tones of saying it and the situations.

I had a talk with John Erskine the first time I met him on this subject of sentences that may look tiresomely alike, short and with short words, yet turn out as calling for all sorts of ways of being said aloud or in the mind's ear, Horatio. I took Emerson's prose and verse as my illustration. Writing is un-boring to the extent that it is dramatic.

In a recent preface to show my aversion to being inter-rupted with notes in reading a poem, I find myself resorting to Emerson again. I wanted to be too carried away for that. There was much of "Brahma" that I didn't get to begin with but I got enough to make me sure I would be back there reading it again some day when I had read more and lived more; and sure enough without help from dictionary or en-cyclopaedia I can now understand every line in it but one or two. It is a long story of many experiences that let me into the secret of:

"But thou, meek lover of the good!
Find me, and turn thy back on heaven."

What baffled me was the Christianity in "Meek lover of the good." I don't like obscurity and obfuscation, but I do like dark sayings I must leave the clearing of to time. And I don't want to be robbed of the pleasure of fathoming depths for myself. It was a moment for me when I saw how Shakespeare set bounds to science when he brought in the North Star, "Whose worth's unknown although his height be taken." Of untold worth: it brings home some that should and some that shouldn't come. Let the psychologist take notice how unsuccessful he has to be.

I owe more to Emerson than anyone else for troubled thoughts about freedom. I had the hurt to get over when I first heard us made fun of by foreigners as the land of the free and the home of the brave. Haven't we won freedom? Is there no such thing as freedom? Well, Emerson says God

> "Would take the sun out of the skies
> Ere freedom out of a man."

and there rings the freedom I choose.

Never mind how and where Emerson disabused me of my notion I may have been brought up to that the truth would make me free. My truth will bind you slave to me. He didn't want converts and followers. He was a Unitarian. I am on record as saying that freedom is nothing but departure—setting forth—leaving things behind, brave origination of the courage to be new. We may not want freedom. But let us not deceive ourselves about what we don't want. Freedom is one jump ahead of formal laws as in planes and even automobiles right now. Let's see the law catch up with us very soon.

Emerson supplies the emancipating formula for giving an attachment up for an attraction, one nationality for another nationality, one love for another love. If you must break free

> "Heartily know,
> When half-gods go
> The gods arrive."

I have seen it invoked in *Harper's Magazine* to excuse disloyalty to our democracy in a time like this. But I am not sure of the reward promised. There is such a thing as getting too transcended. There are limits. Let's not talk socialism. I feel projected out from politics with lines like:

> "Musketaquit, a goblin strong,
> Of shards and flints makes jewels gay;
> They lose their grief who hear his song,
> And where he winds is the day of day.

> So forth and brighter fares my stream,—
> Who drink it shall not thirst again;
> No darkness stains its equal gleam,
> And ages drop in it like rain."

Left to myself I have gradually come to see what Emerson was meaning in "Give all to Love" was Give all to Meaning. The freedom of all freedoms is ours to insist on meaning.

The kind of story Steinbeck likes to tell is about an old labor hero punch drunk from fighting the police in many strikes, beloved by everybody at headquarters as the greatest living hater of tyranny. I take it that the production line was his grievance. The only way he could make it mean anything was to try to ruin it. He took arms and fists against it. No one could have given him that kind of freedom. He saw it as his to seize. He was no freedman; he was a free man. The one inalienable right is to go to destruction in your own way. What's worth living for is worth dying for. What's worth succeeding in is worth failing in.

If you have piled up a great rubbish heap of oily rags in the basement for your doctor's thesis and it won't seem to burst into flame spontaneously, come away quickly and without declaring rebellion. It will cost you only your Ph.D. Union Card and the respect of the Union. But it will hardly be noticed even to your credit in the world. All you have to do is to amount to something anyway. The only reprehensible materiality is the materialism of getting lost in your material so you can't find out yourself what it is all about.

A young fellow came to me to complain of the department of philosophy in his university. "There wasn't a philosopher in it. I can't stand it." He was really complaining of his situation. He wasn't where he could feel real. But I didn't tell him so I didn't go into that. I agreed with him that there wasn't a philosopher in his university—there was hardly ever more than one at a time in the world—and I advised him to quit. Light out for somewhere. He hated to be a quitter. I told him the Bible says, "Quit ye, like men." "Does it?" he said. "Where would I go?" Why anywhere almost. Kamchatka, Madagascar, Brazil. I found him doing well in the educational department of Rio when I was sent on an errand down there by our government several years later. I had taken too much responsibility for him when I sent him glimmering like that. I wrote to him with troubled conscience and got no answer for two whole years. But the story has a happy ending. His departure was not suicidal. I had a post card from him this Christmas to tell me he was on Robinson Crusoe's island Juan Fernandez on his way to Easter Island that it had always been a necessity for him someday to see. I would next hear from him in Chile where he was to be employed in helping restore two colleges. Two! And the colleges were universities!

No subversive myself I think it very Emersonian of me that I am so sympathetic with subversives, rebels, runners out, runners out ahead, eccentrics, and radicals. I don't care how extreme their enthusiasm so long as it doesn't land them in the Russian camp. I always wanted one of them teaching in the next room to me so my work would be cut out for me warning the children taking my courses not to take his courses.

I am disposed to cheat myself and others in favor of any poet I am in love with. I hear people say the more they love anyone the more they see his faults. Nonsense. Love is blind and should be left so. But it hasn't been hidden in what I have said that I am not quite satisfied with the easy way Emerson takes disloyalty. He didn't know or ignored his Blackstone. It is one thing for the deserter and another for the deserted. Loyalty is that for the lack of which your gang will shoot you without benefit of trial by jury. And serves you right. Be as treacherous as you must be for your ideals, but don't expect to be kissed good-bye by the idol you go back on. We don't want to look too foolish, do we? And probably Emerson was too Platonic about evil. It was a mere Τὸ μὴ ὄν that could be disposed of like the butt of a cigarette. In a poem I have called the best Western poem yet he says:

"Unit and universe are round."

Another poem could be made from that to the effect that ideally in thought only is a circle round. In practice, in nature, the circle becomes an oval. As a circle it has one center—Good. As an oval it has two centers—Good and Evil. Thence Monism versus Dualism.

Emerson was a Unitarian because he was too rational to be superstitious and too little a story teller and lover of stories to like gossip and pretty scandal. Nothing very religious can be done for people lacking in superstition. They usually end up abominable agnostics. It takes superstition and the prettiest scandal story of all to make a good Trinitarian. It is the first step in the descent of the spirit into the material-human at the risk of the spirit.

But if Emerson had left us nothing else he would be remembered longer than the Washington Monument for the monument at Concord that he glorified with lines surpassing any other ever written about soldiers:

> "By the rude bridge that arched the flood
> Their flag to April breeze unfurled
> Here once the embattled farmers stood
> And fired the shot heard round the world."

Not even Thermopylae has been celebrated better. I am not a shriner but two things I never happen on unmoved: one, this poem on stone, and the other, the tall shaft seen from Lafayette Park across the White House in Washington.

*Daedalus,* fall 1959

# The Future of Man

IT's the word "challenge" that interests me, of course—the challenge of the future to the prophet—and I am the prophet. I am going to tell you about the future—I'm not going to advocate the future; I'm going to tell you what it will be.

The standing challenge—the great challenge—is of man's originality to his law and order, to his government. And that will always be the challenge—that of man's energy and daring and originality to his law and order. That means that looking ahead into the future with my eyes shut—I see government paired with government for the championship of its era—to see after whom the period will be named, in this era for instance, us or the Russ. Unfortunately, we haven't a very good name for ourselves. All my South American friends object to our calling ourselves America—we shall have to call ourselves "us," to rhyme with "Russ."

Add to that, that there will always be an issue for the two powers to pair off on, and the Lord is the Great Provider; He'll provide the issue. There's always been an issue, a great issue, a grave issue, like the one between Persia and Greece, Rome and Carthage, Christendom and Islam—for every period. We see a great issue today. I never can bear to blackguard an enemy; I like him to be an intelligible enemy, a worthy antagonist.

Next, are we going on to be another kind of people? Young people of our day, in studying anthropology and listening to the anthropologists, think it's such an amusing distance between the monkeys and us that it will only be another amusing distance from us to the superman. It's a field day for all comic strip teasers, you see, every man can make his own comic strip. Let me tell you about that—I know just what's going to happen or not happen. Our self-consciousness is terminal—there's nothing beyond us. Life in us has reached a self-consciousness that terminates the growth.

I saw a little while ago a list of all the thoughts man has had—published in Chicago, I think. There weren't over a hundred or two. I looked for the word evolution, and there it was. I looked for the word growth, the plain word growth, and there it wasn't. Apparently in Chicago growth is not an idea but I take it that evolution comes under the head of growth. Only it has a strange illusory way of making you think it goes on forever. But all growth is limited—the tree of life is limited like a maple tree or an oak tree—they all have a certain height, and they all have a certain life-length. And our tree, the tree Yggdrasil, has reached its growth. It doesn't have to fall down because it's stopped growing. It will go on blossoming and havings its seasons—I'd give it another hundred or two hundred million years. Make that anything you please. It'll go on leaving out and blooming into successions of the doubleness, I foresee, just like the doubleness of the sexes. There'll be two parties always to it, some way. I hope that this tree is self-fertilizing—I guess I hadn't thought of that—and it doesn't need another tree besides it, and in itself has all the doubleness I ask, good and evil, two sexes, one of *them* good and the other evil.

I wish the young people would relieve themselves of the responsibility of attending to the future of our height. There's nothing coming beyond us. The tree Yggdrasil has reached its growth.

Then I want to say another thing about the god who provides the great issues. He's a god of waste, magnificent waste. And waste is another name for generosity of not always being intent on our own advantage, nor too importunate even for a better world. We pour out a libation to him as a symbol of the waste we share in—participate in. Pour it on the ground and you've wasted it; pour it into yourself and you've doubly wasted it. But all in the cause of generosity and relaxation of self interest.

But I think I've said enough about it. There are many details that I had in mind, but I don't want to be too long about it. The point is that the challenge will always be there between man's originality and his law and order, his government. I sometimes think the scientists have got themselves scared; they're afraid they'll run away with themselves they are so original. They needn't worry; the executives will take care of them.

*The Future of Man*, 1959

# The Future of Man
*(unpublished version)*

CHALLENGE seems to be the word. I have never before used it in prose or verse. I should hope the meaning of it hadn't escaped me. There is the challenge of the future to the prophet: guess me. The great challenge, the eternal challenge, is that of man's bursting energy and originality to his own governance. His speed and his traffic police. We become an organized society only as we tell off some of our number to be law-givers and law-enforcers, a blend of general and lawyer, to hold fast the line and turn the rest of us loose for scientists, philosophers, and poets to make the break-through, the revolution, if we can for refreshment. Science is the most formidable in challenge but philosophy has been formidable too. Philosophers have had to be given hemlock and burned at the stake. The party of the holding part, the defender of the state and status, is of course the chief executive. Let us call him king for short and for the purposes of this conclave.

The challenge of science to government takes the form of asking What will you do with our latest? Will you use it as a weapon or a tool or both? If you ignore it, we shall go elsewhere with it and try it on your rivals. If you suppress it, we will do the same.

The challenge of science to the run of us, the small fry intelligentsia, takes the form of asking What are you going to say to our latest? How are you going to take our having hit the moon for Russia? With chagrin rightly. You should hate not to win. Nothing can be done with people who don't mind losing. You are not that bad. It must have been more painful for you to be beaten in the race for the moon than it would have been to lose the races at Melbourne. You seem thrown into consternation and confusion by the truck load of new words for fuel we poured rattling down the chute into your old coal bin in the cellar. Find something to say to our posers. You must learn to sass the Sphinx. It seems a shame to come on you with our new novelties when you are hardly up around after what Darwin, Spencer, and Huxley did to you last century. But I suppose you will be taken care of as you were the last time by the king's editorial writers, column writers, and commentators. Remember how you were helped by being reminded all you were asked to do was change from your old idea that God made man out of mud to the new idea that God made man out of prepared mud.

Now science seems about to ask us what we are going to do about taking in hand our own further evolution. This is some left-over business from the great Darwinian days. Every school boy knows how amusingly short the distance was from monkeys to us. Well it ought not to be much longer from us to supermen. We have the laboratorians ready and willing to tend to this. We can commission them any day to go ahead messing around with rays on genes for mutations or with sperm on ovules for eugenics till they get us somewhere, make something of us for a board or foundation to approve of. But I am asked to be prophetic. As far into the future as I can see with my eyes shut people are still pairing for love and money, perhaps just superstitious enough to leave their direction to what the mystic Karl Marx called historical necessity but what I like to call passionate preference, to the taste there's no disputing about. I foresee no society where artificial insemination won't be in bad taste.

But while I am in the mood to comply, why don't I go on prophesying to the limit? I am in danger of making all this sound as if science were all. It is not all. But it is much. It comes into our lives as domestic science for our hold on the planet, into our deaths with its deadly weapons, bombs and airplanes, for war, and into our souls as pure science for nothing but glory; in which last respect it may be likened unto pure poetry and mysticism. It is man's greatest enterprise. It is the charge of the ethereal into the material. It is our substantiation of our meaning. It can't go too far or deep for me. Still it is not a law unto itself. It comes under the king. There never was a scientist king and there never will be any more than there will be a philosopher king. (The nearest a poet king was Henry VIII who acquired the art in Freshman English under the poet Skelton.) Science is a property. It belongs to us under the king. And the best description of us is the

humanities from of old, the book of the worthies and un-
worthies. The passing science of the moment may contribute
its psychological bit to the book like one of the fleeting ele-
ments recently added to the chemical list. As one of the hu-
manities itself, it is jealous for their dignity and importance. I
see it is getting, it has already got, in such technological
schools as M.I.T., Cal Tech, and Case, so the students can
divide their time between cyclotrons, and listening to gener-
alizations about Socrates and his boys, Alcibiades and Critias;
about Talleyrand and his peace of Vienna; and about the sym-
bolism of Moby Dick.

The view from the top of Ararat is into the vale of prevalure,
where ignorant armies clash by night, more or less ignorant.
Only the general or king can be thought great who can go
into action or before Congress and Parliament on less infor-
mation than he wishes he had. By night and by day too for
the next ten thousand years I see nation pairing with nation
for the championship of the age to see whose king the age
will be named for. It was Greece against Persia, Republican
Rome against Carthage, Caesar's Rome against the world.
And so on down to England against the Continent to outdo
it in colonization. The one the mystic Karl Marx calls histor-
ical necessity can be trusted in to supply the great issues for
us to quarrel about forever. God send that the issues be gen-
uine as they are between us and Russia today. And that they
be not too ignoble.

And how would this be for an idea to wind up with: if we
are thought to have matured to a point where we can take
control of our own evolution to go on with, why can't it be
to stop ourselves in our tracks if there isn't too much the
matter with us as we are. The free-for-all has been very excit-
ing since man began to drag down man and nation nation. I
am tempted to think that we may be that in the tree Yggdrasil
that determines its length of growth. No tree we are ac-
quainted with but has to stop or be stopped or self-stopped
somewhere. The tree hasn't to fall down just because it can't
get any taller. I see it blossom into one dominant civilization
era after era. Its eras are like its seasons, each with a glory of
its own. We are warned not to be too ambitious in our ideas

what it should be. We must take Sunday off. We must let down in tribute to the generosity of waste with now and then a libation on to the ground or down our own gullets where the waste is double. The burnt offering must be burnt to cinders and ashes not servable on the dinner table.

1959

# 'Paris Review' Interview

## with Richard Poirier

FROST: I never write except with a writing board. I've never had a table in my life. And I use all sorts of things. Write on the sole of my shoe.

INTERVIEWER: Why have you never liked a desk? Is it because you've moved around so much and lived in so many places?

FROST: Even when I was younger I never had a desk. I've never had a writing room.

INTERVIEWER: Is Cambridge your home base now pretty much?

FROST: In the winter. But I'm nearly five months in Ripton, Vermont. I make a long summer up there. But this is my office and business place.

INTERVIEWER: Your place in Vermont is near the Bread Loaf School of Writing, isn't it?

FROST: Three miles away. Not so near I know it's there. I'm a way off from it, down the mountain and up a side road. They connect me with it a good deal more than I'm there. I give a lecture at the school and a lecture at the conference. That's about all.

INTERVIEWER: You were a co-founder of the school, weren't you?

FROST: They say that. I think I had more to do with the starting of the conference. In a very casual way, I said to the president, "Why don't you use the place for a little sociability after the school is over?" I thought of no regular business—no pay, no nothing, just inviting literary people, a few, for a week or two. The kitchen staff was still there. But then they started a regular business of it.

INTERVIEWER: When you were in England from 1912 to 1915, did you ever think you might possibly stay there?

FROST: No. No, I went over there to be poor for a while, nothing else. I didn't think of printing a book over there. I'd never offered a book to anyone here. I was thirty-eight years old, wasn't I? Something like that. And I thought the way to a book was the magazines. I hadn't too much luck with them, and nobody ever noticed me except to send me a check now and then. So I didn't think I was ready for a book. But I had written three books when I went over, the amount of three books—*A Boy's Will*, *North of Boston*, and part of the next in a loose-leaf heap.

INTERVIEWER: What were the circumstances of your meeting Pound when you were in England?

FROST: That was through Frank Flint. The early Imagist and translator. He was a friend of Pound and belonged in that little group there. He met me in a bookstore, said "American?" And I said, "Yes. How'd you know?" He said, "Shoes." It was the Poetry Book Shop, Harold Monro's, just being organized. He said, "Poetry?" And I said, "I accept the omen." Then he said, "You should know your fellow countryman, Ezra Pound." And I said, "I've never heard of him." And I hadn't. I'd been skipping literary magazines—I don't ever read them very much—and the gossip, you know, I never paid much attention to. So he said, "I'm going to tell him you're here." And I had a card from Pound afterwards. I didn't use it for two or three months after that.

INTERVIEWER: He saw your book—*A Boy's Will*—just before publication, didn't he? How did that come about?

FROST: The book was already in the publishers' hands, but it hadn't come out when I met Pound, three or four months after he sent me his card. I didn't like the card very well.

INTERVIEWER: What did he say on it?

FROST: Just said, "At home, sometimes." Just like Pound. So I didn't feel that that was a very warm invitation. Then one day walking past Church Walk in Kensington, I took his card out and went in to look for him. And I found him there, a little put out that I hadn't come sooner, in his Poundian way. And then he said, "Flint tells me you have a book." And I said, "Well, I ought to have." He said, "You haven't seen it?" And I said, "No." He said, "What do you say we go and get a copy?" He was eager about being the first one to talk. That's one of the best things you can say about Pound: he wanted to be the first to jump. Didn't call people up on the telephone to see how they were going to jump. He was all silent with eagerness. We walked over to my publisher; he got the book. Didn't show it to me—put it in his pocket. We went back to his room. He said, "You don't mind our liking this?" in his British accent, slightly. And I said, "Oh, go ahead and like it." Pretty soon he laughed at something, and I said I knew where that was in the book, what Pound would laugh at. And then pretty soon he said, "You better run along home, I'm going to review it." And I never touched it. I went home without my book and he kept it. I'd barely seen it in his hands.

INTERVIEWER: He wrote perhaps the first important favorable review, didn't he?

FROST: Yes. It was printed in the States, in Chicago, but it didn't help me much in England. The reviewing of the book there began right away, as soon as it was out. I guess most of those who reviewed it in England didn't know it had already been reviewed in Chicago. It didn't sound as though they did. But his review had something to do with the beginning of my reputation. I've always felt a little romantic about all that—that queer adventure he gave me. You know he had a mixed, a really curious position over there. He was friends with Yeats, Hueffer, and a very few others.

INTERVIEWER: Did you know Hueffer?

FROST: Yes, with him. And Yeats, with him.

INTERVIEWER: How much did you see of Yeats when you were in England?

FROST: Oh, quite a little, with him nearly always—I guess always.

INTERVIEWER: Did you feel when you left London to go live on a farm in Gloucestershire that you were making a choice against the kind of literary society you'd found in the city?

FROST: No, my choices had been not connected with my going to England even. My choice was almost unconscious in those days. I didn't know whether I had any position in the world at all, and I wasn't choosing positions. You see, my instinct was not to belong to any gang, and my instinct was against being confused with the—what do you call them?—they called themselves Georgians, Edwardians, something like that, the people Edward Marsh was interested in. I understand that he speaks of me in his book, but I never saw him.

INTERVIEWER: Was there much of a gang feeling among the literary people you knew in London?

FROST: Yes. Oh, yes. Funny over there. I suppose it's the same over here. I don't know. I don't "belong" here. But they'd say, "Oh, he's that fellow that writes about homely things for that crowd, for those people. Have you anybody like that in America?" As if it were set, you know. Like Masefield—they didn't know Masefield in this gang, but, "Oh, he's that fellow that does this thing, I believe, for that crowd."

INTERVIEWER: Your best friend in those years was Edward Thomas?

FROST: Yes—quite separate again from everybody his age. He was as isolated as I was. Nobody knew he wrote poetry. He didn't write poetry until he started to war, and that had something to do with my life with him. We got to be great friends. No, I had an instinct against belonging to any of those crowds. I've had friends, but very scattering, a scattering over there. You know, I could have . . . Pound had an afternoon meeting once a week with Flint and Aldington and H. D. and at one time Hulme, I think. Hulme started with them. They met every week to rewrite each other's poems.

INTERVIEWER: You saw Hulme occasionally? Was it at these rewriting sessions, or didn't you bother with them?

FROST: Yes, I knew Hulme, knew him quite well. But I never went to one of those meetings. I said to Pound, "What do you do?" He said, "Rewrite each other's poems." And I said, "Why?" He said, "To squeeze the water out of them." "That sounds like a parlor game to me," I said, "and I'm a serious artist"—kidding, you know. And he laughed and he didn't invite me any more.

INTERVIEWER: These personal associations that you had in England with Pound and Edward Thomas and what you call the Georgians—these had nothing to do with your establishing a sense of your own style, did they? You'd already written what were to be nearly the first three volumes of your poetry.

FROST: Two and a half books, you might say. There are some poems out in Huntington Library that I must have written in the nineties. The first one of mine that's still in print was in '90. It's in print still, kicking round.

INTERVIEWER: Not in *A Boy's Will*—the earliest poem published in there was written in '94, I think.

FROST: No, it's not in there. First one I ever *sold* is in there. The first one I ever had printed was the first one I wrote. I never wrote prose or verse till 1890. Before that I wrote Latin and Greek sentences.

INTERVIEWER: Some of the early critics like Garnett and Pound talk a lot about Latin and Greek poetry with reference to yours. You'd read a lot in the classics?

FROST: Probably more Latin and Greek than Pound ever did.

INTERVIEWER: Didn't you teach Latin at one time?

FROST: Yes. When I came back to college after running away, I thought I could stand it if I stuck to Greek and Latin and philosophy. That's all I did those years.

INTERVIEWER: Did you read much in the Romantic poets? Wordsworth, in particular?

FROST: No, you couldn't pin me there. Oh, I read all sorts of things. I said to some Catholic priests the other day when they asked me about reading, I said, "If you understand the word 'catholic,' I was very catholic in my taste."

INTERVIEWER: What sort of things did your mother read to you?

FROST: That I wouldn't be able to tell you. All sorts of things, not too much, but some. She was a very hard-worked person—she supported us. Born in Scotland, but grew up in Columbus, Ohio. She was a teacher in Columbus for seven years—in mathematics. She taught with my father one year after he left Harvard and before he went to California. You know they began to teach in high schools in those days right after coming out of high school themselves. I had teachers like that who didn't go to college. I had two noted teachers in Latin and Greek who weren't college women at all. They taught Fred Robinson. I had the same teachers he had. Fritz Robinson, the old scholar. My mother was just like that. Began teaching at eighteen in the high school, then married along about twenty-five. I'm putting all this together rather lately, finding out strolling round like I do. Just dug up in Pennsylvania the date of her marriage and all that, in Lewistown, Pennsylvania.

INTERVIEWER: Your mother ran a private school in Lawrence, Massachusetts, didn't she?

FROST: Yes, she did, round Lawrence. She had a private school. And I taught in that some, as well as taking some other schools. I'd go out and teach in district schools whenever I felt like springtime.

INTERVIEWER: How old were you then?

FROST: Oh, just after I'd run away from Dartmouth, along there in '93, '4, twenty years old. Every time I'd get sick of the city I'd go out for the springtime and take school for one term. I did that I think two or three times, that same school. Little school with twelve children, about a dozen children, all barefooted. I did newspaper work in Lawrence, too. I followed my father and mother in that, you know. I didn't know what I wanted to do with myself to earn a living. Taught a little, worked on a paper a little, worked on farms a little, that was my own departure. But I just followed my parents in newspaper work. I edited a paper a while—a weekly paper— and then I was on a regular paper. I see its name still up there in Lawrence.

INTERVIEWER: When you started to write poetry, was there any poet that you admired very much?

FROST: I was the enemy of that theory, that idea of Stevenson's that you should play the sedulous ape to anybody. That did more harm to American education than anything ever got out.

INTERVIEWER: Did you ever feel any affinity between your work and any other poet's?

FROST: I'll leave that for somebody else to tell me. I wouldn't know.

INTERVIEWER: But when you read Robinson or Stevens, for example, do you find anything that is familiar to you from your own poetry?

FROST: Wallace Stevens? He was years after me.

INTERVIEWER: I mean in your reading of him, whether or not you felt any—

FROST: Any affinity, you mean? Oh, you couldn't say that. No. Once he said to me, "You write on subjects." And I said, "You write on bric-a-brac." And when he sent me his next book he'd written "S'more bric-a-brac" in it. Just took it good-naturedly. No, I had no affinity with him. We were friends. Oh, gee, miles away. I don't know who you'd connect me with.

INTERVIEWER: Well, you once said in my hearing that Robert Lowell had tried to connect you with Faulkner, told you you were a lot like Faulkner.

FROST: Did I say that?

INTERVIEWER: No, you said that Robert Lowell told you that you were a lot like Faulkner.

FROST: Well, you know what Robert Lowell said once? He said, "My uncle's dialect—the New England dialect, *The Biglow Papers*—was just the same as Burns's, wasn't it?" I said, "Robert! Burns's was not a dialect, Scotch is not a dialect. It's a language." But he'd say anything, Robert, for the hell of it.

INTERVIEWER: You've never, I take it then, been aware of any particular line of preference in your reading?

FROST: Oh, I read 'em all. One of my points of departure is an anthology. I find a poet I admire, and I think, well, there must be a lot to that. Some old one—Shirley, for instance, "The glories of our blood and state"—that sort of splendid poem. I go looking for more. Nothing. Just a couple like that and that's all. I remember certain boys took an interest in certain poems with me in old times. I remember Brower one day in somebody else's class when he was a student at Amherst—Reuben Brower, afterwards the Master of Adams House at Harvard. I remember I said, "Anyone want to read that poem to me?" It was "In going to my naked bed as one that would have slept," Edwards's old poem. He read it so well I said, "I give you A for life." And that's the way we joke with each other. I never had him regularly in a class of mine. I visited other classes up at Amherst and noticed him very early. Goodness sake, the way his voice fell into those lines, the natural way he did that very difficult poem with that old quotation—"The falling out of faithful friends is the renewing of love." I'm very catholic, that's about all you can say. I've hunted. I'm not thorough like the people educated in Germany in the old days. I've none of that. I hate the idea that you ought to read the whole of anybody. But I've done a lot of looking sometimes, read quite a lot.

INTERVIEWER: When you were in England did you find yourself reading the kind of poetry Pound was reading?

FROST: No. Pound was reading the troubadours.

INTERVIEWER: Did you talk to one another about any particular poets?

FROST: He admired at that time, when I first met him, Robinson and de la Mare. He got over admiring de la Mare anyway, and I think he threw out Robinson too. We'd just bring up a couple of little poems. I was around with him quite a little for a few weeks. I was charmed with his ways. He cultivated a certain rudeness to people that he didn't like, just like Willy Whistler. I thought he'd come under the influence of Whistler. They cultivated the French style of boxing. They used to kick you in the teeth.

INTERVIEWER: With grace.

FROST: Yes. You know the song, the nasty song: "They fight with their feet—" Among other things, what Pound did was show me Bohemia.

INTERVIEWER: Was there much Bohemia to see at that time?

FROST: More than I had ever seen. I'd never had any. He'd take me to restaurants and things. Showed me jiu jitsu in a restaurant. Threw me over his head.

INTERVIEWER: Did he do that?

FROST: Wasn't ready for him at all. I was just as strong as he was. He said, "I'll show you, I'll show you. Stand up." So I stood up, gave him my hand. He grabbed my wrist, tipped over backwards and threw me over his head.

INTERVIEWER: How did you like that?

FROST: Oh, it was all right. Everybody in the restaurant stood up. He used to talk about himself as a tennis player. I never played tennis with him. And then he'd show you all these places with these people that specialized in poets that dropped their aitches and things like that. Not like the "beatniks," quite. I remember one occasion they had a poet in who had a poem in the *English Review* on Aphrodite, how he met Aphrodite at Leatherhead. He was coming in and he was a navvy. I don't remember his name, never heard of him again— may have gone on and had books. But he was a real navvy. Came in with his bicycle clips on. Tea party. Everybody horrified in a delighted way, you know. Horror, social horror. Red-necked, thick, heavy-built fellow, strong fellow, you know, like John L. Lewis or somebody. But he was a poet. And then I saw poets made out of whole cloth by Ezra. Ezra thought he did that. Take a fellow that had never written anything and think he could make a poet out of him. We won't go into that.

INTERVIEWER: I wonder about your reaction to such articles as the recent lead article by Karl Shapiro in the *New York Times Book Review* which praised you because presumably you're not guilty of "Modernism" as Pound and Eliot are.

FROST: Is that my telephone? Just wait a second. Halt!

FROST: Where were we? Oh yes, you were trying to trace me.

INTERVIEWER: I wasn't trying to trace you. I was—

FROST: Oh, this thing about Karl Shapiro. Yeah, isn't it funny? So often they ask me—I just been all around, you know, been out West, been all around—and so often they ask me, "What is a modern poet?" I dodge it often, but I said the other night, "A modern poet must be one that speaks to modern people no matter when he lived in the world. That would be one way of describing it. And it would make him more modern, perhaps, if he were *alive* and speaking to modern people."

INTERVIEWER: Yes, but in their way of speaking, Eliot and Pound seem to many people to be writing in a tradition that is very different from yours.

FROST: Yes. I suppose Eliot's isn't as far away as Pound's. Pound seemed to me very like a troubadour, more like the troubadours or a blend of several of them, Bertrand de Born and Arnault Daniel. I never touched that. I don't know Old French. I don't like foreign languages that I haven't had. I don't read translations of things. I like to say dreadful, unpleasant things about Dante. Pound, though, he's supposed to know Old French.

INTERVIEWER: Pound was a good linguist, wasn't he?

FROST: I don't know that. There's a teacher of his down in Florida that taught him at the University of Pennsylvania. He once said to me, "Pound? I had him in Latin, and Pound never knew the difference between a declension and a con-

jugation." He's death on him. Old man, still death on Ezra.
[*Breaks into laughter.*] Pound's gentle art of making enemies.

INTERVIEWER: Do you ever hear from Pound? Do you correspond with him now?

FROST: No. He wrote me a couple of letters when I got him out of jail last year. Very funny little letters, but they were all right.

INTERVIEWER: Whom did you speak to in Washington about that?

FROST: Just the Attorney General. Just settled it with him. I went down twice with Archie and we didn't get anything done because they were of opposite parties, I think. And I don't belong to any party.

INTERVIEWER: Yes, but weren't you named Robert Lee because your father was a stanch Democrat around the time of the Civil War? That makes you a Democrat of sorts, doesn't it?

FROST: Yeah, I'm a Democrat. I was born a Democrat—and been unhappy ever since 1896. Somebody said to me, "What's the difference between that and being a Republican?" Well, I went down after we'd failed, and after Archie thought we'd failed, I just went down alone, walked into the Attorney General's office and said, "I come down here to see what your mood is about Ezra Pound." And two of them spoke up at once. "Our mood's your mood; let's get him out." Just like that, that's all. And I said, "This week?" They said, "This week if you say so. You go get a lawyer, and we'll raise no objection." So, since they were Republicans, I went over and made friends with Thurman Arnold, that good leftish person, for my lawyer. I sat up that night and wrote an appeal to the court that I threw away, and, in the morning, just before I left town, I wrote another one, a shorter one. And that's all there was to it. Ezra thanked me in a very short note that read: "Thanks for what you're doing. A little conversation would be in order." Then signed, in large letters. And then he wrote me another one, a nicer one.

INTERVIEWER: Did you see him before he left for Italy?

FROST: No, no, I didn't want to high-hat him. I wanted him to feel kind of free from me. But he feels, evidently, a little gratitude of some kind. He's not very well, you know.

Some of them didn't want . . . Well, it's a sad business. And he's a poet. I never, I never questioned that. We've been friends all the way along, but I didn't like what he did in wartime. I only heard it second-hand, so I didn't judge it too closely. But it sounded pretty bad. He was very foolish in what he bet on and whenever anybody really loses that way, I don't want to rub it into him.

INTERVIEWER: I've been asking a lot of questions about the relationship of your poetry to other poetry, but of course there are many other non-literary things that have been equally important. You've been very much interested in science, for example.

FROST: Yes, you're influenced by the science of your time, aren't you? Somebody noticed that all through my book there's astronomy.

INTERVIEWER: Like "The Literate Farmer and the Planet Venus"?

FROST: Yes, but it's all through the book, all through the book. Many poems—I can name twenty that have astronomy in them. Somebody noticed that the other day: "Why has nobody ever seen how much you're interested in astronomy?" That's a bias, you could say. One of the earliest books I hovered over, hung around, was called *Our Place among the Infinities*, by an astronomer in England named Proctor, noted astronomer. It's a noted old book. I mention that in one of the poems: I use that expression "our place among the infinities" from that book that I must have read as soon as I read any book, thirteen or fourteen, right in there I began to read. That along with *Scottish Chiefs*. I remember that year when I first began to read a book through. I had a little sister who read everything through, lots of books, everybody's books—very young, precocious. Me, I was—they turned me out of doors for my health.

INTERVIEWER: While we're thinking about science and literature, I wonder if you have any reaction to the fact that Massachusetts Institute of Technology is beginning to offer a number of courses in literature?

FROST: I think they'd better tend to their higher mathematics and higher science. Pure science. They know I think that. I don't mean to criticize them too much. But you see it's like this: the greatest adventure of man is science, the adventure of penetrating into matter, into the material universe. But the adventure is our property, a human property, and the best description of us is the humanities. Maybe the scientists wanted to remind their students that the humanities describe you who are adventuring into science, and science adds very little to that description of you, a little tiny bit. Maybe in psychology, or in something like that, but it's awful little. And so, the scientists to remind their students of all this give them half their time over there in the humanities now. And that seems a little unnecessary. They're worried about us and the pure sciences all the time. They'd better get as far as they can into their own subject. I was over there at the beginning of this and expressed my little doubts about it. I was there with Compton one night—he was sitting on the platform beside me. "We've been short"—I turned to him before the audience—"we've been a little short in pure science, haven't we?" He said, "Perhaps—I'm afraid we may have been." I said, "I think that better be tended to." That's years ago.

INTERVIEWER: You just mentioned psychology. You once taught psychology, didn't you?

FROST: That was entirely a joke. I could teach psychology. I've been asked to join a firm of psychiatrists, you know, and that's more serious. But I went up there to disabuse the Teacher's College of the idea that there is any immediate connection between any psychology and their classroom work, disabuse them of the notion that they could mesmerize a class if they knew enough psychology. That's what they thought.

INTERVIEWER: Weren't you interested at one time in William James?

FROST: Yes, that was partly what drew me back to Harvard. But he was away all the time I was around here. I had Santayana, Royce, and all that philosophy crowd, Munsterberg, George Herbert Palmer, the old poetical one. I had 'em all. But I was there waiting for James, and I lost interest.

INTERVIEWER: Did Santayana interest you very much at that time?

FROST: No, not particularly. Well, yes. I always wondered what he really meant, where he was headed, what it all came to. Followed that for years. I never knew him personally. I never knew anybody personally in college. I was a kind of—went my own way. But I admired him. It was a golden utterance—he was something to listen to, just like his written style. But I wondered what he really meant. I found years afterward somewhere in his words that all was illusion, of two kinds, true and false. And I decided false illusion would be the truth: two negatives make an affirmative.

INTERVIEWER: While we're on things other than poetry that you were and are interested in, we might get onto politics for a moment. I remember one evening your mentioning that Henry Wallace became somehow associated with your poem, "Provide, Provide."

FROST: People exaggerate such things. Henry Wallace was in Washington when I read the poem. Sat right down there in the first row. And when I got to the end of it where it says, "Better to go down dignified—With boughten friendship at your side—Than none at all. Provide, Provide!" I added, "Or somebody else will provide for ya." He smiled; his wife smiled. They were right down there where I could see them.

INTERVIEWER: Well, you don't have a reputation for being a New Dealer.

FROST: They think I'm no New Dealer. But really and truly I'm not, you know, all that clear on it. In "The Death of the Hired Man" that I wrote long, long ago, long before the New Deal, I put it two ways about home. One would be the manly way: "Home is the place where, when you have to go there, They have to take you in." That's the man's feeling about it. And then the wife says, "I should have called it/Something you somehow hadn't to deserve." That's the New Deal, the feminine way of it, the mother way. You don't have to deserve your mother's love. You have to deserve your father's. He's more particular. One's a Republican, one's a Democrat. The father is always a Republican toward his son, and his mother's always a Democrat. Very few have noticed that second thing; they've always noticed the sarcasm, the hardness of the male one.

INTERVIEWER: That poem is often anthologized, and I wonder if you feel that the poems of yours that appear most often in the anthologies represent you very well.

FROST: I'm always pleased when somebody digs up a new

one. I don't know. I leave that in the lap of the gods, as they say.

INTERVIEWER: There are some I seldom see; for example, "A Servant to Servants" or "The Most of It" or "The Subverted Flower." All of these I noticed the other day are omitted, for instance, from Untermeyer's anthology of your poems. Strange, isn't it?

FROST: Well, he was making his own choice. I never said a word to him, never urged him. I remember he said Robinson only did once. Robinson told him, "If you want to please an old man you won't overlook my 'Mr. Flood's Party.' " That is a beautiful poem.

INTERVIEWER: Do you feel that any particular area of your work hasn't been anthologized?

FROST: I wouldn't know that. "The Subverted Flower," for instance, nobody's ever touched. No—I guess it is; it's in Matty's anthology. That's the one he made for the Oxford people.

INTERVIEWER: Yes, but its appearance is extremely rare in any selection of your work. It doesn't seem to fit some people's preconceptions about you. Another neglected poem, and an especially good one, is "Putting In the Seed."

FROST: That's—sure. They leave that sort of thing out; they overlook that sort of thing with me. The only person ever noticed that was a hearty old friend of mine down at the University of Pennsylvania, Cornelius Weygandt. He said, "I know what *that's* about."

INTERVIEWER: Do you ever read that poem in public?

FROST: No, I don't bother with those. No, there are certain ones. I wouldn't read "The Subverted Flower" to anybody outside. It isn't that I'm afraid of them, but I don't want them out. I'm shy about certain things in my books, they're more —I'd rather they'd be read. A woman asked me, "What do you mean by that 'subverted flower'?" I said, "Frigidity in women." She left.

INTERVIEWER: Do you think that it was to correct the public assumption that your poetry is represented by the most anthologized pieces such as "Birches" that Lionel Trilling in his speech at your eighty-fifth birthday emphasized poems of a darker mood?

FROST: I don't know—I might run my eye over my book after Trilling, and wonder why he hadn't seen it sooner: that there's plenty to be dark about, you know. It's full of darkness.

INTERVIEWER: Do you suppose he imagined he was correcting some sort of public ignorance—some general mistake about your work?

FROST: He made the mistake himself. He was admitting he made it himself, wasn't he? He was telling what trouble he'd had to get at me. Sort of a confession, but very pleasant.

INTERVIEWER: That's true, but many admirers of yours did object to his emphasis on the "darkness" or "terror" in your poems.

FROST: Yes, well, he took me a little by surprise that night. He was standing right beside me and I had to get up right after him. Birthday party. And it took me—it didn't hurt me, but I thought at first he was attacking me. Then when he began comparing me to Sophocles and D. H. Lawrence I was completely at sea. What the two of them had to do with me, you know. Might be I might like it about Sophocles, but I'd be puzzled, oh, utterly at sea about D. H. Lawrence. It's all right, though. I had to get up and recite soon after that, and so I was a little puzzled what to recite to illustrate what he was talking about. And right there—new to me: I hadn't read his paper. I'd never read him much. I don't read criticism. You see no magazines in the house.

INTERVIEWER: Did you feel better about his talk when you read his substantiation of it in the *Partisan Review*?

FROST: I read his defense of it. Very clever, very—very interesting. Admired him. He's a very—intellectual man. But I read very little, generally, in the magazines. Hadn't read that Shapiro thing you mentioned. That's news to me what he said. Is he a friend of mine?

INTERVIEWER: Oh, yes. He's a friend of yours, but he's like many friends of yours: he chooses to see in you something more simple than your best friends see. It's a bit like J. Donald Adams, also in the *Times*, angrily defending you against Trilling, only J. Donald Adams doesn't understand you very well either.

FROST: What was Shapiro saying?

INTERVIEWER: He was saying that most modern poetry is obscure and overdifficult, that this is particularly true of Pound and Eliot, but that it isn't true of you.

FROST: Well, I don't want to be difficult. I like to fool—oh, you know, you like to be mischievous. But not in that dull way of just being dogged and doggedly obscure.

INTERVIEWER: The difficulty of your poetry is perhaps in your emphasis on variety in tones of voice. You once said that consciously or unconsciously it was tones of voice that you counted on to double the meaning of every one of your statements.

FROST: Yes, you could do that. Could unsay everything I said, nearly. Talking contraries—it's in one of the poems. Talk by contraries with people you're very close to. They know what you're talking about. This whole thing of suggestiveness and *double entendre* and hinting—comes down to the word "hinting." With people you can trust you can talk in hints and suggestiveness. Families break up when people take hints you don't intend and miss hints you do intend. You can watch that going on, as a psychologist. I don't know. No, don't . . . no don't you . . . don't think of me . . . See, I haven't led a literary life. These fellows, they *really* work away with their prose trying to describe themselves and understand themselves, and so on. I don't do that. I don't want to know too much about myself. It interests me to know that Shapiro thinks I'm not difficult. That's all right. I never wrote a review in my life, never wrote articles. I'm constantly refusing to write articles. These fellows are all literary men. I don't have hours; I don't work at it, you know. I'm not a farmer, that's no pose of mine. But I have farmed some, and I putter around. And I walk and I live with other people. Like to talk a lot. But I haven't had a very literary life, and I'm never very much with the gang. I'm vice-president, no, I'm Honorary President of the Poetry Society of America. Once in a great while I go. And I wish them well. I wish the foundations would take them all, take care of them all.

INTERVIEWER: Speaking of foundations, why do you think big business, so long the object of literary ridicule for being philistine, should now be supporting so much literary effort?

FROST: It's funny they haven't sooner, because most of them have been to college and had poetry pushed into them. About half the reading they do in all languages will be in verse. Just think of it. And so they have a kind of respect for it all and they probably don't mind the abuse they've had from our quarter. They're people who're worried that we just don't have enough imagination—it's the lack of imagination they're afraid of in our system. If we had enough imagination we could lick the Russians. I feel like saying, "Probably we won the Civil War with Emily Dickinson." We didn't even know she was there. Poor little thing.

INTERVIEWER: Would you agree that there are probably more good prizes for poetry today than there are good poets?

FROST: I don't know. I hate to judge that. It's nice for them—it's so nice for them to be interested in us, with their foundations. You don't know what'll come of it. You know the real thing is that the sense of sacrifice and risk is one of the greatest stimuli in the world. And you take that all out of it—take that away from it so that there's no risk in being a poet, I bet you'd lose a lot of the pious spirits. They're in it for the—hell of it. Just the same as these fellows breaking through the sound barrier up there, just the same. I was once asked in public, in front of four or five hundred women, just how I found leisure to write. I said, "Confidentially—since there's only five hundred of you here, and all women—like a sneak I stole some of it, like a man I seized some of it—and I had a little in my tin cup." Sounds as if I'd been a beggar, but I've never been consciously a beggar. I've been at the mercy of . . . I've been a beneficiary around colleges and all. And this is one of the advantages of the American way: I've never had to write a word of thanks to anybody I had a cent from. The colleges came between. Poetry has always been a beggar. Scholars have also been beggars, but they delegate their begging to the president of the college to do for them.

INTERVIEWER: I was suggesting just now that perhaps the number of emoluments for poets greatly exceeds the number of people whose work deserves to be honored. Isn't this a situation in which mediocrity will necessarily be exalted? And won't this make it more rather than less difficult for people to recognize really good achievement when it does occur?

FROST: You know, I was once asked that, and I said I never knew how many disadvantages anyone needed to get anywhere in the world. And you don't know how to measure that. No psychology will ever tell you who needs a whip and who needs a spur to win races. I think the greatest thing about it with me has been this, and I wonder if others think it. I look at a poem as a performance. I look on the poet as a man of prowess, just like an athlete. He's a performer. And the things you can do in a poem are very various. You speak of figures, tones of voice varying all the time. I'm always interested, you know, when I have three or four stanzas, in the way I *lay* the sentences in them. I'd hate to have the sentences all lie the same in the stanzas. Every poem is like that: some sort of achievement in performance. Somebody has said that poetry among other things is the marrow of wit. That's probably way back somewhere—marrow of wit. There's got to be wit. And that's very, very much left out of a lot of this labored stuff. It doesn't sparkle at all. Another thing to say is that every thought, poetical or otherwise, every thought is a feat of association. They tell of old Gibbon—as he was dying he was the same Gibbon at his historical parallels. All thought is a feat of association: having what's in front of you bring up something in your mind that you almost didn't know you knew. Putting this and that together. That click.

INTERVIEWER: Can you give an example of how this feat of association—as you call it—works?

FROST: Well, one of my masques turns on one association like that. God says, "I was just showing off to the Devil, Job." Job looks puzzled about it, distressed a little. God says, "Do you mind?" And, "No, no," he says, "No," in that tone, you know, "No," and so on. That tone is everything, the way you say that "no." I noticed that—that's what made me write that. Just that one thing made that.

INTERVIEWER: Did your other masque—*Masque of Mercy*—have a similar impetus?

FROST: I noticed that the first time in the world's history when mercy is entirely the subject is in Jonah. It does say somewhere earlier in the Bible, "If ten can be found in the city, will you spare it? Ten good people?" But in Jonah there is something worse than that. Jonah is told to go and prophesy against the city—and he *knows* God will let him down. He can't trust God to be unmerciful. You can trust God to be anything but unmerciful. So he ran away and—and got into a whale. That's the point of that and nobody notices it. They miss it.

INTERVIEWER: Why do you suppose, Mr. Frost, that among religious groups the masques had their best reception among Jesuits and rabbis?

FROST: Amusing you say that—that's true. The other, the lesser sects without the law, you see, they don't get it. They're too apt to think there's rebellion in them—what they go through with their parents when they're growing up. But that isn't in them at all, you know. They're not rebellious. They're very doctrinal, very orthodox, both of them. But how'd you notice that? It's amusing to me too. You see, the rabbis have been fine to me and so have the SJ's particularly, all over the country. I've just been in Kansas City staying with them. See, the masques are full of good orthodox doctrine. One of them turns on the thought that evil shows off to good and good shows off to evil. I made a couplet out of that for them in Kansas City, just the way I often do, offhand: "It's from their having stood contrasted/That good and bad so long have lasted."

INTERVIEWER: Making couplets "offhand" is something like writing on schedule, isn't it? I know a young poet who claims he can write every morning from six to nine, presumably before class.

FROST: Well, there's more than one way to skin a cat. I don't know what that would be like, myself. When I get going on something, I don't want to just—you know . . . Very first one I wrote I was walking home from school and I began to make it—a March day—and I was making it all afternoon and making it so I was late at my grandmother's for dinner. I finished it, but it burned right up, just burned right up, you know. And what started that? What burned it? So many talk, I wonder how falsely, about what it costs them, what agony it is to write. I've often been quoted: "No tears in the writer, no tears in the reader. No surprise for the writer, no surprise for the reader." But another distinction I made is: however sad, no grievance, grief without grievance. How could I, how could anyone have a good time with what cost me too much agony, how could they? What do I want to communicate but what a *hell* of a good time I had writing it? The whole thing is performance and prowess and feats of association. Why don't critics talk about those things—what a feat it was to turn that that way, and what a feat it was to remember that, to be reminded of that by this? Why don't they talk about that? Scoring. You've got to *score*. They say not, but you've got to score, in all the realms—theology, politics, astronomy, history, and the country life around you.

INTERVIEWER: What do you think of the performances of the poets who have made your birthplace, San Francisco, into their headquarters?

FROST: Have they? Somebody said I saw a lot of them in Kansas City at the end of my audience. They said, "See that blur over there? That's whiskers." No, I don't know much about that. I'm waiting for them to say something that I can get hold of. The worse the better. I like it anyway, you know. Like you say to somebody, "Say something. Say something." And he says, "I burn."

INTERVIEWER: Do young poets send you things?

FROST: Yes, some—not much, because I don't respond. I don't write letters and all that. But I get a little, and I meet them, talk with them. I get some books. I wonder what they're at. There's one book that sounded as if it might be good, "Aw, hell." The book was called "Aw, hell." Because "aw," the way you say "aw," you know, "Aw, hell!" That might be something.

INTERVIEWER: Most of the titles are funny. One is called *Howl* and another *Gasoline*.

FROST: *Gasoline*, eh? I've seen a little of it, kicking round. I saw a bunch of nine of them in a magazine in Chicago when I was through there. They were all San Franciscans. Nothing I could talk about afterwards, though, either way. I'm always glad of anybody that says anything awful. I can use it. We're all like that. You've got to learn to enjoy a lot of things you don't like. And I'm always ready for somebody to say some outrageous thing. I feel like saying, "Hold that now, long enough for me to go away and tell on you, won't you? Don't go back on it tomorrow." Funny world.

INTERVIEWER: When you look at a new poem that might be sent to you, what is it usually that makes you want to read it all or not want to read it?

FROST: This thing of performance and prowess and feats of association—that's where it all lies. One of my ways of looking at a poem right away it's sent to me, right off, is to see if it's rhymed. Then I know just when to look at it. The rhymes come in pairs, don't they? And nine times out of ten with an ordinary writer, one of two of the terms is better than the other. One makeshift will do, and then they get another that's good, and then another makeshift, and then another one that's good. That is in the realm of performance, that's the deadly test with me. I want to be unable to tell which of those he thought of first. If there's any trick about it, putting the better one first so as to deceive me, I can tell pretty soon. That's all in the performance realm. They can belong to any school of thought they want to, Spinoza or Schopenhauer, it doesn't matter to me. A Cartesian I heard Poe called, a Cartesian philosopher, the other day . . . tsssssss . . .

INTERVIEWER: You once saw a manuscript of Dylan Thomas's where he'd put all the rhymes down first and then backed into them. That's clearly not what you mean by performance, is it?

FROST: See, that's very dreadful. It ought to be that you're thinking forward, with the feeling of strength that you're getting them good all the way, carrying out some intention more felt than thought. It begins. And what it is that guides us— what is it? Young people wonder about that, don't they? But I tell them it's just the same as when you feel a joke coming. You see somebody coming down the street that you're accustomed to abuse, and you feel it rising in you, something to say as you pass each other. Coming over him the same way. And where do these thoughts come from? Where does a thought? Something does it to you. It's him coming toward you that gives you the animus, you know. When they want to know about inspiration, I tell them it's mostly animus.

*The Paris Review*, Summer–Fall 1960

# A Poet's Boyhood

ONE OF my earliest San Francisco memories is political, of crossing the bay to Oakland to see my father off on a train as a delegate to the Democratic National Convention at Cincinnati in 1879 to help nominate Hancock. We were Democrats and very intense ones. I remember my father's disappointment in Hancock's defeat and his even greater disappointment when Hancock as an old friend and fellow soldier of Garfield's went to Garfield's inauguration and shook hands with him in public right on the platform.

Four years later at the age of nine I was marching all over San Francisco in uniform in the great torchlight processions that I thought elected Grover Cleveland. At first I rode on a fire engine pulled by many men on the same loop of rope till it was decided a girl would look better up there and I was taken down to carry my torch on foot in the middle of the loop. The cause was too serious for any vanity on my part either way. As I have said we were Democrats in those days.

My father was chairman of the Democratic City Committee and my health not being very good I was kept out of school and taken down town with him to his office many, many days. I rode around with him in a buggy electioneering and tacking his card to the ceilings of saloons with a silver dollar for tack hammer. I often acted as his errand boy to the City Hall and to the office of the Democratic boss, Buckley, who was my kind friend. I had my lunches free off the saloon counters. I wasn't drinking myself.

Of course I remember a few preliminary earthquakes. I got away before the big one. And there was Woodward's Gardens with its animals, and the Cliff House where the seals yelped. Have I not written poems about both these places? I wish I could get you to read "Once by the Pacific" to yourself before I have to read it to you. It took me a long, long time to get over the idea that the Pacific Ocean was going to be more important in our history than the Atlantic. If I ever got over it. I left the Coast in '85 at the death of my father. (My father, William Prescott Frost, was a newspaper man with papers long

894

discontinued, "The Post" and "The Bulletin.") As late as six or seven years afterwards, I was writing lines like these:

"Europe might sink and the wave of its sinking sweep
And spend itself on our shore and we would not weep.
Our cities would not even turn in their sleep.

Our faces are not that way or should not be.
Our future is in the West on the other sea."

The rest is lost. I wish I could recapture it. It was never published. Many things have happened since to confute me. But I don't know—

Nothing but idyllic politics. Corruption may have been in it. Lincoln Steffens says so. Looking back I can see where it might have come in.

Cambridge Mass
Oct 6 1960
Robert Frost

Brochure announcing reading at
Berkeley Community Theatre,
November 6, 1960

# A New England Tribute

HARD of course to judge of the importance of an event at the time of it, but an election like that, an inauguration like this, may well be looked back on as a turning point in the history of our country, even perhaps in the history of Christendom. It was such a great jump forward toward settling it once for all that the church's reformation both from within and from without had been accomplished; the old agonies and antagonisms were over; it was tacitly conceded that our founders were not far wrong; safety lay in a plurality of denominations and doctrines unenforced by secular law. I come fresh to say this from communion with portraits by Stuart of four of them who are on record to this effect, Washington, Jefferson, Adams, and Madison, enshrined in a temple on the North Shore of Massachusetts.

> "How still a moment may precede
> One that may thrill the world forever.
> To that still moment none would heed
> Man's doom was linked no more to sever."

So someone said of the first Christmas of all seven hundred and sixty three years after the founding of Rome. Such was our gift for Christmas confirmed by vote one hundred and eighty years after the first election.

For New Year's the inauguration might be another gift, a more than New Year's resolution, to make sure of the more than social security of us all in a greater strength, a greater formidability. A little more decisiveness at the points of decision, we don't exactly see where or how. We look forward with confidence to young leadership to show us where and how. We can afford a little stimulation of our will to win all the way from the sports to the sciences and arts.

> We have the Olympic games as yet.
> Where is the Olympic spirit gone?
> Of two such lessons why forget
> The nobler and the manlier one?

896

We have given ourselves before: we may have to give our-
selves again. I have heard the despairers of the Republic say
we may need the discipline of being invaded. Our Revolu-
tion was:

## OUR GIFT OUTRIGHT

The land was ours before we were the land's.
She was our land more than a hundred years
Before we were her people. She was ours
In Massachusetts, in Virginia,
But we were England's, still colonials,
Possessing what we still were unpossessed by,
Possessed by what we now no more possessed.
Something we were withholding made us weak
Until we found it was ourselves
We were withholding from the land of living,
And forthwith found salvation in surrender.
Such as we were we gave ourselves outright
(The deed of gift was many deeds of war)
To the land vaguely realizing westward,
But still unstoried, artless, unenhanced,
Such as she was, such as she will become.

*Official Program of the Inaugural*
*Ceremonies of John F. Kennedy and*
*Lyndon B. Johnson,* 1961

# Ernest Hemingway

ERNEST HEMINGWAY was rough and unsparing with life. He was rough and unsparing with himself. It is like his brave free ways that he should die by accident with a weapon. Fortunately for us, if it is a time to speak of fortune, he gave himself time to make his greatness. His style dominated our story telling long and short. I remember the fascination that made me want to read aloud *The Killers* to everybody that came along. He was a friend I shall miss. The country is in mourning.

The New York Times, July 3, 1961

# On "Choose Something Like a Star"

I AM NOT partial with my poems, any more than a mother with her children. But your choice, "Choose Something Like a Star," is one I like to say.

I seem to fancy it as rather Horatian in its ending. Then I like the two ways of spelling 'staid'; that's playing the words. And I like to mingle science and spirit here—as I do so deliberately in my new book.

But there are things beyond all this which I care more about, and hope we all do.

*Poet's Choice,* 1962

# William Faulkner

I HAD to admire him for the position he won for us in the world as an American. I read him for the deep dark magnificence of his "Tale Told by an Idiot" in the same way I admire the passage in Shakespeare that he takes the title from. His humor has the same macabre quality as in the story of the Choctaw Indians with their negro slaves and even in the story "That Evening Sun." Our personal acquaintance was but slight. My chief recollection would be of my daughter and me seeing him off from Rio de Janeiro, Brazil, to attend his daughter's wedding in Mississippi. I should like to have known him better. Sixty five is too young for a man to retire from the world or from his occupation.

July 1962

# On the Cold War

Dear Mr. Heineman:

The very name of your magazine gives me conscientious qualms for my not having given the attention I should have to who's running the county. I should be writing you an article about that but articles seem nothing I can undertake. I hate a cold war of sustained hate that finds no relief in blood letting but probably it should be regarded as a way of stalling till we find out whether there is really an issue big enough for a big show-down. We are given pause from the dread of the terribleness we feel capable of. I was sometimes like that as a boy with another boy I lived in antipathy with. It clouded my days. But here I am almost writing the article I was going to tell you I couldn't write. My limit seems to be verse and talk. I am dictating this.

    With regrets
    Sincerely yours,
    Robert Frost

*County Government Magazine,*
December 1962

# On Extravagance: A Talk

I THINK the first thing I ought to speak of is all this luxuriance: all in easy chairs and a beautiful hall—and nothing to do but to listen to me. Pretty soft, I call it. Pretty soft.

I was so made that I—though a Vermonter and all that—I never took any stock in the doctrine that "a penny saved is a penny earned." A penny saved is a mean thing, and a penny spent, you know, is a generous thing and a big thing—like this, you see. It took more than a penny to do this. There's nothing mean about it.

And one of the expressions I like best is—in the Bible it is and in poets—they say, "of no mean city am I." That's a great saying, ain't it?—to be "of no mean city," like San Francisco, Boston. People deprecate our beautiful cities, and I go around thinking how many people living in them must say that— "of no mean city am I," you know. How splendid. And "of no mean college am I." (Funny for me to be talking about that.)

And I was thinking—I am going to read to you, of course, principally—I was thinking of the extravagance of the universe, you know, what an *extravagant* universe it is. And the most extravagant thing in it, as far as we know, is man—the most wasteful, spending thing in it—in all his luxuriance, you know. And how stirring it is, the sun and everything. Take a telescope and look as far as you will, you know. How much of a universe was wasted just to produce puny us. It's wonderful, it fills you with awe.

And poetry is a sort of extravagance, in many ways. It's something that people wonder about. What's the need of it?— you know. And the answer is, no need—not particularly. That is, that's the first one.

I've always enjoyed being around colleges, nominally as a professor, you know, and a puzzle to everybody as to what I was doing—whether anything or not, you know. (You'd like to leave that to others. Never would defend myself there.) And people say to me occasionally, "Where *does* poetry come in?" Some of you may be thinking it tonight: "What's it all for? Does it *count*?"

When I catch a man reading my book, red-handed, you know, he usually looks up cheerfully and says, "My wife is a great fan of yours." Puts it off on the women. And I figured that out lately—that there's an indulgence of poetry, a manly indulgence of poetry, that's a good deal like the manly indulgence of women, see. You know, we say that women rule the world. That's a nice way to talk. And we say that poetry rules the world. There's a poem that says:

> We are the music-makers,
>     And we are the dreamers of dreams, . . .
> World-losers and world-forsakers,

and all that. We are "the makers" of the future. We

> Built Nineveh with our sighing,
>     And Babel itself with our mirth;
> And o'erthrew them with prophesying
>     To the old of the new world's worth;

—you see—

> For each age is a dream that is dying,
>     And one that is coming to birth.

That's a big claim, isn't it? An exaggerated claim.

But I look on the universe as a kind of an exaggeration anyway, the whole business, see. That's the way you think of it: great, great, great expense—everybody trying to make it mean something more than it is.

But all poetry asks is to be accorded the same indulgence that women are accorded. And I think the women, the ladies, are perhaps the go-betweens, you know. They're our ambassadors to the men. They break the poetry to the men. And it's a strange thing that men write the poetry more than the women; that is, the world's history is full of men poets and very few women. Women are in the dative case. It's to and for them—the poetry. And then for men and the affairs of men through them. (One knows the story that makes an argument that women really run the world in the end, you know, run everything.)

And I'm not defending at all. I just thought one of the figures of poetry—it's a metaphor, isn't it? you know, various kinds of metaphor—but one of the figures you never hear mentioned is just the one extravagance. See. This is a little extravaganza, this little poem. And to what extent is it excessive? And can you go with it? Some people can't. And sometimes it's a bitter extravagance, like that passage in Shakespeare that so many make their novels out of: life is a tale told by an idiot, signifying nothing, you know. That's an extravagance, of course—of bitterness.

And people hold you. You say something sad or something pessimistic and something cynical, and they forget to allow for the extravagance of poetry—that you're not saying that all the time. That's not a doctrine you're preaching. You loathe anybody that wants you to be either pessimist or optimist. It doesn't belong to it; it doesn't belong at all. Are you happy or are you unhappy? Why are you? You know, you have no right to ask.

The extravagance lies in "it sometimes seems as if." See. That would be a good name of a book: "it sometimes seems as if." Or it says: "if only you knew." You could put that on the cover of a book. "If only I could tell you," you know. "Beyond participation lie my sorrows and beyond relief," you know; and yet you're harping on them, you see, in that way.

I arrived step by step at these things about it all, myself. I've been thinking lately that politics is an extravagance, again, an extravagance about *grievances*. And poetry is an extravagance about *grief*. And grievances are something that can be remedied, and griefs are irremediable, you know. And there you take them with a sort of a happy sadness. You know that they say drink helps—say it does. "Make you happy," the song goes, you know, the college song goes, "Make you happy, make you sad . . . sad . . ." That old thing. How deep those things go.

So I suppose that leads me to say an extravagance. I think I have right here one. Let's see it. It's made out in larger print for me by my publishers. And I remember somebody holding it up for some doctrine that's supposed to be in it, you know. It begins with this kind of a person:

He thought he kept the universe alone;

See, just that one line could be a whole poem, you know.

He thought he kept the universe alone;

That's the way he felt that day.

> For all the voice in answer he could wake
> Was but the mocking echo of his own
> From some tree-hidden cliff across the lake.
> Some morning from the boulder-broken beach
> He would cry out on life, that what it wants
> Is not its own love back in copy speech,
> But counter-love, original response.

See, that's what's one of the terrible things that's lacking, see.

> Is not its own love back in copy speech,
> But counter-love, original response.
> And nothing ever came of what he cried
> Unless it was the embodiment that crashed
> In the cliff's talus on the other side,
> And then in the far distant water splashed,
> But after a time allowed for it to swim,
> Instead of proving human when it neared
> And someone else additional to him,
> As a great buck it powerfully appeared,
> Pushing the crumpled water up ahead,
> And landed pouring like a waterfall,
> And stumbled through the rocks with horny tread,
> And forced the underbrush—and that was all.

That's all he got out of his longing, you see. (And somebody made quite an attack on that as not satisfying the noblest in our nature or something, you know.) He missed it all. All he got was this beautiful thing, didn't he? And then:

> Unless it was the embodiment that crashed
> In the cliff's talus on the other side,
> And then in the far distant water splashed,
> But after a time allowed for it to swim,
> Instead of proving human when it neared

This person expected it to be, I think.

> Instead of proving human when it neared
> And someone else additional to him,

> As a great buck it powerfully appeared,
> Pushing the crumpled water

And he didn't get anything out of that, you know.

> And forced the underbrush—and that was all.

But that's just by way of carrying it over from what I was talking. I usually, you know, talk without any reference to my own poems—talk politics or something.

And then, just thinking of extravagances, back through the years—this is one, with a title like this: "Never Again Would Birds' Song Be the Same." You see, this is another tone of extravagance:

> He would declare and could himself believe

See, this is beginning to be an extravagance right in that line, isn't it?

> He would declare

—you know, defiantly—

> and could himself believe
> That the birds there in all the garden round
> From having heard the daylong voice of Eve
> Had added to their own an oversound,
> Her tone of meaning though without the words.
> Admittedly an eloquence so soft
> Could only have had an influence on birds
> When call or laughter carried it aloft.
> Be that as may be, she was in their song.
> Moreover her voice upon their voices crossed
> Had now persisted in the woods so long
> That probably it never would be lost.
> Never again would birds' song be the same.
> And to do that to birds was why she came.

See. They used to write extravagant things to ladies' eyebrows, you know. See, that's part—one of the parts of poetry.

And now I can see some people are incapable of taking it, that's all. And I'm not picking you out. I do this on a percentage basis. And I can tell by expression of faces how

troubled they are, just about that. I think it's the extravagance
of it that's bothering them. Say in a Mother Goose thing like
this—another kind of extravagance:

> There was a man and he had nought,
>  So the robbers came to rob him;

—naturally. You see, that's an extravagance there.

> There was a man and he had nought,
>  So the robbers came to rob him;
> He climbed up to his chimney-top,
>  And then they thought they had him.

> But he climbed down on t'other side,
>  And so they couldn't find him;
> He ran fourteen miles in fifteen days,
>  And never looked behind him.

See. Now, that's all, you know. If you can't keep up with it,
don't try to.

And then, I could go right on with pretty near everything
I've done. You know, there's always this element of extrava-
gance. It's like snapping the whip, you know. Are you there?
Are you still on?—you know. Are you with it? Or has it
snapped you off?

That's a very emotional one, and then this is one in
thought—a recent one, another kind of tone altogether:

> There was never naught,

—it begins—

> There was always thought.
> But when noticed first
> It was fairly burst
> Into having weight.
> It was in a state
> Of atomic One.
> Matter was begun—
> And in fact complete,
> One and yet discrete
> To conflict and pair.

See? That's a sweeping statement. "To conflict and pair"—
those are the two things.

> Everything was there
> Every single thing
> Waiting was to bring,
> Clear from hydrogen
> All the way to men.
> It was all the tree
> It would ever be,
> Bole and branch and root
> Cunningly minute.
> And this gist of all
> Is so infra-small
> As to blind our eyes
> To its every guise
> And so render nil
> The whole Yggdrasil.
> Out of coming-in
> Into having been!
> So the picture's caught
> Almost next to naught
> But the force of thought.

And my extravagance would go on from there to say that
people think that life is a *result* of certain atoms coming to-
gether, see, instead of being the *cause* that brings the atoms
together. See, there's something to be said about that in the
utter, utter extravagant way.

And then—oh then let's see—another one. This is a poem
that I partly wrote while I was here at Dartmouth in 1892,
and failed with. And I kept a couple of lines of it, and they
came in later. You can see what I was dwelling on. I was dwell-
ing on the Pacific Coast—the shore out at Cliff House, where
I had been as a child.

> The shattered water made a misty din.
> Great waves looked over others coming in,
> And thought of doing something to the shore
> That water never did to land before.
> The clouds were low and hairy in the skies,

Like locks blown forward in the gleam of eyes.
You could not tell, and yet it looked as if
The shore was lucky in being backed by cliff,
The cliff in being backed by continent;
It looked as if a night of dark intent
Was coming, and not only a night, an age.
Someone had better be prepared for rage.
There would be more than ocean-water broken
Before God's last *Put out the Light* was spoken.

That's another one, you see, just the way it *all* is. Some of them probably more than others.

And then sometimes just fooling, you know:

I once had a cow that jumped over the moon,

This poem is called "Lines Written in Dejection on the Eve of Great Success."

I once had a cow that jumped over the moon,
Not on to the moon but over.
I don't know what made her so lunar a loon;
All she'd been having was clover.

That was back in the days of my godmother Goose.
But though we are goosier now,
And all tanked up with mineral juice,
We haven't caught up with my cow.

Same thing, you know.

You know, one of the things about it in the criticism, and where I fail, is in I can enjoy some—oh *great* extravagance, and *abandon*, see. Abandon, especially when it's humorous. (I can show you other things, too; they're not all humorous. But I can enjoy it.) Some of this *solemn* abandon—I don't know what it is they call it, abstract art or something like that. And you know I don't keep up with it. You see, I'm distressed a little. You get left behind, at some age. Don't sympathize with me too much.

And then, take a thing like this:

But God's own descent
Into flesh was meant

> As a demonstration
> That the supreme merit
> Lay in risking spirit
> In substantiation.

See, that's a whole of philosophy. To the very limit, you know.

And it comes out; it doesn't mean it's untruth, you know, this extravagance. For instance, somebody says to me—a great friend—says, "Everything's in the Old Testament that you find in the New." You can tell who he was probably by his saying that.

And I said, "What *is* the height of it?"

"Well," he said, "love your neighbor as yourself."

I said, "Yeah, that's in both of them." Then, just to tease him, I said, "But it isn't good enough."

He said, "What's the matter with it?"

"And *hate* your neighbor as you hate yourself."

He said, "You hate yourself?"

"I wouldn't be religious unless I did." You see, we had an argument—of that kind.

Some people can't go with you. Let them drop; let them fall off. Let the wolves take them. And, you see, in the Bible twice it says—and I quote that in a poem somewhere, I think, yes—twice it says, "these things are said in parables"—said in this way that I'm talking to you about, see, extravagance said in parable—"so the wrong people won't understand them and so get saved." Thoroughly undemocratic, very superior—as when Matthew Arnold says, in a whole sonnet, only those who've given everything and strained every nerve, you know, "mount, and that hardly, to eternal life." 'Taint everybody. It's just those only—the few that have done everything, sacrificed, risked everything, bet their sweet life on what they lived, you know. What a broad one that is: "You bet your sweet life." That's the height of it all, in whatever you do: "bet your sweet life," you know. And only those who have done that to the limit, you know, he says, "mount, and that hardly"—they barely make it, you know—"that hardly, to eternal life."

I like to see you. I like to bother some of you. What do we go round with poetry for? Go round just for kindred spirits some way—not for criticism, not for appreciation, and nothing but just awareness of each other about it all.

Now I'm going to forget all that, but let me say an extravagance of somebody else, another one beside mine. See how rich this is—not mine at all:

> By feathers green, across Casbeen
>     The traveller tracks the Phoenix flown,
> By gems he strew'd in waste and wood,
>     And jewell'd plumes at random thrown:
>
> Till wandering far, by moon and star,
>     They stand beside the funeral pyre,
> Where bursting bright with sanguine light
>     The impulsive bird forgets his sire.

You see, that's something, ain't it.

> Those ashes shine like ruby wine,
>     Like bag of Tyrian murex spilt,
> The claws, the jowl of the flying fowl
>     Are with the glorious anguish gilt.
>
> So fair the sight, so bright the light,
>     Those pilgrim men,

—that track this bird, you know—

> Those pilgrim men, on traffic bent,
>     Drop hands and eyes and merchandise,
>     And are with gazing well content.

That's somebody else, but that's another example—a rich one, lush, lavish.

Then, another kind of thing—not all my own, you know. Take for just the delight in the sound of the two stanzas that I'll say to you—three stanzas, maybe. The way it changes tune with a passion—a religious passion, I guess you'd call it. This is an old poem—old, old poem. It says:

> What if the king, our sovereign lord,
>     Should of his own accord
> Friendly himself invite,

And say 'I'll be your guest tomorrow night,'
How should we stir ourselves, call and command
All hands to work! 'Let no man idle stand!'

'Set me fine Spanish tables in the hall;
See they be fitted all;

Then I skip a little, and it says:

Thus, if a king were coming, would we do;
And 'twere good reason too;
For 'tis a duteous thing
To do all honor to an earthly king,
And after all our travail and our cost,
So he be pleased, to count no labor lost.

And then watch this, the extravagance of this:

But at the coming of the King of Heaven

See, we've talked about the coming of the earthly king.

But at the coming of the King of Heaven
All's set at six and seven;
We wallow in our sin,
Christ cannot find a chamber in the inn.
We entertain Him always as a stranger,
And, as of old, still house Him in the manger.

That's just letting go—saying.

Then, another strange one. You could say this is bad, you know; it lets you down too much. (That doesn't. That's great stuff. That lifts you up.) But suppose someone says:

In either mood, to bless or curse
God bringeth forth the soul of man;
No angel sire, no mother nurse
Can change the work that God began.

One spirit shall be like a star,
He shall delight to honor one:
Another spirit he shall mar:
None may undo what God hath done.

I marred that one a little, didn't I.

Then go back to just in general—see if I've got anything
else there. No. Yeah. This is slippery. No I'll just say them, I
guess—little ones now. Some old ones I'll mix with some new
ones. The first poem I ever read in public, in 1915, was at Tufts
College, and this was it—1915:

> Two roads diverged in a yellow wood,
> And sorry I could not travel both
> And be one traveler, long I stood
> And looked down one as far as I could
> To where it bent in the undergrowth;
>
> Then took the other, as just as fair,
> And having perhaps the better claim,
> Because it was grassy and wanted wear;
> Though as for that the passing there
> Had worn them really about the same,
>
> And both that morning equally lay
> In leaves no step had trodden black.
> Oh, I kept the first for another day!
> Yet knowing how way leads on to way,
> I doubted if I should ever come back.
>
> I shall be telling this with a sigh
> Somewhere ages and ages hence:
> Two roads diverged in a wood, and I—
> I took the one less traveled by,
> And that has made all the difference.

Then—that's an old one—then another old one, quite a
different tone. You see, this one is more casual talking, this
next one:

> Whose woods these are I think I know.
> His house is in the village though;
> He will not see me stopping here
> To watch his woods fill up with snow.

My little horse must think it queer
To stop without a farmhouse near
Between the woods and frozen lake
The darkest evening of the year.

He gives his harness bells a shake
To ask if there is some mistake.
The only other sound's the sweep
Of easy wind and downy flake.

The woods are lovely, dark and deep,
But I have promises to keep,
And miles to go before I sleep,
And miles to go before I sleep.

And that—I won't use the word extravagance again this evening. I swear off. You know sometimes a talk is just trying to run away from one word. If you get started using it you can't get away from it, sometimes.

But then a new one. (See, that's supposed to be a problem poem. I didn't write it for that, but it's supposed to be a problem poem. You see, by analogy you can go off from anything. Someone says that means—"The woods are lovely, dark and deep, / But I have promises to keep"—that means the world is "lovely," life is "lovely, dark and deep," but I must be getting to heaven. You see it's a death poem. You don't mind that? You shouldn't. Let them go.) And then here's a new one. "Away!" this is called, "Away!" Little stanzas, tiny stanzas:

Now I out walking
The world desert,
And my shoe and my stocking
Do me no hurt.

I leave behind
Good friends in town.
Let them get well-wined
And go lie down.

Don't think I leave
For the outer dark
Like Adam and Eve
Put out of the Park.

Forget the myth.
There is no one I
Am put out with
Or put out by.

Unless I'm wrong
I but obey
The urge of a song:
I'm—bound—away!

And I may return
If dissatisfied
With what I learn
From having died.

That's straight goods. They can't do much with that.

And then—just as it happens now, it's nothing to do with anything particular—"Escapist—Never." (These are some of my new ones.) "Escapist—Never."

He is no fugitive—escaped, escaping.
No one has seen him stumble looking back.
His fear is not behind him but beside him
On either hand to make his course perhaps
A crooked straightness yet no less a straightness.
He runs face forward. He is a pursuer.
He seeks a seeker who in his turn seeks
Another still, lost far into the distance.
Any who seek him seek in him the seeker.
His life is a pursuit of a pursuit forever.
It is the future that creates his present.
All is an interminable chain of longing.

Life is all an interminable chain of longing.

Then—just at random now—this about the road up at my

place—it's called "Closed For Good"—used to go right across country past several houses, all gone except mine.

Much as I own I owe
The travellers of the past
Because their to and fro
Has cut this road to last,
I owe them more today
Because they've gone away

And come not back with steed
And chariot to chide
My slowness with their speed
And scare me to one side.
They have found other means
For haste and other scenes.

They leave the road to me
To walk in saying naught
Perhaps but to a tree
Inaudibly in thought,
'From you the road receives
A priming coat of leaves.

'And soon for lack of sun,
The prospects are in white
It will be further done,
But with a coat so light
The shape of leaves will show
Beneath the spread of snow.'

And so on into winter
Till even I have ceased
To come as a foot printer,
And only some slight beast
So mousy or so foxy
Shall print there as my proxy.

That goes with that other one.
    Then I . . . let's see . . . caprice. Sometimes I see some-

thing I want to read to you, and then I think I don't. Here's
another tiny little pessimistic one, if you want to call it that—
"Peril of Hope." It's about our orchards in the spring.

> It is right in there
> Betwixt and between
> The orchard bare
> And the orchard green,
>
> When the orchard's right
> In a flowery burst
> Of pink and white,
> That we fear the worst.
>
> For there's not a clime
> But for all the cost
> Will take that time
> For a night of frost.

What I do it for is the sing-song, there.

Then—this one. Funny fates—adventures—you have with
them. This is called "The Draft Horse."

> With a lantern that wouldn't burn
> In too frail a buggy we drove
> Behind too heavy a horse
> Through a pitch-dark limitless grove.
>
> And a man came out of the trees
> And took our horse by the head
> And reaching back to his ribs
> Deliberately stabbed him dead.
>
> The ponderous beast went down
> With a crack of a broken shaft.
> And the night drew through the trees
> In one long invidious draft.
>
> The most unquestioning pair
> That ever accepted fate
> And the least disposed to ascribe
> Any more than we had to to hate,

> We assumed that the man himself
> Or someone he had to obey
> Wanted us to get down
> And walk the rest of the way.

Then I'll say this one.

> I opened the door so my last look
> Should be taken outside a house and book.

My regular way, the last thing of the night, so I'd take my last look outside of a house and book—

> Before I gave up seeing and slept
> I said I would see how Sirius kept
> His watch-dog eye on what remained
> To be gone into if not explained.
> But scarcely was my door ajar,
> When past the leg I thrust for bar
> Slipped in to be my problem guest,
> Not a heavenly dog made manifest,
> But an earthly dog of the carriage breed;
> Who having failed of the modern speed,
> Now asked asylum—and I was stirred
> To be the one so dog-preferred.
> He dumped himself like a bag of bones,
> He sighed himself a couple of groans,
> And head to tail then firmly curled
> Like swearing off on the traffic world.
> I set him water, I set him food.
> He rolled an eye with gratitude
> (Or merely manners it may have been),
> But never so much as lifted chin.
> His hard tail loudly smacked the floor
> As if beseeching me, "Please, no more
> I can't explain—tonight at least."
> His brow was perceptibly trouble-creased.
> So I spoke in tones of adoption thus:
> "Gustie old boy, Dalmatian Gus,
> You're right, there's nothing to discuss.
> Don't try to tell me what's on your mind,
> The sorrow of having been left behind,

Or the sorrow of having run away.
All that can wait for the light of day.
Meanwhile feel obligation-free.
Nobody has to confide in me."
'Twas too one-sided a dialogue.
And I wasn't sure I was talking dog.
I gave up baffled. And all the same
In fancy, I ratified his name,
Gustie, Dalmatian Gus, that is,
And started shaping my life to his,
And sharing his miles of exercise,
Finding him in his right supplies.

Next morning the minute I was about
He was at the door to be let out
With an air that said, "I have paid my call.
You mustn't feel hurt if now I'm all
For getting back somewhere or further on."
I opened the door and he was gone.
I was to taste in little the grief
That comes of dogs' lives being so brief,
Only a fraction of ours at most.
He might have been the dream of a ghost
In spite of the way his tail had smacked
My floor so hard and matter-of-fact.
And things have been going so strangely since
I wouldn't be too hard to convince,
I might almost claim, he was Sirius
(Think of presuming to call him Gus)
The star itself, Heaven's brightest star,
Not a meteorite, but an avatar,
Who had made this overnight descent
To show by deeds he didn't resent
My having depended on him so long,
And yet done nothing about it in song.
A symbol was all he could hope to convey,
An intimation, a shot of ray,
A meaning I was supposed to seek,
And finding, wasn't supposed to speak.

I would like to read *part* of something to you that's hard
to read. It's in my new book, and I have it here in large print
for my eye. And I thought I'd—and yet these books won't
stay there, they won't. This is in blank verse. You know me
well enough to know I've written in nothing but blank verse
and rhymed verse. (I did write one free verse poem, you know,
and I kept it. I thought it was so smart. A lady said to me
one night, "You've said all sorts of things tonight, Mr. Frost.
Which are you, a conservative or a radical?" And I looked at
her very honestly and earnestly and sincerely, and I said:

> I never dared be radical when young
> For fear it would make me conservative when old.

That's my only free verse poem.)
    This is in blank verse, and the title of it—and the little read-
ing of it's all you're going to get—"How Hard It Is to Keep
from Being King When It's in You and in the Situation." And
you don't know—it's kind of, in a way, political and invidi-
ous—but you wouldn't know who I was driving at, maybe,
maybe you would. But it's an old story.

> The King said to his son: "Enough of this!
> The Kingdom's yours to finish as you please.
> I'm getting out tonight. Here, take the crown."
>
> But the Prince drew away his hand in time
> To avoid what he wasn't sure he wanted.
> So the crown fell and the crown jewels scattered.
> And the Prince answered, picking up the pieces,
> "Sire, I've been looking on and I don't like
> The looks of empire here. I'm leaving with you."
>
> So the two making good their abdication
> Fled from the palace in the guise of men.

They're not ordinary men, that means.

> But they had not walked far into the night
> Before they sat down weary on a bank
> Of dusty weeds to take a drink of stars.

And eyeing one he only wished were his,
Rigel, Bellatrix, or Betelgeuse,
The ex-King said, "Yon star's indifference
Fills me with fear I'll be left to my fate:
I needn't think I have escaped my duty,
For hard it is to keep from being King
When it's in you and in the situation.
Witness how hard it was for Julius Caesar.
He couldn't keep himself from being King.
He had to be stopped by the sword of Brutus.
Only less hard it was for Washington.
My crown shall overtake me, you will see,
It will come rolling after us like a hoop."

"Let's not get superstitious, Sire," the Prince said.
"We should have brought the crown along to
    pawn."
"You're right," the ex-King said, "we'll need some
    money.
How would it be for you to take your father
To the slave auction in some market place
And sell him into slavery? My price
Should be enough to set you up in busines—
Or making verse if that is what you're bent on.
Don't let your father tell you what to be."

The ex-King stood up in the market place
And tried to look ten thousand dollars' worth
To the first buyer coming by who asked

No, that ought to be punctuated different.

To the first buyer coming by who asked
What good he was he boldly said, "I'll tell you:
I know the *Quint*essence of many things.
I know the *Quint*essence of food, I know
The *Quint*essence of jewels, and I know
The *Quint*essence of horses, men, and women."

The eunuch laughed: "Well, that's a lot to know.
And here's a lot of money. Who's the taker?
This larrikin?

That's the son.

      All right. You come along.
You're off to Xanadu to help the cook.
I'll try you in the kitchen first on food
Since you put food first in your repertory.
It seems you call quint*ess*ence *quint*essence."

"I'm a Rhodes scholar—that's the reason why.
I was at college in the Isle of Rhodes."

The slave served his novitiate dish-washing.
He got his first chance to prepare a meal
One day when the chief cook was sick at heart.
(The cook was temperamental like the King)
And the meal made the banqueters exclaim
And the Great King inquire whose work it was.

"A man's out there who claims he knows the secret,
Not of food only but of everything,
Jewels and horses, women, wine, and song."
The King said grandly, "Even as we are fed
See that our slave is also. He's in favor.
Take notice, Haman, he's in favor with us."

There came to court a merchant selling pearls,
A smaller pearl he asked a thousand for,
A larger one he asked five hundred for.
The King sat favoring one pearl for its bigness,
And the other for its costliness
(He seems to have felt limited to one),
Till the ambassadors from Punt or somewhere
Shuffled their feet as if to hint respectfully,
"The choice is not between two pearls, O King,
But between war and peace as we conceive it.
We are impatient for your royal answer."

No estimating how far the entente
Might have deteriorated had not someone
Thought of the kitchen slave and had him in
To put an end to the King's vacillation.

And the slave said, "The small one's worth the price,
But the big one is worthless. Break it open.
My head for it—you'll find the big one hollow.
Permit me"—and he crushed it under his heel
And showed them it contained a live teredo.

"But tell us how you knew," Darius said.

"Oh, from my knowledge of its *quint*essence.
I told you I knew the *quint*essence of jewels.
But anybody could have guessed in this case,
From the pearl's having its own native warmth,
Like flesh, there must be something living in it."

"Feed him another feast of recognition."

And so it went with triumph after triumph
Till on a day the King, being sick at heart
(The King was temperamental like his cook,
But nobody had noticed the connection),
Sent for the ex-King in a private matter.
"You say you know the inwardness of men
As well as of your hundred other things.
Dare to speak out and tell me about myself.
What ails me? Tell me. Why am I unhappy?"

"You're not where you belong. You're not a King
Of royal blood. Your father was a cook."

"You die for that."

                    "No, you go ask your mother."

His mother didn't like the way he put it,
"But yes," she said, "some day I'll tell you, dear.

You have a right to know your pedigree.
You're well descended on your mother's side,
Which is unusual. So many kings
Have married beggar maids from off the streets.
Your mother's folks—"

                                        He stayed to hear no more,
But hastened back to reassure the slave
That if he had him slain it wouldn't be
For having lied but having told the truth.
"At least you ought to die for wizardry.
But let me into it and I will spare you.
How did you know the secret of my birth?"

"If you had been a king of royal blood,
You'd have rewarded me for all I've done
By making me your minister,
Or giving me a nobleman's estate.
But all you thought of giving me was food.
I picked you out a horse called Safety Third
By Safety Second out of Safety First,
Guaranteed to come off safely with you
From all the fights you had a mind to lose.
You could lose battles, you could lose whole wars,
You could lose Asia, Africa, and Europe,
No one could get you: you would come home
    smiling.
You lost your army at Mosul. What happened?
You came companionless, but you came home.
Is it not true? And what was my reward?
This time an all-night banquet, to be sure,
But still food, food. Your one idea was food.
None but a cook's son could be so food-minded.
I knew your father must have been a cook.
I'll bet you anything that's all as King
You think of for your people—feeding them."

But the King said, "Haven't I read somewhere
There is no act more kingly than to give?"

"Yes, but give character and not just food.
A King must give his people character."

"They can't have character unless they're fed."

"You're hopeless," said the slave.

                              "I guess I am;
I am abject before you," said Darius.

And that's where I'll leave it. There's twice as much of it. See
the rest of it, how it comes out—how the cook becomes king
again, becomes king; and the other man wants himself exe-
cuted, the regular king. And I guess I've taken my time with
you—or let me say one or two little things.

Oh yeah—see. So many of them have literary criticism in
them—*in* them. And yet I wouldn't admit it, you know. I try
to hide it. So many of them have politics in them, like that—
that's just *loaded* with politics. I got it out of the Arabian
Nights, of course, the outline of the story. But it's just *loaded*,
*loaded* with politics. And I've bent it, you know, to make it
more so, you see. I'm guilty, and all that.

But now this one:

                    O

(speaking to a star up there)

            O Star (the fairest one in sight),
            We grant your loftiness the right
            To some obscurity of cloud—
            I was about to say of night
            But dark is what brings out your light.
            Some mystery becomes the proud.
            But to be wholly taciturn
            In your reserve is not allowed.
            Say something to us we can learn
            By heart and when alone repeat.
            Say something! And it says, 'I burn.'
            But say with what degree of heat.
            Talk Fahrenheit, talk Centigrade.
            Use language we can comprehend.

> Tell us what elements you blend.
> It gives us strangely little aid,
> But does tell something in the end.
> And steadfast as Keats' Eremite,
> Not even stooping from its sphere,
> It asks a little of us here.
> It asks of us a certain height,
> So when at times the mob is swayed
> To carry praise or blame too far,
> We may take something like a star
> To stay our minds on and be staid.

And by that star I mean the Arabian Nights or Catullus or something in the Bible or something way off or something way off in the woods, and when I've made a mistake in my vote. (You know, we were talking about that today. How many times we voted this way and that by mistake.)

And then see little personal things like this: Do you know the real motivation probably of it all? Take the one line in that, "Some mystery becomes the proud." See, you know where I got that? Out of long efforts to understand contemporary poets. You see, let them be mystery. And that's my generosity—call it that. If I was sure they meant anything to themselves it would be all right.

Now take a little one like this—you see how different my feeling's about it:

> She always had to burn a light
> Beside her attic bed at night.
> It gave bad dreams and troubled sleep,
> But helped the Lord her soul to keep.
> Good gloom on her was thrown away.
> It is on me by night or day,
> Who have, as I foresee, ahead
> The darkest of it still to dread.

Suppose I end on that dark note. Good night.

Dartmouth College Address,<br>November 27, 1962

CHRONOLOGY

NOTE ON THE TEXTS

NOTES

INDEXES

# Chronology

1874    Born on March 26 in San Francisco, California, first child of Isabelle Moodie and William Prescott Frost Jr., and named Robert Lee Frost after Confederate general Robert E. Lee. (Mother, b. 1844 in Alloa, Scotland, was the daughter of a sea captain who died soon after her birth; she was brought up by her father's parents, and after her grandfather's death came to America in 1856 to live with her successful uncle in Columbus, Ohio. Father, b. 1850 in Kingston, New Hampshire, was the only child of an old New England farming family. As a teenager during the Civil War he had run away from home to join the Army of Northern Virginia under Lee, getting as far as Philadelphia before he was caught and sent home. A Phi Beta Kappa graduate of Harvard, he met his wife in Lewistown, Pennsylvania, where they were both teaching; they were married in March 1873. They moved to San Francisco soon after, and father obtained job as a journalist.)

1875    Father becomes city editor of the San Francisco *Daily Evening Post*, edited by social reformer Henry George, a family friend (mother will later write book reviews and poems for the paper).

1876    Travels east in spring with mother, who is expecting another child and is upset with father's drinking and gambling. Sister, Jeanie Florence, is born in grandparents' home in Lawrence, Massachusetts, on June 25. Spends autumn with relatives in Columbus, Ohio. Returns to San Francisco in late November with mother, sister, and mother's old friend, Blanche Rankin ("Aunt Blanche"), who will live with family for four years. Father is diagnosed as consumptive after defeating celebrated walker Dan O'Leary in six-day walking race.

1877–78    Lives in Abbotsford House hotel (family will move often during years in San Francisco, living in both apartments and hotels). Receives religious instruction from mother, who reads stories from the Bible, and attends Sunday school at the Swedenborgian church. Father is stern and short-tempered.

1879        Goes to kindergarten for one day, but suffers severe ner-
            vous pain in stomach and does not return.

1880        Father is elected as delegate to the Democratic National
            Convention in Cincinnati, which nominates General Win-
            field S. Hancock for president, and writes short campaign
            biography of General William S. Rosecrans, who is run-
            ning for Congress. Grandparents visit in summer. Frost
            enters first grade in public school, but soon drops out
            when nervous stomach pain returns and is educated by
            mother for the remainder of the school year; takes walks
            with her around San Francisco to learn the city's geogra-
            phy and history. Accompanies father to campaign events
            in San Francisco. Though Rosecrans wins congressional
            race, father is deeply depressed by defeat of Hancock by
            Republican congressman James A. Garfield in presidential
            election.

1881        Frost enters second grade. Baptized in mother's Sweden-
            borgian church.

1882        Drops out of school in February when nervous pain in
            stomach returns and continues education at home. Goes
            with mother and sister to visit "Aunt Blanche," now mar-
            ried and living in the Napa Valley north of San Francisco.

1883        Enjoys hearing mother tell stories about Joan of Arc and
            characters in the Bible, myths, and fairy tales; she also
            reads aloud from works of Shakespeare, Poe, and George
            MacDonald (mother will later read aloud from *Tom
            Brown's School Days*, Emerson, Burns, Wordsworth, Bry-
            ant, Tennyson, and Longfellow). Sometimes hears voices
            when left alone and is told by mother that he shares her
            gift for "second hearing" and "second sight." Family va-
            cations in summer at Bohemian Club camp in Sausalito
            (father is member). Frost watches with terror while father
            takes long swims in San Francisco Bay. Father continues
            to drink as his health deteriorates.

1884        Accepted in a neighborhood gang after proving his cour-
            age by fighting two boys at once. Works briefly as paper-
            boy. With sister Jeanie, spends six weeks visiting "Aunt
            Blanche" in Napa Valley. Works enthusiastically in cam-

paign of father, who has resigned his newspaper job to run for city tax collector on the Democratic ticket. Father loses election and is deeply depressed; with his health declining, he has difficulty finding and keeping work. Mother publishes children's story *The Land of Crystal*.

1885    Father dies of tuberculosis on May 5, leaving family with only $8 after expenses are paid. Grandfather sends money, and family takes father's body to Lawrence, Massachusetts, for burial. Family lives with grandfather, now retired from job as mill supervisor, and grandmother, a former leader of the local suffragist movement. Frost and Jeanie dislike grandparents' sternness and rigorous discipline and feel homesick for California. Family goes to Amherst, New Hampshire, in summer to stay at the farm of great-aunt Sarah Frost and her husband, Benjamin S. Messer. Frost enjoys living with Messers and helping with berry-picking, but dislikes the local teacher when school begins in fall. Family returns to Lawrence and takes its own apartment. Takes school placement tests and is placed in the third grade, while Jeanie qualifies for the fourth grade. Henry George visits the family while on a lecture tour in the Northeast.

1886    Family moves to nearby Salem Depot, New Hampshire, where mother begins teaching the fifth to eighth grades in the district school. Frost and Jeanie enter the fifth-grade class. Learns to whittle and play baseball and becomes close friends with Charlie Peabody, who teaches him how to climb birches, trap animals, and collect birds' nests. Briefly works in shoe factory, then begins making shoe heels in leather shop of their landlord, Loren Bailey. Learns to box from older men in the shop. Becomes infatuated with Sabra Peabody, Charlie's sister, and writes letters to her. Returns to school in fall.

1887    While mother continues to read aloud from works such as Scott's *Tales of a Grandfather*, Percy's *Reliques*, and *The Poems of Ossian*, Frost begins to enjoy reading on his own, starting with Jane Porter's *The Scottish Chiefs*. Studies geography, arithmetic, history, grammar, and reading in his mother's class. Memorizes Fitz-Greene Halleck's poem "Marco Bozzaris."

1888    Passes entrance examinations for Lawrence High School in June. Commutes with Jeanie by train from Salem Depot. Enrolls in the "classical" (college preparatory) program, taking courses in Latin, Greek history, Roman history, and algebra. Angered when complaints by some parents about mother's lax discipline and favoritism toward high-school bound students forces her resignation from the Salem Depot district school.

1889    Finishes school year at the head of the class, for the first time getting better grades than Jeanie. Pursues interest in Indian lore and history by reading Cooper's Leatherstocking Tales, Mary Hartwell Catherwood's *Romance of Dollard*, and W. H. Prescott's *History of the Conquest of Mexico*. Works on Bailey's farm, and learns to sharpen a scythe and mow hay. Returns to Lawrence High School, taking courses in Greek, Latin, European history, and geometry; befriends older student, Carl Burell, who introduces him to botany, astronomy, and evolutionary theory, as well as works by American humorists Artemus Ward, Josh Billings, Petroleum V. Nasby, and Mark Twain.

1890    After mother obtains teaching job in nearby Methuen, Massachusetts, family returns to Lawrence in February. With help from his mother, Frost earns telescope by selling subscriptions to *The Youth's Companion*. Observes planets and stars, using astronomical maps from the Lawrence Public Library. First published poem, "La Noche Triste," based on episode in Prescott's *Conquest of Mexico*, appears in the Lawrence High School *Bulletin* in April; a second poem, "The Song of the Wave," appears in the *Bulletin* in May. Joins the high school debating society. Finishes school year at the head of his class. During the summer family works at hotel in Ocean Park, Maine, where Frost learns tennis. Takes Greek and Latin composition in the fall.

1891    Passes preliminary entrance examinations for Harvard College in Greek, Latin, Greek history, Roman history, algebra, geometry, and English literature. Elected chief editor of the *Bulletin* for the 1891–92 school year. Publishes poem "A Dream of Julius Cæsar" in May *Bulletin*. Maintains position as head of his class. Spends three weeks in the summer doing odd jobs on farm near Canobie Lake, New Hampshire. Works in the Braithwaite Woolen Mill in Lawrence for 11 hours a day, six days a week until midsummer when the workers force the mills to give Saturday afternoons off. Meets and falls in love with fellow student Elinor Miriam White (b. 1872) during fall. Writes several editorials and articles for the *Bulletin* and plays on high school football team as right end. Jeanie is hospitalized in December with typhoid fever and is forced to drop out of school.

1892    Resigns as editor of the *Bulletin* when his assistants fail to do their share of the work. Begins to read widely in poetry and gives books by Emily Dickinson (*Poems*, first published in 1890) and Edward Rowland Sill to Elinor White. Shares valedictory honors with Elinor at graduation, and delivers address "A Monument to After-Thought Unveiled." Writes lyric for commencement hymn as class poet and is awarded prize for scholastic excellence. Works during summer as clerical assistant at mill in Lawrence. Becomes engaged to Elinor; they exchange rings in private ceremony as a pledge of love. Dependent on grandparents for financial support, enters Dartmouth College instead of Harvard because it is cheaper, and because grandparents blame Harvard for his father's bad habits. Takes courses in Greek, Latin, and mathematics. Buys copy of Francis Turner Palgrave's *Golden Treasury of Songs and Lyrics* and reads intensively on his own in English lyric poetry. Bored by college life and restless, leaves Dartmouth at the end of December.

1893    Takes over mother's unruly eighth-grade class in Methuen for several weeks and canes several students. Quits teaching job to help Elinor's mother and ailing sister Ada; finds house for them in Salem and lives with them through the summer. When Elinor returns from St. Lawrence University in Canton, New York, in April, Frost tries to persuade her to leave college and marry him, but she returns to college in September. Works at the Arlington Woolen Mill in Lawrence, changing carbon filaments in ceiling arc lamps. Studies Shakespeare during spare hours while living with mother and sister in an apartment in Lawrence. Beaten up by former students he had caned earlier in the year.

1894        Quits job at the mill in February. Begins teaching grades
            one through six in Salem. Learns in March that *The In-
            dependent* will publish his poem "My Butterfly: An Elegy"
            and pay him $15 for it. Begins long correspondence with
            Susan Hayes Ward, literary editor of *The Independent*, and
            writes her that his four favorite poems are Keats' "Hype-
            rion," Shelley's "Prometheus," Tennyson's "Morte
            D'Arthur," and Browning's "Saul." Tries unsuccessfully
            to convince Elinor to marry him at once. Works unhappily
            at odd jobs in the summer, convinced that Elinor is
            engaged to another man. Has local printer prepare two
            copies of *Twilight*, containing his poems "Twilight," "My
            Butterfly: An Elegy," "Summering," "The Falls," and
            "An Unhistoric Spot." Goes in the fall to St. Lawrence
            University to present Elinor with a copy, but is thrown
            into despair by her cool reception; destroys his own copy
            and returns home. Still distraught, decides to go to the
            Dismal Swamp on the Virginia–North Carolina border.
            Leaves Lawrence on November 6 and travels by train and
            boat to Norfolk, Virginia, then follows wagon road and
            walks for miles into the swamp at night. Meets a party of
            boatmen at canal lock who agree to take him through
            swamp to Elizabeth City, North Carolina. Stays with boat
            as it crosses Albemarle Sound to Nags Head on the At-
            lantic coast. Begins return journey by hopping freight cars
            from Elizabeth City to Baltimore. Exhausted and fright-
            ened, writes mother for return fare and arrives in Lawrence
            on November 30. Learns that "My Butterfly: An Elegy"
            had appeared in *The Independent* on November 8 (will
            continue to publish poems in the journal).

1895        Works as reporter for the Lawrence *Daily American* and
            *Sentinel*. Tutors students in school started by his mother
            and sister. Rents cabin at Ossipee Mountain, New Hamp-
            shire, to be near Elinor, who has graduated from St.
            Lawrence and is spending the summer with her sister
            Leona White Harvey, a portrait painter. Tutors two stu-
            dents who stay with him for several weeks. Returns to help
            mother find better accommodations for her private school,
            where Elinor begins teaching in fall. Frost teaches at Sa-
            lem district school. Marries Elinor White in Lawrence on
            December 19 in ceremony conducted by Swedenborgian
            pastor.

1896    Lives with Elinor and his mother and sister. Writes poems but feels they are not good enough (writes to Ward: "I fear I am not a poet, or but a very incomprehensible one"). Suffers from nervous ailments and stomach pains. Goes with Elinor on delayed honeymoon to rural Allenstown, New Hampshire, where they rent a cottage near the home of their high school friend Carl Burell. Under Burell's influence, Frost renews his interest in botany; makes frequent collecting forays into the countryside and reads with pleasure Mrs. William Starr Dana's *How to Know the Wild Flowers*. Dismayed when Burell is severely injured while working in a box factory. Returns to Lawrence and helps move mother's school into house on Haverhill Street; Frost and Elinor take apartment on second floor. Teaches older students in mother's school. Son Elliott is born on September 25. Fined $10 in December for hitting a lodger during quarrel.

1897    Publishes poem "Greece," inspired by the Greco-Turkish War, in the Boston *Evening Transcript* on April 30. Spends summer with wife and son in Amesbury, Massachusetts. Passes Harvard College entrance examinations in Greek, Latin, ancient history, English, French, and physical science. With money borrowed from grandfather, enters Harvard as a freshman. Moves into a single room in Cambridge and takes part-time job at a North Cambridge night school. Studies German, English composition, and Latin. Joined by Elinor, Elliott, and his mother-in-law in late fall and moves with them into larger apartment in Cambridge.

1898    Awarded Sewall Scholarship for academic excellence. Spends summer in Amesbury, Massachusetts. Suffers from chills and chest pains, which doctor thinks may be consumption. Returns to Harvard in the fall; Elinor, who is again pregnant, remains in Lawrence. Takes Greek, Latin, and philosophy, studying with George Herbert Palmer, George Santayana, and Hugo Munsterberg, who assigns William James' *Psychology: Briefer Course* as course text. (Frost later says about James: "My greatest inspiration, when I was a student, was a man whose classes I never attended.") Returns to Lawrence once a week to see Elinor and teach evening classes in mother's school.

1899    Continues regular studies and audits Nathaniel Shaler's
        course in historical geology. Suffers recurrence of chest
        pains and chills and worries about Elinor's pregnancy and
        his mother's health. Withdraws from Harvard on March
        31. Daughter Lesley is born on April 28. After doctor warns
        that sedentary work would harm his health, takes up poul-
        try farming with financial help from grandfather. Rents a
        house and barn in Methuen, Massachusetts, and buys 200
        eggs for incubation. Insists that his mother see a doctor,
        and learns that she has advanced cancer; she comes to live
        with family in Methuen.

1900    Enjoys tending chickens. Elliott dies of cholera on July 8
        and is buried in Lawrence. Elinor suffers severe depression.
        Frost's health declines, as recurring chest pains, fevers, and
        frequent nightmares cause him to fear consumption.
        Mother enters sanatorium in Penacook, New Hampshire.
        Frost moves family to 30-acre farm in Derry, New Hamp-
        shire, purchased by grandfather, who arranges to have Carl
        Burell and his grandfather, Jonathan Eastman, move in to
        help with farming chores. Mother dies of cancer on No-
        vember 2 and is buried in Lawrence.

1901    Writes poems at night despite depression, then begins to
        feel better when spring arrives. Botanizes with Burell, of-
        ten taking Lesley along. Reads Thoreau's *Walden* for the
        first time. Grandfather William Prescott Frost dies on July
        10; his will gives Frost a $500 annuity and use of the Derry
        farm for ten years, after which the annuity is to be in-
        creased to $800 and Frost is to be given ownership of the
        farm.

1902    Takes over most of the farming duties in spring when Bu-
        rell leaves after Jonathan Eastman dies. Borrows money
        from old friend Ernest Jewell to expand poultry business.
        Son Carol is born on May 27.

1903    Publishes short story "Trap Nests" in *The Eastern Poul-
        tryman* in February (will publish total of 11 stories and
        articles in the *Poultryman* and in *Farm-Poultry*, 1903–5).
        Vacations in March with family in New York City; makes
        several calls on editors, but is unable to interest them in
        his poetry. Daughter Irma is born on June 27.

1904     Continues to write poetry at night at the kitchen table. Enjoys company of neighbor Napoleon Guay and deepens friendship with poultryman John Hall.

1905     Daughter Marjorie is born on March 28.

1906     Secures part-time position teaching English literature at Pinkerton Academy in Derry. Publishes poem "The Tuft of Flowers" in the Derry *Enterprise* in March. Goes alone to Bethlehem, New Hampshire, in the White Mountains in August to relieve the severe hay fever that increasingly troubles him. Stays with John and Mary Lynch, who become friends. Assumes full-time teaching post at Pinkerton Academy. Works on poems in sonnet form.

1907–8     Writes poem "The Later Minstrel" for the Pinkerton celebration of the 100th anniversary of Longfellow's birth. Contracts pneumonia in March and is sick throughout the spring term. Daughter Elinor Bettina is born on June 18 and dies on June 21, 1907. Takes family to Bethlehem, New Hampshire, in August 1907, where they stay with the Lynches for six weeks (will also visit in 1908). Resumes teaching at Pinkerton; one of his students, John Bartlett, will become a lifelong friend and correspondent. Continues to write poems at night.

1909     Impresses Henry C. Morrison, New Hampshire superintendent of public instruction, when he visits Pinkerton; Morrison arranges for Frost to lecture about his teaching methods before several conventions of New Hampshire teachers. Poem "Into Mine Own" appears in *New England Magazine* in May. Sells remaining poultry and moves family from the farm to apartment in nearby Derry Village. Takes family on camping and botanizing trip to Lake Willoughby in Vermont. Supervises *The Pinkerton Critic*, student literary magazine.

1910     Directs students in series of five plays (Marlowe's *Doctor Faustus*, Milton's *Comus*, Sheridan's *The Rivals*, and Yeats' *The Land of Heart's Desire* and *Cathleen ni Houlihan*). Revises English curriculum for the Pinkerton Academy and develops program emphasizing an informal, conversational teaching style. (Writes in school catalog: "The general aim of the course in English is twofold: to bring our students under the *influence* of the great books, and to teach them the *satisfactions* of superior speech.") Father-in-law Edwin White dies of heart disease while visiting Frost family on May 26. Family vacations in Bethlehem in August.

1911    Accepts offer to teach at State Normal School and moves family to Plymouth. Teaches courses in education and psychology; assigns works by Pestalozzi, Rousseau, Plato, and William James' *Psychology: Briefer Course* and *Talks to Teachers on Psychology and to Students on Some of Life's Ideals*. Befriends Sidney Cox, a young teacher at Plymouth High School (will often write to him in later years). Sells the Derry farm in November. Sews together a booklet of seventeen poems and sends it to Susan Hayes Ward, literary editor of *The Independent*, as a Christmas gift. (Writes to her: "It represents . . . not the long deferred forward movement you are living in wait for, but only the grim stand it was necessary for me to make until I gather myself together. The forward movement is to begin next year.") Visits the Wards in New York City during Christmas vacation. Reads Henri Bergson's *Creative Evolution* en route.

1912    Decides to live in England for a few years and devote himself to writing full time. Resigns teaching position and sails from Boston with family on August 23. Stays in London for a week before renting a cottage in Beaconsfield, Buckinghamshire, 20 miles north of London. Prepares manuscript of *A Boy's Will* in October and submits it to London firm of David Nutt and Company, which accepts it for publication.

1913    Attends opening in January of Harold Monro's Poetry Bookshop in Kensington, where he meets poet Frank S. Flint, who introduces him to Ezra Pound. *A Boy's Will* is published on April 1 and is favorably reviewed by Pound in *Poetry*, Flint in *Poetry and Drama*, and Norman Douglas in *The English Review*. Through Pound, meets Richard Aldington, Hilda Doolittle, Ford Hermann Hueffer (Ford Madox Ford), May Sinclair, Ernest Rhys, and William Butler Yeats (who tells Pound that *A Boy's Will* is "the best poetry written in America for a long time"). Frost meets with T. E. Hulme and Flint to discuss poetics; begins to set down ideas about "the sounds of sense with all their irregularity of accent across the regular beat of the metre" in series of letters to American friends John Bartlett and Sidney Cox. Writes to Bartlett: "there is a kind of success called 'of esteem' and it butters no parsnips. It means a success with the critical few who are supposed to know. But really to arrive where I can stand on my legs as a poet and nothing else I must get outside that circle to the general reader who buys books in their thousands. I may not be able to do that. I believe in doing it—dont you doubt me there. I want to be a poet for all sorts and kinds. I could never make a merit of being caviare to the crowd the way my quasi-friend Pound does. I want to reach out, and would if it were a thing I could do by taking thought." Friendship with Pound is strained ("He says I must write something much more like *vers libre* or he will let me perish by neglect. He really threatens"). Vacations with family in Scotland. Resumes literary contacts in London, meeting Walter de la Mare, Rupert Brooke, Lawrence Binyon, W. H. Davies, Wilfred Gibson, Lascelles Abercrombie, and Robert Bridges, and attending weekly gatherings at homes of Hulme and Yeats. Forms close friendship with essayist and critic Edward Thomas.

1914    Moves family to old house near Dymock, Gloucestershire, to be near friends Gibson and Abercrombie. *North of Boston* is published on May 15 by David Nutt and Company and is favorably reviewed in *The Nation* (London), *The Outlook*, *The Times Literary Supplement*, *Pall Mall Gazette*, *The English Review*, *The Bookman*, *The Daily News*, and other periodicals. Spends much time with Thomas and encourages him to write poetry. Becomes friends with Gloucestershire barrister and botanist John W. Haines. Amused when local people think he may be a spy after the outbreak of World War I in August. Moves in with Abercrombie family to save expenses during the winter. Learns that New York publishing firm of Henry Holt and Company will publish his books in the United States. Decides to return to America, borrowing money from friends to help finance passage. Worries that review of *North of Boston* by Pound in *Poetry* may cause Americans to consider him to be one of Pound's "party of American literary refugees."

1915    Sails from Liverpool on February 13 with family and Edward Thomas's 15-year-old son, Mervyn (who is to visit friends in New Hampshire). Arrives in New York February 23 and learns that *North of Boston* was published by Henry Holt and Company on February 20. Remains in New York City while family goes to the John Lynch farm in Bethlehem, New Hampshire. Meets with Holt editor Alfred Harcourt and editors of the *The New Republic*, which had recently published "The Death of the Hired Man" and a favorable review of *North of Boston* by Amy Lowell. Visits sister Jeanie, now teaching in Pennsylvania and increasingly troubled, and convinces her to attend college (she will receive B.A. from the University of Michigan in 1918). Travels to Boston, and meets critic and anthologist William Stanley Braithwaite, *Atlantic Monthly* editor Ellery Sedgwick, Amy Lowell, and John Gould Fletcher. Rejoins family in Bethlehem. *A Boy's Will* is published by Henry Holt and Company in April; Frost is surprised by number of good reviews. Buys farm in Franconia, New Hampshire. Suffers great nervousness while addressing Boston Authors' Club in May, but feels more at ease when reading poems "Birches," "The Road Not Taken," and "The Sound of Trees" at Tufts College. Meets poet Edwin Arlington Robinson, whom he admires, and poet, critic, and anthologist Louis Untermeyer, a correspondent of Abercrombie, who becomes an intimate lifelong friend. Moves to farm in Franconia in June. Writes poems on a homemade writing board that attaches to a chair. Learns that *North of Boston* is selling very well. Sends children to public school (they had been educated at home since the family left Plymouth). Visits William Dean Howells at offices of *Harper's Magazine* in September. Frightened when Elinor, who is pregnant and has a weak heart, becomes very ill; she recovers after miscarriage.

1916    Gives talks and readings in Massachusetts, New Hampshire, Pennsylvania, and New York City. Reads "Bonfire" and "The Ax-Helve" at Harvard College. Elected to the National Institute of Arts and Letters. Visits New York to inscribe copies of *Mountain Interval*, published by Holt on November 27. Accepts offer from Alexander Meiklejohn, president of Amherst College, to teach for one semester at salary of $2,000.

1917    Moves family to Amherst, Massachusetts, in January.
        Begins teaching courses in poetry appreciation and in
        pre-Shakespearean drama. *A Way Out*, one-act play, is
        published in *The Seven Arts*. Continues to give talks and
        readings. Deeply grieved by death of Edward Thomas,
        killed by an artillery shell in France on April 9 at the battle
        of Arras, but is grateful that his efforts to have Thomas's
        poems published in America have been successful. Accepts
        offer to extend teaching appointment at Amherst. Returns
        with family to Franconia for the summer. Lesley enters
        Wellesley College. Frost wins $100 prize given by *Poetry:
        A Magazine of Verse* for "Snow."

1918    Meets Vachel Lindsay, Sara Teasdale, and James Oppen-
        heim at party given by Untermeyer in New York. Awarded
        honorary M.A. degree by Amherst College in May; reap-
        pointed professor of English with teaching responsibilities
        limited to the first semester of each year. Pleased when
        Lesley leaves college after her freshman year to do war
        work in an aircraft factory. Spends summer in Franconia.
        During national epidemic Frost suffers severe case of in-
        fluenza that lasts for months.

1919    Attends the premiere performance of his play *A Way Out*
        given by Amherst students in Northampton, Massachu-
        setts, on February 24. Elected president of the New Eng-
        land Poetry Club. During visit to New York City, where
        Lesley is now a student at Barnard College, meets and
        becomes friends with Ridgely Torrence and Padraic
        Colum. Returns to Franconia with family in April. Con-
        tinues to give talks and readings during fall semester at
        Amherst.

1920    Resigns position at Amherst College in February over dis-
        agreements with President Meiklejohn, whom Frost con-
        siders too morally permissive, and to devote more time to
        writing poetry. Learns on March 31 that sister Jeanie, who
        has exhibited symptoms of paranoia for several years, was
        arrested in Portland, Maine, on March 25 for disturbing
        the peace and was pronounced insane by an attending
        physician. Goes to Portland and commits Jeanie to the
        state mental hospital at Augusta, Maine (will continue to
        visit her in hospital). Sells property in Franconia and buys

farm in South Shaftsbury, Vermont, near homes of friends Sarah Cleghorn and Dorothy Canfield Fisher. Moves with family in October into 18th-century farmhouse ("Stone Cottage") and makes plans to raise apples with his son Carol. Begins serving as consulting editor for Henry Holt and Company at a salary of $100 per month. Takes occasional trips to New York City, often accompanied by Elinor.

1921    Continues to give talks and readings; now receives at least $100 plus expenses for each. Spends one week in March as "poet in residence" at Queens University in Kingston, Ontario. Plants apple orchard and pine trees with Carol. Enjoys drives with horse and buggy. Reads in July at newly established Bread Loaf School of English in Ripton, Vermont, beginning long association with the school. After accepting a one-year, $5,000 fellowship at the University of Michigan, moves with family in October to Ann Arbor (Marjorie remains in high school in Bennington). Though no specific duties are assigned, finds schedule busy with advising students, giving talks, and dining out.

1922    Helps students arrange a successful poets' lecture series which includes Padraic Colum, Carl Sandburg, Louis Untermeyer, Amy Lowell, and Vachel Lindsay. Awarded honorary M.A. by the University of Michigan. Named Poet Laureate of Vermont by the state League of Women's Clubs. Returns to South Shaftsbury. Hikes with children for 65 miles along the Long Trail in the Green Mountains, then walks 50 miles along an easier route when he is unable to keep up with them. Fellowship at the University of Michigan is renewed for another year. Visits the South, lecturing in Texas, Louisiana, and Missouri in November. Returns to Ann Arbor exhausted and ill. Spends Christmas at South Shaftsbury farm.

1923    Returns to Ann Arbor in early February. Invites Hamlin Garland, Dorothy Canfield Fisher, and Untermeyer to campus as guest lecturers. *Selected Poems* is published by Henry Holt on March 15. Suffers another bout of influenza. Awarded honorary LHD by the University of Vermont. Accepts appointment as professor of English at Amherst College after Meiklejohn is dismissed as

president by the trustees. Teaches one course on philo-
sophical judgments and another based on readings from
Melville, Thoreau, Emerson, Gibbon, and others. Dis-
cusses quantum theory with Danish physicist Niels Bohr
when Bohr lectures at Amherst in October. Gives Carol
the South Shaftsbury farm as a wedding present when he
marries Lillian LaBatt on November 3. *New Hampshire*,
with woodcuts by J. J. Lankes, is published by Henry Holt
on November 15.

1924    Awarded the Pulitzer Prize for *New Hampshire* in May.
Travels to Pittsfield, Massachusetts, to help Lesley and
Marjorie, who are opening a bookstore. Receives Hon-
orary Litt.D. degrees from Middlebury College and Yale
University. Spends a week at the Bread Loaf School of
English in July. Grandson William Prescott Frost, son of
Carol and Lillian, is born on October 15. Gives notice to
Amherst of his acceptance of lifetime appointment at Uni-
versity of Michigan as Fellow in Letters, with no teaching
obligations (appointment begins in autumn 1925).

1925    Attends "Fiftieth Birthday Dinner" given by friends in-
cluding Untermeyer, Dorothy Canfield Fisher, Frederick
Melcher, Willa Cather, Irita and Carl Van Doren, Elinor
Wylie, and Wilbur L. Cross, in New York City on March
26 (Frost believes he was born in 1875). Writes obituary
tribute to Amy Lowell for *The Christian Science Monitor*
in May. Goes to Ann Arbor in late September to begin
new appointment despite Elinor's concern about their
children's health and their distance from them. Continues
to give readings and talks, often returning home exhausted
and ill. Joins Elinor in Pittsfield in December when Mar-
jorie is hospitalized, suffering from pneumonia, a peri-
cardiac infection, chronic appendicitis, and nervous ex-
haustion.

1926    Returns to Ann Arbor in late January after spending two
weeks at Amherst and giving talks at Bryn Mawr and
Union College. Joined in spring by Elinor, Marjorie, and
Irma, who has left art school in New York. When Amherst
president George Daniel Olds visits Ann Arbor in May,
Frost accepts his offer to rejoin college faculty as a part-
time professor of English, with salary of $5,000 a year and

no obligation to teach formal classes. Awarded honorary Litt.D. by Bowdoin College (continues to receive honorary degrees for the rest of his life). Returns to farm in South Shaftsbury. Participates in inaugural session of the Bread Loaf Writers' Conference. Continues to make annual stays in Franconia during late-summer hay-fever season. Pleased by marriage of daughter Irma to John Paine Cone in Franconia on October 15. Spends two weeks lecturing and meeting with students at Wesleyan University.

1927    Moves to Amherst in January, where he teaches for ten weeks before visiting Michigan, Dartmouth, and Bowdoin for short stays. Rents house for summer in North Bennington, Vermont. Grandson Jack is born to Irma and John Cone. Goes with Elinor and Marjorie to Baltimore, where Marjorie enters Johns Hopkins Hospital for ten weeks of treatment. Frost returns with Elinor to Amherst.

1928    Signs new contract with Holt providing for royalty increase from 15 to 20 percent after 5,000 copies of a book are sold, as well as a $2,000 advance and monthly payments of $250 for the next five years. Dismayed when Irma, who is unhappy living on farm in Kansas, returns home with her baby; John Cone soon follows. Buys them a small farm in North Bennington. Sails for France with Elinor and Marjorie on August 4. Leaves Marjorie with friends of Dorothy Fisher in Sèvres, and goes to England with Elinor, who is exhausted and depressed. Spends time in Gloucestershire with John W. Haines, returning to places they had explored with Edward Thomas. Sees old friends in London. Travels alone to Dublin to visit Padraic Colum and George Russell ("Æ") and to see Yeats. Reads in London at Harold Monro's bookstore and meets T. S. Eliot for the first time before visiting friends in Scotland. Returns to America in late November. Learns that Lesley, who had married James Dwight Francis in September, is unhappy and contemplating divorce. *West-Running Brook*, with woodcuts by J. J. Lankes, is published November 19 by Holt, which also brings out an expanded edition of *Selected Poems.*

1929    Permits Marjorie to begin nursing school at Johns Hopkins. Lives in North Bennington while overseeing work on newly purchased 150-acre "Gully Farm" in South Shaftsbury, about a mile away from "Stone Cottage." Grandchild Elinor Frost Francis, first child of Lesley and Dwight Francis, is born. Participates in the Bread Loaf Writers' Conference in August. Sister Jeanie dies in state mental hospital in Augusta, Maine, on September 7; Frost and Carol arrange and attend her funeral and interment at Lawrence, Massachusetts. Frost and Elinor move into "Gully" farmhouse.

1930      *Collected Poems* published in November by Holt. Elected to membership in the American Academy of Arts and Letters. Goes with Elinor to Baltimore in December to see Marjorie, who is hospitalized with tuberculosis.

1931      Decides with doctors that Marjorie should enter sanatorium in Boulder, Colorado, near home of his friend John Bartlett. Delivers six lectures at the New School for Social Research in New York City, and continues to make appearances at other colleges. Awarded Pulitzer Prize for *Collected Poems* in June. Goes to Montauk, Long Island, where grandchild, Lesley Lee Francis, Lesley's second daughter, is born on June 20 (Lesley's divorce from Dwight Francis becomes final soon after). Visits Marjorie in Boulder during summer and lectures at the University of Denver and the University of Colorado. Travels with Elinor to Monrovia, California, where Carol and his family have moved because of Lillian's tuberculosis. Visits San Francisco and tries to locate childhood scenes. Returns to South Shaftsbury. Receives Russell Loines Poetry Prize from the National Institute of Arts and Letters in December.

1932      Moves into newly purchased house in Amherst in February. Travels to Boulder with Elinor to meet Marjorie's fiancé, archaeology student Willard Fraser, then goes with Marjorie to California to visit Carol and his family in Monrovia. Attends Olympic Games in Los Angeles in August. Delivers lectures at several colleges. Returns to South Shaftsbury in October. Attends dinner given for T. S. Eliot at the St. Botolph Club in Boston; is displeased by Eliot's slighting remarks concerning Robert Burns and other Scottish poets.

1933 Continues heavy lecture schedule to earn extra money for his children's expenses. Joined by Elinor in Texas, where he delivers ten public lectures and readings in eleven days in late April. Marjorie marries Willard Fraser in Billings, Montana, on June 3; Frost is too exhausted to attend wedding.

1934 Granddaughter Marjorie Robin Fraser is born on March 16. Frost and Elinor go to Billings in April after learning that Marjorie is very ill with puerperal fever. Arranges to have Marjorie flown to the Mayo Clinic in Rochester, Minnesota. Although she receives intensive course of serum injections and blood transfusions, Marjorie remains delirious and dies on May 2. After her burial in Billings, Frost returns to Amherst with Elinor, Willard, and baby Robin; writes Untermeyer: "The noblest of us all is dead and has taken our hearts out of the world with her." Family keeps Robin, who is cared for by Lillian (now recovered from her tuberculosis) at Stone Cottage until the fall. Elinor, depressed and exhausted, suffers severe attack of angina pectoris in early November. On doctor's orders, Frost and Elinor go in early December to Key West, Florida, where they are later joined by Carol and his family.

1935 Meets Wallace Stevens, who is also staying in Key West. Gives lecture at the University of Miami. Returns north with Elinor in late March. After Edwin Arlington Robinson's death in April, Frost agrees to write preface to his last book, *King Jasper*. Lectures at the Rocky Mountain Writers' Conference in Boulder to give Elinor opportunity to see granddaughter Robin. Speaks in Santa Fe, New Mexico, at request of Witter Bynner. Gives first of many talks at Agnes Scott College, Decatur, Georgia, in November. With Elinor, rents house for winter in Coconut Grove, Florida; joined at Christmas by Carol and Lesley and their families.

1936 Privately publishes *Franconia*, a small volume of Marjorie's poems. Lectures again at the Winter Institute of Literature at Miami, where he becomes friends with Bernard DeVoto. Leaves Florida with Elinor for Cambridge in late February to begin appointment as Charles Eliot Norton Professor of Poetry at Harvard University. Delivers series of six lectures on "The Renewal of Words" to overflow audiences of more than a thousand. Becomes close friends with Theodore Morrison, Harvard tutor and director of the Bread Loaf Writers' Conference, and his wife, Kathleen, who host receptions at their home after his lectures. *A Further Range*, published by Holt on May 20, is made a selection of the Book-of-the-Month Club. Suffers severe case of shingles in late August and is unable to complete two poems intended to be read at Harvard ceremonies in the fall. Spends winter in San Antonio, Texas, with Elinor; they are joined for the holidays by Willard, Robin, Lesley, Carol, and their families.

1937    Returns to Amherst in March. Wins Pulitzer Prize for *A Further Range*. Elected to membership in the American Philosophical Society. Continues to lecture widely and win awards. Spends hay-fever season in Concord Corners, Vermont, where he has purchased two houses. Elinor undergoes surgery for breast cancer in Springfield, Massachusetts, in early October; Frost writes to Untermeyer that she "has been the unspoken half of everything I ever wrote." After her strength slowly returns, goes with Elinor to Gainesville, Florida, to spend the winter; they are again joined by family.

1938    Elinor dies of heart failure in Gainesville on March 20. Frost collapses and is unable to attend cremation. Remains in Gainesville until mid-April and is visited by friends Hervey Allen and Louis Untermeyer. Arranges memorial service on April 22 in Johnson Chapel, Amherst College, where he has often read. Continues lecturing. Resigns position at Amherst College in June, sells Amherst house, and returns to South Shaftsbury. Elected to the Harvard Board of Overseers. Accepts invitation from Kathleen Morrison to go with her to the West Dover, Vermont, vacation home of the Nathaniel Sage family. Asks Kathleen Morrison to marry him; she refuses. Attends Bread Loaf Writers' Conference, where his continuing emotional instability draws attention. Frost is delighted when Kathleen Morrison agrees to work for him as a paid secretary and take care of arranging lecture appearances (she will continue to do so for remainder of Frost's life). Moves to apartment in Boston in October. After Frost threatens to leave Henry Holt, the firm offers him a new contract which guarantees a 20 percent royalty on all books sold and raises his monthly payment to $300.

1939     Awarded the Gold Medal by the National Institute of Arts and Letters in New York on January 18. Goes to Key West, where he is joined by the Morrisons for two weeks. Visits Hervey Allen's estate in Coconut Grove. Carol and family arrive to spend the winter nearby. Frost takes first plane trip, flying to Cuba with Paul and Mary Engle for short stay. Enlarged edition of *Collected Poems*, with preface "The Figure a Poem Makes," is published by Holt on February 17. Returns to Boston from Florida in late February. Goes on extensive reading and lecturing tour in the East, Midwest, and Mountain States. Accepts two-year appointment as Ralph Waldo Emerson Fellow in Poetry at Harvard in May. Decides to purchase the Homer Noble Farm in Ripton, Vermont, located within walking distance of Bread Loaf. Designates Lawrance Thompson, whom he had first met in the late 1920s, as his "official" biographer on condition that the biography appear only after his death. Begins teaching weekly course in poetry held in Adams House at Harvard. Suffers painful attack of acidosis in December.

1940     Undergoes surgery for hemorrhoids. Travels to Key West with Kathleen Morrison, who remains for two weeks until Thompson arrives. Frost dines with Wallace Stevens in Key West and visits Hervey Allen in South Miami. Returns to Boston in mid-March in improved health. Arranges to buy five acres of land near Allen's house in South Miami in May. Moves into the cabin at the Homer Noble Farm for the summer while the Morrisons occupy the main house. Joins Carol and 15-year-old grandson Prescott in South Shaftsbury while Lillian undergoes surgery in early October. Tries to talk his son, whose long-standing depression and suspiciousness have become more acute since Elinor's death, out of his suicidal thoughts. Returns to Boston thinking crisis is over, and is horrified when Carol commits suicide with a deer-hunting rifle on October 9. Returns to South Shaftsbury immediately to make funeral arrangements and to be with Prescott, who had discovered his father's body. Writes about Carol to Untermeyer: "I took the wrong way with him. I tried many ways and every single one of them was wrong."

1941      Goes to South Miami for the winter and plants grove of orange trees on his land there (orchard eventually includes grapefruit, mango, loquat, and banana trees). Becomes close friends with Hyde Cox. Moves in March to newly purchased house at 35 Brewster Street in Cambridge (will continue to live there for the remainder of his life, spending summers at the Homer Noble Farm and winters in South Miami). On March 26, his birthday, visits exhibition of his works arranged by Lesley at the Library of Congress in Washington, D.C., to coincide with his talk there on "The Role of a Poet in a Democracy." Accepts offer from Harvard of a fellowship in American Civilization with stipend of $3,000; duties consist of holding informal talks with students in all seven of the college's residential houses. Reads poem "The Lesson for Today" at Harvard. Continues extensive schedule of lectures. With Lillian and Prescott, buries urns containing Carol's and Elinor's ashes in family burial plot purchased in the cemetery of the First Congregational Church in Old Bennington. Reads three unpublished poems, including "The Gift Outright," at College of William and Mary in December.

1942      Has two small prefabricated houses built on his land in South Miami, which he names "Pencil Pines." *A Witness Tree*, dedicated to Kathleen Morrison "for her part in it," is published by Holt on April 23; sales reach 10,000 copies within two months.

1943      Enjoys gardening at Pencil Pines and on the Homer Noble Farm. Continues to lecture, although war has reduced invitations. Awarded Pulitzer Prize for *A Witness Tree* in May, becoming the first person to receive the Prize four times. Accepts appointment at Dartmouth College as George Ticknor Fellow in the Humanities, with $2,500 stipend and $500 for expenses. Duties include informal teaching and advising students from Friday afternoon through Sunday. Pleased by the large Dartmouth exhibition of his books and manuscripts, compiled by friend Ray Nash. Hospitalized in December with serious case of pneumonia.

1944        Travels with Kathleen Morrison to Pencil Pines for the
            winter (Lillian and Prescott, who is attending the Univer-
            sity of Miami, now live on the property for the remainder
            of the year). Lectures widely throughout the Midwest, but
            finds wartime travel difficult. Continues to participate in
            the Bread Loaf Writers' Conference. Learns that Irma,
            who is showing signs of mental instability similar to
            Jeanie's, and John Cone have separated.

1945        Meets John Dewey in Key West. *A Masque of Reason* is
            published by Holt on March 26. Reads at Amherst College
            for the first time since resigning in 1938. Works on *A Masque
            of Mercy* during the summer. Returns to Dartmouth as
            Ticknor Fellow and spends several weeks each term con-
            ducting informal seminars with limited enrollment.

1946        Arranges for Irma and her six-year-old son Harold to stay
            in Ripton during the summer (Jacky, her 19-year-old son,
            is in the army). As her mental condition deteriorates, Frost
            has difficulty finding satisfactory lodging for her; consults
            his friend, poet and psychiatrist Merrill Moore, about her
            case. Modern Library publishes an edition of *Collected
            Poems* with recently written preface, "The Constant
            Symbol."

1947        Purchases house for Irma and Harold in Acton, Massa-
            chusetts. Travels to Berkeley in March to receive his 17th
            honorary degree. Attends gala birthday party in San Fran-
            cisco, revisits old childhood scenes, and visits "Aunt
            Blanche," who is now nearly 100 years old. Lectures in
            Southern California before returning home in April. En-
            joys surprise visit from T. S. Eliot in Cambridge in early
            May. *Steeple Bush* is published by Holt on May 28; Frost
            waits anxiously for reviews and suffers pains in his chest
            and arms after reading critical review in *Time*. Learns that
            Irma's condition has worsened and worries about Harold.
            After consulting with grandson Jacky (now out of the
            army) and Merrill Moore, who both advise medical care,
            Frost has Irma committed to the state mental hospital in
            Concord, New Hampshire, in August. *A Masque of Mercy*
            is published by Holt in November.

1948        Enjoys working at Dartmouth but feels closer to Amherst
            and accepts offer made in November to return there as

Simpson Lecturer in Literature with a salary of $3,500. Duties include delivering a lecture each year to the entire college, visiting classes, and holding informal seminars and conferences for one month each semester (will hold the lectureship until his death).

1949    Angered by award of Bollingen Prize to Ezra Pound, now confined to a mental hospital and under indictment for treason for his radio broadcasts from Italy during World War II. Deeply gratified when *Complete Poems of Robert Frost 1949*, published by Holt on May 30, receives good reviews and sells very well.

1950    U.S. Senate adopts resolution honoring Frost on his 75th birthday (actually his 76th). Begins friendship with Edward Connery Lathem, a senior at Dartmouth College (Lathem later becomes a posthumous editor of Frost's work). Attends conference held in his honor at Kenyon College in October.

1951    Continues to give readings and lectures; because of worsening eyesight, now often recites poems, including those of other poets, from memory. Has cancerous lesion removed from upper right side of his face.

1952    Attends funeral of old friend Sidney Cox in Hanover on January 6. Lesley marries Joseph W. Ballantine, a retired diplomat and teacher, on August 23.

1953    Awarded the Fellowship of the Academy of American Poets, with a stipend of $5,000 in March. Undergoes surgery in late December for a recurrence of facial skin cancer.

1954    Invited to the White House by his friend, former New Hampshire governor Sherman Adams, who is now serving as chief of staff to President Eisenhower. Attends series of 80th birthday celebrations (has now learned that he was born in 1874), including a dinner given by Holt at the Waldorf-Astoria and a dinner given by old friends in Amherst. Holt publishes *Aforesaid*, new selection of his poems, in limited edition of 650 copies. Convinced by Lesley that he would be serving his country, travels with her to Brazil as a delegate to the World Congress of Writers held in São Paulo, August 4–19. Lectures and reads to enthusiastic audiences in São Paulo and Rio de Janeiro, then returns to the United States by way of Lima, Peru.

1955–56    Vermont state legislature names mountain in Ripton after Frost in May 1955. Frost has patchwork quilts made from 26 academic hoods he has received along with honorary degrees. Continues to give readings.

1957    Frost, T. S. Eliot, and Ernest Hemingway sign letter, drafted by Archibald MacLeish, asking Attorney General Herbert Brownell to drop the treason indictment against Ezra Pound. Accompanied by Lawrance Thompson, Frost travels to England on a "good will mission" under the auspices of the Department of State. Gives readings at the University of London, then goes to Cambridge, Durham, and Manchester. Sees granddaughter Lesley Lee Francis in London. Awarded honorary Litt.D. degrees by Oxford and Cambridge, becoming only the third American (after Henry Wadsworth Longfellow and James Russell Lowell) to receive honors from both universities in the same year. Tours Dymock region of Gloucestershire, where he lived in 1914–15. Meets W. H. Auden, E. M. Forster, Stephen Spender, C. Day Lewis, and Graham Greene. Attends dinner in his honor at the English Speaking Union in London. T. S. Eliot, offering a toast, calls Frost "*the* most eminent, the most distinguished" living Anglo-American poet, and says: "I think that there are two kinds of local feeling in poetry. There is one kind which makes that poetry only accessible to people who had the same background, to whom it means a great deal. And there is another kind which can go with universality: the relation of Dante to Florence, of Shakespeare to Warwickshire, of Goethe to the Rhineland, the relation of Robert Frost to New England. He has that universality." Frost visits "The Bungalow" in Beaconsfield, where he lived from 1912 to 1914. Travels to Dublin, Ireland, where he receives honorary degree from the National University. Returns to America on June 20. Becomes actively involved in effort to free Ezra Pound, traveling to Washington in July and October to discuss case with MacLeish and Deputy Attorney General William P. Rogers.

1958      Invited by President Eisenhower to the White House on February 27. Discusses Pound case with Sherman Adams and Rogers, who is now attorney general, before attending dinner party hosted by Eisenhower. Meets again with Rogers on April 14, and is told that the government is ready to drop the charges against Pound. Drafts statement in support of Pound's release for use at court hearing on April 18 that ends with the dismissal of the indictment (Pound is discharged from federal mental hospital on May 7). Frost is appointed in May to be Consultant in Poetry to the Library of Congress. Receives Emerson-Thoreau Medal of the American Academy of Arts and Sciences; delivers address "On Emerson."

1959      Predicts in March that Senator John F. Kennedy will win the 1960 presidential election. Attends dinner held in honor of his 85th birthday at Waldorf-Astoria Hotel, at which he hears Lionel Trilling deliver an assessment of his work. Before reciting his poems after dinner, Frost admits to nervousness caused by Trilling's speech. (Trilling had remarked: "The universe that he conceives is a terrifying universe. . . . Read 'Neither Out Far Nor In Deep,' which often seems to me the most perfect poem of our time, and see if you are warmed by anything in it except the energy with which emptiness is perceived.") Appointed to three-year term as Honorary Consultant in the Humanities at the Library of Congress.

1960      Continues to teach at Amherst and Bread Loaf and to maintain intensive schedule of lectures. Testifies before Senate subcommittee in favor of a bill to establish a National Academy of Culture. Congress passes bill awarding Frost a gold medal in recognition of his poetry. Pleased when John F. Kennedy, now president-elect, invites him to take part in inaugural ceremonies.

1961      Writes new poem for inauguration on January 20, but is unable to read it in glare of bright sunlight and recites only "The Gift Outright." Accompanied by Thompson, travels in March under auspices of the State Department to Israel and Greece. Lectures at Hebrew University in Jerusalem and explores the city, including the Jordanian sector (crossing of the frontier is made possible by the

American consulate). Delivers three lectures in Athens and climbs the Acropolis. Goes on to London and attends party given in his honor by U.S. Ambassador David Bruce. Feeling sick and exhausted, Frost cuts trip short and returns to America. Enjoys lecturing in the State Department auditorium on May 1, where he is introduced by his friend Secretary of the Interior Stewart Udall to an audience of ambassadors, senators, generals, and cabinet officers. Vermont state legislature names Frost "Poet Laureate of Vermont."

1962    Attends dedication of "Robert Lee Frost Elementary School" in Lawrence, Massachusetts, in January. Falls seriously ill with pneumonia and is hospitalized in South Miami in February. *In the Clearing* is published by Holt, Rinehart and Winston, on his birthday, March 26. Goes to White House to receive from President Kennedy the gold medal voted him by Congress in 1960, then attends birthday dinner with over 200 guests; speakers include Chief Justice Earl Warren, Robert Penn Warren, Adlai Stevenson, Justice Felix Frankfurter, and Mark Van Doren. At the invitation of President Kennedy, travels in late August to the Soviet Union as part of cultural exchange program sponsored by the State Department, accompanied by friend Frederick B. Adams Jr., director of the Morgan Library, and Franklin D. Reeve, a young professor of Russian literature who acts as his interpreter. Gives public readings in Leningrad and Moscow and meets poets Anna Akhmatova, Yevgeny Yevtushenko, and Andrei Voznesensky, as well as Andrei Tvardovsky, poet and influential editor of literary journal *Novy Mir*. Travels to Gagra, resort on the Black Sea coast of Georgia, to meet with Soviet Premier Nikita Khruschev. Exhausted and ill, Frost is too weak to leave his guest house, and Khruschev comes to visit him; they talk for 90 minutes. Returns to America still suffering from exhaustion and tells press on arrival that Khruschev "said we were too liberal to fight," causing a controversy that strains friendship with Kennedy. Travels widely to lecture and read. Learns that an anonymous donor has given $3.5 million for construction of The Robert Frost Library at Amherst. Participates in National Poetry Festival at the Library of Congress during the Cuban missile crisis in October, and admits that Khruschev had not said the words he had attributed to him. Gives talk at Ford Hall Forum in Boston on December 2. Persuaded by Kathleen Morrison, enters Peter Bent Brigham Hospital in Boston on December 3 for observation and tests. Undergoes prostate operation on December 10; doctors find cancer in his prostate and bladder. Suffers pulmonary embolism on December 23.

1963 Learns on January 3 that he has been awarded the Bollingen Prize for Poetry by committee that includes John Hall Wheelock, Allen Tate, Louise Bogan, Richard Eberhart, and Robert Lowell. Suffers another pulmonary embolism on January 7. Mind remains clear and doctors allow visitors. Dies shortly after midnight on January 29. Private memorial service for friends and family is held in the Appleton Chapel in Harvard Yard on January 31, and public service is held at Johnson Chapel, Amherst College, on February 17. Ashes are interred in the Frost family plot in Old Bennington on June 16.

# Note on the Texts

This volume contains two published collections of poetry by Robert Frost, *Complete Poems* (1949) and *In the Clearing* (1962), as well as a selection of 94 uncollected poems, arranged by the approximate date of their composition, including 17 that are printed here for the first time. Following the poems, this volume presents three plays, *A Way Out*, *In an Art Factory*, and *The Guardeen*, and a selection of 88 lectures, essays, stories, and letters.

Frost published ten volumes of new poetry between 1913 and 1947: *A Boy's Will* (London: David Nutt, 1913), *North of Boston* (London: David Nutt, 1914), *Mountain Interval* (New York: Henry Holt, 1916), *New Hampshire* (New York: Henry Holt, 1923), *West-Running Brook* (New York: Henry Holt, 1928), *A Further Range* (New York: Henry Holt, 1936), *A Witness Tree* (New York: Henry Holt, 1942), *A Masque of Reason* (New York: Henry Holt, 1945), *Steeple Bush* (New York: Henry Holt, 1947), and *A Masque of Mercy* (New York: Henry Holt, 1947). In addition, two volumes of *Collected Poems* were published by Henry Holt in 1930 and 1939. *Complete Poems of Robert Frost 1949* (New York: Henry Holt, 1949) collected Frost's ten previously published volumes of new poetry, along with three new poems contained in a section titled "An Afterword."

In preparing the 1930 *Collected Poems*, Frost made several textual changes that were retained in *Complete Poems*. One poem, "In Hardwood Groves," was added to *A Boy's Will*, but three others, "Asking for Roses," "In Equal Sacrifice," and "Spoils of the Dead" were deleted; Frost also removed the commentary that had originally appeared in the table of contents (see note 15.1 in this volume). "Good Hours," a poem that had appeared in the 1915 first American edition of *North of Boston*, but not the 1914 first English edition, was included in the text of *North of Boston* in *Collected Poems*, while "The Pasture," originally the prologue to *North of Boston*, was used as the introductory poem for the entire collection. The footnotes and section titles that had appeared in the first edition of *New Hampshire* were deleted, as were the section titles used in the first edition of *West-Running Brook*; and three poems, "The Lovely Shall Be Choosers," "What Fifty Said," and "The Egg and the Machine," were added to *West-Running Brook*. Other differences between the texts printed in the first editions of Frost's poetry and those printed in *Complete Poems* involve the deletion of dedications, notes, and dates, minor changes in wording, and some alterations in punctuation (a number of the significant differences are shown in the notes to this volume). *Complete Poems of Robert Frost 1949* was published by Henry Holt and

Company on May 30, 1949. The text printed here is that of the first printing of the first American edition.

Frost published only one volume of new poetry after 1949. *In the Clearing* (1962) contained 38 new poems, as well as a revised version of "Closed for Good," originally published in "An Afterword" in *Complete Poems*; and another previously published poem, "The Gift Outright" from *A Witness Tree*, was incorporated into "For John F. Kennedy His Inauguration." The text of *In the Clearing* printed here is that of the first printing of the first American edition, published by Holt, Rinehart and Winston on March 26, 1962.

In addition to the poems included in *Complete Poems* and *In the Clearing*, Frost published other poems that he chose not to collect (poems that originally appeared in various newspapers, periodicals, anthologies, and pamphlets, and in his early volumes of poetry). He also left unpublished poems in manuscript, many of them in letters to friends. This volume includes a large selection of the unpublished poems, including 17 printed here from holograph manuscript for the first time: "A Summer's Garden," "A Winter's Night," "Love Being All One," "Midsummer Birds," "The Mill City," "What Thing a Bird Would Love," "Pussy-willow Time," "Pursuit of the Word," "The Rain Bath," "New Grief," "Winter Winds," "Dear Stark Young: Winter has beaten Summer in fight," "Traces," "Waste or Cod Fish Eggs," "Wanton Waste," "Sym-ball-ism," and "Her husband gave her a ring." Other holograph manuscripts have been used here in cases where there are errors in the published texts of poems not collected by Frost. (The sources of the texts of Frost's uncollected poems printed in this volume are listed below.)

Besides *A Masque of Reason* and *A Masque of Mercy* (included in *Complete Poems*), Frost wrote three plays, only one of which was published in his lifetime. *A Way Out* was first printed in the magazine *The Seven Arts* in February 1917. It was subsequently printed in *More One-Act Plays by Modern Authors* (New York: Harcourt, Brace, 1927), edited by Helen Louise Cohen, and in a limited edition of 485 copies published by The Harbor Press in 1929. Although Frost did not revise the play after its publication in *The Seven Arts*, he did write a short preface for the Harbor Press edition (the preface is printed on page 713 of this volume). The text included here is that of *The Seven Arts* printing.

Frost began another play, *In an Art Factory*, in the 1920s and worked on it over a period of years. A holograph manuscript of the play is in the Clifton Waller Barrett Collection in the Alderman Library of the University of Virginia, and a typescript, prepared from the holograph manuscript sometime after 1938, is in the Dartmouth College Library. Because the typescript contains several errors of tran-

scription, the text printed here is from the holograph manuscript,
with the exception of the words "you dago" (page 588, line 18 in this
volume), which appear only in the typescript. A third play, *The Guar-
deen*, was written between 1939 and 1942. A draft holograph manu-
script and a revised holograph manuscript are in the Clifton Waller
Barrett Collection in the Alderman Library of the University of Vir-
ginia. The text printed here is that of the revised holograph manu-
script. *In an Art Factory* and *The Guardeen* are printed with permis-
sion of Massachusetts Review Inc. The texts of *In an Art Factory*
and *The Guardeen* printed here have been stylistically formatted to
conform with *A Way Out*, which was published during Frost's
lifetime.

Aside from the early writings published in the Lawrence High
School *Bulletin* and in agricultural magazines and the stories written
for his daughter Lesley, most of Frost's prose that is included here—
essays, lectures, prefaces, tributes to other writers, and public state-
ments—bears directly on his work as a poet. The letters selected here
from his extensive correspondence deal primarily with poetry.

The texts of 62 of the 88 prose writings included in this volume
are taken from Mark S. Richardson, "The Collected Prose of Robert
Frost: A New Critical Edition" (New Brunswick: Rutgers University
doctoral dissertation, 1993). In cases where a typescript of a work
Frost prepared for publication is extant, Richardson used the type-
script as his text; where a typescript was not extant, Richardson
printed the published text or, in a few cases, used Frost's holograph
manuscript as his text. In cases of lectures that Frost did not prepare
for publication, Richardson derived his texts whenever possible from
audio recordings; if no recording was extant, Richardson used either
a published version or an unpublished transcription for his text.

The following is a list of the poems and prose writings included in
this volume in the sections titled "Uncollected Poems" and "Lec-
tures, Essays, Stories, and Letters," giving the source of each text.
The most common sources are indicated by these abbreviations:

*Barrett*    Robert Frost Collection (#6261), Clifton Waller Barrett
             Collection, Manuscripts Division, Special Collections
             Department, the Alderman Library of the University of
             Virginia. Reprinted by permission of the Estate of Rob-
             ert Frost and the Alderman Library of the University
             of Virginia.

*Dartmouth*  Dartmouth College Library. Reprinted by permission
             of the Estate of Robert Frost and the Dartmouth Col-
             lege Library.

*Huntington*   Huntington Library, San Marino, California. Reprinted
by permission of the Estate of Robert Frost and the
Huntington Library.

*Letters*   *Selected Letters of Robert Frost* (New York: Holt, Rine-
hart and Winston, 1964), edited by Lawrance Thomp-
son. Copyright © 1964 by Lawrance Thompson and
Holt, Rinehart and Winston, Inc. Reprinted by per-
mission of the Estate of Robert Frost and the publisher.

*Richardson*   Mark S. Richardson, "The Collected Prose of Robert
Frost: A New Critical Edition" (New Brunswick: Rut-
gers University doctoral dissertation, 1993). Reprinted
by permission.

*Thompson*   Lawrance Thompson, *Robert Frost: The Early Years,
1874–1915* (New York: Holt, Rinehart and Winston,
1966); *Robert Frost: The Years of Triumph, 1915–1938*
(New York: Holt, Rinehart and Winston, 1970). Copy-
right © 1966, 1970 by Lawrance Thompson; copyright
© 1966, 1970 by the Estate of Robert Frost. Reprinted
by permission of Henry Holt and Co.

*Untermeyer*   *The Letters of Robert Frost to Louis Untermeyer*, edited
by Louis Untermeyer (New York: Holt, Rinehart and
Winston, 1963), © 1963 by Louis Untermeyer, © 1991
by Laurence S. Untermeyer. Reprinted by arrangement
with Henry Holt and Co.

UNCOLLECTED POEMS

La Noche Triste. Lawrence High School *Bulletin*, April 1890.
Song of the Wave. Lawrence High School *Bulletin*, May 1890.
A Dream of Julius Cæsar. Lawrence High School *Bulletin*, May 1891.
Our Camp. Lawrence High School *Bulletin*, September 1891.
Clear and Colder. Holograph manuscript, *Huntington*.
The Sachem of the Clouds. Lawrence *Daily American*, November 2, 1891.
Parting. Lawrence High School *Bulletin*, December 1891.
Down the Brook . . . and Back. Lawrence High School *Bulletin*, December
    1891.
The Traitor. *The Phillips Andover Mirror*, June 1892.
Class Hymn. Lawrence High School *Bulletin*, June 1892.
Twilight. *Twilight* (1894), privately printed by Frost.
Summering. *Twilight* (1894), privately printed by Frost.

The Falls. *Twilight* (1894), privately printed by Frost.

An Unhistoric Spot. *Twilight* (1894), privately printed by Frost.

The Birds Do Thus. *The Independent*, August 20, 1896.

A Summer's Garden. Holograph manuscript, *Huntington*.

Cæsar's Lost Transport Ships. *The Independent*, January 14, 1897.

Greece. *The Boston Evening Transcript*, April 30, 1897.

Warning. *The Independent*, September 9, 1897.

God's Garden. *The Boston Evening Transcript*, June 23, 1898.

The Rubaiyat of Carl Burell. *Thompson, 1874–1915*, 545–46.

The reason of my perfect ease. *Untermeyer*, 381.

Evensong. Holograph manuscript, *Barrett*.

Despair. Holograph manuscript, *Huntington*.

Old Age. *Untermeyer*, 30–31.

A Winter's Night. Holograph manuscript, *Huntington*.

Love Being All One. Holograph manuscript, *Huntington*.

Midsummer Birds. Holograph manuscript, *Huntington*.

The Mill City. Holograph manuscript, *Huntington*.

What Thing a Bird Would Love. Holograph manuscript, *Huntington*.

When the Speed Comes. Holograph manuscript, *Huntington*.

The Later Minstrel. Broadside printing for chapel service at Pinkerton Academy, February 1907.

The Lost Faith. *The Derry News*, March 1, 1907.

Genealogical. Holograph manuscript, *Huntington*.

The Parlor Joke. *A Miscellany of American Poetry, 1920* (New York: Harcourt, Brace and Company, 1920), edited by Louis Untermeyer, 25–28. Reprinted by permission of the Estate of Robert Frost.

My Giving. Holograph manuscript, *Huntington*.

On the Sale of My Farm. Holograph manuscript, *Huntington*.

Pussy-willow Time. Holograph manuscript, *Huntington*.

Pursuit of the Word. Holograph manuscript, *Huntington*.

The Rain Bath. Holograph manuscript, *Huntington*.

New Grief. Holograph manuscript, *Huntington*.

Winter Winds. Holograph manuscript, *Huntington*.

In England. *Thompson, 1874–1915*, 395–96.

Good Relief. Holograph manuscript, *Barrett*.

In Equal Sacrifice. *A Boy's Will* (London: David Nutt, 1913).

Asking for Roses. *A Boy's Will* (London: David Nutt, 1913).

Spoils of the Dead. *A Boy's Will* (London: David Nutt, 1913).

Poets Are Born Not Made. *Thompson, 1874–1915*, 420.

I am a Mede and Persian. *Thompson, 1874–1915*, 421–23.

Flower Guidance. *Thompson, 1874–1915*, 584.

Nothing ever so sincere. William Pritchard, *Frost: A Literary Life Reconsidered* (Oxford and New York: Oxford University Press, 1984), 128. Reprinted by permission of the Estate of Robert Frost.

Dear Stark Young: Winter has beaten Summer in fight. Typescript, *Dartmouth*.

On Talk of Peace at This Time. *Robert Frost 100* (Boston: David R. Godine, 1974), compiled by Edward Connery Lathem. Reprinted by permission of the Estate of Robert Frost and David R. Godine Publishers Inc. © 1974.

One Favored Acorn. Typescript, *Dartmouth.*

Forest Flowers. *The Pinkerton Annual 1917.* Reprinted by permission of the Estate of Robert Frost.

The Seven Arts. *Untermeyer*, 60.

For Allan/ Who wanted to see how I wrote a poem. Holograph manuscript, *Dartmouth.*

Fish-Leap Fall. *Untermeyer*, 90–91.

On the Inflation of the Currency. Holograph manuscript, *Barrett.*

A Correction. David McCord, ed., *What Cheer: An Anthology of American and British Humorous and Witty Verse* (New York: Coward-McCann, 1945), edited by David McCord, 103. Reprinted by permission of the Estate of Robert Frost.

Oh thou that spinnest the wheel. *Letters*, 306.

The Pans. Holograph manuscript, *Barrett.*

The Cow's in the Corn. *The Cow's in the Corn: A One-Act Irish Play in Rhyme* (Gaylordsville, New York: The Slide Mountain Press, 1929). Reprinted by permission of the Estate of Robert Frost.

The Middletown Murder. *The Saturday Review of Literature*, October 13, 1928. Reprinted by permission. © 1928, Saturday Review Publications, Ltd.

Lowes took the obvious position. *Thompson, 1915–1938*, 382.

Trouble Rhyming. *Untermeyer*, 206.

Dear Louis: The telescope has come. *Untermeyer*, 215–16.

A man is as tall as his height. *Untermeyer*, 211.

The Offer. *Untermeyer*, 228.

Let Congress See To It. *Untermeyer*, 229.

A Restoration. *Robert Frost: Poetry and Prose* (New York: Holt, Rinehart and Winston, 1972), edited by Edward Connery Lathem and Lawrance Thompson, 310–11. Copyright © 1972 by Henry Holt and Co. Reprinted by arrangement with Henry Holt and Co.

A little kingdom. *The Robert Frost Collection in the Watkinson Library* (Hartford: Watkinson Library, Trinity College, 1974), compiled by Marian G. M. Clarke. Reprinted by permission of the Estate of Robert Frost and the Watkinson Library, Trinity College.

Winter Ownership. *The New York Herald Tribune Magazine*, March 4, 1934. © 1934, New York Herald Tribune Inc. All rights reserved. Reprinted by permission.

I only go. *Thompson, 1915–1938*, 424.

Pride of Ancestry. Holograph manuscript, *Barrett.*

Dear Leonard Bacon. *Robert Frost: Poetry and Prose* (New York: Holt, Rinehart and Winston, 1972), edited by Edward Connery Lathem and Lawrance Thompson, 311–12. Copyright © 1972 by Henry Holt and Co. Reprinted by arrangement with Henry Holt and Co.

Unless I call it a pewter tray. Charles Jay Connick, *Adventures in Light and Color* (New York: Random House, 1937), 92. Reprinted by permission of the Estate of Robert Frost.

To prayer I think I go. *Untermeyer*, 331.

Traces. Typescript, *Dartmouth*.

Let's Not Think. Typescript, McCain Library, Agnes Scott College, Decatur, Georgia. Reprinted by permission of the Estate of Robert Frost and McCain Library, Agnes Scott College.

Dear Louis: I'd rather there had been no war at all. *Untermeyer*, 335–40.

Ten Thirty A.M. Holograph dedication to Earle J. Bernheimer, *Barrett*.

Were that star shining there by name. *Robert Frost at Agnes Scott College* (Decatur, Georgia: McCain Library, Agnes Scott College, 1963), compiled by Edna Hanley Byers, 4. Reprinted by permission of the Estate of Robert Frost and McCain Library, Agnes Scott College.

A Bed in the Barn. *Robert Frost: A Descriptive Catalogue of Books and Manuscripts in the Clifton Waller Barrett Library, University of Virginia* (Charlottesville: University Press of Virginia, 1974), edited by Joan St. C. Crane, 188–89. Reprinted by permission of the Estate of Robert Frost and the Associates of the University Library.

Pares Continuas Fututiones. *Letters*, 549.

Waste or Cod Fish Eggs. Typescript, *Dartmouth*.

Wanton Waste. Holograph manuscript, *Barrett*.

Sym-ball-ism. Typewritten notes by Lawrance Thompson, *Barrett*.

Her husband gave her a ring. Typewritten notes by Lawrance Thompson, *Barrett*.

The Prophet. *A Remembrance Collection of New Poems* (New York: Holt, Rinehart and Winston, 1959). Reprinted by permission of the Estate of Robert Frost.

Marx and Engels. *A Remembrance Collection of New Poems* (New York: Holt, Rinehart and Winston, 1959). Reprinted by permission of the Estate of Robert Frost.

For travelers going sidereal. Typescript, *Dartmouth*.

The purpose of the universal plan. *Poetry*, November 1961. Reprinted by permission of the Estate of Robert Frost.

The Prophets Really Do Prophesy as Mystics / The Commentators Merely by Statistics. Booklet printed as Frost's Christmas card for 1962. Reprinted by permission of the Estate of Robert Frost and *Poetry* magazine.


## LECTURES, ESSAYS, STORIES, AND LETTERS

Petra and Its Surroundings. *Richardson*, 14–16.

A Monument to After-Thought Unveiled. *Richardson*, 29–31.

The Question of a Feather. *Richardson*, 51–56.

The Original and Only. *Richardson*, 62–65.

The Cockerel Buying Habit. *Richardson*, 74–76.

Dalkins' Little Indulgence: A Christmas Story. *Richardson*, 84–90.

Children's Stories: Schneider and the Woodchuck; Schneider and the Little
  Bird; The Wise Men. *Stories for Lesley* (Charlottesville: The University Press
  of Virginia, 1984), edited by Roger D. Sell. Reprinted by permission of the
  Estate of Robert Frost and the Bibliographic Society of the University of
  Virginia.
The Pinkerton Academy English Curriculum. *Richardson*, 96–97.
To John T. Bartlett, July 4, 1913. Holograph manuscript, *Barrett.*
To John T. Bartlett, c. November 5, 1913. Holograph manuscript, *Barrett.*
To Sidney Cox, January 19, 1914. Holograph manuscript, *Dartmouth.*
To John T. Bartlett, February 22, 1914. Holograph manuscript, *Barrett.*
To John Cournos, July 8, 1914. Holograph manuscript, Watkinson Library,
  Trinity College, Hartford, Connecticut. Reprinted by permission of the Es-
  tate of Robert Frost and Watkinson Library, Trinity College.
To Sidney Cox, December 1914. Holograph manuscript, *Dartmouth.*
To William Braithwaite, March 22, 1915. Holograph manuscript, Abernethy
  Library of American Literature, Middlebury College. Reprinted by permis-
  sion of the Estate of Robert Frost and Middlebury College.
"The Imagining Ear." Elaine Barry, *Robert Frost on Writing* (New Brunswick:
  Rutgers University Press, 1973), 142–44. Copyright © 1973 by Rutgers, The
  State University. Reprinted by permission of Rutgers University Press.
To Walter Pritchard Eaton, September 18, 1915. Holograph manuscript,
  *Barrett.*
To Louis Untermeyer, January 1, 1917. *Untermeyer*, 47–48.
To Régis Michaud, c. January 1918. Holograph inscription, *Dartmouth.*
The Unmade Word, Or Fetching and Far-Fetching. Elaine Barry, *Robert Frost
  on Writing* (New Brunswick: Rutgers University Press, 1973), 144–48.
  Copyright © 1973 by Rutgers, The State University. Reprinted by permis-
  sion of Rutgers University Press.
Address to the Amherst Alumni Council. *Richardson*, 99–101.
Some Definitions. *Richardson*, 104. First published in *Robert Frost: the Man
  and His Work* (New York: Henry Holt and Co., 1923); reprinted by ar-
  rangement with Henry Holt and Co.
To Louis Untermeyer, March 10, 1924. Holograph manuscript in the Louis
  Untermeyer Papers at the Library of Congress. Reprinted by permission of
  the Estate of Robert Frost.
Preface to *Memoirs of the Notorious Stephen Burroughs. Richardson*, 105–8.
  Reprinted by permission of the Estate of Robert Frost.
Introduction to *The Arts Anthology: Dartmouth Verse. Richardson*, 110–11. Re-
  printed by permission of the Estate of Robert Frost.
Tribute to Percy MacKaye. *Richardson*, 120. Reprinted by permission of the
  Estate of Robert Frost and the Dartmouth College Library.
The Poetry of Amy Lowell. *Richardson*, 109. Reprinted by permission of the
  Estate of Robert Frost.
Preface to *A Way Out. Richardson*, 122. Reprinted by permission of the Estate
  of Robert Frost.
To Sidney Cox, c. September 19, 1929. Holograph manuscript, *Dartmouth.*

To Kimball Flaccus, October 26, 1930. Holograph manuscript, *Dartmouth.*

Education by Poetry: A Meditative Monologue. *Richardson*, 125–36. Reprinted by permission of the Estate of Robert Frost.

To Sidney Cox, c. April 19, 1932. *Robert Frost and Sidney Cox: Forty Years of Friendship* (Hanover, New Hampshire: University Press of New England, 1981), edited by William R. Evans, 203–4. Reprinted by permission of the Estate of Robert Frost.

On "Birches." *Richardson*, 138. Reprinted by permission of the Estate of Robert Frost.

To Wilbert Snow, c. May 16, 1933. *Letters*, 393–94.

To Lesley Frost Francis, 1934. Holograph manuscript, *Barrett.*

To *Books We Like. Richardson*, 157–58. Reprinted by permission of the Estate of Robert Frost and the Massachusetts Library Association.

Letter to *The Amherst Student. Richardson*, 139–40. Reprinted by permission of the Estate of Robert Frost and *The Amherst Student.*

Introduction to E. A. Robinson's *King Jasper. Richardson*, 141–48. Copyright 1935, and renewed © 1936, by Macmillan Publishing Co. Reprinted by permission of Simon & Schuster, Inc.

Introduction to Sarah Cleghorn's *Threescore. Richardson*, 159–62. Reprinted by permission of the Estate of Robert Frost.

To Louis Untermeyer, November 25, 1936. *Untermeyer*, 284–85.

What Became of New England? *Richardson*, 163–66. Reprinted by permission of the Estate of Robert Frost.

Poverty and Poetry. *Richardson*, 167–76. Reprinted by permission of the Estate of Robert Frost and the Friends of the Princeton University Library; first published in *Biblia* 9:1 (Feb. 1938), forerunner of *The Princeton University Library Chronicle.*

The Poet's Next of Kin in College. *Richardson*, 177–81. Reprinted by permission of the Estate of Robert Frost and the Friends of the Princeton University Library; first published in *Biblia* 9:1 (Feb. 1938), forerunner of *The Princeton University Library Chronicle.*

To Robert P. T. Coffin, February 24, 1938. *Letters*, 461–63.

The Figure a Poem Makes. *Richardson*, 187–90. First published in *Collected Poems 1939* (New York: Henry Holt and Co., 1939). Copyright © 1939, 1967 by Henry Holt, Inc.; copyright © 1967 by Lesley Frost Ballantine. Reprinted by permission of Henry Holt, Inc.

Remarks on Receiving the Gold Medal. *Richardson*, 191–92. Reprinted by permission of the Estate of Robert Frost and the American Academy and Institute of Arts and Letters; first published in the *National Institute News Bulletin*, vol. 5 (1939).

The Doctrine of Excursions. *Richardson*, 184–86. Reprinted by permission of the Estate of Robert Frost, the Dartmouth College Library, and Middlebury College.

Preface to Poems in *This Is My Best. Richardson*, 193–94. Reprinted by permission of the Estate of Robert Frost and the Dartmouth College Library.

Preface to "The Death of the Hired Man." *Richardson*, 199. Reprinted by permission of the Estate of Robert Frost and the Associates of the University Library, University of Virginia.

The Constant Symbol. *Richardson*, 200–5. Reprinted by permission of the Estate of Robert Frost and *Atlantic Monthly*.

"Sermon" at Rockdale Avenue Temple. *Richardson*, 206–9. Reprinted by permission of the Estate of Robert Frost.

Speaking of Loyalty. *Richardson*, 210–15. Reprinted by permission of the Estate of Robert Frost.

A Romantic Chasm. *Richardson*, 217–19. Published in *Selected Prose of Robert Frost*, edited by Hyde Cox and Edward Connery Lathem, copyright © 1966 by Henry Holt and Co. Reprinted by arrangement with Henry Holt and Co.

Preface to Poems in *The World's Best*. *Richardson*, 221. Reprinted by permission of the Estate of Robert Frost.

Poetry and School. *Richardson*, 222–26. Reprinted by permission of the Estate of Robert Frost and *Atlantic Monthly*.

On the Poems of Hervey Allen. *Richardson*, 227. Published in *The Family Letters of Robert Frost and Elinor Frost* (Albany: SUNY Press, 1972), edited by Arnold Grade. Reprinted by permission of the Estate of Robert Frost and the State University of New York Press.

"Reading Poems at Tufts." *Richardson*, 228. Reprinted by permission of the Estate of Robert Frost and Tufts University.

The Hear-Say Ballad. *Richardson*, 229–30. Reprinted by permission of the Estate of Robert Frost and the Dartmouth College Library.

The Prerequisites. *Richardson*, 231–33. Published in *Robert Frost: Poetry and Prose* (New York: Holt, Rinehart and Winston, 1972), edited by Edward Connery Lathem and Lawrance Thompson; copyright © 1972 by Henry Holt and Co. Reprinted by arrangement with Henry Holt and Co.

To the Poets of Japan. *Richardson*, 234. Reprinted by permission of the Estate of Robert Frost and the Dartmouth College Library.

On Taking Poetry. Reginald Cook, *Robert Frost: A Living Voice* (Amherst: The University of Massachusetts Press, 1974), 75–87. Reprinted by permission of the Estate of Robert Frost and the University of Massachusetts Press.

"Caveat Poeta." *Richardson*, 245–46. Reprinted by permission of the Estate of Robert Frost and the Dartmouth College Library.

A Perfect Day—A Day of Prowess. *Richardson*, 256–59. Reprinted by permission of the Estate of Robert Frost.

Maturity No Object. *Richardson*, 261–64. Published in *The New Poets of England and America* by Donald Hall, Robert Pack and Louis Simpson, copyright © 1957 by Meridian Books, Inc. Reprinted by permission of the Estate of Robert Frost and Dutton Signet, a division of Penguin Books, USA, Inc.

Preface to *A Swinger of Birches*, by Sidney Cox. *Richardson*, 265–66. Reprinted by permission of New York University Press.

To the Poets of Korea. *Richardson*, 260. Reprinted by permission of the Estate of Robert Frost and the Dartmouth College Library.

"What Worries You Most About America Today?" *Richardson*, 267. Reprinted by permission of *Esquire* Magazine.

Merrill Moore. *Richardson*, 268–69. Reprinted by permission of the Estate of Robert Frost and Harvard University.

The Case of the United States versus Ezra Pound. *Richardson*, 270. Reprinted by permission of Jones Library, Amherst College.

On Being Appointed Consultant to the Library of Congress. *Richardson*, 271–72. Reprinted by permission of the Estate of Robert Frost and the Dartmouth College Library.

The Way There. *Richardson*, 273–74. Reprinted by permission of the Estate of Robert Frost and the Dartmouth College Library.

Preface to an Expanded *North of Boston*. *Richardson*, 275. Reprinted by permission of the Estate of Robert Frost and the Dartmouth College Library.

Dorothy Canfield. *Richardson*, 277–78. Reprinted by permission of the Estate of Robert Frost and the Book-of-the-Month Club; published in *Dorothy Canfield Fisher: In Memoriam* (Book-of-the-Month Club, 1972).

"Books That Have Meant the Most." *Richardson*, 279. Copyrighted Chicago Tribune Company. All rights reserved. Used with permission.

Conversations on the Craft of Poetry. *Interviews with Robert Frost* (New York: Holt, Rinehart and Winston, 1966), edited by Edward Connery Latham, 199–206. Reprinted by permission of the Estate of Robert Frost.

On Emerson. *Richardson*, 280–86. Reprinted by permission of *Daedalus, Journal of the American Academy of Arts and Sciences*, from the issue "Quantity and Quality," Fall 1959 (88:4).

The Future of Man. *Richardson*, 287–88. Reprinted by permission of the Estate of Robert Frost and Joseph E. Seagram & Sons, Inc.; originally presented at "The Future of Man," a symposium sponsored by Joseph E. Seagram & Sons on the dedication of its headquarters building at 375 Park Avenue, September 29, 1959.

The Future of Man (unpublished version). *Richardson*, 289–92. Reprinted by permission of the Estate of Robert Frost and the Dartmouth College Library.

*Paris Review* Interview, with Richard Poirier. *Writers at Work: The Paris Review Interviews, Second Series* (New York: The Viking Press, 1963), edited by George Plimpton, 11–34. Reprinted by permission of *Paris Review*.

A Poet's Boyhood. *Richardson*, 300–1. Reprinted by permission of the Estate of Robert Frost.

A New England Tribute. *Richardson*, 302–3. Reprinted by permission of the Estate of Robert Frost and the Dartmouth College Library.

Ernest Hemingway. *Richardson*, 319. Reprinted by permission of the Estate of Robert Frost and the Dartmouth College Library.

On "Choose Something Like a Star." *Richardson*, 320. Reprinted by permission of the Estate of Robert Frost.

William Faulkner. *Richardson*, 321. Reprinted by permission of the Estate of Robert Frost and the Dartmouth College Library.

On the Cold War. *Richardson*, 350. Reprinted by permission of the Estate of Robert Frost and the Dartmouth College Library.

On Extravagance: A Talk. *Richardson*, 328–49. Reprinted by permission of the Estate of Robert Frost and the Dartmouth College Library.

The following is a list of pages where a stanza break coincides with the foot of the page (except where such breaks are apparent from the stanzaic structure of the poem): 36, 156, 167, 187, 261, 276, 289, 306, 449, 498, 528, 536.

This volume presents the texts of the printings chosen for inclusion here but does not attempt to reproduce features of their typographic design. The texts are printed without alteration, except for the correction of typographical and holographical errors. Spelling, punctuation, and capitalization are often expressive features, and they are not altered, even when inconsistent or irregular. Some of the typographical errors listed here have been determined by collating the text of *Complete Poems* with editions of Frost's individual volumes of poetry. The following is a list of typographical and holographical errors corrected, cited by page and line number: 3.7, young; 20.3, these; 20.10, pane; 46.15, manv; 48.30, warm; 54.23, no; 65.7, vou; 68.39, play; 72.15, biscuit; 110.20, stove.; 115.23, speed; 132.31, clothes.; 162.21, beside; 181.22, him; 202.7, muffled; 209.30, things; 222.10, again; 239.19, Overdog.; 252.11, feet.; 268.3, walking; 290.21–22, (missing stanza break); 291.3, socialism; 295.32, under; 338.1, bed; 405.28, again.; 406.8, star-crossed,; 408.11, nothing; 412.28, O'Neil; 457.2, land.; 465.21 quintessence; 485.14, Beseiged; 494.3, meadows,; 495.3 tthe; 495.5, death; 495.11, lawn.; 512.19, rythm; 512.20, soldiers; 515.2, somewhere.; 515.15, anacronism; 536.24, Shut your eyes!; 538.9, (right); 539.1, Kate.; 540.16, thats'; 549.32, quite; 558.20, siderial; 561.18, birth.; 576.4, visable; 581.2, cumberous; 583.27, His is; 590.15, conceed; 597.2, your; 607.28, rabledom; 607.28, you're; 611.6, canabalism; 615.18, Mr Horn; 615.29, theives; 615.32, Mr Horn; 619.14, me.; 664.22, Swineburn; 664.27, conciously; 675.23, only only; 691.4, the were; 693.11, the the; 703.10, Huebsh; 704.15, developement; 714.21, I keeps; 732.12, Bayarov.

# Notes

In the notes below, the reference numbers denote page and line of this volume (the line count includes titles and headings). No note is made for material included in standard desk-reference books such as *Webster's Collegiate* and *Webster's Biographical* dictionaries. Biblical quotations are keyed to the King James Version. Quotations from Shakespeare are keyed to *The Riverside Shakespeare*, ed. G. Blakemore Evans (Boston: Houghton Mifflin, 1974). Footnotes in the text were in the originals. For more detailed notes, references to other studies, and further biographical background than is in the Chronology, see: *Family Letters of Robert Frost and Elinor Frost*, ed. Arnold Grade (Albany: State University of New York Press, 1972); *The Letters of Robert Frost to Louis Untermeyer*, ed. Untermeyer (New York: Holt, Rinehart and Winston, 1963); *Robert Frost and Sidney Cox: Forty Years of Friendship*, ed. William R. Evans (Hanover, New Hampshire: University Press of New England, 1981); *Selected Letters of Robert Frost*, ed. Lawrance Thompson (New York: Holt, Rinehart, and Winston, 1964); Lawrance Thompson, *Robert Frost: The Early Years, 1874–1915*, *Robert Frost: The Years of Triumph, 1915–38*, and Thompson and R. H. Winnick, *Robert Frost: The Later Years, 1938–63* (New York: Holt, Rinehart and Winston, 1966, 1970, 1976); *Newdick's Season of Frost: An Interrupted Biography of Robert Frost*, ed. William A. Sutton (Albany: State University of New York Press, 1976).

COMPLETE POEMS OF ROBERT FROST 1949

1.1–4    COMPLETE . . . 1949   For "The Figure a Poem Makes," which appeared as a preface in *Complete Poems*, see pages 776–78 in this volume.

3.1    *The Pasture*]   This poem was published in italics as the prologue to *North of Boston* (1914). Beginning with *Collected Poems* (1930), Frost used it as the introductory poem to all editions of his collected poems.

15.1    A BOY'S WILL]   Cf. Henry Wadsworth Longfellow, "My Lost Youth" (1858): "A boy's will is the wind's will, / And the thoughts of youth are long, long thoughts." *A Boy's Will* was first published in 1913 in London by David Nutt with the dedication "To E.M.F." (Elinor Miriam Frost). It included three poems ("In Equal Sacrifice," "Asking for Roses," and "Spoils of the Dead," pages 524.1–527.20 in this volume) that were left out of the collected editions of Frost's poems, and did not include "In Hardwood Groves," which was added for the collected editions. (Frost included "Asking for Roses" in the 1934 edition of *A Boy's Will*, but not the other three poems.) Later collected editions, including *Complete Poems 1949*, follow the 1930 *Collected Poems* contents for *A Boy's Will*. The 1913 table of contents included notes that were dropped from later editions; it reads:

PART I

*Into My Own* The youth is persuaded that he will be rather more than less himself for having forsworn the world.

*Ghost House* He is happy in the society of his choosing.

*My November Guest* He is in love with being misunderstood.

*Love and a Question* He is in doubt whether to admit real trouble to a place beside the hearth with love.

*A Late Walk* He courts the autumnal mood.

*Stars* There is no oversight of human affairs.

*Storm Fear* He is afraid of his own isolation.

*Wind and Window Flower* Out of the winter things he fashions a story of modern love.

*To the Thawing Wind* He calls on change through the violence of the elements.

*A Prayer in Spring* He discovers that the greatness of love lies not in forward-looking thoughts;

*Flower Gathering* nor yet in any spur it may be to ambition.

*Rose Pogonias* He is no dissenter from the ritualism of nature;

*Asking For Roses* nor from the ritualism of youth which is make-believe.

*Waiting—Afield at Dusk* He arrives at the turn of the year.

*In a Vale* Out of old longings he fashions a story.

*A Dream Pang* He is shown by a dream how really well it is with him.

*In Neglect* He is scornful of folk his scorn cannot reach.

*The Vantage Point* And again scornful, but there is no one hurt.

*Mowing* He takes up life simply with the small tasks.

*Going For Water*

PART II

*Revelation* He resolves to become intelligible, at least to himself, since there is no help else;

*The Trial by Existence* and to know definitely what he thinks about the soul;

*In Equal Sacrifice* about love;

*The Tuft of Flowers* about fellowship;

*Spoils of the Dead* about death;

*Pan With Us* about art (his own);

*The Demiurge's Laugh* about science.

PART III

*Now Close the Windows* It is time to make an end of speaking.

*A Line-Storm Song* It is the autumnal mood with a difference.

*October* He sees days slipping from him that were the best for what they were.

*My Butterfly* There are things that can never be the same.

*Reluctance*

15.6    the edge of doom] Cf. Shakespeare's Sonnet 116 ("Let me not to the marriage of true minds"), lines 11–12: "Love alters not with his brief hours and weeks, / But bears it out even to the edge of doom."

22.22    *Rose Pogonias*]    Also known as snakemouth pogonias, small bog orchids of the eastern United States with pink flowers, suggesting the open mouth of a snake, and spear-shaped leaves.

24.8    worn book . . . song]    *Golden Treasury of the Best Songs and Lyrical Poems in the English Language* (1861; rev. 1897), edited by Francis Turner Palgrave, one of Frost's favorite anthologies.

26.28    a bright green snake]    Cf. Samuel Taylor Coleridge's "Christabel" (1816), line 549, where a bard reports his surprise in a dream: "When lo! I saw a bright green snake."

28.15    Wide fields of asphodel fore'er,]    The asphodel, a plant of the lily family with a yellow flower, is associated with death; in Greek myths, the favorites of the gods lived on in Elysium, also known as the Plain of Asphodel, and delighted in the flower.

39.1    NORTH OF BOSTON]    First published in 1914 with the dedication "To E.M.F. THIS BOOK OF PEOPLE" and "The Pasture" as a prologue (see note 3.1).

39.2    *Mending Wall*]    In the original edition of *North of Boston* this poem is preceded by a note: "*Mending Wall* takes up the theme where *A Tuft of Flowers* in *A Boy's Will* laid it down."

60.23–31    the principle . . . Welshman got it planted]    In the Declaration of Independence (adopted July 4, 1776). In his *Autobiography*, Jefferson wrote that, according to family tradition, his father's ancestors came to America from Wales.

61.11–17    Creed . . . Hades"]    The Apostle's Creed, where "hell" was sometimes translated "Hades."

76.7–8    'You riddle . . . Viola.]    In Shakespeare, *Twelfth Night*, I.v.278–80, Viola, disguised as a page, replies when asked about her parentage: "Above my fortunes, yet my state is well: I am a gentleman."

79.20–21    Nausicaä . . . adventurously]    In Homer's *Odyssey*, Book VI, the Phaecian princess alone among her companions is not frightened on encountering the naked, shipwrecked Odysseus, but befriends him and guides him to her father, who eventually returns him to Ithaca.

86.34    Crystal Palace, London]    A huge building of glass and iron built in Hyde Park, London, to house the Great Exhibition of 1851; in 1854 it was moved to Sydenham, south of London, where it was used for public entertainments, including poultry exhibitions. It burned down in 1936.

93.1    *The Self-Seeker*]    The poem is based on a serious accident suffered by Carl Burell while he was working in a box-making factory in 1895.

93.14    You . . . orchids down.]    Burell was writing a book on flowers indigenous to New Hampshire, and at the time of his accident was investigating local varieties of the orchid.

93.15 blessed feet?] Cf. Shakespeare, *1 Henry IV*, I.i.24–26: " . . . holy fields / Over whose acres walked those blessed feet / Which 1400 years ago were nailed for our advantage to the cross."

95.29–30 Burroughs . . . *reginæ*] John Burroughs (1837–1921), American naturalist and author; *Cyprepedium reginæ* means "Queen's orchid."

102.1 *Good Hours*] Not in the first English edition of *North of Boston* (1914); Frost added the poem in the American edition (1915), where it is set at the end in italics.

103.1 MOUNTAIN INTERVAL] An interval, or intervale, is New England usage for low-lying land, especially along a watercourse. *Mountain Interval* was published in 1916 in New York by Henry Holt with a dedication: "TO YOU who least need reminding that before this interval of the South Branch under black mountains, there was another interval, the Upper at Plymouth, where we walked in spring beyond the covered bridge; but that the first interval of all was the old farm, our brook interval, so called by the man we had it from in sale." As in *North of Boston*, the first and last poems in the collection ("The Road Not Taken" and "The Sound of the Trees") were set in italic type in the original edition.

115.26 the Hyla breed] Any of a breed of tree frogs, called spring peepers, that on spring nights sound like a ringing bell.

116.8 *Oven Bird*] A North American warbler, sometimes called a "teacher bird," whose dome-shaped nest resembles an oven and whose call sounds like "teacher, teacher."

121.33 orchid Calypso.'] A delicate bog herb probably named for the mythical nymph Calypso, a beautiful goddess of silence who reigned on the island of Ogygia and offered Odysseus eternal life and youth if he would cease wandering and stay with her forever.

131.1 'Out, Out—'] Shakespeare, *Macbeth*, V.v.23: "Out, out, brief candle!"—from Macbeth's speech on the death of his wife.

151.1 NEW HAMPSHIRE] First published 1923 in New York by Henry Holt with the subtitle *A Poem with Notes and Grace Notes*, it was dedicated: "To Vermont and Michigan" and the final poem was set in italic type. As originally published, *New Hampshire* was divided into three sections: "New Hampshire," containing the title poem; "Notes," containing the thirteen poems from "A Star in a Stone Boat" to "I Will Sing You One-O"; and "Grace Notes," containing the remaining thirty lyrics of the volume. Several footnotes to "New Hampshire" and to other poems link lines in them to later poems in the same book, and in some cases to specific lines in other poems; these notes are given below.

151.9 The having anything to sell] In the original edition of *New Hampshire*, a footnote reads: "Cf. page 173, 'The Axe-Helve.' " (The page and line numbers in Frost's notes have been changed to coincide with the present volume.)

151.32    Volstead Act.] Named after Andrew Volstead, Republican congressman from Minnesota, the act enforced the Eighteenth Amendment, which prohibited the manufacture, sale, and transportation of intoxicating liquors within the United States. The amendment was in effect from 1920 until its repeal in 1933.

152.34    Purse] Franklin Pierce (1804–69), president of the United States 1853–57.

153.1–3    Daniel Webster . . . Dartmouth] Born on a farm in Salisbury, New Hampshire, Webster (1782–1852) was precociously intelligent but poor at farmwork. He attended Exeter Academy, where he was to shy too make a declamation before his class, but excelled in oratory and debate while a student at Dartmouth College, 1797–1801. In 1818 he represented the Dartmouth College trustees before the U.S. Supreme Court in *Dartmouth College* v. *Woodward*, arguing that the college was a private corporation and that the recent revocation of its corporate charter by the New Hampshire legislature violated Article I, section 10, of the Constitution by impairing the obligation of contract. When the Supreme Court ruled in favor of the college in 1819, Webster was hailed as America's greatest lawyer.

153.10    Isles of Shoals] Nine small rocky islands, once fishing villages, about 10 miles southeast of Portsmouth, New Hampshire.

154.6    New Hampshire gold—] In the original edition of *New Hampshire*, Frost noted: "Cf. page 162.15, 'A Star in a Stone-boat.' "

154.23    witch—old style.] In the original edition of *New Hampshire*, Frost noted: "Cf. page 187, 'The Witch of Coös.' "

154.33    S'ciety for Psychical Research] Founded in London in 1882 to study mental phenomena not explainable by accepted principles of science; the American branch was founded in 1890.

155.4    Skipper Ireson's Ride] Title of a ballad (1857) by John Greenleaf Whittier, based on a fragment of rhyme that he heard from one of his old schoolmates; it relates that Ireson, for the abandonment of the passengers on his sinking ship, was "tarred, feathered, and carried in a cart / By the women of Marblehead."

155.9    There quality] In the original edition of *New Hampshire*, a footnote reads: "'Cf. page 165.33, 'The Census Taker;' page 166.27, 'The Star-Splitter;' and 163.3 'A Star in a Stone-boat.' "

155.25    reach of man] In the original edition of *New Hampshire*, a footnote reads: "Cf. page 182, 'Wild Grapes.' "

155.32    any other thing?] In the original edition of *New Hampshire*, a footnote reads: "Cf. page 196, 'A Fountain, a Bottle, a Donkey's Ears and Some Books.' "

156.2    In many Marches.]    In the original edition of *New Hampshire*, a footnote reads: "Cf. page 168, 'Maple.' "

156.19    Election]    In the original edition of *New Hampshire* a footnote reads: "Cf. page 192, 'The Pauper Witch of Grafton.' "

156.22–23    Wilson . . . Hughes]    The Democratic incumbent, Woodrow Wilson, defeated the Republican candidate, Charles Evans Hughes, in the 1916 presidential election, winning 277 out of 531 electoral votes.

156.33    without population.]    In the original edition of *New Hampshire*, a footnote reads: "Cf. page 164, 'The Census Taker.' "

157.4–5    'The God . . . men.']    Emerson's "Ode, Inscribed to W. H. Channing," lines 24–26.

157.6    Another Massachusetts poet]    Amy Lowell (1874–1925). See also "On Emerson," page 861.21–25 in this volume.

157.24    goes on round me.]    In the original edition of *New Hampshire*, footnoted: "Cf. page 176, 'The Grindstone.' "

157.28–29    Marlowe . . . out of it.']    Christopher Marlowe, *The Tragical History of Doctor Faustus* (1604), scene three.

158.7    Hall]    John Hall, a poultryman, lived in Atkinson, New Hampshire; Frost met him at a poultry show in Amesbury, Massachusetts, in 1899.

158.7    Gay]    In the original edition of *New Hampshire* a footnote reads: "Cf. page 173, 'The Axe-Helve.' " Napolean Guay (pronounced, and sometimes spelled, "Gay") of Derry, New Hampshire, was a French-Canadian farmer who inspired "The Ax-Helve" and "Mending Wall."

158.8    Bartlett]    John T. Bartlett, a favorite student of Frost's at Pinkerton Academy in Derry, where Frost taught from 1906 to 1911. Bartlett later wrote several articles about Frost.

158.9    Lynch]    John Lynch, an Irish-born farmer of Bethlehem, New Hampshire, with whom the Frosts stayed several times.

158.14    wish them worse]    In the original edition of *New Hampshire* a footnote reads: "Cf. page 166, 'The Star-Splitter.' "

158.15–16    How . . . Russian novel in America]    Cf. the comments of William Dean Howells (1837–1920) in *My Literary Passions* (1910), "Criticism and Fiction," XXI, which reads in part: " . . . it is one of the reflections suggested by Dostoïevsky's novel *The Crime and the Punishment*, that whoever struck a note so profoundly tragic in American fiction would do a false and mistaken thing . . . very few American novelists have been led out to be shot, or finally exiled to the rigors of a winter at Duluth . . . Our novelists, therefore, concern themselves with the more smiling aspects of life, which are the more American . . . "

159.3    Moosilauke]   Mount Moosilauke in Grafton County, western New Hampshire. In the original edition of *New Hampshire*, Frost noted: "Cf. page 194.13–40, 'The Pauper Witch of Grafton.' "

159.6–7    Bryan . . . chorus.]   After resigning in 1915 as secretary of state under Woodrow Wilson, William Jennings Bryan (1860–1925) became a popular circuit lecturer at religious assemblies, speaking for a literal interpretation of the Bible and urging legislative bodies to ban the teaching of Darwinian evolution; in 1925, he would be a prosecuting attorney in the John Scopes "monkey trial."

159.9    John L. Darwin]   Charles Darwin's name is combined with that of American boxer John L. Sullivan (1858–1918), known as "the great John L.," world heavyweight champion 1882–92. In the original edition of *New Hampshire* a footnote reads: "Cf. line 5, page 184, 'Wild Grapes.' "

159.13    telescope]   In the original edition of *New Hampshire*, Frost noted: "Cf. page 166, 'The Star-Splitter.' "

159.34    Lincoln, Lafayette, and Liberty]   Mountains in New Hampshire's Franconian Range.

160.17    log-jam.]   In the original edition of *New Hampshire* a footnote to this phrase reads: "Cf. page 178, 'Paul's Wife.' "

160.35    Mewling . . . arms.']   Cf. Jaques' speech on the ages of man in Shakespeare's *As You Like It*, II.vii.143–44: "At first, the infant, / Mewling and puking in the nurse's arms . . . "

160.36    don't have to choose.']   In the original edition of *New Hampshire*, footnoted: "Cf. page 195, 'An Empty Threat.' "

161.6    'Nature is cruel, man is sick of blood;]   Matthew Arnold, *Man and Nature*.

161.8    Birnam Wood!]   In Shakespeare's *Macbeth*, V.v.33–45, Birnan Wood seems to move as Macbeth's foes, using leafy boughs as camouflage, advance on his castle.

161.14    nature starts,]   In the original edition of *New Hampshire*, Frost noted: "Cf. page 196, 'A Fountain, a Bottle, a Donkey's Ears and Some Books.' "

161.18–19    'a foiled . . . wanderer,']   Arnold, "Sohrab and Rustum" (1853), line 888.

161.19–20    'took dejectedly . . . throne.']   Cf. Arnold's "The Scholar-Gypsy" (1853), lines 183–84.

161.23–24    Ahaz . . . green trees]   Cf. 2 Kings 16:4 and 2 Chronicles 28:4; the heathen practice is condemned in Deuteronomy 12:2.

162.9    *Stone-Boat*]   A low, flat sled used for transporting stones.

162.10    Lincoln MacVeagh]    MacVeagh was with the trade department of Henry Holt and Company, and had arranged for the publication and illustration of *New Hampshire*. At their first meeting in 1920, MacVeagh had delighted Frost with his appreciation of classical elements in Frost's poetry.

162.26    Bird of Paradise's tail]    The Bird of Paradise is a tropical bird prized for its brilliantly colored plumes.

168.13    we ever said.]    In the original edition of *New Hampshire*, a footnote reads: "Cf. page 162, 'A Star in a Stone-boat;' and page 201, 'I Will Sing You One-O.' "

171.23    'Wave offering,]    A peace offering waved before the Lord; for example, in Numbers 5, 6, 18, and 20, Leviticus 7, 8, 9, 10, 14, and 23, Exodus 29.

182.26    *Wild Grapes*]    For a comment by Frost on the poem in the essay "The Way There," see pages 847.33–848.6 in this volume.

183.3    Eurydice]    In classical mythology, Eurydice disappears into the underworld as Orpheus, ordered not to look while leading her out of Hades, turns toward her when they come in sight of the upper regions.

183.18    Leif . . . German]    Explorer Leif Ericson (fl. A.D. 1000), of an Icelandic family, was driven off course and by luck became the first known discoverer of a land rich in grapes, timber, and self-cultivating wheat that he called "Vinland," or "Wineland, the Good," in North America, possibly some part of Nova Scotia. He carried back to Greenland specimens of wild, grape-bearing vines. His claims, for which there is no contemporaneous written record, were supported by Adam of Bremen (Germany) in *Gesta Hamma-burgenis Ecclesiae Pontificum* (1595).

187.30    COÖS]    Coos County in northern New Hampshire.

188.10    the Sioux Control]    A U.S. agent in charge of the affairs of the Sioux Indian tribe.

190.35    *The Wild Colonial Boy*]    Australian folksong.

192.8    GRAFTON]    County in central New Hampshire.

194.25    Rogers' Rangers]    Rangers commanded by Robert Rogers (1731–95) in the Seven Years' War (1756–63).

196.29    Dalton]    Town about 15 miles southeast of Concord, New Hampshire.

197.2    Kinsman]    Mountain west of Franconia Notch, New Hampshire.

205.10–11    *E. T. . . . poems*]    British essayist Edward Thomas (1878–1917), a close friend of Frost's in England, began writing poetry with Frost's encouragement. He joined the army in 1915, the year Frost returned to the United States. Several of Thomas's poems were published pseudonomously from 1915 to 1917 and Frost succeeded in having a collection of Thomas's poems published in America.

205.24    Vimy Ridge] Captured by Canadian and British troops, April 9–10, 1917, during the battle of Arras. Thomas, who was serving with the Royal Garrison Artillery, was killed by a German shell on April 9, several miles south of the ridge.

224.1    WEST-RUNNING BROOK] The first edition (1928), dedicated "To E.M.F." (Elinor Miriam Frost), was divided into six sections, some followed by epigraphs: "I / SPRING POOLS / *From snow that melted only yesterday*" (containing the first eleven poems of the volume); "II / FIAT NOX / *Let the night be too dark for me to see / Into the future. Let what will be be.*" (containing the next ten poems); "III / WEST-RUNNING BROOK" (containing the title poem); "IV / SAND DUNES" (containing the next six poems); "V / OVER BACK" (containing the next four poems); and "VI / MY NATIVE SIMILE / '*The sevenfold sophie of Minerve.*' " (containing the remaining seven poems). The edition did not include "The Lovely Shall Be Choosers," "What Fifty Said," and "The Egg and the Machine," which Frost first added for *Collected Poems* (1930). Frost also included notes in the first edition associating poems with particular dates: "On Going Unnoticed" is dated "1901." "A Peck of Gold" and "Once by the Pacific" are each dated "As of about 1880." "Bereft" is dated: "As of about 1893." "The Thatch" is dated: "As of 1914," and "The Flower Boat" is dated: "Very Early." These notes were dropped for the collected editions.

227.14–15    *Ridgley Torrence . . . 'Hesperides'*] Torrence (1875–1950) was an American poet, dramatist, journalist, and editor; the poems in *Hesperides* (1925) express his transcendental faith.

229.15    *Put out the Light*] Cf. Shakespeare, *Othello*, V.ii.7, "Put out the light, and then put out the light . . . " from Othello's speech in which he contemplates murdering Desdemona.

233.9    feather-hammer] Northern flicker, a woodpecker.

237.29    Some say] Frost, in a speech at Bryn Mawr in 1926, is reported to have referred to Havelock Ellis' calling life a dance, and to have disagreed with the sentiment. Ellis (1859–1939), English physician and writer, was the author of *The Dance of Life* (1923). Pierouet and Pierouette are idealized clowns in French pantomime.

241.9    George's bank] Georges Bank is a submerged sandbank and fishing ground about 150 miles northeast of Nantucket, Massachusetts, known for its dangerous crosscurrents and fog.

241.13    Happy Isles] Or Fortunate, or Blessed, Isles, thought to be at the farthest western reaches of the world; in classical myth sometimes the same as Elysium (see note 28.15) and the Hesperides.

249.1    A FURTHER RANGE]   First published in 1936 with the dedication: "To E.F. / for what it may mean to her that beyond the White Mountains were the Green; beyond both were the Rockies, the Sierras, and, in thought, the Andes and the Himalayas—range beyond range even into the realm of government and religion."

255.13    Sewell]   Franklane L. Sewell (d. 1945) was considered the foremost illustrator of game birds and fowl of his time; his work appeared in journals including *The Eastern Poultryman* and *Farm-Poultry*.

258.1    *The Gold Hesperidee*]   In Greek myth, the golden apples given by Gaea to Hera grew in the garden of the Hesperidae, three daughters of Atlas who guarded them with the help of a dragon. In various myths, the precious apples were stolen from the garden by Atlas, by Aphrodite, and by Hercules, who put the dragon to sleep. The tree on which they grew sometimes symbolized the tree of life.

259.17–18    Ahaz . . . passage]   Cf. note 161.23–24.

259.24    wasn't . . . Gath]   Gath was a city of the Philistines; cf. 2 Samuel 1:19–20: " . . . how the mighty are fallen! / Tell it not in Gath, publish it not in the streets of Askelon; lest the daughters of the Philistine rejoice, lest the daughters of the uncircumcised triumph."

266.24    *Woodward's Gardens*]   A favorite visiting spot of Frost with his mother and sister when they lived in San Francisco, the garden occupied an entire block from Mission to Valencia Streets and included a zoo, amusements, and botanical exhibitions.

268.7    Cliff House]   Hotel and restaurant on the Pacific shoreline in San Francisco.

272.21    approval stamp]   Cf. *The Good Housekeeping* magazine's "Stamp of Approval," which was awarded to various consumer products.

273.8    *The Master Speed*]   Written as a wedding present for Irma Frost and John Cone, who were married October 15, 1926.

275.1 *Design*]    A version titled "In White," written in early 1912, reads:

> A dented spider like a snowdrop white
> On a white Heal-all, holding up a moth
> Like a white piece of lifeless satin cloth—
> Saw ever curious eye so strange a sight?
> Portent in little, assorted death and blight
> Like the ingredients of a witches' broth?
> The beady spider, the flower like a froth,
> And the moth carried like a paper kite.

What had that flower to do with being white,
The blue Brunella every child's delight?
What brought the kindred spider to that height?
(Make we no thesis of the miller's plight.)
What but design of darkness and of night?
Design, design! Do I use the word aright?

277.4    (All . . . Mather)]   "All my eye and Betty Martin" is an old saying meaning "Nonsense!" Although Cotton Mather (1663–1728) believed that possessed persons should be treated by prayer and fasting, he countenanced the Salem, Massachusetts, witchcraft trials in 1692, when 19 persons were executed, 150 imprisoned, and more than 50 confessed under duress. He later wrote that the methods of the trials were unfair.

283.1    *Divés'*]   Dives (Latin for "rich") is the name popularly given the unnamed rich man in the parable of the rich man and the beggar Lazarus (Luke 16:19–31).

284.4    A king]   Atahuallpa.

286.32    the Vale of Cashmere]   The Vale of Kashmir, along the Jhelum River, is known for its abundant crops.

286.34    Pamir]   The Pamirs is a mountainous region in central Asia sometimes called "the roof of the world," partly bordering Kashmir; the name literally means "valley at the foot of a mountain peak," and has special reference to a glacial valley at an altitude of 12,000–14,000 feet.

288.3    We two . . . Malvern]   The poem is based on an experience shared with Edward Thomas (see note 205.10–11) while walking on the slopes of the Malvern Hills in central England in August 1914.

288.23    I alone . . . to tell]   Cf. Job 1:15–19, where four messengers bring Job news of disasters that have befallen him and his family, saying: "I only am escaped alone to tell thee."

289.3–4    Tityrus . . . Melibeous]   Cf. Virgil's first Eclogue where Tityrus, a poet who loves farming, and Meliboeus, who has just lost his farm, discuss the plight of the farmer; the eclogues were written after Virgil's farm was confiscated in 42 B.C.

290.12    Whittier's luck . . . Ireson]   See note 155.4. In a headnote appended to the poem in the Riverside edition of his collected works (1888), Whittier wrote that Samuel Roads Jr.'s *The History of Marblehead* (1879) had presented evidence of Ireson's innocence, and that he was "glad for the sake of truth and justice that the real facts are given . . . I certainly would not knowingly do injustice to any one, dead or living."

293.17    pinxit]   Latin: "painted it."

299.3–4      Mas d'Azil . . . wheel]   Le Mas d'Azil, a commune of southern France, is the site of a cave, discovered 1887, containing cultural artifacts including pebbles with painted lines, dots, and geometric figures, from the early Mesolithic Period at the end of the last glacial age.

301.1      A WITNESS TREE]   First published in 1942 with the dedication: "To K.M. / For Her Part In It." Kathleen Morrison was Frost's secretary and manager after 1938.

301.9      Witness Tree]   In surveying newly settled land, the location of stakes marking the corners of a property were carved on so-called Witness-trees after a portion of the bark was removed.

301.15      MOODIE]   Spelling of the maiden name of Frost's mother.

301.17–20      Zaccheus . . . PRIMER]   In *The New England Primer*, a Calvinist school book compiled c. 1683 by Benjamin Harris, these untitled lines, based on Luke 19:1–4, are the paradigm of the letter Z.

302.21      Cyb'laean]   Cybele, goddess of the mountains, fertility, earth, and the forces of nature, was worshipped under the guise of a stone said to have fallen from heaven, and was usually represented as pregnant and wearing a crown of turrets or with her head covered by a tower. Her relationship to her favorite, Atys, who castrated himself, was seen as that between the earth and the sun; priests in the ecstatic Cybelean cult, which originated in Phrygia, castrated themselves.

312.9–10      *The Discovery . . . Hackluyt*]   Madeira, off the coast of Morocco north of the Canary Islands, according to legend was discovered by Robert Machin, or Macham, around 1344 after the boat in which he was fleeing England for Brittany with Anna Dorset, or d'Arfet, was blown off course by a gale. Richard Hakluyt (1552?–1616) was an English geographer, translator, and author whose works include *Principall Navigations, Voiages, and Discoveries of the English Nation* (1589; 1598–1600).

315.34–35      bay . . . named for him]   Machico.

317.21      *(Boethian)*]   Amicus Manlius Severinus Boethius (c. A.D. 480–524), a Roman philosopher, consul, and translator of the logical treatises of Aristotle, was executed on suspicion of opposing Gothic rule in Rome. While in prison, he wrote *Consolations of Philosophy*. In it, consolation is found by applying reason to the problems and disasters of life.

318.27      Dione]   A nymph, mother of Aphrodite, who was also sometimes called Dione.

318.28      *ver . . . floribus*]   From *Levis exsurgit Zephirus*, based on Horace, by a poet of the 12th or 13th century, in K. Breul's *The Cambridge Songs* (1915); the phrase may be translated: "Spring sprinkles the earth with flowers." The poem later appeared in *The Goliard Poets* (1949), translated by George F. Whicher and dedicated to Frost.

318.32    Master of the Palace School]    Alcuin (732?–804), an ecclesiastic, teacher, and scholar of York, brought Anglo-Saxon learning to the continent around 781 when he became head of the Palace school of Charles I (768–814), later known as Charlemagne; he organized a liberal educational system, also served as Charles' teacher and adviser, and is credited with preserving writings that might otherwise have been lost in the Dark Ages. In 796 he resigned to become abbot of a monastery in Tours. The author of theological, philosophical, and hagiographical works, grammars, treatises, numerous letters, and poems, Alcuin was the leader of the short-lived Carolingian renaissance, but his particular influence on the ecclesiastical and judicial reforms of Charlemagne is debated, and he has been largely remembered more as a scholar and teacher than as an original thinker.

320.29    Roland, Olivier]    Roland, perhaps a nephew of Charlemagne, and his friend Olivier were among the 12 Paladins, the principal companions in arms, of Charlemagne. They were killed at the battle of Roncesvilles and later celebrated in legends, notably *Song of Roland*.

321.27    his Epitaph.]    Charlemagne left no funeral instructions; the epitaph written for him may be translated: "In this tomb lies the body of Charles, the Great and Orthodox Emperor, who gloriously extended the kingdom of the Franks, and reigned prosperously for forty-seven years. He died at the age of seventy, in the year of our Lord 814, the 7th Indiction, on the 28th day of January."

322.21    your doctrine of Memento Mori]    Alcuin wrote his own epitaph, which became a model for others; the Latin may be translated in part: "Here, I beg you, pause for a while, wayfarer, / And carefully ponder my words in your heart, / That you may understand your fate in my shadow: / The form of your body will be changed as was mine. / What you are now, famous in the world, I have been, wayfarer, / And what I am now, so you will be. / I was wont to seek the joys of the world in vain desire; / Now I am ashes and dust, and food for worms. / Remember therefore to take better care of your soul / Than of your body, because that survives, and this perishes. / Why do you look for possessions? You see in what a little cavern / This tomb holds me: Yours will be equally small. / Why are you eager to deck your body in Tyrian purple / Which soon, in the dust, the hungry worm will devour? / As flowers perish when the menacing wind comes / So also your flesh and all your glory perish . . . " It ends: "My name was Alcuine; wisdom I always loved. / Pour out prayers for me when you quietly read this inscription." Cf. Luitpold Wallach, *Alcuin and Charlemagne: A Study in Carolingian Literature* (Ithaca: Cornell University Press, 1968), pp. 264–65.

323.7    Dwarf cornel . . . maianthemum,]    Perennials: dwarf-cornel is the bunchberry; golden thread (or goldthread), is a delicate herb with a bright gold root; maianthemum is a plant of the *Liliaceae* family, such as false lily of the valley, with small white flowers.

325.21   Shelleyan dejection]   Cf. Shelley's "Stanzas Written in Dejection" (1818).

327.1   *The Rabbit Hunter*]   When this poem was included with those sent to Susan Hayes Ward for Christmas 1911 (see note 518.20), it was titled "Death" and began with six lines that Frost cut from this version; the present lines are unchanged except for slight differences in punctuation. The six dropped lines read: "In the narrow way, / Where it comes down / One wooded hill / To climb the next, / Under the frown / Of gathering night,".

328.3   Balearic sling]   The Balearic Islands in the Mediterranean were supposedly so-named because their ancient inhabitants excelled in slinging and archery (*beleares* is Greek for "throw").

329.1   QUANTULA]   Latin: How little? How small?

329.17   *Boeotian*]   Boeotia, a province of ancient Greece, was legendary for the dull-wittedness of its inhabitants whom the Athenians held to be more interested in physical prowess than mental excellence.

330.25   Islands of the Blessèd]   See note 241.13.

335.33   Serious]   The bright star Sirius in the constellation Canus Major.

338.33   pterodix]   A pterodactyl (literally wing-finger), an extinct order of flying reptile.

339.1   STEEPLE BUSH]   First published in 1947 with the dedication: "For / Prescott * John * Elinor * Lesley Lee / Robin and Harold," Frost's grandchildren. The notes included in the original edition were deleted in *Complete Poems*; they are given below.

340.5   their wooden rings]   "Ripton rings" (note in the original edition of *Steeple Bush*). Ripton, Vermont, site of the Bread Loaf School, where Frost lived in summers from 1939.

340.18   spes alit agricolam]   "Hope nourishes the farmer," from Latin poet Albius Tibullus (c. 60–19 B.C.), *Elegies*, II.vi.21, which reads *agricolas* (farmers).

341.21   serial ordeal]   A succession of trials, as those meant to test the virtue of the knights of King Arthur in their quest for the Holy Grail.

341.37   lost . . . find yourself]   Cf. Matthew 10:38–39, Mark 8:34–35.

342.2   harness gall]   Sore or granulating skin wound caused by the constant irritation of the harness; a gall is also a barren spot in a field where springwater oozes up.

342.21   can't get saved . . . St. Mark]   Cf. Mark 4:11–12 (also, Matthew 13:10–13).

343.12–15   Lucretius . . . love.]   Titus Lucretius Carus (c. 99–c. 55 B.C.) set forth the atomic theory of Epicurus to explain the phenomena of the world in *De rerum natura* (*Of the Nature of Things*), a philosophical didactic poem that maintains in part that the world is governed not by capricious agencies, but by an infinitely various combination of atoms that constitute creation. It begins with an invocation to "nurturing Venus" who is described as the creative force of nature, then depicts Epicurus, praised as the first Greek to take a stand against religion and objectively study the nature of things, setting out in mind and imagination "to traverse the immeasurable universe . . . " (Book I, lines 1, 62–72).

344.31     in forma pauperis]     Latin: "in the form of a pauper," a British legal term used when a poor person had just cause to bring a suit for his defense and was granted counsel by the court without the usual fees.

348.10     Etookashoo and Couldlooktoo]     " . . . who accompanied Dr. Cook to the North Pole" (note in the original edition of *Steeple Bush*).

349.11     *The Fear of God*]     "Acknowledgment to the Papyrus Prisse" (note in the original editon of *Steeple Bush*).

351.1     *The Courage to Be New*]     "No one cavils at their killing / And being killed for speed. / Then why be so unwilling / They should do as much for creed?" (Note in the original edition of *Steeple Bush*.)

351.18     *Iota Subscript*]     Lower case "i" is the smallest letter of the Greek alphabet.

354.30     *Rogers Group*]     American artist John Rogers (1829–1904) created small group sculptures illustrating historical, literary, and humorous subjects; thousands of plaster reproductions were sold.

357.13     *Lake Poets*]     Term applied especially to William Wordsworth, Samuel Taylor Coleridge, and Robert Southey, who lived for a time in the picturesque Lake District of northwest England. The term Lake School was first used derisively by the *Edinburgh Review* in 1817 for poets who lived there and sought inspiration from nature; Byron in the preface to *Don Juan* (1819–24) refers to "all those Lakers."

357.14     'Nature I . . . Art.']     Walter Savage Landor (1775–1864), "I Strove With None" (1853): "I strove with none, for none was worth my strife; / Nature I loved; and next to Nature, Art. / I warmed both hands before the fire of life; / It sinks, and I am ready to depart."

357.15     Dean]     Professor Howard Mumford Jones of the Harvard University English Department, with whom Frost had a running disagreement over the interpretation of the word "Nature" in Landor's quatrain.

358.2     *Haec Fabula Docet*]     Latin: "The fable teaches these things." In the original edition of *Steeple Bush*, a note reads: "—Alternatively / The Moral is it hardly need be shown / All those who try to go it sole alone, / Or with the independence of Vermont / Are absolutely sure to come to want."

362.16    *U. S. 1946 King's X*]   "—Recent Riptonian" (Frost's note in the original edition of *Steeple Bush*); see also note 340.5. The poem refers to the atomic bomb, developed by the United States during World War II and used against Hiroshima and Nagasaki in August 1945. The U.S. introduced a plan in the United Nations in June 1946 to institute international controls over atomic energy and prevent the spread of atomic weapons; the following month the United States tested two atomic bombs in the Pacific.

362.21    *The Ingenuities of Debt*]   "—PreFranconian" (Frost's note in the original edition of *Steeple Bush*).

362.27    Ctesiphon]   A ruined city 20 miles southeast of Baghdad, Iraq, formerly the capital of ancient Parthia and later of the Sassanid empire. It is famous for a huge vaulted hall, the remains of a palace, known as the Taq-e Kosra (Throne of Khosru I).

363.17–18    as Shakespeare . . . out]   *As You Like It*, IV.i.75–76: "Very good orators when they are out, they will spit."

365.2    *Choose . . . Star*]   Frost changed the title to "Take Something Like a Star" (and "choose" to "take" in the penultimate line) for *Selected Poems* (1963).

365.20    Keats' Eremite]   An eremite is a hermit or recluse. John Keats' "Bright Star" begins: "Bright star, would I were steadfast as thou art— / Not in lone splendour hung aloft the night / And watching, with eternal lids apart, / Like nature's patient, sleepless Eremite . . . "

366.1    *Closed for Good*]   For the version in *In the Clearing* (1962), see page 429 in this volume.

367.23    Bradford]   In Vermont, near the Connecticut River.

369.4    Why Tecumseh?]   In his *Memoirs*, Sherman wrote that his father "caught a fancy for the great chief of the Shawnees" during the War of 1812 and "insisted on engrafting the name 'Tecumseh' on the usual family list."

370.33    Shall I . . . enough]   Cf. Milton's *Comus: A Masque*, lines 779–80.

371.9    'So . . . believe it.']   Cf. Shakespeare's *Hamlet*, I.i.165.

372.8    the Burning Bush]   Cf. Exodus 3:2: "Behold the bush burned with fire and was not consumed . . . " Cf. also Acts 7:30: "And when forty days were expired, there appeared to him in the wilderness of mount Sinai an angel of the Lord in a flame of fire in a bush."

372.25    Blake's picture]   British poet William Blake (1757–1827) was an engraver whose illustrations of his own works and for the *Book of Job* and the *Divine Comedy* include representations of God.

373.8    Court of Love]   An association of lords and ladies, believed to have existed in Provence and Languedoc in the time of the troubadours, that decided questions of gallantry and love.

373.14–15    Suffer . . . Waller says.]   Edmund Waller (1606–87), in whose song "Go, Lovely Rose" a rose is sent to a lady and told to "Bid her come forth, / Suffer herself to be desired, / And not blush so to be admired."

374.34    Thyatira]   Cf. Revelation 1:11, 2:18–29. Thyatira, an ancient city of Lydia, is one of the Seven Churches of Asia that in Revelation 1–3 receive messages prophesying the final judgment, God's victory through Christ over evil in the world, and the coming of a new age.

375.18    the witch of Endor]   Cf. 1 Samuel 28:4–14.

376.10    Segub.]   In 1 Kings 16:34, King Hiel loses his youngest son, Segub, when he raises the gates of Jericho; God's "curse" on the man who rebuilds the city is foretold in Joshua 6:26.

376.15    What . . . husband say?]   Job's wife counsels him: "Dost thou still retain thine integrity? curse God and die" (Job 2:9).

378.15    Kipling . . . Hosts]   Rudyard Kipling (1865–1936), "Recessional" (1899), lines 5, 11, 23.

379.14–15    originality, . . . angels]   In Shakespeare's *Henry VIII*, III.ii.440–41, Thomas Cardinal Wolsey counsels Cromwell: "fling away ambition! / By that sin fell the angels . . . "

382.26    only four?]   In a message to Congress, January 6, 1941, President Franklin Roosevelt said that "we look forward to a world founded on four basic human freedoms": freedom of speech and religion, and freedom from want and from fear.

382.29–30    twenty questions]   Game in which players try to identify the subject one of them has in mind by asking up to 20 questions.

383.9    chapters . . . Two.]   Of the book of Job.

383.25–27    rays . . . Western poem]   Cf. Ralph Waldo Emerson, "Uriel," lines 21–24: " 'Line in nature is not found; / Unit and universe are round; / In vain produced, all rays return; / Evil will bless, and ice will burn.' "

384.13–14    your comforters . . . pain.]   In Job 2:11–32:1, three friends come to comfort and mourn with Job, then counsel and berate him, believing that God would not have afflicted him if he had not been a sinner. In Job 42:7, God says they "have not spoken of me the thing that is right, as Job hath."

386.23–24    the one Milton . . . blindness.]   In *Paradise Lost*, Book III, lines 50–55, Milton writes that, although blindness has shut out one entrance of wisdom, "So much the rather thou Celestial light / Shine inward, and the mind through all her powers / Irradiate, there plant eyes, . . . that I may see and tell / Of things invisible to mortal sight."

388.9     *chapter forty-three*]  Job consists of 42 chapters.

390.24     Brook Farm]  Cooperative community established in 1841 near West Roxbury, Massachusetts, by the Transcendentalist Club. It became the American center of Fourierism around 1843 and was dissolved in 1847.

391.20–21     Jonas Dove . . . Jonah]  Jonas is an alternate spelling of Jonah from the Hebrew word "Yonah," which means "dove."

393.21–22     Mr. Flood . . . will.]  In Edwin Arlington Robinson (1869–1935), "Mr. Flood's Party," stanza 2, Eben Flood, alone under a harvest moon, thus responds to his own suggestion of drinking a toast.

393.29–394.1     I've lost . . . city evil.]  In Jonah 3–4, Jonah finally obeys God and prophesies that Nineveh will be overthrown; when its people repent, God, to Jonah's displeasure, spares the city.

394.5     You naughty . . . pie.]  Cf. "Three Little Kittens," a nursery rhyme.

394.23     The Wandering Jew]  Legendary figure condemned to perpetual wandering for, variously, striking Jesus on the day of His crucifixion, or refusing to help carry His cross.

396.11     I'm—bound—away.]  From the chorus of the old chantey *Shenandoah.*

398.27     *script . . . Belshezaar's feast*]  In Daniel 5, at a splendid feast given by Belshazaar, regent of Babylon, during the siege of his kingdom, the prophecy of Babylon's overthrow and Belshazaar's death is miraculously written on a wall.

400.23     Great Books]  An educational program centered on the reading of "great books" as a way of attaining a unified philosophical view of the universe was advanced at the University of Chicago during the tenure of Robert Maynard Hutchens, its president, 1929–45, and chancellor, 1945–51; in 1946 Hutchens took a year off to promote the study of "great books" and by 1947 adult education courses based on them were being established throughout the country.

401.8     My tongue's . . . True Thomas]  Cf. stanza 18, line 1, of "Thomas the Rhymer," 15th-century ballad about a man called "True Thomas" collected in *The Oxford Book of English Verse*, edited by Arthur Quiller-Couch.

401.10     Bohning]  Henry George Bohn (1796–1884) was a London publisher of inexpensive editions of works of theology, literature, philosophy, science, ecclesiastics, and translations of Latin and Greek classics.

404.14–16    Justice . . . shine,]   *Paradise Lost*, Book 3, lines 132–34: "In Mercy and Justice both, / Through Heav'n and Earth, so shall my glorie excel, / But Mercy first and last shall brightest shine."

406.17–19    Itzas . . . well.]   At Chichen-Itza, ancient Mexican city of the Mayan Itza group, sacrifices were made to the gods of the *cenotes* (wells).

406.22    butt of malmsey]   According to an old chronicle, George, Duke of Clarence, was murdered in the Tower of London in 1478 by being drowned in a butt (cask) of malmsey (a strong, sweet wine); a version of the story is in Shakespeare's *Richard III*, I.iv.270.

407.1    Vae Victi]   Latin: "Woe to the Vanquished." Jackson asserted the power of the president to remove appointed federal office-holders. His policy was denounced by his opponents as instituting a "spoils" system, but hailed by his supporters as upholding popular control over the government.

407.2    'Turn the rascals out']   Liberal Republican campaign slogan of Horace Greeley when he ran against the incumbent president, Ulysses S. Grant, in 1872.

407.5–8    Bel's favorite poet . . . Poses)]   Cf. William Butler Yeats (1865–1939) *A Vision* (1925), in which 28 rotating phases of life are founded on a notion of 28 psychological types, each of which exhibits an antithetical relation between its Will and its Mask.

407.9–13    the Nazarene . . . violence.]   Cf. William Butler Yeats (1865–1939), "Two Songs from a Play" (1928), stanza 3 (in line 2 of the stanza, "He" refers to Dionysus): "In pity for man's darkening thought / He walked that room and issued thence / In Galilean turbulence; / The Babylonian starlight brought / A fabulous formless darkness in; / Odour of blood when Christ was slain / Made all Platonic tolerance vain / And vain all Doric discipline."

407.16    old Chaos]   Hesiod in *Theogony* introduced the idea that Chaos ("gaping void") was the first power to come into being and that he gave birth to Erebus (a deity of Hell), and Night; later writers describe Chaos as filled with warring atoms, and the source of the first generation of gods.

407.25    the Sermon]   Matthew 5:1–7:27.

411.3    Martin]   Martin Luther (1483–1546).

412.11    a Roman Pantheon]   The Roman Pantheon, a temple dedicated to all the gods, was built on the orders of Agrippa in 27 B.C. and rebuilt by Hadrain, A.D. 120–124. In 609 it became a church dedicated to all the martyrs. Now called Sancta Maria della Rotunda, the structure is still known as the Pantheon. The light entering from its dome is said to resemble a "sudden revelation."

412.23–24    furnace . . . Abednego]   Daniel 3:12–30.

412.28    Jeffers and O'Neill]   Robinson Jeffers (1887–1962) and Eugene O'Neill (1888–1953).

IN THE CLEARING

419.2    "*And wait . . . I may.*"]   Line from *The Pasture*, page 3.4 in this volume; see also note 3.1.

427.14    Alfred Edwards]   Edwards became a close friend of Frost's after joining Henry Holt and Company in 1945; he would serve as the executor of Frost's estate.

429.1    *Closed For Good*]   For the earlier version, see page 366 in this volume.

431.23    Culebra Cut]   Former name of the Gaillard Cut, the southeast section of the Panama Canal.

440.1    *Version*]   A version of the poem, which Edward Connery Lathem based on the texts of several variant holographs, particularly one inscribed " 'Version' corrected / R.F. / for Bacon Collamore" in a copy of *In The Clearing* in Trinity College Library at Hartford, Connecticut, appears in the 1969 Lathem edition of *The Poetry of Robert Frost*. Lathem drew lines 9, 10, and 13–16 from manuscript and styled them to make them consistent with the text in *In the Clearing*; he also emended "His" to "the" in line 11, below, and "its" to "Her" in line 12, to follow the holograph text inscribed to Collamore, and removed the comma after "non-existence" in line 8. In the Lathem edition, "Version" reads:

> Once there was an Archer,
> And there was a minute
> When He shot a shaft
> On a New Departure.
> Then He must have laughed:
> Comedy was in it.
> For the game He hunted
> Was the non-existence
> Of the Phoenix pullet
> (The Μὴ ὄν of Plato),
> And the shaft got blunted
> On her non-resistance,
> Like a dum-dum bullet—
> Did in fact get splattered
> Like a ripe tomato.
> That's how matter mattered.

The Greek Μὴ ὄν means "non-existence."

441.1    *Kitty Hawk*]   Orville and Wilbur Wright made their first successful flight at Kill Devil Hills near Kitty Hawk, North Carolina, in 1903.

441.2    *Huntington Cairnses*]   Frost began the poem after visiting Cairns, a lawyer and author, and his wife, Florence, in Kitty Hawk, North Carolina, in 1953.

442.22    Alastor]   Cf. "Alastor, or the Spirit of Solitude" (1816), by Percy Bysshe Shelley.

442.40    tower shaft]   A 60-foot granite shaft with a beacon was erected during Hoover's administration in 1932 at Kill Devil Hills, North Carolina, site of the Wright brothers' first successful flight.

443.17–18    dark Hatteras . . . Roanoke]   Cape Hatteras, off the North Carolina coast at a dangerous navigational point in the Atlantic, was the site of a 193-foot lighthouse that had to be abandoned in 1936 when the ocean came too close. Another lighthouse was erected further inland. The colony at Roanoke Island, established by Raleigh in 1585, was abandoned after ten months; a second colony was established in 1587, but by 1591 its inhabitants had disappeared.

444.38    Theodosia Burr]   Theodosia Burr Alston (1783–1813), only child of Aaron Burr, who attended her father's trial for treason in 1807 and whose charm was said to have helped sway the court in his favor. Burr fled to England after his acquittal, but returned to New York in 1812. Theodosia sailed from South Carolina on December 30, 1812, to visit him. The ship was probably lost during a storm off the Carolina coast in January, but legends held that its passengers were killed when it was either captured by pirates, or driven ashore by the storm and plundered by thieves who worked the Carolina coast.

445.17    "And the moon was full,"]   Alfred Tennyson, "The Passing of Arthur," line 180.

446.11–12    What Catullus . . . Somewhat (aliquid)]   Cf. poem 1, lines 3–4, in which Catullus refers to his verse: " . . . *namque tu solebas / meas esse aliquid putare nugas,*" which may be translated: "for you have been accustomed to hold that there is somewhat in my trifles."

447.35–37    slab . . . Moab]   The Moabite stone, discovered 1868 at Dhiban, a ruined city of Palestine, is a block of black basalt with a 34-line inscription in Moabite alphabet dating from the 9th century B.C.; the oldest extant Semitic inscription, it is an account of the wars of Mesha, king of Moab (fl. c. 850 B.C.), including those against kings of Israel (cf. 2 Kings 3).

451.15    the *mens animi.*]   See note 807.8.

453.22    Darius Green]   Cf. "Darius Green and His Flying-Machine," a light poem by John Townsend Trowbridge (1827–1916).

455.19    When the orchard's right]   This reads "When the boughs are right" in *Selected Poems* (1963).

455.21    Of all that's white,]   In *Selected Poems* (1963): "Of pink and white,"; the change was retained in later printings of *In the Clearing.*

457.25    *The Bad Island—Easter*]   Easter Island, a small volcanic island off
the coast of Chile in the Pacific, is the site of monolithic stone heads carved
from compressed volcanic ash. According to legend, the original islanders ar-
rived in two canoes, and it was sometimes assumed, based on a kind of ancient
hieroglyphic writing engraved on wooden tablets, that they had come from
Egypt. The island was discovered by Dutch admiral Jacob Roggeveen on
Easter Sunday of 1722; it was annexed to Chile in 1888.

459.23    "Shine, . . . republic."]   End of line 6 of Jeffers' poem of that
title.

459.25    Cumaean Sibyl]   Legendary prophetess whose cavern was at Cu-
mae, an ancient city near Naples, and whose oracles were collected in the
Sibylline Books.

461.17    the unblinking four]   Mars, Venus, Jupiter, and Mercury.

461.22    "I wish . . . might"]   "Star Wish" ("Star light, star bright"),
author unknown, line 3.

461.31    the Arcadians]   The people of Arcadia, a mountainous region in
central Peloponnesus that according to legend was the birthplace of Zeus,
claimed to be the world's oldest race.

461.35–36    As Keats (or was it Milton?) . . . Caf.]   Cf. Keats' *Hyperion*
(2:52–54): " . . . Nearest him / Asia, born of most enormous Caf, / Who
cost her mother Tellus keener pangs / Though feminine, than any of her
sons . . . " Keats said that he left *Hyperion* unfinished because Milton had
come to dominate his writing. Keats probably took the name Caf from *Vathek,
an Arabian Tale,* by William Beckford, translated into English in 1786, where
Kaf is identified with the Caucasus.

462.4    a plant called the silphion]   An extinct plant known from Greek
writings; its gum resin, called laser, was used in medicines.

462.34    Ararat]   A mountain in eastern Turkey said to be the resting place
of Noah's Ark.

463.18    Rigel, Bellatrix, . . . Betelgeuse]   Stars of the first magnitude in
the constellation Orion.

464.15    Xanadu]   In Coleridge's "Kubla Kahn" (1816), the place where
the Khan decrees "a stately pleasure dome."

465.5    Punt]   Ancient Egyptian name for a part of Africa, probably on the
Somali coast, from which the Egyptians imported slaves and gold, myrrh,
incense, ebony, fruits, and animals.

466.31    Mosul]   City in Iraq, devasted by the Mongols in the 13th century.

468.19–20    Seven . . . Homer begged]   From one of many versions of an
ancient Greek rhyme: "Seven cities contend about being the birthplace of
Homer: / Smyrna, Rhodes, Colophon, Salamas, Ios, Argos, Athens."

468.22    The Seven Freedoms]   Cf. note 382.26.

468.24    Cos.)]   Or Kos, a Greek island in the Aegean closely allied to the
Ptolemaic dynasty in Egypt. In ancient times it was a favorite abode of writers,
the birthplace of Hippocrates, Philitas, perhaps Ptolemy II, and Theocritis,
and site of the hospital of the Asclepiadae who claimed to have descended
from the god Asclepius.

474.19–20    HYDE . . . CROW ISLAND]   Edward Hyde Cox called his
house on the shore in Manchester, Massachusetts, "Crow Island."

476.24    Ahmed S. Bokhari]   An official of the United Nations who, in
1956, invited Frost to write a poem to be inscribed on a block of iron in the
Meditation Room at U.N. Headquarters; he rejected Frost's couplet.

## UNCOLLECTED POEMS

485.1    *La Noche Triste*]   Traditional name for the night of June 30–July 1,
1520, when Spanish forces under Hernando Cortés (1485–1547) suffered
heavy losses while retreating from Tenochtitlán. The details of the poem are drawn
from William Prescott's *The History of the Conquest of Mexico* (1843), Vol. 2,
chap. 3.

485.2    TENOCHTITLAN]   Ancient name for Mexico City, capital of the
Aztec Empire. Cortés arrived there on November 8, 1519, and took Monte-
zuma hostage a week later.

487.3    Leon]   General Juan Valazquez de Leon.

487.27    Alvarado]   Pedro de Alvarado (d. 1541), a lieutenant of Cortés'.

497.3    Lorna]   Cf. the heroine of R. D. Blackmore's popular novel *Lorna
Doone* (1869).

498.1    *Class Hymn*]   Written for the Lawrence High School commence-
ment exercises, 1892.

499.8    I would arise . . . go on—]   Cf. William Butler Yeats, "The Lake
Isle of Innisfree," which begins: "I will arise and go now, and go to Innis-
free . . . "

502.7    *Greece*]   Agitation in Greece for the annexation of Crete, then un-
der Ottoman rule, led to the Greco-Turkish war of 1897. Greece was defeated,
but Crete was eventually made independent and in 1913 was absorbed by
Greece.

505.2    making boxes]   See note 93.1.

511.17    *The Later Minstrel*]   Written to commemorate the centennial of the
birth of Longfellow (1807–82).

511.28    Who sang . . . Youth,]   See note 15.1.

511.29    The Secret of the Sea]   Title of a poem by Longfellow.

513.31    Malvern Hill]   In the last engagement of the Seven Days' Battles fought near Richmond, Confederate General Robert E. Lee attacked the retreating Army of the Potomac at Malvern Hill, Virginia, on July 1, 1862. The attack was defeated by massed Union artillery, and the Confederates lost more than 5,000 men killed and wounded.

515.8    *virumque cano*]   Cf. Virgil's *Aeneid*, I.1: "Arma virumque cano"— "Arms and the man I sing."

515.18    Philip the Chief's son]   Metacomet, sachem of the Wampanoags, was called King Philip by the English; following his death at the end of King Philip's War (1675–76), his young son and widow were sent to the West Indies as slaves.

516.10    *The Parlor Joke*]   Sent with a letter dated March 21, 1920, to Louis Untermeyer, with the following note: "Patented 1910 by R. (L.) Frost."

518.20–521.20    *My Giving . . . Winter Winds*]   These seven poems were included in a booklet that Frost sewed together and sent as a 1911 Christmas gift to Susan Hayes Ward.

519.8    *On the Sale of My Farm*]   Written on the occasion of Frost's sale of the farm in Derry, New Hampshire.

523.29    Kickapoo]   North American Indian group that was eventually resettled on reservations in Oklahoma and Kansas.

524.1–526.10    *In Equal . . . Dead*]   See 15.1 for the earlier publication history of "In Equal Sacrifice," "Asking for Roses," and "Spoils of the Dead," and notes to them in the table of contents, in *A Boy's Will* (1913).

526.2–4    Old Herrick . . . roses.']   Cf. Robert Herrick (1591–1674), "To the Virgins, to Make Much of Time," which begins: "Gather ye rosebuds while ye may . . . "

527.24    my father-in-letters]   Ezra Pound.

528.12    twins]   Hilda Doolittle (H.D.) and her husband Richard Aldington, whose imagist poems Pound had published.

528.15    I am a Mede and Persian]   The law of the Medes and the Persians is proverbially harsh and inflexible; cf. Daniel 6:12. Frost sent the poem, which he considered sending to Ezra Pound, in a letter to F. S. Flint in late July 1913. Flint wrote back that the poem might annoy Pound, and Frost apparently did not send it.

528.17    you]   Ezra Pound.

529.1    You reviewed me]   Pound reviewed *A Boy's Will* in *Poetry* (May 1913).

529.20    two American editors.]   H. L. Mencken, editor of *The Smart Set*, and Harriet Monroe, editor of *Poetry*.

530.19    Stark Young]    Young (1881–1963), a dramatist, novelist, and theater critic, taught at Amherst College from 1915 to 1920 and was partly responsible for bringing Frost to the college's faculty in 1917. The two had met in April 1916 when Frost gave a reading at Amherst College.

531.12    *On Talk of Peace at This Time*]    This poem was inscribed in a copy of *Mountain Interval* (1916) given to Mark Anthony DeWolfe Howe in December 1916.

533.1    *Forest Flowers*]    An earlier version of this poem titled "Tutelary Elves" was sent to Susan Hayes Ward in 1911.

533.11    *The Seven Arts*]    Sent with a letter to Louis Untermeyer in November 1917. *The Seven Arts* (Nov. 1916–Oct. 1917) was a monthly magazine on whose editorial board Untermeyer had served.

533.16    a-Bourneing]    After *Seven Arts* published a series of pacifist essays by Randolph S. Bourne (1886–1918), public reaction caused its financial backer, Mrs. A. K. Rankine, to withdraw her subsidy, and the magazine failed.

533.18    For Allan]    Sent to Allan Neilson, son of William Allan Neilson, president of Smith College.

534.1    *Fish-Leap Fall*]    Sent with a letter dated June 30 to Louis Untermeyer, who noted in *The Letters of Robert Frost to Louis Untermeyer:* "Robert toyed with the idea of putting this in a section entitled 'Over Back' (a subtitle he subsequently used in *A Witness Tree*)."

536.1–21    Oh thou . . . neck.]    In a January 1925 letter to Leonidas W. Payne Jr., after joking about the slowness of trains in Texas, Frost introduced these two poems with a note: "And yet speed is a thing I can see the beauty of and intend to write a poem in free verse on if ever I am tempted to write anything in free verse. Let's see how do you write the stuff . . ."

536.24    Patmos]    Island in the Aegean Sea used by the Romans as a place of exile; according to Revelation 1:9, John wrote the Book of Revelation there.

537.9    *The Cow's in the Corn*]    The Slide Mountain Press edition (Gaylordsville, 1929), printed and bound in 91 copies by James and Hilda Wells, includes a dedication to them, a statement on rights ("Stage and amateur rights for this play are owned and controlled by the author. No public performance or reading may be given without his written consent. / All rights reserved, including that of translation into foreign languages including that of the Scandinavians, the Agerbaijans and the Karafutoanei"), and an Introduction: "This, my sole contribution to the Celtic Drama (no one so unromantic as not to have made at least one) illustrates the latter day tendency of all drama to become smaller and smaller and to be acted in smaller and smaller theatres to smaller and smaller audiences. / R. F." The title is drawn from the nursery rhyme "Little Boy Blue."

542.1    Lowes]    Literary critic and Harvard professor John Livingston Lowes (1867–1945), whose works include *The Road to Xanadu* (1927), a study of Coleridge; during a conversation with Frost, Lowes is reported to have said that poetry "is one texture of quotations" written out of all the books a poet has read, and "it is my pleasure to come after you and trace it to its sources."

542.17 *Trouble Rhyming*] Sent to Untermeyer in a letter dated October 1, 1930; in *The Letters of Robert Frost to Louis Untermeyer*, Untermeyer notes: "In the 1920's I had become acquainted with Burges Johnson . . . a writer of light verse who, in 1931, compiled a New Rhyming Dictionary and Poets' Handbook . . . From time to time he planned 'projects' to show what a series of arbitrarily rhymed words might suggest to different poets." In 1930 Johnson gave a list of 14 such words, which were to provide the basis for a sonnet, to Untermeyer and Frost. Untermeyer continues: "I don't know what happened to my example of word-juggling; I think I took it at least half seriously. But although Robert willingly complied, he burlesqued the whole idea."

542.24 Truslow Adams] James Truslow Adams (1878–1949), American historian.

543.1 Dear Louis:] Sent to Untermeyer October 26, 1931.

543.8 E. A. Robinson's last book] *Matthias at the Door* (1931).

543.22–23 other fellow's . . . art] Cf. Shakespeare's sonnet 29 ("When in disgrace with Fortune and men's eyes") line 7: "Desiring this man's art, and that man's scope".

543.29 a Denverite] Colorado poet, author, and journalist Thomas Hornsby Ferril.

544.13 *Let Congress See To It*] See note 442.40.

544.19 *A Restoration*] Sent to poet and Harvard professor Robert Hillyer in September 1932 in response to Hillyer's article "Robert Frost 'Lacks Power' " (*New England Quarterly*, April 1932), which defended Frost against his critics.

544.28 "O Ra . . . Horus] This, and other references in the poem, are a play on Hillyer's *The Coming Forth By Day* (1923), whose title is a name for ancient Egyptian funerary texts concerning safe passage to and through judgment before the gods.

548.14 Dear Leonard Bacon:] Written in acknowledgment of Bacon's book of satirical poetry *Rhyme and Punishment* (1936), which he dedicated to Frost.

548.32 Peace Dale] Bacon's home town in Rhode Island.

549.36 Sweet Singer of Michigan] Name by which Julia A. Moore (1847–1920) became known after the publication of *The Sweet Singer of Michigan Salutes the Public* (1876), poems said to be so bad they possessed a touch of genius. Ogden Nash (1902–71) claimed to have "humorously employed the mannerisms of her bad verse."

550.1 Unless . . . a pewter tray] Written in acknowledgment of a stained-glass medallion that Charles Jay Connick made in response to Frost's "Stopping by Woods on a Snowy Evening." The poem was first published above a plate depicting the medallion in Connick's *Adventures in Light and Color* (1937).

552.1–2 Dear Louis: . . . war at all] Sent to Untermeyer on August 12, 1944, after Untermeyer, then senior editor of publications for the Office of War Information, asked Frost to participate in the war effort as a writer.

553.28 Kay] Kathleen Morrison, Frost's secretary and manager.

553.36 Larry] Lawrance Thompson (1906–73) who later wrote an "official" biography of Frost (3 vols., 1966, 1970, 1977).

553.38 four freedoms] See note 382.26.

554.35 Lee] Richard Henry Lee (1732–94), American Revolutionary statesman.

554.39 Groton.] Prestigious boys' preparatory school in northeastern Massachusetts, attended by Franklin Delano Roosevelt from 1896 to 1900.

555.31 Your Adirondacs] Untermeyer owned a house in the Adirondack Mountains.

556.12 She who . . . great authority] Kathleen Morrison.

556.29–557.10 Ten . . . Barn] *Ten Thirty A.M.* and *A Bed in the Barn* appear in an early manuscript of Frost's collection *Steeple Bush;* he omitted the poems from the book before its publication.

558.1 *Pares Continuas Fututiones*] In a letter to Louis Henry Cohn dated September 21, 1951, in which Frost enclosed this limerick, he noted that the title referred to Catullus' poem number 31; there, lines 9–10 read: "*sed domi maneas paresque nobis / nouem continuas fututiones*" which may be translated "but stay at home and prepare yourself for / nine consecutive copulations."

558.2 Harvard Neo Malthushian] In the letter to Cohn, Frost wrote that James B. Conant, a former professor of chemistry and president of Harvard University (1933–53), as a "mouthpiece" for science had "undertaken for it to make the planet less uncomfortably crowded with a new kind of manna . . . a contraceptive to be taken by mouth so we can stop breeding without having to stop futution."

558.12 Their totem symbol] The cod is a state emblem of Massachusetts.

560.19 For travelers going sidereal] This poem was originally intended for inclusion in Frost's collection *In the Clearing* (1962).

## PLAYS

571.9–10     cities of the plain]  Sodom and Gomorrah (cf. Genesis 13:12, 19: 25, 29).

576.1     *In an Art Factory*]  The holograph notebook in which this play appears includes a note that reads: "It should be said that this play was written many years ago and has been kept over for publication and possible presentation when I should have done one or two others I intended for its companions. I have read it a few times aloud. Two or three references to public events and personages date it approximately. I remember reading it to Jean and Louis Untermeyer when it was new. It is easy to see what I have been antagonized by all along. I moved the theme off into another art—for objectivity I suppose. I made Campbell out of my talks with and about such people as Faggi Partridge Taft Du Chene Chapin etc. / R.F. / Ripton June 22, 1951 / This is the only copy in hand. Kay Morrison has a copy in her typing." Alfeo Faggi was an Italian-born American sculptor, Lorado Taft, a sculptor and writer, Aroldo du Chêne, a sculptor who made a bust of Frost in 1920, and James Chapin, a painter who made drawings of some of Frost's children.

582.1–2     Solomon . . . child.]  Cf. I Kings 3:16–27.

583.3     Claussen's work]  Probably landscape and figure painter Sir George Clausen (1852–1944), a professor at the Royal Academy in London and author of *Aims and Ideals in Art* (1906), whose works include "The Gleaners Returning," "The Plowman's Breakfast," and "A Winter's Day."

589.1     *The Guardeen*]  In the holograph manuscript, an inscription under the cast of characters reads: "Second Version / for Earle Bernheimer / from his friend / Robert Frost / Cambridge Mass Jan 12 1942".

597.5     Quit ye like men.]  Cf. 1 Samuel 4:9, 1 Corinthians 16:13.

600.22–23     democrat]  A democrat carriage is a light four-wheeled horse-drawn cart with two sets of double seats.

605.8–9     Sherman Act.]  The Sherman Antitrust Act, enacted 1890.

## LECTURES, ESSAYS, STORIES, AND LETTERS

633.1     *Petra*]  Ancient city, now in present-day Jordan, situated in a valley west of ancient Edom (60 miles north of Aqabah), which is reached by passage through a gorge called the Siq.

633.2–3     Mt. Hor . . . Aaron]  Cf. Numbers 20:23–29.

633.6–8     warlike . . . passage.]  The Edomites, descendants of Isaac's eldest son, Esau, refused the Israelites passage through their land during the exodus (Numbers 20:14–21).

636.1     *A Monument . . . Unveiled*]  Frost's high school valedictory speech.

662.9     Horatius . . . Rustum]   Poems by, respectively, Thomas Babington Macaulay (1800–59) in *Lays of Ancient Rome* and Matthew Arnold (1822–88).

662.19     Golden Treasury]   See note 24.8.

662.23–24     Gareth . . . Arthur]   Poems in Alfred Lord Tennyson's Arthurian cycle *The Idylls of the King* (1859–72).

662.33     Kenilworth]   Novel (1821) by Walter Scott.

663.3     Woolley's Handbook]   *College Handbook of Composition* by Edwin Campbell Woolley (1878–1916).

663.12–13     Jonson's Silent Woman]   Ben Jonson's play *Epicoene; or, The Silent Woman* (1609).

664.1     *John T. Bartlett*]   See note 158.8.

664.2–4     The Bungs . . . Bucks]   The Bungalow (Frost's nickname for his cottage), Beaconsfield, Buckinghamshire.

664.6     T. P.'s]   *T. P.'s Weekly* (1902–16), English literary periodical founded by Thomas Power O'Connor (1848–1929).

664.7     Buckley]   Reginald Buckley, assistant editor at *T. P.'s Weekly*.

667.20     Margaret]   Bartlett's wife.

668.7     caviare . . . crowd]   Cf. Hamlet's speech to the players in II.ii.434–439: "I heard thee speak me a speech once, but / it was never acted, or if it was, not above once; for / the play, I remember, pleas'd not the million, 'twas / caviary to the general, but it was—as I receiv'd it, and / others, whose judgments in such matters cried in the / top of mine—an excellent play, . . . "

668.17     Trevelyan]   Robert Calverley Trevelyan (1872–1951), translator of Greek plays and writer of light verse.

668.23     Q's]   Q was the pen name of Sir Arthur Quiller-Couch (1863–1944), journalist, author, and editor of anthologies including *The Oxford Book of Victorian Verse* and *The Oxford Book of English Verse*.

668.24     The Georgian Anthology]   *Georgian Poetry 1911–1912*, edited by Edward Marsh.

668.29     Mrs. Nutt]   M. L. Nutt, widow of David Nutt's son, Alfred T. Nutt, had inherited the publishing firm.

671.29–30     Poetry and Drama]   *Poetry and Drama* (1913–14), edited by Harold Munro, published Frost's poems and reviews of his work.

673.24     District of Columbia]   The Bartletts lived in Vancouver, British Columbia.

674.21     John Cournos]   Cournos (1881–1966), a Russian-born American, lived in England, 1912–30, and became a novelist.

675.36    A Patch of Old Snow]   Cf. "A Patch of Old Snow" in *Mountain Interval*, page 107.

676.20–21    (Asking for Roses.)]   This poem was removed from some later editions of *A Boy's Will*. See page 525 in this volume and note 15.1.

677.10    Henry Horne]   Henry Dow, a character in Frost's play *The Guardeen*, is based on Henry Horne. See page 589 in this volume.

678.23    nasty . . . Alford]   John Alford reviewed 16 volumes of American poetry in *Poetry and Drama*, December 1913. Frost was not among the poets reviewed.

680.6–7    Hueffer's article]   "Mr. Robert Frost and *North of Boston*," in *The Outlook* (London), June 27, 1914. Ford Madox Ford (b. Ford Hermann Hueffer) first wrote under the name Ford Madox Hueffer.

682.17    Keats . . . ode.]   Cf. "Ode to a Nightingale," stanza 7.

682.23    Castle Garden]   Originally a fort called Castle Clinton on the Battery in New York City, and named Castle Garden after it was made into an opera house and amusement hall in 1823, the structure served as an immigrant processing station from 1855 to 1892, before Ellis Island was opened; after World War II it became Castle Clinton National Monument.

682.37    Hatch]   Clarence Hatch, Cox's former student at Dartmouth.

684.1    *William Braithwaite*]   Braithwaite (1878–1962) was an African-American poet, anthologist, and critic whose book reviews appeared in *The Boston Transcript*, *Atlantic Monthly*, and *North American Review*.

684.8–11    pages 1 . . . 49.]   The poems in the order listed are: "Into My Own," "Ghost House," "My November Guest," "A Late Walk," "Storm Fear," "Flower-Gathering," "In a Vale," "A Dream Pang," "In Neglect," "Mowing," "Going for Water," "The Tuft of Flowers," "The Demiurge's Laugh," "Now Close the Windows," "October," "My Butterfly," and "Reluctance."

686.11    quotation . . . Nation]   The article, "A New Voice," written by Lascelles Abercrombie, was published in London on June 13, 1914.

687.2    MR. BROWNE]   George H. Browne was headmaster of Browne and Nichols School.

687.27–28    T.E. Brown's]   English poet Thomas Edward Brown (1830–97).

687.29–30    "Who dreamed . . . dream"]   "The Rose of the World," line 1.

690.1    *Walter Pritchard Eaton*]   Eaton (1878–1957) was a New York drama critic and author of books on theater and the New England countryside; he was one of the summer visitors Frost met at Franconia.

690.11    N.H. Dole]    Nathan Haskell Dole (1852–1935), a poet, novelist, essayist, editor, and translator of Daudet and Tolstoy among others.

690.13    Pooie]    Ernest Poole (1880–1950), Chicago-born New York novelist and social reformer.

690.21–22    article . . . The Atlantic]    "A New American Poet," by Edward Garnett, *The Atlantic Monthly*, August 1915.

692.13    Bergson and Fabre]    Cf. French philosopher Henri Bergson's *Creative Evolution* (1907; English translation, 1911). Jean Henri Fabre (1823–1915), French entomologist whose observation of insects led him to oppose the theory of evolution, wrote of his findings in *Annales des sciences naturelles* (1855–58) and *Souvenirs entomologiques* (1879–1907; English translation 1912).

692.30    Lowell]    Amy Lowell (1874–1925).

693.1    *Régis Michaud*]    Michaud (1880–1939), associate professor of French at Smith College, 1917–19; Frost met him in Amherst.

703.10    Huebsch]    Benjamin W. Huebsch (1876–1964) published books under his own imprint from 1906 until he joined the newly formed Viking Press in 1925.

703.15–16    Lincoln MacVeagh]    MacVeagh, an editor, publisher, writer, and later diplomat, was with Henry Holt & Co. before becoming president of Dial Press, Inc., 1924–33.

703.22    Maurice Firuski]    Bookseller of The Dunster House Bookshop in Cambridge, Massachusetts.

704.26    Jean]    Poet Jean Starr Untermeyer (1886–1970).

704.30–31    Mrs Olds, . . . Presidents]    Marion Leland Olds' husband, George Daniel Olds, was president of Amherst College, 1924–27.

705.2–3    '*Memoirs . . . Stephen Burroughs*']    Published first in 1811. Stephen Burroughs (1765–1840) served in the army, which he deserted, and attended Dartmouth College, which he left without a diploma; he became "notorious" for impersonating an ordained minister with plagiarized sermons and for counterfeiting. Burroughs later went to Canada, converted to Roman Catholicism, and became a respected tutor of the sons of wealthy Catholics.

705.26    the Leanders']    In the *Memoirs* Burroughs' friends in Pelham are called the "Lysanders."

706.24    Melchizedek]    Melchizedek's priesthood is discussed in Hebrews 7; see also Genesis 14:18–20 and Psalm 110:4.

708.2    W. R. Brown]    Warren R. Brown, Amherst real-estate agent.

709.31–36    "The Village" . . . Sleep"]    "The Village Daily" was written by Richard Eberhart; "The Ski Jumper" by A. W. Edson; "Underneath Sleep" was published anonymously.

711.1  *MacKaye*]  MacKaye had helped Frost get his appointment as Poet in Residence at the University of Michigan; MacKaye had himself been awarded a fellowship by Miami University (Oxford, Ohio) in 1920, and then began a campaign on behalf of artists, starting with an article published in *The Forum* in June 1921 called "University Fellowships in the Creative Arts."

714.22  Mrs William Rose Benet]  American poet and novelist Elinor Wylie (1885–1928).

722.10–11  Someone visiting Gibbon]  Edward Gibbon's friend, John Baker Holroyd (1735–1821), 1st Earl of Sheffield, who reported, "The parallels which he drew, and the comparisons which he made, between the leading men of this country, were sketched in his best manner, and were infinitely interesting." Gibbon died several weeks after this visit on January 16, 1794.

724.23–24  one . . . "Odyssey"]  Book V.

729.13–14  your . . . me]  The manuscript of *A Swinger of Birches: A Portrait of Robert Frost*, published posthumously in 1957; Cox's shorter book was *Robert Frost: Original Ordinary Man* (1929).

729.31  one very great.]  "Death the Leveller."

730.1  the Gilchrist book]  Marie Gilchrist's *Writing Poetry: Suggestions for Young Writers* (Houghton Mifflin, 1932).

732.1  *Wilbert Snow*]  Poet and professor of English at Wesleyan University in Connecticut, and a close friend of Frost's.

732.3–7  The Hungry . . . Flood]  Poems in Snow's book *Down East* (1932).

732.28–30  George Meredith . . . within."]  The conclusion of "Love's Grave": "In tragic life, God wot, / No villain need be! Passions spin the plot: / We are betray'd by what is false within."

734.15  Mrs Sheffield]  Ada, wife of Alfred Dwight Sheffield.

735.3–4  in Reed . . . Form]  Herbert Read, *Form in Modern Poetry* (1932).

735.11  Richards]  Ivor Armstrong Richards (1893–1979), English literary critic.

736.1  her opera]  *Four Saints in Three Acts*, which premiered in Hartford, Connecticut, on February 8, 1934; a number of performances followed in New York and in Chicago.

736.4  "The bailey . . . bell"]  Anonymous poem, variously titled "The Maidens Came" or "The Bridal Morning."

736.12  long poem . . . Perse]  *Anabase* (1924) by Saint-John Perse, pseudonym of Alexis Saint-Léger Léger (1887–1975), French diplomat and poet; T. S. Eliot's translation appeared in 1930.

737.2      This song . . . boys]   See note 736.12

737.5      "Desiring . . . scope"]   From Sonnet 29 ("When in disgrace with
Fortune and men's eyes . . . "); Eliot has "this man's gift."

738.3      Palmer's translation]   George Herbert Palmer (1842–1933), *The
Odyssey of Homer* (1884).

738.28     *The Prisoner of Zenda*]   Novel (1894) by Sir Anthony Hope
Hawkins (1863–1933), who wrote under the pseudonym "Anthony Hope."

738.36     *Books We Like*]   *Books We Like; Sixty-Two Answers To the Question:
'Please choose, and give reasons for your choice, ten books, exclusive of the Bible
and Shakespeare, dictionaries, encyclopedias, and other ordinary reference books,
that you believe should be in every public library'*, edited, and with a preface,
by Edward Weeks (Boston: Massachusetts Library Association, 1936).

739.3–4    STUDENT . . . my age.]   Response to birthday greetings from
Amherst College students.

744.38–39  Miniver . . . about it.]   From Robinson's "Miniver Cheevy."

745.14–15  One pauses . . . played—]   From Robinson's "Flammonde."

745.16     His death]   Robinson died on April 6, 1935.

745.23–24  Once a man . . . minute.]   From Robinson's "Old King
Cole."

745.35–37  The games . . . through.]   From Robinson's sonnet "Dear
Friends."

746.1      He speaks . . . skill.]   In "George Crabbe": "Of his plain excel-
lence and stubborn skill / There yet remains what fashion cannot kill, /
Though years have thinned the laurel from his brows."

746.24–29  The miller's . . . say.]   From "The Mill."

747.17–18  golden . . . Sheaves."]   Cf. the closing lines of the poem: "A
thousand golden sheaves were lying there, / Shining and still, but not for
long to stay— / As if a thousand girls with golden hair / Might rise from
where they slept and go away."

747.31–32  The inscrutable . . . thing]   Cf. "The Rat": "As often as he
let himself be seen / We pitied him, or scorned him, or deplored / The
inscrutable profusion of the Lord / Who shaped as one of us a thing so
mean—"

747.37     immedicable woes]   The phrase is from the once vastly popular
poem "The Man With a Hoe," by Edwin Markham (1852–1940).

748.1–2    play's the thing . . . All virtue in "as if."]   Cf. Shakespeare's *Hamlet*, II.ii.604: "the play's the thing / Wherein I'll catch the conscience of the King," and *As You Like It*, V.iv.98–103: "I knew when seven justices could not take up a quarrel, but when the parties were met themselves, one of them thought of an If, as, 'If you said so, then I said so'; and they shook hands and swore brothers. Your If is the only peacemaker; much virtue in If."

748.3–4    As if . . . done.]   From Robinson's "The Dark Hills."

749.7    Childe Roland . . . Tower]   A reference to Robert Browning's "Childe Roland to the Dark Tower Came," under which Browning notes: "See Edgar's song in *Lear*." Cf. Shakespeare's *King Lear*, III.iv.182.

749.10–12    "May . . . fraud."]   Cf. Ralph Waldo Emerson, "Berrying," lines 1–3; in Emerson, line three ends "fraud and force,'."

749.21–22    a novelist . . . a poet.]   The novelist is Dorothy Canfield Fisher (1879–1958); the essayist is Zephine Humphrey Fahenstock; the "saintly poet" is Cleghorn.

749.26    Cleghorn's poem]   "The Golf Links" (*New-York Tribune*, 1915): "The golf links lie so near the mill / That almost every day / The laboring children can look out / And see the men at play."

751.1–3    One . . . northward]   "Harriet Tubman," a ballad.

751.15    (see page 110)]   On this page in *Threescore* Cleghorn discusses how much can be accomplished by writing letters to the editors of newspapers.

753.9    I . . . English]   John Masefield took Frost's place as Phi Beta Kappa poet and in the Harvard Tercentenary exercises.

753.10    Billy Phelps]   William Lyon Phelps (1865–1943), former professor of English at Yale University.

753.28    his Rosiness]   Franklin Delano Roosevelt.

754.5    Shaw and Butler]   George Bernard Shaw and Samuel Butler (1825–1902).

754.15–16    Larry . . . Esther]   The adopted sons and third wife of Untermeyer.

755.1    What . . . England?]   Robert S. Nedwick of Ohio State University English department prepared a typescript from a stenographic record of this speech and published it with Frost's approval, though Frost took no part in its preparation.

755.3    Western Reserve]   A section of land in the northeast corner of Ohio reserved by the state of Connecticut when it ceded the rest of its western land claim to the United States in 1786. In 1800 Connecticut transferred jurisdiction over the Western Reserve to the federal government, and it became part of the newly created Ohio territory.

755.15–16    a book . . . society]   A reference to Amy Lowell's review of *North of Boston*, published in *The New Republic*, February 20, 1915: "Mr. Frost's book reveals a disease which is eating into the vitals of our New England life, at least in its rural communities."

755.17    A distinguished critic]   In a notebook entry bearing the heading "What Became of New England?" Frost attributes these sentiments to novelist and critic Ford Madox Ford (1873–1939), who spent much of the last years of his life in America.

758.22–33    Strong . . . wide.]   From Christopher Smart (1722–71), "A Song to David."

759.1    *Poverty and Poetry*]   "Poverty and Poetry" and "The Poet's Next of Kin in College" are texts prepared from stenographic records by Lawrance Thompson, who explains that he "edited" the talks "heavily, and even took the liberty of compressing sentences . . . "

759.10–11    *A Book of People*]   See note 39.1.

759.14    one . . . acted]   "The Death of the Hired Man" and "Home Burial" were performed in Boston in 1915.

760.14–15    Bill . . . strike]   William Haywood (1869–1928), American labor leader and organizer for the Industrial Workers of the World, helped organize a successful strike in the winter of 1912 against Lawrence, Massachusetts, textile mill owners who had lowered wages after agreeing to shorten hours.

761.4    "Let not . . . asunder,"]   Cf. Matthew 19:6.

765.34    "counter-revolutionary"]   Cf. Rolfe Humphries's review of *A Further Range* (1936) in *New Masses*, August 11, 1936.

768.1    *The Poet's . . . College*]   See note 759.1 above.

769.21    a literary-scientific-research man]   Literary critic John Livingston Lowes, author of *The Road to Xanadu* and other works.

770.11–12    One of . . . friends]   Edward Morgan Lewis (1872–1936), born in Wales, was pitcher for the Boston National League baseball team, 1896–1900, and Boston's American League team, 1901, then taught at his alma mater, Williams College, and in 1927 became president of the University of New Hampshire.

773.1    *Robert P. T. Coffin*]   Coffin (1892–1953), a Maine poet and novelist, had asked for notes on a talk Frost had given at the annual dinner of the Poetry Society of America on April 1, 1937.

773.27    the Harvard invitation]   Contrary to established practice, Frost never published his Charles Eliot Norton lectures, and no transcription is known to be extant.

774.34    Molly Colum] Colum (1885–1957) was an Irish author and educator whose works include *From These Roots* (1937); she and her husband, poet Padraic Colum (1881–1972), came to the United States in 1914.

779.21–22    O Time . . . art thou.] From Thomas William Parsons (1819–92), "On a Bust of Dante."

782.23    Hoosac Tunnel] Railroad tunnel extending 4.73 miles through the Hoosac Mountains of western Massachusetts, completed in 1875.

783.24    This selection] The sixteen poems chosen for inclusion were: "The Need of Being Versed in Country Things," "Come In," "The Onset," "Stopping By Woods On a Snowy Evening," "On a Tree Fallen Across the Road," "The Woodpile," "Willful Homing," "A Blue Ribbon at Amesbury," "Two Tramps in Mud Time," "A Prayer in Spring," "Mowing," "A Drumlin Woodchuck," "Sitting By a Bush in Broad Sunlight," "Sand Dunes," "A Soldier," "The Gift Outright."

783.30–31    divinity . . . ends] Cf. *Hamlet* V.ii.9–10: "that should learn us / There's a divinity that shapes our ends."

783.31    building . . . knew] Cf. Ralph Waldo Emerson's "The Problem," line 23: "He builded better than he knew."

785.1–2    *Preface . . . Hired Man*'] This preface was written for a textbook, *American Authors Today*, edited by Whit Burnett and Charles Slatkin, (1947), but the editors decided to write their own introduction and Frost's preface was not published during his lifetime.

787.2    Viennese] The reference is to Sigmund Freud.

787.3–4    gregarious . . . sex.] Cf. Herbert Read's *Form in Modern Poetry* (1932): "There are many instincts besides the sex instinct, and if any one instinct is more in question than another, I think it is probably the gregarious instinct." Grex is the Latin root for gregarious.

787.7    Terence's answer] Cf. Terence (185–159 B.C.), *Heauton Timoroumenos* ("The Self-Tormenter"), line 77: "I am a man: I hold that nothing human is alien to me."

788.29    as Blake says] Cf. William Blake's (1757–1827) poem "Love's Secret" in *The Oxford Book of English Verse* edited by Quiller-Couch, which begins "Never seek to tell thy love" (in another version of Blake, "seek" reads "pain").

789.7–8    "When . . . eyes."] Shakespeare, Sonnet 29, line 1.

789.13    by what jutting points of rock] Cf. lines 49–51 of Tennyson's "Morte d'Arthur": "He, stepping down / By zig-zag paths, and juts of pointed rock, / Came on the shining levels of the lake."

789.37–38    "I intended . . . Sonnet."] Henry Austin Dobson (1840–1924), "Urceus Exit," lines 1–2.

789.40    Rose]   The woman who figures in "Urceus Exit."

792.3–4    Rabbi Reichert]   Rabbi Victor Reichert prepared this text from an audio-recording of the sermon.

792.13    *That*]   In his preface to the Spiral Press edition of Frost's "Sermon," Rabbi Reichert noted that a cornucopia filled with vegetables and tropical fruits was placed on the pulpit near the lectern from which Frost spoke.

796.1    *Speaking of Loyalty*]   George Whicher prepared a transcript of this talk and submitted it to Frost to be revised for publication. Some of Whicher's original footnotes to the first appearance of the talk in the *Amherst Graduates' Quarterly* are given below.

796.2    CHARLIE COLE . . . Whicher]   Charles Cole was president of Amherst College and George Whicher was a professor of English there.

796.3–4    a brand new college]   Whicher noted: "See Walter Hendricks' article, 'Marlboro College,' in the May, 1948, *Quarterly*."

797.8    article . . . *Magazine.*]   "Who Is Loyal to America?" by Henry Steele Commager, September 1947.

797.19–21    Heartily . . . arrive.]   Last lines of Ralph Waldo Emerson's "Give All To Love."

798.18–31    It's about . . . Astarte.]   Whicher noted: "The episode as recorded by the Carthaginian navigator who first came in contact with pygmies (not anthropoid apes) on the coast of Sierra Leone runs as follows in *The Periplus* of Hanno, translated from the Greek by Wilfred H. Schoff (Philadelphia, 1912), p. 5: 'In the recess of this bay there was an island, like the former one, having a lake, in which there was another island full of savage men. There were women, too, in even greater number. They had hairy bodies, and the interpreters called them Gorrilae. When we pursued them we were unable to take any of the men; for they all escaped, by climbing the steep places, and defending themselves with stones; but we took three of the women, who bit and scratched their leaders, and would not follow us. So we killed them and flayed them, and brought their skins to Carthage. For we did not voyage further, provisions failing us.' "

799.5–7    "Poetry . . . detrimental."]   Whicher noted: " 'Diction and sound seem to be dominant; meaning, on the other hand, has been held to be nonessential (and in some few cases even detrimental) to true poetry.' *Columbia Encyclopedia* (New York, 1935), p. 1412."

799.17    Merrimack River]   Whicher noted: " 'In 1764 the Connecticut River was established as the western boundary, with the present Vermont belonging to New York. The dispute between Vermont and New Hampshire as to the exact line of demarcation continued into the 20th century.' *Columbia Encyclopedia*, art. 'New Hampshire.' "

800.9–14    Ah, when . . . season?]  Last stanza of "Reluctance."

801.1    Pease]  Arthur Stanley Pease, former president of Amherst and, at this time, chairman of the Harvard Latin Department.

802.1    *A Romantic Chasm*]  Cf. Samuel Taylor Coleridge's "Kubla Kahn," line 12: "But O, that deep romantic chasm . . . "

802.5    had . . . Kipling]  Cf. Rudyard Kipling's "An American," lines 37–44: "Inopportune, shrill-accented, / The acrid Asiatic mirth / That leaves him, careless 'mid his dead, / The scandal of the elder earth. // How shall he clear himself, how reach / Your bar or weighed defence prefer— / A brother hedged with alien speech / And lacking all interpreter?"

802.14–15    his great book]  *The American Language* (1919; rev. 1921, 1923, 1936; supplementary vols., 1945, 1948).

802.26    Jack Haines]  English barrister and amateur botanist.

802.35    Mark Curtius]  When a huge chasm suddenly opened in the forum and an oracle proclaimed that it would be sealed only after Rome had thrown into it its most precious treasure, Curtius (fl. 362 B.C.) armed himself, mounted his horse, and leaped into the gulf, which then closed.

803.9–10    Ivor Brown]  Brown (1891–1974) was an English journalist and author who wrote primarily on drama, but also edited "word-anthologies," including *A Word in Your Ear* (1942).

803.10    Sursanure]  Heals outwardly but not inwardly.

803.32–33    Phoebus . . . trembling ears),]  Cf. Milton's "Lycidas" (1638), lines 76–78: "But not the praise, / *Phoebus* repli'd, and touched my trembling ears; / Fame is no plant that grows on mortal soil . . . "

803.37    "entertain . . . stranger"]  Cf. "Preparations," penultimate line, in which the anonymous poet speaks of Christ: "We entertain Him only as a stranger," (*The Oxford Book of English Verse*, ed. Quiller-Couch).

805.10    a few]  Frost chose for inclusion: "The Need of Being Versed in Country Things," "The Mountain," "The Road Not Taken," "The Grind-stone," "The Gift Outright," "One Step Backward Taken."

807.8    Catullus . . . *mens animi*]  Cf. Catullus's poem number 65, line 4. Frost discussed and translated the phrase more than once. In a talk at Kenyon College in 1950, he said: "mens—mind, and animus—the spirit, see . . . And I suppose that's what we've been talking about today. The order—mens is the order—mens, the order of my wildness . . . see that's the way I translate enterprise of the spirit . . . that's the animus, that's the enterprise, that's the spirit that breaks the form." At Oxford in 1957, Frost said: "Poetry is the thoughts of the heart. I'm sure that's what Catullus meant by *mens animi*. Poetry is hyphenated, like so many British names. It's a thought-felt thing.

Poetry is the thing that laughs and cries about everything as it's going on—
and makes you take it. A momentary stay against confusion . . . "

810.22    a book heard round the world]   *Anthony Adverse* (1933), a pica-
resque historical romance set at the end of the 18th century, was translated
into at least nine languages and by 1946 had sold two million copies.

812.2–5    "AN ORDINARY . . . ignorance."]   From Joseph Addison's essay
on the ballad "Chevy Chase" (numbered 70 in the collected *Spectator* series),
published May 21, 1711.

812.23–24    Child . . . Mrs. Flanders]   Francis James Child (1825–96), pro-
fessor at Harvard University, 1851–96, edited *English and Scottish Ballads* (8
vols., 1857–58) and *English and Scottish Popular Ballads* (5 vols. 1883–98); Helen
Hartness Flanders was editor of *Ballads Migrant in New England.*

814.16    "Brahma"]   By Ralph Waldo Emerson.

815.38    Yidags]   In a June 1953 talk at the Bread Loaf School of English,
Frost identifies the name "Yidag" as belonging to Hindu mythology: "The
things you can get born into, you know, are angels, human beings, animals,
purgatorians, titans, and yedigs. That's it." The alternate spelling is Lawrance
Thompson's, who transcribed the talk from a tape recording.

817.1    *To the Poets of Japan*]   This brief message bears no title. Frost's ref-
erence to his age (eighty) dates the message in 1954.

830.1    "*Caveat Poeta*"]   Never published during Frost's lifetime. With the
typescript of "Caveat Poeta" in the Dartmouth College Library is a cover
sheet with the following paragraph dictated by Frost to his secretary, Kathleen
Morrison: "It should be amusing to people that I should be the one asked
to answer for the harm done by the educational system to the fine arts—I
who never went to school and college more than six years of my life and have
nothing to do with them except as a teacher in them now and then and the
object of their lavish patronage. Very extraordinary, nothing like it in the
world's history."

830.29    Meccano.]   An instructional game played with miniature metal
parts from which engineering models are constructed.

832.1    *A Perfect . . . Prowess*]   This essay appeared with the headnote:
"The All-Star Game is an All-American Affair." *Sports Illustrated* invited Frost
to sit in the stands in Washington, D.C., as guest columnist.

832.10    Boyer . . . catches]   Ken Boyer, third baseman for the St. Louis
Cardinals.

832.13    Berra]   Lawrence Peter "Yogi" Berra, catcher for the New York
Yankees.

832.32    Ed Lewis]   See note 770.11–12.

833.12      Anson]    Adrian Constantine "Cap" Anson (1852–1922), first base-
man, played for Chicago's National League club, 1876–97, and was elected to
the Hall of Fame in 1939.

833.28      Clark . . . field]    Griffith Stadium in Washington, D.C., where the
Senators played from 1911 to 1960, was named for Clark "The Old Fox"
Griffith (1869–1955), baseball pitcher, manager, and owner of the Senators.

833.30      Walter Johnson]    Walter Perry "The Big Train" Johnson (1887–
1946), pitcher for the Senators, 1907–27.

833.32      Gabby Street]    Charles Evard "Gabby" Street (1882–1951), catcher,
played for National and American League teams, 1904–12, 1931, and was a
manager, 1929–33, 1938.

833.35      Howard Schmitt]    A friend of Frost's from Hamburg, New York,
just south of Buffalo.

833.37–38      Temple of the Redlegs]    John Ellis "Johnny" Temple (b. 1928),
second baseman for the Cincinnati Reds.

836.4–5      Shakespeare . . . ripe.]    Cf. *As You Like It*, III.ii.119–120.

838.20      an article . . . *New Republic*]    "The Sincerity of Robert Frost,"
August 25, 1917.

840.1      *To . . . Korea*]    The *Korea Times*, an English-language paper pub-
lished in Seoul, published a letter from Frost with the article: "Dear Miss
Moh: Nothing but the charm of your visit could have inspired me to so much
of a message as the enclosed to people I have never met and know so little
about. I can't name names and I can't quote poems. My sympathy has to be
very general. You may see how much more political than literary it is likely
to be under the circumstances. Wouldn't it be great if we could have an era
of peace all over the world so that we could come and go with each other on
nothing but errands like yours to America. Robert Frost." Moh had been on
a five-month tour in the United States at the invitation of the State Depart-
ment, during which she visited Frost in Boston.

841.1–2      *"What . . . Today?"*]    A headnote by Dean Brelis to the *Esquire*
symposium, titled "Top Brass of America's intellectual capital give answers to
a key question of our time / What Worries You Most About America Today?",
reads in part: "In a time when brain power measures the rise and fall of a
nation, the lasting strength of a people is its capacity to think, to plan for the
future. In the average-sized American city of Cambridge, Massachusetts, the
thinking that is taking place now may well determine the survival of the
United States . . . *Esquire* has asked some of the great minds in America's
intellectual center to tell what worries them most about America—to help
chart the course of national survival."

842.12      Dudley Fitts]    Fitts (1903–68) was an educator, a translator of
Greeks including Aristophanes, Euripides, and Sophocles, and a poet.

842.16        physician . . . artist]   Moore (1903–57), a practicing psychiatrist in
Boston, published a number of collections of his sonnets, including *The Noise
that Time Makes* (1929), *Six Sides to a Man* (1935), *One Thousand Autobio-
graphical Sonnets* (1938), and *Clinical Sonnets* (1949).

843.8–9        "L'Allegro" and "Il Penseroso"]   Poems by John Milton.

843.10–11      "The Ballad of the Revenge."]   Tennyson's "The Revenge: a
Ballad of the Fleet."

843.17        laws of Petrillo]   Labor leader James Caesar Petrillo (1892–1984)
was president of the American Federation of Musicians, 1940–58.

843.19        Squantum]   Peninsular projection into Boston Harbor at the
mouth of the Neponset River.

844.1–3        *The Case . . . Pound*]   In July 1943, Pound (1885–1972), who was
living in Italy, was indicted in absentia for treason for making radio broadcasts
in support of the Axis powers. He was returned to the United States in No-
vember 1945 and in February 1946 found unfit to plead by reason of insanity
and remanded to St. Elizabeth's federal psychiatric hospital in Washington,
D.C. Court hearings in April 1958 resulted in the dismissal of the indictment
against him.

844.8–10       I append . . . predicament.]   *A Casebook on Ezra Pound* (1959),
edited by William Van O'Connor, includes statements (compiled by Archibald
MacLeish) from T. S. Eliot, Ernest Hemingway, MacLeish, W. H. Auden, Van
Wyck Brooks, John Dos Passos, Robert Fitzgerald, Marianne Moore, Carl
Sandburg, Allen Tate, and Dag Hammerskjöld.

844.21–22      Dr. Overholser]   Dr. Winfred Overholser, superintendent of
St. Elizabeth's.

845.1–2        *On Being . . . Congress*]   The appointment was announced at a
press conference at the Library on May 21, 1958.

845.13        Flanders and Aiken]   Ralph Edward Flanders (1880–1970), a me-
chanical engineer, served as U.S. senator from Vermont, 1946–58; George
David Aiken (1892–1984), a farmer, served 1940–50 and 1956–75.

845.19–20      a small . . . Rosecrans]   *William Starke Rosecrans, His Life
and Public Services* (San Francisco: Democratic Congressional Committee,
1880), a campaign biography. Rosecrans (1819–98) had been a major general
in the Union Army; he served in the U.S. House of Representatives, 1881–85.

847.1        *The Way There*]   Preface to a proposed publication of selections of
Frost's poems for younger readers, which was to have included: "Questioning
Faces," "Birches," "The Pasture," "Last Word of a Bluebird," "Locked
Out," "Going For Water," "A Tuft of Flowers," "Dust of Snow," "Gath-
ering Leaves," "Stopping By Woods on a Snowy Evening," "Looking for a
Sunset Bird in Winter," "Spring Pools," "Blue Butterfly Day," "A Drumlin

Woodchuck," "The Runaway," "A Peck of Gold," "A Time To Talk," "Blueberries," "A Minor Bird," "Lodged," "Christmas Trees," "Good Hours," "A Record Stride," "The Need of Being Versed in Country Things," "A Young Birch," "Wild Grapes," "Mowing."

848.5    Susan Hayes Ward]   Ward was literary editor of *The Independent*, which published a number of Frost's early poems.

848.8–9    published . . . thing]   "La Noche Triste" appeared in the Lawrence High School *Bulletin* in 1890.

848.12    Nicasio]   A town in Marin County, California, that Frost visited as a child.

849.5–6    one . . . Caesar]   "A Dream of Julius Cæsar."

849.7    Meliboeus]   A shepherd in Virgil's first Eclogue.

850.17    Basques]   Canfield did relief work in the Basque region of France during World War I; she drew on the experience in *Basque People* (1931), a collection of short stories.

850.22    Book . . . Club]   Canfield served on the editorial board of the Book-of-the-Month Club from 1926 until her death in 1957.

850.35    granddaughter]   Marjorie Robin Fraser, Marjorie's daughter.

852.8    "Incidents . . . Stevens]   Stevens (1805–52) was an important early explorer of the Mayan ruins.

853.2    WITHERS]   Kenny Withers, an editor at Holt, Rinehart and Winston.

853.13    WARREN]   Novelist Robert Penn Warren.

853.30    BROOKS]   Literary critic Cleanth Brooks; Brooks collaborated with Warren on *Understanding Poetry* (1938), *Understanding Fiction*, and other critical works.

854.29    "What . . . lies?"]   *The Canterbury Tales*, "The Wife of Bath's Prologue," line 302.

854.33–35    Since . . . bean.]   "Merciles Beaute: A Tripel Roundel," lines 27–29.

860.1    *On Emerson*]   Originally delivered as a speech before the American Academy of Arts and Sciences, October 8, 1958, when the Academy awarded the Emerson-Thoreau Medal to Frost.

860.9–10    Fred Melcher]   Frederic Gresham Melcher (1879–1963), co-editor of *Publishers Weekly*, 1918–58.

860.22–23    Emerson . . . ways.]   In "Swedenborg; or, The Mystic," in *Representative Men*, Emerson quotes from Robert Burns' "Address to the Deil": "O wad ye tak a thought, and mend!"

860.30–31    St. John Perse]   See note 736.12.

861.9    "Cut . . . bleed,"]   Cf. "Montaigne; or, the Skeptic" in *Representative Men*: "Cut these words, and they would bleed; they are vascular and alive."

861.18–20    "The God . . . men]   See note 157.4–5.

862.6    Ivor . . . hundred]   English literary critic and linguist I. A. Richards (1893–1979) developed "Basic English," short for "British, American, Scientific, International, Commercial English," a theoretical universal language that draws on a fundamental list of 850 English words.

862.17    in the mind's ear, Horatio.]   Cf. Shakespeare's *Hamlet*, I.ii.186. When asked where he saw his father, Hamlet replies: "In my mind's eye, Horatio."

862.20    a recent preface]   "The Prerequisites" in *Aforesaid* (1954), a selection of Frost's poems.

862.38    "Whose . . . taken."]   Sonnet 19 ("Let not the marriage of true minds").

863.9–10    "Would . . . man."]   Cf. "Ode Sung in the Town Hall, Concord, July 4, 1857," last lines.

863.26–28    "Heartily . . . arrive."]   "Give All to Love," last lines.

863.29    invoked . . . *Magazine*]   See note 797.8.

863.34–864.4    "Musketaquit, . . . rain."]   "Two Rivers," final stanzas.

864.36    "Quit ye like men."]   Cf. 1 Samuel 4:9, 1 Corinthians 16:13.

865.30–31    a mere Tὸ μὴ ὄν]   A mere "that which is not"; a non-entity.

865.32–33    best . . . round."]   See note 383.25–27 to Frost's *Masque of Reason*.

866.13–16    By the . . . world."]   "Hymn Sung at the Completion of the Concord Monument, April 19, 1836," first stanza.

866.13    Thermopylae]   A small pass leading from Thessaly into Locris and Pocis, celebrated in Herodotus's *Histories*, Book 7, as the site of a battle between Xerxes and the Greeks in 480 B.C., where a vastly outnumbered band of Spartans were annihilated by the Persian army after they refused to surrender the pass.

866.19    the tall shaft]   The Washington Monument.

867.1    *The Future of Man*]   Contribution to a symposium on "the future of man" sponsored by Joseph E. Seagram and Sons, Inc., on the occasion of the dedication of the Seagram Building, 375 Park Avenue, New York City. Other panelists included Bertrand Russell, Julian Huxley, Ashley Montagu, and Hermann J. Muller.

871.12    Ararat]   See note 462.34

871.13    where . . . night.]   Matthew Arnold, "Dover Beach," last line.

873.2    *Richard Poirier*]   Poirier was teaching at Harvard at the time this interview was conducted.

874.13    Poetry . . . Monro's]   Poet and editor Monro (1879–1932) began the Poetry Bookshop in 1913 to promote the sale of poetry and poetry readings; Monro published the *Georgian Poetry* series and *Poetry and Drama* at the Bookshop.

875.21    Hueffer]   See note 680.6–7.

875.39–40    Edward . . . book]   *A Number of People* (1939).

877.34–35    Fred Robinson]   Fred Norris Robinson (b. 1871) taught Celtic philology and medieval literature at Harvard University. Part of his education was in Germany.

878.23–24    Stevenson's . . . ape]   Robert Louis Stevenson, *Memories and Portraits*, Chapter 4, "A College Magazine": "I have thus played the sedulous ape to Hazlitt, to Lamb, to Wordsworth, to Sir Thomas Browne, to Defoe, to Hawthorne, to Montaigne, to Baudelaire, and to Obermann."

879.11–12    My uncle's . . . Papers]   *The Biglow Papers* by James Russell Lowell (1819–91), collected 1848 and 1867, are satirical letters in verse written in Yankee dialect.

879.20–21    Shirley . . . state"]   James Shirley (1596–1666), "Death of the Leveller."

879.28–36    "In going . . . of love."]   Cf. Richard Edwards (?1523–66), variously titled "In going to my naked bed" or "Amantium Irae," lines 1 and 8.

881.3    John L. Lewis]   See note 159.9.

882.11    Archie]   Archibald MacLeish (1892–1982).

883.23–24    *Our . . . Infinities*]   By Richard Anthony Proctor (1837–88).

884.15    Compton]   Karl Taylor Compton (1887–1954), physicist and president of M.I.T., 1930–48.

886.17    Matty's anthology.]   F. O. Matthiessen edited *The Oxford Book of American Verse* (1950).

887.27–28    his talk . . . Review?]   Published in the Summer 1959 issue.

887.36–38    J. Donald Adams . . . Trilling]   The article appeared in Adams' column "Speaking of Books," *The New York Times Book Review*, April 12, 1959.

890.20    Gibbon]   See note 722.10–11.

890.38 Bible . . . ten] See Genesis 18:32.

892.30 *Howl . . . Gasoline.*] Allen Ginsberg's *Howl and Other Poems* (1956) and Gregory Corso's *Gasoline* (1958).

893.36 animus] See note 807.8.

894.1 *A Poet's Boyhood*] This essay appeared in a brochure announcing a reading held at the Berkeley Community Theatre, Berkeley, California, on November 6, 1960: *Dana Attractions Inc. Presents In Person America's Poet Laureate Robert Frost Reading from his own Works* (Berkeley: Dana Attractions, 1960).

894.26 Democratic boss, Buckley] Chris Buckley (also known as "Blind White Devil").

894.32 Have I . . . places?] "At Woodward's Gardens" and "Once by the Pacific."

896.1 *A New England Tribute*] A title suggested by the Kennedy-Johnson Inaugural Committee to complement Walter Prescott Webb's article, titled "A Southwestern Tribute," which also appears in the published inaugural program.

896.4–5 a turning . . . Christendom.] John F. Kennedy was the first Roman Catholic to be elected president of the U.S.

896.16–19 "How still . . . sever."] From the penultimate stanza of Alfred Domett (1811–87), "A Christmas Hymn, 1837."

897.21 will become.] Originally "would become"; Frost changed the wording at Kennedy's request.

898.1 *Ernest Hemingway*] This tribute, at the time of Hemingway's suicide, appeared among others under the general title "Authors and Critics Appraise Works."

899.8 my new book.] *In the Clearing.*

900.1 *William Faulkner*] From Kathleen Morrison's manuscript of Frost's dictated remarks. This may be the letter Frost sent to Oxford, Mississippi, after Faulkner's death on July 6, 1962. No published version has been found.

900.4 "Tale . . . Idiot"] *The Sound and the Fury* (1929) takes its title from *Macbeth* V.v.24–28: "Life's but a walking shadow, . . . a tale / Told by an idiot, full of sound and fury, / Signifying nothing."

900.7 Choctaw . . . slaves] "A Justice."

901.2 Mr. Heineman] James H. Heineman. The letter appeared as part of an informal symposium on the theme "The Cold War Is Being Won."

901.3 name . . . magazine] The magazine was an official publication of the State of New York.

902.2–3    all this luxuriance]    Frost delivered the lecture at the newly built Hopkins Center at Dartmouth College.

902.12    "of no . . . I."]    Cf. Paul, of Tarsus, in Acts 21:39.

903.9–19    We are . . . birth.]    Cf. Arthur William Edgar O'Shaughnessy (1844–81), "Ode," lines 1–2, 5, 19–24.

904.5–7    that . . . nothing]    See note 900.4.

909.35–910.4    But God's . . . substantiation.]    From "Kitty Hawk," Part two. See page 441 in this volume.

910.23    "These . . . parables]    See note 342.21

910.27–29    Matthew . . . life."]    "Immortality."

911.6–24    By feathers . . . content.]    Frost quotes Arthur Christopher Benson (1862–1925), "The Phoenix," with some variants.

911.32–912.21    What . . . manger.]    Cf. "Preparations," lines 1–8, 19–30; see also note 803.37.

911.26–33    In either mood . . . done.]    Cf. "Doom" by Arthur William Edgar O'Shaughnessy.

# Index of Titles and First Lines

# Index of Prose Titles

CATALOGING INFORMATION

Frost, Robert, 1874–1963.
  (Selections. 1995)
  Collected poems, prose, and plays / Robert Frost.
    p.  cm. — (The Library of America ; 81)
  Contents: Complete poems 1949 — In the clearing —
Uncollected poems — Plays — Selected prose.
   I. Title.   II. Title: Collected poems, prose, and plays.
III. Series.
PS 3511.R94A6   1995     94–43693
811'.52—dc20
ISBN 1–883011–06–X

# THE LIBRARY OF AMERICA SERIES

1. Herman Melville, *Typee, Omoo, Mardi* (1982)
2. Nathaniel Hawthorne, *Tales and Sketches* (1982)
3. Walt Whitman, *Poetry and Prose* (1982)
4. Harriet Beecher Stowe, *Three Novels* (1982)
5. Mark Twain, *Mississippi Writings* (1982)
6. Jack London, *Novels and Stories* (1982)
7. Jack London, *Novels and Social Writings* (1982)
8. William Dean Howells, *Novels 1875–1886* (1982)
9. Herman Melville, *Redburn, White-Jacket, Moby-Dick* (1983)
10. Nathaniel Hawthorne, *Collected Novels* (1983)
11. Francis Parkman, *France and England in North America* vol. I, (1983)
12. Francis Parkman, *France and England in North America* vol. II, (1983)
13. Henry James, *Novels 1871–1880* (1983)
14. Henry Adams, *Novels, Mont Saint Michel, The Education* (1983)
15. Ralph Waldo Emerson, *Essays and Lectures* (1983)
16. Washington Irving, *History, Tales and Sketches* (1983)
17. Thomas Jefferson, *Writings* (1984)
18. Stephen Crane, *Prose and Poetry* (1984)
19. Edgar Allan Poe, *Poetry and Tales* (1984)
20. Edgar Allan Poe, *Essays and Reviews* (1984)
21. Mark Twain, *The Innocents Abroad, Roughing It* (1984)
22. Henry James, *Essays, American & English Writers* (1984)
23. Henry James, *European Writers & The Prefaces* (1984)
24. Herman Melville, *Pierre, Israel Potter, The Confidence-Man, Tales & Billy Budd* (1985)
25. William Faulkner, *Novels 1930–1935* (1985)
26. James Fenimore Cooper, *The Leatherstocking Tales* vol. I, (1985)
27. James Fenimore Cooper, *The Leatherstocking Tales* vol. II, (1985)
28. Henry David Thoreau, *A Week, Walden, The Maine Woods, Cape Cod* (1985)
29. Henry James, *Novels 1881–1886* (1985)
30. Edith Wharton, *Novels* (1986)
31. Henry Adams, *History of the United States during the Administrations of Jefferson* (1986)
32. Henry Adams, *History of the United States during the Administrations of Madison* (1986)
33. Frank Norris, *Novels and Essays* (1986)
34. W. E. B. Du Bois, *Writings* (1986)
35. Willa Cather, *Early Novels and Stories* (1987)
36. Theodore Dreiser, *Sister Carrie, Jennie Gerhardt, Twelve Men* (1987)
37. Benjamin Franklin, *Writings* (1987)
38. William James, *Writings 1902–1910* (1987)
39. Flannery O'Connor, *Collected Works* (1988)
40. Eugene O'Neill, *Complete Plays 1913–1920* (1988)
41. Eugene O'Neill, *Complete Plays 1920–1931* (1988)
42. Eugene O'Neill, *Complete Plays 1932–1943* (1988)
43. Henry James, *Novels 1886–1890* (1989)
44. William Dean Howells, *Novels 1886–1888* (1989)
45. Abraham Lincoln, *Speeches and Writings 1832–1858* (1989)
46. Abraham Lincoln, *Speeches and Writings 1859–1865* (1989)
47. Edith Wharton, *Novellas and Other Writings* (1990)
48. William Faulkner, *Novels 1936–1940* (1990)
49. Willa Cather, *Later Novels* (1990)
50. Ulysses S. Grant, *Personal Memoirs and Selected Letters* (1990)
51. William Tecumseh Sherman, *Memoirs* (1990)
52. Washington Irving, *Bracebridge Hall, Tales of a Traveller, The Alhambra* (1991)
53. Francis Parkman, *The Oregon Trail, The Conspiracy of Pontiac* (1991)
54. James Fenimore Cooper, *Sea Tales: The Pilot, The Red Rover* (1991)

*This book is set in 10 point Linotron Galliard,*
*a face designed for photocomposition by Matthew Carter*
*and based on the sixteenth-century face Granjon. The paper is*
*acid-free Ecusta Nyalite and meets the requirements for permanence*
*of the American National Standards Institute. The binding*
*material is Brillianta, a woven rayon cloth made by*
*Van Heek-Scholco Textielfabrieken, Holland.*
*The composition is by The Clarinda*
*Company. Printing and binding by*
*R.R.Donnelley & Sons Company.*
*Designed by Bruce Campbell.*

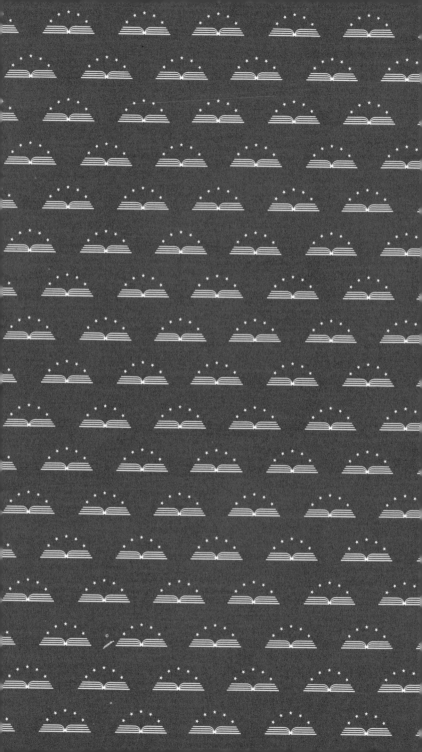